CIVIL RIGHTS
IN THE
UNITED STATES

CIVIL RIGHTS

—— IN THE ——

UNITED STATES

Edited by

WALDO E. MARTIN, JR.
Department of History
University of California, Berkeley

and

PATRICIA SULLIVAN
W. E. B. Du Bois Institute
Harvard University

VOLUME 2

MACMILLAN REFERENCE USA
An Imprint of The Gale Group
NEW YORK

Macmillan Library Reference USA
1633 Broadway
New York, NY 10019

PRINTED IN THE UNITED STATES OF AMERICA

Printing Number
1 2 3 4 5 6 7 8 9 10

Library of Congress Cataloging-in-Publication Data
Civil rights in the United States / Waldo E. Martin, Jr., Patricia Sullivan, editors.
 p. cm.
 "Volume 1."
 Includes bibliographical references and index.
 ISBN 0-02-864765-3 (set)—ISBN 0-02-864763-7 (vol. 1)
 1. Minorities—Civil rights—United States—History—Encyclopedias.
2. Afro-Americans—Civil rights—History—Encyclopedias. 3. Civil rights
movements—United States—History—Encyclopedias. 4. United States—Race
relations—Encyclopedias. 5. United States—Ethnic relations—Encyclopedias.
I. Martin, Waldo E., 1951– II. Sullivan, Patricia.

E184.A1 C47 2000
323′.0973′03—dc21
                                        99-057548

This paper meets the requirements of ANSI-NISO Z39.48-1992 (Permanence of Paper).

L

Labor Movement

The labor movement in the United States is predicated on the assumption that employers are at odds with employees; that only through a collective voice—combined with strikes or boycotts—can workers realize better conditions of employment. The labor movement seeks to achieve its goals through unions. At various times, and to its own detriment, the labor movement excluded from its ranks the unskilled, women, people of color, and immigrants.

The modern labor movement began at the end of the eighteenth century when journeymen became separated from master mechanics by the emergence of large firms that threatened the occupational mobility characteristic of craft production before the American Revolution. Changes in production and distribution created economic conditions in which a working class, or people wholly dependent on wages for their existence, began to appear. Though the pace of economic change varied by trade and location, by the 1830s the modern labor movement had established itself and had institutions protecting working-class interests on the job and at the ballot box.

As fast as journeymen organized to defend themselves, employers created institutions to challenge the rights of working people. Using a combination of violence, the courts, and superior economic means, employers struggled to maintain managerial control over wages and over terms and conditions of employment. They were particularly successful at using the courts to limit the power of worker associations, successfully arguing that strikes and boycotts were conspiracies against the commonweal.

Throughout most of the nineteenth century the labor movement worked on both political and job-related issues. Before 1886, workers generally divided the world into those who produced things for a living and those who did not. The task of the labor movement was to protect the producing classes on the job and to ensure a government free from the corrupting influence of moneyed interests who threatened democracy while exploiting producers. The most significant union taking this position was the KNIGHTS OF LABOR. Founded in 1869, the Knights grew in number from 19,000 in 1881 to 700,000 in 1886, winning several major strikes and demanding the eight-hour day. The Knights were uniquely inclusive, welcoming to their ranks women as well as blacks. The Knights went into rapid decline after 1886 following another round of employer resistance. The Knights of Labor is an early example of industrial unionism that sought to include all workers in an industry within a single union. Craft unionism, on the other hand, concerns itself with workers who perform a single craft or trade.

As the Knights declined, Samuel Gompers, of the Cigar Makers Union, founded the American Federation of Labor (AFL) in 1886 as an umbrella organization of craft unions. Almost uninterrupted, Gompers headed the AFL until 1924. Wary of government and employer resistance, and a strong believer in craft unionism, Gompers steered the AFL away from direct involvement in politics and from organizing the unskilled. With slightly less than 200,000 members in 1886, the AFL grew to 4.25 million in 1919. Craft

417

Union leader Samuel Gompers. (CORBIS/Bettmann)

unionism did not go unchallenged during Gompers's reign, as the American Railway Union (1893), headed by Eugene Debs, and the INDUSTRIAL WORKERS OF THE WORLD (1905), contested the idea. Moreover, within the AFL a strong socialist element existed that challenged the nonpartisanship of Gompers.

In response to the AFL and other unions, employers again took the offensive, utilizing methods that had proved successful in the past. Taking advantage of antitrust laws to restrain unions, giant corporations and small businesses used the courts to limit the power of organized labor and, when necessary, turned to violence to crush the labor movement. Not until the NEW DEAL of Franklin ROOSEVELT (1933–1945) would the labor movement be relatively safe from the violence of American employers and the open hostility of the courts.

In 1933, during the Great Depression, Congress passed the National Industrial Recovery Act, whose Section 7(a) granted workers the "right to bargain collectively through representatives of their own choosing" and prohibited employers from "interference, restraint, or coercion." Though the Act was declared unconstitutional in 1935, the provisions of 7(a) were renewed by the National Labor Relations Act (NLRA) that same year. During the years of the Great Depression, the craft orientation of the AFL was successfully challenged by members within its own ranks. The emergence of the Congress of Industrial Organizations (CIO), founded by United Mine Workers president John L. Lewis in 1935, led to the reorganization of mass-production industries such as steel, auto, and rubber as workers tested the meaning of the new laws with innovative job actions like the sit-down strike. These unions included unskilled and craft workers, bargained for benefits, and participated in national politics. In 1955 the AFL and CIO merged.

The achievements of the post-1933 labor movement are many. Organized labor is wholly or partly responsible for: the eight-hour day with time and a half for overtime; the minimum wage; Social Security; Medicare; occupational health and safety; paid vacation; fair employment practices laws; unemployment insurance; health and pension benefits; and higher wages. Though not always helpful in the struggle for equal rights, organized labor, particularly the United Auto Workers under Walter Reuther, played a critical role in the civil rights movements of the 1950s and 1960s, providing financial and political support.

United Auto Workers Union leader Walter Reuther testifies before a Senate subcommittee in 1981. (AP/ Wide World Photos)

Since the AFL-CIO merger, organized labor has been in decline. The combined effects of the Red Scare and anticommunism, the difficulty of organizing a new work force with many more women and people of color, the loss of manufacturing jobs in the face of the global economy, unimaginative and lethargic unions, and another round of employer and governmental reaction during the REAGAN years have acted to hurt the labor movement. One bright spot has been the increase in union membership among public employees. Since 1995, the AFL-CIO has put renewed energy and resources into organizing, with some success. The official mission of the AFL-CIO in 1999 is to "improve the lives of working families—to bring economic justice to the workplace and social justice to the nation."

BIBLIOGRAPHY

Baron, Eva, ed. *Work Engendered: Toward a New History of American Labor.* 1991.

Dubofsky, Melvyn, and Warren Van Tine, eds. *Labor Leaders in America.* 1987.

Fink, Gary M., and Merle E. Reed, eds. *Race, Class, and Community in Southern Labor History.* 1994.

Frisch, Michael H., and Daniel J. Walkowitz, eds. *Working-Class America: Essays on Labor, Community, and American Society.* 1983.

Geoghegan, Thomas. *Which Side Are You On? Trying to Be for Labor When It's Flat on Its Back.* 1991.

James, Dante J., producer. *A. Philip Randolph: For Jobs & Freedom,* California Newsreel, San Francisco. 1995.

Kessler-Harris, Alice. *Out to Work: A History of Wage-Earning Women in the United States.* 1982.

Laurie, Bruce. *Artisan into Worker: Labor in Nineteenth-Century America.* 1989.

Leab, Daniel J., ed. *The Labor History Reader.* 1985.

Salvatore, Nick. *Eugene V. Debs: Citizen and Socialist.* 1982.

Zieger, Robert H. *Organized Labor in the Twentieth-century South.* 1991.

Jeffrey Kolnick

La Flesche, Francis ("Frank")

(1857–1932), anthropologist.

A member of the Omaha Tribe of Nebraska, Frank La Flesche became a leading anthropological writer and authority on the culture and traditions of the Omahas, Osage, and other Plains tribes.

Born on the Omaha Reservation in northeastern Nebraska and educated at the Presbyterian Mission School there, Frank La Flesche served as an important intermediary for non-Indian ethnographers such as James Owen Dorsey and Alice C. Fletcher, who studied and recorded Plains Indian cultures during the last decades of the nineteenth century. He collaborated with Fletcher to produce *The Omaha Tribe* (1911), a massive anthropological record of the tribe's cultural traditions, which remains one of the most comprehensive and oft-cited studies of Plains Indian culture. Fletcher informally "adopted" La Flesche in 1881, and his service as an aide and translator in her misguided 1883 campaign for the "allotment" of Omaha tribal land to individual tribal members is a particularly controversial episode. The allotment of Omaha lands ultimately resulted in the tribe's loss of tens of thousands of acres, and served as an unfortunate model for the General Allotment Act of 1887 (DAWES ACT), which mandated the "privatization" of Indian lands all over the country.

La Flesche spent most of his adult life in Washington, D.C., serving as a clerk, interpreter, and writer for the Indian Bureau and the Bureau of Ethnography. His legacy among modern Omahas is somewhat tainted not only by his role in the allotment program, but also by his participation in the transfer of sacred tribal artifacts to eastern museums. Some of those items have been recovered by the Omahas in the 1990s. Despite his clouded legacy, La Flesche's work preserved for the tribe a wealth of information about its traditions and cultural practices that might well have been lost without his efforts.

BIBLIOGRAPHY

Boughter, Judith. *Betraying the Omaha Nation, 1790–1916.* 1998.

Mark, Joan. *A Stranger in Her Native Land; Alice Fletcher and the American Indians.* 1988.

Riddington, Robin, and Dennis Hastings. *Blessing for a Long Time: The Sacred Pole of the Omaha Tribe.* 1997.

Mark R. Scherer

Lampkin, Daisy

(ca. 1884–1965), civil rights activist.

Daisy Lampkin was widely known for her work with the NATIONAL ASSOCIATION FOR THE ADVANCEMENT OF COLORED PEOPLE (NAACP) as regional field secretary (1930–1935), national field secretary (1935–1947), and board of directors member (1947–1965); yet her more than half-century struggle for racial justice and women's rights extended beyond the civil rights organization.

Born Daisy Elizabeth Adams, she was the only child of George and Rosa Anne Proctor Adams. In 1909, Daisy joined the WOMAN SUFFRAGE MOVEMENT in Pittsburgh, becoming president of the Negro Women's Franchise League in 1915. She married William Lampkin of Rome, Georgia, in 1912. The following year she became a successful subscription saleswoman for the

Pittsburgh *Courier*, one of the most influential black newspapers in the country, and later was its vice president (1929–1965). Lampkin was in the forefront of numerous black women's organizations, including the NATIONAL ASSOCIATION OF COLORED WOMEN, the NATIONAL COUNCIL OF NEGRO WOMEN (as a cofounder), Delta Sigma Theta sorority, the Links, and the Lucy Stone Civic League, and was active in both the DEMOCRATIC PARTY and the REPUBLICAN PARTY. She was active in the Republican Party during the 1920s but joined the Democrats during the NEW DEAL era. (In 1952 she returned to the Republican Party camp when the Democrats ran a segregationist, John Sparkman, for U.S. vice president.)

In the 1930s, Lampkin developed a unique and highly successful NAACP membership campaign strategy—a team method centered around black churches—and traveled widely throughout the country enrolling new members, sometimes attending as many as forty meetings in one month. Her contacts with black women's groups gave her considerable leverage within the NAACP; conversely, she also utilized this female associational network to promote the NAACP, illustrating the importance of African-American women's organizations in fueling NAACP expansion. Tireless and self-sacrificing to the end of her life, Lampkin suffered a stroke while on an NAACP business trip in 1964, and died several months later.

BIBLIOGRAPHY

Daisy Lampkin Papers. Privately held in Verona, Pennsylvania, by Edna B. McKenzie, who is at work on a biography tentatively titled "Service Well Done: The Life of Daisy Lampkin."

Giddings, Paula. *When and Where I Enter: The Impact of Race and Sex on Black Women in America*. 1985.

Hill, Lisa Beth. "Daisy Lampkin." In *Notable Black American Women* , edited by Jessie Carney Smith. 1992.

McKenzie, Edna B. "Daisy Lampkin: A Life of Love and Service." *Pennsylvania Heritage* IX (3) (Summer 1983).

McKenzie, Edna B. "Daisy Lampkin." In *Black Women in America: An Historical Encyclopedia*, vol. I, edited by Darlene Clark Hine. 1993.

NAACP Papers. Library of Congress, Washington, D.C.

Pittsburgh Courier, March 20, 1965, 1.

Christina Greene

La Raza Unida Party

See Raza Unida Party, La.

Las Gorras Blancas

See Gorras Blancas, Las

Lau v. Nichols (1974)

In *Lau v. Nichols* (1974), the SUPREME COURT unanimously held that Chinese-speaking San Francisco school children were entitled to remedial assistance because their lack of English language proficiency prevented them from taking advantage of public educational programs conducted in English. The Court reasoned that Title VI of the CIVIL RIGHTS ACT OF 1964 prohibited institutions receiving federal funds from maintaining programs and policies that had the effect of racial or ethnic discrimination. Accordingly, "merely providing curriculum, teachers and textbooks" identical to that received by English-fluent students without accounting for the language barrier "effectively foreclosed [Chinese-speaking children] from any meaningful education" and thus made "a mockery of public education."

The Court did not mandate a specific remedy. However, following *Lau* the U.S. Department of Education required schools that had failed to offer equal treatment to adopt what came to be known as the "*Lau* Remedies": teaching students English while instructing them in other subjects in their native language to prevent them from falling behind academically.

The case reflected several important political developments. *Lau* was a major victory for the growing Asian-American civil rights movement. Although the *Lau* plaintiffs spoke Chinese, the decision probably had the greatest impact on Spanish-speaking students, a much larger group. *Lau* also foreshadowed increasing concern for the problem of social participation by language minorities, as represented by, for example, the 1975 amendment to the VOTING RIGHTS ACT OF 1965, an amendment that made it easier for non–English-speaking citizens to vote.

Lau's conclusion that Title VI prohibited programs that had a discriminatory effect without discriminatory intent has been called into question by later cases. However, CONGRESS essentially codified *Lau* when it passed the Equal Educational Opportunities Act of 1974.

Lau's recognition of legal rights generated a reaction among the voters. In 1998, Californians passed Proposition 227, amending the Education Code to require that most limited-English-proficiency students be "immersed" in all-English classrooms shortly after entering school.

BIBLIOGRAPHY

An, Gi Hyun. "The Right To Bilingual Education: Providing Equal Educational Opportunity for Limited English Proficient Children in a Pluralist, Multicultural Society." *Georgetown Immigration Law Journal* 11 (1996): 133–165.

Crawford, James, ed. *Language Loyalties: A Sourcebook on the Official English Controversy*. 1992.

Lau v. Nichols, 414 U.S. 563 (1974).
Wang, L. Ling Chi. "Lau v. Nichols: History of a Struggle for Equal and Quality Education." In *Counterpoint: Perspectives on Asian America*, edited by Emma Gee. 1976.

Gabriel J. Chin
Chris K. Iijima

Lawson, James Morris, Jr.

(1928–), minister, civil rights leader, advocate of nonviolent civil disobedience.

A native of Uniontown, Pennsylvania, James Morris Lawson spent time in a federal prison in the early 1950s for his refusal to serve in the armed forces during the Korean War. He later graduated from Baldwin-Wallace College in Berea, Ohio. Lawson then attended the Vanderbilt University Divinity School, but did not graduate, instead earning a bachelor of sacred theology degree from Boston University in 1960. In the mid-1950s, Lawson, an ordained United Methodist minister and a pacifist, had traveled to India to study GANDHI's techniques of nonviolent civil disobedience. Divinity student Lawson was dismissed from Vanderbilt for teaching CIVIL DISOBEDIENCE workshops to college students in Nashville. The dismissal caused a crisis of conscience among the divinity faculty, who persuaded Vanderbilt Chancellor Harvie Branscomb to invite Lawson to return to the school; but by that time Lawson had transferred to Boston University.

After graduating from Boston University, Lawson accepted a pastorate in Memphis and worked actively for the STUDENT NONVIOLENT COORDINATING COMMITTEE (SNCC), an offshoot of the SOUTHERN CHRISTIAN LEADERSHIP CONFERENCE (SCLC). James Lawson worked with most of the leading civil rights groups during the 1960s. He wrote SNCC's statement of purpose when it was founded in April 1960 at Shaw University in Raleigh, North Carolina, and he took part in the FREEDOM RIDES that tried to desegregate interstate bus station facilities in the South. After 1961, the "Turks" in SNCC rejected their first statement of purpose, which had placed much emphasis on love and nonviolence; and the revolutionary members of SNCC increasingly crowded out the religionists such as Lawson and Martin Luther KING, JR. The leaders of SNCC believed that the problems of black people were racial and social in character, not religious or spiritual, and that clergy leadership was too conciliatory and impractical. Lawson's influence with SNCC, like King's, was rejected after 1961, in a conflict that gave rise to calls for BLACK POWER.

In 1968, Lawson helped to organize the MEMPHIS SANITATION WORKERS STRIKE. He hoped that the presence of invited participant Martin Luther King, Jr., would bring national attention to the plight of the garbage collectors. Tragically, some of the black workers, unable to gain shelter from a heavy rain in an office with white coworkers, found shelter in the back of a garbage truck, where one of them was accidentally crushed to death by the truck's compactor. The media's focus on the garbage workers, which Lawson had wanted, abruptly shifted when Martin Luther King was fatally shot. Ironically, James Lawson later officiated at the prison wedding of King-assassin James Earl Ray. And in yet another irony, in 1996, James Lawson—then a Los Angeles, California, minister—returned to Vanderbilt University to receive the Divinity School's first Distinguished Alumnus Award.

Lawson believed that nonviolence was spiritual and should be adopted as a way of life. His conviction, along with Martin Luther King's, that nonviolence was spiritual and would ultimately triumph over RACISM helped to transform the civil rights movement from a regional movement to a mass movement.

BIBLIOGRAPHY
Broderick, Francis, ed. *Negro Protest in the Twentieth Century*. 1966.
Farmer, James, and Don E. Carleton. *Lay Bare the Heart: An Autobiography of the Civil Rights Movement*. 1998.
Forman, James, and Julian Bond. *The Making of Black Revolutionaries*. 1997.
Vanderbilt Magazine 801(4) (Winter 1999): 13.

Claude Hargrove

Lazarus, Julius

(1918–), photographer.

Born into a working-class Austrian Jewish family at the end of WORLD WAR II, Julius Lazarus fled Vienna in 1938 in the wake of the terror that followed the Nazi *Anschluss* (annexation) of Austria. Active in labor and progressive circles after the war, Lazarus, a skilled ironworker until a wartime service injury made it impossible for him to continue his work, became a freelance photographer of civil rights, civil liberties, and labor protests. In the late 1940s, his photographs of civil rights protests, labor demonstrations against the Taft-Hartley Law, and demonstrations against the Mundt-Nixon bill, which required all Communist Party members and front organizations to register with the U.S. government—a precursor of what would be called MCCARTHYISM after 1950—appeared widely in labor and left publications. Traveling with W. E. B. DU BOIS and Paul ROBESON to a left-sponsored World Peace Congress in Paris in 1949, Lazarus photographed intellectuals from all over the world drawn together by their opposition to RACISM, COLONIALISM, the COLD WAR, and the nuclear arms race threat to peace.

Working as a photographer in Eastern Europe between 1949 and 1953, Lazarus took photographs of the restoration of the Warsaw Ghetto and events at various world youth festivals. Also, deeply moving photographs that he had taken earlier of slum HOUSING conditions in Harlem were published widely in the press of the world's socialist nations. Like his friend Paul Robeson four years earlier, Lazarus lost his passport when he returned to the United States in 1953, but continued his work as a photographer of such events as the National Deliverance Day of Prayer support rally for the MONTGOMERY BUS BOYCOTT in 1956 and the "Lift Every Voice" concert, protesting racist and anti-Semitic policies at Metropolitan Life Insurance Company's Parkchester Housing Development in New York.

Settling on Cape Cod, Massachusetts, in the 1960s, Lazarus continued to work until his failing eyesight in 1980 marked the end of his career as an active photographer. His photographic archive, now in the Special Collections of the Alexander Library of Rutgers University, is a rich and vital source for understanding the activists of the American Left and their contributions to the struggle for civil rights and social equality in the United States.

BIBLIOGRAPHY

Julius Lazarus Collection. Alexander Library, Rutgers University, New Brunswick, N.J.

Trojan, Judith. "Pictures from a Revolution." *Rutgers Magazine* (Fall 1997): 32–33.

Norman Markowitz

LDF

See NAACP Legal Defense and Educational Fund.

Leadership Conference on Civil Rights

The Leadership Conference of Civil Rights (LCCR)— a broad coalition of civil rights, labor, civic, and religious groups—was founded in 1950 as a national lobbying group in support of civil rights legislation.

The LCCR strengthened the political base established in Washington by the NATIONAL ASSOCIATION FOR THE ADVANCEMENT OF COLORED PEOPLE (NAACP). Throughout the 1960s, the endeavors of the LCCR and the NAACP were closely interrelated; Clarence Mitchell, Jr., director of the Washington bureau of the NAACP, was also legislative chairman of the LCCR. Through its broad constituencies and the work of its staff and affiliated organizational representatives on Capitol Hill, the LCCR played a pivotal role in shaping and securing civil rights legislation, from the tepid CIVIL RIGHTS ACT OF 1957 through the major legislation of the 1960s.

By 1960, the LCCR included more than seventy organizations. As growing mass protests and violent white resistance focused national attention on the South's racial caste system, LCCR's efforts began to bear fruit. While the LCCR staff and representatives strategized and lobbied legislators for a strong civil rights bill on Capitol Hill, LCCR orchestrated grassroots campaigns through church and union affiliates, building a vocal and expanding base of national support for the enactment of the CIVIL RIGHTS ACT OF 1964. The LCCR–NAACP legislative network played a critical role in securing the VOTING RIGHTS ACT of 1965 and the Civil Rights Act of 1968 (see FAIR HOUSING ACT).

In recent decades, the LCCR has grown to include more than 185 national organizations. It has become a clearinghouse for the concerns of a variety of groups that have suffered discrimination due to ethnicity, sexual preference, gender, and physical disabilities. The LCCR continues to monitor Congress and lobby for legislation that advances equal opportunity, human rights, and social justice for all citizens.

BIBLIOGRAPHY

Watson, Denton L. *Lion in the Lobby: Clarence Mitchell, Jr.'s Struggle for The Passage of Civil Rights Laws.* 1990.

Whalen, Charles, and Barbara Whalen. *The Longest Debate: A Legislative History of the 1964 Civil RIghts Act.* 1985.

Patricia Sullivan

League of United Latin American Citizens

Founded in 1929 in TEXAS, the League of United Latin American Citizens (LULAC) is the oldest Mexican-American civil rights association in the United States. LULAC was formed in a merger of the various Mexican-American organizations existing at that time in Texas. Concerned over the level of fractionalization between groups and interested in political unity, Ben Garza of the Sons of America and M. C. Gonzales of the Knights of America approached leaders of the remaining groups and organized a convention, held on February 17, 1929, that resulted in formation of the League of United Latin American Citizens under the leadership of Alonso Perales.

The goal of the organization was to achieve increased equality for Mexican Americans within American mainstream society by their being acculturated politically without losing their Mexican traditions and customs. Members sought to achieve their goals by addressing issues of SEGREGATION and discrimination. They protested against segregation in movie theaters, swimming pools, restaurants, hospitals, and the Texas State Prison in Huntsville. In 1941, they protested against discrimination by the Southern Pacific Railroad, which refused to provide skilled apprenticeships to Mexican Americans, and they fought for equal job opportunities for WORLD WAR II veterans.

In *Hernandez v. State of Texas* in 1954, LULAC addressed the exclusion of Mexican Americans from jury duty, arguing that defendants' FOURTEENTH AMENDMENT rights were being violated through this discriminatory practice. Although the lower courts did not side with them, the U.S. SUPREME COURT ruled on May 3, 1954 that the defendant had not received a fair trial owing to discrimination in the jury selection process. The decision also denied previous arguments made in the lower courts that the Fourteenth Amendment applied only to African Americans and Anglos.

LULAC was also a pioneer in fighting segregation of schools in the Southwest. In 1930, the organization fought against the segregation of Mexican children in Del Rio, Texas. LULAC obtained a court injunction prohibiting the use of recently approved funding to build a new school for Mexican-American children. The local court ruled in favor of LULAC. However, a state appellate court overturned the injunction, arguing that, in this particular case, the separation of Mexican-American children was purely for instructional reasons and not based on race. The court did rule that school segregation based on race was unconstitutional. LULAC addressed this issue once again in 1946 in the *Westminster* case in California, a class action suit against school districts in Orange County. The local court again ruled in their favor. The courts would favor LULAC's claims in similar cases filed in Texas in 1948 and 1954.

Although officially LULAC's membership excluded Mexican nationals and adopted English as the official language, this did not necessarily result in the alienation of Mexican nationals, as LULAC aimed to Americanize them by offering English and citizenship courses. However, the exclusion of Mexican nationals did become problematic during LULAC protests against the BRACERO PROGRAM, which provided temporary contract labor, primarily for agribusiness. LULAC argued that these programs exploited immigrant workers in addition to discriminating against native-born Mexican farmworkers by providing unfair labor competition. Frustrated by their failure to shut down the program, they supported mass arrests and deportations by the Immigration Service in Operation Wetback.

Women held significant roles within the organization. In 1932, LULAC incorporated women's auxiliaries, and among the prominent women leaders was J. C. Machuca of El Paso, who organized the first Ladies' Council. Some of the women's efforts included working in orphanages and health clinics. They also registered voters, raised money for college scholarships, and taught English and citizenship courses to Mexican nationals.

Until the late 1950s, LULAC had distinguished itself as an organization that did not favor special programs for Mexican Americans, as part of a continuing effort to refuse to be labeled a "minority" organization. This all changed, however, in 1957 under the administration of Felix Tijerina, who implemented the Little School of 400, designed to teach English to Mexican-American preschool children before they entered the public school system. Tijerina achieved state funding for such programs, defining them as state-sponsored programs specifically for Mexican Americans. The Little School of 400 became the model for the HEAD START programs begun in the 1960s. During the political movements of the 1960s, when "minoritized" groups were demanding compensatory programs, LULAC added its voice, making similar demands for Mexican Americans and further minoritizing the organization. Other programs achieved by LULAC included job placement centers, SER-Jobs for Progress, started in 1965. Although the change to minority status led to the alienation of the older leadership, LULAC continued to spread throughout the United States, and it furthered its efforts against discrimination and educational inequality by including Puerto Ricans and Cuban Americans in its membership in the late twentieth century.

Timeline

1929 Organization is founded in Texas.
1930 Protesters desegregate various public places throughout Texas, including swimming pools, restaurants, and movie theaters.
1931 *Salvatierra v. Del Rio Independent School District* is won, against segregation of schools in Texas.
1932 Ladies auxiliaries are incorporated.
1946 *Mendez v. Westminster* case is won, against segregation of schools in California.
1948 *Delgado v. Bastrop Independent School District* is filed, which ended the segregation of schools in Texas
1954 *Hernandez v. the State of Texas* wins the right for Mexican Americans to serve on juries and de-

nies the exclusion of Mexican Americans from the Fourteenth Amendment.

1957   The Little School of 400, a program for Mexican-American preschool children to teach them English, is implemented.

1960   The Little School of 400 becomes Project Head Start under the Lyndon B. Johnson administration.

1965   SER–Jobs for Progress, job placement centers, are piloted by LULAC.

BIBLIOGRAPHY

Acuña, Rudy. *Occupied America: A History of Chicanos.* 1988.

Garcia, Mario. *Mexican Americans.* 1989.

Griswold del Castillo, Richard, and Arnoldo de Leon. *North to Aztlan: A History of Mexican Americans in the United States.* 1996.

Muñoz, Carlos. *Youth, Identity, Power.* 1989.

Ortiz, Frank. "About LULAC." (www.lulac.org).

Elizabeth Garcia

Feminist leader M. W. Parks of the League of Women Voters. (CORBIS/Bettmann)

League of Women Voters

The League of Women Voters (LWV) is the offspring of the NATIONAL AMERICAN WOMAN SUFFRAGE ASSOCIATION (NAWSA), a leading force in the suffrage campaign. In 1919, Carrie Chapman CATT, final president of NAWSA, had proposed the formation of an organization to keep woman suffragists united after the vote was secured, and the League of Women Voters (LWV) was born in February 1921 at an NAWSA convention honoring the ratification of the NINETEENTH AMENDMENT. Nonetheless, only a small percentage of NAWSA membership joined LWV and, unlike NAWSA, LWV did not focus exclusively on one issue but embraced a large number of social programs and reforms.

Initially these included projects to increase voter participation and awareness, food and public hygiene programs, and initiatives to promote the welfare of children, as well as proposals addressing the rights of women and their needs in the work force. In 1923 the organization stated its goals as the advancement of pacifism, the improvement of government social programs, and the promotion of women's rights. In the face of opposition from varying political establishments, the LWV was forced to withdraw some of its more overtly feminist goals, such as its attempt to create a female voting bloc. Subsequently the League focused on increasing the effectiveness of the political process, the education of women voters being a secondary objective. Accordingly, the League typically favored a gradual, nonradical approach for achieving progress in women's rights, and avoided issues that were controversial to any segment of its membership.

In its early years, the LWV worked most actively for disarmament and for labor issues. Its predominantly upper- and middle-class background notwithstanding, the League welcomed support from working women. The LWV was a leading advocate of protective laws for women in the work force, for example laws extending special types of protection to working women, such as limitations on the amount of weight they could lift while on the job. More militant feminists actually frowned upon protective laws, as they impeded the possible passage of an EQUAL RIGHTS AMENDMENT and the creation of a truly gender-blind legal code.

The LWV was conscientiously nonpartisan and shunned political endorsements; however, it did offer its advocacy of specific pieces of legislation. In conjunction with several other women's organizations, the LWV pushed for passage of the 1921 Sheppard–Towner Maternity and Infancy Protection Act, which granted funds to mothers and infants, and the 1922

Cable Act, which made women's citizenship to some degree independent of that of their husbands.

Feminists of later generations offer a divided assessment of the role of the LWV. Some believe the organization seemed to suggest that women were uniquely in need of special training to compensate for their lack of familiarity with the political process; these feminists argue that the LWV's concern for women's issues was lukewarm. Others applaud the LWV's attempt to keep the issue of voting prominent in women's minds and endorse Carrie Chapman Catt's vision of an organization that would help to integrate women into the existing political structure rather than to segregate them into entirely female institutions. The LWV viewed the vote, if actively used, as a tool sufficient in-and-of-itself for achieving all other political aims.

In the second half of the twentieth century, the League had abandoned much of its political activism and became an established part of the landscape of women's organizations.

BIBLIOGRAPHY

Brumbaugh, Sarah B. *Democratic Experience and Education in the National League of Women Voters.* 1946.
Chafe, William Henry. *The Paradox of Change: American Women in the Twentieth Century.* 1991.
Frost-Knappman, Elizabeth, with Sarah Kurian. *The ABC–Clio Companion to Women's Progress in America.* 1994.
Holt, Judith, and Ellen Levine. *Rebirth of Feminism.* 1971.
Young, Louise M. *In the Public Interest: The League of Women Voters, 1920–1970.* 1989.

Sarah Kurian

Lebrón, Lolita

(1919–), political activist, feminist, and poet.

Lolita Lebrón (Dolores "Lolita" Lebrón Soto) is best known for leading an armed attack against members of the U.S. CONGRESS on March 1, 1954. She, along with Andrés Figueroa Cordero, Rafael Cancel Miranda, and Irvin Flores Rodríguez, belonged to the militant Puerto Rican Nationalist Party (known in Puerto Rico as Partido Nacionalista Puertorriqueño), although all four nationalists then resided in New York City. On the morning of March 1 they boarded a train to Washington, D.C., eventually making their way to the visitors' gallery of the House of Representatives. There they unfurled a Puerto Rican flag, shouted "Long live free Puerto Rico!" and started shooting at members of Congress, five of whom were wounded. They did this to bring COLONIALISM in Puerto Rico to the attention of the world.

Lolita Lebrón was born on November 19, 1919 in Lares, Puerto Rico, a mountain town in the coffee-growing, western region of the island. Lares is also the cradle of the independence movement because on September 23, 1868 an armed uprising known in Spanish as "El Grito de Lares" resulted in a short-lived Puerto Rican declaration of independence from Spain.

The daughter of Gonzalo Lebrón Bernal and Rafaela Soto Luciano, Lolita came from a stable family that was essentially of Spanish heritage, which also included her brothers Augusto, Julio, and Gonzalo.

Lolita Lebrón's support for self-determination and the independence of Puerto Rico developed naturally because her parents were members of the Puerto Rican Liberal Party, which advocated sovereignty for the island. It is believed that the 1937 "Ponce Massacre," in which the Puerto Rican police killed twenty-one Nationalist Party members and injured two hundred more, aroused Lolita's interest in militant nationalism. Her joining the Nationalist Party was delayed by an early romantic relationship that produced a daughter but ended soon thereafter.

In 1940, at age twenty-one, Lolita left Puerto Rico to settle in New York City after breaking up with her common-law husband. In New York, she was employed as a sewing-machine operator, joining the ranks of hundreds of Puerto Rican women and men who integrated the garment industry. Concurrently, she was also witness to the massive migration of Puerto Ricans to New York. Lolita Lebrón saw that her compatriots were victims of exploitation. To improve her skills, in the hope of leaving the factory job, Lolita enrolled in evening classes at George Washington High School. At age twenty-three, she gave birth to a son from a short-lived marriage that ended in divorce.

By the early 1940s, Lolita had developed a genuine interest in the Nationalist Party and had begun to contribute to their work in New York. She formally joined the party in 1946, declaring her solidarity with the party leader, Pedro ALBIZU CAMPOS, a Harvard-educated lawyer identified with militant Puerto Rican nationalism. Albizu was incarcerated several times, beginning in 1936, but had been released in 1943 because of a heart ailment. From 1943 to 1947 Albizu also lived in New York, at a time when Nationalist activism was surging, but Lolita did not have the opportunity to meet him.

By 1950, a proposed change in the status of Puerto Rico motivated the Nationalists to attempt an assassination of President Harry TRUMAN. The "commandos" (Oscar Collazo and Griselio Torresola) who attacked Blair House, the temporary presidential residence, came from the New York branch of the party, where Lolita Lebrón was among the leaders.

Four years later, Lolita Lebrón led the assault on Congress. In addition to the four participants in this attack, eleven other U.S.-based Nationalists were arrested. Another group was taken into custody in Puerto Rico, including Pedro Albizu Campos. After the trial, Lolita Lebrón was sentenced to sixteen to fifty years in prison. All three men were sentenced to terms of a minimum of twenty-five to a maximum of seventy-five years. All except Andrés Figueroa Cordero remained incarcerated until 1979, when President Jimmy CARTER pardoned them and Oscar Collazo, who was jailed in 1950. Figueroa Cordero had been released earlier, suffering with an advance stage of cancer.

While in custody, Lolita Lebrón lost both of her children. Her son was the victim of a drowning when she was initially confined. Her daughter was killed in an automobile accident while Lolita was imprisoned in the federal penitentiary for women in Alderson, West Virginia. These two experiences may have helped to heighten her devotion to Catholicism. In prison she devoted herself to the work of the Church, as well as serving as a counselor to recently imprisoned women. Lolita was also a poet and successfully published a number of poems.

Upon her release from prison in 1979, after twenty-five years of incarceration, Lolita returned to Puerto Rico with the other four Nationalists to massive demonstrations of support from many sectors of the population. Since then, she has continued to be active with the Nationalist Party and other causes. An avowed Christian and a feminist, Lolita Lebrón has remarried and is a sought-after speaker, both in Puerto Rico and abroad.

Although a Nationalist Party leader, Lolita no longer espouses the confrontational strategies that were trademarks of her party. She is committed to self-determination and independence for Puerto Rico through peaceful means. Her shift to nonviolence is attributed, in part, to her Catholic faith and to the belief that much blood has been shed on behalf of the nationalist struggle for sovereignty. Recently, Lolita Lebrón was elected president of the Puerto Rican Nationalist Party. Ironically, she replaced Laura Meneses Albizu, the granddaughter of Dr. Pedro Albizu Campos.

BIBLIOGRAPHY

Ribes-Tovar, Federico. *Lolita Lebrón: La Prisionera*. 1974.
Torres, Andrés, and José E. Velázquez. *The Puerto Rican Movement: Voices from the Diaspora*. 1998.
Wagenheim, Kal, and Olga Jiménez de Wagenheim. *The Puerto Ricans: A Documentary History*. 1973.

Basilio Serrano

Lee, Herbert

(1912–1961), civil rights martyr.

Herbert Lee, an illiterate black farmer, husband, and father of nine children, was born and raised in Amite County, Mississippi. When his boyhood friend E. W. Steptoe founded the Amite County, Mississippi, chapter of the NATIONAL ASSOCIATION FOR THE ADVANCEMENT OF COLORED PEOPLE (NAACP) in 1954, Lee was one of its charter members. For several years he helped maintain the viability of the organization while resisting attempts at economic and physical intimidation from local white supremacists.

To protect his family, Lee refused to allow his children to accept employment from whites and did his shopping across the state line in Louisiana rather than endure the indignities that were ingrained in the racial tradition in southwestern MISSISSIPPI. When Robert MOSES and the STUDENT NONVIOLENT COORDINATING COMMITTEE (SNCC) began a voter registration campaign in Amite County, Lee was the first local black to attempt to register. He also inflamed local whites by driving SNCC workers about the county as they recruited potential voters.

At nine o'clock in the morning of September 25, 1961 (three months into SNCC's drive), Herbert Lee was shot and killed by white State Representative E. H. Hurst near a cotton gin in rural Liberty, Mississippi. An investigation by the local coroner's jury found that Hurst had acted in self-defense and the jury immediately released him. However, several black witnesses reported that Hurst had targeted Lee because of his economic prosperity as well as his civil rights activities.

Lee's murder brought SNCC's voter registration drive to a temporary halt. The message was clear: challenging white supremacy in Mississippi could get a man killed.

BIBLIOGRAPHY

Dittmer, John. *Local People*. 1994.
Payne, Charles. *I've Got the Light of Freedom*. 1994.
Zinn, Howard. *SNCC: The New Abolitionists*. 1964.

Homer Douglass Hill

Legal Defense and Educational Fund

See NAACP Legal Defense and Educational Fund

Lewis, John

(1940–), civil rights leader and U.S. congressman.

John Lewis was born near Troy, Alabama. His mother was a maid and his father farmed on rented land. As

Representative John Lewis of Georgia stands before the U.S. Capitol on May 21, 1998. (AP/Wide World Photos)

a child, Lewis was a strict vegetarian and a strong Christian; one of his most traumatic teenage memories was the accidental drowning of a chicken during an attempted baptism. At 17, Lewis gained a scholarship to the American Baptist Theological Seminary in Nashville. While there, he came under the influence of Vanderbilt student Jim Lawson and began attending nonviolent workshops where students discussed Jesus, Gandhi, and the MONTGOMERY BUS BOYCOTT.

Consequently, Lewis took a leading role in the Nashville sit-in movement in 1960, which successfully desegregated the city's lunch-counters. The following year Lewis was the only participant in both legs of the FREEDOM RIDE and he joined the board of the STUDENT NONVIOLENT COORDINATING COMMITTEE (SNCC).

Among student activists, Lewis gained a reputation for extreme courage, suffering arrest over forty times, and being beaten on numerous occasions. One SNCC colleague, Worth Long, commented aptly that "John would not just follow you into the lion's den, he would lead you into it." Lewis was also one of the most fervent exponents of SNCC's original devotion to nonviolence

and interracial activism. He shared with his hero, Martin Luther KING, JR., the belief that means and ends could not be separated. For Lewis, the goal was the "beloved community," a redeemed society which was at peace with itself.

Such a philosophy infused Lewis's activities as SNCC's third chairman, from June 1963. As chairman, Lewis was also the most militant of the so-called "big six" civil rights leaders who cochaired the MARCH ON WASHINGTON of 1963. In his draft speech, Lewis described America "as a place of cheap political leaders" and called for protesters to "crack the South into a thousand pieces." Although he toned down his actual speech under pressure from the other leaders, Lewis still asked the famous question, "I want to know— which side is the federal government on?"

However, Lewis's continued insistence on nonviolence, interracial cooperation, and his unswerving loyalty to King eventually alienated him from the growing radical elements in SNCC. In 1966 he was replaced by Stokely Carmichael as SNCC chairman and he resigned from the organization when it adopted BLACK POWER ideology shortly afterward.

Lewis continued to campaign for civil rights through less confrontational means. While he was director of the VOTER EDUCATION PROJECT, nearly four million minority persons (primarily blacks) were added to the voter rolls. In 1977, President Jimmy CARTER appointed Lewis as director of Volunteers in Service to America.

In 1981, Lewis launched his political career, gaining election to the Atlanta city council. Five years later he defeated former SNCC colleague Julian Bond in the election to represent Georgia's Fifth Congressional District, which encompassed metropolitan Atlanta. In 1991, Lewis became Chief Democratic Party whip and the following year he seconded the nomination of Al Gore for vice president. In 1996, Lewis was unopposed in his bid for a sixth term as congressman from Georgia.

BIBLIOGRAPHY

Lewis, John. *Walking with the Wind: A Memoir of the Movement.* 1998.
Time Magazine. December 29, 1975.
Transcribed interviews held at Civil Rights Documentation Project, Howard University, Washington D.C., and at the Martin Luther King, Jr., Center for Nonviolent Social Change, Atlanta, GA.

Stephen Tuck

Liberalism

Liberalism has been one of the most malleable concepts in American politics. Its meaning has changed dramatically since the eighteenth century, when the term came into common use. Those who consider themselves liberals, moreover, have not espoused a sharply defined agenda; on the contrary, they have promoted divergent, even clashing, policies and programs.

Liberalism began in the 1700s in France and Britain as a defense of individual liberties, which liberals believed were threatened by the power of monarchy. Drawing on the European example, Americans made liberalism—particularly its language of "inalienable rights"—the centerpiece of their revolt against the British crown. When the revolution succeeded, American liberals transferred their fear of the king to the republic's leaders. The new nation's government must be carefully limited, they said, to assure Americans the ability to exercise their rights fully.

As the nation industrialized in the nineteenth century, liberals extended their faith in limited government to the economic realm. Again drawing on the European example, they argued that the free play of market forces best assured individuals their rights and provided them with economic opportunity. Government, therefore, should play a minimal role in economic affairs, perhaps helping businesses to expand but certainly not regulating their actions. By the close of the nineteenth century, the liberal doctrine had infused almost every level of American government.

By then, however, a new generation of politically active Americans had begun to transform liberalism in the most profound way. Industrialization had extended so far, these "progressives" contended, that it threatened the health of American society. The progressives did not agree on the way in which industrialization threatened the nation. Some believed that the massive concentration of capital in a few hands gave businessmen the power to undermine individual rights and opportunity. Others feared that business power corrupted democratic institutions. Still others were concerned with the social changes industrialization had wrought. They worried, for instance, that the immigrants whom industrialization had attracted to the nation would not adjust to life in the United States, and that the working class was becoming alienated from the American political system. Whatever their understanding of the nation's problems, the progressives agreed that the government needed to spearhead the search for solutions. The progressives thus reversed a basic tenet of their predecessors' liberalism, rejecting limited government and embracing an activist state.

The progressives' vision of the activist state, however, remained circumscribed in some important respects. Most progressives believed that government policy should be set not by democratic processes but by experts, who could fashion rational solutions to specific problems. More important, they did not believe that government should wield its power to transform economic, social, and political relations in a fundamental way. State action should not challenge capitalism, they said, but rather should strengthen it by correcting its abuses. The government need not empower the nation's weakest citizens but rather should help them meet their immediate needs. Government reform should not pit economic or social groups against each other but should instead seek to integrate those on the margins of society into the mainstream.

The progressive brand of liberalism enjoyed widespread success in the first two decades of the twentieth century, as reformers on the municipal, state, and federal levels laid the groundwork for the activist state. Those efforts stalled in the immediate aftermath of WORLD WAR I, only to be revived, this time under the label of New Deal liberalism (see NEW DEAL AND DEPRESSION) during the 1930s. Led by President Franklin D. ROOSEVELT, the liberals of that era undertook a sweeping reform of American capitalism, in the process creating the nation's welfare state.

Neither the progressives nor the New Dealers built strong records in support of civil rights. To be sure, some early twentieth-century liberals were appalled by the destruction of African-American rights under JIM CROW and sought to use the government, particularly the courts, to restore those rights. These liberals were responsible for one of the signal events of civil rights history, the founding in 1909 of the NATIONAL ASSOCIATION FOR THE ADVANCEMENT OF COLORED PEOPLE (NAACP), an organization that still bears the liberals' stamp.

Most liberals, however, refused to endorse black rights. Indeed, some of the most important progressives promoted racial discrimination. President Woodrow Wilson, for instance, extended SEGREGATION throughout the federal government. Many other reformers simply chose to ignore the issue. They did so for a variety of reasons: they were convinced that it was immaterial to the economic problems they considered their primary concern; they believed racial problems to be immune to the sort of rational solutions they favored; they thought civil rights was impossible to address politically, as white Southerners would block any meaningful federal action. Franklin Roosevelt stands as the foremost example of liberal temporizing on civil rights. Anxious to maintain Southern congressional support for his economic programs, Roosevelt countenanced racial discrimination in many New Deal programs. He refused to support the most basic protection of civil rights, most notably a bill to make LYNCHING a federal offense. Also, during WORLD WAR II, he explicitly approved one of the worst violations of civil liberties in the nation's history, the internment of 120,000 Japanese Americans.

Only in the years after World War II, as liberalism underwent yet another great transformation, did liberals throw their support behind the civil rights struggle. A convergence of events triggered the change. As more and more Americans enjoyed the fruits of economic expansion in the first two and a half decades after the war, liberals became less concerned with economic affairs. At the same time, they became more aware of the costs of racial supremacy as they confronted the horrors of the German death camps. The exigencies of the COLD WAR, particularly the superpowers' competition for the loyalty of non-European nations, heightened the liberals' concern about the stain of American RACISM. Finally, African Americans' mounting civil rights activism, in both North and South, forced the issue into the center of public debate, leaving liberals no choice but to take a stand. Together, these events led liberals to replace economics with civil rights as the most pressing of their domestic concerns.

For the most part, the civil rights agenda of post–World War II liberals fit within the broad framework they had developed during the course of the twentieth century. They favored using government power to attack the specific barriers—VOTING RIGHTS restrictions, SEGREGATION of schools and other public facilities, discriminatory EMPLOYMENT practices—that prevented African Americans from securing EQUALITY before the law and enjoying equality of opportunity. The weapons they used in their attacks relied on the power of experts: investigatory panels, mediation services, voting registrars. They believed that, once the barriers were destroyed, African Americans should and would be integrated into white society.

Armed with these beliefs, liberals became powerful allies of the Southern civil rights struggle of the 1950s and early 1960s, itself committed to securing legal equality and assuring INTEGRATION. The alliance reached its apex in the mid-1960s, when liberals were instrumental in helping civil rights activists win passage of the CIVIL RIGHTS ACT OF 1964 and the VOTING RIGHTS ACT OF 1965 the legal embodiments of the liberal civil rights program.

Liberals often found it difficult to support other aspects of the multifaceted civil rights struggle of the 1950s and 1960s. Few were comfortable with demands for black empowerment, and many liberals recoiled when African Americans forcefully asserted their dissatisfaction with existing power relations. Liberal policymakers struggled mightily to address the pervasive problem of African-American poverty, particularly by strengthening the welfare state, but their efforts were hamstrung by their commitment to working within the economic order. By the second half of the 1960s, these tensions had driven a wedge between liberals and key sections of the black FREEDOM movement.

As conflict mounted, liberals struggled to adjust their program. By the late 1960s, liberal politicians had become much more open to African-American political participation within their ranks. Many liberals had concluded that it was not enough to assure African Americans equality of opportunity; public policy should seek to provide black Americans "equality of outcome" with white Americans, particularly in economics. They had endorsed aggressive programs, such as AFFIRMATIVE ACTION, that they hoped could achieve that result.

These changes reshaped liberalism once again, making it a movement that African Americans themselves helped to define by their participation and their votes. This transformation carried a heavy political price. Liberals continued to define national policy on racial matters throughout the 1970s. From the late 1960s on, however, conservative politicians used racial appeals to undermine white support for liberalism (see CONSERVATISM; George WALLACE). That proved to be a powerful tactic, particularly in combination with other appeals: by the 1980s, liberalism had been overwhelmed by the conservative tide. That tide has become so powerful in recent years that it has swept away some of the most vital liberal policies, most notably the welfare state as liberals had defined it.

Liberals now struggle to find a way to regain a voice in public affairs. Some reformers call for a return to the liberalism of the New Deal era by putting a premium on economic issues and avoiding divisive racial issues. Others argue that liberalism needs to sustain, even expand, the commitments it made to the African-American cause. The outcome of these debates is not clear. Nor is it clear that no matter what form it takes, liberalism can regain the power it formerly held to shape the national agenda.

BIBLIOGRAPHY

Edsall, Thomas Byrne, and Mary D. Edsall. *Chain Reaction: The Impact of Race, Rights, and Taxes on American Politics.* 1991.

Fine, Sidney. *Laissez-Faire and the General Welfare State: A Study of Conflict in American Thought, 1865–1901.* 1956.

Gerstle, Gary. "The Protean Character of American Liberalism." *American Historical Review* 99 (1994): 1043–1073.

Graham, Hugh Davis. *The Civil Rights Era: Origins and Development of National Policy, 1960–1972.* 1990.

Martin, John Frederick. *Civil Rights and the Crisis of Liberalism: The Democratic Party, 1945–1976.* 1979.

Matusow, Alan. *The Unraveling of America: A History of Liberalism in the 1960s.* 1984.

Myrdal, Gunnar. *An American Dilemma: The Negro Problem and Modern Democracy*. 1944.

Patterson, James T. *Grand Expectations: The United States, 1945–1974*. 1996.

Schlesinger, Arthur, Jr. *The Vital Center: The Politics of Freedom*. 1949.

Sitkoff, Harvard. *A New Deal for Blacks: The Emergence of Civil Rights as a National Issue*. 1978.

Sitkoff, Harvard. *The Struggle for Black Equality, 1945–1992*. 1993.

Sleeper, Jim. *Liberal Racism: How Fixating on Race Subverts the American Dream*. 1997.

Stern, Marc. *Calculating Visions: Kennedy, Johnson, and Civil Rights*. 1992.

Sullivan, Patricia. *Days of Hope: Race and Democracy in the New Deal Era*. 1996.

Kevin Boyle

Liberty Party

The Liberty Party was the first American political organization to actively oppose slavery through electoral politics. The party was formed in 1839 and conducted vigorous presidential campaigns in 1840 and 1844. The party never gained the support of the followers of the nation's best-known abolitionist, William Lloyd Garrison, because the Garrisonians refused to participate in elections. Moreover, as a single-issue party, the Liberty Party failed to attract mainstream citizens who opposed slavery but were also concerned about other political and economic issues. The party laid the groundwork for future successful antislavery political movements, however.

In 1840 the Liberty Party ran James Gillespie Birney, a former slaveowner turned abolitionist, for president. The party called for the abolition of slavery in all federal territories and the District of Columbia and a complete ban on the interstate slave trade. Such a platform was a radical break with American presidential politics. Birney won only about seven thousand votes in 1840.

In 1844 Birney won about 62,000 votes, over 2 percent of all votes cast. The party received votes in four-fifths of the counties in the North, suggesting at least the breadth of antislavery political support. Birney won some sixteen thousand votes in New York State. James K. Polk, who won the election, carried New York by only five thousand votes. Had most of the Liberty Party votes gone to Henry Clay, the Whig candidate, Clay would have carried New York, and with it the election. Had all Liberty voters, nationwide, supported Clay, he would have surpassed Polk in the national popular vote. There is no reason to believe, however, that the antislavery Liberty Party voters would have supported the slaveholder Clay over the slaveholder

Polk. It is just as likely they would have sat out the election.

In 1848, as a result of the Mexican War, the more broad-based Free Soil Party emerged, with former president Martin Van Buren as its candidate. Most Liberty Party activists became Free-Soilers in 1848, and in 1854 helped organize the radical wing of the new Republican Party.

BIBLIOGRAPHY

Sewell, Richard H. *Ballots for Freedom: Antislavery Politics in the United States, 1837–1860*. 1976.

Smith, Theodore Clarke. *The Liberty and Free Soil Parties in the Northwest*. 1897.

Steward, James B. *Holy Warriors*. 1976.

Paul Finkelman

Literature and Civil Rights

American writers have long been engaged in the struggle to combat social inequality and injustice. At certain times in U.S. history, this engagement has been more pronounced as literary artists have positioned themselves and their work on the front line of civil rights activism. From the abolitionist movement of the mid-nineteenth century to the civil rights movement of the mid-twentieth, writers have left us a rich legacy of socially conscious and politically charged narratives that have profoundly changed the way we view the promises of American life.

Although the first great commingling of literature and civil rights began with the abolitionist movement, early American writers were acutely aware of other social-justice issues. Poet Philip Freneau's *The British Prison-Ship* (1781) is perhaps the earliest example, and popular writers as temperamentally diverse as James Fenimore Cooper and Catharine Maria Sedgwick used their fiction to plead for social change. Later writers, such as Rebecca Harding Davis (*Life in the Iron Mills*, 1861) and William Dean Howells (*A Hazard of New Fortunes*, 1890), prefigured the concerns that would be expressed more fully—and more radically—in the socialist fiction of the next century. But it was with the rise of abolitionism that nineteenth-century American literature voiced its most impassioned concern for social justice. The first great American literary genre, the slave narrative, came out of this movement, and it is difficult to imagine our literature without such biographical works as Frederick DOUGLASS's *Narrative* (1845) or Harriet Jacobs's *Incidents in the Life of a Slave Girl* (1861). Fiction was also enriched by this movement; from it came the century's most popular and influential novel, Harriet Beecher Stowe's *Uncle Tom's Cabin* (1852), as well as the first African-American novel, William Wells Brown's *Clotel* (1853). Consider too that the movement also attracted the energies of Ralph Waldo Emerson, Herman Melville, Henry David Thoreau, Walt Whitman, and John Greenleaf Whittier, and the effect of the abolitionist cause on American literature cannot be overestimated.

The early twentieth century saw the next important confluence of literature and civil rights. Here, the issues had less to do with race than with economics. Frank Norris (*The Octopus*, 1901), Upton Sinclair (*The Jungle*, 1906) and socialist Jack London (*The Iron Heel*, 1908) fired the first shots at "robber baron" capitalism. Sinclair's and London's novels were rather flatly polemical. Eventually, more literally accomplished writers crafted works that were politically radical, socially sensitive, and aesthetically complex. Jean Toomer's *Cane* (1923), Countee Cullen's poem "The Black Christ" (1929), Erskine Caldwell's *God's Little Acre* (1933), Clifford Odets's play *Waiting for Lefty* (1935), Zora Neale Hurston's *Their Eyes Were Watching God* (1937), John Steinbeck's *The Grapes of Wrath* (1939), and Richard Wright's *Native Son* (1940) are all significant artistic contributions to American literature. Furthermore, as a result of their activist politics, many of these radical writers also placed themselves and their work at the service of diverse civil rights causes: freedom for political radicals Nicola Sacco and Bartolomeo Vanzetti, acquittal for the Scottsboro boys

Author Zora Neale Hurston. (Library of Congress)

(see SCOTTSBORO CASE), justice for the coal miners in Harlan County, Kentucky, and so on.

The civil liberties issues that arose amidst the red scare of the post–World War II era (see MCCARTHY-ISM; CENSORSHIP; COLD WAR) gave rise to such searchingly symbolic works as Arthur Miller's play *The Crucible* (1953), which used the witchhunts of the New England past as a symbolic commentary on contemporary events, or Ray Bradbury's *Fahrenheit 451* (1953) which suggested a similarly symbolic dystopian near-future in which all books are burned as expressions of subversive individuality, and E. L. Doctorow's *The Book of Daniel* (1971), which looked retrospectively at the life and times of the Rosenberg family, executed for treason in the early 1950s. The Vietnam War in turn has inspired such works as Norman Mailer's *The Armies of the Night* (1968) and *Miami and the Siege of Chicago* (1969) and many volumes or poetry by the likes of Robert Bly, Robert Duncan, and others.

But neither the Cold War/red scare nor the Vietnam disaster generated the kind of sustained, widespread artistic response that flourished in anticipation of, in response to, or in the wake of the civil rights movement (1954–1968). In many ways, this literature had deep roots. In 1901, black American author Charles Chesnutt fashioned a moving protest novel, *The Marrow of Tradition*, inspired by the 1898 Wilmington, North Carolina, race riots, and the repeated violation of African-Americans' civil rights by lynch mobs (see LYNCHINGS) inspired such diverse writers as Theodore Dreiser ("Nigger Jeff," 1901), Claude McKay ("If We Must Die," 1919), William Faulkner ("Dry September," 1931), Langston HUGHES's "Christ in Alabama" (1931, a poem inspired by the aforementioned Scottsboro case), and Lillian SMITH (*Strange Fruit*, 1944), among many others.

At the brink of the full flourishing of the modern civil rights movement, we find such important works as William Faulkner's *Intruder in the Dust* (1948) or Ralph Ellison's *The Invisible Man* (1952). When the movement began in earnest, ca. 1954 or thereabout, the artistic response was forceful. William Melvin Kelley (*A Different Drummer*, 1959), poet Gwendolyn Brooks ("The Chicago Defender Sends a Man to Little Rock," 1960), James BALDWIN (essays and *Blues for Mister Charlie*, 1964), Alex Haley (*The Autobiography of Malcolm X*, 1965), John O. Killens (*'Sippi*, 1967), poet Nikki Giovanni (*Black Feeling/Black Talk*, 1968), and Margaret WALKER (*Prophets for a New Day*, 1970) all produced artistically and socially significant work. Perhaps more surprisingly, many white Southerners wrote sympathetically about the black freedom struggle. Some works, such as Jesse Hill Ford's Pulitzer prize–winning *Liberation of Lord Byron Jones* (1964), have lost their staying power, but others, such as Elizabeth

Novelist Ralph Ellison in the New York offices of his publisher in 1964. (AP/Wide World Photos)

Spencer's *Voice at the Back Door* (1956), Lettie Rogers's *Birthright* (1957), and Eudora Welty's short-story masterpiece "Where Is This Voice Coming From?" (1964), remain minor classics of Southern fiction. Curiously, the two most influential works of the period—Lorraine HANSBERRY's *Raisin in the Sun* (1959) and Harper Lee's *To Kill a Mockingbird* (1960)—raise civil rights issues but do so by focusing on events occurring before the movement. However, to read these narratives as independent of their historical moment is to underappreciate their full import and impact.

In the end, the modern civil rights movement never produced a work of fiction comparable in influence or social impact to *Uncle Tom's Cabin* or *The Jungle.* Nonetheless, works such as Alice Walker's *Meridian* (1976), Ernest Gaines's *In My Father's House* (1978), Shelby Foote's *September, September* (1977), Octavia Butler's "Patternist" science fiction tetralogy (1977–1984) Lewis Nordan's *Wolf Whistle* (1993), Julius Lester's *All Our Wounds Forgiven* (1994), and John Grisham's *The*

Chamber (1994) prove that the movement remains fertile ground for the American literary imagination. While novelists, poets, and playwrights will continue to till this soil well into the twenty-first century, there will no doubt arise a next great effort to secure rights for the (perhaps newly) disenfranchised.

BIBLIOGRAPHY

Aaron, Daniel. *Writers on the Left: Episodes in American Literary Communism.* 1961.
Elliott, Emory, ed. *The Columbia Literary History of the United States.* 1988.
Gates, Henry Louis, Jr., and Nellie Y. McKay, eds. *Norton Anthology of African American Literature.* 1997.
Karl, Frederick R. *American Fictions, 1940–1980.* 1983.
Watkins, Floyd C. *The Death of Art: Black and White in the Recent Southern Novel.* 1970.

Christopher Metress

Little, Malcolm

See Malcolm X.

Little Rock Nine

Nine black teenagers broke the color line at a public high school in Little Rock, ARKANSAS, in September 1957. The youths had voluntarily transferred to the formerly all-white Central High as part of a city plan to comply with a 1955 Supreme Court ruling that school boards make a "prompt and reasonable start" to desegregate "with all deliberate speed." Little Rock then widely appeared poised to lead Southern communities in peacefully integrating public education. Instead the Little Rock Nine, as the media dubbed the black students, were repeatedly harassed by segregationists incited by Arkansas Governor Orval E. FAUBUS.

After failing to get a federal court to delay school integration, ostensibly to avoid racial violence, Governor Faubus ordered the Arkansas National Guard to bar black students from Central High. On September 4, 1957, the state NATIONAL ASSOCIATION FOR THE ADVANCEMENT OF COLORED PEOPLE (NAACP) president, Daisy BATES, shepherded eight black students to the school, but they were turned away by guardsmen at bayonet point. The ninth student, fifteen-year-old Elizabeth Eckford, was jeered, cursed, and threatened by a white mob, and narrowly escaped injury. Ten days later President Dwight D. EISENHOWER hosted Faubus at his summer home in Rhode Island, urging the governor to end his obstruction of court orders. But even after a federal judge secured the withdrawal of Arkansas guardsmen and local police escorted the black students to school, Faubus remained defiant.

Eight of the nine students who were the first to attend a previously all-white high school in Little Rock, Arkansas. (CORBIS/Bettmann)

On September 23 the Little Rock Nine were spirited into Central High but then evacuated from the school by police due to the presence of several thousand white vigilantes. On September 24, in response to an urgent plea from the mayor of Little Rock, President Eisenhower reluctantly federalized the Arkansas National Guard and dispatched Army troops to protect the students, explaining on national television, "Mob rule cannot be allowed to override the decisions of our courts." The following morning soldiers from the 101st Airborne Division accompanied the Little Rock Nine into Central High.

Army troops stayed for over two months to curb threats of mob violence at Central High, and federalized Guard units remained until the school year ended in May 1958. The black students nonetheless suffered persistent harassment by an organized minority inside and outside the school. One of the Little Rock Nine, Minniejean Brown, lost her temper after repeated verbal and physical provocations and was expelled in February 1958 for exchanging racial epithets with a white girl (who remained a student in good standing). During the following school year, 1958–1959, the Little Rock Nine received no formal education because the city closed its schools rather than face down segregationist threats. Only in August 1959, after the Supreme

Court outlawed such "evasive schemes," did the public high schools reopen on an integrated basis.

The prolonged ordeal of the black students brought limited tangible gains for the civil rights movement. President Eisenhower never endorsed the Supreme Court's call for school desegregation, while in Arkansas, Governor Faubus traded on his segregationist laurels to win reelection overwhelmingly in 1958 and in four subsequent campaigns. By 1960 just 6.4 percent of Southern black school children (and 0.2 percent of those in the Deep South) attended classes with whites. Still, the Little Rock Nine became internationally renowned symbols of black courage in seeking racial justice. Ernest Green, the first black student to graduate from Central High, in May 1958, recalled savoring the event as a landmark for black rights, saying, "I knew that once I . . . received that diploma, I had cracked the wall."

BIBLIOGRAPHY

Ashmore, Harry S. *Hearts and Minds: The Anatomy of Racism from Roosevelt to Reagan.* 1982.
Bates, Daisy. *The Long Shadow of Little Rock: A Memoir.* 1962.
Beals, Melba Pattillo. *Warriors Don't Cry.* 1994.
Freyer, Tony. *The Little Rock Crisis: A Constitutional Interpretation.* 1984.

Williams, Juan. *Eyes on the Prize: America's Civil Rights Years, 1954–1965.* 1987.

Robert Weisbrot

Liuzzo, Viola Fauver Gregg

(1925–1965), civil rights activist and martyr.

A homemaker from Detroit, Viola Liuzzo was murdered by members of the KU KLUX KLAN after participating in the third Selma-to-Montgomery March.

Born in California, Pennsylvania, Viola Fauver Gregg was the daughter of a disabled miner and a teacher. The family moved to Tennessee and Georgia during the Great Depression before Viola's mother found factory work in Detroit during World War II. Viola had two unsuccessful marriages before she married Teamsters Union local official Anthony James Liuzzo in 1950. The Liuzzos had three children plus two others from Viola's second marriage.

A high school dropout, Viola Liuzzo renewed her education at Detroit's Carnegie Institute and then at Wayne State University in 1962, where she joined the student movement for civil rights. Liuzzo decided to leave Detroit to join the Selma-to-Montgomery March of March 21–22, 1965, after which she volunteered to drive marchers back to Selma. On the night of March 25, passing Ku Klux Klansmen fatally shot Liuzzo beside her African-American passenger. President Lyndon JOHNSON announced her death on national television, calling for federal voting rights legislation, which he signed August 6. William Eaton, Collie LeRoy Wilkins, and Eugene Thomas were acquitted of murder but were convicted of federal civil rights violations that December, each earning ten-year prison sentences.

In 1979, Liuzzo's children unsuccessfully sued the federal government for negligence, claiming that the FEDERAL BUREAU OF INVESTIGATION (FBI) knew of planned violence thanks to informant Gary Thomas Rowe, who accompanied the three convicted Klansmen when the murder occurred.

BIBLIOGRAPHY

Mendelsohn, Jack. *The Martyrs: Sixteen Who Gave Their Lives for Racial Justice.* 1966.

Siegel, Beatrice. *Murder on the Highway: The Viola Liuzzo Story.* 1993.

Wesley Brian Borucki

Lodge Election Bill

See Federal Election Bill of 1890.

Lopez Tijerina, Reies

See Tijerina, Reies Lopez

Lorde, Audre

(1934–1992), poet.

Audre Geraldine Lorde was born in Harlem, New York City, on February 18, 1934, of middle-class immigrant parents from Grenada. She earned a bachelor's degree in library science from Hunter College in 1959 and a master's from Columbia University in 1961, and afterward worked as a librarian in New York City.

A published poet even before her graduation from Hunter High School, in 1968 Lorde won a National Endowment for the Arts grant as a poet-in-residence at Tougaloo College, in Mississippi. Her first book of poetry, *The First Cities* (1968), introduced her nationally as a noteworthy black female poet. The collection was praised for its freshness and "quiet" introspection. *Cables to Rage* (1970), her second book of poems, however, introduced readers to her harsh social criticism, and in 1972 she received a Creative Artists Public Service grant.

In *From a Land Where Other People Live* (1973), nominated for the National Book Award, Lorde became an advocate for Third World peoples, linking their oppression to those of minority groups in U.S. cities, such as New York and Detroit. For her, art involved truth-telling and bearing witness, speaking "the truth as I see it," she said. She condemned racism, sexism, homophobia, and other forms of oppression, and was often considered antiestablishment because of her vehement criticism of established society.

Audre Lorde reading from her work. (© Marilyn Humphries/Impact Visuals/PNI)

Lorde saw herself as a composite of multiple identities, the "different 'people' within my identity." She referred to herself as a "Black, Woman, and Poet" or a "Black lesbian feminist mother of two." Later, her exploration of these multiple identities had a tremendous impact on feminist discourse on race, gender, sexuality, and nationalism. Although she is more frequently associated with feminism, Audre Lorde was also a civil rights activist who fought for the dignity of black people and expressed anguish over the loss of that dignity. Her works were informed by both the collective experiences of black people and her own personal experiences. Black racial and cultural heritages, including African and West Indian cultures and histories, play central roles in her works. In *Black Unicorn* (1978), she returned to her African heritage, invoking Seboulisa, a mythic goddess, as a source of cultural, sexual, and spiritual strength and renewal. Her book *The Cancer Journals* (1980) traces her personal struggle with cancer, whereas *Zami: A New Spelling of my Name* (1984), her "biomythography," explores a young teenage girl's struggle with her latent homosexuality and growing up.

By her death at fifty-eight in 1992, Audre Lorde had published a large body of work in poetry, fiction, lectures and speeches, and critical essays. She had taught at the John Jay College of Criminal Justice, as well as Lehman and Hunter colleges, and helped found Kitchen Table: Women of Color Press (1982), devoted to publishing works by ethnic women. She was also named the Poet Laureate of the State of New York in 1991, a year before her death. Some works on Lorde include Mari Evans's *Black Women Writers, 1950–1980* (1984) and Claudia Tate's *Black Women Writers at Work* (1988).

BIBLIOGRAPHY

Annas, Pamela. "A Poetry of Survival: Unnaming and Renaming in the Poetry of Audre Lorde, Pat Parker, Sylvia Plath, and Adrienne Rich." *Colby Library Quarterly* 18 (1992).
Evans, Mari. *Black Women Writers, 1950–1980.* 1984.
Lorde, Audre. *The Cancer Journals.* 1980.
Lorde, Audre. *Zami: A New Spelling of My Name.* 1984.
Tate, Claudia. *Black Women Writers at Work.* 1988.

Maureen N. Eke

Louisiana

Since their arrival as slaves in Louisiana in 1709, people of African descent have pushed for justice and humane treatment. Indeed, the struggle for freedom occurred on the African continent and in the holds of slave ships. Resistance and opportunities to seek freedom involved escape or suicide. Gwendolyn Midlo Hall's *African in Colonial Louisiana: The Development of Afro-Creole Culture in the Eighteenth Century* (1992) tells of the French Governor, Etienne de Perier, opposing Indian slavery to stop Indian/black alliances. Africans were the most economically salutary commodity brought to the struggling French and subsequently Spanish colony of Louisiana. Their technologies of rice production, processing of indigo, farming, and metal working were more advanced than those of European settlers and planters.

Since no legal avenues for civil or human rights were available to those enslaved in colonial Louisiana, they resisted by forming alliances with Indians; this practice was especially prevalent among Africans of the Bambara ethnic group. It was during the late 1720s, when large numbers of Bambaras were loaded aboard slave ships, that their tradition of resistance, the *fadenya* principle, validated above all in troubled times, was forged. They revolted at sea and this spirit of resistance continued after their arrival in Louisiana. The group maintained an organized language community, and formed alliances with the Indian nations who were in revolt against their French captives, conspiring to take charge of the colony. Also, escape took many forms: maroon societies escaped and ran away to Havana, up the Mississippi River, to Texas, or to military outposts on the Red River. Physical attacks on masters represented another form of resistance. Even after Louisiana became a Spanish colony in 1766 (though remaining French in culture), these various forms of rebellion continued.

Participation in the military offered an avenue to freedom. Blacks sometimes acquired their freedom through acts of bravery in the war against Indians under the French. According to Roland C. McConnell in *Negro Troops of Antebellum Louisiana: A History of the Battalion of Free Men of Color* (1968), military service offered opportunities for those enslaved and those already free. Blacks were organized into a company with their own officers during the second Chickasaw war, and there was an assurance that the government depended upon them for its defense. To African Americans, this service would continue to lay the foundation for a further claim to full equality, especially since they had helped recuse Louisiana from destruction by Natchez and Chickasaw Indians, formidable enemies. This military service would continue under the Spanish and early American leadership in Louisiana. Eighty free persons of color accompanied Don Bernardo de Galvez in 1779 in support of his goal of driving the British from the Gulf of Mexico and the banks of the

Mississippi during the American Revolution. These actions furthered blacks' claims for civil rights.

Although there was no decrease in the desire of African Americans to participate in the military as a way to further their claims to rights, there was a marked decline in the enthusiastic reception for this desire under the American regime. Historian Roland McConnell argues that African Americans' struggle for American recognition of their rights was difficult because of the constant fear of slave revolt or of slaves uniting with free people of color. Despite this fear, blacks were called upon to serve during the War of 1812 by General Andrew Jackson and saw duty in the Battle of New Orleans in 1815. Throughout the antebellum period and during the Civil War, the legacy of military service would provide a foundation for the civil rights struggle. After a short-lived association between free blacks and the Confederate cause, a certain fighting spirit would be enlisted full-fledged in support of the Union war efforts. The courage of the native guard regiments (1st and 3rd) at Port Hudson would begin a new chapter in the assessment of capabilities of black soldiers. After this engagement, black novelist and intellectual William Wells Brown, in *The Black Man: His Antecedents, His Genius and His Achievements*, (1863) observed that no race hater would henceforth withhold black rights on the argument that blacks would not fight. While between 180,000 and 200,000 blacks served nationwide in the Union Army, Louisiana provided approximately 24,000 troops, the largest number enlisted by any state.

After emancipation, the record of African-American military service would provide a steppingstone to political participation and a demand for total civil rights during the RECONSTRUCTION era. As part of presidential Reconstruction, formulated by Abraham Lincoln, there was an immediate call for voting rights for educated and propertied free blacks. Despite this appeal, those who wrote the state constitution of 1864 rejected such a request. U.S. congressional leaders, sometimes called Radicals (see RADICAL REPUBLICANS), gained a majority in Congress following the 1866 elections, and the Reconstruction plans of President Andrew Johnson came under attack—especially the amnesty for confederates proposed by Johnson himself. Congressional leaders moved to impeach the president (a strategy that failed), but their program, labelled congressional Reconstruction, was enacted. The mainstay of this program was the Reconstruction Acts of 1867, calling for military districts, registration of blacks as voters, and new state constitutions.

The Louisiana Constitutional Convention was held from November 1867 to March 1868. The ninety-eight delegates, evenly divided into forty-nine blacks and forty-nine whites, held a majority who supported Article 13 (of the new constitution) as proposed by one of the leading black delegates, P. B. S. Pinchback. The article called for integration within public conveyances and public accommodations. Other provisions of the Louisiana constitution urged the adoption of a Bill of Rights, the first constitution in the states's history to obtain laws of this kind, and state-supported integrated public education. Subsequently, the FOURTEENTH and FIFTEENTH AMENDMENTS would bring national recognition of citizenship and voting privileges. After ratification of the constitution by voters, state officials were elected.

Throughout Reconstruction in Louisiana, blacks comprised roughly one-third of the state legislature, despite the fact that they were a slight majority in the population. This combined membership of black and white leaders was solidly in back of the changing of the status quo in Louisiana, and black legislators were especially active in this regard. Their civil rights efforts were centered around strengthening Article 13. One provision of the Act of 1869 contained an exemplary clause, whereby violators of Article 13 could be forced to forfeit their business licenses as well as be subject to monetary fines. Other efforts called for innkeepers and managers of places of public amusement to offer equal accommodations.

During the 1870s Louisiana's civil rights laws were some of the most progressive and far-reaching in the entire South. They had secured the rights of blacks to first-class accommodations on public conveyances, in theaters, and taverns. The black press, especially the *New Orleans Tribune*, supported these civil rights activities without reservation. In urban areas blacks tested some of the laws, although in rural areas the daily toil of survival consumed most of the energies of potential testers. The violent paramilitary group, the KU KLUX KLAN, opposed these laws and those testing them.

A small number of financially capable black men and women tested state and federal accommodation laws. Chief among them were Josephine Dubuclet Decuir and Homer Plessy. Their efforts reached the U.S. SUPREME COURT. In the case known as *Hall v. Decuir*, Josephine Decuir tested the public accommodation provision of a state civil rights law. A descendent of free people of color and sister of Antoine Dubuclet, the highly competent state treasurer during Reconstruction, Decuir sought her rightful place for accommodation as a lady on a first-class coach and was not denied. In 1875, Decuir was aboard a Mississippi steamboat en route from New Orleans to Vicksburg, Mississippi, and was told she would need to comply with the company policy of dual accommodations. Her destination was Hermitage, a landing on the Louisiana bank of the Mississippi. She had intended to test the

A Norman Rockwell painting showing six-year-old Ruby Bridges being escorted to school. Bridges was the first African-American student to attend the William Frantz Elementary School in New Orleans in 1960. (Reproduced by Permission of the Norman Rockwell Family Trust/Photo courtesy of The Norman Rockwell Museum at Stockbridge)

validity of an 1869 Louisiana statute that prohibited segregation in interstate commerce. The passenger was actually making an intrastate trip. Although the Louisiana State Supreme Court upheld the District Court's favorable ruling awarding Decuir one thousand dollars, the U.S. Supreme Court in an 1878 decision (*Hall v. Decuir*) invalidated the state court ruling as placing an undue burden on interstate commerce in prohibiting segregation in interstate commerce.

The case involving Homer Plessy would have significance on civil rights far beyond the boundaries of the state and would shape aspects of race relations for generations. A progressive segment of the African-American community of New Orleans organized finances and tested a Louisiana statute, passed in 1890, providing for "all railway companies carrying passengers in their separate but equal accommodations for the white and colored races. . . . " Called the Citizens' Committee to Test the Constitutionality of the Separate Car Law, men and women of means, descendants of free blacks, questioned this law. Their publication, the *New Orleans Crusader*, was inaugurated and a white Northern lawyer, Albion W. Tourgee, was hired. Plessy, who was actually seven-eighths Caucasian and one-eighth black, purchased a ticket to travel between two cities in Louisiana. Entering the coach reserved for whites, he was ordered by the conductor to sit in the colored section, and upon his refusal was arrested, and

charged with violating the statute. The Supreme Court rendered a decision known as PLESSY V. FERGUSON in 1896, confirming "separate but equal." The only dissenter was Justice Louis Harlan who argued that the Constitution was "color blind." Shortly after this decision there appeared the segregationist provision in the new Louisiana Constitution of 1898, called the "grandfather clause," that basically eliminated the effects of the Fourteenth and Fifteenth Amendments. These events would close the door on civil rights gains of the Reconstruction era.

Blacks continued to seek democracy and civil rights. The membership of Louisiana blacks in chapters of Marcus Garvey's UNIVERSAL NEGRO IMPROVEMENT ORGANIZATION (UNIA) was the highest in the nation. The NATIONAL ASSOCIATION FOR THE ADVANCEMENT OF COLORED PEOPLE (NAACP), National Urban League, and similar organizations had a high rate of Louisiana representation. The New Orleans branch of the NAACP was founded in 1915 and immediately provided a vehicle for opposing racial discrimination. The NAACP had many notable successes during the early years. In 1930, lawyers hired by the NAACP assisted in the prosecution of Charles Guerard, a white man who shot and killed a fourteen-year-old black girl, Mattie McCray, who had resisted his sexual advances. At the trial, an all-white jury found Guerard guilty. In *Race and Democracy: The Civil Rights*

Struggle in Louisiana, 1915–1972 (1995), Adam Fairclough writes that this was probably the first time that a white person had been sentenced to death for the murder of a black person. Throughout the 1920s and 1930s blacks pushed hard for voting privileges and educational opportunities. Voting leagues, such as the Seventh Ward Civic League, the Eighth Ward Civic League, as well as the citywide Federation of Civic Leagues were prominent in New Orleans. This pattern would gradually become a factor in other areas of the state.

Violence against blacks was a common occurrence in Louisiana and the South throughout the 1930s and 1940s. Dr. A. C. Terrence was the lone black registered voter in Opelousas. When other blacks tried to register they were beaten. Adam Fairclough's *Race and Democracy* tells of the sheriff of Beinville Parish leading a mob to lynch Nelson Cash after taking him from the jail; three of the four lynchings in 1933 involved the complicity of law officials. These lynchings occurred in Opelousas (Pointée Coupée) and Assumption Parishes. The following year Jerome Wilson was lynched in Washington Parish, and in 1938 W. C. Williams, a nineteen-year-old black youth, was lynched near Ruston, Louisiana. (See LYNCHING.) These brutal activities were catalysts for the growth of the NAACP. Even during the waning years of the Great Depression, branches were established in Jennings, Plaquemine, and Lake Charles, while the reorganization of the NAACP revived dormant branches in Shreveport and Lake Providence. By 1940, Baton Rouge, the capital city, had a branch of the NAACP with eight hundred members. The survival of these branches was due to dedicated professional members, such as insurance agent Benjamin Stanley in Baton Rouge and Dr. Rivers Frederick of New Orleans. Many teachers held clandestine membership.

The man who argued most of the civil rights cases in Louisiana for the NAACP was Alexander Pierre Turead. Known as "Mr. Civil Rights," he joined the organization in 1922. A close ally of Thurgood MARSHALL, he would argue cases centered on pay equalization for teachers (the McKelpin case) and the integration of buses, parks, and public buildings. He represented the first Louisiana students to be arrested in the sit-in movement of 1960. Others instrumental in the NAACP's litigations were David E. Byrd, J. K. Haynes, and Arthur J. Chapital. Organizations participating in the civil rights struggle included the Prince Hall Masons, black newspapers, college students and faculty, the Louisiana Civil Rights Congress led by Dr. Oakley Johnson, and some Catholic Church leaders. The 1950s saw black demand for dignity and opportunity throughout Louisiana and the South. In 1951 parents and children in Alexandria picketed the parish courthouse in opposition to School Board-sanctioned pol-

icy of delaying schools' opening until cotton picking was completed. In Lafayette in 1953 black children boycotted a newly opened high school because facilities failed to measure up to those of the white high school. In June 1953, the Baton Rouge Bus boycott, which would be the precursor for the 1957 MONTGOMERY BUS BOYCOTT in Alabama, provided concessions to black bus riders. Although they achieved only half a loaf, the black community had experienced cooperation and unity.

The 1960s witnessed the ascendency of college students as the most vital players in the civil rights movement nationwide and particularly in Louisiana. Students at Southern University and Agricultural and Mechanical College questioned segregation and restriction on voting rights in a major way during 1960–1962. Beginning in early March 1960, students sought a more proactive and activist university in their drive for "equal rights." By late March seven university students were arrested after sitting at the lunch counter of the Kress Store in Baton Rouge, and were taken into custody by police authorities. The following day saw "wildcat" efforts at another store in Baton Rouge and at the Greyhound bus station. Boycotting of classes and a march to the state capitol of over 1500 students forced university president Felton G. Clark to act. Facing his most severe challenge as president, he would play the role of Abraham Lincoln in the Civil War crisis and seek to "preserve the Union"—Southern University—even if it meant expelling the students in question to satisfy the all-white state Board of Education, according to Louis Lomax's *The Negro Revolt* (1962). Another series of "antisegregation protests" came in December and January 1961–1962, and witnessed approximately 1500 students participating in an orderly demonstration downtown. Eight students were expelled. Civil rights organizations such as the CONGRESS OF RACIAL EQUALITY as (CORE) and the NAACP were actively advising students and others throughout the state. In New Orleans, Plaquemine, Clinton, and Bogulusa, there were similar protests. Ku Klux Klan membership increased.

Two events of the 1960s civil rights movement activities commanded international attention—the New Orleans school crisis of 1960–1961 and the Bogulusa movement. New Orleans saw the federal government chaperon and protect the entry of Ruby Bridges into a New Orleans elementary school. In Bogulusa, Governor John J. McKeithen and the state's leading businessmen confronted implications of the CIVIL RIGHTS ACT OF 1964. In the case of *Hicks v. Knight*, attorney Nils Douglas filed suit to compel police to protect black demonstrators instead of harassing them. The U.S. Justice Department intervened to seek a judgment of criminal and civil contempt against local police officials. Other suits sought integration of Bogulusa restaurants and injunctions against the Klan and some of its members. Violence and unrest continued in Bogulusa but the Civil Rights Act of 1964 had given the federal government the necessary tool to intervene, protect demonstrators, and prevent violence. The protest march from Bogulusa to Baton Rouge in 1967 was conducted without major violence or death and probably represented the culmination of a decade-long struggle against fear.

After women and blacks gained political and social rights, the decades of the 1970s, 1980s and 1990s witnessed a quest for economic rights and gains. This struggle was not without challenges, as illustrated by the Weber case of 1987. The case involved a white worker (Weber) seeking to obtain a Baake-inspired ruling, which had seriously challenged affirmative actions in higher education. (See AFFIRMATIVE ACTION.) Weber brought suit against the employment practices of the Kaiser Aluminum and Chemical Company plant in Geismar, in part designed to provide opportunities for blacks. The U.S. Supreme Court upheld the right of an employer to promote blacks to higher positions to achieve affirmative action goals even if that meant bypassing white candidates with greater seniority. (See BAAKE, REGENTS OF THE UNIVERSITY OF CALIFORNIA V.)

BIBLIOGRAPHY

Blassingame, John W. *Black New Orleans, 1860–1880.* 1973.
Blaustein, Albert, and Sangrando, eds. *Civil Rights and Black America: A Documentary History.* 1968.
Farmer, James. *Lay Bare the Heart: An Autobiography of the Civil Rights Movement.* 1985.
Fischer, Roger A. *The Segregation Struggle in Louisiana, 1862–1877.* 1974.
Franklin, John Hope, and Alfred A. Moss, Jr. *From Slavery to Freedom: A History of African Americans.* 1998.
Jemison, Theodore J., Jr. *The T. J. Jemison Story.* 1994.
Logan, Rayford W. *The Betrayal of the Negro: From Rutherford B. Hayes to Woodrow Wilson.* 1965.
Ross, Michael A. "Justice Miller's Reconstruction: *The Slaughter-House Cases,* Health Codes and Civil Rights in New Orleans, 1861–1873." *The Journal of Southern History* 64 (1998): 649–677.
Taylor, Joe Gray. *Louisiana Reconstructed, 1863–1877.* 1974.
Vincent, Charles. *Black Legislators in Louisiana During Reconstruction.* 1976.
Vincent, Charles. *A Centennial History of Southern University and A & M College, 1880–1980.* 1981.

Charles Vincent

Loving v. Virginia (1967)

The U.S. Supreme Court decision in *Loving v. Virginia* overturned state laws forbidding interracial marriage. Such antimiscegenation laws were key tools in ensuring the subordination of people of color. At various times thirty-seven states had laws banning miscegenation. All thirty-seven forbade marriage between European Americans and African Americans; fifteen prohibited other racial combinations, usually involving whites and Asians.

Richard Loving and Mildred Jeter were residents of Central Point, an insular district in rural Virginia where nearly everyone was about the same color and black and white had quietly mixed for generations. Neither family nor community objected to the match, so they went off to Washington, D.C., where interracial marriage was legal, to be wed. On returning from their honeymoon, they were rousted out of bed by an irate sheriff, arrested, tried, and sentenced to a year in prison. The angry judge suspended their sentences on the condition that they stay out of Virginia for the next twenty-five years. The Lovings appealed the decision, and after nine years won the right to live in Virginia as husband and wife.

There was a modest increase in the rate of black-white intermarriage, and larger percentage increases in the rates for Asian-white and some other combinations, beginning in the 1960s and continuing through the 1990s. The *Loving* decision does not seem to have been the cause of this trend; rather, *Loving* and the intermarriage increase were both results of the general softening of interracial social boundaries that followed the civil rights movement of the 1950s and '60s.

BIBLIOGRAPHY

Booker, Simeon. "Couple that Rocked the Courts." *Ebony* (September 1967): 78–84.
Sickels, Robert. *Race, Marriage, and the Law.* 1972.
Spickard, Paul R. *Mixed Blood: Intermarriage and Ethnic Identity in Twentieth-Century America.* 1989.

Paul Spickard

Lowndes County Black Panther Party

The Lowndes County Freedom Organization (LCFO), also known as the BLACK PANTHER PARTY, was one of the first political parties to develop near the end of the civil rights movement. LCFO was formed within the black struggle to acquire and use the vote as a power base within black belt ALABAMA. LCFO, with its slogan "Pull the lever for the Black Panther and go on home," emerged to challenge white dominance in a predominantly black county characterized as "a truly totalitarian society—the epitome of the tight, insulated police state."

Black voting rights activities had begun in Selma, Alabama in early 1963. By January 1965, Martin Luther KING, JR., and the SOUTHERN CHRISTIAN LEADERSHIP CONFERENCE (SCLC) had brought national media attention to the Selma struggle. Nightly mass rallies and marches to Selma's courthouse were frequent. In February 1965 more than 3,000 marchers were arrested in Selma. On February 3, in the nearby town of Marion, 700 black children were arrested for marching around the courthouse. In a bloody beating of more than 200 marchers in Marion, state troopers beat and shot 26 year-old Jimmy Lee Jackson as he came to the aid of his mother, Viola Jackson. Jimmy Lee Jackson died eight days later at Good Samaritan Hospital in Selma. No one was charged or convicted for Jackson's murder.

The murder of Jimmy Lee Jackson was the catalyst for the Selma-to-Montgomery March in March 1965. On the afternoon of March 7, 1965, 2,000 marchers, led by SCLC's Hosea Williams and Student Nonviolent Coordinating Committee's (SNCC's) John Lewis and Robert Mants, were trampled and beaten by Alabama deputies and state troopers on the orders of Selma's infamous Sheriff Jim Clark and Major John Cloud. On March 9, Martin Luther King, Jr., joined 3,000 marchers who confronted a police barricade outside Selma. King led the marchers in prayer and instructed them to retreat. After the abortive march, three white ministers who had joined the march were attacked by a local Selma white crowd. One of the ministers, the Reverend James Reeb, died a few days later.

The murder of Reeb brought immediate national response. Contrary to the official silence following the murder of Jimmy Lee Jackson, President Lyndon B. Johnson telephoned Reeb's widow, Marie, and Vice-President Hubert Humphrey attended Reeb's funeral. Four days after Reeb's death President Johnson delivered the voting rights bill to Congress. Johnson also delivered a national television speech in which he declared the struggle in Selma to be "part of a larger movement." No one was ever convicted for Reeb's murder.

Despite internal strategic and tactical differences between the SCLC and the SNCC, the Selma to Montgomery march finally occurred March 21, 1965. At least 25,000 marchers, black and white, made it to Alabama's capital on March 25. After the rally, Mrs. Viola Liuzzo, a white homemaker from Detroit, was shot and killed in Lowndes County, while driving to Montgomery after transporting marchers back to Selma. Three of Mrs. Liuzzo's murderers were eventually found guilty and given maximum prison sentences of ten years each.

The murders of Jackson, Reeb, and Liuzzo, and the brutal beatings on the Edmund Pettus Bridge, led SNCC workers to reconsider the tactic of nonviolent direct action. Led by Stokely Carmichael (now known as Kwame Ture) SNCC would help form the Lowndes County Freedom Organization—The Black Panther Party. The Black Panther Party launched an intensive effort to register black people to vote and run black candidates for public office.

Lowndes County is located between Selma and Montgomery. Its black residents were poor, landless, and economically and politically dependent on elite white plantation owners. Eighty-six white families owned 90 percent of the land in the county and controlled the government. Lowndes County is in the heart of Alabama's black belt. Black people far outnumbered whites. Eighty-percent of Lowndes County was black. The average black income was $985 per year. Black people were largely unregistered to vote, because of a literary test. Black people also were lukewarm to civil rights activity.

Carmichael's efforts to organize the Black Panther Party would test his belief that indigenous, poor, and uneducated black people should make their own decisions and provide leadership to their local struggle. He believed that organizations such as SNCC should make their skills and talents available to rural black people. Carmichael and other SNCC workers proceeded to identify and organize a group of self-reliant and militant Lowndes County black leaders.

The campaign to register black residents of Lowndes county was accelerated by the passage of the 1965 Voting Rights Act. The increase in black registration intensified white resistance. On August 20, 1965, a white deputy sheriff in Hayneville shot and killed Jonathan Daniels, a white seminary student from Keene, New Hampshire. Daniels's murder led Carmichael to declare that "we're going to tear this county up. Then we're going to build it back, brick by brick, until it's a fit place for human beings."

After Daniels's death, Carmichael and SNCC came to question the utility of Lowndes County black residents registering as Democrats. After much discussion and deliberation, SNCC decided to create an independent political party. A provision in Alabama law allowed for the formation of political parties at the county level. Nominating conventions could be held to nominate independent candidates. If candidates received 20 percent of the vote cast in county elections then their party would gain official recognition.

In March 1966, Carmichael, SNCC, and Lowndes County black residents formed the Lowndes County Freedom Organization (LCFO). The organization was also known as the Black Panther Party because it used a picture of a black panther as its official mascot. John Hulett, a thirty-seven-year-old father of seven, and long-time Lowndes County political activist, who in 1965 had formed the Lowndes County Christian Movement for Human Rights as an affiliate of the South Christian Leadership Conference, was chosen as its chairman. LCFO's main objective was to acquire political power for the black residents of Lowndes

County. SNCC workers believed that political power was the first step to independence and freedom.

The LCFO ran a candidate for the offices of sheriff, coroner, tax assessor, tax collector, and three school board seats. Though all seven LCFO candidates lost, the efforts to seize political power in Lowndes County demonstrated a belief in the new philosophy of BLACK POWER: "that in Lowndes County, Alabama, a black sheriff can end police brutality. A black tax assessor and tax collector and county board of revenue can lay, collect, and channel tax monies for the building of better roads and schools serving black people." In 1969 John Hulett was elected Sheriff of Lowndes County, marking a major victory in LCFO's long struggle to "use power to exercise control."

"Bloody Lowndes" County, Alabama, was not only the testing ground for a new militant civil rights leadership but it also ushered in the era of "Black Power." The rallying cry to "Pull the lever for the Black Panther and go on home" symbolized a new phrase in the Southern black freedom struggle and gave black people throughout the United States a political model to follow.

BIBLIOGRAPHY

Allen, Robert L. *Black Awakening In Capitalist America: An Analytic History.* 1969.
Carmichael, Stokely, and Charles V. Hamilton. *Black Power: The Politics of Liberation in America.* 1967.
Carson, Clayborne. *In Struggle: SNCC and the Black Awakening of the 1960s.* 1981.

Rickey Hill

Loyalty Oaths

Loyalty oaths have a long and ignominious history. They test compliance of belief and loyalty to the sovereign, which is why they are sometimes called "test oaths." Henry VII used them to eliminate followers of the Roman Catholic Church. They were common in both military and civilian settings during the founding generation. In the 1832–1833 NULLIFICATION controversy, SOUTH CAROLINA compelled its officials to swear primary loyalty to the state, not the nation. Loyalty oaths became omnipresent during the Civil War. The Confederacy linked them to the passes required for travel. The Union used oaths to identify security risks. Taking an oath was the only alternative captives and hostile civilians had to indefinite imprisonment.

In 1867, the SUPREME COURT seemingly limited the reach of loyalty oaths. At issue in *Cummings v. Missouri* and *Ex parte Garland* were a Missouri law that required persons in various occupations to swear that they had not aided or sympathized with the rebellion and a fed-

eral statute that forced attorneys who practiced in federal courts to swear that they had not supported the Confederacy. The Court ruled both enactments as being unconstitutional ex post facto laws and bills of attainder.

During the Red Scare that followed World War I, thirty-two states had loyalty oath requirements for teachers. This was but a prelude to the loyalty-security hysteria after World War II. One study concluded that loyalty oaths and checks were applied to 13.5 million persons—one-fifth of the nation's workforce—as a condition of employment. Oaths aimed to purge public employment and licensed occupations from communist or subversive influences proliferated. Like earlier oaths, they required takers to renounce certain beliefs, words, or acts. Sometimes only the imagination of their drafters limited the oaths. In California, a three-year-old girl was hired as a model at a public college. Her mother was told that the girl could not be paid unless she signed a loyalty oath. Since the girl could not write, she was never paid. In Indiana, no one could perform as a professional wrestler, a barber, or a junk dealer without taking a loyalty oath. Cedars of Lebanon Hospital in Los Angeles barred seven doctors as loyalty risks.

The Supreme Court in the 1950s sustained the constitutionality of oaths. In a 1951 case (*Garner v. Board of Public Works*), the majority analogized a municipality (Los Angeles) that had a loyalty oath program for its employees to a private employer and held that the latter was as free as the former to consider the political beliefs of applicants in determining their fitness for work. "From time immemorial," the Court wrote in 1952, "one's reputation has been determined by the company he keeps."

Justice Hugo L. BLACK and William O. Douglas continually dissented from these decisions, stressing that the constitutional test should be overt acts violating a valid statute. "History attests, the efficacy of that instrument [the test oath] for inflicting penalties and disability on obnoxious minorities," Justice Black noted when the Court in 1950 upheld the non-Communist affidavit provision required of labor union officers under the Taft–Hartley Act.

Gradually, however, as the loyalty mania waned, the Court changed its mind. In 1956 in *Pennsylvania v. Nelson*, it reaffirmed federal primacy in sedition laws, thereby invalidating criminal statutes in more than forty states. This helped to lay the groundwork for a series of decisions in the 1960s that declared unconstitutional as violating the First Amendment several loyalty oaths barely different from those it had upheld. Government employment, the Court ruled, may not be conditioned on an oath that one has not engaged, nor will engage, in speech that is constitutionally protected, such as criticizing institutions of government, discussing political doctrines that approve the overthrow of certain forms of government, or sponsoring candidates for political office. The cumulative impact of the Court's decisions has made it almost impossible for government to impose a loyalty oath with teeth on its employees.

Benjamin Franklin in 1776 expressed the common sense of the matter when he wrote, "I have never regarded oaths otherwise than as the last recourse of liars."

BIBLIOGRAPHY

Cook, Fred J. *The Nightmare Decade.* 1971.
Hyman, Harold M. *To Try Men's Souls: Loyalty Tests in American History.* 1959.
"Loyalty Oaths." *Yale Law Journal* 77 (1968):739.
Reitman, Alan, ed. *The Pulse of Freedom: American Liberties: 1920–1970s.* 1971.

Roger K. Newman

Lucy Foster, Autherine

(1929–   ), civil rights activist.

Born in Shiloh, ALABAMA, in 1929, Autherine Lucy attended Selma University and Miles College in Birmingham, graduating in 1952. The following summer, she and a friend, Polly Myers, decided that a degree from Miles College was not sufficient, and they sought admission to obtain a second undergraduate degree from the University of Alabama in Tuscaloosa. They were initially admitted for the semester beginning in September 1952, but when it was discovered that they were not white, the admission was revoked.

Lucy and Myers then contacted the NATIONAL ASSOCIATION FOR THE ADVANCEMENT OF COLORED PEOPLE (NAACP) for legal assistance in the fight to gain admittance to the segregated institution (see SEGREGATION). Eventually they won a court order restraining the university from rejecting applications on the basis of race. When it was discovered that Myers had conceived a child prior to wedlock, she was again rejected by the university as unsuitable, but Lucy was granted admission on January 30, 1956. In February she began attending classes, accompanied by the dean of women and a police escort. On the third day of classes she was assaulted by a riotous mob that hurled eggs and rocks at her and shouted death threats. The Alabama riot was the first instance of violence at the university in connection with such an admission. Citing safety concerns, the university suspended Lucy that same day. The NAACP quickly filed suit and the university was shortly ordered by a federal court to

Autherine Lucy Foster sits in a federal court house in Birmingham, Alabama, on February 20, 1956, awaiting a district judge's decision on whether to reinstate her as a student at the University of Alabama. She had been expelled by the university on February 6 after threats of violence on campus. (AP/ Wide World Photos)

reinstate her and to take measures to ensure her safety and that of other students. The university then expelled her again on February 29, charging that the language of the lawsuit filed against them had been so extreme as to constitute a deliberate attempt to slander or malign the institution's character. At this point, Lucy and the NAACP decided not to pursue the case further. In April 1956, Lucy married Hugh Foster, a divinity student she had met while attending Miles College, and became known as Autherine Lucy Foster. She briefly remained involved as a civil rights activist for several months thereafter, but eventually withdrew from active involvement in the movement. She had difficulty obtaining a teaching job for some time thereafter because of her notoriety, but was eventually hired as a public school teacher in Alabama in 1974.

Still later, in April 1988, Autherine Lucy's 1956 expulsion was annulled by the University of Alabama, and Autherine Lucy Foster enrolled in the university's graduate program in elementary education, receiving an M.A. degree in 1992.

BIBLIOGRAPHY

Miles, Tiya. "Autherine Juanita Lucy Foster." In *Black Women in the United States: An Historical Encyclopedia*, edited by Darlene Clark Hine. 1993.

Woodward, C. Vann. *The Strange Career of Jim Crow*, 3rd rev. ed. 1974.

Rochelle C. Hayes

Lynch, John Roy

(1847–1939), former slave and U.S. congressman.

John Roy Lynch became the first and only black Mississippian to serve in the United States House of Representatives during RECONSTRUCTION.

Lynch was born on a plantation in Louisiana and sold to a Natchez, Mississippi, slaveowner in 1863. He received his freedom from occupying Union forces in 1864 and quickly became politically active in the Republican Party after the onset of Congressional Reconstruction in 1967. Lynch began his formal political career as a Justice of Peace for Adams County in 1869. In 1870, he won election to the Mississippi House of Representatives, and in 1872 he became Speaker of the House. At the urging of local and national Republican leaders, he ran for the U.S. House seat in the Sixth District in 1872 and was elected. He was reelected in 1875, defeated in 1876, was victorious again in 1880, and was defeated once again in 1882. During his first term in the House, Lynch spoke repeatedly and forthrightly in favor of the CIVIL RIGHTS ACT OF 1875, and his enthusiastic support of this bill fueled the conservative white opposition, which led to his first defeat. After his third and last term in the House, he managed his property in Mississippi, entered private law practice and participated actively in local, state, and national Republican affairs, serving as a delegate to four national conventions (1884, 1888, 1892, and 1900). At the 1884 convention, Lynch gave the keynote address. He also embarked upon a military career by enlisting in the Army as a paymaster during the Spanish American War and serving as an officer until 1911.

In 1913, Lynch began the historical debate on the nature of the Reconstruction era with the publication of *The Facts of Reconstruction*. In this work Lynch, as both eyewitness and active participant, attacked the prevailing view of Congressional Reconstruction, which emphasized the freedmen's supposed unfitness for political participation and the resulting corruption of southern governments under black and white Republican rule. Conservative whites often used this interpretation to justify the "redemption" of Southern state governments and the resultant end of Congressional Reconstruction in the 1870s as well as the im-

plementation and maintenance of white supremacy in the following decades. Historians such as James Ford Rhodes and William A. Dunning promoted general acceptance of this demeaning perspective in scholarly circles. Although Lynch's work received little serious attention at the time of its publication, he provided the earliest serious challenge to this perspective (the "Dunning school") by emphasizing the positive accomplishments of both blacks and whites who served in office during this era. In succeeding decades Lynch's views were more broadly accepted and have became foundational to most contemporary interpretations of Reconstruction. Lynch died in Chicago, Illinois, soon after completing his autobiography, *Reminiscences of an Active Life*. He was buried at Arlington National Cemetery.

BIBLIOGRAPHY

Franklin, John Hope. "John Roy Lynch: Republican Stalwart from Mississippi." In *Southern Black Leaders of Reconstruction*, edited by Howard Rabinowitz. 1982.

Lynch, John Roy. *The Facts of Reconstruction*, edited by William C. Harris. 1970.

Stephen C. Messer

Lynching

Lynching is a term applied to various forms of summary punishment inflicted by self-appointed groups without regard to established legal procedures. Although not uniquely American, lynching has been conspicuous throughout American history and has been one graphic measure of the oppression of African Americans.

The term "lynching" probably had its origins during the Revolutionary War when Charles Lynch (1736–1796), a Virginia patriot, conducted a campaign of violence against suspected loyalists. In subsequent decades, popular tribunals throughout the nation periodically punished transgressors of community standards. After the Civil War, lynching became a chronic feature of southern life. Lynch mobs there continued to execute alleged wrongdoers long after lynching had become a rarity elsewhere in the nation. Between 1880 and 1930 southern mobs lynched an estimated 723 whites and 3,220 blacks. Mobs elsewhere executed approximately 630 whites and 124 blacks. The blatant connection between lynching and racism in the South became glaring over time. Outside the South and border states, 83 percent of mob victims were white. In the South and the border states, in contrast, 85 percent of lynching victims were black. Between 1880 and 1930, the proportion of

Tom Shipp and Abe Smith were lynched at Marion, Indiana, on August 7, 1930. (CORBIS/Bettmann)

lynching victims in the South who were white decreased from 32 percent to 9 percent.

For African Americans, lynching was one of the most intolerable manifestations of their oppression. Because local, state, and federal officials often either ignored or endorsed lynching, voluntary reform organizations comprised the only consistent opposition to the practice. African Americans devised a variety of informal responses to lynchings, ranging from flight from lynching-prone areas to outright protest, even including armed resistance to white mobs. But organized opposition by southern blacks was always difficult and dangerous. Even so, from the 1880s until the 1950s, Frederick DOUGLASS, Ida WELLS, Walter WHITE, and a succession of black leaders denounced lynchings. During the 1890s Wells exposed the shibboleths that whites used to justify their violence. Black newspaper editors, such as Robert S. Abbott of the Chicago *Defender,* hammered away at the barbarism of white lynchers and the craven complicity of law officers and public officials. After the founding of the NATIONAL ASSOCIATION FOR THE ADVANCEMENT OF COLORED PEOPLE (NAACP) in 1909, W. E. B. DU BOIS used its journal, *The Crisis,* to insist that the struggle for black equality could not be separated from the campaign to end lynching.

After WORLD WAR I, a small but influential group of white Southern moderates organized the COMMISSION ON INTERRACIAL COOPERATION (CIC) to improve race relations in the South. The CIC for the first time mobilized well-placed southern whites to prevent lynchings. From the ranks of the organization emerged the Association of Southern Women for the

Prevention of Lynching (ASWPL), which worked through white women's church and civic groups to educate public opinion against lynching. Yet, consistent with the moderate principles that guided them, neither CIC nor the ASWPL supported legislation to make lynching a federal crime.

A federal antilynching statute remained a major goal of African-American activists for decades. Throughout the 1920s and 1930s the NAACP lobbied tirelessly for an antilynching bill. But, beginning in April 1918, each antilynching statute went down to defeat because of either southern Democratic opposition or fitful Republican commitment. Antilynching activists were no more successful in prodding President Franklin D. ROOSEVELT's administration to support antilynching legislation. But, beginning during WORLD WAR II, the Justice Department took tentative steps to punish lynchers by interpreting the "equal protection" clause of the FOURTEENTH AMENDMENT as grounds for federal intervention in racially motivated violence. For the first time, the threat of the federal prosecution of lynchers loomed as a possibility. That possibility turned to certainty after the passage of the CIVIL RIGHTS ACT OF 1964, which finally empowered the federal government to prosecute participants in lynchings.

Increasing federal opposition, relentless African-American activism, and the weakening of traditional forms of racial domination in the South during the twentieth century most likely explain the decline in lynching. A gradual decline in lynching in the South during the 1920s was followed by an even more marked decline after 1930. Lynching virtually ceased as a regular occurrence during the 1950s, although the murders of various civil rights activists by white supremacists during the 1960s displayed some of the hallmarks of lynchings. Yet, even as recently as 1981, KU KLUX KLAN members in Alabama lynched a black youth.

BIBLIOGRAPHY

Brundage, W. Fitzhugh. *Lynching in the New South: Georgia and Virginia, 1880–1930.* 1993.

Brundage, W. Fitzhugh. *Under Sentence of Death: Essays on Lynching in the South.* 1997.

Moses, Norton H. *Lynching and Vigilantism in the United States: An Annotated Bibliography.* 1997.

Shapiro, Herbert. *White Violence and Black Response: From Reconstruction to Montgomery.* 1988.

Tolnay, Stewart E., and E. M. Beck, *A Festival of Violence: An Analysis of Southern Lynchings, 1882–1930.* 1995.

Zangrando, Robert L. *The NAACP Crusade Against Lynching, 1909–1950.* 1980.

W. Fitzhugh Brundage

Lyon, Phyllis A.

(1924–), gay/lesbian movement founder.

Phyllis Lyon earned a degree in journalism from the University of California at Berkeley in 1946. With this as a tool, she spearheaded an informational campaign to increase lesbian rights that had nothing short of a revolutionary impact on lesbian and gay activism in the United States (see GAY AND LESBIAN RIGHTS). In 1955, she co-founded the DAUGHTERS OF BILITIS with Del MARTIN, her partner. While Martin ran the organization, Lyon edited its monthly publication, *The Ladder*, from 1956 to 1969. With her typewriter, Lyon inspired a cultural shift in lesbian activism. Each issue contained political commentary, literature, book reviews, and information about scientific research that was relevant to lesbian lives. Lyon was particularly interested in sex research and later earned a degree in education from the Institute for Advanced Study of Human Sexuality (IASHS). She has lectured widely, both at the IASHS, where she worked as a professor, 1976–1987, and at universities across the United States.

In 1972 Lyon co-authored (with Martin) *Lesbian/Woman*, a book that traces the history of the Daughters of Bilitis and asserts a feminist analysis of lesbian activism. Published initially by Bantam, *Lesbian/Woman* was republished in 1995 to popular acclaim. Lyon has also been active in San Francisco politics. In 1964 she co-founded the San Francisco Council on Religion and the Homosexual, which brought the struggle for lesbian and gay civil rights to the attention of local pastors and ministers—a powerful cohort in city politics. With this support, in 1965 Lyon co-founded Citizen's Alert, a coalition of civil rights organizations that worked to combat police violence and harassment, particularly in San Francisco's Tenderloin district. In 1972, she helped organize the city's Alice B. Toklas Lesbian and Gay Democratic Club, addressing a long-standing desire to see lesbian and gay activism reach mainstream politics. In 1976 she was appointed chair of San Francisco's Human Rights Commission, where she served, along with Del Martin, until 1983.

Phyllis Lyon has received numerous honors and awards. San Francisco's Women's Alternative Health Services renamed itself the Lyon-Martin Clinic in 1980 to celebrate the contributions both Lyon and Martin have made to women's health, and the two women have been honored as Grand Marshals in Gay Pride celebrations in San Francisco, Sacramento, and Los Angeles. Lyon and Martin donated their archives to the San Francisco Gay and Lesbian Historical Society of Northern California in 1996.

BIBLIOGRAPHY
Martin, Del, and Phyllis Lyon. *Lesbian/Woman*, rev. ed. 1991.

Nan Alamilla Boyd

M

Maine

Annexed by Massachusetts in the 1650s and made a free state by the terms of the Missouri Compromise (1820), Maine had some early investments in slavery and institutional segregation. Maine has struggled with racial reconciliation, and 1955 to 1975 were watershed years for African Americans. With the highest black population returns since the 1870 census, these decades were marked by a sharp resurgence in NATIONAL ASSOCIATION FOR THE ADVANCEMENT OF COLORED PEOPLE (NAACP) membership and protest in cities including Bangor, Brunswick, Lewiston, and Portland. As in the civil rights tradition, the church was a stabilizing community force. Prominent civic leaders included Leonard Cummings, Alberta Jackson, Jean Sampson, and Gerald Talbot, a former president of the Portland NAACP and the first black state legislator (1972). Activists strived to dismantle de facto segregation in Maine's housing market and to create equal access to employment beyond the racial caste of menial labor. This public practice offered few blacks opportunities for stability or advance, and helped hinder the growth of communities in a state where blacks have consistently represented less than 1 percent of the population.

Other Mainers were involved in and benefited from the civil rights movement, including French-Canadian, Jewish, Native American, and Irish Catholic residents, some of whom have also been objects of harassment by local KU KLUX KLAN contingencies. In 1965 Maine signed its Fair Housing Bill into law and in 1971 it established a Human Rights Commission to prevent discrimination in employment, housing, public accommodations, and credit. Recent civil rights protests have confronted discrimination against gays and lesbians, and although a 1997 statewide referendum defeated protection for gays and lesbians in these domains, some cities have retained these rights at the municipal level.

BIBLIOGRAPHY

Anchor of the Soul: A Documentary About Black History in Maine. Produced by Shoshana Hoose and Karine Odlin. Video.

Gerald E. Talbot Collection. African American Archives of Maine, University of Southern Maine Library, Portland, Me.

Lumpkins, Charles L. "Civil-Rights Activism in Maine, 1945–1971." *Maine History* 36 (1997): 70–85.

Miller, Eben Simmons. "Resistance in 'Pioneer Territory': The Maine NAACP and the Pursuit of Fair Housing Legislation." *Maine History* 36 (1997): 86–105.

Maureen Elgersman Lee

Malcolm X

(1925–1965), black nationalist and human rights spokesman.

Malcolm X was born Malcolm Little in Omaha, Nebraska, on May 19, 1925. His father, Earl Little, was a Baptist preacher, deeply influenced by the racial separatism of Marcus GARVEY's UNIVERSAL NEGRO IMPROVEMENT ASSOCIATION. His mother, Louise, was born in Grenada and spent much of her early life

Malcolm X addresses a rally in Harlem, New York, in 1963. (CORBIS)

rearing children. Malcolm's childhood was disrupted by familial trauma on a number of occasions. His father was killed by a streetcar in 1931, perhaps a victim of white supremacists; his mother was declared legally insane in 1939 and committed to a mental hospital in Kalamazoo, Michigan. Around this time, Malcolm dropped out of school, lived in several foster homes in Lansing, Michigan, and finally relocated to Boston to live with his sister Ella. With an incomplete education and few marketable skills, Malcolm became involved in an assortment of criminal activities in Boston and New York, ranging from gambling and procuring women to drug peddling and theft. In 1946, he was indicted for larceny and other offenses and served six and a half years in Massachusetts prisons before being released in August 1952.

While incarcerated, Malcolm learned about the NATION OF ISLAM, a quasi-Islamic movement that advocated black separatism, an ascetic moral code, and self-help. Its leader, Elijah MUHAMMAD, counseled Malcolm through letters to give up his vices and encouraged him to make use of the prison library, take pride in being black, and join the Nation of Islam. After being paroled, Malcolm rose swiftly in the Muslim movement. He was instrumental in organizing mosques throughout the country and attracting young people to the Nation. His skills as an organizer were only surpassed by his oratorical powers, which had been greatly enhanced by his study of elocution, etymology, and other disciplines while in prison. In 1953, Malcolm received the surname X from Elijah Muham-

mad, which symbolized both the African ancestral name that he could never know and the break he had made with his self-destructive past. A year later, Malcolm was named minister of New York Mosque No. 7, which soon became the largest cell of Muslims in the country.

Like Elijah Muhammad, Malcolm was, for most of his life, on the margins of the modern civil rights movement, which had been launched by the Supreme Court decision in BROWN V. BOARD OF EDUCATION (1954). The Nation of Islam's cultural and territorial separatism, anti-Christian rhetoric, racial chauvinism, and assertion of the right to self-defense were antithetical to the tactics, goals, and ethos of most civil rights leaders. Nonetheless, Malcolm was a vital voice in the national discourse over the future of African Americans, largely playing an adversarial role vis-à-vis Martin Luther KING, JR., and other leaders.

Malcolm forced African Americans to seriously question the value of integration into a society that had historically thrived on their economic exploitation, tolerated their political disfranchisement, and codified a stigmatizing system of racial segregation. He did not believe that sit-ins, marches, or other tactics of civil rights activists were effective tools with which to gain rights, especially when confronted with violent resistance in the South. In 1963, when the federal government failed to immediately respond to televised police brutality against nonviolent demonstrators in Birmingham, Alabama, Malcolm lambasted the KENNEDY administration for its inaction. He subjected the

MARCH ON WASHINGTON later that year to similar ridicule, characterizing it as more of a choreographed media event than a militant protest for civil rights. The racist terrorism against African Americans in the South, ranging from church bombings to the open assassination of civil rights activists, convinced him that the civil rights movement could not change deepseated racial hatred and decades-long patterns of discrimination in America.

Malcolm X left the Nation of Islam in March 1964, following a protracted and humiliating "silencing" that Elijah Muhammad had imposed upon him for impolitic comments made in the wake of the Kennedy assassination. In addition to this punishment, internal jealousies, scandals, ideological differences, and even death threats had disaffected Malcolm to the point that he sought to philosophically reinvent himself following his departure from the Nation. Throughout 1964, Malcolm traveled widely in Africa and the Middle East, using the customary *hajj* to Mecca as a platform to both renounce the racial theology of Elijah Muhammad and to embrace al-Islam.

After leaving the Nation of Islam, Malcolm did not abandon all of his black nationalist convictions; he still talked of black-sponsored business ventures, black-run schools, and a cultural revitalization of African-American communities. However, he did consciously move closer to the agenda of civil rights leaders, something that he had wanted to do for years, but could not for fear of arousing the ire of Elijah Muhammad. By mid-1964, Malcolm endorsed a number of civil rights tactics, including rent strikes, boycotts, and cooperation with sympathetic whites. Similarly, the goals of Dr. King—whom he met only once in March 1964—and others, such as the attainment of voting rights and the ending to legalized forms of racial discrimination, became more palatable to him and were incorporated into the charter of his newly formed ORGANIZATION OF AFRO-AMERICAN UNITY (OAAU). At the invitation of young militants, Malcolm traveled to the South in early 1965 and delivered a speech that endorsed many of the goals of the civil rights movement. By this time, his analysis of the racial situation in America had broadened to include comparisons to anticolonial struggles in Africa and Asia, socialist theory, and human rights concerns. He admittedly thought that black nationalism was too narrow a concept to describe his evolving philosophical leanings. However, by the end of his life, he had yet to formulate a coherent ideology that tied together the various beliefs and ideas that were shaping his views.

Malcolm X was assassinated February 21, 1965, during a talk in the Audubon Ballroom in New York. The details of any plot to kill Malcolm X are vague, though individuals affiliated with the Nation of Islam were charged with the crime. The significance of Malcolm X to the civil rights movement lies in his willingness to question the strategies and objectives of the leadership. He, and the Nation of Islam, may have facilitated the successes of Dr. King and other leaders by showing Americans that there were black leaders who had not bought into the merits of nonviolence or integration and who would, if given the chance, take the civil rights movement into a very different direction.

BIBLIOGRAPHY

Breitman, George, ed. *Malcolm X Speaks.* 1965.
Carson, Clayborne, et al. *Malcolm X: The FBI File.* 1991.
Clark, Steve, ed. *Malcolm X: February 1965, the Last Speeches.* 1992.
Clegg, Claude A., III. *An Original Man: The Life and Times of Elijah Muhammad.* 1997.
Cone, James. *Martin & Malcolm & America: A Dream or a Nightmare.* 1991.
Goldman, Peter. *The Death and Life of Malcolm X.* 1976.
Lincoln, C. Eric. *The Black Muslims in America.* 1961.
Malcolm X (with Alex Haley). *The Autobiography of Malcolm X.* 1965.
"Malcolm X: Make It Plain." PBS documentary. 1994.
Perry, Bruce. *Malcolm: The Life of a Man Who Changed Black America.* 1991.

Claude A. Clegg

Marcantonio, Vito

(1902–1954), U.S. congressman.

Vito Marcantonio was born in 1902 in an East Harlem tenement and grew up in the same neighborhood as Fiorello LaGuardia, whom he met during his senior year of high school. From this chance encounter grew a lifelong personal and political alliance that would prove to be crucial to Marcantonio's public career. He went on to study law and upon graduation went to work in LaGuardia's legal office. His basic philosophy was that it was the government's duty to provide for those who, through no fault of their own, could not sustain themselves. His forceful advocacy of a welfare state would mark him as perhaps the most progressive member of CONGRESS.

Marcantonio initially ran for Congress as a Republican, then eventually became the most prominent member of the American Labor Party, a New York–based reform party with strong ties to the COMMUNIST PARTY USA and various socialist groups. First elected to Congress in 1934, he was defeated in 1936 and then won reelection in 1938. He would serve until 1950, when he lost as a result of his opposition to both the KOREAN WAR and the Marshall Plan—and because he was perceived by many as being, if not an out-and-out Red, then at least a Communist sympathizer.

Motivated by a genuine concern for the downtrodden, Marcantonio embraced a host of causes considered radical for the time. He became a strong supporter of tenants' rights, and he lobbied tirelessly on behalf of those he thought were being bilked by sadistic landlords and a system that did not respond to tenants' needs. Recognizing the critical need for low-cost urban HOUSING, he fought hard to increase federal funding in this area. The congressman worked throughout his career to pass legislation that would eliminate the poll tax, and he tried to use the authority of the FAIR EMPLOYMENT PRACTICE COMMITTEE to end discriminatory hiring practices. He remained a staunch supporter of organized labor during his tenure.

Marcantonio was one of the first to show an interest in the welfare of Puerto Rican Americans, both those living on the mainland and those on the island. He advocated the use of bilingual education, and the extension of protective legislation, including the minimum wage, to include the island. He further advocated the opening of Puerto Rico's sugar trade to buyers other than U.S. merchants. Within his own district, he made sure that his own staffers hired bilingual assistants, and that they were attentive to the special needs of Hispanic Americans. Marcantonio opposed all manner of racial quotas and restrictions on IMMIGRATION, indicating that he identified with the plight of all minority Americans.

Vito Marcantonio died of a heart attack in 1954.

BIBLIOGRAPHY
Schaffer, Alan. *Vito Marcantonio: Radical in Congress.* 1966.

Robert W. Nill

The Rev. Dr. Martin Luther King, Jr., acknowledges the crowd at the Lincoln Memorial after giving his "I Have a Dream" speech during the March on Washington, D.C., on August 28, 1963. (AP/Wide World Photos)

March on Washington (1963)

On Wednesday, August 28, 1963, approximately 300,000 protesters rallied at the Lincoln Memorial in the March on Washington for Jobs and Freedom, the largest civil rights demonstration in American history. The march culminated months of intensifying local civil rights struggles throughout the South (and in some northern cities), most prominent being the Birmingham, Alabama, movement led by the Rev. Dr. Martin Luther KING, JR.

The march was initiated by veteran black leader A. Philip RANDOLPH, head of the BROTHERHOOD OF SLEEPING CAR PORTERS and an AFL-CIO vice president. Randolph's threatened march on Washington in June 1941 had compelled President Franklin D. ROOSEVELT to ban racial discrimination in the war industry. In late 1962 Randolph proposed a mass protest, during the centennial of the EMANCIPATION PROCLAMATION, to draw attention to black unemployment and poverty. But as Randolph gained support for the march from fellow black leaders Roy WILKINS, (NATIONAL ASSOCIATION FOR THE ADVANCEMENT OF COLORED PEOPLE [NAACP]), Whitney YOUNG, JR. (NATIONAL URBAN LEAGUE), and King, its main focus shifted from economic demands to enactment of a strong civil rights law barring segregation, which the Birmingham movement had made a high priority for President John F. KENNEDY and congressional liberals. Randolph chose his protégé Bayard RUSTIN to direct the organizing campaign, overriding opposition by Wilkins and other leaders concerned about Rustin's left-wing past and homosexuality. When civil rights leaders met with President Kennedy at the White House on June 22, 1963, Randolph challenged the President's effort to stop the march; Kennedy feared disorder that might jeopardize the civil rights bill. Four weeks later he publicly endorsed the protest.

Over the summer Rustin and Randolph built a broad coalition of civil rights groups, liberal clergy, and labor unions spearheaded by the United Auto Workers. The AFL-CIO, however, refused to endorse the march. The coalition's outreach brought participants to Washington from all over the country on twenty-two chartered trains, nearly 2,000 charter buses, and thousands of carpools. The mass assembly was estimated to be about three-quarters black, one-quarter white and Latino. Many poor African Americans were bussed from the Deep South.

As the marchers surrounded the long reflecting pool between the Lincoln Memorial and the Washington Monument, Randolph helped to resolve a last-minute conflict. Moderate speakers, backed by Attorney General Robert KENNEDY, objected to a militant address by John LEWIS of the STUDENT NONVIOLENT COORDINATING COMMITTEE (SNCC) that attacked the civil rights bill for neglecting voting rights and failing to deal with southern police brutality. Meeting in a small room behind Lincoln's statue, Randolph, King, and others persuaded Lewis to temper his rhetoric. Climaxing the hot afternoon of freedom songs, numerous speeches by civil rights and religious leaders, and spirituals sung by Marian Anderson and Mahalia Jackson, King delivered an address whose extemporaneous conclusion set forth his vibrant dream of racial justice. Considered one of the greatest orations in U.S. history, the celebrated speech solidified King's position as the preeminent African-American leader.

Televised live to a nationwide audience, the peaceful rally displayed to CONGRESS and the public the united face and nonviolent character of the interracial civil rights movement just as it reached its peak of influence. It helped transform the civil rights struggle from a southern to a national movement and placed it at the center of American politics. The mass protest had a major impact on congressional passage of the CIVIL RIGHTS ACT OF 1964.

BIBLIOGRAPHY

Anderson, Jervis. *Bayard Rustin: Troubles I've Seen.* 1997.
Council for United Civil Rights Leadership. "We Shall Overcome!" Audiorecording of the March on Washington. 1963.
Garrow, David J. *Bearing the Cross.* 1986.
Pfeffer, Paula F. *A. Philip Randolph, Pioneer of the Civil Rights Movement.* 1990.

Stewart Burns

March on Washington Movement

Although most Americans had recovered from the throes of the Great Depression by 1940, African Amer-

icans, as the "first fired and last hired," still suffered 25 percent unemployment. With the outbreak of war in Europe, many companies initiated intensive training programs to manufacture war supplies. African Americans were excluded from those opportunities and were confined to employment primarily in service and unskilled positions. Black men were also segregated in the Army, restricted to menial service in the Navy, and barred from the other branches of the military.

Less than two weeks after President Franklin D. ROOSEVELT signed the 1940 Selective Service Act into law, the NATIONAL URBAN LEAGUE's T. Arnold Hill, BROTHERHOOD OF SLEEPING CAR PORTERS' A. Philip RANDOLPH, and the NAACP's Walter WHITE met with the President to discuss the Armed Forces' use of black manpower. The War Department issued a statement after the meeting that affirmed its policy of segregating black soldiers and that implied the black leaders' acquiesence in the policy.

To show their disagreement with the policy and to impress the White House with their indignation, Randolph in January 1941 proposed that African Americans stage a March on Washington against discrimination in defense industries and the military. A March on Washington Committee (MOWC) was organized and selected July 1 as the date for the demonstration. The MOWC excluded white participation in the march for fear of Communist Party infiltration and disruption similar to what Randolph had recently experienced as president of the NATIONAL NEGRO CONGRESS. He explained that the MOWC was not anti-white but problack. Moreover, a black effort was needed to mobilize African Americans, to instill faith in themselves, and to foster a sense of self-reliance.

Randolph initially announced that 10,000 Negroes would march, a figure that soon grew to 100,000. New York's Mayor Fiorello H. La Guardia and Eleanor Roosevelt tried to persuade the MOWC to call off the march, but the organizers stood fast. Numerous black fraternal, labor, and social groups as well as the black press endorsed the march. After meeting with Randolph, White, and labor organizers Frank R. Crosswaith and Layle Lane, President Roosevelt on June 25, 1941 issued Executive Order 8802 banning discrimination in employment by defense industries and the government and establishing a FAIR EMPLOYMENT PRACTICES COMMITTEE (FEPC) to investigate compliance with the order. The MOWC canceled the march, having achieved most of its objectives.

The MOWC started as a temporary coalition of black organizations with limited objectives. Randolph continued the MOWC to keep pressure on the White House to enforce its directive, which many African Americans hailed as the greatest presidential order

since Abraham Lincoln's EMANCIPATION PROCLAMA-
TION. The MOWC soon evolved into the March on
Washington Movement (MOWM), a grass roots orga-
nization with dues-paying members.

The MOWM staged huge rallies in major cities during the summer of 1942, with "blackouts" in black
neighborhoods that closed stores, had shades drawn,
and all activity at a standstill. Not since Marcus GARVEY
packed Madison Square Garden with a crowd of
25,000 in 1920 did as many African Americans attend
a meeting in New York City. When the MOWM became
a membership organization, the NATIONAL ASSOCIA-
TION FOR THE ADVANCEMENT OF COLORED PEOPLE
(NAACP), NATIONAL URBAN LEAGUE, and other organizations withdrew support. It survived primarily
with assistance from the Brotherhood of Sleeping Car
Porters.

In December, 1942, the MOWM announced that it
would use Gandhian tactics of mass civil disobedience
to end racial segregation in public accommodations.
The 1943 race riots in Detroit and Harlem, however,
dampened enthusiasm for mass demonstrations. The
MOWM declined after 1943 and disappeared a few
years later. It had achieved success in Executive Order
8802 with the help of many black organizations, but
once it became a potential rival, it lost their support
and could not sustain itself as a grass-roots organization based on mass mobilization and demonstrations.

BIBLIOGRAPHY

Bracey, John H., Jr., and August Meier. "Allies or Adver-
saries?: The NAACP, A. Philip Randolph and the 1941
March on Washington." *The Georgia Historical Quarterly*
75 (1991): 1–17.

Garfinkel, Herbert. *When Negroes March: The March on
Washington Movement in the Organizational Politics for
FEPC.* 1959.

Pfeffer, Paula F. *A. Philip Randolph, Pioneer of the Civil Rights
Movement.* 1990.

Ruchames, Louis. *Race, Jobs & Politics: The Story of FEPC.*
1953.

Robert L. Harris, Jr.

Marshall, Thurgood

(1908–1993), civil rights lawyer, Supreme Court
justice.

Thurgood Marshall was born in Baltimore, Maryland.
His mother, a school teacher and homemaker, and
his father, a steward at an exclusive country club, provided Marshall with a comfortable upbringing but
could not shelter him from the indignities of growing
up in a segregated society. Marshall graduated from
Lincoln University (Pennsylvania) in 1930 and went
on to the Howard University Law School. Graduating

*On October 2, 1967, Thurgood Marshall, the great-
grandson of a slave, became the first African-
American Supreme Court justice. He served on the
Court until 1991. (Archive Photos/APA)*

first in his class in 1933, Marshall found a mentor in
law school dean Charles Hamilton HOUSTON, who
taught his students to see law as a form of social engineering.

Marshall struggled to establish a private law practice in Depression-era Baltimore, devoting a great deal
of time and effort to invigorating the local chapter of
the NATIONAL ASSOCIATION FOR THE ADVANCEMENT
OF COLORED PEOPLE (NAACP). In 1936 Houston arranged to have Marshall hired by the NAACP's Legal
Defense Fund, which Houston then headed (see
NAACP LEGAL DEFENSE AND EDUCATION FUND).
When Houston left the fund in 1939, Marshall became
its chief lawyer, a position he held until 1961.

Marshall played a number of roles at the Legal Defense Fund. A superb trial lawyer, Marshall defended
several African Americans accused of murder. He also
conducted trials of challenges to various aspects of
the southern system of SEGREGATION, including suits
against school systems that paid African-American
teachers less than they paid whites. Marshall became

a talented appellate advocate as well, eventually arguing nearly thirty cases before the SUPREME COURT, most of them successfully. His style was informal and relaxed, and he typically sought to persuade judges that the positions he was advancing represented the sound common sense of the situation.

Marshall's most important role was to coordinate the general attack on segregation, particularly in southern schools. Pursuing a strategy initially laid out by Houston, Marshall began by challenging segregated education at the university level. When the Supreme Court agreed (*Sweatt v. Painter*, 1950), Marshall turned the attention of his legal team to elementary and secondary education. Carefully handling the sometimes fractious group of lawyers, Marshall deployed legal teams to three states and the District of Columbia, and himself handled the trial of the South Carolina desegregation case.

In 1896 the Supreme Court had held that segregated facilities were constitutional if they were equal (PLESSY V. FERGUSON). Marshall's efforts were directed at showing that segregated schools could not possibly be equal. Focusing primarily on the material differences between the schools for whites and African Americans, he also relied on what the Supreme Court had called "intangible" differences in quality. More controversially, he allowed the lawyers to introduce evidence from social psychologist Kenneth Clark that African-American children had lower self-esteem in segregated schools.

The Supreme Court held segregation unconstitutional in 1954 (BROWN V. BOARD OF EDUCATION). For the remainder of the 1950s Marshall's role changed. He devoted a great deal of time raising funds to support lawsuits attempting to bring about real desegregation. Faced with a concerted challenge by southern legislators and attorneys-general to thwart the NAACP's activities, Marshall also had to spend time defending the NAACP against attacks.

By 1961 Marshall decided the time had come for him to move on. His first wife, Buster, had died early in 1955. He married Cecilia Suyatt in December 1955, and by 1961 they had two young sons. Marshall wanted to spend more time with his family. He also found himself increasingly out-of-step with a civil rights movement becoming more interested in demonstrations and SIT-INS than with litigation. President John F. KENNEDY wanted to increase the number of African-American federal judges, and Marshall was a natural choice. After resisting efforts to appoint him to the federal trial court, Marshall accepted an appointment of the prestigious Court of Appeals for the Second Circuit in New York, where he served until 1965.

President Lyndon JOHNSON also saw political advantage in Marshall's promotion. Naming him Solicitor-General (the government's representative in the Supreme Court) in 1965, Johnson then maneuvered to get Justice Tom C. Clark to resign in 1967 so that he could nominate Marshall to the Supreme Court. In announcing Marshall's appointment, Johnson said, "[I]t is the right thing to do, the right time to do it, the right man and the right place."

Joining the liberal Warren Court in 1967 (see WARREN, Earl), Marshall expected to be part of a liberal majority for a long time. The Court's composition rapidly changed, and by 1972 Marshall found himself part of a beleaguered minority defending traditional liberal constitutional positions. He rarely had the opportunity to write important civil rights opinions. His dissents, however, were often eloquent statements of a liberalism on race issues that many in the nation had abandoned.

His experience made him acutely aware of the social reality that underlay apparently technical questions. Responding to Justice Harry Blackmun's suggestion that it would be relatively easy for poor people to pay a $50 filing fee in bankruptcy cases, Marshall wrote, "[N]o one who has had close contact with poor people can fail to understand how close to the margin of survival many of them are. . . . It is perfectly proper for judges to disagree about what the Constitution requires. But it is disgraceful for an interpretation of the Constitution to be premised upon unfounded assumptions about how people live" (*United States v. Kras*, 1973).

Marshall strongly defended AFFIRMATIVE ACTION programs when the Court invalidated Richmond's affirmative action program for construction contracts in *City of Richmond v. J.A. Croson* (1989). Marshall found "deep irony" in the Court's concern about the fairness of an affirmative action program adopted by a city council whose majority was African American. For Marshall, "[w]hen the . . . leaders of cities with histories of pervasive discrimination testify that past discrimination has infected one of their industries, armchair cynicism . . . has no place."

Marshall retired in 1991, feeling the effects of age. His colleagues recounted his role as a raconteur on the Court, who used his folksy stories to bring some home-spun truths to the attention of justices who were sometimes isolated from the real world in which constitutional law operated. His death in 1993 led to an outpouring of public sentiment, provoked by the passing of a symbol of racial liberalism when that ideology's time seemed to have ended.

BIBLIOGRAPHY

Kluger, Richard. *Simple Justice.* 1976.

NAACP Papers, Library of Congress, Manuscript Division, Washington, D.C.

Thurgood Marshall Papers, Library of Congress, Manuscript Division, Library of Congress, Washington, D.C.

Tushnet, Mark. *Making Civil Rights Law: Thurgood Marshall and the Supreme Court, 1936–1961.* 1994.
Tushnet, Mark. *Making Constitutional Law: Thurgood Marshall and the Supreme Court, 1961–1991.* 1997.

Mark Tushnet

Martin, Dorothy L. ("Del")

(1921–   ), gay/lesbian movement founder.

Del Martin was the co-founder along with Phyllis Lyon (her partner for over 40 years) of the DAUGHTERS OF BILITIS (DOB), the first lesbian rights organization in the United States. Martin served as president of the organization from 1955 to 1962, and under her leadership DOB grew into a national organization with chapters in over twelve U.S. cities. Through her columns in DOB's monthly publication, *The Ladder*, Martin articulated a lesbian civil rights agenda that stretched from anti-violence to health care and political representation (see GAY AND LESBIAN RIGHTS). Through the 1960s, Martin also worked to build coalitions between lesbian and gay civil rights organizations. In 1966, she helped found the North American Committee of Homophile Organizations (NACHO), and at its inception she asserted a strong and uncompromising feminist position. In this way, Martin positioned feminist concerns as central rather than secondary to lesbian and gay civil rights, paralleling feminist responses to the sexism of civil rights and New Left organizations.

Martin increasingly understood anti-lesbianism and HOMOPHOBIA to be the product of sexism and misogyny. She co-authored (with Lyon) *Lesbian/Woman*, a book that explained the feminism behind lesbian activism. Published in 1972, the book was excerpted in *Ms.* magazine, and it won the Gay Book Award from the American Library Association. Republished in 1991, *Lesbian/Woman* has been widely read by a generation of activists and scholars.

Through the 1970s, Martin also worked tirelessly to fight domestic violence. In 1975 she was co-founder of the Coalition for Justice for Battered Women; in 1976 she helped found San Francisco's La Casas de las Madres battered women's shelter; and in 1977 she co-founded the California Coalition Against Domestic Violence. Drawing from these experiences, she authored *Battered Wives*, published in 1976 and revised in 1981; this informational text has been widely used in classrooms and to train shelter volunteers. Because of her activism and visibility as a lesbian and feminist, Martin was appointed chair of San Francisco's Commission on Crime Control and Violence Prevention. She also sits on the San Francisco Human Rights Commission. She has won many awards and honors, including the American Civil Liberties Union's Earl Warren Civil Liberties Award. Martin's archives and the organization records of the Daughters of Bilitis are located in San Francisco at the Gay and Lesbian Historical Society of Northern California.

BIBLIOGRAPHY
Martin, Del, and Phyllis Lyon. *Lesbian/Woman*, rev. ed. 1991.

Nan Alamilla Boyd

Martínez, Elizabeth "Betita"

(1925–   ), Chicana activist, writer, editor.

A major Chicana essayist, campus lecturer, and activist, Elizabeth "Betita" Martínez was born Elizabeth Sutherland, of Oaxacan ancestry, and raised in Washington, D.C. She has dedicated forty years to working for civil rights and social justice, writing six books and dozens of articles on these subjects. Throughout her career she has worked across national boundaries and race lines, approaching civil rights from a broad socioeconomic and political standpoint. After graduating from Swarthmore College, she studied economics in New York City and later Ethnic Studies at San Francisco State University. Through extensive travels to Eastern Europe, the Soviet Union, China, Mexico, Guatemala, and Vietnam, Martínez has sought a global, multicultural perspective on civil and human rights.

Her views perhaps first took shape in the 1950s at the United Nations Secretariat, where she was involved in research on COLONIALISM. Later, visits to Cuba from 1959 to 1961 inspired her dedication to the universal struggle for human rights, dignity, and equality. Her reflections on women, education, housing, work, and race relations appear in *The Youngest Revolution: A Personal Report on Cuba* (1969).

As an editor at Simon & Schuster, Martínez sponsored books that reflected the times with their emphasis on social justice. One of these was *The Movement* (1964), which illustrates the black civil rights movement with photographs and is narrated by playwright Lorraine HANSBERRY. Royalties from the sale of *The Movement* benefited the STUDENT NONVIOLENT COORDINATING COMMITTEE (SNCC).

Serving first as a volunteer, Martínez became a full-time staff member and ultimately directed SNCC's New York office, which fund-raised, demonstrated, and created publicity for the cause in the South. In that work, she collaborated with noted black activists such as Stokely CARMICHAEL (later known as Kwame Toure), SNCC chairman, and Julian BOND, now chairman of the NATIONAL ASSOCIATION FOR THE ADVANCEMENT OF COLORED PEOPLE. In 1964, Martínez also served in the historic Mississippi Summer Project (see FREEDOM SUMMER; VOTING RIGHTS) to register voters and establish FREEDOM SCHOOLS. Gathering letters by summer project volunteers, she edited and published this correspondence in *Letters from Mississippi* (1965).

Martínez sees the black civil rights movement as a major force for nationwide change in the 1960s, and she has actively contributed to parallel struggles in other communities of color. By 1968, she had moved to New Mexico during the height of the CHICANO MOVEMENT, where she supported the ALIANZA FEDERAL DE PUEBLOS LIBRES (Federal Alliance of Free City States) to recover lands lost by Hispanics in the United States–Mexico War in the nineteenth century. For the next five years, she wrote about civil rights for the bilingual Chicano movement newspaper *El Grito del Norte* (The Cry of the North), which she cofounded. Martínez went on to cofound and direct the Chicano Communications Center (CCC) in Albuquerque, which educated grass-roots Mexican Americans about their history and culture (1973–1976).

While at the CCC, she published a pivotal work, *450 Years of Chicano History in Pictures/450 Años del Pueblo Chicano* (1976), which has been revised as *500 Years of Chicano History* (1991). Used nationwide by teachers and community organizations, this bilingual volume represents one of Martínez's greatest contributions to understanding Mexican-American civil rights. Beginning with the pre–Columbian period, the text offers signposts of Chicano history, including Spanish colonialism, the birth of the *mestizo* (mixed breed), Mexico's war of independence, and the war between the United States and Mexico, ending with the 1848 Treaty of Guadalupe-Hidalgo, which made half of Mexico into today's American Southwest. The book documents the lives of Chicano and Chicana workers, students, and communities across the country, including barrio leader Rodolfo "Corky" GONZALES in Denver and farm workers' organizer César CHÁVEZ in California.

In 1984 the issue of land rights surfaced again in Martínez's work when she coedited *Guatemala: Tyranny on Trial*. This sourcebook exposes the genocidal practices against peasants that occurred under the authority of the Guatemalan army, the CIA, and the U.S. military from the 1950s to the 1990s. It gathers together firsthand accounts from Guatemalans, including the indigenous activist and Nobel Peace Prize winner Rigoberta Menchú.

Pursuing civil rights and social justice during the Reagan Administration, Martínez ran for governor of California in 1982, and she exposed the backlash against the gains for women and people of color that had been made in the 1960s by the Peace and Freedom Party ticket. More recently she has argued for immigrant rights, noting that Mexican workers and other recent arrivals have become scapegoats for a score of social problems. She sees that not only whites are complicit in denying civil rights to immigrants, but that Latinos and blacks can denigrate newcomers as well. Articles on this topic, and on organized RACISM, CLASS inequity and SEXISM, appear in her latest book, *De Colores Means All of Us: Latina Views for a Multi-Colored Century* (1998). Here Martínez analyzes past and present struggles of Latinos in the city, the fields, on the job, and in the schools, and reviews the status of Latino civil rights in the United States.

In 1997 Martínez founded the Institute for MultiRacial Justice in the Bay Area with other leading activists of color including Angela DAVIS. A resource center to build alliances among people of color in order to win civil and human rights, the institute seeks to combat racism and to counter divisiveness. Martínez is the organization's cochair, serves as a mentor for youths in the Bay area, and teaches Women's Studies at California State University at Hayward. She has one daughter, Tessa Martínez, who has taken the struggle for civil rights into the arts as cofounder of the Latina Theater Lab in San Francisco.

BIBLIOGRAPHY

Prior to 1969, Martínez published under the byline of Elizabeth Sutherland, her maiden name. Subsequently, she has used two bylines: Elizabeth Sutherland Martínez and Elizabeth Martínez.

500 Years of Chicano History/500 Años del Pueblo Chicano. 1991.

Jonas, Susanne, Ed McCaughan, and Elizabeth Sutherland Martínez, eds. *Guatemala: Tyranny on Trial, Testimony of the Permanent People's Tribunal.* 1984.

Lopéz y Rivas, Gilberto. *The Chicanos: Life and Struggles of the Mexican Minority in the United States*, edited and translated by Elizabeth Martínez. 1973.

Martínez, Elizabeth. "Chicanas and Mexicanas Within a Transnational Working Class: Theoretical Perspectives." In *Between Borders: Essays on Mexicana/Chicana History*, edited by Adelaida Del Castillo. 1990.

Martínez, Elizabeth. *De Colores Means All of Us: Latina Views for a Multi-Colored Century.* 1998.

Martínez, Elizabeth. "Scapegoating Immigrants." In *Immigration: Debating the Issues*, edited by Nicholas Capaldi. 1997.

Martínez, Elizabeth Sutherland, and Enriqueta Longeaux y Vásquez. *Viva La Raza: The Struggle of the Mexican-American People.* 1974.

Sutherland, Elizabeth. *The Youngest Revolution: A Personal Report on Cuba.* 1969.

Sutherland, Elizabeth, ed. *Letters from Mississippi.* 1965.

Luz Elena Ramirez

Maryland

The struggle for civil rights, social and economic justice, and human dignity in Maryland reveals over a century of protest. In this northernmost southern state and the home of black abolitionists Harriet Tubman and Frederick Douglass, the seeds of black resistance seasonally produced fruits of success. The uphill struggle, which is still incomplete, bespeaks the desire and the mettle of people who fought for inclusion in a society that presupposed, yet withheld, democracy.

The demise of slavery in Maryland (even in a state that boasted the largest free urban black population in the 1860s) did not bring unfettered freedom. While black men gained the franchise in 1870 with the Fifteenth Amendment (and without the state legislature's support), racial prejudice circumscribed black Marylanders' lives. Former slaves and free people experienced conscripted labor, vandalism of their homes and churches, and intimidation when they tried to testify in court. By the 1920s, this border state, which strategically aligned itself with the Union cause, continued to deny black women and men in rural and urban areas their civil and human rights. In general, Maryland sought to maintain the status quo along both race and gender lines. For example, despite pressure by suffragettes, Maryland legislators refused to approve the Nineteenth Amendment that gave women the franchise in 1920.

Maryland boasted one of the country's largest Ku Klux Klan state memberships. In Baltimore, its largest city and major trading port, racial ghettoes were formed, partially the result of a 1911 municipal ordinance—the nation's first law designed to establish segregated white and black residential blocks. (Local and federal urban and housing policies would fortify and expand segregation.) Many public accommodations excluded black people, who also occupied the most menial, dirty, service-oriented, and labor-intensive jobs. From the 1880s well into the 1930s, mob violence stained the state's landscape crimson. In 1933, Euel Lee, a sixty-year-old man falsely accused of murdering a white family on the Eastern Shore, was executed despite protests. That same year, 5,000 whites, in a public spectacle at the Somerset County courthouse, burned to death George Armwood, who was charged with assaulting an elderly white woman.

While black women and men struggled on a daily basis, the circumstances of the late 1920s and 1930s—racial segregation, physical terrorism, and economic exclusion during a period of depression—helped heighten and galvanize anew black activism. Baltimore became the state's center for civil rights protests. The city had black religious coalitions, geographically distinct black communities, and was home to the renowned black newspaper, the *Afro-American*. Baltimore also had interracial branches of the Urban League, the Communist Party (which defended Euel Lee), and the Socialist Party (which organized under the slogan "Black and White, Unite and Fight"). (See Communist Party USA.) Even more striking was the central role of black women and youth in the black freedom struggles.

In Baltimore, the City-Wide Young People's Forum, founded in 1931 to educate the community on issues and led by Juanita Jackson, represented just one group that boycotted whites stores, several of which, as a result, began to hire black people. In the 1942, the Baltimore NAACP (by then the second largest chapter in the nation), resuscitated by Lillie Carroll Jackson, Juanita Jackson's mother, organized a march to Annapolis to protest police brutality.

Direct action campaigns continued but would wane in the 1940s as a primary strategy, only to reemerge feverishly in the 1960s. The post-World War II strategy of the NAACP, in particular, took on a gradualist tenor: litigation and voter registration drives. Organizers who believed "your vote is your ticket to freedom" encouraged Maryland's black community to exercise the franchise. In 1954, black votes sent the first black delegate, Harry Cole, of Baltimore, to the state legislature. In 1958, two black women, Verda Welcome and Irma Dixon, were elected; and Woman Power, Inc., a civic and political black women's organization, was founded in Baltimore by Ethel P. Rich and Victorine Adams (who also formed the Colored Democratic Women in 1946 to mobilize the black vote for racially progressive candidates.)

Successful Maryland-based lawsuits such as the *Murray v. University of Maryland* 1935 law school admission case and the equalization of teachers' salaries statewide by 1941 provided precedents for the national NAACP's assault on discrimination. Black women and men, particularly from Baltimore, led the local fight against Jim Crow and secured leadership positions in national civil rights groups. Baltimore lawyer Thurgood Marshall, the first black U.S. Supreme Court Justice, argued the Brown v. Board of Education (1954) case. Clarence Mitchell, Jr., and Juanita Jackson Mitchell, the husband-wife duo, became the chief lobbyist and the youth coordinator, respectively, for the national NAACP.

By the late 1940s and 1950s, gradualism was the order of the day in both strategy and process. The barriers of exclusion to some theaters, hospitals, restaurants, and department stores began to weaken under black pressure and a racially moderate Republican governor, Theodore McKeldin. However, the fact of equality remained a challenge despite such access, appointments to state commissions, representation in the General Assembly, and de jure legal equality in the wake of the *Brown* decision. Local and state policies in response to *Brown*, such as "freedom of choice" in segregated public housing complexes and schools, actually helped more to preserve the status quo than to promote integration.

The early 1960s again witnessed demonstrations against those businesses that remained loyal to the racial edifice of segregation. Morgan State College students sat in at lunch counters in Baltimore and Maryland State College students followed suit in Salisbury. By the mid-1960s, as restaurants, stores, amusement parks, and theaters began to open up, the freedom struggle moved beyond issues of legal equality and access to public facilities to economic injustice.

In the early 1960s, Gloria H. Richardson, of the Cambridge Nonviolent Action Committee, led one of the first grassroots direct action movements outside the Deep South. The Richardson-led Cambridge movement, one of the first major nationwide movements (1962) led by a woman, presaged economic battles and urban uprisings soon to come (in 1963 and again in 1967). The Cambridge Movement focused on housing, unemployment, health care, and sanitation, and in doing so met the wrath of the political power structure and police force.

By 1966, the CONGRESS OF RACIAL EQUALITY (CORE), which made Baltimore a "target city," and the Baltimore-based Union for Jobs and Income Now (U-JOIN) focused on the redistribution of power and economic resources. Numerous grassroots groups—organizing around the rights of blacks, women, poor people, and tenants—emerged, such as the Mother Rescuers from Poverty (1966) and the Baltimore Housing Authority's Resident Advisory Board (1968). By 1968, the year Baltimore erupted in fire after the murder of Dr. Martin Luther KING, JR., the proliferation of rights-based groups questioned legal equality as a cure for discrimination.

White feminist groups followed a trail blazed by black women and men in struggle. For despite gaining the vote and property rights as wives in the early to mid-1900s, many white women discovered that they still experienced legal and political status inequality. They, like black women, faced powerful male dominance in the home and workplace. The Maryland chapter of the NATIONAL ORGANIZATION OF WOMEN (NOW), composed mostly of white female suburbanites, focused on economic and educational equality, and established daycare centers, abortion centers, and battered women shelters in Anne Arundel County and Baltimore. In 1968 in Baltimore, three married white women started the Marxist journal *Women: A Journal of Liberation*, and the women's liberation movement took an antisexist, antiracist, antiwar rhetorical stance and called for the radical restructuring of society. (See WOMEN AND CIVIL RIGHTS STRUGGLES.)

Between 1865 and the late 1970s, the struggles against exclusion and discrimination have rendered victories, particularly in the realm of traditional civil rights. Even so, it is clear that *legal* equality has not made obsolete the necessity for ongoing struggles against racism and sexism, poverty and inadequate educational systems, limited job and housing opportunities, and the assaults on reproductive rights and political representation. At the start of the twenty-first century, activists are also waging battles to protect the civil rights of the disabled; gay, lesbian, bisexual, and transgender persons; and prisoners.

In the 1980s and 1990s, the American Civil Liberties Union (ACLU) of Maryland filed and won a series of black voting rights cases that led to redistricting on the Eastern Shore. The ACLU also secured increased educational funding for Baltimore city schools in 1997. Even so, the 1990s have ushered in new challenges. A lawsuit, *Kirwan v. Podberesky*, filed by a University of Maryland College Park student resulted in the dismantling of the university's minority scholarships programs.

While Baltimore city provides domestic partner benefits and the state took steps in 1998 and 1999 toward decriminalizing gay and lesbian lives by striking down its sodomy and oral sex statutes with regard to consensual sex, Maryland laws still fail to offer basic protections to gay, lesbian, bisexual, and transgender people. In 1999, the General Assembly was considering an Anti-Discrimination Bill and Hate Crimes Bill to expand the state's anti-discrimination laws to cover sexual orientation. In addition, the ACLU remained embroiled in two lawsuits: the *Carmen Thompson et al.* case against the Baltimore Housing Authority, the mayor, and the Department of Housing and Urban Development for racial discrimination in administering the city's low-income federal housing program; and the "driving while black" case (also supported by the Maryland NAACP) against the Maryland State Police for its use of racial profiling in stopping motorists.

BIBLIOGRAPHY

Articles and Books

Argersinger, JoAnn E. *Toward a New Deal in Baltimore.* 1988.

Arnold, Joseph L. "Baltimore: Southern Culture and a Northern Economy." In *Snowbelt Cities: Metropolitan Politics in the Northeast and Midwest Since World War II*, edited by Richard M. Bernard. 1990.

Brock, Annette K. "Gloria Richardson and the Cambridge Movement." In *Women in the Civil Rights Move-*

ment: *Trailblazers & Torchbearers, 1941–1965*, edited by Vicki L. Crawford, Jacqueline Anne Rouse, and Barbara Woods. 1990.

Callcott, George H. *Maryland & America, 1940 to 1980.* 1985.

Fee, Elizabeth, Linda Shopes, and Linda Zeidman, eds. *The Baltimore Book: New Views of Local History.* 1991.

Fields, Barbara. *Slavery and Freedom on the Middle Ground: Maryland During the Nineteenth Century.* 1985.

Skotnes, Andor. *The Black Freedom Movement and the Workers' Movement in Baltimore, 1930–1939.* 1991.

Skotnes, Arnold, "'Buy Where You Can Work': Boycotting for Jobs in African-American Baltimore, 1933–34." *Journal of Social History* 27 (1994): 735–761.

Collections/Documents

African American Vertical File Collection. Enoch Pratt Free Library, Baltimore, Md. This 55,000-item collection includes newspaper clippings from local newspapers including the *Baltimore Afro-American* and *Baltimore Times*, some pamphlets and leaflets and other documents cataloguing important names, organizations, events, places, topics and themes in black Baltimore and America.

Governor Theodore McKeldin–Dr. Lillie May Jackson Project. Maryland Historical Society, Baltimore, Md. This oral history project is an inquiry into the civil rights activities of McKeldin and Jackson during the mid-twentieth century. It is a collection of over eighty interviews conducted between 1975 and 1977 with McKeldin and Jackson, and with people who knew and worked with them. Theodore McKeldin's mayoralty in Baltimore and gubernatorial administrations in Maryland between the 1940s and 1960s.

Is Baltimore Burning? Documents for the Classroom, Maryland State Archives, Annapolis, Md.

Maryland Vertical File Collection. Enoch Pratt Free Library, Baltimore, Md. This collection includes newspaper clippings from Baltimore's newspapers (including the *Baltimore Sun, Evening Sun,* and the now-defunct *News-Post* and *News American*), some pamphlets, and leaflets, bibliographies, reports, government publications and other documents cataloguing important names, organizations, events, places, topics and themes in primarily Baltimore and Maryland.

Documentary/Film

The Road to Brown. Public Broadcasting System (PBS) version, a presentation of The University of Virginia. Film: California Newsreel, San Francisco. ca. 1990.

Rhonda Y. Williams

Mason, Lucy Randolph

(1882–1959), labor movement activist.

Born July 26, 1882, near Alexandria, Virginia, Lucy Randolph Mason became one of the reformers critical to the development of the labor and civil rights movements in the American South. The daughter of an Episcopal minister and a reformer of distinguished southern lineage, Mason nonetheless lacked the means for extensive schooling.

After working as a legal stenographer during her twenties, Mason gained a prominent position within her local (Richmond, Va.) YWCA. (See YOUNG MEN'S CHRISTIAN ASSOCIATION AND YOUNG WOMEN'S CHRISTIAN ASSOCIATION.) Her growing concern for workers' rights was most evident in the feminist portion of political activism, and sometimes involved her in controversy. Following her work as a member of the Union Label League, which promoted the sale of products made by unionized workers, Samuel Gompers named her, in 1917, state chairman of the Committee of Women in Industry of the wartime National Advisory Committee on Labor. Mason interrupted her YWCA activities for five years, from 1918 to 1923, during which time she took care of her father, who was ill, and became involved with a local WOMAN SUFFRAGE organization, seeing female enfranchisement as essential for the enactment of other progressive reforms.

During her tenure as YWCA general secretary (1923–1932), Mason expanded her agenda to include African-American rights and economic well-being. She protested a local SEGREGATION law in Virginia and in 1928 served on a commission, comprised of both blacks and whites, that reviewed the statuses of African-Americans. The commission evolved into the Richmond Urban League, in which Mason also played a leading role. The National Consumers' League (NCL), an organization that was influential in the area of labor reform, admired Mason's work. Under the leadership of Florence Kelley, the NCL supported Mason financially as she formed the Southern Committee on Women and Children in Industry. Mason lobbied on behalf of labor legislation and authored the highly regarded *Standards for Workers in Southern Industry*, a pamphlet published in 1931.

In 1932 Mason assumed Kelley's role as general secretary of the National Consumers' League, and helped to focus more of the organization's attention on the South. As the ROOSEVELT administration was highly sympathetic to labor causes, the NCL gained influence with prominent officials in the NEW DEAL government. Mason's contact with the Congress of Industrial Organizations (CIO; see AFL–CIO) reinforced her belief in the unity of all workers regardless of gender, race, or trade, and from the late 1930s to the early 1950s she acted as a public spokesperson for the CIO in the South. Although the success of her efforts varied with the political climate, she was by this time an extremely experienced and well-connected organizer, whose personal clout and ability to attract public attention helped deter violent opposition to unionization and African-American rights.

Historians view Lucy Randolph Mason as a critical force in the growth of political liberalism in the South and the creation of liberal southern institutions, especially because of her access to prominent figures in government, education, religion, and the media, as well as to members of popular volunteer organizations. Although her life's work stressed practical achievement, her principal legacy is an ideological one: she helped foster the notion that economic justice was an integral part of true democracy, and her emphasis on interracial unity, in part an outgrowth of her Christian faith, played a role in the intellectual genesis of the civil rights movement of the 1960s.

Mason died in 1959 in Atlanta, Georgia, six years after retiring from her political activities. Her autobiography, *To Win These Rights* (1952), chronicled her career as a political activist.

BIBLIOGRAPHY

Carnes, Mark C., and John A. Garraty, eds. *American National Biography* (1999).

Griffith, Barbara. *The Crisis of American Labor: Operation Dixie and the Defeat of the CIO*. 1988.

Reed, Linda. *Simple Decency and Common Sense: The Southern Conference Movement, 1938–1963*. 1991.

Salmond, John. *Miss Lucy of the CIO*. 1988.

Sarah Kurian

Massachusetts

Massachusetts has been at the forefront of American states in protecting the civil rights of its citizens. However, the long road to freedom and equality has been marked with a few bumps and potholes. The first blacks arrived in the Massachusetts Bay Colony in 1638 with Puritan colonists. When the colony adopted a Body of Liberties in 1641, it allowed blacks and Native Americans to be enslaved. This occurred despite Puritan religious beliefs that slavery was morally wrong. In 1656, the colony banned blacks from owning weapons, and in 1705 prohibited interracial marriage; ministers who performed such a ceremony faced a heavy fine. Of course, slavery had its opponents. Anti-slavery activists, led by James Otis, convinced the colonial legislature to pass a law banning slavery in 1771, but English Royal Governor Thomas Hutchinson rejected it. Many blacks, including runaway and freed slaves, came to the New Bedford area, attracted by the Quaker settlement's opposition to slavery there. Throughout the 1700s, blacks served among the crews of whale ships that operated out of the port of New Bedford. Notable among these was Crispus Attucks, a runaway slave who spent twenty years as a whaler and merchant seaman before being killed by British soldiers in the Boston Massacre of 1770. By the time the American colonies declared independence from England in 1776, there were about 5,250 blacks in Massachusetts (about 1.5 percent of the population).

During the 1770s, African Americans in Massachusetts made a concerted effort to end slavery. In 1773, a group of slaves unsuccessfully petitioned the colonial House of Representatives for EMANCIPATION. Another petition was filed in the state legislature in 1777, but the House refused to act on it. Also in 1777, eight black Bostonians petitioned the general court of Massachusetts to abolish slavery, and again the effort failed. However, the state constitution that was adopted in 1780 contained a provision that seemed to bar slavery. Using that provision, a runaway slave sued his "owner" for freedom in 1781. Two years later, the Massachusetts Supreme Court ruled that the U.S. Constitution did ban slavery and declared that all men were "born free and equal." Although slavery continued in the state, it gradually decreased and, by 1790, all blacks there were free. Discrimination, however, continued well into the 1800s as the number of white immigrants (mostly Irish) to the state increased and viewed black residents as economic competition. Blacks found it increasingly difficult to find employment or were hired only for the most menial jobs at bare wages.

As slavery flourished in the southern states, Massachusetts, and particularly Boston, became a hotbed for abolition. In 1833, a coalition of blacks and whites founded the American Anti-Slavery Society in Boston. In 1838, a Maryland slave, Frederick DOUGLASS, fled to Massachusetts and settled in New Bedford. In 1841, Douglass spoke about his experiences as a slave at an abolitionist meeting in Nantucket. For the next four years he traveled as a lecturer for the Massachusetts Anti-Slavery Society. In 1847, he founded the abolitionist newspaper *North Star*. In 1843, the state repealed its ban on interracial marriage. The second half of the nineteenth century saw substantial progress in civil rights, with the first blacks being elected to the state legislature. In Boston, the schools became integrated in 1855 following a lawsuit filed by Benjamin Roberts, a black parent. Massachusetts passed a civil rights act in 1865, and by 1895 had banned racial discrimination in all public facilities. All-black military units from Massachusetts fought courageously in the Civil War and Spanish-American War.

During the early years of the twentieth century, Boston's black population had bifurcated, to some degree, into two distinct societies. Boston was the hub of an African-American elite, composed of such prominent figures as William Henry Lewis, Josephine St.

Pierre Ruffin, Angelina Weld Grimké, Maria Baldwin, and William Monroe TROTTER. Many of this group had attended Harvard University. It included W. E. B DU BOIS, born in Great Barrington, who was a leading member of the group during his years at Harvard University. The "colored elite"—as they referred to themselves—were an aristocracy of talent, were highly educated, and intellectually gifted. Trotter was founding editor of the *Boston Guardian*. It was the *Guardian* that enabled Trotter to promote his views on civil rights and, most notably, to launch his campaign against black leader Booker T. WASHINGTON, leading proponent of assimilationist ideology and, in Trotter's view, the nation's chief impediment to racial equality. It was from his Boston stronghold that Trotter launched his campaign, which consequently propelled him into a national spotlight and established him as a race leader and advocate of "radical" civil rights ideas. Trotter subsequently helped to found such organizations as the NIAGARA MOVEMENT and the Boston Committee to Advance the Cause of the Negro (which in 1910 became the first branch of the NAACP). Trotter continually used the *Guardian* to point out the cruelties, and the absurdities, of racial discrimination. In the 1920s, Trotter led a successful campaign for the integration of the staffs of all city hospitals.

Massachusetts's black population increased markedly during World War II as industrial jobs in defense industries were opening up; however, blacks still represent less than 5 percent of the state's population. Most live in Boston, with many still trapped in inner-city poverty. Other blacks have settled in such places as Springfield and Worcester, both of which were sites of racial conflict during the 1960s. Massachusetts harbors a terrible paradox—the state is and has always been, allegedly, one of the most liberal in the nation, yet Boston has been a site of tremendous racial enmity.

The city of Boston became a civil rights battleground during the 1970s. In 1974, a federal judge declared that Boston's public schools must be integrated. When the school district refused to act on the ruling, federal and state authorities decided to integrate the schools by BUSING black students to predominantly white schools (see SCHOOL DESEGREGATION). Protests by whites, often accompanied by violence, ensued. However, integration became established and within a few years the violence subsided. Racial tensions remain deep-seated, particularly in Boston. A 1985 survey of local social and civil rights workers by the University of Massachusetts in Boston found that 77 percent believed race relations had remained unchanged or worsened since 1982. And racial violence has escalated against other ethnic minority groups, including Chinese and Vietnamese. In 1986, voters defeated a non-binding ballot measure to allow ten mostly black legislative districts in Boston to secede and form a new city called Mandela (after the South African leaders). A wave of racial unrest at the University of Massachusetts led to a 1992 report by a federal civil rights panel calling for more minority recruitment and multicultural studies at the school (see MULTICULTURALISM).

Pilgrim society held women to be inferior, as well as subservient, to men, and forbade them from voting or participating in any political decisions. Independence from England and statehood did not improve the status of women. The Massachusetts Constitution, adopted in 1780, denied women the right to vote. The first substantial challenge to male domination in Massachusetts came in 1850, when Worcester hosted the first national women's rights convention. Two of the most famous WOMAN SUFFRAGE leaders, Susan B. ANTHONY and Lucy STONE, hailed from Massachusetts. In 1847, Stone had become the first Massachusetts woman to earn a college degree. Women did not gain the right to vote until the NINETEENTH AMENDMENT to the U.S. Constitution was approved in 1920. Civil rights for women again came to the foreground in the 1970s with the proposed EQUAL RIGHTS AMENDMENT, which Massachusetts ratified in 1972.

GAY AND LESBIAN RIGHTS became an issue in Massachusetts in the 1970s. In 1979, the state supreme court ruled that citizens could not file discrimination claims based on sexual orientation. However, the state legislature passed a gay rights measure in 1989 banning discrimination against gays in HOUSING, EMPLOYMENT, and credit, becoming only the second state to do so. Massachusetts was the first state to elect openly gay congressmen: Gerry E. Studds (1973–1997) and Barney Frank (1981–   ). In 1993, the Massachusetts Supreme Court ruled that a lesbian couple could legally adopt a child, opening the way for additional gay adoptions.

BIBLIOGRAPHY

Abbott, Lyman. "Why Women Do Not Wish the Suffrage." *Atlantic Monthly* 92 (September 1903): 289–296.
Bull, Chris. "A Clean Sweep" (Gay Legislation in New England). *The Advocate* 738 (July 22, 1997): 35–36.
Greene, Lorenzo. *The Negro in Colonial New England*. 1942.
Hampton, Henry, and Steve Fayer. *Voices of Freedom*. 1990.
Kerr, Andrea M. *Lucy Stone: Speaking Out for Equality*. 1992.
Piersen, William D. *Black Yankees: The Development of an Afro-American Subculture in Eighteenth Century New England*. 1988.
Reidy, Joseph P. "Negro Election Day and Black Community Life in New England, 1750–1860." *Marxist Perspectives* 1 (Fall 1978).
Salzman, Jack, David Lionel Smith, and Cornel West, eds. *Encyclopedia of African-American Culture and History*. 1996.

Starr-Lebeau, Gretchen D. *American Eras* (Series). 1997.

Ken R. Wells

Massive Resistance

On May 17, 1954, the United States SUPREME COURT ruled unanimously in BROWN V. BOARD OF EDUCATION that segregated public schools were unconstitutional. Separate schools for blacks and whites had long been the rule in much of the United States, and the Court's ruling came as unwelcomed news to many whites. While schools in the North had already experienced DESEGREGATION to some degree, schools throughout the South enforced a rigid color line that had kept black and white schools separate for generations. The *Brown* decision represented the greatest threat to white supremacy since RECONSTRUCTION, and even the most optimistic observers understood that the vast majority of white southerners still favored SEGREGA-TION, and that many of them were prepared to resort to whatever means were necessary to maintain it.

Newspaper editorials from across the nation tended to reflect the mood of their constituencies, and opinions in the South were decidedly different from those in the North. While most editorials called upon readers to remain calm, and several others (mainly in the North) praised the decision, many southern newspapers were defiant, some going so far as to predict violence if the federal government tried to enforce desegregation in the South. An increasing number of whites—especially white southern politicians—began to rail against the evils of school "integration." ("Integration" generally implies a greater degree of social interaction than "desegregation," and white southern politicians often deliberately conflated the two terms so as to strengthen opposition to *Brown*.)

On February 24, 1956, U.S. Senator Harry F. BYRD of VIRGINIA, one of the South's most influential segregationists, issued a statement from Washington, D.C., in which he first used the phrase "massive resistance": "If we can organize the Southern States for massive resistance to this order [*Brown*] I think that in time the rest of the country will realize that racial integration is not going to be accepted in the South." The very next month, Senator Byrd and SOUTH CARO-LINA's Senator J. Strom THURMOND, another die-hard segregationist, took the lead in drafting the "SOUTHERN MANIFESTO." Eventually signed by 92 of the 106 southern members of the U.S. CONGRESS, the "Southern Manifesto" condemned the *Brown* decision as an unwarranted intrusion by the federal government into local matters and vowed to use "every lawful means" to resist its implementation. During the first three months of 1956, the legislatures of ALABAMA,

GEORGIA, MISSISSIPPI, South Carolina, and Virginia— five of the most defiant states—enacted a total of forty-two prosegregation statutes.

Over the next several months, one southern state after another passed a series of measures aimed at preventing school desegregation. Five states amended their compulsory public school attendance laws so that no white child would be forced to attend a desegregated school. Four states passed legislation to withhold state funding from schools that desegregated. Eight states passed various "interposition" resolutions urging defiance of the *Brown* decision, even to the point of authorizing the governor to close the schools. Ten states passed laws intended to cripple the NA-TIONAL ASSOCIATION FOR THE ADVANCEMENT OF COL-ORED PEOPLE. The NAACP had been in the forefront of the school desegregation battle, and was a frequent target of segregationists, who regarded it as sinister and communist-inspired. While much of this legislation was genuinely intended to prevent desegregation, some of the laws—having been drafted hastily and out of anger—bordered on the ridiculous, and were meant to be more of a statement than an actual policy. For example, the Georgia House of Delegates passed a resolution demanding a return to segregation in the armed forces, the impeachment of Supreme Court justices, and the nullification of the THIRTEENTH and FOURTEENTH AMENDMENTS.

Perhaps the best-known example of massive resistance to school desegregation occurred in Little Rock, ARKANSAS, in the fall of 1957. Arkansas governor Orval FAUBUS had defied the courts by refusing to allow nine black students to enroll at Central High School. In a brazen display of defiance, he ordered 250 National Guardsmen to prevent the black students from entering the school. When the students arrived at the school, they were greeted by an angry white mob. As the violence in Little Rock escalated, President Dwight D. EISENHOWER (who had never publicly endorsed the *Brown* decision) was compelled to assert the supremacy of federal law by dispatching more than a thousand members of the 101st Airborne Division to Little Rock, and he ordered the Arkansas National Guard to protect the nine black students, the so-called LITTLE ROCK NINE. For the remainder of the year, federal troops were stationed at the school. Once the school year had ended, Governor Faubus renewed his political posturing. Even after the Supreme Court ruled unanimously in September 1958 that school desegregation must proceed in Little Rock, Faubus responded by shutting down all public schools in Little Rock for the 1958–1959 school year. In a Gallup Poll taken in late 1958, Americans selected Faubus as one of their ten most admired men. In the gubernatorial contest that fall he won reelection by a landslide, and remained virtually unbeatable in Arkansas politics for the better part of a decade. Faubus, along with Governors Ross Barnett of Mississippi and George WALLACE of Alabama, as well as a host of others, became representative of white southern politicians who rose to national prominence because of their unabashed opposition to school desegregation.

With the notable exception of Prince Edward County, Virginia, where the public schools remained closed from 1959 until 1964, massive resistance quietly came to an end in the early 1960s. By then, crafty southern politicians realized that open defiance of federal law was no longer feasible or necessary. Massive resistance gradually gave way to "passive resistance," wherein local school districts merely gave the appearance of complying with *Brown*, when in fact their desegregation plans were nothing more than sophisticated schemes designed to forestall actual implementation. As a result, most southern school districts did not achieve significant desegregation until the early 1970s, and by then the full impact of *Brown* had already been blunted by determined segregationists. Despite the Supreme Court's noble intentions in 1954, "massive resistance" had demonstrated the depth of white resentment to school desegregation and the willingness of some to defy federal law in the pursuit of their objectives.

BIBLIOGRAPHY

Bartley, Numan V. *The Rise of Massive Resistance: Race and Politics in the South During the 1950s.* 1969.

Bass, Jack, and Walter Devries. *The Transformation of Southern Politics: Social Change and Political Consequence Since 1945.* 1976.

Douglas, Davison M. *Reading, Writing & Race: The Desegregation of the Charlotte Schools.* 1995.

Ely, James W. *The Crisis of Conservative Virginia: The Byrd Organization and the Politics of Massive Resistance.* 1971.

Klarman, Michael J. "How *Brown* Changed Race Relations: The Backlash Thesis." *Journal of American History* 81 (1994): 81–118.

Martin, John B. *The Deep South Says "Never."* 1957.

Murphy, Walter F. "The South Counterattacks: The Anti-NAACP Laws." *Western Political Quarterly* 12 (June 1959): 371–90.

Muse, Benjamin. *Ten Years of Prelude: The Story of Integration Since the Supreme Court's 1954 Decision.* 1964.

Pratt, Robert A. *The Color of Their Skin: Education and Race in Richmond, Virginia, 1954–89.* 1992.

Smith, Robert (Bob) Collins. *They Closed Their Schools: Prince Edward County, Virginia, 1951–1964.* 1965.

Robert A. Pratt

Mattachine Society

The Mattachine Society was not only the first organization to advocate for homosexual rights in the United States, but also the first to put forth the idea that homosexuals were a minority group which suffered from injustice and oppression. Five men living in southern California established the organization in 1950, although one of these men, Harry Hay, is generally recognized as its main founder. Hay named the society after a group of unmarried men in medieval France who performed as masked dancers.

The Communist Party backgrounds of some of Mattachine's founders shaped their political analysis, leading them to conclude that homosexuals needed to reject the idea that they were simply individuals with personal problems, and instead develop a group consciousness from which to build a movement for social change. Mattachine's leaders also recognized that their group shared with the Communist Party a need for secrecy of membership, given the hostility in cold war America toward both Communists and homosexuals. Consequently, Mattachine's founders decided to organize the group into a complex, hierarchical, secret structure patterned after the Communist Party's structure.

Men comprised the bulk of Mattachine's membership, and this influenced the first political campaign the organization led. In 1952 police arrested one of the founding members, Dale Jennings, for lewd behavior in a park. Rather than quietly submitting to the legal penalties as was the norm in such cases, Jennings challenged the arrest, charging that the police had accosted and entrapped him. Mattachine printed and distributed leaflets protesting police entrapment and soliciting contributions for a legal defense fund. The case went to trial, the jury deadlocked, and the district attorney dropped the charges. This first victory for the organization led to a rapid expansion in membership across California, and soon, across the country.

As the organization grew it began to meet with internal dissent. The Communist affiliation of its founders, its secretive leadership structure, and its radical political analysis met with increasing criticism, exploding into a rejection of the founders and the establishment of a new leadership core in 1953. Subsequently, the group moved away from collective action and toward trying to persuade the general public that homosexuals were as respectable as any other American citizens. The group's membership in this period declined, but its newsletter, *The Mattachine Review* as well as *ONE* magazine, an independent publication that was originally affiliated with the organization, enjoyed a wide circulation.

By 1960 the New York City chapter of the group was the biggest in the country. Continued in-fighting between members and chapters led, in 1961, to a dissolution of the national organization, making each chapter independent.

Several of the Mattachine groups on the East Coast stepped up their political engagement in the 1960s. Taking some of their inspiration and techniques from the African-American civil rights movement, the New York and Washington Mattachine societies allied with other East Coast gay and lesbian groups to hold protests and pickets, lobby the medical establishment to depathologize homosexuality, and seek to end civil service discrimination against homosexuals. The resurgence of this more politically engaged, radical stream culminated in the emergence of gay liberation in the late 1960s, a phenomenon often associated with the STONEWALL RIOT of 1969.

BIBLIOGRAPHY

D'Emilio, John. *Sexual Politics, Sexual Communities: The Making of a Homosexual Minority in the United States, 1940–70.* 1983.

Katz, Jonathan. *Gay American History: Lesbians and Gay Men in the U.S.A.: A Documentary History*, rev. ed. 1992.

Sears, James T. *Lonely Hunters: An Oral History of Lesbian and Gay Southern Life, 1948–68.* 1997.

Timmons, Stuart. *The Trouble with Harry Hay: Founder of the Modern Gay Movement.* 1990.

Pippa Holloway

Mays, Benjamin Elijah

(1894–1984), educator.

Benjamin Elijah Mays was an educator who by personal example and as president of Morehouse College (1940–1967) influenced a generation of black leaders.

Born in Greenwood County, South Carolina, Mays attended high school at South Carolina A&M College and received his B.A. from Bates College (1920), and his M.A. (1925) and Ph.D. (1935) from the University of Chicago. He held a variety of posts in his early career, including Executive Secretary of the Tampa Urban League (1926–1928), National Secretary of the YMCA (1928–1930), and chief investigator for a study of black churches (1930–1932). May's two most significant positions were the deanship at Howard University School of Religion (1934–1940) and the presidency of Morehouse College (1940–1967).

Mays contributed to the civil rights movement as an early activist and mentor. He set an example by living according to his principles and taking individual stands against SEGREGATION. He also worked with the interracial movement, including the COMMISSION ON INTERRACIAL COOPERATION, the Association of Southern Women for the Prevention of Lynching, and

Benjamin E. Mays, center, with hands resting on table, meets with President John Kennedy and others in the Oval Office in 1962.

the SOUTHERN REGIONAL COUNCIL, which he helped found. More important, as president of Morehouse College he influenced, through his leadership, friendship, and weekly chapel sermons, a number of later leaders, including foremost Martin Luther KING, JR., whose eulogy he performed, but also Julian BOND, Samuel Dubois Cook, Maynard Jackson, Lonnie King, and Andrew YOUNG. In his later life Mays served as president of the Atlanta Board of Education and helped oversee the desegregation of the school system.

BIBLIOGRAPHY

Colston, Freddie C. "Dr. Benjamin E. Mays: His Impact as Spiritual and Intellectual Mentor of Martin Luther King, Jr." *The Black Scholar* 23 (2) (1993): 6–15.

Matthews, Verner R. "The Concept of Racial Justice of Benjamin Elijah Mays (1895–1984) [sic] and Its Relevance to Christian Education in the Black Church." Ph.D. dissertation, New York University. 1991.

Mays, Benjamin Elijah. *The Negro's God as Reflected in His Literature.* 1938.

Mays, Benjamin Elijah. *Born to Rebel.* 1971.

Mays, Benjamin Elijah, with Joseph William Nicholson. *The Negro's Church.* 1933.

Mays, Benjamin Elijah, with Joseph William Nicholson. *Seeking to Be Christian in Race Relations.* 1965.

Preskill, Stephen. "Combative Spirituality and the Life of Benjamin E. Mays." *Biography* 19 (4) (1996): 404–416.

Tracy E. K'Meyer

McCarran–Walter Immigration Act

The McCarran–Walter Immigration Act of 1952 was a typical piece of COLD WAR–era legislation. Since it was essentially a continuation of the quota system established in the 1920s, President Harry S. TRUMAN vetoed it, in part because "it discriminates, deliberately and intentionally, against many of the peoples of the world." It was passed over his veto. The law added harsh anticommunist provisions that barred distinguished visitors, such as the French philosopher Jean-Paul Sartre, on the grounds of their "subversive" political associations, and expanded the grounds for political deportation. It also charged immigrants from colonies to the quota of their mother country, but limited the number from any colony to 100 per year and mitigated chiefly against Afro-Caribbeans, such as Jamaicans, who had heretofore been able to enter the United States relatively freely. This had the unexpected effect of spurring the migrations of Afro-Caribbeans to the United Kingdom. And it broadened the family reunification provisions of existing law, un-

President Lyndon B. Johnson signing the repeal of the McCarran-Walter Immigration Act. (LBJ Library Collections)

der which the families of American citizens could enter without "numerical restriction"—that is, over and above the quota numbers.

But amid these largely reactionary provisions, the law ended the discrimination against Asians in the NATURALIZATION laws and made naturalization, for the first time, color-blind. The reasons for the passage of such a provision—which Truman applauded in his veto message—were complex. Many in CONGRESS—but far from a majority—were intellectually committed to at least formal equality. But perhaps even more of those who favored the liberalized naturalization provisions were cold warriors who had begun to understand that it was difficult for the United States to be the true "leader of the free world" while one of its basic laws barred a majority of the world's peoples from naturalization.

The McCarran–Walter Act had one totally unexpected consequence. The combination of two of its provisions—color-blind naturalization and broadened family reunification—set in train the vast increase in immigration from Asia that is often credited solely to the admittedly liberal IMMIGRATION ACT OF 1965.

BIBLIOGRAPHY

Daniels, Roger. *Coming to America: A History of Immigration and Ethnicity in American Life.* 1990.
Reimers, David. *Still the Golden Door: The Third World Comes to America,* 2nd ed. 1992.

Roger Daniels

Senator Joseph McCarthy, chairman of the Senate Investigations Subcommittee, at a Washington, D.C., press conference in 1954. (Photos/APA)

McCarthyism

In February 1950, as COLD WAR tensions intensified, Senator Joseph McCarthy of Wisconsin charged that recent foreign policy reverses could be explained by the presence of communists in the U.S. State Department, and he began naming names. He could not substantiate his charges and never exposed a single spy, but the careers of many were ruined. McCarthyism is the term that came to be applied to such irresponsible accusations.

The outbreak of the KOREAN WAR that summer deepened a red scare in which not only government employees but other individuals and groups too could be accused of communist sympathies. Liberal politicians, often sympathetic to civil rights, were particularly vulnerable to such charges, as were celebrities in the entertainment industry. In Florida in 1950 the New Dealer Claude Pepper lost his seat in the U.S. Senate following attacks on his "Red Record," and in California Richard NIXON won a seat after depicting his liberal Democratic opponent (actress Helen Gahagan Douglas) as "the Pink Lady." Civil rights organizations were impugned similarly as abettors of communism. The CONGRESS OF RACIAL EQUALITY (CORE) succumbed early to Cold War pressures, prohibiting "communist-controlled" groups in 1948 from affiliating with it, and in 1950 the NATIONAL ASSOCIATION FOR THE ADVANCEMENT OF COLORED PEOPLE (NAACP) resolved to expel any communist-led branches. These harassed organizations ensured their own survival by distancing themselves from the Communist Party, but at the cost of compromising their records on civil liberties. The weakening of McCarthyism from about 1954 on eased the reemergence of the civil rights movement.

BIBLIOGRAPHY

Heale, M. J. *American Anticommunism: Combating the Enemy Within, 1830–1970.* 1990.
Powers, Richard Gid. *Not Without Honor: The History of American Anticommunism.* 1995.
Schrecker, Ellen. *Many Choices: McCarthyism in America.* 1998.

M. J. Heale

McKissick, Floyd Bixler

(1922–1991), lawyer and civil rights leader.

Floyd McKissick, who served as the national director of the CONGRESS OF RACIAL EQUALITY (CORE) (1966–1969), a developer of Soul City (1971–1980), and a state district court judge (1990–1991), contributed widely to DESEGREGATION, black empowerment, and the justice system.

McKissick emerged as a leader in the southern freedom struggle. He was a native of Asheville, NORTH CAROLINA, where he attended one of the state's few high schools for blacks. His father, a bellhop, and mother encouraged the child to be independent. When a white policeman arrested Floyd for directing traffic around his Boy Scout troop's roller-skating contest, Asheville's branch of the NATIONAL ASSOCIATION FOR THE ADVANCEMENT OF COLORED PEOPLE (NAACP) protested, and he joined the group. He attended Morehouse College, in Atlanta, before joining the Army in 1942. Advancing to sergeant, he earned five battle stars and the Purple Heart in WORLD WAR II.

While earning A.B. and LL.B. degrees at Durham's North Carolina College (NCC), McKissick battled JIM CROW by nonviolent direct action. He briefly accompanied CORE's interracial team, which endured threats and some arrests, on the North Carolina leg of its 1947 bus Journey of Reconciliation. In 1949, when NCC law students picketed in Raleigh over unequal facilities, he took legal action. *McKissick v. Carmichael* (1951), won in the U.S. Court of Appeals for the FOURTH CIRCUIT, made him the University of North Carolina Law School's first black student. As counsel for North Carolina's NAACP he sued for the Durham public schools to desegregate under the 1954 BROWN V. BOARD OF EDUCATION decision (plaintiffs included his five children), and summoned the state to enforce the CIVIL RIGHTS ACT OF 1957. He represented black pastor and SOUTHERN CHRISTIAN LEADERSHIP CONFERENCE (SCLC) board member Douglas E. Moore, who faced prosecution for leading a 1957 Durham sit-in. McKissick and Moore's youth nonviolence workshops foreshadowed the 1960s student movement.

McKissick became nationally controversial in the 1960s. As NCC's NAACP–CORE advisor and North Carolina CORE organizer, he used mass activism to forge RACE and CLASS inclusion. He led the 1962 Freedom Highways Campaign, an offspring of the 1961 FREEDOM RIDES. Targeting segregated Howard Johnson's restaurants, the campaign fueled massive Piedmont SIT-INS in 1963. Black nationalism permeated CORE's ranks, meantime, and McKissick embraced it. In 1963, debating liberation strategies with NATION OF ISLAM minister MALCOLM X, McKissick justified INTE-GRATION, peaceful protest, and judicial reform even as persistent black poverty and police brutality angered him. By 1966 he preached BLACK POWER, self-defense, and racial separatism. White liberals steadily quit CORE. Yet in his moderate *Three-Fifths of a Man* (1969), McKissick advocated black economic power via corporate and governmental assistance.

That strategy underlay Soul City, covering 3,400 acres one mile off U.S. Route 1 between Warrenton and Manson in rural Warren County, North Carolina. McKissick Enterprises, a supporter of President Richard M. NIXON's reelection, financed its development from 1971 to 1978 through federally guaranteed loans, grants, and contracts totaling $31 million. Infrastructures, including a water treatment plant, were completed, and hope abounded. But job-creating industries did not materialize, and housing construction dragged. The town also incurred damaging federal audits and U.S. Senator Jesse A. Helms's opposition, defaulting on its loans in 1980. In 1988, the community had a fire station, health clinic, preschool center, recreation complex, and forty-one homeowners, McKissick among them.

Republican Governor James G. Martin appointed McKissick to a North Carolina district court judgeship in 1990, the culmination of an exemplary legal career.

BIBLIOGRAPHY

Carson, Clayborne. *In Struggle: SNCC and the Black Awakening of the 1960s.* 1981.
Davidson, Osha Gray. *The Best of Enemies: Race and Redemption in the New South.* 1996.
McKissick, Floyd B. *Three-Fifths of a Man.* 1969.
Meier, August, and Elliott Rudwick. *CORE: A Study in the Civil Rights Movement.* 1975.
"Soul City." *North Carolina Collection Clipping File* 64 (1979): 1038–1081; ibid. 155 (1979): 642–707. North Carolina Collection, Louis Round Wilson Library of the University of North Carolina at Chapel Hill.
Van Deburg, William L. *New Day in Babylon: The Black Power Movement and American Culture, 1965–1975.* 1992.

Raymond Gavins

Means, Russell

(1939–   ), Indian activist and leader of the American Indian Movement's 1973 takeover of Wounded Knee.

Russell Means, a Lakota/Oglala, was born on the Pine Ridge Reservation in South Dakota, but spent most of his childhood off the reservation in California. He joined the AMERICAN INDIAN MOVEMENT (AIM) in 1970 and quickly assumed a leadership role. The goals of the movement were to draw attention to the injus-

Russell Means, leader of the American Indian Movement, testifies before a special investigative committee of the Senate Select Committee on Capitol Hill, January 31, 1993. (AP/Wide World Photos)

tices American Indians suffered at the hands of state and federal governments, especially the BUREAU OF INDIAN AFFAIRS (BIA), to win back Indian sovereignty by the enforcement of treaties, and to ease the economic plight of Indians on the reservations. Means helped to get national media exposure by taking part in demonstrations at Mount Rushmore in 1970 and later that year, at Plymouth Plantation. The TRAIL OF BROKEN TREATIES in 1972 brought Indians from across the United States to Washington, D.C., to sit in at the BIA building.

The representatives of the Oglala nation especially wanted to have the government uphold the Fort Laramie 1868 treaty, which honored the Lakota nation's claims to its homelands in the northern Plains, with the sacred grounds of the Paha Sapa, the Black Hills. The WOUNDED KNEE OCCUPATION, a siege lasting from February to May 1973, was led by Means for that purpose and also with the hope of securing the removal of Richard Wilson from power over Pine Ridge Reservation. Wilson had ruled with an iron fist and with the support of the BIA. Federal marshals fortified the BIA Building on the reservation and called in massive firepower. The subsequent trial of Means and his AIM colleague Dennis BANKS and their acquittal focused attention on the behavior of the FEDERAL BUREAU OF INVESTIGATION (FBI) during and after the siege.

Means defeated Wilson for political control of Pine Ridge reservation in 1974, but maneuvering (and perhaps fraud) by Wilson led to Means's victory being overturned.

Means was a traditional dancer, and as such it was important to him not merely to ensure political rights, such as Lakota sovereignty, but also the religious and cultural rejuvenation of Indians. One of the first activists to wear traditional Indian clothing and braids, he strove to bring back Indian pride and spirituality to his own people.

Means survived four attempts on his life, including a stabbing in prison, where he served a year after being found guilty of "rioting to obstruct justice." After his release in 1979, he became part of the Black Hills Alliance, an environmentalist action group that succeeded in stopping strip mining in the area. Means then started a camp as part of his mission to reclaim Indian sovereignty of the Black Hills. "Yellow Thunder Camp" was an embodiment of a traditional Indian lifestyle, and Means lived there until 1983. He tried to run again for Pine Ridge president in 1984, but his ex-convict status led to his candidacy being ruled ineligible.

Still an influential figure, Means played the role of Chingachgook in the movie *The Last of The Mohicans* in 1991. He has continued to work through the legal system for redress and for Indian independence.

BIBLIOGRAPHY
Matthiessen, Peter. *In the Spirit of Crazy Horse.* 1983.
Means, Russell, with Marvin J. Wolf. *Where White Men Fear To Tread: The Autobiography of Russell Means.* 1995.

Noeleen McIlvenna

M.E.Ch.A.

See Movimiento Estudiantil Chicano de Aztlan

Meier, August

(1923–   ), historian.

August Meier, a pioneering scholar of African-American history and supporter of the civil rights movement, was born in Newark, New Jersey, of German and Jewish ancestry. In 1945, following his graduation from Oberlin College, Meier took a teaching position at Tougaloo College, a black institution in Mississippi, where he taught classes in Negro history. In 1948, Meier left Tougaloo for doctoral studies at Columbia University. While completing his dissertation, Meier held research positions at Howard and Fisk universities and contributed black history essays to THE CRISIS and other publications. Meanwhile, in 1951 and 1956, he served as secretary of the Newark branch of the NATIONAL ASSOCIATION FOR THE ADVANCEMENT OF COLORED PEOPLE (NAACP), where his status as a white activist brought him unusual visibility within the organization.

In 1957, after receiving his Ph.D., Meier became a professor at Morgan State University in Baltimore. In 1960, when the SIT-INS began, Meier became advisor to a nonviolent action group, the Civic Interest Group, loosely affiliated with the STUDENT NONVIOLENT COORDINATING COMMITTEE (SNCC), and he participated in numerous demonstrations. He also wrote critical analyses of the civil rights movement for publications such as *New Politics.*

In 1963, after he published *Negro Thought in America, 1880–1915,* Meier took a position at Roosevelt University in Chicago and scaled back his protest activities. In ensuing years, during which period he taught at Kent State University in Chicago, he became known for the scholarly studies of black protest he wrote with his colleague Elliott Rudwick, notably *From Plantation to Ghetto* (1966), *CORE* (1973), and *Along the Color Line* (1976). These works historically treated both integrationist and nationalist theories.

BIBLIOGRAPHY
Meier, August. *A White Scholar and the Black Community, 1945–1965.* 1992.
Meier, August, and Elliott Rudwick. *CORE: A Study in The Civil Rights Movement, 1942–1968.* 1973.

Greg Robinson

Memphis Civil Rights Museum

See National Civil Rights Museum

Memphis Sanitation Workers' Strike of 1968

On February 12, 1968, thirteen hundred black sanitation workers walked off the job in Memphis, TENNESSEE. Few suspected the strike would escalate into one of the climactic struggles of the 1960s. By the time their strike ended with a contract sixty-four days later, the tenor of labor and race relations in Memphis had changed forever. The struggle of the poorest of black workers for fair wages and union benefits revived a dormant labor movement, and reignited a black freedom movement in the city that had never come to full heat. The workers themselves provided the main leadership for this uprising of the urban poor, but they were joined by preachers, students, teachers, and the black middle class, creating one of the most vibrant all-class movements for social justice and racial improvement seen anywhere in the South.

Memphis had long been ruled by paternalistic city administrations that had nearly crushed both union and civil rights organizing. From before WORLD WAR I to the 1950s, political boss E. H. Crump created a repressive system of one-man rule. Craft unions had excluded African Americans from the best jobs, and long-standing racism among white workers and the wave of anticommunist hysteria after WORLD WAR II had limited the impact of industrial unions and the growth of social change organizations. The NATIONAL ASSOCIATION FOR THE ADVANCEMENT OF COLORED PEOPLE (NAACP) operated virtually underground until the 1950s. But change began to come in the early 1960s, as NAACP-led picketing and SIT-INS desegregated public facilities, with only minor clashes with white authorities. In Tennessee, blacks retained voting rights, although under onerous conditions imposed by the poll tax. As early as 1964, blacks were able to elect an African American to the state legislature, and by 1967 they had elected three blacks to city government when an at-large voting system was eliminated. The white power structure, however, believed that change had gone far enough, and frustrations brewed as economic conditions deteriorated in a predominantly poor black community.

In a city of 540,000 people, some 40 percent of them black, nearly 60 percent of African Americans lived below the poverty line. Blacks suffered disproportionately high mortality rates and deficits in basic education in a highly segregated school system. Mechanization undercut jobs in cotton production in the rural areas and factory employment in the city, worsening the plight of the working poor. Political progress was stymied by a split in the black vote in 1967, which allowed the election of Mayor Henry Loeb, a Republican fiscal conservative. Loeb's election and that of Republican Dan Kuykendall signaled a shift to the right and a hardening of racial lines among the city's white voters.

Under these conditions, African Americans quickly came to see the sanitation strike of 1968 as symbolic of the strivings of the working poor and a representation of the general demand by African Americans for civil equality and economic opportunity. Members of the American Federation of State, County, and Municipal Employees (AFSCME) Local 1733 first sought the city's recognition of their right to union representation, without which they could do little about their work conditions. But Mayor Loeb refused to accept their right to bargain. Long before Loeb's election, union leader T. O. Jones and others had been fired and blacklisted for union activities; he and other sanitation workers had been asking the city for union recognition and for a resolution of their many grievances since 1963.

Local members say that Local 1733 was named after thirty-three fired workers, and they made their right to belong to a union their core strike demand. They placed this demand within the context framed by Rev. Albert Hibbler, a rank and file member of the union who coined the slogan that came to represent the nature of the Memphis struggle. "I Am a Man" called for the recognition of the humanity of African Americans and their right to represent themselves through the union of their choice.

Sanitation workers had many grievances. They lived below the poverty level, many of them qualifying for welfare while working full-time jobs. They received almost no health care benefits, pensions, or vacations, worked in filthy conditions, and lacked a place to eat lunch or to shower after days when they carried leaky garbage tubs that spilled maggots and refuse on them. White supervisors called black men "boys" and sent them home without pay for being even a moment late for work.

The 1968 walkout occurred spontaneously after supervisors sent blacks home without pay during a rainstorm, while keeping white supervisors on at full pay.

A malfunctioning garbage compacter had recently crushed two black men to death, highlighting the unsafe conditions; the city's failure to pay significant benefits fueled the men's rage at conditions they could no longer tolerate. Union activist Taylor Rogers, who became the president of Local 1733 after the strike, later recalled that "we just got tired" of such treatment and walked out. They did so in the dead of winter, not the best time to call a sanitation strike, without consulting the national union. Nonetheless, AFSME soon sent representatives in to assist them.

The strike polarized the city racially after police attacked a march by sanitation workers and ministers to city hall only a few days into the strike. Indiscriminate beatings and macings of prominent blacks by the city's police galvanized strike support among black ministers and the civil rights community, as most whites rallied to the mayor's effort to suppress the strike. Daily mass meetings, picketing, and a boycott of Memphis businesses and commercial newspapers (which African Americans thought consistently distorted the facts and issues in the strike), jointly organized by black workers and black ministers, highlighted the strike's importance not only to workers but to the whole black community. The strike turned into an impressive mass movement, as white resistance and continuing police brutality also made it an increasingly stark racial confrontation reminiscent of the tumultuous battles in Montgomery, Birmingham, St. Augustine, Selma, and other centers of the Southern struggle.

A month into the strike, Dr. Martin Luther KING, JR., came to Memphis at the request of his longtime ally Rev. James LAWSON, who pastored Centenary United Methodist Church in Memphis. King was in the midst of organizing the POOR PEOPLE'S CAMPAIGN, an effort to take the grievances of the poor directly to the seat of national government in Washington, D.C. Roy WILKINS and Bayard RUSTIN had already spoken in Memphis; but King's March 18 speech focused national media attention on the strike for the first time and gave a lift to the strikers, who were growing discouraged. King's participation also led to increased strike support by national and local trade unions as well as the civil rights community.

King's reception in Memphis raised his hopes that a focus on the plight of the unemployed poor and the working poor could revive and unify the flagging social movements of the late 1960s. By the time King returned to Memphis for a mass march on March 28, however, tensions in Memphis had risen to a fever pitch, BLACK POWER advocates and youth had become increasingly incensed at police brutality, and were impatient with mass marches. King arrived late when a bomb threat delayed his air transportation, making an impatient crowd increasingly restless. Window breaking during the march, apparently instigated by by-standers and perhaps some marchers, touched off a police riot. Leaders could no longer maintain discipline, and, fearing the worst, Rev. Lawson forced King to leave and turned the march around. The police, however, savagely beat the protesters and went on a rampage throughout Memphis's black community. Confronting unarmed sixteen-year-old Larry Payne in a nearby housing project, a police officer shot him to death, claiming that he thought he was reaching for a weapon. Meanwhile, at the request of Mayor Loeb, four thousand National Guard members occupied the city.

In the aftermath of these incidents, the national media overwhelmingly pinned responsibility for violence in Memphis on King, while a Memphis court enjoined him from leading further marches. This turn of events threatened to destroy the credibility of King's campaign for a nonviolent poor people's march on Washington, and forced him to return to Memphis and to seek a lifting of the court injunction and to lead a mass nonviolent march. An exhausted King spoke at a mass meeting in Mason Temple on the night of April 3. He dramatically reviewed his life in the freedom struggle, called for support of a worldwide "human rights revolution," and, in an emotional climax to the speech, prophesied that "I may not get there with you, but I want you to know tonight that we as a people will get to the promised land."

King's April 4 assassination at the Lorraine Motel, for which James Earl Ray was later convicted and sentenced to life imprisonment, led to massive riots all over the United States. Turmoil in the streets of Memphis was muted, however. On April 7 some eight thousand Memphians, most of them white, expressed their concern about what was happening in their city. A completely silent mass of twenty thousand to forty thousand people from Memphis and all over the United States marched through the streets of Memphis in silent outrage and grief on April 8.

King's death forced the city to negotiate. President Lyndon JOHNSON called Tennessee Governor Buford Ellington and pressured him into allowing a representative of the city to meet with and recognize Local 1733, and to create a means to check off union dues from workers' pay checks. The victory of Local 1733 initiated a wave of public employee union organizing among black workers in other parts of the South. In Memphis, AFSCME became the largest union local, providing the strength needed to spread public employee unionism and increase black voter registration. Wages for sanitation workers climbed and work conditions improved dramatically. African-American workers took on a higher profile in the labor movement and as voters. Civil rights leaders such as Mem-phis NAACP Director Maxine Smith became increasingly active in school board and other issues. The African-American community continued its pressure to open up jobs in previously forbidden zones of white-collar employment and in the police force, and protested continuing police brutality. In 1991, an expanding black population and political activism led to the election of African-American Willie Herrenton as mayor, as Memphians attempted to reconcile the city's history of racial polarization by creating the NATIONAL CIVIL RIGHTS MUSEUM at the Lorraine Motel, scene of Dr. King's martyrdom.

These improvements came at a great cost, however. Ever since April 4, 1968, the nation has struggled to draw meaning from King's death. In celebrating his January 15 birthday, the country's memory has focused mainly on King's speech at the Lincoln Monument in 1963, not on his leadership of the poor and workers in 1968. The sanitation strike and the Poor People's Campaign of 1968 have remained part of an unresolved and almost unmentioned legacy of the freedom movement's struggle to address the demands of poor people, in the midst of the growing racial and economic disparities of the global economy at the dawn of the twenty-first century.

BIBLIOGRAPHY

Beifus, Joan T. *At the River I Stand: Memphis, the 1968 Strike, and Martin Luther King.* 1985.

Honey, Michael K. *Southern Labor and Black Civil Rights: Organizing Memphis Workers.* 1993.

Honey, Michael K. *Black Workers Remember, An Oral History: Segregation, Industrial Unionism, and the Freedom Struggle.* 1998.

Honey, Michael K. "Martin Luther King, Jr., the Crisis of the Black Working Class, and the Memphis Sanitation Strike." In *Southern Labor in Transition, 1940–1995,* edited by Robert H. Zieger. 1999.

Ross, Steven, Allison Graham, and David Appleby. "At the River I Stand," a Public Broadcasting Service documentary. 1993.

Michael Honey

Menominee DRUMS

Menominee DRUMS (Determination of Rights and Unity for Menominee Shareholders) was an activist group founded by Menominee people in response to problems following the official "termination" of that tribe. Formed in 1969, it had become a dominant political force by the early 1970s, and in 1973 it achieved the restoration of the Menominee Nation as a federally recognized tribe. In its tactics, membership, and ultimate objectives, Menominee DRUMS shared a number of characteristics with other American Indian activist, or RED POWER, organizations and, along with groups such as the AMERICAN INDIAN MOVEMENT (AIM), it spearheaded the movement for tribal self-determination.

Termination policy derived from post–WORLD WAR II social and political conditions that effectively eroded support for distinctive Indian communities and promoted assimilation by linking the end of reservations with "liberating" Indians from oppressive conditions. In policymaking circles, support for termination gathered force in the late 1940s and culminated on August 1, 1953, when the U.S. CONGRESS passed House Concurrent Resolution 108, thus establishing termination as official policy.

The Menominee Tribe of WISCONSIN quickly emerged as the "test case" for termination. This determination was based upon several factors: the existence of an apparently assimilated governing "elite," a decades-long history of operating a logging and lumbering enterprise, a tribal fund holding substantial deposits, and the $7.6 million settlement of a lawsuit alleging federal mismanagement of tribal timberlands. Even though most Menominees opposed termination, policymakers pressed on and succeeded in generating an affirmative vote in 1953. This result, however, derived from a duplicitous process when Senator Arthur V. Watkins (R-Utah), a vigorous termination proponent, manipulated the vote by threatening to withhold congressional appropriation of the award money unless Menominees approved termination. When Menominees discovered that Watkins had acted improperly, they lobbied unsuccessfully for a second vote.

The U.S. Congress passed the Menominee Termination Act (P. L. 83-399) on June 17, 1954, and on May 1, 1961 the reservation ceased to exist. Menominee County became Wisconsin's seventy-second county, and, with the exception of educational services (handled by neighboring counties), then became responsible for social services previously handled (at least in part) by the BUREAU OF INDIAN AFFAIRS. To manage resources and property formally in the hands of the tribe, the act created Menominee Enterprises Incorporated (MEI), a corporation that also came to dominate governmental functions. Each Menominee enrolled as of 1954 (when the rolls were "closed") received one hundred shares of MEI stock and a $3,000 bond. MEI was governed by a voting trust and board of directors, theoretically granting Menominee shareholders some influence over the way it conducted business. The reality was quite different, however, as MEI actually concentrated authority into very few hands and enhanced the influence of First Wisconsin Trust Company, which held the shares of minors and others who chose to sell.

Termination proved nothing short of a disaster. Hampered by a fifty-year-old mill, an end to government contracts, and a slump in the housing market, the lumbering enterprise quickly fell into the red. Menominee County found it virtually impossible to meet the needs of its residents, and its one major taxpaying entity, MEI, proved unable to generate anywhere near the necessary funds. In response, the MEI board of directors attempted to raise money by requiring homeowners to purchase land upon which their houses stood, reducing employment at the mill and, most controversially, inaugurating the "Lake of the Menominees" (LOM) project, a plan to develop county lakefront properties and sell homesites to non-Menominees. These moves were compounded by the progressive loss of Menominee influence over MEI and hence county governance as individual Menominees began selling their shares and bonds in order to raise money and, in some cases, reduce their financial holding to qualify for state welfare payments.

Worsening conditions, particularly the LOM project, stimulated a sharp reaction and ultimately the creation of Menominee DRUMS. The organization seems to have originated in Milwaukee and Chicago, a product of the same conditions that led to the creation of the NATIONAL INDIAN YOUTH COUNCIL and the American Indian Movement. Led by a younger generation of educated Indians such as James White and Ada Deer, Menominee DRUMS devised a several-pronged strategy that included public demonstrations, political lobbying, litigation, and fundraising. Denounced as "outside agitators" by non-Indian landowners and political figures as well as the Menominee governing elite, DRUMS nevertheless generated funding and legal assistance and found a presence within the county. At the same time, Ada Deer directed behind-the-scenes political lobbying efforts, and James White organized public demonstrations, including the very successful "March for Justice" from the county to the state capitol in Madison on October 2, 1971. This activity galvanized public opinion against Menominee termination and earned for DRUMS several political allies, including Governor Patrick Lucey.

DRUMS also labored to take control of MEI by forwarding a slate of candidates for elected positions on the corporation's board of directors. They accomplished this goal by 1972, and with control of county governance came an acceleration of efforts to reverse termination outright and to bring full restoration of Menominee tribal status. Intensive lobbying and a more generous political climate (compared with the 1950s) ultimately led to passage of the Menominee Restoration Act in 1973 (P. L. 93-197), a signature event in the tribe's history and in the evolution of U.S. Indian policy from termination to self-determination.

Aided by the NATIVE AMERICAN RIGHTS FUND (NARF), DRUMS members wrote the initial draft of the restoration bill, and its final draft included most of the organization's demands, even as it compromised on the rights of non-Menominee landowners (whose property rights were not affected). Nevertheless, the Menominee reservation reappeared, and with that official recognition of the tribe's right to self-determination.

Today's Menominee Reservation shows the effects of DRUMS activity. A new corporation, Menominee Tribal Enterprises (MTE), has taken the place of MEI but functions in the interests of the tribal community, not as an agent for its dissolution. The community population is growing, as are opportunities, and Menominees are justifiably proud of their role in reversing termination even as they remember hardships caused by that ill-advised policy. Ada Deer's work is honored in the tribe's casino–hotel complex, and she now occupies a faculty position with the University of Wisconsin after having served as Assistant Secretary of the Interior for Indian Affairs from 1993 to 1997.

BIBLIOGRAPHY

Beck, David Robert Martin. "Siege and Survival: Menominee Responses to an Encroaching World." Ph.D. dissertation, University of Illinois, Chicago, 1994.

Fixico, Donald L. *Termination and Relocation: Federal Indian Policy, 1945–1960.* 1986.

Fowler, S. Verna. "Menominee." In *Encyclopedia of North American Indians,* edited by Frederick E. Hoxie. 1996.

Kelly, Lawrence C. "United States Indian Policies, 1900–1980." In *History of Indian–White Relations,* edited by Wilcomb E. Washburn, Vol. 4, *Handbook of North American Indians,* William C. Sturtevant, general ed. 1988.

Menominee Tribal Enterprises. *The Menominee Forest Management Tradition: History, Principles and Practices.* 1997.

Peroff, Nicholas. *Menominee DRUMS: Tribal Termination and Restoration, 1954–1974.* 1982.

Philp, Kenneth R., ed. *Indian Self-Rule: First-Hand Accounts of Indian–White Relations from Roosevelt to Reagan.* 1983.

Spindler, Louise S. "Menominee." In *Northeast,* edited by Bruce G. Trigger, Vol. 15, *Handbook of North American Indians,* William C. Sturtevant, general ed. 1978.

Brian C. Hosmer

A civil rights activist while a student, James Meredith defied segregation in 1962 to enroll at the University of Mississippi. In 1963 he became the first black to be graduated from the university. (AP/Wide World Photos)

Meredith, James

(1933–   ), first African American to attend the University of Mississippi.

J. H. Meredith was born into a poor family on a central MISSISSIPPI farm during the nadir of the Great Depression. In 1950, upon graduating from high school, he volunteered for service in the U.S. Air Force. While in the service, he changed his name to "James Howard" Meredith, claiming he felt divinely inspired to become a new person, one who was to help free his people from the oppressive discrimination so prevalent in America at the time. During his nine years in the Air Force, he achieved the rank of sergeant. He also pursued a college education through correspondence courses and extensions of various institutions, including the universities of Kansas and Maryland.

In 1960, Meredith returned to the family farm in Mississippi, hoping to continue his education in his home state. Well aware that no African American had ever been admitted to Mississippi's only university, "Ole Miss" in Oxford, Meredith made it his mission to be the first. After John F. KENNEDY was elected president in November 1960, Meredith believed the time was right to bring the civil rights movement to Mississippi. On January 21, 1961, one day after Kennedy was inaugurated, Meredith, twenty-nine years old, applied for admission to Ole Miss.

The battle to integrate Ole Miss started slowly and bureaucratically, as the university repeatedly denied Meredith admission, citing various technicalities of school policy. Meredith, who was unquestionably qualified to enroll, then sought the help of the NATIONAL ASSOCIATION FOR THE ADVANCEMENT OF COLORED PEOPLE (NAACP) to fight the university in federal court. After more than a year of trials and appeals, Meredith finally got a favorable federal court ruling, and Ole Miss was forced to allow him to matriculate. Mississippi Governor Ross Barnett, however, in defiance of the court order, vowed to block Meredith's admission by any means necessary, thus setting up a showdown between the federal government and the State of Mississippi in September 1962. The Kennedy administration thus found itself in the precarious position of hoping to promote civil rights while simultaneously wanting to keep peace in the South. Threatening Barnett in public while carefully negotiating with him in secret, the administration convinced the governor to back down and allow Meredith to enter the university peacefully.

On September 30, 1962, in an international media spectacle, federal marshals escorted Meredith from Memphis, Tennessee, to Oxford. Upon his arrival on campus, two thousand white protesters greeted the hopeful student with epithets, rocks, and ultimately firearms. In the ensuring riot, two people were killed, and nearly four hundred others were injured. President Kennedy ordered more than twenty thousand federal troops to Oxford to quell the riot. Meredith, unharmed, followed through with his matriculation and attended classes under armed guard. On August 18, 1963, after less than one year of study, he graduated with a baccalaureate degree from the University of Mississippi. In so doing, he helped to hasten the demise of racial discrimination in Southern higher education and to open arguably the most racially divided state in the nation to INTEGRATION.

Soon after graduating, Meredith moved to Nigeria and later to New York, where he continued his education. In June 1966, however, believing his work for civil rights in Mississippi not yet complete, he organized a march from Memphis to Jackson, hoping to prove to thousands of doubtful fellow black Mississippians that they need no longer fear white racist attacks in the state. Unfortunately, having just left Memphis and crossed the state line, Meredith was shot, ironically, by a white gunman from Tennessee. While Meredith was recovering from the wound, other civil rights leaders, including Martin Luther KING, JR., of the SOUTHERN CHRISTIAN LEADERSHIP CONFERENCE (SCLC) and Stokely CARMICHAEL of the STUDENT NONVIOLENT COORDINATING COMMITTEE (SNCC), continued the march on his behalf. The Meredith march ultimately damaged rather than helped the cause of civil rights, however, as the marchers became bitterly divided over whether they should continue with the peaceful demonstration that King advocated or adopt Carmichael's radical BLACK POWER philosophy.

In subsequent years, James Meredith has become a controversial figure. His espousal of conservative Republican politics has lost him the admiration of African Americans, and his authorship of a series of self-published books about Mississippi history has not advanced his reputation in scholarly circles.

BIBLIOGRAPHY

Johnston, Erle. *Mississippi's Defiant Years, 1953–1973.* 1990.

Meredith, James. *Three Years in Mississippi.* 1966.

Meredith, James. *Mississippi: A Volume of Ten Books.* 1995.

Sewell, George A., and Margaret L. Dwight. *Mississippi Black History Makers.* 1977.

Silver, James W. *Mississippi: The Closed Society.* 1964.

Williams, Juan. *Eyes on the Prize: American Civil Rights Years, 1954–1968* (video). 1987.

Thomas Adams Upchurch

Mexican American Legal Defense and Educational Fund

In the 1960s, during a period when many racial minorities advocated for greater group solidarity and for additional protection of their civil and legal rights based on the gains of the civil rights movement, numerous organizations were founded throughout the country. For the nation's second-largest minority population—Mexican Americans—this too was a period of intense organizational development, and the founding of the Mexican American Legal Defense and Educational Fund (MALDEF) in 1967 must be viewed within the broader national context of civil rights advocacy. The origin of MALDEF was also part and parcel of the so-called CHICANO MOVEMENT, a mobilization among Mexican-origin people in the United States that gave rise to an ethnic/cultural renaissance and progressive political orientation for social change. Patterned in similar ways to the NAACP's Legal Defense Fund (LDF), MALDEF developed, over time, into the most important legal rights advocacy organization for Mexican Americans.

Founded by a group of Mexican-American civil rights attorneys and activists in San Antonio, TEXAS, headed by Pete Tijerina, and with assistance from Jack Greenberg of the NAACP-LDF, MALDEF was incorporated in 1967. With initial funding from the Ford Foundation, MALDEF set up shop a year later in San Antonio with Tijerina serving as the first executive director and lawyer Mario Obledo as general counsel. From the beginning, MALDEF's goal was to combat discriminatory treatment against Mexican Americans in Texas and elsewhere in the Southwest, the region where historically the great majority of Mexican-origin people resided. A small but committed staff of attorneys and other professionals laid the foundation, early on, by litigating several important court cases involving, for example, the segregation of Mexican-American schoolchildren and an unequal educational finance system in Texas, the gerrymandering of electoral districting that affected Mexican-American voter participation, and the discriminatory practices by certain employers both in Texas and in California.

Between 1969 and 1973 the organization opened regional field offices in Albuquerque, Denver, Los Angeles, and Washington, D.C. (an office was later opened in Chicago in 1980) and, in 1970, MALDEF moved its main office to San Francisco where Obledo served for three years in a position that combined the executive directorship with general counsel. The appointment as president and general counsel in 1973 of Vilma Martinez, formerly with the NAACP-LDF and a MALDEF staff attorney since 1968, ushered in a ten-year period of consolidation, growth, and maturation for the organization. During the decade of Martinez's leadership, MALDEF stabilized its funding base by attracting additional foundation and corporate grants while maintaining significant financial support from the Ford Foundation. New sources of support, in turn, permitted MALDEF to expand the scope of its work by developing a public policy and research capability and new initiatives in the areas of Chicana rights, public policy information dissemination, and leadership development. All the while, MALDEF focused its work on institutionalizing the organization's civil rights agenda for Mexican Americans and other Hispanics in the United States. Through its Voting Rights Project and Employment Litigation Project, MALDEF worked to establish important legal benchmarks using precedent-setting court cases to protect the civil and voting rights of Mexican Americans.

Through the 1980s and 1990s, MALDEF participated in and/or led the way in many court cases that resulted in important gains for Mexican Americans in a variety of areas. The organization played a key role in advocating for the inclusion of Hispanics in the reauthorization of the Voting Rights Act in 1975 and for the extension of this legislation in the early 1980s. In a case argued before the U.S. Supreme Court in 1982, it successfully defended the rights of children of undocumented immigrant families to a free public education in 1982 (*Doe v. Plyler*). In 1990 MALDEF, together with the U.S. Department of Justice, won a critically important voting rights-related case (*Garza v. Los Angeles County Board of Supervisors*). This legal victory resulted in changing the district boundaries of Los Angeles County's most powerful political body and in the first election in the twentieth century of a Spanish-surnamed person to the Board.

The litigation and advocacy role of MALDEF has remained constant over the years though the leadership has changed and new issues have moved to center stage in state and local public policy arenas. After the resignation of Martinez in 1982, MALDEF's veteran voting rights attorney Joaquín Avila ably assumed the position for three years. Since 1985 the organization has been headed by Antonia Hernandez, the second Chicana to lead MALDEF for more than a decade. MALDEF is an organization with its headquarters in California, a state with nearly ten million Hispanics (approximately a third of the total population) who are facing a political and racial climate in the 1990s reflected in policies that have reversed affirmative action, contested the rights of immigrants, and rescinded bilingual educational programs. MALDEF's advocacy role in defense of the rights of Mexican Americans and other Hispanics has intensified the challenge for one of the nation's most important civil rights-oriented organizations.

BIBLIOGRAPHY

Avila, Joaquín G. *The Political Integration of Racial and Ethnic Minorities.* Tenth Annual Ernesto Galarza Commemorative Lecture. Stanford Center for Chicano Research. Stanford University. 1997.

"Chicano! The History of the Mexican American Civil Rights Movement." A four-part Public Broadcast Service documentary series produced by the National Latino Communications Center and Galan Productions. 1996.

Gallegos, Herman E., and Michael O'Neill, eds. *Hispanics and the Nonprofit Sector.* 1991.

Gómez-Quiñones, Juan. *Chicano Politics: Reality and Promise 1940–1990.* 1990.

Hernandez, Antonia. *Latinos in the Decade of the 90's: A Political Coming of Age.* Eighth Annual Ernesto Galarza Commemorative Lecture. Stanford Center for Chicano Research. Stanford University. 1993.

Meier, Matt S. *Mexican American Biographies: A Historical Dictionary, 1836–1987.* 1988.

Research Guide to the Records of the Mexican American Legal Defense and Educational Fund and Puerto Rican Legal Defense and Education Fund, compiled and edited by Theresa Mesa Casey and Pedro Hernandez. The MALDEF organizational records from 1968 through 1983 are located in the Department of Special Collections in Green Library at Stanford University. The MALDEF collection contains 1,600 linear feet of records relating to all aspects of the organization's work. 1996.

Rosales, F. Arturo. *Chicano! The History of the Mexican American Civil Rights Movement* (based on the PBS documentary series). 1996.

Albert Camarillo

Mexican-American Student Organizations

In the mid-1960s, the formation of Mexican-American student organizations emerged as part of the Chicano student movement. This campus-based movement was organized by these groups throughout colleges and universities in the American South and Midwest. Primarily comprised of working-class students, they sought to expand educational opportunities for Mexican Americans through recruitment and retention programs. They also demanded the establishment of academic programs focusing on the study of Mexican Americans. In addition to serving as a political tool to further their struggles for educational equality and civil rights, these groups functioned to develop their Chicano identity.

By the fall of 1967, several groups had been organized on campuses in CALIFORNIA, TEXAS, and ARIZONA. Among these were the United Mexican American Students, the Mexican American Student Confederation, the Mexican American Student Organization, and the Mexican-American Youth Organizations. In 1968, students began to make their demands heard through more aggressive tactics, beginning with the Third World Liberation Front strike at San Francisco State College. Mexican-American students participated in this strike, which demanded ethnic studies programs and open admissions to students of color. In 1969, students at the University of California, Berkeley, followed suit, and formed their own Third World Liberation Front. Mexican-American students took a leading role in the strike, which lasted for four months. The students demanded a Third World College with departments of Mexican-, Asian-, and African-American studies. They also demanded the increased recruitment of students of color and the hiring of Third World faculty.

Although their main struggles surrounded educational issues, they expanded their political involvement beyond their college campuses. They sponsored events in support of César CHÁVEZ and the UNITED FARM WORKERS' labor struggles. They organized student caravans to take food to Delano, the headquarters of the United Farm Workers. They also brought key leaders of the CHICANO MOVEMENT, such as Reies Lopez TIJERINA and Corky GONZALES, to speak at their campuses. The United Mexican American Students participated in the organization of high school blowouts in 1968, where students walked out of their classes in protest of racist school policies and teachers. In addition, the Mexican-American Student Confederation at the University of California, Berkeley, took over the office of Charles Hitch, the president of the University of California system, to protest his refusal to discontinue the purchase of grapes in support of the United Farm Workers' struggles.

The student movement culminated in the 1969 Denver Youth Conference, with development of the political plan for the Chicano movement, the Plan Espiritual de Aztlan, which subsequently was followed by many student organizations. The first opportunity to take practical action occurred at the Santa Barbara conference, also in 1969, sponsored by the Coordinating Council on Higher Education. Seeking to implement the ideologies of nationalism and unity among Chicanos, the students decided to merge their organizations and sought a name that would express their educational concerns as well as their newly formed identities as Chicanos. The students finally merged under the name MOVIMIENTO ESTUDIANTIL CHICANO DE AZTLAN (MECHA).

BIBLIOGRAPHY

Gomez Quiñones, Juan. *Chicano Politics: Reality and Promise, 1940–1990.* 1990.

Muñoz, Carlos. *Youth, Identity, Power.* 1989.

Elizabeth Garcia

MFDP

See Mississippi Freedom Democratic Party

Michigan

The twenty-sixth state, admitted to the Union on January 26, 1837, Michigan has had a mixed civil rights record marred by urban riots and isolation between cities and suburbs. Even before statehood, Michigan had a distinct anti-slavery tradition; slavery was prohibited there by the Northwest Ordinance of 1787. Later, in 1832, Laura Smith Haviland and Elizabeth Margaret Chandler established the Logan Female Anti-Slavery Society in Lenawee County, site of

Michigan's first "station" on the Underground Railroad to Canada. While living in Battle Creek, former slave Sojourner Truth also promoted the anti-slavery movement.

In Michigan, women also sought greater political rights for themselves, particularly VOTING RIGHTS. In 1846, Ernestine Rose addressed the Michigan legislature for WOMAN SUFFRAGE, but not until the mid-1850s did the legislature consider Lenawee County women's numerous petitions seriously. Sojourner Truth spoke before the Women's Rights Convention in Akron, Ohio, in 1851. In 1866 Michigan's first woman suffrage bill failed by one vote. Although the legislature allowed women to vote in school elections in 1867, the state only granted general female suffrage slowly. Proposed state constitutional amendments failed in 1874, 1912, and 1913 referenda. Finally, in 1917, Governor Albert Sleeper signed legislation giving Michigan women voting rights in presidential elections. Another referendum for a state constitutional amendment passed in 1918, and on June 10, 1919, Michigan became the second state to ratify the NINETEENTH AMENDMENT to the U.S. Constitution for woman suffrage. Leading the national suffrage movement was Anna Howard Shaw of Big Rapids, president of the NATIONAL AMERICAN WOMAN SUFFRAGE ASSOCIATION, who became the first female recipient of the U.S. Distinguished Service Medal for her service as chairwoman of the Women's Committee of the Council of National Defense during World War I.

Later Michigan women campaigned actively for the EQUAL RIGHTS AMENDMENT (ERA), which Michigan Representative Martha Griffiths reintroduced in Congress. Michigan was one of twenty-two states that ratified the ERA in 1972, within a year of congressional approval. The ERA ultimately failed ratification by the requisite thirty-eight states. Other Michigan women distinguished themselves in the civil rights struggle. Detroiter Viola LIUZZO was murdered by Ku Klux Klansmen while assisting black participants in the Selma-to-Montgomery March of 1965. Petoskey resident Waunetta Dominic co-founded in 1948 the Northern Michigan Ottawa Association to protect Native Americans' TREATY RIGHTS.

Michigan's Chippewa, Ottawa, and Potawatomi populations have struggled to maintain their cultural identity. After the War of 1812, white settlers' pressure on Michigan's Indians for land became immense. The Ottawa and Chippewa tribes ceded most of Michigan's territory to the U.S. government with several treaties, most notably the treaties of Saginaw (1819), Washington (1836), La Pointe (1842), and Detroit (1855). In exchange, Natives received annuities, hunting and fishing rights on ceded lands, and land allotments dispersed among several townships. Although their complete removal was averted, whites frequently swindled the Indians out of these lands. Only the Saginaw Chippewa received a reservation in a treaty of 1864. Cultural identity was further endangered as wartime jobs in the twentieth century drew Native Americans to the cities.

Recently Indian communities have been rejuvenated somewhat. Aided by the CARTER administration, Michigan tribes acquired more land, established businesses, and gained greater control over education, housing, and health care. They also fought for resources in court: In 1971 a state court in *People v. Jondreau* allowed the Keweenaw Bay Indian Community to fish without restriction by Michigan laws. In 1975 Indians of the Mar Shunk neighborhood of Saulte Sainte Marie won $6 million as part of a lawsuit against the City for improvements in infrastructure. The federal court for Michigan's Western District ruled in *United States v. Michigan* (1981) that treaties and federal laws made after the 1836 treaty did not affect Chippewas' fishing rights in areas ceded under that treaty. The court reaffirmed tribes' rights to regulate by law their own members—rights guaranteed by Congress in 1934.

The "Great Migration" of African Americans brought about by the mechanization and depression of Southern agriculture and Northern industrial employment booms during the world wars made race relations in Michigan a critical issue. Michigan's African-American population grew from 17,115 (6.1 percent) in 1910 to 208,345 (4 percent) in 1940 and to 1,289,012 in 1990 (13.9 percent). Most of this growth occurred in industrial cities like Detroit and Flint. Racial tensions first erupted from these changes in Detroit on June 20–21, 1943. A race riot resulted in thirty-four deaths and 700 injuries. Some promise surfaced from the destruction, as CBS paid unprecedented attention to racial problems in its radio broadcast "*An Open Letter to the American People.*"

Detroit's racial problems did not improve, however. Increasing poverty again made the city the scene of rioting in 1967, despite Mayor Jerry Cavanagh's progressive reputation. Arrests of eighty blacks in a police raid on a speakeasy sparked violence on July 23. As in 1943, the Michigan National Guard and federal troops intervened. A week of mayhem resulted in forty deaths (thirty-two black), 2,250 injuries, and property losses estimated at $250 million. Smaller riots soon occurred in Pontiac, Grand Rapids, Kalamazoo, Albion, Flint, and Saginaw.

The riots disclosed the dissatisfaction behind Michigan's progressive image. Under the state constitution of 1963, Michigan established the first civil rights commission at the state level, but the NATIONAL ASSOCIATION FOR THE ADVANCEMENT OF COLORED PEOPLE

(NAACP) opposed the commission's slow apparatus for fighting HOUSING discrimination. Northern, urban African Americans wanted not only civil rights but also economic opportunities. The 1943 and 1967 riots also symbolized the isolation between central cities and predominantly white suburbs. African Americans constituted 63.1 percent of Detroit's population but 20.5 percent of the tri-county metropolitan population in 1980. The state and Detroit's suburbs successfully fought a metropolitan busing plan for school desegregation in the U.S. Supreme Court case MILLIKEN v. BRADLEY (1974). Abrasive rhetoric from Detroit's first black mayor, Coleman Young (1974–1994), and high crime rates further alienated white suburbanites.

In November 1992, the fatal beating of a black motorist, Malice Green, by white Detroit police officers who suspected Green of drug possession again threatened peace in the city. Officers Walter Budzyn and Larry Nevers were convicted of second-degree murder and imprisoned in 1993. Budzyn was again convicted in 1998 after the Michigan Supreme Court granted a new trial. Fortunately the city stayed quiet.

BIBLIOGRAPHY

Cleland, Charles E. *Rites of Conquest: The History and Culture of Michigan's Native Americans.* 1992.

"Deep Trouble." *Time* 41 (June 28, 1943): 19.

Fine, Sidney. *Violence in the Model City: The Cavanagh Administration, Race Relations, and the Detroit Riot of 1967.* 1989.

Goldman, Peter. "An American Tragedy, 1967—Detroit." *Newsweek* 70 (August 7, 1967): 18–26.

Harley, Rachel Brett, and Betty MacDowell. *Michigan Women: Firsts and Founders*, Vol. 2. 1995.

Kalodner, Howard I., and James J. Fishman, eds. *Limits of Justice: The Courts' Role in School Desegregation.* 1978.

Michigan Special Commission on Urban Problems. *Urban Growth & Problems; Report to Governor George Romney.* 1968.

Michigan Supreme Court. *Final Report of the Michigan Supreme Court Task Force on Racial/Ethnic Issues in the Courts.* 1989.

"Outspoken Broadcast." *Time* 42 (August 9, 1943): 62.

Sturm, Albert L., and Margaret Whitaker. *Implementing a New Constitution: The Michigan Experience.* 1968.

Young, Coleman, and Lonnie Wheeler. *Hard Stuff: The Autobiography of Coleman Young.* 1994.

Wes Borucki

Migration

As recently as 1910, almost 90 percent of African Americans in the United States lived in the South, and more than 78 percent of southern blacks lived in rural areas. From the end of the Civil War, there had been some migration of blacks from rural to urban areas and from agricultural regions to coal-mining areas in Alabama, Tennessee, Kentucky, and West Virginia. The migration escalated and shifted somewhat in the years prior to WORLD WAR I, as blacks sought new employment opportunities in growing southern and border state communities such as New Orleans, Birmingham, Atlanta, Norfolk, and Louisville. There was also the beginning of substantial migration to northern cities such as Chicago, Philadelphia, and New York. Blacks from the Deep South tended to head for Chicago, while those in the upper South were more likely to relocate to Philadelphia or New York. During World War I and the early 1920s, the migration escalated into the first great migratory wave of the twentieth century. Migratory destinations became more widespread, as huge numbers of blacks left the South for cities throughout the Midwest, Great Lakes region, and Northeast. (There was also a smaller but substantial migration to one key point on the West Coast, Los Angeles, involving not only blacks but whites as well.) The number of black migrants was disproportionately male, to such an extent that black men outnumbered black women in many cities of these key migratory areas by a ratio of 140 to 100. The male-female imbalance in these key urban centers was not fully alleviated until WORLD WAR II.

The second great migratory wave occurred during the 1940s, when more than 1.2 million African-Americans migrated out of the rural South, mostly to Northern cities. This second great exodus reshaped many aspects of postwar America, from popular music to industrial labor relations. In American literature, for instance, both Richard Wright's *Native Son* (1947) and Ralph Ellison's *Invisible Man* (1940) depict the confrontation between the displaced southern black working class and the urban North to which it was drawn (see LITERATURE AND CIVIL RIGHTS).

This migration involved both "pull" and "push" factors. The most important "push" factor was the lack of opportunity for southern blacks. In the mid-1940s inventors and tinkers were trying to build a mechanical cotton-picker. By the late 1940s they had succeeded. One mechanical cotton-picker replaced as many as fifty workers. This loss of jobs was compounded by the discovery of new synthetic fibers such as rayon and nylon, which depressed the cotton market. A final "push" factor was the desire of many southern black people to get out from under the social SEGREGATION of the JIM CROW South. Refusals to "move to the back of the bus" on the part of black patrons (including black servicemen in uniform) sparked numerous confrontations in the 1940s.

The main "pull" factor was the higher wages in the North, especially in the new mass-production industries. About 75 percent of the black migrants settled in California, Illinois, Michigan, New York, Ohio, and Pennsylvania—manufacturing states with well-established unions. Thanks to pressure on the administration of President Franklin D. ROOSEVELT from black labor leader A. Philip RANDOLPH in 1941, black workers were eventually hired in war production jobs. Many were represented by CIO unions, a new branch of the LABOR MOVEMENT committed to "organizing the unorganized" and less encumbered by the racially exclusionary practices of older trade unions (see also AFL-CIO; UNIONS). During the 1940s more than half a million black workers became members of the CIO unions.

Migration from the South spurred racial conflict as blacks and whites competed over scarce resources, as demonstrated by events in Detroit, Michigan. HOUSING was scarce in the city. Both whites and blacks paid high prices for housing, but blacks were restricted to a small segment of the city characterized by dilapidated housing stock. Tensions increased as blacks moved into white neighborhoods. White home owners organized to prevent blacks from buying in white neighborhoods and even tried to exclude blacks from public housing. The Detroit Sojourner Truth public housing project was the scene of a violent confrontation in the summer of 1942.

Jobs were another potentially explosive issue. In 1943 a series of "hate strikes" erupted at the Packard Motor Car Company (among others) when white United Autoworkers (UAW) union members walked off the job to protest the hiring of black workers. The union leadership was obliged to tell the white workers that they must either go back to work with the black workers or lose their jobs. The most frightening manifestation of racial animosity took place on a hot June Sunday in 1943, when a bloody riot broke out at Belle Isle, Detroit's main recreational park. Twenty-five blacks and nine whites died.

Although Detroit appears to have had the most violent reaction to the influx of black migrants, there were similar incidents in other large Northern cities such as Chicago. When competition between blacks and whites over scarce housing was superimposed on their rivalry in other areas—jobs, schools, and even recreational space—the result was a worsening of already bitter race relations in the city. The single factor that brought together these different levels of economic and cultural conflict was the great migration of black workers during World War II.

See also IMMIGRATION AND IMMIGRANTS.

BIBLIOGRAPHY

Adler, Bill. *Land of Opportunity: One Family's Quest for the American Dream in the Age of Crack.* 1995.

Capeci, Dominic J., Jr. *Race Relations in Wartime Detroit.* 1984.
Denby, Charles. *Indignant Heart: A Black Worker's Journal.* 1978.
Hirsch, Arnold. *The Making of the Second Ghetto: Race and Housing in Chicago, 1940–1960.* 1983.
Lemann, Nicolas. *The Promised Land: The Great Black Migration and How It Changed America.* 1991.
Sugrue, Thomas J. *The Origins of the Urban Crisis: Race and Inequality in Postwar Detroit.* 1996.

R. David Riddle

Milliken v. Bradley I (1974) and Milliken v. Bradley II (1977)

The *Milliken* case began when the parents of Ronald Bradley, a black grade-school student living in Detroit, sued the school system after he was assigned to a kindergarten class that was 97 percent black. Prior to this assignment, the Detroit Public Schools had undergone years of litigation and had agreed to desegregate. Because of Detroit's population disparities (in 1970, approximately 64 percent of enrolled students were black), the most feasible DESEGREGATION plans resulted in most schools being 75 to 90 percent black. In addition, the three-county area surrounding the city of Detroit had eighty-six independent school districts, which by 1970 had attracted much of the white middle- and upper-class tax base to the surrounding suburbs. This "white flight" made it increasingly difficult for the city of Detroit to desegregate without forcing suburban schools to participate as well.

The U.S. District Court (Eastern District of Michigan) agreed that effectively desegregating the Detroit Public Schools would involve disregarding traditional school district boundaries and creating an interdistrict desegregation plan. (This proposal was not a new one; many urban areas had made similar proposals. In fact, the SUPREME COURT in *School Board of Richmond v. State Board of Education* [1973] had been unable to determine whether a district court had the authority to require three school districts to merge in order to eliminate the racial SEGREGATION found in one district.) The court ordered a metropolitan remedy that consolidated the Detroit Public Schools with fifty-three suburban districts. The remedy proposed busing between the city and the suburbs, with both groups of students sharing the burden of travel over the course of their education. The District Court found that the State of MICHIGAN had contributed to racial segregation of the predominately black city and the white suburbs by (1) failing to subsidize transportation of Detroit students, (2) requiring state approval of new school building plans, and (3) legislating against voluntary integration plans in Detroit. The Appellate Court (for the Sixth Circuit) ruled that desegregating the Detroit Public Schools required redefining the traditional boundaries between suburban and city school districts; consequently, it upheld the constitutionality of the metropolitan desegregation plan.

In 1974, the Supreme Court once again found itself faced with the question of the legitimacy of forcing multiple school districts to participate in desegregation when de jure segregation (segregation maintained by law) exists in only one district. In his majority opinion, Chief Justice Warren Burger found no evidence that the discrimination existing in the Detroit schools was based on unconstitutional actions of the outlying districts. Consequently, the Court decided that a federal court could not impose a multidistrict remedy unless each school district had engaged in unconstitutional segregationist behaviors. In his dissent, Justice Thurgood MARSHALL pointed out that the fear of Northern white suburbanites had triggered a state and national political backlash against desegregation plans. "Today's holding, I fear, is more a reflection of a perceived public mood that we have gone far enough in enforcing the Constitution's guarantee of equal justice than it is the product of neutral principles of law. In the short run, it may seem to be the easier course to allow our great metropolitan areas to be divided up each into two cities—one white, the other black—but it is a course, I predict, our people will ultimately regret" (814–815). The *Milliken I* decision prevented public school desegregation from becoming a reality in many communities by limiting the power of the federal court judges to intervene in urban areas and narrowing the implementation options of metropolitan desegregation plans. *Milliken I* marked the limits of the Supreme Court's willingness to directly intervene in state and local governance, even for the purposes of enforcing the requirements of the FOURTEENTH AMENDMENT.

After the Supreme Court rejected interdistrict desegregation in Detroit, the Supreme Court in *Milliken II* unanimously recognized in 1977 the authority of federal district court judges to order state governments to fund programs for remediating damages resulting from illegal segregation. The U.S. District Court ordered the State of Michigan to pay for additional programs "essential to the effort to combat the effects of segregation." Because the State of Michigan shared in the responsibility for the de jure segregation of the schools, it shared in the price of correcting these violations. Since this decision, the federal courts have been able to order state governments to finance remedies designed to overcome the consequences of segregation and unequal education; however, because of *Milliken I* many school districts remain segregated and underfunded.

BIBLIOGRAPHY

Bell, Derrick. "Running and Busing in Twentieth-Century America." *Journal of Law and Education* 4 (Jan. 1975): 214–217.

Cooper, Phillip J. "*Milliken* v. *Bradley*: The Detroit Busing Case." *Hard Judicial Choices: Federal District Court Judges and State and Local Officials*, 1988: 105–135.

Milliken v. Bradley, U.S. 717 (1974).

Milliken v. Bradley, 433 U.S. 267 (1977).

Missouri v. Jenkins, 115 S.Ct. 2038 (1995).

Orfield, Gary. *Must We Bus? Segregated Schools and National Policy*, 1978.

School Board of Richmond v. State Board of Education, 412 U.S. 92 (1973).

United States Commission on Civil Rights. *Milliken v. Bradley: The Implications for Metropolitan Desegregation.* 1974.

Wilkinson, J. Harvie, III. "Busing the Suburbs: *Milliken* v. *Bradley*." *From Brown to Bakke: The Supreme Court and School Integration: 1954–1978*. 1979: 216–249.

Michelle Donaldson Deardorff

Million Man March

On October 16, 1995, a vast throng of black men converged on the Mall in Washington, D.C., to participate in "a day of atonement," called there by the Reverends Louis FARRAKHAN and Benjamin Chavez. Months of controversy and excitement heralded the event, as some observers criticized the anti-Semitic record of Farrakhan's organization, the NATION OF ISLAM, and others decried the march's exclusive focus on men as a promotion of patriarchy.

Unlike most previous marches on Washington, this march was not called to reveal injustices or to win new federal policies. Instead, organizers presented the event as a public opportunity for African-American men to experience personal transformation and to acknowledge individual responsibility. This approach drew on conservative ideologies of self-help and traditions of evangelical Christianity.

Debates about the significance of the march centered on the number and the motivations of the attendees. There was a high turnout because of media coverage and the event's grassroots organization and coalition building. On the day of the march, organizers claimed to have reached their goal of one million marchers, but federal officials estimated that around 600,000 people were present. The ensuing cantankerous debate showed the importance of numbers as an index of a march's success.

At the Million Man March in Washington, D.C., on October 16, 1995, tens of thousands of black men from across the United States gathered to pledge racial unity and self-improvement. (AP/Wide World Photos)

The motivation of the participants was equally controversial. Many of them declared their support for the black separatism that Farrakhan espoused. Others, however, responded to the social and cultural conditions of the 1990s. Black men were experiencing disproportionate unemployment and massive rates of incarceration; and they saw media images depicting them as criminals, drug users, and irresponsible fathers. Consequently, for many marchers the event was an opportunity to show African-American men as responsible, motivated, and united. Thus, their march became an assertion of the right of African Americans to present their own self-images.

BIBLIOGRAPHY

Bythewood, Reggie R., scriptwriter, and Spike Lee, director. *Get on the Bus* (film). 1997.

Madhubuti, Haki R., and Maulana Karenga, eds. *Million Man March, Day of Absence: A Commemorative Anthology; Speeches, Commentary, Photography, Poetry, Illustrations, Documents.* 1996.

Pickney, Darryl. "Slouching Towards Washington." *New York Review of Books*, pp. 73–81, Dec. 21, 1995.

Walker, Clarence E. "March to Nowhere." *Red Pepper* 19 (Dec. 1995): 24–25.

Lucy G. Barber

Minnesota

When Minnesota achieved statehood in 1858, VOTING RIGHTS extended to persons of mixed white and Na-

tive American blood and Native Americans who adopted white customs, a policy that did nothing to mollify the Dakota Sioux, whose complaints intensified due to increasing numbers of federal and state violations to treaty agreements, culminating in the U.S.–Dakota War of 1862, which occurred in southwestern Minnesota. In consequence, the government facilitated the massive relocation of Sioux to other states.

Meanwhile, the new state constitution denied voting rights to Minnesota blacks. Despite the 1857 U.S. SUPREME COURT decision in DRED SCOTT V. SANDFORD that held black rights to be unconstitutional in all states and territories, the Minnesota REPUBLICAN PARTY remained determined to submit the issue to the state electorate. The DEMOCRATIC PARTY helped to defeat two statewide referenda. In 1868 the Republicans finally prevailed in establishing suffrage rights for black males in Minnesota, predating congressional adoption of the FIFTEENTH AMENDMENT by two years. On January 1, 1869, the Sons of Freedom, Minnesota's first black civil rights organization, was founded.

Nevertheless, discrimination continued. In 1873, Henry Robinson initiated a discrimination suit against the Milwaukee and St. Paul Railway Company and lost the jury verdict. Similar cases, springing up throughout the country, prompted Congress to pass a public accommodations bill in 1875 that banned such discrimination. When additional discrimination cases that tested the new law came before the U.S. Supreme

Court in a collected from called the *Civil Rights Cases*, the Court held in 1883 that Congress was unauthorized by the THIRTEENTH AMENDMENT and FOURTEENTH AMENDMENT to enact such far-reaching legislation (see also CIVIL RIGHTS DECISION OF 1883). Minnesota, like other states across the nation, passed its own equal rights and accommodations bill in 1885. To secure their rights the small black community relied on the Republican Party, which dominated state government well into the twentieth century. In 1897, the legislature enacted a civil rights law and later hosted a convention in the state capitol for the newly formed Minnesota Protective and Industrial League, an organization intended to monitor civil rights infringements and promote projects that improved the general quality of life. As race relations worsened across the nation, black life in Minnesota was relatively peaceful. In 1899, Republican John Francis Wheaton, Minnesota's first black legislator, sponsored a bill that successfully expanded the state's Civil Rights Act of 1897.

After 1900, national civil rights activities spread to Minnesota. On July 9, 1902, Booker T. WASHINGTON and W. E. B. DU BOIS spoke at a meeting of the National Afro-American Council (NAAC), which convened at the state capitol. (See NATIONAL AFRO-AMERICAN LEAGUE, the NAAC's predecessor.) Although a split ensued between supporters of Washington and Du Bois, both factions remained active. Washington's supporters took over the leadership of the St. Paul chapter of the NAAC, while others joined Du Bois in organizing the NIAGARA MOVEMENT in 1905 and the NATIONAL ASSOCIATION FOR THE ADVANCEMENT OF COLORED PEOPLE (NAACP) in 1909. The St. Paul Chapter of the NAACP was founded in 1912. It successfully lobbied to defeat a bill that prohibited black-white marriages. From 1912 to 1920, interracial violence increased almost everywhere except in Minnesota. In 1920, however, three black men were lynched in the port city of Duluth. The following year, the legislature, with support from J. A. Burnquist, Minnesota's governor and president of the St. Paul chapter of the NAACP, passed an antilynching law (see LYNCHING). Two years later, the St. Paul branch of the NATIONAL URBAN LEAGUE was formed to combat HOUSING and EMPLOYMENT discrimination.

By the middle of the twentieth century, the number of racial minorities increased in Minnesota. The need for civil rights protection likewise expanded. In 1947, Minneapolis Mayor Hubert H. HUMPHREY championed a fair employment city ordinance that banned discrimination based on race, color, and creed, the first of its kind in the nation. After Congress enacted U.S. Public Law 280 in 1953, which transfered civil and criminal jurisdiction over Native American land from federal to state courts, Minnesota, one of five states so charged, assumed responsibility for monitoring Native American civil rights. In 1955, the legislature created the statewide Fair Employment Practices Commission. The Minnesota Human Rights Commission was formed in 1956 to identify discriminatory practices against African-American, Hispanic, and Asian-Pacific Minnesotans. In 1957, the legislature declared decent housing to be a fundamental a civil right.

The vibrant period of liberation politics for racial minorities and women made an impact on the country during the 1960s and 1970s. In Minnesota, the Democratic-controlled legislature, in the liberal tradition of Hubert Humphrey, enacted laws that reflected the trend by expanding antidiscrimination measures for women in 1967 and 1969 (see WOMEN AND CIVIL RIGHTS STRUGGLES), and for the disabled in 1973 (see DISABILITY RIGHTS). In 1974, the legislature banned neighborhood "redlining" by the finance industry. In 1981, it increased punitive damages for human rights violations from $1,000 to $6,000 and empowered the state commissioner to issue temporary restraining orders. Bidders for state contracts were required by law to have certified AFFIRMATIVE ACTION plans, and in 1982 the legislature enacted a comparable-worth statute that sought to eliminate pay disparities by gender in public sector jobs, and in 1993 the Human Rights Act was extended to cover sexual preference (see GAY AND LESBIAN RIGHTS).

BIBLIOGRAPHY

Blegen, Theodore C. *Minnesota: A History of the State.* 1975.
Folwell, William Watts. *A History of Minnesota*, Vols. 1 and 2. 1961.
Golden, Kevin J. "The Independent Development of Civil Rights in Minnesota: 1849–1910." *William Mitchell Law Review* 17 (1991): 449–466.
Green, William D. "Race and Segregation in St. Paul Schools, 1848–1869." *Minnesota History* 55, no. 4 (1996): 138–149.
Green, William D. "Minnesota's Long Road to Black Suffrage, 1849–1868." *Minnesota History* 56, no. 2 (1998): 68–84.
Hoffbeck, Steven R. "'Victories Yet to Win': Charles W. Scrutchin, Bemidji's Black Activist Attorney." *Minnesota History* 55, no. 2 (1996): 59–75.
Reichard, Gary W. "Mayor Hubert Humphrey." *Minnesota History* 56, no. 2 (1998): 50–67.
Spangler, Earl. *The Negro in Minnesota.* 1961.
Taylor, David V. "Blacks." In *They Chose Minnesota, A Survey of the State's Ethnic Groups*, edited by June Drenning Holmquist. 1981.

William Green

Mississippi

In the early nineteenth century, Mississippi appeared to be a land of boundless opportunity. Low land prices and fertile soils made the state alluring to farmers from the Atlantic Seaboard states. Despite its reputation for providing opportunity to some citizens, Mississippi has, throughout its history, denied many residents equality of opportunity in political, social, and economic life. No other state better deserves a reputation for resistance to civil rights reform than Mississippi.

Mississippi entered the union with a constitution that restricted suffrage to white male taxpayers, and thus property holders, over the age of twenty-one. The restrictive VOTING RIGHTS measures incorporated in the 1817 constitution remained in force until the constitutional convention of 1832. The voting rights clause in the 1832 constitution permitted white manhood suffrage. The impetus for suffrage reform was the opening of Choctaw homelands to white settlement and the influx of white immigrants from the East Coast. Political leaders, including aristocratic and undemocratic ones such as John A. Quitman, knew that the pleas of new arrivals for white manhood suffrage could be ignored only at the peril of revolution. A further broadening of suffrage would not come until 1868, when mandated by the federal government.

Immediately after the Civil War, when required to rewrite their constitution, white Mississippians refused to grant to ex-slaves the privileges of citizenship, much less the right to vote. In 1866, Mississippi adopted a BLACK CODE that restricted ex-slaves' mobility, access to economic opportunity, and political expression. Reacting to the legislation, CONGRESS invalidated the 1865 constitution and required the adoption of universal manhood suffrage. The election of delegates to the 1868 constitutional convention was the first biracial election in Mississippi history, and consequently, a large number of liberal-minded members of the REPUBLICAN PARTY, backed by ex-slaves, were elected as delegates to the convention. The 1868 constitution extended to African Americans the privileges of citizenship, including the right to testify in court, the right to own property, and the right to vote. The 1868 elections were significant because black men voted for the first time, and because great violence—perpetrated by the KU KLUX KLAN and the DEMOCRATIC PARTY—occurred. Largely owing to violence against black and white Republicans as well as the waning interest of the federal government, RECONSTRUCTION in Mississippi ended in 1875.

Between 1875 and 1890, Mississippi took steps to eliminate post–Civil War achievements in civil rights reform. Violence accompanied elections, undermining the Reconstruction-era efforts of the federal government to establish the citizenship of ex-slaves. African Americans and Republicans remained targets of political demagoguery; and whites, especially ordinary farmers, who challenged Democratic Party authority under alternative banners also fell victim to it. Ostensibly for the purpose of curbing electoral violence, Mississippi convened a constitutional convention in 1890. Various methods of voting rights restrictions were suggested during the convention. Some delegates proposed multivoting schemes based on the amount of property a citizen owned; others wanted literacy tests to be used to restrict the vote. Members of the Women's Christian Temperance Union advocated WOMAN SUFFRAGE as a means of outnumbering blacks at the polls. Eventually, Senator James Z. George wrote into the constitution clauses that required registrants to pay a poll tax and pass a literacy test, though local registrars had broad discretion to apply an understanding test to "illiterates." The suffrage restrictions were intended to evade the FOURTEENTH and FIFTEENTH AMENDMENTS and to remove African Americans and dissident whites from the political process. The 1890 constitution accomplished its goals. Participation in elections plummeted, but not without consequences. The discontent of common whites eventually resulted in the 1902 primary law, which established a system of white-only primary elections and empowered virulently racist politicians such as James Vardaman and Theodore BILBO.

From 1875 to 1890, there was a wholesale attack on Reconstruction-era civil rights reforms. Local governments and businesses restricted the privileges of citizenship available to African Americans. During the 1870s, railroad companies in Mississippi segregated black and white passengers. Ham Carter, a former slave and black politician, sued the Mississippi Central Railroad Company for forcing him to ride in the second-class compartment solely because of his race. His suit was unsuccessful, but his action testifies to the fact that SEGREGATION was a way of life before formal laws and ordinances appeared to mandate it. African Americans experienced restrictions on their economic liberty as well. The 1868 crop-lien law, which permitted money lenders to confiscate the crops of debtors, hindered the economic options available to both black and white sharecroppers. Furthermore, rural blacks, especially those who worked in lumber mills, fell victim to violent acts committed by whites envious of their success in achieving economic independence. During the early 1890s and again ten years later, an organization known as the "Whitecaps" attempted to chase African Americans from the southern part of the state.

By 1900, black Mississippians seem to have been subjected to a new form of slavery. They did not vote in large numbers; they faced tremendous and arbitrary violence; the vast majority existed in abject poverty. Yet, when segregated from the mainstream of

American life, some black Mississippians responded by creating a world similar to the white one from which they were excluded. Mississippi cities saw the birth of successful black-owned businesses, including banks, pharmacies, newspapers, realty companies, theaters, and bakeries. The largest single black-owned business in the state was the Mississippi Life Insurance Company, founded in 1908 by Dr. W. A. Attaway and Wayne Wellington Cox. To some extent, black-owned businesses often thrived during the age of JIM CROW because their greatest asset for business growth was the ill will of whites. Nonetheless, at the same time, other black Mississippians responded to segregation, disfranchisement, and violence by moving out of Mississippi. Between 1910 and 1920, an estimated 148,500 black Mississippians fled the state, and the trend persisted. Neither the NEW DEAL, which failed to lift rural blacks out of poverty and at the same time provided an impetus for replacing black farm labor with machinery, nor the economic prosperity fostered by WORLD WAR II slowed the tide of black migration. During the 1940s, some 314,200 black Mississippians left the state.

World War II marked the beginning of the modern civil rights movement in Mississippi. Many black veterans, among them Charles EVERS and Medgar EVERS, returned from overseas assignments committed to gaining the liberty so long denied them. The initial attempt by the Evers brothers to vote in the 1946 primary election at Decatur ended in a bitter confrontation, but other black Mississippians succeeded in exerting their political might. The NATIONAL ASSOCIATION FOR THE ADVANCEMENT OF COLORED PEOPLE (NAACP) and the Progressive Voters' League rallied nearly two hundred black Mississippians—farmers, businessmen, sharecroppers, and day laborers—to testify against Senator Bilbo, who had exhorted whites to meet with violence every black intending to cast a ballot in the primary election. Bilbo considered the action of black Mississippians, who were responding to the recent SUPREME COURT *Smith v. Allwright* decision, to be a blatant challenge to WHITE SUPREMACY. Only a fraction of the five thousand registered blacks in Mississippi voted in 1946. Yet, in response to the testimony of Mississippi blacks, the Senate refused to seat Bilbo.

Throughout the 1940s and 1950s, atrocities against African Americans mounted as sentiment for civil rights reform grew, and every incident heightened the desire of blacks and white moderates for change. Civil rights reform finally occurred in three broad arenas: EDUCATION, economic opportunity and public accommodations, and politics. Support for ending Mississippi's segregated system of public schools became open and widespread among blacks in the 1940s, as the U.S. SUPREME COURT moved toward ending segregation in higher education. By the early 1950s, the state legislature even considered abolishing public education in anticipation of court-ordered desegregation. When the Supreme Court handed down its BROWN V. BOARD OF EDUCATION decision in 1954, the reaction in Mississippi was predictable. Blacks petitioned school boards to desegregate, and school boards refused their pleas. Individual whites fired petitioners from their jobs, called in bank loans, and attacked petitioners. Robert Patterson of Sunflower County organized the WHITE CITIZENS' COUNCIL to harass petitioners and to encourage the state to resist the desegregation order. For fifteen years, despite decisions by the Supreme Court and the FIFTH CIRCUIT Court of Appeals, Mississippi refused to desegregate its schools. Not even the September 1962 riot that occurred at Oxford, when federal authorities and white citizens clashed over the admission of James MEREDITH to the University of Mississippi, convinced whites that resistance to civil rights reform was impossible. Only in 1969, when the Supreme Court handed down its *Alexander v. Holmes County* decision did a war-weary Mississippi finally end legally mandated segregation in public secondary schools.

The battle over equal access to economic opportunity and public accommodations began in 1960. In March, students at Tougaloo College staged a SIT-IN at the Jackson Public Library, which led the state president of the NAACP, Aaron HENRY, to launch "Operation Mississippi," a program that encouraged black students to attempt to desegregate public facilities. Almost overnight, young African Americans tried to desegregate the Jackson zoo, swimming pools, public parks, trains, and theaters. In Biloxi, Dr. Gilbert Mason and other NAACP members attempted to desegregate the beach, but the protesters were met with violence. Within weeks, however, the U.S. Justice Department, acting under the aegis of the CIVIL RIGHTS ACT OF 1957, desegregated the Biloxi beach. Taking their cue from a boycott of downtown businesses in Clarksdale, the north Jackson NAACP chapter built on the effort of students to end segregation and discriminatory practices in downtown businesses. The Jackson movement achieved a state of high drama in May 1963, when Anne Moody and two other students attempted to desegregate Woolworth's lunch counter. Soon massive demonstrations filled the streets of the capital. Police arrested hundreds of students. In early June, as protests continued, Byron de la Beckwith assassinated Medgar Evers. At the urging of Justice Department officials, the city of Jackson offered to hire six black police officers and to promote several sanitation department employees. The offer did not appease protesters, but by the summer of 1963 many Jackson residents began refocusing their energies on gaining full voting rights.

In the summer of 1964, a coalition of civil rights organizations descended on Mississippi. The FREEDOM SUMMER project brought to Mississippi hundreds of college students, who operated voter education drives and FREEDOM SCHOOLS. At the start of Freedom Summer, three civil rights volunteers—James CHANEY, Andrew GOODMAN, and Michael SCHWERNER—were murdered in Neshoba County. The killers, who were police officers and Klansmen, were convicted of violating the civil rights of the three men. At McComb, which had been the scene of a STUDENT NONVIOLENT COORDINATING COMMITTEE (SNCC) project in 1961, the return of civil rights reformers resulted in daily and flagrant violence. Local whites bombed and burned property in the black community. In the Delta, Freedom Summer produced the MISSISSIPPI FREEDOM DEMOCRATIC PARTY (MFDP), a biracial alternative to the lily-white Democratic Party. The MFDP staged elections for delegates to the national Democratic Party convention and attempted to gain seats at the Atlantic City gathering. President Lyndon JOHNSON balked at seating the MFDP delegation, but the convention speech of sharecropper Fannie Lou HAMER swayed the party to grant credentials to four MFDP delegates. The travails of Freedom Summer and MFDP also testified to the need for legislation to protect black voting rights. In 1965, CONGRESS passed the most significant piece of legislation in the modern crusade for civil rights: the VOTING RIGHTS ACT. Operating under the act, the Justice Department undermined the ability of Mississippi voter registrars to discriminate. Almost overnight, large numbers of African Americans began voting; and as they did, resistance to access in public accommodations and education withered.

Ultimately, the involvement of the federal government and the will of local African Americans forced Mississippi to work toward its potential as a land of opportunity for all—but the struggle continues. Today, more African-American Mississippians live beneath the poverty level than whites. Although black politicians, such as Bennie Thompson and Mike Espy, have won seats in Congress, state and local politics have an undercurrent of race-conscious rhetoric. Furthermore, urban school districts continue to grapple with making school INTEGRATION meaningful in the face of white flight and the lifting of decades-old court-ordered desegregation decrees. Likewise, although an ever-increasing number of African-American college students attend predominantly white institutions, the graduation rate for black students lags far behind that of their white classmates. On the other hand, there are signs that Mississippi has changed over the past three decades. In a symbolic gesture, the Mississippi legislature in 1995 voted unanimously to ratify the THIRTEENTH AMENDMENT, abolishing slavery—yet it is noteworthy that the state has never taken the same step to approve the constitutional amendment granting women the right to vote. The 1990s also saw two notorious assassins brought to justice: Byron de la Beckwith was convicted for the murder of Medgar Evers, and Sam Bowers, one of the conspirators in the Philadelphia murders, was convicted for his role in the 1966 murder of voting rights activist Vernon Dahmer.

BIBLIOGRAPHY

Bond, Bradley G. *Political Culture in the Nineteenth-Century South: Mississippi, 1830–1900.* 1995.

Curry, Constance. *Silver Rights.* 1995.

Dittmer, John. *Local People: The Struggle for Civil Rights in Mississippi.* 1994.

Harris, William C. *Presidential Reconstruction in Mississippi.* 1967.

Harris, William C. *The Day of the Carpetbagger: Republican Reconstruction in Mississippi.* 1977.

McMillen, Neil R. *The Citizens Council: Organized Resistance to the Second Reconstruction, 1954–1964.* 1971.

McMillen, Neil R. *Dark Journey: Black Mississippians in the Age of Jim Crow.* 1989.

Moody, Anne. *Coming of Age in Mississippi.* 1968.

Payne, Charles M. *I've Got the Light of Freedom: The Organizing Tradition and the Mississippi Freedom Struggle.* 1995.

Silver, James W. *Mississippi: The Closed Society.* 1964.

Bradley G. Bond

Mississippi Freedom Democratic Party

One of the strengths of the civil rights movement was the variety of tactics its forces employed. From the 1954 legal attack that culminated in BROWN V. BOARD OF EDUCATION, to the impromptu SIT-INS in 1960, which led restaurants and other businesses to desegregate in many parts of the South, to the FREEDOM RIDES of 1961, which forced the U.S. government to confront SEGREGATION in interstate transportation and to recognize the growing violence of the white racist reaction, the innovative spirit of the movement won many battles. But although the civil rights movement was flexible and innovative, by the mid-1960s it still lacked the political power to define and defend a new racial status quo.

Attempting to change this fact, in 1964 the STUDENT NONVIOLENT COORDINATING COMMITTEE (SNCC) organized its 1964 FREEDOM SUMMER campaign in MISSISSIPPI. One of the goals of Freedom Summer was to bring attention to the discriminatory practices of that state's DEMOCRATIC PARTY. African

Members of the Mississippi Freedom Democratic Party—Fannie Lou Hamer, Victoria Gray, and Annie Devine—hold a telegram from House Speaker John McCormick granting them permission to take seats during the House floor debate, Washington, D.C., August 17, 1965.

Americans were barred from any meaningful participation in the party—effectively disenfranchised in a state where Democratic candidates won nearly every election. The MISSISSIPPI FREEDOM DEMOCRATIC PARTY (MFDP) was established by SNCC as an African-American alternative to the regular Democratic Party. While other Freedom Summer volunteers organized voter registration drives for African Americans and taught at FREEDOM SCHOOLS, the MFDP organized mock elections for Democratic Party officials. Over 17,000 African Americans voted in these elections and selected sixty-eight delegates to represent Mississippi at the 1964 Democratic National Convention.

The Democrats' 1964 convention in Atlantic City, New Jersey, was expected to be a smoothly orchestrated nomination of President Lyndon B. JOHNSON. However, the credentials fight between the MFDP delegates and the all-white delegation from the state's official Democratic Party disrupted this celebration. The MFDP demanded to be the sole Mississippi delegates at the national convention. Testifying before the convention's Credentials Committee, MFDP delegates spoke of the discriminatory practices of Mississippi's party and of the violence and discrimination that African Americans in Mississippi faced when they tried to exercise their rights. The televised testimony of Fannie Lou HAMER about the beatings she had endured at the hands of whites because of her activism was particularly moving. Concerned at the possibility of a walkout by the Southern delegations if the MFDP's demands were met, President Johnson sought a compromise. He sent Vice President Hubert HUMPHREY and Senator Walter Mondale of Minnesota to offer the

MFDP two "at large" delegate seats, with the understanding that in the future the Democratic Party would not seat all-white delegations. The MFDP delegation rejected this compromise and denounced the Democratic Party. Provided with floor passes by sympathetic members of other delegations, many MFDP delegates staged a sit-in protest on the convention floor, only to be removed by security guards. Ironically, all but three of the all-white Mississippi delegation had already stormed out of the convention.

Although the MFDP failed in its immediate goal of gaining seats at the 1964 convention, it was very successful in raising awareness of the Democratic Party's discriminatory practices, as well as highlighting the poor conditions for African Americans in the state of Mississippi. At the strife-torn 1968 convention in Chicago, another all-white Mississippi delegation was turned away by the national party, prompting reforms of the Mississippi Democratic Party to eliminate discriminatory practices.

BIBLIOGRAPHY

Carson, Clayborne, David J. Garrow, Gerald Gill, Vincent Harding, and Darlene Clark Hine, eds. *The Eyes on the Prize Civil Rights Reader: Documents, Speeches, and Firsthand Accounts from the Black Freedom Struggle.* 1991.

Chalmers, David. *And the Crooked Places Made Straight: The Struggle for Social Change in the 1960s.* 1996.

O'Neill, William L. *Coming Apart: An Informal History of America in the 1960s.* 1975.

Radosh, Ronald. *Divided They Fell: The Demise of the Democratic Party, 1964–1996.* 1996.

Schulman, Bruce J. *Lyndon B. Johnson and American Liberalism: A Brief Biography with Documents.* 1995.

Sitkoff, Harvard. *The Struggle for Black Equality, 1954–1980.* 1981.

Williams, Juan. *Eyes on the Prize: America's Civil Rights Years, 1954–1965.* 1987.

R. David Riddle

Missouri

Classified as a border, southern, western state, and a former slave state, with a black population of 11 percent, Missouri is a microcosm of America. Since its very beginning, the state of Missouri has been a mirror of the civil rights struggle in this country. The uneasy Compromise of 1820, followed by the Dred Scott case (see DRED SCOTT V. SANDFORD) in 1857, foreshadowed the American Civil War. Missouri was a Union sympathizer but remained a slave state, though it did not secede in 1861. Early during RECONSTRUCTION, Missouri's 1865 constitution ended slavery but required a segregated educational system (see SEGREGATION), prohibited racial intermarriage, and mandated the maintenance of separate libraries, public parks, and playgrounds. In the 1890 *Grundy* decision, Missouri Supreme Court Justice Francis M. Black alleged that "color carries with it natural peculiarities that justified the separation of blacks and whites."

Of particular importance to the African-American community was EDUCATION. Following the Civil War, in 1866 soldiers of the 62nd and 65th Colored Infantries raised funds to establish Lincoln University in Jefferson City as an institution of higher education for Missouri blacks. The Missouri legislature, in 1921, granted the college university status in an attempt to equalize the educational and training opportunities for blacks. Missouri was also the first state to pay out-of-state tuition for black students to attend graduate and professional schools. In 1907, Nathaniel C. Bruce followed his mentor, Booker T. WASHINGTON and established the Bartlett Agricultural and Industrial School. Annie Turnbo Malone received a patent for the hot comb in 1900; she opened the Poro Beauty College in St. Louis in 1917, the first school for "studying and teaching of black cosmetology." Throughout the state, African-American children attended segregated public schools that were often miles from their homes.

In the 1930s, Missouri was the focus of the NATIONAL ASSOCIATION FOR THE ADVANCEMENT OF COLORED PEOPLE's national campaign to equalize education. Lloyd Lionel Gaines, a twenty-five-year-old St. Louis resident and an honors graduate of Lincoln University, wanted to attend law school. The University of Missouri in Columbia rejected his application for admission in 1935. In *Gaines v. Canada* (1938), the U.S. Supreme Court ruled that Gaines must be admitted to the University of Missouri Law School or the state must provide him with an equivalent education as mandated by the 1896 PLESSY V. FERGUSON decision. Therefore, the state chose the "separate but equal" route and established a black law school in St. Louis. Gaines never attended the school; he disappeared from his Chicago boardinghouse for reasons unknown. Nonetheless he played a vital role in SCHOOL DESEGREGATION. After his precedent, Lucille Bluford, editor of the *Kansas City Call*, brought a successful lawsuit against the University of Missouri's journalism school, but was unable to attend when the school was closed because of WORLD WAR II. Finally, in 1950, Gus Tolver Ridgel of Poplar Bluff was admitted to the graduate program in economics, becoming the first African American to desegregate the University of Missouri—two years after St. Louis University opened its doors to African Americans.

Beyond the educational arena, black Missourians fought for their political rights as well. After the Civil War, James Milton Turner, an educator and minister

to Liberia, was pivotal in amassing the black vote for the RADICAL REPUBLICANS, yet by 1878 the REPUBLICAN PARTY would not support him for an election bid for Missouri's Third Congressional District. In 1921, Walthall M. Moore was the first African American elected to the Missouri Legislature. Instead of white patronage, St. Louis blacks had organized through the Citizens Liberty League and the Missouri Negro Republican League to get their candidate into office. Across the state in Kansas City, African Americans benefited from the patronage of Tom Pendergast. And Missouri's native son, President Harry S. TRUMAN, desegregated the U.S. Armed Forces when he issued Executive Order 9981 (see PRESIDENT'S COMMITTEE ON CIVIL RIGHTS) on July 26, 1948—a precursor to the modern Civil Rights Movement.

In 1962, DeVerne Lee Calloway became the first African-American woman elected as a state representative to Missouri's legislature. Ironically, the 1962 election was Calloway's first attempt to run for political office. While her husband, Ernest, was president of the NAACP, Mrs. Calloway worked directly with the black communities, where she encouraged the masses of people to organize for their rights. During the 1950s, Calloway was active in the SIT-INS to desegregate lunch counters and department stores in downtown St. Louis. In the seven years preceding her election, the Calloways were responsible for securing over 1,600 new NAACP members and personally raising more than $7,000 for the NAACP coffers. This experience led directly to Calloway running for political office on the Democratic ticket in 1962, when a vacancy occurred because of illness in the Thirteenth District. The most significant elements of Mrs. Calloway's platform included social welfare, industrial development in the urban core, improved race relations, and education. Calloway served for twenty years before retiring.

By 1969, Missouri had the second-largest number of blacks serving in state and national legislative bodies.

In 1962, Freedom Incorporated was founded in Kansas City by two black businessmen, Leon Jordan and Bruce R. Watkins. In 1965, seven of Freedom Incorporated's eight candidates were elected to state offices. At the national level, Missouri has elected two black congressmen: Democrats William L. Clay, Sr., in 1968 and Alan D. Wheat in 1982.

As early as 1890, nearly 50 percent of African Americans lived in Missouri cities, primarily in St. Louis and Kansas City. After slavery and reconstruction through the early twentieth century, black workers found positions as janitors, domestics, and artisans, but they knew that freedom and property ownership were closely correlated, so whenever possible, they purchased land and started their own businesses. In 1910, Dr. J. E. Perry founded the Provident Hospital for blacks in Kansas City. Due to segregated and cramped living conditions (see HOUSING) as well as poor health care, African Americans did not live as long an average as their white counterparts. Perry's efforts helped to close this gap; he was ably supported by many black women, who raised funds to keep the hospital solvent in times of crisis.

Black women in Missouri were thus essential to the improvement of the African-American community. These women reformers galvanized community resources to meet the vast needs of their people, provided leadership, and exemplified the honor and dignity of African-American womanhood. Josephine Silone Yates, a teacher in Kansas City, served as third president of the NATIONAL ASSOCIATION OF COLORED WOMEN (NACW), 1901–1906. The NACW was composed of middle-class black women who represented the local, state, regional, and national concerns of all African Americans.

African Americans were sometimes subject to violence merely because they had dared to succeed. For example, James T. Scott was unjustly accused of rape and hanged by a vigilante mob at the Stewart Road Bridge near the University of Missouri in 1923. As Ida B. Wells-Barnett (see Ida B. WELLS) revealed in *A Red Record* and other writings, "Lynching represented a tool of social control used to impede black progress, especially economic progress."

In 1939, Missouri was again in the national spotlight, when black farm workers in southeastern Missouri went on strike to protest sharecropping and the tenant farm system. The farmers' plight was ameliorated through donations from across the country and from the local communities. In 1940 Missouri farmers were helped to buy land near Poplar Bluff through the Farm Security Administration.

African-American cultural strivings prospered in Missouri in spite of racial and economic oppression. After Reconstruction, John William "Blind" Boone of Warrensburg was an early ragtime musician; other famous musicians included Scott Joplin of Sedalia and W. C. Handy. Missouri became a center for jazz music. A group called The Missourians featured Cab Calloway, and Count Basie was a piano player in Kansas City during the 1920s. Finally, the writer Langston HUGHES was born in Missouri.

In the new millennium, civil rights in Missouri have not reached their full meaning as intended by the American Constitution. However, as early as the late 1940s, desegregation occurred in HOUSING with the *Shelley v. Kraemer* case in St. Louis. During the 1950s and 1960s, schools and public accommodations slowly began to desegregate, mostly through the nonviolent

efforts of the NAACP, the National Urban League, the CONGRESS OF RACIAL EQUALITY (CORE), and many smaller grass-roots organizations. In 1968, protests broke out across the state. The Kansas City riots in particular epitomized the frustration that African Americans felt toward their unequal treatment—spotlighted by the recent assassination of the Rev. Dr. Martin Luther KING, JR. While Kansas City elected its first black mayor, the Reverend Emmanuel Cleaver II, in 1991, the city is still one of the most residentially and educationally segregated cities in this country.

BIBLIOGRAPHY

Adams, Patricia. "Fighting for Democracy in St. Louis: Civil Rights During World War II." *Missouri Historical Review* 80 (October 1985).

Capeci, Dominic J. *The Lynching of Cleo Wright.* 1998.

Cook, Delia Crutchfield. "Shadow Across the Columns: The Bittersweet Legacy of African Americans at the University of Missouri." Ph.D. diss., University of Missouri-Columbia. 1996.

Greene, Lorenzo J., Gary Kremer, and Antonio F. Holland. *Report to the United States Commission on Civil Rights on Desegregation of Schools in Missouri.* 1959.

Greene, Lorenzo J., Gary Kremer, and Antonio F. Holland. *Missouri's Black Heritage,* rev. ed. 1993.

Higginbotham, A. Leon, Jr. "Race, Sex, Education and Missouri Jurisprudence: *Shelley v. Kraemer* in a Historical Perspective." *Washington University Law Quarterly* 67 (Fall 1989): 674–708.

Kremer, Gary. *James Milton Turner and the Promise of America: The Public Life of a Post–Civil War Black Leader.* 1991.

Strickland, Arvarh E. "The Plight of the People in the Sharecroppers' Demonstration in Southeast Missouri." *Missouri Historical Review* 81 (July 1987).

Wilson, Thomas D. "Chester A. Franklin and Harry S. Truman: An African American Conservative and the 'Conversion' of the Future President." *Missouri Historical Review* 88 (1993): 48–77.

Delia Crutchfield Cook

Mitchell, Clarence, Jr.

(1911–1984), NAACP director.

Clarence Mitchell, Jr., was director of the NATIONAL ASSOCIATION FOR THE ADVANCEMENT OF COLORED PEOPLE (NAACP) Washington, D.C., Bureau.

The third of ten children, he was born in Baltimore, Maryland, the son of Clarence Maurice Mitchell, a waiter and musician, and Elsie Davis Ruff. In 1937 he married activist Juanita Jackson, also born in Baltimore, the daughter of Keiffer Albert and Lillie May Jackson. They had four sons—Clarence III, Keiffer Jackson, Michael Bowen, and George Davis.

Mitchell attended the old Douglass High School in Baltimore and in 1932 he received his A.B. degree from Lincoln University in Pennsylvania. He was a reporter for the *Baltimore Afro-American* from 1933 to 1936, after which he spent a year as a NATIONAL URBAN LEAGUE fellow at the Atlanta School of Social Work. In 1940 he did additional graduate work at the University of Minnesota School of Social Work. In 1963, he was awarded L. L. B. and J. D. degrees from the University of Maryland Law School. He was a member of the bar of the state of Maryland, the U. S. District Court for the district of Maryland, the U.S. Court of Appeals, and for the Fourth Circuit the U.S. SUPREME COURT.

In 1937 he was Maryland State Director of the Negro National Youth Administration and in 1938 was named executive secretary of the National Urban League branch in St. Paul, Minnesota, where he established his expertise in labor questions. In 1941 he became field assistant in the labor division of the Office of Production Management in Washington, D.C. From 1943 to 1945 he was assistant director of field operations of the FAIR EMPLOYMENT PRACTICES COMMITTEE (FEPC), subsequently he became director of the division. The following year, after Congress killed the FEPC, he became labor secretary for the NAACP, working in the Washington Bureau.

Upon becoming director of the NAACP Washington Bureau in 1950, Mitchell assumed full command of the struggle for passage of civil rights laws. His chief mission was to encourage government to adopt constructive civil rights policies, often by garnering presidential leadership for the cause. His strategies included enlisting organized labor as a key force in the struggle on Capitol Hill, organizing bipartisan coalitions of liberals and conservatives in both houses of Congress, and mobilizing the NAACP branch network as a mighty political machine.

To keep the FEPC idea alive, he helped to persuade Presidents TRUMAN, EISENHOWER, KENNEDY, and JOHNSON to issue executive orders barring discrimination in employment. He similarly won an end to segregation on military posts in the South, and contributed significantly to ending segregation in the armed services.

He won his first victory in Congress with passage of the CIVIL RIGHTS ACT OF 1957. He next helped to win passage of the CIVIL RIGHTS ACT OF 1960, the CIVIL RIGHTS ACT OF 1964, the VOTING RIGHTS ACT OF 1965, the FAIR HOUSING ACT, and all strengthening amendments, until his retirement in 1978.

Popularly called the "101st senator," he was awarded the NAACP Spingarn Medal in 1969. President CARTER awarded him the Medal of Freedom in 1980.

BIBLIOGRAPHY

Mitchell, Clarence, Jr. "Democrats v. Dixiecrats." *The Nation* 175 (September 27, 1952): 268–271.

Mitchell, Clarence, Jr. "The Status of Racial Integration in the Armed Services." *Journal of Negro Education* (Summer 1954): 208–213.

Mitchell, Clarence, Jr. "The Warren Court and Congress: A Civil Rights Partnership." Booklet reprinted from *Nebraska Law Review* 48 (1968): 91–128.

Watson, Denton L. *Lion in the Lobby, Clarence Mitchell, Jr.'s Struggle for the Passage of Civil Rights Laws.* 1990.

Denton L. Watson

Montana

The first major influx of non-native settlers into Montana occurred during the Civil War, ensuring that the debate over civil rights would be prominent in early Montana politics. The fact that Montana had a relatively sparse population and a small number of minorities helped prevent severe civil rights abuses such as those that occurred in the Deep South, but RACISM was institutionalized in Montana from its inception as a territory in 1864.

The right to vote was denied to blacks by the first Montana Territorial Assembly in 1864. This situation was remedied when the U.S. CONGRESS passed the Territorial Suffrage Act of 1867, which granted voting rights to African Americans in the Western territories two years before the adoption of the FIFTEENTH AMENDMENT. In the same year Helena became the first Montana city to allow blacks to vote in a municipal election. While many of the city's black male residents cast ballots, others were deterred by an election-day riot in which one black voter was killed. In the years that followed, Helena blacks apparently exercised their voting rights without serious opposition.

In 1872 the Montana Territorial Legislature passed a law stipulating separate educational facilities for black and white children. In Helena, this led to the creation of a separate school for African-American children in 1875. Elsewhere in the state, the law effectively barred black children from public education. Though the law was fought by the African-American community and other progressive forces in Helena, it was the cost of maintaining separate educational facilities and overcrowding in the white schools that brought the defeat of segregated education in municipal elections in 1882. In 1883, the Territorial Legislature followed suit, voting to end segregation in Montana schools, but it was not until 1895 that the original segregationist law was taken off the books.

The last major piece of antiblack legislation passed by the Montana Legislature was a 1909 law banning interracial marriages. Opposition to this law inspired the formation of the Afro-American Protective League in April 1909, to bring political pressure in defense of blacks' rights. As the twentieth century wore on, and Montana's black population shrank to a fraction of 1 percent of the total population, the issue of civil rights for African Americans mostly dropped from public view in the state.

Montana's Chinese residents, who made up almost 10 percent of the state's population in 1870, suffered some of the most severe civil rights abuses of any of Montana's minority groups. As early as 1872 the Territorial Legislature passed a law prohibiting the sale of placer mining lands to aliens (the immigration status of most Chinese at that time). Though thrown out by the Montana Supreme Court, this law represented the first of many attempts to drive the Chinese from Montana through economic strangulation. The Montana Constitutional Convention in 1889 debated, though did not pass, a statute barring corporations from hiring any "Chinese or Mongolians" either directly or indirectly. In 1885 and again in 1897, organized labor in Butte proclaimed a boycott of Chinese businesses and any business that employed Chinese labor. Chinese living in Montana won a number of court battles in the Montana Supreme Court upholding their civil rights in the years following the first Exclusion Act of 1882, which barred the immigration of Chinese contract laborers; but they found the court not so willing to uphold their rights against the racism of Montana society. Increasingly unable to secure a living in Montana, discriminated against at every turn, and without further immigration from China because of a racist national immigration policy, the Chinese population declined steadily in Montana. From a numerical high of 2,532 in 1890 it decreased to 1,285 in 1910, and by 1940 there were only 258 people of Chinese descent living in Montana.

In the struggle for equal rights for women, Montana has seen two notable victories. Women won the right to vote in Montana elections in 1914, joining the women of just ten other western states. Following this victory, Jeannette Rankin, the leader of the WOMAN SUFFRAGE MOVEMENT in Montana, ran for and won a seat in the House of Representatives of the United States in 1916, becoming the first female member of Congress in U.S. history.

The rights of Montana's large and diverse Native American population, which constitutes about 6 percent of Montana's population today, have been mostly determined by federal policy. Since the 1930s, the Indian tribes on Montana's seven reservations have won back many of the tribal rights that were stripped from them by the DAWES ACT of 1887 and other federal mandates around the turn of the century. Although

Native Americans have gained a greater degree of jurisdiction over their own affairs, they generally have been unable to find a solution to the crushing poverty that grips Montana's reservations. Still suffering from the legacy of exploitative government policy, the quest for Native American rights in the twenty-first century must address the economic conditions on Montana's reservations.

In 1974, the Montana legislature passed the Human Rights Act, making discrimination on the basis of race, color, religion, sex, or national origin illegal in all public accommodations. As the twentieth century drew to a close, however, Montana's population was still overwhelmingly white. If Native Americans (the majority of whom live on or near a reservation) are excluded, whites made up 98.6% of the population at the 1990 census. While there are benign explanations for this racial imbalance, one result is that Montana has attracted more than its share of vocal racists over the years, making the state less attractive as a home for people of color. Many Montanans are hopeful, however, that other demographic pressures will intervene in the next century to help make Montana more representative of America's cultural diversity.

BIBLIOGRAPHY

Giles, Kevin J. *Flight of the Dove: The Story of Jeanette Rankin.* 1980.

Lang, William L. "The Nearly Forgotten Blacks on Last Chance Gulch, 1900–1912." *Pacific Northwest Quarterly* 70 (1979): 50–57.

Malone, Michael P., Richard B. Roeder, and William L. Lang. *Montana: A History of Two Centuries*, rev. ed. 1991.

Smurr, J. W. "Jim Crow Out West." *Historical Essays on Montana and the Northwest*, edited by J. W. Smurr and K. Ross Toole. 1957.

Swartout, Robert R., Jr. "From Kwantung to Big Sky: The Chinese Experience in Montana." *Montana* 38 (Winter 1988): 42–53.

Taylor, Quintard. *In Search of the Racial Frontier: African Americans in the American West, 1528–1990.* 1998.

Wunder, John R. "The Law and Chinese in Frontier Montana." *Montana* 30 (Summer 1980): 16–31.

Matthew Millikan

Montgomery Bus Boycott

The Montgomery Bus Boycott of 1955–1956 is widely regarded as the event that began the modern civil rights movement. That may overstate the case, but the 381-day boycott was the first sustained mass protest against JIM CROW segregation; it launched the civil rights careers of Martin Luther KING, JR., Ralph David

Rosa Parks being fingerprinted in Montgomery, Alabama, on February 22, 1956. Her refusal to move to the segregated back section of a city bus sparked the Montgomery bus boycott. (AP/Wide World Photos)

ABERNATHY, and Fred D. GRAY; and it made a world-wide hero of a small, quiet woman named Rosa PARKS.

African-American citizens in many cities had complained bitterly for years about the way they were treated on segregated city buses. In early 1955, Sarah Mae Flemming sued the city of Columbia, South Carolina, over its segregated bus seating and, in July 1955, the U.S. FOURTH CIRCUIT Court of Appeals ruled in the case that segregated seating was unconstitutional. In July 1955, James M. Ritter refused a driver's order to move to the rear of a Richmond, VIRGINIA, bus and was fined $10.

In Montgomery, ALABAMA, bus-related disputes were common. On March 2, 1955, teenager Claudette Colvin was arrested for violating the same segregation law that Mrs. Parks ran afoul of on December 1, 1955. Colvin was the first person to plead not guilty to such a charge. Her attorney, Fred Gray, raised constitutional issues in her defense, but she was convicted. The Women's Political Council (WPC), headed by JoAnn Robinson and Mary Fair Burks, had written letters to

city officials protesting the lack of black bus drivers, rudeness on the part of white drivers, and the seating policies in general. But the arrest of Parks, the secretary of the local NAACP, galvanized local black leaders, including E. D. NIXON, who bailed her out of jail, and the members of the WPC who, on December 2, wrote and disseminated a flyer calling for a boycott for December 5, the day Parks was to be tried in municipal court. As the news spread, other leaders joined in and a meeting was held to plan a one-day boycott. Ministers announced the boycott on Sunday, December 4, and, on the morning of December 5, the boycott was almost completely observed by Montgomery's black citizens. Mrs. Parks was convicted and fined $10. That afternoon, the leaders met to form the MONTGOMERY IMPROVEMENT ASSOCIATION, and King, then 26, was elected president. A meeting held that evening at the Holt Street Baptist Church was attended by more than 5,000 people, who proclaimed their willingness to stay off the buses as long as necessary. The initial demands of the boycott leaders did not include changing the segregation law itself but sought courtesy, hiring of at least some black drivers, and a first-come, first-seated policy, with whites filling the buses from the front and blacks from the rear. Bus company officials, facing mounting losses, were eager to compromise, but intransigence on the part of city officials and rising violence against black citizens—including bombings, beatings, and petty harassment—led attorney Gray, then 25, to attack the segregation ordinance itself. This strategy ultimately succeeded. Meanwhile, the nation was focused on the philosophy and strategy of nonviolence being articulated through King's powerful oratory, along with the quiet perseverance of the black citizens of a city that a hundred years earlier had been the birthplace of the Confederacy.

BIBLIOGRAPHY

Branch, Taylor. *Parting the Waters.* 1988.
Burns, Stewart, ed. *Daybreak of Freedom.* 1997.
Gray, Fred. *Bus Ride to Justice.* 1995.
Raines, Howell. *My Soul Is Rested.* 1977.
Sikora, Frank. *The Judge.* 1992.
Thornton, J. Mills. "Challenge and Response in the Montgomery Bus Boycott of 1955–56." *Alabama Review* (July 1980).

Horace Randall Williams

Montgomery Improvement Association

The Montgomery Improvement Association (MIA) was organized on December 5, 1955, following the conviction of Rosa L. PARKS for refusing to yield her seat on a segregated Montgomery, ALABAMA, city bus. Parks had been arrested four days earlier, and local black leaders, notably E. D. NIXON and JoAnn Robinson, had seized on her case as a way to improve the treatment of black citizens, to some extent the result of a 1900 segregation ordinance that required blacks to stand if their seats were needed by white passengers. On December 2, Robinson's Women's Political Council, consisting mostly of professors at Alabama State College, distributed flyers calling for a boycott of the buses on the morning Parks was to appear in court (see MONTGOMERY BUS BOYCOTT). Over the next few days, various black leaders met at least twice to plan the protest. On the morning of December 5, the boycott was almost total. Predictably, Parks was convicted and, that afternoon, a large group of leaders met in the basement of Dexter Avenue Baptist Church to consider further action. The group voted to support a sustained protest and formed itself into the Montgomery Improvement Association. Martin Luther KING, JR., the 26-year-old pastor of the Dexter Avenue church,

was elected president. Ralph D. ABERNATHY was elected vice president, and Nixon was elected treasurer. Rufus Lewis was named to head a transportation committee, which, over the coming months, would grow into a well-organized car pool system with as many as 200 vehicles and extensive routes. With the eloquent King as spokesperson, the MIA held meetings with Montgomery city officials in an effort to negotiate an end to the boycott. But city officials were unyielding in their support for segregation, and the MIA gradually adopted a two-pronged strategy: its legal team, led by Fred D. GRAY, challenged the segregation law in federal court, while the MIA itself organized alternative transportation, raised funds, conducted a local and national publicity campaign, and kept up the enthusiasm of local black citizens. This last was achieved primarily through weekly mass meetings hosted at various African-American churches. These meetings combined powerful preaching and singing with reports to the people on the progress of the boycott. Staying off the buses was no small matter because, at that time, few black citizens owned private automobiles and many, especially women domestic workers, lived in black west Montgomery but worked in the homes of white people in east Montgomery. Yet for more than a year, the boycott was effectively supported. Blacks returned to the buses on December 20, 1956, after the U.S. Supreme Court let stand a lower court ruling forbidding segregated bus seating. The MIA spawned the SOUTHERN CHRISTIAN LEADERSHIP CONFERENCE, headed by King, who left Montgomery in 1957 to lead the civil rights movement on a national level. In the years after the boycott, the MIA has continued to meet monthly. It has been led since 1968 by Johnnie CARR. Today, the organization concerns itself largely with an annual scholarship award, with anniversaries of the boycott, and with advisory roles in the creation of museums recognizing the bus boycott and other civil rights milestones.

BIBLIOGRAPHY

Branch, Taylor. *Parting the Waters.* 1988.
Burns, Stewart, ed. *Daybreak of Freedom.* 1997.
Gray, Fred. *Bus Ride to Justice.* 1995.
Raines, Howell. *My Soul Is Rested.* 1977.
Sikora, Frank. *The Judge.* 1992.
Thornton, J. Mills. "Challenge and Response in the Montgomery Bus Boycott of 1955–56." *Alabama Review* (July 1980).
Williams, Randall. *Johnnie: The Life of Johnnie Rebecca Carr.* 1995.
Williams, Randall, ed. *The Children Coming On.* 1998.

Horace Randall Williams

Moore, Amzie

(1912–1982), political activist.

A political organizer from the Mississippi Delta, Amzie Moore helped guide STUDENT NONVIOLENT COORDINATING COMMITTEE (SNCC) activists in their voter registration and black citizenship campaigns of the 1960s. Moore, driven by the idea that such campaigns were the key to changing black life in the Delta, first began registering black voters prior to being drafted in 1942. However, his experience as a segregated WORLD WAR II Army draftee bolstered his resolve to change the conditions of black life in the Delta. The awful contradiction of fighting for freedom abroad while suffering oppression at home made Moore more determined than ever to fight racial injustice.

In 1951, Moore helped initiate the Regional Council of Negro Leadership, an organization that promoted voter registration, as well as boycotts of businesses that did not provide for black customers. In 1955, Moore became the president of the Cleveland, Mississippi, chapter of the NATIONAL ASSOCIATION FOR THE ADVANCEMENT OF COLORED PEOPLE (NAACP). Despite acts of violence and severe economic reprisals from the local WHITE CITIZENS' COUNCIL, Moore remained a forceful defender of black rights throughout the 1950s.

Moore's activism was revived by the student movement of the early 1960s. When approached by SNCC activist Robert MOSES, Moore helped map out a voter registration plan for student activists in Mississippi (see VOTING RIGHTS). By opening his home to the movement, Moore provided shelter, relative safety, and an organizing base for SNCC activists. Moore was part of a cohort of older activists excited about the prospect of working with young people who could realize their ideas. To this end, they shared their historical knowledge, personal experiences, and contacts, and offered their personal credibility to help launch a successful civil rights campaign in the Mississippi Delta.

BIBLIOGRAPHY

Amzie Moore Papers. Social Action Collection, State Historical Society of Wisconsin.

Garvey, Michael. "An Oral History with Amzie Moore." Mississippi Oral History Program, University of Southern Mississippi. 1981.

Payne, Charles. I've Got the Light of Freedom: The Organizing Tradition and the Mississippi Struggle. 1995.

Raines, Howell. My Soul Is Rested. 1977.

Blair L. Murphy

Moore, Harry Tyson

(1905–1951), educator and civil rights martyr.

Born in Houston, Florida (near Live Oak), the son of S. Johnny Moore and Rosalea A. Tyson, Harry T. Moore spent most of his early years in Suwannee County, in north Florida. After graduating from Florida Normal Institute (Live Oak), he received his certificate and began his teaching career. He later received his A.A. (1936) and B.S. (1951) degrees from Bethune-Cookman College, in Daytona Beach. Moore married Harriette V. Sims, and to them were born daughters Annie Rosalea and Juanita Evangeline.

Moore was employed by the school board of Brevard County from 1925 to 1946, serving as both a teacher and a principal. Because textbooks did not portray African Americans in a favorable role, he often utilized black newspapers for teaching purposes. Also he strongly emphasized the implications of the Constitution for his students.

As the founder and president of the Brevard County branch of the NATIONAL ASSOCIATION FOR THE ADVANCEMENT OF COLORED PEOPLE (NAACP) and as regional president of the Florida State Teachers Association, Moore led the state campaign for equal salaries for black teachers and for general improvement in the schools. His strong stance for civil rights led to his dismissal by the school board. After his firing, Moore devoted full time to the pursuit of racial EQUALITY. Encouraged by the civil rights successes of his local branch, he organized and became president of the Florida Conference of NAACP Chapters in 1941 and served as executive secretary from 1946 to his death in 1951. During his tenure, he organized and nurtured local branches throughout the state and raised money for the operation of his office.

In addition to his NAACP post, Moore served as executive secretary of the Progressive Voters' League of Florida (1946–1951), an organization that he helped to found. In his dual role, he was instrumental in defeating a bill that would have converted the DEMOCRATIC PARTY into a private white club and another bill that would have required a literacy test as a prerequisite for voting. Moore also played a direct and influential role in politics. His voter registration campaigns and his granting of political endorsements often led to the election of candidates who were friendly to progressive causes, which translated into a more enlightened attitude regarding issues of concern to African Americans—equalization of salaries for teachers, anti–poll-tax legislation, hiring of black policemen, and so on.

At a time when many African Americans appeared willing to accept police brutality and mob violence as their fate, Moore spoke out boldly against these evils. He complained to the governor about LYNCHING and called for the suspension of public officials who allowed these mob activities to take place. He denounced STATES' RIGHTS as an ineffective doctrine and lobbied for federal intervention to protect the VOTING RIGHTS of blacks and to ensure for them equal opportunities in EDUCATION and EMPLOYMENT.

Because Moore displayed courage in fighting for racial equality, the KU KLUX KLAN and other segregationists made him their target. On Christmas night of 1951, race haters achieved their goal by setting off a bomb under his bedroom, killing him almost instantly. His wife, a loyal supporter in the struggle, died several days later. His bold leadership in the campaign for racial equality may be viewed as a prelude to the civil rights revolution that followed his death.

BIBLIOGRAPHY

Clark, James C. "Civil Rights Leader Harry T. Moore and the Ku Klux Klan in Florida." *Florida Historical Quarterly* (October 1994): 166–183.
Green, Ben. *Before His Time: The Untold Story of Harry T. Moore, America's First Civil Rights Martyr.* 1999.

Jake C. Miller

Mora, Magdalena

(1952–1981), labor activist, feminist, and scholar.

Magdalena Mora courageously supported and defended Mexican immigrant workers throughout her short life. Mora's profound sympathies toward the working class were the product of experience and study. In 1962, Mora's family immigrated to the United States from the state of Michoacán, Mexico. The family settled in San Jose, California, where Mora spent summers working in the fields, and, later, while a student at the University of California, Berkeley, in area canneries. On the Berkeley campus, Mora pursued a bachelor's degree in economics and became immersed in Chicano student protest politics. After graduating in 1974, Mora helped found the Oakland affiliate of the Centro de Acción Social Autónoma–Hermandad General de Trabajadores (Center for Autonomous Social Action–General Brotherhood of Workers). Best known by its acronym, CASA, the organization vigorously defended immigrant rights.

Becoming one of the most dynamic and energetic CASA members in California, Mora directed a successful strike of mostly women workers against the Toltec Food Corporation in Richmond, California, in 1975. Interested particularly in the plight of women laborers, Mora wrote articles that contributed a feminist perspective to CASA's publication, *Sin Fronteras* (*Without Borders*). After CASA disbanded in 1978, Mora enrolled at the University of California, Los Angeles to study Chicana/o history. With graduate student Adelaida R. del Castillo, she immediately began to compile *Mexican Women in the United States*, an anthology published in 1980. Diagnosed with a brain tumor in January 1979, Mora continued her studies and activism almost until her death two years later.

BIBLIOGRAPHY

Editorial Prensa Sembradora. *Raiz Fuerte Que No Se Arranca: The Life of a Luchadora.* A collection of testimonials voiced at a gathering of friends and colleagues to honor Mora after her death.
Mora, Magdalena. "The Tolteca Strike: Mexican Women and the Struggle for Unionization." In *Mexican Immigrant Workers in the United States.* 1981.

Lorena Oropeza

Moreno, Luisa

(1906–1992), labor organizer.

A passionate labor organizer during the 1930s and 1940s, Moreno improved conditions for countless workers, especially women employed in California's food processing industry. Born in Guatemala to a well-to-do family, Moreno attended grammar school in the United States and immigrated to that country in 1928. At the start of the Depression, Moreno was living in New York City, where she found employment in a garment factory in order to support her artist husband and infant daughter. The work as a sewing machine operator—and on-the-job exposure to Puerto Rican socialists—radicalized her.

Moreno, now divorced and a single mother, traveled the country as a professional organizer for the American Federation of Labor and later for the nascent Congress of Industrial Organizations. Particularly interested in the plight of ethnic Mexican workers in the southwest, Moreno participated in the 1938 pecan shellers' strike in San Antonio. Also in 1938, Moreno devoted herself to organizing El Congreso Nacional de Pueblo de Habla Española (National Spanish-Speaking Congress), the country's first pan-Latino civil rights organization. From 1941 to 1947, Moreno was an international vice-president of the militant United Cannery, Agricultural, Packing and Allied Workers of America (UCAPAWA). A powerful speaker in English and Spanish, Moreno helped negotiate and defend food industry contracts that delivered higher wages, safer facilities, and, in one case, a work-site nursery. In 1948, the Immigration and Naturalization Service began proceedings against Moreno, whose activism was considered suspect—part of the anticommunist hysteria that followed World War II. Threatened with deportation, Moreno left the country in 1950.

BIBLIOGRAPHY

Larralde, Carlos C., and Richard Griswold del Castillo. "A Hispanic Civil Rights Leader in San Diego." *Journal of San Diego History* 11 (1995): 284–311.
Ruiz, Vicki L. *Cannery Women, Cannery Lives.* 1987.
Ruiz, Vicki L. "Luisa Moreno." In *The Reader's Guide to American History,* edited by Eric Foner and John A. Garraty. 1991.

Lorena Oropeza

Morgan v. Virginia (1946)

In 1946, the U.S. SUPREME COURT ruled that Virginia's law mandating racially segregated public buses was unconstitutional when applied to interstate passengers. Irene Morgan had been traveling from Virginia to Maryland on July 16, 1944, when she was arrested for refusing to move further back so that white passengers could be seated. While paying a hundred-dollar fine for resisting arrest, she hired Richmond NATIONAL ASSOCIATION FOR THE ADVANCEMENT OF COLORED PEOPLE (NAACP) lawyer Spottswood Robinson to appeal her conviction and ten dollar fine on the segregation charge. After losing before the Virginia Supreme Court of Appeals, she appealed to the U.S. Supreme Court. There NAACP lawyers William HASTIE and Thurgood MARSHALL, with Robinson's assistance, argued that Virginia's segregation law was unconstitutional when applied to interstate passengers because it put an undue burden on interstate commerce. The possible confusion arising from variations among the states regarding segregation laws and methods of racial identification, and the possibility of repeated seat changes on a single trip convinced the Court, by a seven to one margin, to rule for Morgan. Precedent for the decision was set in *Hall v. DeCuir* (1877), in which the Court overturned a Louisiana law requiring integration using the same logic.

Though the Morgan victory inspired the 1947 Journey of Reconciliation, forerunner of the 1961 FREEDOM RIDES, the decision made little practical difference in the experiences of most blacks on public buses. In most instances, the overturned state laws were simply replaced by bus company regulations mandating the same practices.

BIBLIOGRAPHY

Barnes, Catherine. *Journey from Jim Crow: The Desegregation of Southern Transit.* 1983.
Morgan v. Commonwealth, 184 VA 24, 34 S. E. 2d 491 (1945).
Morgan v. Virginia, 328 U.S. 373, 66 S. Ct. 1050, 90 L. Ed. 1317 (1946).
Ware, Gilbert. *William Hastie: Grace Under Pressure.* 1984.

Kara Miles Turner

Moses, Robert Parris

(1935–), educator and civil rights activist.

Robert Parris Moses is best known for his civil rights work with the STUDENT NONVIOLENT COORDINATING COMMITTEE (SNCC) in MISSISSIPPI and the Algebra Project teaching math literacy.

Raised in Harlem, Bob Moses graduated from Hamilton College in 1956 and completed an M.A. in philosophy from Harvard a year later. Teaching math in New York City, Moses was inspired by the southern student sit-in movement and spent the summer of 1960 volunteering in Atlanta. He met SNCC founder and longtime civil rights activist Ella BAKER, who encouraged Moses to join SNCC and travel to Mississippi. There Mississippi activist and businessman Amzie MOORE convinced him that voter registration was the key to achieving full citizenship for African Americans. Moses returned to Mississippi in 1961 to implement Moore's plan through the slow process of door-to-door canvassing, literacy and citizenship classes, and inspiring potential applicants, drawing on Baker's example. Like Baker and many in SNCC, Moses became known for his community organizing approach which included faith in local leaders and perseverance in the face of apparently insurmountable barriers. Seemingly fearless, Moses led by example and persisted despite being jailed, beaten, and shot at.

When friends and colleagues were murdered for their civil rights work, Moses helped envision and carry out the 1964 FREEDOM SUMMER, which brought hundreds of volunteers to the state to teach in freedom schools, work on voter registration, and organize the MISSISSIPPI FREEDOM DEMOCRATIC PARTY (MFDP). An alternative political party created to challenge the state's all-white Democratic party, the MFDP provided African Americans access to politics even when white officials kept them from registering. Moreover, disheartened by the failure of the law to protect African Americans in Mississippi, Moses believed that white northern volunteers would bring the laws and attention of the rest of the country into Mississippi with them.

When three civil rights workers were murdered (including two whites), massive publicity forced the FEDERAL BUREAU OF INVESTIGATION (FBI) to mount an aggressive investigation of these deaths, though African Americans murdered and found dead throughout the summer were still ignored by law and the media.

As a result of this, and the Democratic Party's rejection of the MFDP's bid to be seated instead of the Mississippi regulars at the 1964 Convention, Moses and other civil rights workers grew increasingly disillusioned.

Over the next two years, Moses tried to escape his growing influence in the movement, left SNCC, protested the VIETNAM WAR, and, as a conscientious objector, went to Canada to avoid the draft. He moved to Tanzania in 1968, teaching math there until returning to the United States in 1976 when President Jimmy CARTER pardoned draft resisters.

In the 1980s, Moses returned to community organizing in the tradition of Ella Baker through volunteer work in his daughter's school. With parents and teachers, he developed the Algebra Project to teach math literacy to prepare students for advanced high school math. Like voter registration in the 1960s, Moses saw math literacy as a requirement for full citizenship. According to Moses and others in the Algebra Project, it, like the Mississippi movement, is based on the leadership and empowerment of grassroots people and the principle of working within the context of one's life.

BIBLIOGRAPHY

Burner, Eric. *And Gently He Shall Lead Them: Robert Parris Moses and the Civil Rights Movement in Mississippi.* 1994.

Carson, Clayborne. *In Struggle: SNCC and the Black Awakening of the 1960s.* 1981.

Dittmer, John. *Local People: The Struggle for Civil Rights in Mississippi.* 1995.

Field, Connie, and Marilyn Mulford. *Freedom on My Mind.* Film. California Newsreel. 1994.

Moses, Robert P., Mieko Kamii, Susan McAllister Swap, and Jeffrey Howard. "The Algebra Project: Organizing in the Spirit of Ella Baker." *Harvard Educational Review* 59, 4 (1989): 423–442.

Robert P. Moses

Mothers of East Los Angeles

Community activism often requires a catalyst for action. In the early 1980s, the state of CALIFORNIA proposed the construction of a new state prison in the East Los Angeles neighborhood of Boyle Heights. State highway construction and housing projects had already disrupted the neighborhood, and residents, especially a group of mothers, were furious. A priest at the neighborhood Resurrection Catholic Church spurred a group of women to organize in protest of the proposed prison project.

Mothers of East Los Angeles (MELA) was formed in 1984, and their weekly protest marches against the prison project attracted around 3,000 participants.

Statewide and national attention was drawn to the neighborhood, and eventually the prison project was cancelled. Unfortunately, the original group of women split at the celebration party. The Mothers of East Los Angeles–Santa Isabel (MELA-SI), or Madres del Este de Los Angeles–Santa Isabel, formed around Santa Isabel Catholic Church. Both groups claim the rights to the name Mothers of East Los Angeles, both claim to be the original group, and both are incorporated non-profit organizations.

Fortunately for the East Los Angeles community, both groups continue to provide active support for community needs and projects. MELA fights against adult businesses, has advocated for a subway project, and builds low-income housing. MELA-SI has raised and distributed hundreds of thousands of dollars in scholarships, run graffiti cleanup programs, conserved water through the distribution of free low flush toilets, and provided field trip opportunities for local youth to Mono Lake. Both MELA and MELA-SI are active participants in Los Angeles area environmental and community improvement projects.

BIBLIOGRAPHY

"Group Raises $20,000 for College Scholarships." *Los Angeles Times* (February 18, 1998).

Madres del Este do Los Angeles Santa Isabel. Cited online at www.clnet.ucr.edu/community/intercambios/melasi/.

"The Mothers' Saga: How a Movement Split in Two." *Los Angeles Times* (August 29, 1999).

Southern California Non-profit Organizations Working for Sustainability. Cited online at www.scced.org/scced/sust_orgs/urbanorg.html.

Michael Dawson

Motley, Constance Baker

(1921–   ), lawyer and judge.

Counsel for the NATIONAL ASSOCIATION FOR THE ADVANCEMENT OF COLORED PEOPLE (NAACP), civil rights leader, and the first black woman federal judge, Constance Baker Motley was a leader in the DESEGREGATION of schools in MISSISSIPPI, GEORGIA, ALABAMA, and other bastions of southern racial segregation in the 1950s and 1960s. An expert in constitutional law, Motley fought for the rights of black students to attend public schools and won nine of ten cases she argued before the U.S. SUPREME COURT. With courage and determination, Motley litigated milestone cases in school desegregation, including those of black plaintiffs Autherine LUCY at the University of Alabama in 1956, James MEREDITH at the University of Mississippi

Constance Baker Motley with President Lyndon B. Johnson. In 1966, Motley became the first black woman to be appointed to a federal judgeship in the United States. (AP/Wide World Photos)

in 1960, and Charlayne Hunter-Gault and Hamilton Homes at the University of Georgia in 1961.

Constance Baker was born in 1921 in New Haven, Connecticut, to Rachel and Willoughby Baker, immigrants from the Caribbean island of Nevis. Members of her family and most of the blacks in her community were employed in service and domestic work at Yale University and in the homes of affluent white families in New Haven. With financial support of benefactor Clarence Blakeslee, who was impressed by her youthful confidence and insight into her community's problems, Constance Baker was able to begin college in 1941 at Fisk University in Nashville, Tennessee. From there, she transferred to New York University and graduated with a B.S. degree in economics in 1943. She entered Columbia University and earned a law degree in 1946; in the same year, she married Joel Wilson Motley, an insurance broker.

Constance Motley's role as a leader in the civil rights movement began after she was appointed by NAACP Chief Counsel Thurgood MARSHALL to be associate counsel for the NAACP LEGAL DEFENSE AND EDUCATIONAL FUND. She served in this position for twenty years, 1945–1965. Motley spent many hours preparing briefs, devising strategy, and preparing plaintiffs for civil rights cases. In 1954, she assisted Marshall in litigating the Supreme Court's famous BROWN V. BOARD OF EDUCATION decision, which declared racial SEGREGATION in public schools to be un-lawful. Judge Motley practiced civil rights law at a time when it was rare to see a black woman lawyer in a southern courtroom. She demonstrated that the law could be called into use as an instrument for social change and racial justice.

In 1963, Motley entered electoral politics by completing the unexpired term of New York state senator James Watson. A year later, she was elected to a full term and became the first black woman New York state senator, and the first woman borough president of Manhattan. In 1966, Motley was nominated by President Lyndon B. JOHNSON to sit on the federal bench. In spite of considerable opposition from Southern senators, she was confirmed and became the first black woman federal judge in the United States. In 1982, Motley was named chief judge of the U.S. Southern District of New York, thus becoming the highest-ranking black woman jurist in the United States. Although the significance of Constance Baker Motley and other black women lawyers as leaders in the civil rights movement has been obscured by the lack of public visibility of tedious courtroom litigations, Motley stands alongside Thurgood Marshall and Charles Hamilton HOUSTON as a masterful legal tactician in the civil rights struggle.

BIBLIOGRAPHY

Barnett, Bernice McNair. "Invisible Southern Black Women Leaders of the Civil Rights Movement and the

Triple Constraints of Gender, Race, and Class." *Gender and Society* 7, 2 (1993): 162–182.

Barnett, Bernice McNair. *Sisters in Struggle: Invisible Black Women Leaders of the Civil Rights Movement, 1945–1970.* Forthcoming.
Motley, Constance Baker. "The Role of Law in Effecting Social Change." *Crisis* 85, 1 (1978): 24–28.
Motley, Constance Baker. Interview with Bernice McNair Barnett, November 1990.
Motley, Constance Baker. "My Personal Debt to Thurgood Marshall." *Yale Law Review*, 1991.

Bernice McNair Barnett

Moton, Robert Russa

(1867–1940), educator.

Robert Moton, Booker T. WASHINGTON's successor as leader of southern blacks, was born and raised in Virginia, and attended the Hampton Institute in Hampton, Va. During this time, he also studied law and obtained a license to practice. Following his graduation in 1890, Moton became Commandant of Hampton's Cadet Corps, and took the title "Major," which he retained for the rest of his life.

During his years at Hampton, Moton became a close follower of Washington's philosophy of black self-help, accommodation with SEGREGATION, and disavowal of civil rights. In 1915, following Washington's death, Moton was named to his position as principal of the Tuskegee Institute. During the 1920s, Moton developed a college curriculum for Tuskegee and tripled the Institute's endowment.

Meanwhile, Moton became a nationwide spokesperson for southern black conservatism, although he was never the commanding figure Washington had been. While he generally opposed civil rights activism, in 1923 he successfully lobbied for the establishment of an all-black Veterans Administration hospital in Tuskegee, and he led defense efforts when the hospital was threatened by the KU KLUX KLAN. Moton's greatest contribution to civil rights was the book *What the Negro Thinks* (1930), in which he bluntly denounced the injustice of legal segregation and the humiliations it imposed on blacks. However, Moton did not advocate racial INTEGRATION, but instead the strengthening of black institutions in order to build blacks' self-worth. His book won Moton the coveted Spingarn Medal from the NATIONAL ASSOCIATION FOR THE ADVANCEMENT OF COLORED PEOPLE (NAACP) in 1932. In 1935 Moton retired and returned to Virginia. He died in 1940.

BIBLIOGRAPHY
Eisenstadt, Peter. "Southern Black Conservatism, 1865–1945." In *Black Conservatism: Essays in Intellectual and Political History*, edited by Peter Eisenstadt. 1998.
Norell, Robert J. *Reaping the Whirlwind: The Civil Rights Movement in Tuskegee.* 1983.

Greg Robinson

Mount Rushmore Protests

U.S. violation of the 1868 Fort Laramie Treaty and the resulting Black Hills land claim of the Sioux Nation was a centerpiece of American Indian dissent throughout the twentieth century. Although the bulk of such activities took place in court until the late 1960s, the "direct action" approach taken by the civil rights and antiwar movements had by then begun to produce other modes of Indian political expression.

The first signs of this in Sioux country came in June 1970, when a small group of local Oglala Lakotas assembled to protest federal impoundment of the Sheep Mountain area of the Pine Ridge Reservation, in SOUTH DAKOTA. Oglala elders soon suggested that a similar action be undertaken at the Mount Rushmore National Monument, in the Black Hills, to draw public attention to the question of the Lakotas' broader land rights.

In September, a contingent of the AMERICAN INDIAN MOVEMENT (AIM) headed by Russell MEANS, an Oglala, arrived to conduct the demonstration. Although it was anticipated that the event would consist mainly of speechmaking in the monument's public viewing area, AIM members surprised everyone by quickly climbing atop the massive portrait of four presidents carved by sculptor Gutzon Borglum into the face of the mountain itself. The occupation, which was sustained until December, garnered national television coverage of Sioux grievances for the first time.

On June 6, 1971, AIM returned to Mount Rushmore. This time, federal personnel subjected the demonstrators to mass arrest, injuring several. This, too, resulted in extensive media coverage, however; so the activists once again achieved their objectives. The lessons of the Mount Rushmore protests were lost on neither the Lakota traditionals nor AIM leaders such as Means, and would help shape a mutual style of confrontation politics culminating in the seventy-one–day armed standoff at WOUNDED KNEE in 1973.

BIBLIOGRAPHY
Johnson, Troy, Joane Nagel, and Duane Champaign, eds. *American Indian Activism: Alcatraz to the Longest Walk.* 1997.
Means, Russell, with Marvin J. Wolf. *Where White Men Fear to Tread: The Autobiography of Russell Means.* 1995.
Smith, Paul Chaat, and Robert Allen Warrior. *Like a Hurricane: The American Indian Movement from Alcatraz to Wounded Knee.* 1996.

Weyler, Rex. *Blood of the Land: The Government and Corporate War Against the American Indian Movement*, 2nd ed. 1992.

Ward Churchill

Movement for Independence–Puerto Rican Socialist Party

The Movement for Independence (MPI) was founded in Puerto Rico in 1959. In 1964, the organization made its presence felt in New York through a sector comprised of proindependence intellectuals. Originally it functioned as a support group for the independence movement on the island. However, by the late 1960s, the organization began to transform itself into a Marxist–Leninist party, as members recognized that in order to mobilize the migrant Puerto Rican population in favor of independence they would need to address their relevant issues.

By 1971, the organization had renamed itself the Puerto Rican Socialist Party (PSP). The membership was comprised of labor organizers, intellectuals, college students, and factory workers. The organization grew steadily, creating branches in New Jersey, Connecticut, Chicago, Boston, San Francisco, and Los Angeles. The party's first congress was held in the United States in 1973. A political plan was adopted and documented under the title "Entre las Entrañas" ("From the Belly of the Beast"). The party's goal became to link the island independence movement with mainland Puerto Rican struggles for democratic rights.

Some of the group's initial activities included supporting Puerto Rican student movements, organizing Puerto Rican workers in the steel plants of Gary, Indiana, and participating in housing struggles in Boston and New York City. Members addressed independence by mobilizing to free five Nationalist Puerto Rican prisoners and through continuing circulation of the island-based newspaper *Claridad* and its subsequent bilingual supplement, *Bilingual Claridad*. These efforts, however, were not considered sufficient by the party's central branch on the island.

In 1973 and 1974, the island branch called for the organization of mass solidarity events, increasing the group's visibility on the question of independence. On October 27, 1974, a National Day of Solidarity was celebrated, mobilizing twenty thousand people. The U.S. branch began to criticize the sole focus on independence, and the following year the organization's efforts were refocused on mainland concerns. In 1975, the party ran candidates in New York's Lower East Side for positions on the community school board. In New Jersey, members protested against cutbacks in education and social services to senior citizens. In 1976, the focus shifted once again to mass solidarity events. The July 4 Coalition was formed to organize antibicentennial celebrations as a protest against U.S. imperialism.

Along with infiltration of the organization by agents provocateurs and continuous intimidation by the FEDERAL BUREAU OF INVESTIGATION, these mass solidarity events led to the decline of the organization. Members, burned out by the amount of work involved in organizing these events, began to leave the group. The leaders of the U.S. branch became critical of the group's island leaders for not addressing the concerns of the mainland population. In 1982, an ideological split arose within the island branch between those who supported Marxist–Leninist ideology and those who wanted to move away from it. As a result, many of the branches on the mainland stopped functioning. Finally, in 1995, the party in Puerto Rico dissolved itself and initiated formation of the New Independence Movement, returning to the original goals of the MPI.

BIBLIOGRAPHY

Rivera, Carmen Vivian. "Our Movement: One Woman's Story." In *The Puerto Rican Movement: Voices from the Diaspora*, edited by Andrés Torres and José E. Velazquez. 1998.

Velazquez, José E. "Coming Full Circle: The Puerto Rican Socialist Party, U.S. Branch." In *The Puerto Rican Movement: Voices from the Diaspora*, edited by Andrés Torres and José E. Velazquez. 1998.

Elizabeth Garcia

Movement for National Liberation

See Movimiento de Liberacíon Nacional

Movimiento de Liberacíon Nacional

In 1898, the United States gained political control of Puerto Rico from Spain in the Treaty of Paris. Thus began a long period of economic development and exploitation of the island's resources along with the granting of U.S. citizenship to its residents. Socioeconomic reform to improve living conditions of Puerto Ricans began in the 1940s with the first Puerto Rican–born governor gaining leadership in 1946 under U.S. appointment. Puerto Rico became a self-governing commonwealth in 1952 with its own constitution, approved by the U.S. CONGRESS. Also in the 1950s, immigration to the United States of Puerto Ricans seeking greater economic opportunities significantly increased, mostly to the larger cities.

Many Puerto Ricans believed the Puerto Rican political changes were a sham to perpetuate U.S. colonialistic activities. In 1967, Puerto Ricans voted to retain commonwealth status, rather than seeking U.S. statehood or independence. In reaction, the Movimiento de Liberacíon Nacional (MLN), known in English as the Movement for National Liberation, emerged in 1977 in Chicago with membership spreading elsewhere, including New York by the 1980s. The MLN, loosely associated with other organizations, sought independence for Puerto Rico. Connections with the clandestine Armed Forces of National Liberation (FALN) resulted in several MLN members being imprisoned for failing to cooperate with investigations of FALN. Though the Puerto Rican independence movement became associated with a number of terrorist bombings in the United States, the MLN established social programs, including day care, to garner support for its political goals. However, with many Puerto Rican nationalists held in prison until a 1999 pardon was issued by President Bill Clinton, the political issue of independence waned.

BIBLIOGRAPHY

Barreto, Amilcar Antonio. *Language, Elites, and the State: Nationalism in Puerto Rico and Quebec.* 1998.

Fernandez, Ronald. *Puerto Rico: The Disenchanted Island.* 1992.

Richard C. Hanes

Movimiento Estudiantil Chicano de Aztlán

Chicano political activists in the American Southwest wrote a manifesto entitled "El Plan de Santa Barbara" in April 1968, at a conference in Santa Barbara, California. The manifesto explains an attitude and commitment to a cultural movement for the betterment of Chicanos in the United States. From this plan, chapters of Movimiento Estudiantil Chicano de Aztlán (M.E.Ch.A.) have been formed in many communities and on college and high school campuses.

M.E.Ch.A. is not widely publicized or recognized in the mainstream media, and its activities and goals are not widely understood. The document upon which the organization is founded can be interpreted on the one hand to be a prescription for revolution, while on the other hand, it can be interpreted as describing a goal for economic and cultural independence. Non-Chicano readers have voiced concern over language some would call inflammatory. The term "Aztlán," for example, is an Aztec word for a mythical place M.E.Ch.A. defines as the southwestern United States—a place it regards as in need of liberation.

El Plan de Santa Barbara promotes the concept of a cultural identity for the Chicano people. It describes the term "Hispanic" as pejorative and an attempt by the white majority to anglicize a native culture. The manifesto sees self-determination for the Chicano people as the only means for obtaining socioeconomic justice. It promotes the unification of the Chicano people for the struggle toward individual and community improvement. A central tenet of the manifesto is the importance of education: education for the individual and for the community. Therefore, the principle goals of M.E.Ch.A. focus on providing and encouraging higher education opportunities for Chicanos and Chicanas, and educating the Chicano community on civil rights.

During the California election campaign of 1994, an initiative was on the ballot to restrict the access of public services to illegal immigrants. That initiative, Proposition 187, was widely believed by many Chicanos to be racist in nature, but it passed with over 58 percent of the vote. Chicano organizations sued to prevent implementation of the initiative and court actions have blocked its implementation.

Among their activities, in 1996, M.E.Ch.A. worked to organize a march of activists from Sacramento to San Diego, culminating at the Republican National Convention, which was held in San Diego in August 1996. The goal of the march was to raise community awareness of the problems with Proposition 187, and to demonstrate the political power of the Chicano community.

M.E.Ch.A. frequently posts documents of its manifesto and goals at Chicano public meetings and activities and organizes marches, public meetings, and demonstrations. M.E.Ch.A. is also actively involved in promoting higher education to its constituents, including active solicitation of students to attend colleges with M.E.Ch.A. chapters. It is working to form a national political party that would represent the sentiments of the Chicano community.

BIBLIOGRAPHY

Arizona Parents for Traditional Education Home Page. Cited online at www.theriver.com/Public/tucson_parents_edu_forum/MECHA.html.

"Chicano Group Will Celebrate." *San Diego Union-Tribune* (September 30, 1994).

"El Plan De Aztlán." MEChA Website. Cited online at gladstone.uoregon.edu/~mecha/plan.html.

MEChA Website. Cited online at www.stanford.edu/group/MEChA.

MEChA Website. Cited online at www-rohan.sdsu.edu/dept/mecha/index.html.

"Prospective Students Delighted by Calls From SDSU Undergrads." *San Diego Union-Tribune* (February 21, 1993).

Michael Dawson

Movimiento Pro Independencia

See Movement for Independence–Puerto Rican
Socialist Party

MPI

See Movement for Independence–Puerto Rican
Socialist Party

Muhammad, Elijah

(1897–1975), religious leader and head of the
Nation of Islam.

Elijah Muhammad was born Elijah Poole in Sanders-
ville, Georgia, in October 1897. His father, William,
worked as a sharecropper and a Baptist minister; his
mother, Mariah, labored as a domestic for local whites.
After the Poole family moved to Cordele, Georgia, in
1900, Elijah and his siblings contributed to the family's
income by working odd jobs. During his life in Georgia, Elijah was employed in a number of capacities,
ranging from selling firewood in Cordele to employment as a gang laborer with the Southern Railroad
Company in Macon. Largely due to the financial
needs of his family, Elijah spent very little time in

*Elijah Muhammad, leader of the Nation of Islam, in
the 1950s.* (Archive Photos)

school, reaching the eighth grade at best. On separate
occasions, Elijah witnessed the aftermath of two lynchings, which embittered him enough to leave the state.
In 1923, he and his wife Clara, along with their two
children, departed for Detroit, Michigan, in search of
a better life.

Elijah, though poorly educated, was able to find
work in the automobile industry in Detroit prior to
the Great Depression. However, by the early 1930s, he
was unemployed and unable to provide for his growing family. Consequently, the Pooles went onto the welfare roll, and Elijah turned to alcohol. In 1931, Elijah
became an early follower of Wallace D. Fard, who had
founded the NATION OF ISLAM a year earlier. Throughout poverty-stricken black Detroit, Fard spread the
message of the Nation of Islam (or Muslims), which
preached, among other beliefs, that blacks were the
"Original People," whites were devils, and that America would be destroyed by a "Mother Plane" (a space-
ship piloted by black scientists) so that the righteous
black people could be restored to their former glory.
He also encouraged moral reform and economic self-
help among his African-American following. After
Fard disappeared in 1934, Elijah Poole, renamed Elijah Muhammad, assumed the leadership of the Nation
of Islam. While a number of people left the movement
after Muhammad proclaimed that Fard had been "Allah in person" and that he had been appointed by Fard
as the "Messenger of Allah," Muhammad was able to
retain a small but loyal core of followers.

Over the next two decades, Elijah Muhammad and
the Nation of Islam faced a number of trials. Muhammad, who had relocated the movement's headquarters
to Chicago, was persecuted by the FEDERAL BUREAU
OF INVESTIGATION (FBI) and imprisoned during the
1940s for evading the draft. After his release from
prison in 1946, he took the Nation of Islam into the
realm of business and real estate, purchasing a farm,
a restaurant, and a bakery. As the organization increased in size, talented people such as MALCOLM X,
a former convict-turned-believer, came into the Muslim movement and enhanced its popularity among
African-Americans discontented with the slow pace of
social change. In 1959, Elijah Muhammad made a *hajj*,
or pilgrimage, to Mecca, Saudi Arabia, and began to
attract the attention, largely negative, of the national
media.

Elijah Muhammad was a vocal critic of the leadership, methods, and objectives of the civil rights movement. By 1960, the Nation of Islam was demanding a
separate state for African Americans, and thus saw little value in the goal of integration or the strenuous
efforts that Dr. Martin Luther KING, JR., and others
were making toward racial reconciliation. Muhammad
was particularly critical of civil disobedience, especially
in instances where vigilante violence and police bru-

tality against black people were going unchecked by legal authorities in places like Mississippi and Alabama. Additionally, he excoriated civil rights leaders for misleading African Americans into believing that America would someday extend "freedom, justice, and equality" to the descendants of former slaves.

Though the rhetoric of the Nation of Islam was interpreted by many as anti-American and subversive, the organization was, in fact, quite conservative. Throughout his leadership of the Muslim movement, Muhammad advocated a puritanical moral code, shunned electoral politics and overt forms of dissident activism, and encouraged capitalist enterprises among blacks. Actually, the FBI, which sought to curb all forms of black activism, was much more concerned about the goals of mainstream civil rights organizations than those of the Muslims.

During the 1960s, the Nation of Islam grew greatly in size. Despite a number of organizational crises caused by state repression, ideological divisions, the departure and subsequent assassination of Malcolm X, and a number of damaging scandals, Muhammad's message of economic initiative, racial separatism, and moral uplift drew tens of thousands of people into the movement in the wake of the BLACK POWER era. When Muhammad died in 1975, the Nation of Islam had seventy-five mosques throughout the country and assets in excess of forty million dollars. Given his four-decade reign over the Muslim movement, few leaders have had the kind of prolonged impact on black consciousness and racial pride that Elijah Muhammad had.

BIBLIOGRAPHY

Beynon, Erdmann D. "The Voodoo Cult Among Negro Migrants in Detroit." *American Journal of Sociology* 43, 6 (May 1938): 894–907.

Clegg, Claude A., III. *An Original Man: The Life and Times of Elijah Muhammad.* 1997.

Essien-Udom, E. U. *Black Nationalism: A Search for an Identity in America.* 1962.

Lincoln, C. Eric. *The Black Muslims in America.* 1961.

Lomax, Louis E. *When the Word Is Given.* 1963.

Malcolm X (with Alex Haley). *The Autobiography of Malcolm X.* 1965.

Muhammad, Elijah. Uline Arena Address. Washington, D.C., May 31, 1959.

Muhammad, Elijah. *Message to the Blackman in America.* 1965.

Claude A. Clegg

Multiculturalism

Multiculturalism is a result not only of the civil rights movement but also of the new immigration policies of the 1960s, which have significantly changed the de-

mographics of certain regions in the United States (see IMMIGRANTS AND IMMIGRATION). It is also related to a growing interest on the part of liberals and the Left to redefine American nationalism after the debacle in Vietnam and is largely an ideology about cultural and racial assimilation. Clearly opposed to older notions of nationalism espoused by Robert E. Park, which offered the view of a melting pot or a transformation of the immigrant into an American through a process of acculturation over a few generations, multiculturalism began to emerge in the late 1960s and early 1970s as, increasingly, social thinkers like Daniel Patrick Moynihan, Nathan Glazer, and Michael Novak began to talk about "unmeltable ethnics" and the persistence of ethnic identification in the United States despite several generations of exposure to the assimilation process.

What intensified this thinking was the civil rights and BLACK POWER movements, which, in the first instance, accused the United States of being a white nation or of having historically espoused a "white" nationalism and, in the second instance, encouraged African Americans to see themselves as a justly proud and distinct group, separate in traditions, outlook, values, and interests from the white majority. Certainly the persistent criticisms of INTEGRATION as a goal in the civil rights movement spurred this sort of thinking—coupled as they were with the urban riots of the mid-1960s and the failure of the movement (as seen by many young blacks) to overturn RACISM, end social and economic injustice, and bring about equity. Moreover, it must be remembered that although there has been a process of assimilation in the United States, particularly or perhaps exclusively for whites, there was for them also a fairly strong tradition of separatism—from the Mormons and the Shakers to the Confederacy. In short, after 1965, increasing numbers of blacks began to think that some assertive form of racial self-consciousness and racialized culture was good.

No doubt the public policy of AFFIRMATIVE ACTION also sparked this trend. Although affirmative action did not recognize cultures or their worth, it was a public policy based on a fundamental understanding of the cultural and political history of groups and individuals and their goal to better divide society's spoils, privileges, and rewards in recognition of those in the past who had been unfairly denied them. This policy obviously has led to more group consciousness, which only magnifies the tendency toward racial self-consciousness and the ideal of a group's racialized culture. The emergence of BLACK STUDIES programs at this time also fueled the rise of multiculturalism, as these programs saw their intellectual mission as the refutation of white scholarship or a scholarship that was seen as being based on the idea of white and bourgeois norms, as well as on a Eurocentric view of American culture and society.

Multiculturalism has three basic tenets: first, that group consciousness—highly developed racial, ethnic, or even gender or sexuality consciousness—is good and is the fundamental component of individual human identity; second, that the majority group, whites, are naturally inclined to racist and intolerant beliefs and that to cure this they must be taught to understand and appreciate—not merely tolerate—other expressions of group consciousness and group traditions; third, that American nationalism is not a melting pot but a mosaic or quilt made up of different colors and all of equal importance. The United States is thus not a synthesis of specific European cultures, but a collection of different (equally valuable) cultures, some unfairly and brutally repressed by the European hegemony—a practice that is not merely to be deplored but to be fought against.

Multiculturalism has certainly been aided in its emergence by the rise of structuralism and postmodernism, intellectual theories that suggest there is no central truth in the world, that reality is most accurately located in the perceptions of those on the margins, and that human relationships are nothing but various expressions of power. The critics of multiculturalism say that this view largely reduces people to sociological categories and oversimplifies the nature of human identity. Further, critics contend that multiculturalism is inherently divisive, will lead to social disruption, and will exacerbate cultural tendencies toward separatism.

BIBLIOGRAPHY

Auerbach, S., ed. *Encyclopedia of Multiculturalism*, 6 vols. 1994.
Parillo, Vincent N. *Diversity in America*. 1996.
Salett, Elizabeth Pathy, and Diane R. Koslow, eds. *Race, Ethnicity, and Self: Identity in Multicultural Perspective*. 1994.

Gerald Early

Murieta, Joaquín, and Vásquez, Tiburcio

Bandits.

While Joaquín Murieta (?–1853?)—California's legendary bandit king—may or may not have existed as one single person, Tiburcio Vásquez (1835–1875) lived a well-documented life as a bandit that breathed life into many of the Murieta legends. Both have been described as "social bandits" to explain their resistance to the brutal exploitation of the Spanish-speaking Californians in the second half of the nineteenth century.

The legends of Joaquín Murieta arose from intense bandit activity in 1852–1853, after the native Californians had been driven out of the gold fields by Anglo-Americans and other foreigners who had "rushed" into the area following the gold strikes in 1849. Variously described as of Californian, Mexican, or Chilean origin, the bandit Joaquín terrorized much of California, causing the appointment of special ranger groups to track down "Joaquí" and his bandits, which led to the claimed killing of Joaquín Murieta in 1853. Yellow Bird (John Rollin Ridge), a Cherokee newspaperman, wrote a book beginning the romantization of the bandit Joaquín the very next year. Since then Joaquín Murieta has time and again been used to dramatize the struggles of the oppressed against the oppressors. Writers from Chilean poet Pablo Neruda to Chicano activist Rodolfo "Corky" GONZÁLEZ (*I Am Joaquín*) have helped perpetuate the legend.

Tiburcio Vásquez, born in Monterey county, began a long and active career as a cattle rustler, stagecoach robber, and ultimately convicted murderer just a few years after the death of Joaquín. Finally captured in 1874 after the biggest manhunt in nineteenth-century California history, Vásquez was tried and executed in 1875. After his final capture Vásquez eloquently described his life in crime as a reaction to the injustices visited upon California society by the Yankee invaders.

BIBLIOGRAPHY

Castillo, Pedro, and Albert Camarillo, eds. *Furia y Muerte: Los Bandidos Chicanos*. Monograph No. 4. Aztlán Publications. 1973.
Neruda, Pablo. *Splendor and Death of Joaquín Murieta*. 1972.
Pitt, Leonard. *The Decline of the Californios, A Social History of Spanish-Speaking Californians, 1846–1890*. 1966.
Sawyer, Eugene Taylor. *The Life and Career of Tiburcio Vásquez*. 1944.
Yellow Bird, pseud., John Rollin Ridge. *The Life and Adventures of Joaquín Murieta, the Celebrated California Bandit*. 1955.

Ward S. Albro

Murray, Anna Pauline ("Pauli")

(1910–1985), civil rights and women's rights activist, writer, priest.

Pauli Murray was born in Baltimore, Maryland, to William Henry and Agnes Georgiana Fitzgerald Murray. When she was three years old, her mother died and her father's health did not allow him to care for his six children. Pauli's aunt, Pauline Fitzgerald Dame, adopted her and moved her to North Carolina, where she attended the public schools in Durham, graduating from Hillside High School in 1926. In 1928, she

Portrait of Pauli Murray, ca. 1940. (CORBIS/
Bettmann)

entered Hunter College in New York City, but her
studies were interrupted briefly by the Great Depression and were not completed until 1933 (see NEW
DEAL AND DEPRESSION). This period would, however,
allow her to work under the auspices of the federal
Writers Project Administration and would introduce
her to many writers and artists. She soon became great
friends with First Lady Eleanor ROOSEVELT, and the
two of them would work together on a variety of
causes.

Murray began her civil rights activism in 1938, when
she applied for admission to the graduate school at
the University of North Carolina, Chapel Hill. Denied
admission because of her color, she wrote a series of
editorials that criticized the university. She was subsequently accepted at Howard University's law school in
Washington, D.C., becoming the only female member
of her class. During her years there, she and her fellow
students staged SIT-INS at local restaurants, protesting
the JIM CROW laws of the nation's capital. For several
years Murray also had to endure the sexism of her
male counterparts, but in 1944 she graduated with an
LL.B. degree. Again she encountered the color bias at
Harvard University when she attempted to do advanced law studies there. Ultimately she enrolled at

the University of California's Boalt Hall of Law (Berkeley) and earned an LL.M. degree in 1945. In 1951 she
authored one of the most widely used references on
civil rights law: *States' Law on Race and Color.* In 1965,
Yale University's law school awarded Murray a doctor
of juridical science degree, the first such degree to be
awarded to an African American. She was admitted to
practice law in New York, California, and before the
U.S. Supreme Court. During the 1950s her work with
the Commission on Law and Social Action was short-
lived, and she opened a private law practice in New
York City. Then, with a less-than-thriving practice,
Murray decided to turn to teaching—the profession
of her aunt, and one she had once been determined
to avoid.

The early years of the 1960s gave Murray the opportunity to visit and then teach in Ghana. She accepted a position as senior lecturer and created and
taught a course in constitutional and administrative
law at the Ghana Law School in Accra. At the same
time she coauthored *The Constitution and Government
of Ghana.* Murray returned to America in time to witness the BLACK POWER nationalist movement, especially on college campuses. In 1967–1968, she served
as vice president of Benedict College in Columbia,
South Carolina, and from 1968 to 1973 she taught at
Brandeis University. She witnessed the black students'
takeover of her office building at Brandeis. In 1972
she was called into the ministry. She applied for admission to holy orders in the Episcopal Church and
entered the seminary, graduating in 1976 with a master of divinity degree. In 1977 she was ordained the
first African-American female priest of the Episcopal
Church at the National Cathedral in Washington, D.C.
By the time of her death in 1985, Murray had received
many awards and honors. In 1945 the National Council of Negro Women listed her among twelve of the
most outstanding women in American life; *Mademoiselle* magazine named her Woman of the Year in 1947.

Murray often found herself, as she wrote, taking the
"lonely and unpopular position of calling for a broad,
inclusive expression of feminism at a time when many
prominent Negro women felt impelled to subordinate
their claims as women . . . " She stated, "I argued that
black women can neither postpone nor subordinate
the fight against discrimination to the Black Revolution. . . . As a matter of survival black women [must]
insist upon equal opportunities without regard to sex
in training, education and employment. . . . The outlook for their children will be bleak unless they are
encouraged in every way to develop their potential
skills and earning power. I saw the liberation of black
women in terms of feminist solidarity across racial
lines."

Murray authored several autobiographical works, including *Proud Shoes: The Story of an American Family* (1956); *Song in a Weary Throat: An American Pilgrimage* (1987), reissued as *Pauli Murray: The Autobiography of a Black Activist, Feminist, Lawyer, Priest, and Poet* (1989); and her prized collection of poems, *Dark Testament and Other Poems* (1970).

BIBLIOGRAPHY

Hine, Darlene Clark, et al., eds. *Black Women in America: An Historical Encyclopedia.* 1993.
Smith, Jessie C., ed. *Notable Black American Women.* 1992.

Jacqueline A. Rouse

Museum of African American History

Established in 1965 by Dr. Charles Wright, the International Afro-American Museum (IAAM)—as it was then called—was the first of its kind in Detroit. Starting on the city's West Side, after two changes of venue and one change of name, the Museum of African American History (MAAH) occupied its latest home as the largest museum of its type on April 12, 1997.

Wright, a black obstetrician and gynecologist, was inspired to start the museum after visiting a World War II memorial in Denmark. Envisioning an international African-American history center for the Motor City, he located the museum in a small house on West Grand Boulevard, where it quickly outgrew its confines. A year after opening, a mobile IAAM took to the road. The IAAM obtained land from the city to build a larger building in 1978, but raising money for the new, multi-million-dollar facility was difficult. Eight years later, a partnership with the city of Detroit secured sufficient funding, and after changing its name to the Museum of African American History, groundbreaking for the new site took place on May 21, 1985.

Like its predecessor, the new 28,000-square-foot building soon proved insufficient. In 1992, city voters approved a bond issue to finance construction of the present, 120,000-square-foot facility. After breaking ground in August 1993, and after an additional $10-million bond was approved by voters, the new site at 315 East Warren opened on April 12, 1997.

The museum's exhibits include the 16,000-square-foot core presentation, "Of the People: The African American Experience." Rotating galleries focus on African-American art, history, and culture. The museum's striking exterior architecture is complemented inside by an equally striking set of life-sized human castings, depicted as quartered on a slave ship.

BIBLIOGRAPHY

Anderson, Kelly L. "Celebrations Begin for New African American Museum." *Detroit News,* April 12, 1997.
The Museum of African American History Webpage (http://www.maah-detroit.org). June 14, 1999.

Gregory L. Parker

Magón, Ricardo and Enrique Flores

See Flores Magón, Ricardo and Enrique

Music

When thinking of the music associated with the civil rights movement in the United States in the twentieth century, one almost inevitably recalls grainy black-and-white newsreels featuring Dr. Martin Luther KING marching arm-in-arm with supporters, singing freedom songs such as "We Shall Overcome." While these events and songs were important and influential, many often overlook the wide array of styles of both leadership and music within the civil rights movement itself. These differences reflected the various strategies and positions of leaders and artists committed to racial equality in the United States, yet who were not necessarily in agreement as to how to achieve that goal. Just as it is much too simplistic to identify the civil rights struggle only with Dr. King and his extraordinary efforts, a discussion of the music of the civil rights movement would be incomplete without reviewing the wide scope and flavor of political songs and music which continues to evolve. Without a doubt, however, the constant and perhaps enduring musical reminder of the civil rights movement is "We Shall Overcome."

"We Shall Overcome"

The hymn itself had been in use in the United States for an entire century before it became the anthem of the civil rights movement. Generally traced to "I'll Overcome, Some Day," "We Shall Overcome" was composed in the late 1910s by the Reverend C. A. Tindley. (Tindley's work had a major influence on modern gospel music—a genre of sacred music that would later be heavily identified with the civil rights movement.) Later, the song was used by striking tobacco workers in SOUTH CAROLINA as a method of voicing their demands to their company in 1945. During the strike, two new lines were added to the words ("We will win our rights" and "We will overcome"). Two of the picketers later attended the HIGHLANDER FOLK SCHOOL in the Tennessee mountains, which trained labor and civil rights organizers. There the two picketers passed the song to other attendees, including a folksinger who, in turn, taught it to the founding conference of the STUDENT NONVIOLENT COORDINATING COMMITTEE (SNCC) in 1959. Singer Pete Seeger is credited with substituting the words "We shall overcome" for "We will overcome" in the song.

Civil rights leaders, workers, and demonstrators adopted "We Shall Overcome"; its words were heard at countless sit-ins, freedom rides, marches, and rallies during the 1960s. All across the nation, in the face of beatings, imprisonment, and harassment, the song served as a quietly defiant and demanding inspiration to those seeking racial justice and equality. During the MARCH ON WASHINGTON in the summer of 1963, a quarter of a million people sang the hymn led by Joan Baez. As the song rang out from the Lincoln Memorial, it became the anthem of the civil rights movement. Demands for equal rights and federal protection of those rights began to increase, and in 1965 a presidential address containing the familiar phrase of the song helped move a government to action.

On March 15, 1965, President Lyndon JOHNSON addressed a joint session of CONGRESS. A few days earlier, the nation watched as civil rights marchers approached the Edmund Pettus Bridge in Selma, Alabama. The workers were subsequently beaten by white police officers as a white mob cheered. The president recognized that something had to be done and utilized the bully pulpit of his office to its fullest extent. President Johnson outlined his desire for comprehensive legislation and emphasized the moral duty that he and the rest of the nation shared in erasing the stain of violence and discrimination from the land. "This time, on this issue, there must be no delay, no hesitation, and no compromise." Johnson then took his declaration further than any American president had ever gone in aligning with the efforts of African Americans to live in freedom: "Their cause must be our cause too. Because it is all of us who must overcome the crippling legacy of bigotry and injustice." Johnson paused and the next few words caused a crescendo heard throughout the nation: "And we *shall* overcome." Johnson had not only taken up the cause of civil rights; he had sounded its battle hymn as well. The simple words of a simple song had become the rallying cry of the most powerful man in the world. Watching the speech on television, Martin Luther King wept at Johnson's words.

"What's Going On?"

Not everyone shared the belief or the hope that nonviolent social protest and action by Congress and the president would even begin to afford African Americans the ability to live in the United States as free and equal citizens. Many blacks were impatient

Joan Baez sang "We Shall Overcome" from the steps of the Lincoln Memorial, with a quarter of a million people joining in, during the 1963 March on Washington.

with the techniques of this faction of the civil rights movement, and they were convinced that any strides that were made through legislation regarding the practices of discriminatory institutions and individuals would be small and relatively ineffective. Leaders like MALCOLM X and Huey NEWTON represented segments of people dissatisfied with the leadership of King, and with what they saw as parsimony from the federal government. These leaders appealed to the mounting frustration of inaction and nonviolent resistance in the face of immense brutality and criminal activity against African Americans. Likewise, a different type of music typified and amplified this growing alienation associated with being black in the United States.

The BLACK POWER movement was nationalistic in ideology and advocated self-help and self-promotion rather than waiting for the federal government or state government to dole out rights in slow fashion. Many musical artists echoed these sentiments in their work. Some, like Marvin Gaye, went against the wishes of their own studios by blazing new trails in their work and taking political stands. Gaye, who at the end of the 1960s had emerged as a popular moneymaker and star for Motown Records, went against his clean-cut romantic pop image and began writing and recording protest songs. Gaye's influential "What's Going On" album, recorded in 1971, dealt with such volatile issues as racism and the continued struggle for civil rights, opposition to the Vietnam War, environmental awareness, and corrupt politics that turned citizenship into cynicism. Gaye's album was a bold step and began a trend followed by several of his contemporaries.

Many black artists of this era adopted a nationalistic ideology and more and more began to identify with their African heritage in dress and hairstyle. The lyrics to many songs demonstrated the commitment of many influential stars to the Black Power movement and its rhetoric of uplift, pride, action, and self-awareness. Aretha Franklin's "Respect," "We're A Winner" by Curtis Mayfield and the Impressions, "Give More Power to the People" by the Chi-Lites, and a number of singles by James Brown characterized the tenor of the times. Much of the music embodied the rhythmic structure and conventions of gospel music (which was, of course, the root of protest songs such as "We Shall Overcome") but expressed an explicit impatience with the order of things in contrast to the songs that had come before.

Fight the Power

In the years following the civil rights and Black Power movements, life for African Americans (especially in urban areas) did not improve very much. The 1970s and 1980s were periods of high unemployment, increasing poverty, and the breakdown of educational opportunities and quality of life. Gang violence and so-called "black-on-black" crime rose to unprecedented levels, creating a perilous situation in cities all over the nation. Out of this despair and cultural breakdown came the roots of a new musical force and another level of politically charged music and art that introduced a new generation of young people to black nationalism, self-awareness, and the condemnation of social injustice. Rap combines the methods of oral tradition with the latest in music production technology; the use of synthesizers, and sampling from prerecorded tracks from artists like James Brown and George Clinton. Rap is a very diverse genre, yet it has made a significant political and cultural impact.

Many rap artists and groups echo the sentiments of the Black Power movement; figures such as Malcolm X, Marcus GARVEY, and the modern-day Nation of Islam are often invoked and are a source of inspiration. Artists and groups who are politically focused include Public Enemy, Boogie Down Productions, and X Clan, among others. Some rappers espouse some of the teachings of the controversial Minister Louis FARRAKHAN of the NATION OF ISLAM in their rhymes. Farrakhan has been dismissed by many blacks and whites who say his teachings and views are racist and generally disruptive to racial harmony. His nationalistic messages, however, resonate with many rap artists, such as Chuck D of Public Enemy, who addresses Farrakhan's detractors in the single "Don't Believe the Hype" by imploring "Don't tell me that you understand/Until you hear the man." Many rappers who communicate political messages also focus on positive uplift of black Americans, racial pride, and the acquisition of knowledge of history, so as to learn about the enormous contributions that Africans and people of African descent have made during the history of mankind.

Rap has been involved in the political arena many times since its explosion onto the American scene. Many rap groups use explicit lyrics and vivid descriptions of violence to get their point across, and thus many rappers and groups have been used as examples of the need to cut down on such material. Advocates such as Tipper Gore—who campaigns for warning labels on albums featuring explicit material—and William Bennett and Senator Joe Lieberman—who press record companies and motion picture studios to cease producing violent and explicit productions—often point to rap as one area of entertainment that pushes the limit too far. During the 1992 presidential campaign, then-governor Bill CLINTON pointed to the lyrics of rapper Sister Souljah, which suggested that in the wake of incidents of police violence against blacks that there be a measure of revenge against white people. Clinton, a Democratic Party candidate who won the presidency that year, criticized her remarks in a speech to Operation PUSH, which is run by Rev. Jesse JACKSON. Coverage of the incident and subsequent debate over the many issues that it raised showed how significant rap had become, and that it was a potent political vehicle.

Epilogue

The civil rights movement in the United States has taken on many forms and functions over the years of the twentieth century, and the music identified with that movement can be seen as a parallel to that change. "We Shall Overcome" is still most closely identified with the civil rights movement in the minds of many Americans, but there have been many different musical expressions for the different eras and philosophies that encompass the struggle for civil rights for all Americans. These different incarnations of expression have impacted the highest levels of political and social dialogue in the United States and will most likely continue to do so.

BIBLIOGRAPHY

Branch, Taylor. *Parting the Waters: America in the King Years 1954–63*. 1988.

Caro, Robert A. *Means of Ascent*. 1990.

Friedberg, Harris. "Motown." In *Encyclopedia of African-American Culture and History*, Volume 4, edited by Jack Salzman, David Lionel Smith, and Cornel West. 1996.

Maultsby, Portia K. "Music." In *Encyclopedia of African-American Culture and History*, Volume 4, edited by Jack Salzman, David Lionel Smith, and Cornel West. 1996.

Sanger, Kerran L. *When the Spirit Says Sing!: The Role of Freedom Songs in the Civil Rights Movement*. 1995.

Matthew May

N

NAACP

See National Association for the Advancement of Colored People.

NAACP Legal Defense and Educational Fund, Inc.

The NAACP Legal Defense and Educational Fund, Inc. (LDF, also known as the "Inc. Fund") was the chief command center in the legal struggle for civil rights during the last half of the twentieth century. Incorporated in 1940 by the NATIONAL ASSOCIATION FOR THE ADVANCEMENT OF COLORED PEOPLE (NAACP) to administer tax-exempt donations for legal work, the LDF had a formally separate organizational and financial structure from the NAACP. However, the LDF's board of directors and organizational strategy overlapped with the parent group.

In its early years, under the leadership of director-counsel Thurgood MARSHALL, the LDF devoted most of its limited resources to civil rights litigation and to defending African-Americans in cases that presented clear evidence of racial discrimination. LDF attorneys—including Marshall, Franklin Williams, Constance Baker MOTLEY, Jack GREENBERG, and Robert CARTER—spent much of their time on the road, performing the arduous and often dangerous work of defending blacks in criminal cases in small southern towns. Although they frequently lost cases in lower courts, they won many appeals, and their presence at the trials helped assure fair procedure and reasonable criminal sentencing.

Meanwhile, the LDF won a series of important civil rights victories in cases before the SUPREME COURT. For example, in SMITH V. ALLWRIGHT (1944), the Court ruled that "white primary" elections that excluded blacks were unconstitutional. In 1948, the Court ruled in *Shelley v. Kraemer* that "restrictive covenants" forbidding sale of property to blacks in restricted areas were not legally enforceable.

The LDF's most important contribution, however, was its successful strategy of incremental challenge to SEGREGATION in the field of education. Without directly attacking the doctrine of "separate but equal" established in PLESSY V. FERGUSON (1896), the LDF successfully argued a series of lawsuits, including *Sipuel v. Oklahoma State Regents* (1948), *McLaurin v. Oklahoma State Regents* (1950), and *Sweatt v. Painter* (1950), in which the Court ruled that segregation of graduate and law school facilities resulted in discrimination. Having established this principle, the LDF then directly challenged public school segregation, and brought the cases that resulted in the Supreme Court's epochal school desegregation decision in BROWN V. BOARD OF EDUCATION (1954).

In 1956, shortly after the *Brown* decision, interpersonal and organizational disputes led to a complete separation of LDF and the NAACP. In the years that followed, LDF concentrated its energies on school DESEGREGATION, designing desegregation plans and bringing lawsuits to force recalcitrant southerners to comply with the Supreme Court ruling. Eventually, LDF attorneys were forced to litigate in a dozen

The team of lawyers of the NAACP Legal Defense and Educational Fund, who were rewarded with the 1954 Supreme Court decision in Brown v. Board of Education *that "separate but equal" schools were "inherently unequal."* (AP/Wide World Photos)

southern states. Although it won some notable Supreme Court victories, including *Cooper v. Aaron* (1958), which ordered the admission of nine black students to Little Rock, Arkansas's Central High School, the process of integration was slow and frustrating. Meanwhile, LDF attorneys also participated in defending civil rights protesters, and in 1958, its attorneys won *Gayle v. Browder*, the Supreme Court bus segregation case that grew out of the MONTGOMERY BUS BOYCOTT. In more recent years, under the direction of Julius Chambers and Elaine Ruth Jones, LDF has been notable for fighting death penalty cases and for its defense of AFFIRMATIVE ACTION programs.

BIBLIOGRAPHY

Greenberg, Jack. *Crusaders in the Courts.* 1994.
Kluger, Richard. *Simple Justice.* 1976.
Tushnet, Mark V. *Making Civil Rights Law.* 1994.

Greg Robinson

Nash, Diane Bevel

(1938–   ), civil rights activist.

Leader of the Nashville Student Movement for DESEG-REGATION, Diane Nash was one of the founders of the STUDENT NONVIOLENT COORDINATING COMMITTEE (SNCC) and is an advocate of nonviolent civil disobedience. Nash attended Howard University in Washington, D.C., for a year and transferred to Fisk University in Nashville, Tennessee, where she encountered rigid segregation for the first time and was shocked. She approached James Lawson's Nashville workshop on nonviolent civil disobedience with extreme doubt, but quickly absorbed Lawson's teachings and became a true believer. She also saw nonviolence as a "way of life" with deep spiritual implications for self-transformation. Nash soon emerged as the leader of the Nashville Student Movement, a group that included John LEWIS and Marion Barry. She organized SIT-INS at Woolworth's, Walgreen's, Kress's, Harvey's, and other city department stores.

Nash worked with Ella BAKER in founding SNCC, an offshoot of the SCLC (Southern Christian Leadership Conference); Baker was executive director of SCLC. Despite Nash's leadership abilities and the egalitarian mood of participatory democracy, gender conventions were strong in the civil rights movement and a titled position for a woman usually indicated a clerical role. Nonetheless, Nash and more than two hundred delegates met at Shaw University in Raleigh, North Carolina, from April 16 to 18, 1960, to organize SNCC and to ensure that the viewpoints of students in the movement would be listened to by older leaders. The student leaders found fault with clergy leadership, especially that of James Lawson and Martin Luther KING, JR. Many of the more radical students had only tepid support for nonviolence. In the years after 1961, SNCC had tenuous ties to the SCLC. SNCC's members continued to be among the bravest and most effective activists in the South, especially as combatants in direct action.

Nash was married in 1961 to James Bevel, one of the original leaders in the Nashville Student Movement and a student at Baptist Theological Seminary. Nash retained her last name and took her husband's name as her middle name. James Bevel was soon appointed field secretary for the entire state of MISSISSIPPI for the SCLC; Nash herself also worked for the SCLC, in a salaried staff position. In 1965, the SCLC gave Diane Bevel Nash and her husband its highest honor: the Rosa PARKS Award for their outstanding achievements in the field of civil rights.

Diane Nash's civil rights activism led her to the peace movement and FEMINISM. During the next thirty years she continued to work for a variety of causes that affected jobs (see EMPLOYMENT), HOUSING, and other civil rights, especially among African Americans in Chicago. Nash's full embrace of nonviolence helped to shape the forms of civil rights protest in the early 1960s, which continues to resonate in America.

BIBLIOGRAPHY

Crawford, Vicki, ed. *Women in the Civil Rights Movement: Trailblazers and Torchbearers, 1941–1965.* 1993.
Hine, Clark Darlene, ed. *Black Women in America: An Historical Encyclopedia.* 1994.
Hough, J. C. *Black Power and White Protestants: A Christian Response to the New Negro Pluralism.* 1977.
Lewis, John. *Walking with the Wind: A Memoir of the Movement.* 1998.

Claude Hargrove

National Afro-American League

The National Afro-American League (NAAL) was proposed by journalist Timothy Thomas FORTUNE through the pages of his newspaper, the *New York Age,* in May 1887. Fortune, a former slave, conceived the NAAL as a way to combat disfranchisement, LYNCHING, and the penitentiary system in the South as well as inadequate funding for EDUCATION and discrimination against blacks in public accommodations and transportation nationally. He encouraged the League to use the media, the pulpit, public meetings, and the courts to combat these "abominations" in the face of the FOURTEENTH and FIFTEENTH AMENDMENTS. Established as a national civil rights entity in January 1890, the principles and objectives of the NAAL anticipated the NIAGARA MOVEMENT, the NATIONAL ASSOCIATION FOR THE ADVANCEMENT OF COLORED PEOPLE (NAACP), and the national Negro Business League. The NAAL's constituency was primarily from the Northeast and the Midwest. Encouraged by the presence of a small, though determined Southern delegation at its organizing convention in Chicago, the NAAL's hopes for a base in the South never materialized.

The NAAL supported and advocated development of solidarity among African Americans of diverse backgrounds. It also pushed for separate black economic development, especially black banks, job bureaus, and cooperative business enterprises. Moderately successful in some locales, the NAAL was never significant nationally. Despite efforts to reorganize as the National Afro-American Council in 1898, the group never received support from the black masses and was defunct by 1908. Often relegated to minor historical significance, its support for civil rights, participation of both men *and* women, and a black nationalist agenda make the NAAL a trailblazer that set precedents for later civil rights activism.

BIBLIOGRAPHY

Franklin, John Hope, and Alfred E. Moss. *From Slavery to Freedom,* 7th ed. 1994.
Nieman, Donald G. *Promises to Keep: African Americans and the Constitutional Order, 1776 to the Present.* 1991.
Renfro, G. Herbert. "Is the Afro-American League a Failure?" *Literary Digest* (August 3, 1892).
Thornbrough, Emma Lou. "The National Afro-American League, 1887–1908." *Journal of Southern History* 27 (November 1961): 495–512.

Homer Douglass Hill

National American Woman Suffrage Association

The founding of the National American Woman Suffrage Association (NAWSA), the leading organization in the fight for female enfranchisement, marked the birth of a united and purely feminist social movement in the United States. It was formed in 1890, out of the reconciliation of two rival factions in the women's rights movement: the AMERICAN WOMAN SUFFRAGE ASSOCIATION (AWSA) and the National Woman Suffrage Association (NWSA). Headed by Lucy STONE, AWSA represented moderate feminists whose agenda included racial issues as well as WOMAN SUFFRAGE; NWSA membership included women such as Elizabeth Cady STANTON and Susan B. ANTHONY, who were single-mindedly dedicated to securing the vote for women. NAWSA clearly seemed to reflect the militancy of the latter organization, especially because of the influence of young, educated, professional women.

The merger was achieved in part through the efforts of Alice Stone Blackwell, daughter of Lucy Stone and Henry Blackwell, who would continue to hold a prominent position in NAWSA for almost all of its life-span of nearly three decades. Lucy Stone became chairwoman of NAWSA's executive committee. Elizabeth Cady Stanton and Susan B. Antony were the group's first and second presidents, respectively, although NAWSA would distance itself from Stanton in the mid-1890s because of her publication of a critique of the Christian scriptures. Anthony herself was not immune from controversy. It occurred sometimes over organizational issues—for example, she unsuccessfully voiced objections to Alice Blackwell's suggestion of a biannual convention in the capital. More significantly, it occurred because of her ambiguous attitude toward racial issues. During her 1892 to 1900 presidency, she feared the loss of support from Southern white women and concealed her own disdain for RACISM.

NAWSA inherited some of the divisiveness of its parent bodies, and its members continued to argue about the question of whether they should pursue suffrage victories in individual states or seek ratification of a federal amendment. Susan B. Anthony yielded to some of her state-oriented colleagues, and, after the 1893 suffrage victory for women in Colorado, she participated in unsuccessful campaigns in New York (1894) and California (1896).

In 1900, Carrie Chapman CATT, a former educator and journalist, became president of NAWSA upon the recommendation of Susan B. Anthony. Catt, who had been a member of NAWSA ever since the year of its founding, had extensive experience in dealing with CONGRESS on the proposed amendment on female enfranchisement. In her initial four-year tenure as president, she continued to provide the shrewdness and enthusiasm she had exhibited as director of NAWSA's national committee—which coordinated the efforts of local suffragists—a body that she herself had conceived. Catt resigned the NAWSA presidency because of the ill health of her husband and a growing commitment to international suffrage—although she continued to work for the American woman suffrage campaign during WORLD WAR I.

Beginning in 1904, NAWSA was headed by Anna Howard Shaw, a former clergywoman and physician, who had previously served as a vice president of the organization. Her support later collapsed, in part because of competition from the followers of Alice PAUL, a factor that Catt sought to address in resuming the presidency of NAWSA in 1915.

A member of NAWSA since 1912, Paul founded the organization's congressional committee, which represented the views of militant young women and clashed with the NAWSA leadership because of their advocacy of a federal amendment rather than a state-oriented strategy. Paul formed the Congressional Union to fol-

low the federal strategy more fully, and was replaced as head of the congressional committee. When the Congressional Union merged with another body to form the NATIONAL WOMAN'S PARTY, in 1916, Paul withdrew from NAWSA altogether.

In her second presidency, Catt sought to bring new energy to NAWSA and to reconcile the state and federal approaches. During her second term, which would last through the passage of the NINETEENTH AMENDMENT, NAWSA experienced its greatest growth and launched its most successful strategy, Catt's "Winning Plan," which was ultimately the plan most responsible for the success of the suffrage campaign. Formulated in 1916 and introduced secretly at a meeting of the executive committee following NAWSA's convention that year, the Winning Plan was structured on the assumption that federal and state efforts would complement each other, as representatives from states that passed female suffrage legislation were likely to support a national amendment. Catt sought additional state victories before sending the federal amendment to the legislatures; specifically she sought to win New York and one southern state, thus breaking the solidarity of the East Coast. She also sought victories in Iowa, South Dakota, North Dakota, Nebraska, and Maine. In thirty-six states there was a special strategy in place. Suffragists were also asked to become more cooperative with one another in their efforts and to work more energetically.

NAWSA's nonconfrontational approach to government officials and partisan support for the Wilson administration were in contrast to the tactics of its rival organization, Alice Paul's Congressional Union for Woman Suffrage. NAWSA members were awarded government jobs and offered political support; Alice Paul's supporters, on the other hand, were arrested for picketing the White House, claimed political prisoner status, and consistently attacked Democrats, anti-suffrage or otherwise (because they always faulted the party in power and moreover held the national DEMOCRATIC PARTY responsible for not endorsing suffrage). Nonetheless, both NAWSA and the Congressional Union can share credit for the 1920 ratification of the Nineteenth Amendment.

Following the ratification of the suffrage amendment, a large percentage of the NAWSA membership founded a new organization, the LEAGUE OF WOMEN VOTERS, at a NAWSA convention. The League's formation, in 1921, represented the fulfillment of Carrie Chapman Catt's vision of a nonpartisan organization designed to keep women active on political issues, by creating a vehicle for them to serve as advocates for FEMINISM, PACIFISM, better government, and improved social programs.

BIBLIOGRAPHY

Anthony, Katharine. *Susan B. Anthony: Her Personal History and Her Era.* 1954.

Catt, Carrie Chapman, and Nettie Rogers Shuler. *Woman Suffrage and Politics.* 1923.

DuBois, Ellen Carol. *Feminism and Suffrage: The Emergence of an Independent Women's Movement in America, 1848–1869.* 1978.

DuBois, Ellen Carol. *Elizabeth Cady Stanton/Susan B. Anthony: Correspondence, Writings, Speeches.* 1981.

Flexner, Eleanor. *Century of Struggle: The Woman's Rights Movement in the United States,* rev. ed. 1975.

Frost-Knappman, Elizabeth, with Sarah Kurian. *The ABC-Clio Companion to Women's Progress in America.* 1994.

Kraditor, Aileen S. *The Ideas of the Woman Suffrage Movement, 1890–1920.* 1981.

Sarah Kurian

National Association for the Advancement of Colored People

The National Association for the Advancement of Colored People (NAACP) is the oldest and largest civil rights organization in the United States. It engineered and sponsored the legal campaign that culminated with the 1954 Supreme Court decision in BROWN V. BOARD OF EDUCATION and played a leading role in shaping the civil rights legislation of the 1960s. But its historical significance goes deeper. From its founding in 1909, up through the 1960s, the NAACP provided the primary organizational and institutional foundation from which the struggle to secure full CITIZENSHIP for black Americans was mounted, organized, debated, and sustained.

Early Decades, 1909–1930

In 1908, the antiblack terror that had ensured the triumph of JIM CROW in the South erupted in a brutal race riot in Springfield, Illinois, the home of Abraham Lincoln. Northern white reformers were stunned by the encroachment of southern racial mores, and they resolved to counter the steady deterioration of race relations. Under the leadership of Oswald Garrison Villard, Mary White Ovington, William English Walling, and other white progressives, several hundred whites and blacks joined in New York in 1909 to establish the National Association for the Advancement of Colored People. Although the NAACP began as an elite, mostly white group of progressive reformers, W. E. B. Du Bois, leader of the anti–Booker T. WASHINGTON faction and founder of the militant NIAGARA MOVEMENT, played an active role from the beginning. He became director of publicity and research and edited *The* CRISIS, the official organ of the NAACP. The

Crisis quickly became the voice of the organization's goals, with a circulation of ten thousand during its first year and one hundred thousand ten years later. The association established a centralized organizational structure, dominated by the national office, but it promoted its membership growth through the establishment of branches around the country.

From the beginning, the NAACP concerned itself with efforts to protect the legal rights of blacks by publicizing and prosecuting cases involving PEONAGE, racial SEGREGATION, police brutality, and the denial of political rights. In 1913, a Legal Committee was established, headed by Arthur Spingarn. Major SUPREME COURT victories during the organization's first decade included *Guinn v. United States* (1915), which outlawed the use of a "grandfather clause" to limit black voting, and *Buchanan v. Warley* (1917), which ruled that

Since its inception in 1909, the National Association for the Advancement of Colored People (NAACP) has become the most important civil rights organization in the United States. NAACP President Kweisi Mfume (center) leads demonstrators to the steps of the U.S. Supreme Court in an effort to promote the hiring of more minority law clerks at the Supreme Court. (AP/Wide World Photos)

residential segregation ordinances were unconstitutional.

WORLD WAR I and the accompanying "Great Migration" of Southern blacks to industrial jobs in the urban North altered the social and political landscape of black America and created new opportunities and challenges for the NAACP. In the spring of 1917, as the United States prepared for entry into the war, the NAACP convened a national meeting of black leaders and representatives from black organizations to develop a policy regarding black participation in the ARMED FORCES. A consensus emerged calling for blacks to enlist in the Army and support the war effort, regardless of the persistence of racial segregation. A major effort, spearheaded by NAACP board chairman Joel Spingarn, secured the establishment of a separate training camp for black officers in Des Moines, Iowa. While many blacks opposed what amounted to a compromise or consensus, the NAACP ultimately endorsed it because it was the only way to ensure that black officers would be commissioned.

During the war years, thirty-one new NAACP branches were established, and overall membership increased to 91,000 from 9,200. The new branches served as a vehicle for local black protest, particularly in the South. Black domestic workers in Atlanta turned to the NAACP for support in their struggle against "work or fight laws," a tool to control black labor. In many parts of the country, NAACP branches, along with new organizations such as the League for Democracy, channeled the determination of returning black veterans to secure the democracy they had fought for abroad.

Meanwhile the NAACP continued to protest the persistent antiblack violence that scarred the nation. During 1917 lynch mobs murdered at least thirty-eight African Americans (see LYNCHING), and some forty blacks lost their lives in a bloody riot in East St. Louis, Missouri, sparked by the employment of blacks as strike breakers in a local factory (see EAST ST. LOUIS RACE RIOTS). The NAACP sponsored a silent protest parade down New York's Fifth Avenue; fifteen thousand marched, protesting these outrages with signs asking President Woodrow Wilson to "make America safe for Democracy." Yet black men returning from the war were met by a nationwide wave of violence and repression, collectively described as the RED SUMMER of 1919. In Elaine, Arkansas, twelve black union activists who defended themselves from a white mob were tried and sentenced to death. In the face of such terror and violence, the NAACP launched a systematic legal, political, and educational campaign. Its efforts focused around securing legislation making lynching a federal crime. Two antilynching bills (see ANTI-LYNCHING CAMPAIGN) were introduced in Congress

in 1918, providing a rallying point for NAACP efforts. In 1919 the association sponsored a national Anti-Lynching Conference in New York and published a report, *Thirty Years of Lynching in the United States, 1889–1918.*

The 1920s were a time of transition and consolidation for the NAACP. The "New Negro" movement of that decade heightened black militancy and racial consciousness. In 1921, James Weldon JOHNSON became the first black executive secretary of the NAACP, signaling a transition to black leadership that would be complete by the early 1930s. Marcus GARVEY and his UNIVERSAL NEGRO IMPROVEMENT ASSOCIATION, with appeals to black pride and the promotion of economic self-help, challenged the NAACP's emphasis on integration and exposed its inherent class bias (at least at the national level). While W. E. B. Du Bois emerged as one of Garvey's severest critics, Charles Hamilton HOUSTON, who would become the NAACP's legal director, contended that Garvey "made a permanent contribution in teaching the simple dignity of being black."

The NAACP's Legal Committee was by now inundated with requests for assistance—far beyond what its resources could handle. Among the association's legal victories, however, three were particularly notable. In *Moore v. Dempsey* (1923), the Supreme Court overturned the conviction of twelve Arkansas sharecroppers and union activists who had been sentenced to death. In 1925 the NAACP employed Clarence Darrow and Arthur Garfield Hays to defend Ossian Sweet and several others accused of murdering a white man while defending Sweet's home in Detroit from a white mob; all were acquitted. In 1927 the NAACP won its first major victory in the fight against the all-white primary when the Supreme Court ruled in *Nixon v. Herndon* that a Texas state law excluding blacks from voting in the Democratic primary was unconstitutional.

New Deal Era, 1930–1950

In 1930 the NAACP—along with the American Federation of Labor (see AFL-CIO)—actively opposed President Herbert Hoover's nomination of FOURTH CIRCUIT Judge John J. PARKER to the U.S. Supreme Court because Parker had allegedly claimed that "the participation of Negroes in politics is a source of evil and danger." In the process, blacks were energized politically, severing their longtime allegiance to the REPUBLICAN PARTY. Yet, as the NAACP was coming of age in the national political arena, its weakness at the local level, particularly in the South, was exposed with the SCOTTSBORO CASE. The organization's failure to respond to the hasty conviction and sentencing of the nine young black men accused of raping two white women in Alabama contrasted with the swift action of the International Labor Defense (ILD), the legal arm of the COMMUNIST PARTY USA; the ILD's intervention undoubtedly saved the lives of the men. NAACP lawyer Charles HOUSTON observed that the Communist Party worked directly among the sharecroppers and the unemployed, "offering them full and complete brotherhood." In the decade that followed, Houston would push the NAACP to pursue a more grass-roots agenda.

In 1933, in the midst of the Great Depression, Robert C. WEAVER and John P. Davis, recent graduates of Harvard University, attended hearings on the new administration's National Recovery Act, a cornerstone of the early New Deal (see NEW DEAL AND DEPRESSION). Calling themselves the Negro Industrial League, Weaver and Davis succeeded in defeating plans for a racial wage differential. In light of their success, the NAACP established the Joint Committee on Economic Recovery, a coalition of black organizations, to monitor New Deal legislation and lobby for the fair inclusion of blacks. Meanwhile, the NAACP secured a place in the coalition of labor and liberal groups that developed around the democratic initiatives of the administration of Franklin D. ROOSEVELT. Walter Francis WHITE established a close working relationship with First Lady Eleanor ROOSEVELT, succeeding in enlisting her support in the Anti-Lynching Campaign. President Franklin Roosevelt was sympathetic, but failed to support the necessary legislation, citing the inevitable opposition of powerful southerners in Congress. Still, Mrs. Roosevelt continued to support White and the efforts of the NAACP, helping to solidify the broad New Deal coalition that played such a pivotal role in the 1936 election. That year, a majority of black voters abandoned the Republican Party and joined with labor and ethnic urban voters in swelling the vote for FDR. This new coalition of voters eclipsed the dominance of Southern whites in the DEMOCRATIC PARTY.

Charles Houston, a graduate of Harvard Law School who had transformed Howard University into a laboratory for developing civil rights law, in 1933 became the first director of a broad-based legal campaign funded by a grant from the American Fund for Public Service. Under his leadership, the NAACP embarked upon a protracted attack on racial discrimination in public education that would culminate with the *Brown* decision two decades later. In 1938, however, the organization won its first major legal victory in the campaign when the U.S. Supreme Court ruled in *Missouri ex. rel. Gaines v. Canada* that African-American Lloyd Gaines must be admitted to the University of Missouri Law School. It was the first crack in the legal wall of the southern caste system. The NAACP's legal campaign now sought, slowly and deliberately, to establish its roots in local communities.

In endless rounds of meetings with groups throughout the South, Houston and Thurgood MARSHALL, who succeeded Houston as director of the campaign in 1938, explained to blacks the mechanics of the legal fight, its political significance, and its relationship to broader community concerns, routinely encouraging people to persist in their efforts to register and vote and to organize political clubs. The work of Houston and Marshall expanded and strengthened the network of NAACP branches throughout the South and other parts of the nation. In 1944 the long fight against the all-white primary was finally victorious with the U.S. Supreme Court's ruling in SMITH V. ALLWRIGHT. In *Irene v. Morgan*, two years later, the Court outlawed the segregation of interstate travel.

Blacks' expectations and activism escalated in response to WORLD WAR II. In the spring of 1941, Walter White joined A. Philip RANDOLPH in demanding desegregation of the armed forces and federal action to ensure that African Americans had equal access to federally funded defense jobs. After Randolph threatened to lead a march on Washington (see MARCH ON WASHINGTON MOVEMENT) if the government failed to act, the Roosevelt administration compromised, issuing an executive order that required fair employment in defense jobs—to be monitored by the Fair Employment Practices Committee (FEPC). The FEPC lacked any enforcement power, however.

African-Americans' migration from the rural South to centers of defense production swelled during the war years, and widespread patterns of racial discrimination persisted. But black workers, with the support of the NAACP and the NATIONAL NEGRO CONGRESS (NNC), took advantage of the new opportunities inherent in the no-discrimination policy promoted by the industrial UNIONISM of the CIO. Indeed, organized labor became a primary battleground in the emerging civil rights movement (see LABOR MOVEMENT). A new partnership between major unions like the United Automobile Workers and the NAACP emerged during these years, one that was held together in large part by a common enemy: the white supremacist, anti-union southern bloc in Congress.

NAACP membership grew to nearly two hundred thousand during the war years, the rate of increase in the South exceeding that in other parts of the country by three times. The growth in membership there paralleled the rapid increase in black voter registration, particularly in the wake of the 1944 Supreme Court ruling, *Smith v. Allwright*, which overturned the all-white primary. Further, the vibrant network of politically active NAACP branches helped energize the national office. As the leading civil rights organization with a presence in Washington, the NAACP was positioned to expand on the DOUBLE V CAMPAIGN and place the black struggle for freedom in America in a global context. Walter White traveled extensively during the war, investigating the conditions of black soldiers who served abroad and racial discrimination in the Caribbean. A vocal critic of British imperialism, he linked the struggle for civil rights in America to the decolonization movements in India and Africa (see COLONIALISM). In 1945, White, Du Bois, and Mary McLeod BETHUNE represented the NAACP at the United Nations Conference in San Francisco. In 1947 Du Bois prepared "An Appeal to the World," a detailed statement on racial discrimination in the United States, seeking redress in the United Nations.

Most African Americans had been drawn to the Democratic Party by Franklin Roosevelt and the New Deal. This allegiance seemed less secure after FDR's death in April 1945; during his first year in office, President Harry S. TRUMAN did little to engage the hopes of blacks. When the Democrats lost the congressional midterm elections in 1946, however, it became clear that the black vote could not be taken for granted and, indeed, could easily determine the outcome of the 1948 presidential race. Late in 1946, Truman appointed the PRESIDENT'S COMMITTEE ON CIVIL RIGHTS, partially in response to the lynching of two war veterans and their wives in Georgia. The following spring, he issued the committee's report, "To Serve These Rights," which called for antilynching legislation and strong federal action in support of civil rights. At about this time Truman became the first president to address a meeting of the NAACP, signaling his identification publicly with the organization.

While the Truman administration embraced the cause of civil rights in the spring of 1947, the president issued an executive order establishing a loyalty program (see LOYALTY OATHS) that had a chilling effect on those who fought for CIVIL LIBERTIES. As a companion to the Truman Doctrine, which committed the United States to containing the spread of communism abroad, the loyalty program made suspect any criticism of the United States or of U.S. foreign policy. The national NAACP quickly accommodated the political realities of the COLD WAR: White withdrew the organization's support for Du Bois's "Appeal," and the national board passed a resolution supporting the Truman Doctrine and the Marshall Plan. In 1948 the NAACP ousted Du Bois from the organization for publicly supporting the presidential candidacy of Henry WALLACE, an active supporter of civil rights but a staunch critic of the Cold War. That year the Democratic Party adopted a civil rights plank at its convention, and, shortly thereafter, Truman issued an executive order mandating the desegregation of the nation's armed forces. While Henry Wallace broke new ground with his interracial campaign through the Deep South, Truman won a majority of the black vote in 1948 and narrowly clinched the presidential election. By accommodating the political imperatives of Cold War liberalism, the NAACP also reinforced its legitimacy in national political circles. In 1949 the NAACP broadened the national coalition for civil rights legislation with the establishment of the LEADERSHIP CONFERENCE ON CIVIL RIGHTS (LCCR), which included labor, religious groups, and liberal organizations. At the same time, the NAACP attempted to purge its ranks of suspected communists and communist sympathizers and retreated from its bold support of the world's decolonization struggles.

Civil Rights Era, 1950–1968

The foundation of the NAACP's program remained anchored in the cumulative gains of its legal campaign and in its extensive network of branches. In 1950, two major Supreme Court decisions, *Sweatt v. Painter* from Texas and *McLaurin v. Oklahoma*, paved the way for a direct challenge to the *Plessy* doctrine of "separate but equal." Over the next three years the NAACP brought five major cases from South Carolina, Virginia, the District of Columbia, Kansas, and Delaware before the U.S. Supreme Court, challenging racial segregation in elementary and secondary schools. These cases were argued under the umbrella of *Brown v. Board of Education*. The Department of Justice filed an amicus (friend of the court) brief in support of the NAACP side in the case, arguing that racial discrimination "furnishes grist for the Communist propaganda mills." On May 17, 1954, in a unanimous decision, the Court outlawed racial segregation in public schools, proclaiming that "separate educational facilities are inherently unequal." A year later, the Court issued a second ruling, commonly referred to as *Brown II*, concerning the implementation of the decision. While urging "all deliberate speed," the Court left it for the federal district courts to determine the pace and timing of SCHOOL DESEGREGATION in light of local circumstances. White Southerners took this as an invitation to resist. They waged a campaign of MASSIVE RESISTANCE to block implementation of the *Brown* ruling and to drive the NAACP from the South. Arkansas governor Orval FAUBUS's bold defiance of a court order to admit nine black students (see LITTLE ROCK NINE) to Central High School in Little Rock compelled President Dwight EISENHOWER to send federal troops to escort the nine students into school and to maintain order. A year later Faubus closed the schools in Little Rock rather than preside over their integration—a tactic used throughout the Deep South and in Prince Edward County, Virginia.

After the *Brown* decision, NAACP branches became the targets of city councils and state legislatures determined to expose their membership lists and restrict their ability to function. In Alabama, the NAACP was effectively outlawed for nearly ten years. In the wake of the Montgomery Bus Boycott, local activists established the Montgomery Improvement Association to preside over that event, which became a model for Martin Luther King, Jr.'s, Southern Christian Leadership Conference (SCLC). While King's leadership and the unyielding boycott drew most of the media attention, it was NAACP lawyers who finally defeated bus segregation in Montgomery through a Supreme Court ruling, *Browder v. Gayle.* Moreover, NAACP branches remained a vital source of support for civil rights activity throughout the South—even in Mississippi, where Medgar Evers, Amzie Moore, and others maintained a spirited resistance.

Within a year after the *Brown* decision, Walter White died and was succeeded as executive secretary of the NAACP by Roy Wilkins. In 1956 the NAACP Legal Defense and Educational Fund (LDEF) split off from the organization. Robert L. Carter, a lawyer who had been Thurgood Marshall's assistant since the early 1940s, became the NAACP's general counsel and established a new legal department. Under Carter's direction, the legal office broadened its challenge to de facto school segregation in the North; in 1960 it would win a major Voting Rights case, *Gomillion v. Lightfoot* (see Charles Gomillion), opening the way for federal intervention in securing fair electoral practices. Working largely through the Leadership Conference on Civil Rights, which the NAACP's Clarence Mitchell directed, Wilkins and other NAACP officials played a pivotal role in lobbying Congress for civil rights legislation. In 1957, the first Civil Rights Act was passed since Reconstruction. While it was weak, it provided some leverage for expanding voter participation in the South and for exposing the legal, extralegal, and violent methods used to bar African Americans from voting. Another civil rights act was passed in 1960, only slightly modifying the voting rights provisions of the 1957 act. At the same time, NAACP labor secretary Herbert Hill mounted a sustained campaign against racial discrimination on the part of organized labor. Through litigation and publicity, Hill pressured the government as well as corporations and individual unions to open up job opportunities for blacks.

In the aftermath of the student Sit-Ins of 1960, direct-action protests brought national and international attention to the American South, providing a critical lever in the final assault on the segregation system. Indeed, the leadership of Martin Luther King, Jr., and the young shock troops of the Student Non-violent Coordinating Committee (SNCC) energized and broadened the ranks of the civil rights movement during a time when the NAACP was under constant attack from local and state officials throughout the South. Nevertheless, in many parts of the South and the rest of the nation, NAACP members provided the backbone of the struggle. By 1963, NAACP membership had surpassed four hundred thousand, making it the largest U.S. civil rights organization and, as August Meier and John Bracey have observed, it was "the only civil rights organization that was funded primarily by the black community."

Meanwhile, the national leadership of the NAACP continued to play a critical role in mediating between the pressures exerted at the grass-roots level and the legislative process in Washington. This reached a critical turning point in 1963, as the violence in Birmingham, Alabama (see Birmingham Campaign), and the March on Washington heightened the demands for presidential action. Roy Wilkins and Clarence Mitchell were uniquely positioned to pressure the administration of John F. Kennedy and allies in Congress to reap full benefits of this historic moment. Following the assassination of Kennedy, Lyndon B. Johnson carried Kennedy's initiatives forward and, with the full support of NAACP and LCCR lobbyists, secured passage of the Civil Rights Act of 1964. In addition to outlawing racial segregation in public places, the act included (largely due to the efforts of Herbert Hill and the NAACP) in Title VII a strong equal-opportunities provision. In the year that followed, NAACP strategists pushed for legislation protecting voting rights while King and SNCC mobilized a protest in Selma. The violent police riot that broke out during the first Selma march pushed Johnson to act on Voting Rights; NAACP lobbyists helped facilitate the passage of a strong Voting Rights Act in August 1965.

Five days after President Johnson signed the Voting Rights Act, a racial rebellion exploded in the Watts area of Los Angeles (see Watts Riot). Black riots in Detroit, Washington, D.C., New York, and other cities signaled the depths of black rage and despair in Northern urban areas. Now, with the end of state-imposed segregation, civil rights leaders faced the centuries-old patterns of racial exclusion and discrimination that were woven into the fabric of national life. King's efforts to apply the tactics used in the Southern struggle in Chicago failed (see Chicago Campaign of 1966), while the appeal of Black Power further eclipsed the ideal of integration. In 1968, in the immediate aftermath of King's assassination, President Johnson signed the Fair Housing Act with the critical support of NAACP and LCCR lobbyists. Less than a year later, however, Richard Nixon became president, signaling a new era of conservative politics.

"Post–Civil Rights Era"

In the aftermath of the judicial and legislative victories of the 1950s and 1960s, the NAACP faced new challenges in the ongoing struggle for racial justice and equality. Primary among these were the application and enforcement of the laws barring racial discrimination in schools, HOUSING, and EMPLOYMENT. While Hill continued to pressure organized labor to break down racial barriers to African Americans, he and other NAACP lawyers worked with businesses and government officials in developing and implementing minority hiring programs in compliance with the civil rights acts. As in the past, NAACP branches continued to be the primary forces fighting police brutality and racial discrimination in cities and towns across the nation, and most often it was they who took the initiative in implementing the process of desegregation in schools. After the Supreme Court ruling in *Swann v. Charlotte-Mecklenberg* (1971), busing became a major tool for breaking down racial barriers in the schools. In Boston, after a decade-long fight to gain equal access to public school resources, the local NAACP chapter won a federal court order mandating BUSING in order to achieve racial integration of the city's public schools. The violent white Bostonian resistance to the court order was reminiscent of Massive Resistance in the Deep South. "Busing" quickly became a buzzword among conservatives who were leading the retreat from the civil rights gains of the 1960s.

At the national level, the NAACP at times appeared to be adrift and unsure of its mission in a post–civil rights era. In some ways, it was a victim of its own successes. The dramatic increase of the number of elected black officials in the aftermath of the Voting Rights Act vastly expanded the range of black political leadership at the local, state, and national levels. During the 1970s the organization went through a major transition in leadership with the retirement of Roy Wilkins in 1976 and Clarence Mitchell in 1978. When Benjamin Hooks became executive director in 1977, the organization suffered from financial problems, as well as from the challenge of charting a direction to secure the gains of the 1960s and meet the institutionalized manifestations of racial discrimination and inequality. During the Reagan administration in the 1980s, just holding the line on civil rights gains absorbed much of the organization's energy. In 1993, Benjamin Chavis succeeded Hooks as NAACP executive secretary. The youthful Chavis, many thought, would energize the organization and broaden its appeal to young people. Chavis's short term was wracked with controversy. He made a determined effort to bring young people into the organization and focused the NAACP's attention on the problem of environ-

mental RACISM—an issue with great resonance for many African Americans. Reminiscent of the early history of the organization, Chavis hosted a black leadership conference in an effort to join blacks around a unified program; but his inclusion of NATION OF ISLAM leader Louis FARRAKHAN stirred much criticism, especially when Chavis refused to denounce Minister Farrakhan's anti-Semitic views. In August 1994, deep in debt, the NAACP removed Chavis as executive director.

The crisis that engulfed the NAACP during Chavis's term led to much discussion in the media and among blacks about the role of the NAACP in a "post–civil rights" era. In her service as chairman of the NAACP board (1995–1998), Myrle Evers Williams revived the spirit of the organization and restored hope in its future. The appointment of Kwisi Mfume, the distinguished congressman and leader of the CONGRESSIONAL BLACK CAUCUS, as executive secretary in 1995 also marked a new departure for the organization. Under Mfume and Evers Williams the NAACP regained a measure of financial health while restoring its public image. In 1998, former SNCC activist Julian BOND succeeded Evers Williams as chairman of the board. Bond's deep commitment to the organization, its history, and its future, serves as a bridge to the twenty-first century.

BIBLIOGRAPHY

Fairclough, Adam. *Race and Democracy: The Civil Rights Movement in Louisiana, 1915–1972.* 1995.

Goings, Kenneth. *The NAACP Comes of Age: The Defeat of Judge John J. Parker.* 1990.

Grant, Joanne. *Freedom Bound: A Biography of Ella Baker.* 1998.

Kellog, Charles Flint. *NAACP: A History of the National Association for the Advancement of Colored People, 1909–1920.* 1967.

Lewis, David Levering. *W. E. B. Du Bois: Biography of a Race, 1868–1919.* 1993.

McNeil, Genna Rae. *Groundwork: Charles Hamilton Houston and the Struggle for Civil Rights.* 1983.

Meier, August, and John Bracey, Jr. "The NAACP as a Reform Movement: 1909–1965—'To Reach the Conscience of America.'" *Journal of Southern History* (February 1993).

Meier, August, and Elliot Rudwick. "The Rise of the Black Secretariat in the NAACP, 1909–1935." In *Along the Color Line: Explorations in the Black Experience.* 1976.

Pitre, Merline. *In Struggle Against Jim Crow: Lulu B. White and the NAACP, 1900–1957.* 1999.

Reed, Christopher. *The Chicago NAACP and the Rise of Black Professional Leadership, 1910–1966.* 1997.

Ross, D. Joyce. *J. E. Spingarn and the Rise of the NAACP.* 1972.

Tushnet, Mark. *The NAACP's Legal Strategy Against Segregation, 1925–1950.* 1987.

Watson, Denton. *Lion in the Lobby: Clarence Mitchell, Jr.'s Struggle for the Passage of Civil Rights Laws.* 1990.

White, Walter. *A Man Called White.* 1948.

Wilkins, Roy, with Tom Matthews. *Standing Fast: The Autobiography of Roy Wilkins.* 1970.

Zangrando, Robert. *The NAACP Crusade Against Lynching, 1909–1950.* 1960.

Patricia Sullivan

National Association of Colored Women

The National Association of Colored Women (NACW) was founded in Washington, D.C., in 1896 as a result of the merger of two African-American club women's federations. The Colored Women's League, a coalition of 113 organizations chartered in 1892 and led by Margaret Murray Washington, dean of women at Tuskegee Institute, and the National Federation of Afro-American Women, an alliance of 85 organizations established in 1895 and headed by educator and activist Mary Church TERRELL, united to create the first national secular race-based organization. Members elected Mary Church Terrell to serve as the first president. This newly merged federation of black club women predated the birth of the NATIONAL ASSOCIATION FOR THE ADVANCEMENT OF COLORED PEOPLE (NAACP) by fifteen years and drew upon a longstanding tradition of black female political and social activism rooted in older African-American female associations and mutual aid societies. Shortly after it was founded, the NACW had 5,000 members. By the 1920s it had attracted 100,000 members.

The black women who formed the backbone of the NACW were largely middle-class professional women educated at premier schools such as Oberlin College. Many of them were involved in teaching or other social service organizations. Local and state affiliates of the NACW undertook a variety of projects, including setting up kindergartens, helping female migrants from the South to find employment, assisting the elderly, creating child care programs, teaching domestic science, promoting female suffrage, and supporting the civil rights agenda of the NAACP. The organization published a monthly newsletter called the *National Notes.* Prominent women in the organization such as Mary Church Terrell, Ida B. WELLS, and Anna Julia Cooper also made it their objective to challenge public attacks on the character and morality of black women.

The NACW was both radical and conservative in nature. The organization was highly critical of LYNCHING and called for better race relations in the JIM CROW South. It advocated boycotts of segregated facilities, condemned Booker T. WASHINGTON for his conciliatory attitude toward the violation of black civil and political rights, and did not take an active stand against interracial marriage. The NACW provided black women a forum for public commentary and national leadership that had not previously existed. However, these club women did not significantly challenge Victorian notions of womanhood or entrenched middle-class values. The federation's motto "Lifting as We Climb" reflected their commitment to the moral uplift of their race. Members of the NACW aimed to make black women better wives and mothers, and homes the breeding ground of virtue and self-improvement.

During the 1930s the federation suffered from financial instability and declining membership. The need for federal assistance during the Great DEPRESSION had made the ideology of self-help and moral uplift seem anachronistic. The NACW continued to be active by supporting the National Recovery Act and forging ties with such groups as the AFL-CIO. However, with the establishment of a new national umbrella organization in 1935 called the NATIONAL COUNCIL OF NEGRO WOMEN, the NACW moved to a secondary role. The NACW still endures as the twenty-first century dawns, primarily focusing on education and social service.

BIBLIOGRAPHY

Davis, Angela Y. *Women, Race and Class,* 1983.

Giddings, Paula. *When and Where I Enter: The Impact of Black Women on Race and Sex in America,* 1984.

Hamilton, Tullia Kay Brown. "The National Association of Colored Women, 1896–1920." Ph.D. dissertation. Emory University, 1978.

Jones, Beverly W. "Mary Church Terrell and the National Association of Colored Women, 1896 to 1901." *Journal of Negro History* 67 (1982): 20–33.

Kendricks, Ruby M. "'They Also Serve': The National Association of Colored Women, Inc." *Negro History Bulletin* 42 (Mar. 1954): 171–175.

Shaw, Stephanie J. "Black Club Women and the Creation of the National Association of Colored Women." *Journal of Women's History* 3 (1991): 10–25.

Natalie J. Ring

National Baptist Convention

Formed in 1895, the National Baptist Convention, U.S.A. (NBC) survived the schisms that produced rival Baptist conventions in 1897, 1915 (when it incorporated), and 1961. Today, it is the largest of all African-American denominations and organizations. Its 7,500,000 members comprise almost a third of blacks belonging to Christian churches and nearly a quarter of the entire black population.

It emerged as a bellwether of racial hope and struggle. Before World War I the convention was outspoken on temperance and education, supporting perhaps 100 schools (elementary, secondary, and collegiate). The million-member auxiliary Woman's Convention (WC) conducted educational, missionary, and reform work of great social significance. In 1909, led by Nannie Helen Burroughs (1879–1961), the WC opened a National Training School for Women and Girls in Washington, D.C. Self-help did not block protest, however, as NBC affiliates demonstrated against lynching, Jim Crow streetcars, job discrimination, and unequal public relief. During World War II the convention's state associations played a key role in expanding the membership of the NATIONAL ASSOCIATION FOR THE ADVANCEMENT OF COLORED PEOPLE (NAACP). They also promoted voting rights campaigns following the 1944 antiwhite primary decision in SMITH v. ALLWRIGHT.

Yet the civil rights and Black Power movements deepened generational and ideological differences between the NBC's leaders. From 1953 to 1982 president Joseph H. Jackson (1900–1990) advocated blacks' self-development, which included legal steps to win equal opportunity. But he opposed mass demonstrations and the emerging leadership of Martin Luther KING, JR., who became a national officer in 1958. After failing to unseat Jackson in 1961, King and other activists formed the Progressive National Baptist Convention. Theodore J. Jemison (b. 1918), Jackson's successor and a civil rights movement veteran, launched a successful nationwide voter registration campaign.

BIBLIOGRAPHY

Fitts, Leroy. *A History of Black Baptists.* 1985.
Garrow, David J. *Bearing the Cross: Martin Luther King, Jr., and the Southern Christian Leadership Conference.* 1988.
Higginbotham, Evelyn Brooks. *Righteous Discontent: The Women's Movement in the Black Baptist Church, 1880–1920.* 1993.
Lincoln, C. Eric, and Lawrence H. Mamiya. *The Black Church in the African American Experience.* 1990.
Paris, Peter J. *Black Religious Leaders: Conflict in Unity.* 1991.

Raymond Gavins

National Bar Association

The National Bar Association (NBA) was formally organized by African-American lawyers in 1925 in Des Moines, Iowa, having as its mission "to advance the science of jurisprudence, uphold the honor of the legal profession, promote social intercourse among the members of the American Bar and protect the civil and political rights of all citizens of the several states and of the United States." The organization was needed because for sixty-six years black lawyers were barred from membership in the American Bar Association (ABA).

The first black bar association in the United States was formed in Greenville, Mississippi, in 1891; subsequently the founding of black bar groups throughout the nation became known as the Greenville Movement. As the roots of the Greenville Movement took hold, so did the need for black lawyers to organize at the national level. The National Negro Bar Association (NNBA)—formed in 1909 as an auxiliary of the National Negro Business League (NNBL), which was founded in 1900 by Booker T. WASHINGTON—preceded the National Bar Association. In 1919, black lawyers began a formal split from the NNBL, as the NNBA wanted to take more aggressive actions to combat RACISM in America than did the NNBL. The refusal of the American Bar Association to admit African-American attorneys during the 1920s, solely because of their race, also provided an impetus for the formation of the NBA.

George H. Woodson of the Iowa Negro Bar Association is credited with being instrumental in forming the NBA. In February 1925, Woodson and several other lawyers invited African-American attorneys from around the United States to a meeting in Des Moines. On August 1, 1925, twelve African-American lawyers from the United States and the Virgin Islands, including Gertrude Elzora Durden Rush, the sole female attorney in attendance, formed the NBA in Des Moines. The board of directors (now the board of governors) was composed of seven members from seven different regions of the country.

During the second annual meeting, Carl F. Phillips of Washington, D.C., called on the NBA "to unite themselves in one solid body to fight legally the cause of the Race against unjust discrimination, prejudice and segregation." Despite its primary focus on issues affecting the African-American community, membership in the NBA has been open to attorneys of all races from its inception. In the early years, the NBA formed committees to deal with international law, legal education, professional ethics, uniform state laws, jurisprudence, law reform, legal aid, and crime. The presence of women in the American bar (there were twenty-five women attorneys in the entire country in 1928) was highlighted during the fourth annual meeting by the participation of Chicago attorney Edith Sampson. Women have held various national offices in the NBA; and in 1981, the NBA elected its first woman president, Arnette Rhinehart Hubbard.

Throughout the years, the NBA has taken a stand on issues affecting African-Americans. In the 1940s the group campaigned for DESEGREGATION of the armed forces and the admission of black lawyers into the American Bar Association, and it criticized the federal government's failure to hire black lawyers and appoint black judges. In recent years, the NBA has supported AFFIRMATIVE ACTION and vigorously fought against EMPLOYMENT discrimination.

The NBA publishes the *National Bar Journal*, a scholarly legal periodical. The formation of the *Journal* during the 1940s created a national platform for African-American attorneys and professors to share their views with their constituents.

In 1943, the American Bar Association (ABA) officially began to accept African-American members, but it did not actually welcome them until the 1950s and 1960s. In the face of these changes, there was some concern about whether the NBA should continue, but the leaders recognized that there remained a need to promote the rights of African-American in the United States.

The NBA meets annually in the United States and abroad. In 1999, the NBA had seventeen thousand members and eighty-seven affiliate chapters in the United States, Canada, the United Kingdom, Africa, and the Caribbean.

BIBLIOGRAPHY

Articles of Incorporation of the National Bar Association, Article II. "Our Origin." *National Bar Journal* 2 (1944): 161, 163.

National Bar Association, Internet Legal Resources. "National Bar Association Perspective." (www.nationalbar. org/nbapers.html). 1999.

Segal, Geraldine R. *Blacks in the Law*. 1983.

Smith, J. Clay. *Emancipation: The Making of the Black Lawyer, 1844–1944*. 1993.

Smith, J. Clay, ed. *Rebels in Law: Voices in History of Black Women Lawyers*. 1998.

Wendy Brown Scott

National Civil Rights Museum

The National Civil Rights Museum in Memphis, TENNESSEE, built at the Lorraine Motel site of Dr. Martin Luther KING, JR.'s, assassination has put the history of the Southern freedom struggle into the travel guides. It is among the most successful public history vehicles commemorating the searing civil rights movements of the 1950s and 1960s. Others include the BIRMINGHAM CIVIL RIGHTS INSTITUTE in Alabama (across from the Sixteenth Street Baptist Church where four black girls were killed by a bomb planted by white supremacists in 1963); the SOUTHERN POVERTY LAW CENTER monument to slain civil rights martyrs in Montgomery, Alabama; a museum devoted to the voting rights battle

in Selma, Alabama; and the King Center, a complex of buildings on Auburn Avenue in Atlanta, which tell about the life of Dr. King, his family, and his community.

The creation of vehicles for a public history of the movement did not happen without a struggle. In Memphis, the city tried for many years to forget April 4, 1968. King's death on that date during a strike of black sanitation workers cast a pall over the city, which went into a deepening malaise during the 1970s and 1980s due to plant closings and the city's bad image. Urban decay surrounded the Lorraine Motel, which became a habitat for the urban poor, prostitutes, and drug addicts. Yet visitors from outside the city persisted in coming to the Lorraine to see where Dr. King died and to pay their respects to him and the movement he represented.

How King and the city's struggle over the right of workers to union representation should be remembered became a point of contention. "People did not want out of town visitors to come and see this side of Memphis," said Juanita Moore, the museum's first director and an experienced hand in African-American museum work. "White Memphians felt that you just tear it down and put up a marker and that would be it." Most blacks, who now make up more than 50 percent of the city's population, thought people should see the poverty King struggled to end in the last year of his life, and should learn about the movement he represented. Just as in life, in death King continued to be a focal point of conflicting black and white visions of what the city should be.

Black community activists and the American Federation of State, County, and Municipal Employees (AFSCME) Local 1733, the union which King supported in 1968, worked for over seven years to bring the museum into being. Walter Bailey, owner of the motel, created his own shrine to King, in the room where King was to have spent the night and on the balcony outside, where King was shot down. When Bailey was about to lose the motel because he could no longer pay taxes on it, he called Charles Scruggs, general manger of black-run radio station WDIA. Scruggs and the station launched a campaign to save the Lorraine, and Local 1733 and international units of AFSCME pledged $25,000. Others in the city raised $128,000 to buy the motel at the auction block in 1982. Judge D'Army Bailey, Tri-State Bank President Jesse Turner, and others formed the Lorraine Civil Rights Museum Foundation, which spearheaded more than seven years of struggle to convince city, state, and county governments to fund construction of the museum, which finally opened in September 1991.

Museum professionals concerned about preserving the legacy of the civil rights movement played critical roles in bringing the vision of the museum's founders to completion. Ben Wallace, former head of exhibits at the Smithsonian Institution, as well as designers from Kansas City and numerous historical consultants, built exhibits aimed at creating a feeling of being there and participating in the struggle. In the MONT-GOMERY BUS BOYCOTT section of the exhibit, visitors board a bus, and when they sit down behind the sculpted forms of Rosa Parks and a bus driver, a recording tells them to "go to the back of the bus." This sets off confusing impulses as to whether to go along in order not to ruin the "display" or to disobey the order. Wherever visitors sit, they are able to think for a moment about the dilemma many black people found themselves in every day prior to the desegregation of transportation facilities. In an exhibit on the Greensboro lunch counter SIT-INS, visitors sit down with sculpted protestors as a screen displays footage of interviews with black and white southerners supporting or opposing segregation; another screen shows whites dousing black and white students with ketchup and beating them to the ground for trying to be served. "I'm sorry, we're not allowed to serve niggers in here," a waitress on one screen explains to visitors.

The exhibit on the movement in Birmingham, Alabama, likewise puts the observer in the center of the action. Films, played through the windows of a life-sized storefront, show police cars rushing forward, jets of water from fire hoses knocking people down, and children being arrested, while crowd noise roars and sirens scream from behind. Visitors curious enough to look through a wire screen into the audio hole in the wall see themselves mirrored through the bars of a jail. This jarring and disconcerting exhibit then leads the visitors to a sterile-looking prison cell, which evokes King's detention and his "Letter from a Birmingham Jail."

Toward the end of the exhibit, which includes many other vignettes on the history of the movement, sculpted National Guard troops point bayonets toward black strikers holding picket signs saying "I Am a Man"—the trenchant cry for recognition taken up by the MEMPHIS SANITATION WORKERS' STRIKE OF 1968. A few feet farther on, visitors arrive at King's motel room, outside of which films on the sanitation strike play on television monitors. Finally, reaching the balcony where King died, approaching it from inside the hotel, visitors experience again the feelings of pain, grief, and rage that many felt in 1968. From the outside of the motel, one can look up to the spot where King was shot and to the rooming house from which authorities believe the shot came, as well as at other areas around the site where assassins may have concealed themselves.

The museum, as the organizers of the exhibits intended, creates a space in which visitors can go back in time and, to a limited extent, experience the history of the place. People from all national and ethnic backgrounds, including many tourists from abroad and visitors from all over the United States, as well as Memphians, mingle in a way they rarely if ever could in King's lifetime. As an introduction to the museum, a film raises some of the questions King addressed, asking visitors to consider together the meaning of the words "democracy" and "equality."

Special programs have extended this educational thrust beyond the exhibits. A three-day national retrospective on the meaning of the movement and King's life and work was held on the twenty-fifth anniversary of his death in 1993. During that three-day event, leaders from all parts of the movement participated, including Bob MOSES, C. T. Vivian, Dorothy COTTON, Charles McDew, Rosa PARKS, and many local and regional activists. Academic commentators, including Cornell West, offered their perspectives as well, in a program co-chaired by civil rights scholars and activists Julian BOND, Linda Reed, and Michael Honey. Later on, the city itself launched a more massive commemoration than this, marking the thirtieth year since King's death.

The legacy and the message of the movement in Memphis and the South can hardly be ignored. They have become a part of the tourism industry that is reviving the city's downtown and Beale Street, home of the blues, where there are other museums and exhibits as well as night spots. The National Civil Rights Museum has also undergone an expansion. In its early years its isolated location made it easy to miss, but the museum purchased the rooming house from which James Earl Ray presumably fired the fatal shot, and extended the grounds of the museum to connect with major streets.

Through events and exhibits, the museum has become a centerpiece of tourism in Memphis, as the city tries to turn its tragedies into something from which people can learn. Some believe that turning the site into an educational and tourism vehicle trivializes King's memory. Jackie Smith, a former resident of the hotel who used to lead people on informal tours of the assassination site, year after year has held a lone vigil outside the hotel, protesting that it should have become a place providing poor people and students with educational and housing services. To what extent the museum should represent the ongoing civil rights movement is still debated. But the museum clearly carries forward the story of the black freedom struggle to many uninitiated and otherwise uninformed people. Many students, young people, and visitors from out of state and from outside the United States find the experience the museum offers to be transformative. For some, it opens up a world of history they know little about, and initiates new thinking about interracialism and the struggle for change today.

In Memphis, the museum has also played an important role in bringing people together. "I think that people in Memphis are very proud of the fact that they have moved past thinking of Memphis as just the place where King was assassinated to a place where they can come and learn more about the civil rights movement itself, as you pay your respects to King and his memory," says Juanita Moore. Civil rights monuments and museums, people such as Ms. Moore believe, should not become strictly a matter of tourism. Many of the very people who opposed the movement itself prefer to see the movement turned into "history," something outside of the bounds of current battles.

Beverly Robertson, following Ms. Moore as the museum's director, and numerous others continue to develop the museum as a living memory of the people who took part in the struggle for equal rights. The museum allows the voices of the masses of civil rights activists whom most people have not heard of to come to the fore. "It is the site of the assassination of King, but it is not a memorial to King," Moore suggests. "It is a civil rights museum. It is a memorial to all of the people that participated in that movement. It is not just about a few great people, or a few people everybody knows, it is about a lot of folks." And it is not only about the past, but how the freedom movement's legacy is to be carried on for current and future generations.

BIBLIOGRAPHY

Parts of this article appeared in a previously published interview with Juanita Moore. Michael Honey. "Doing Public History at the National Civil Rights Museum: A Conversation with Juanita Moore." *Public Historian* 17 (1) (Winter 1995): 71–84.

Michael Honey

National Colored Labor Union

Founded in 1869, the National Colored Labor Union (NCLU) was the first nationwide organization to merge African-American working-class issues with a civil rights agenda. The NCLU closely aligned itself with the REPUBLICAN PARTY and hence followed a different path from that of the National Labor Union (NLU), organized in 1866 largely by white workers. The history of the NCLU, however, remains closely interwoven with that of the NLU. Relations between the NCLU and the NLU were tenuous at best, as differences in objectives between white and black la-

bor hampered a unified working-class movement. Whereas white labor focused on the CLASS struggle, the African-American leadership of the NCLU downplayed class conflict and insisted on civil rights agitation combined with interracial working-class cooperation. The NCLU advocated full citizenship rights, free EDUCATION, and worker cooperatives, and aimed to acquire property for the rank and file. In addition, black labor activists remained suspicious of the white working-class's virulent RACISM. Contributing to the ideological differences was the fact that prominent NCLU leaders such as John Mercer Langston and P. B. S. Pinchback were Republican politicians. In contrast, the NLU opposed the Republicans as agents of capitalism, and supported an independent working-class political party. Finally, although the white leadership of the NLU argued for interracial cooperation, the rank and file proved intransigent on the race question. The NCLU's insistence upon merging civil rights issues with labor organizing illustrates the complexity of the black working-class experience in the years immediately following the Civil War. The NCLU's final convention in 1872 repudiated the NLU and declared itself solidly behind the Republican Party.

BIBLIOGRAPHY

Foner, Philip, and Ronald L. Lewis, eds. *Black Workers: A Documentary History from Colonial Times to the Present.* 1989.

Spero, Sterling, and Abram L. Harris. *The Black Worker.* 1931.

Charles Franklin Lee

National Committee to Abolish the Poll Tax

First created in 1939 as an outgrowth of the SOUTHERN CONFERENCE FOR HUMAN WELFARE's (SCHW's) Civil Rights Committee, the National Committee to Abolish the Poll Tax (NCAPT) lobbied for the repeal of poll taxes that limited the electorate and restricted participatory democracy in the South. This effort was only part of a larger attempt by the SCHW to combat racism and fight for an expanded role for African Americans in Southern society.

Though often portrayed as radicals—sometimes even as communist sympathizers—in contemporary accounts, the leadership of the SCHW was primarily comprised of middle-class white southerners who believed that the impetus for racial justice in the South had to come from southerners themselves. Despite the limits of the southern liberalism, the organization was vocal and active in their attempt to transform

Costumed activist demonstrating against the poll tax in New York City in 1946. (UPI/CORBIS-Bettmann)

southern political culture and combat institutionalized racism.

As the idea behind the abolition of the poll tax was populist in nature—far more whites were disfranchised by such laws than blacks—the leadership of the SCHW believed the poll tax issue would offer the opportunity for a southern working-class solidarity on which they would later build a foundation for expanded civil rights for African Americans.

Among the most important leaders in the effort to abolish the poll tax was Virginia Foster DURR of Birmingham, Alabama. As vice-chairman of the SCHW's Civil Rights Committee, Durr's activism helped carry the issue to state legislatures and the United States CONGRESS. In 1941, the Committee separated from the Southern Conference and became the National

Committee to Abolish the Poll Tax (NCAPT). As the war years wore on, the effort to abolish the poll tax gathered momentum, winning friends and supporters from a wide variety of individuals and organizations, including Claude Pepper, Mary McLeod BETHUNE, George Norris, Vito MARCANTONIO, John L. LEWIS, Sidney Hillman, numerous churches, labor and civil rights organizations, and women's groups.

Between 1940 and 1948, the Committee helped to introduce bills against the use of the poll tax in federal and some state elections. By the mid-1940s, the issue was being hotly debated in regional and national newspapers. The Committee had succeeded in making the campaign to abolish the poll tax a populist crusade, as print media across America warned that democracy was dead or dying in the American South. But in concentrating so heavily on the poll tax—the repeal of which would do little to increase African American participation in the electoral process—SCHW, NCAPT, and southern liberals missed several opportunities to fight for black suffrage. In the end, the effort collapsed in the post-war anti-Communist backwash that nearly overwhelmed the American left. There were few short-term results and most southern states continued to use the poll tax until it was prohibited with the adoption of the Twenty-Fourth Amendment in 1964.

In the aftermath of the Committee's collapse, it became obvious that southern liberals in the Jim Crow South could not, and in some cases would not, bring about the kinds of changes necessary to establish racial justice themselves. They did, however, keep alive the idea that the majority of the white South would one day come to terms with the race problem and—as both good Christians and good southerners—find some solution to racial injustice. Nevertheless, NCAPT's efforts helped to turn most white southerners against the poll tax by the late 1940s and forced the United States Congress to revisit the issue of voting rights for the first time in sixty years.

BIBLIOGRAPHY

Barnard, Hollinger F., ed. *Outside the Magic Circle: The Autobiography of Virginia Foster Durr.* 1985.

Dunbar, Anthony P. *Against the Grain: Southern Radicals and Prophets, 1929–1959.* 1981.

Dykeman, Wilma, and James Stokely. *Seeds of Southern Change: The Life of Will Alexander.* 1962.

Egerton, John. *Speak Now Against the Day: The Generation Before the Civil Rights Movement.* 1994.

Singal, Daniel Joseph. *The War Within: From Victorian to Modernist Thought in the South, 1919–1945.* 1982.

Sosna, Morton. *In Search of the Silent South: Southern Liberals and the Race Issue.* 1977.

Sullivan, Patricia. *Days of Hope: Race and Democracy in the New Deal Era.* 1996.

J. Wayne Jones

National Congress for Puerto Rican Rights

After Puerto Rico became a U.S. possession following the Spanish-American War in 1898, existing labor movements on the island established ties with U.S. labor. Strong ties among Puerto Rican homeland and U.S. labor organizations have continued into the twenty-first century.

Early twentieth century Puerto Rican migrations to the United States produced workers for the cigar shops in New York City and Miami. Later, immigrants (see IMMIGRATION AND IMMIGRANTS) went to work in the textile and garment industries, munitions factories and shipyards, meatpacking, and service industries. Discrimination in the labor movements in these industries tended to force Puerto Rican immigrants to form their own labor organizations. Within Puerto Rican communities in the United States, militant labor organizations became strong, especially in New York City, where over 40 percent of Puerto Rican immigrants resided.

During the 1970s, however, the poor economic conditions in New York and the flight of manufacturing jobs to nonunionized states in the American Southwest and to Central America prompted the establishment of radical organizations such as the Young Lords Party, El COMITÉ (or MINP), and the PUERTO RICAN SOCIALIST PARTY. These organizations fought RACISM and poverty among Puerto Rican workers. They also helped link up Puerto Rican efforts with those of African Americans and other minorities.

In 1981, the NATIONAL CONGRESS FOR PUERTO RICAN RIGHTS (NCPRR) was founded in the Bronx borough of New York City. Chapters have since been established in Boston, Philadelphia, and San Francisco. The NCPRR advocates human and civil rights for Puerto Ricans. It strives to educate its members and the community on Puerto Rican issues and to develop leadership. It also organizes local and national campaigns to further its goals. The NCPRR is a volunteer organization that, in order to maintain independence, does not accept government funding. The NCPRR has been a party to lawsuits and other efforts to promote civil rights, including a high-profile suit to disband a New York City police unit accused of civil rights violations. It works with other Puerto Rican and civil rights groups to organize marches and protests for matters of concern. Examples include successful efforts against a waste incinerator project at Mott Haven

(Bronx, New York) and the Harlem River Rail Yard Project, as well as efforts in support of such organizations as the South Bronx Clean Air Coalition.

In 1996, the NCPRR established a committee, the Puerto Rico Collective (PRC) to focus on the hundredth anniversary of what NCPRR members term the U.S. colonization of Puerto Rico. The efforts of the PRC have been caught up in the minority struggle for Puerto Rican statehood or independence, issues that are unresolved on the island as well as in the Puerto Rican communities of the United States.

BIBLIOGRAPHY

Figueroa, Hector. "Puerto Rican Workers: A Profile." *NACLA Report on the Americas* (November/December 1996).

Gardiner, Beth. "Suit Demands New York Disband Elite Police Unit." *Bergen Record* (March 9, 1999).

Kersten, Jason. "Young Lords Grow Old, Legacy Lives On." *Bronx Beat Online* (April 1, 1996). Website at http://bronx-beat.jrn.columbia.edu/previous/040196/lords.html

"National Congress for Puerto Rican Rights." Website at http://www.columbia.edu/~rmg36/NCPRR.html

Michael Dawson

National Congress of American Indians

The National Congress of American Indians (NCAI), arguably the most important Indian rights organization in American history, is also the oldest and largest national Indian organization. The SOCIETY FOR AMERICAN INDIANS (SAI), established in 1911, preceded the NCAI as an organization dedicated to addressing Indian issues with membership limited to Indians, but internecine conflicts, financial difficulties, and failure to build grassroots support among reservation communities contributed to its demise in the 1920s. The NCAI forged its reputation for successful lobbying in the 1940s, expanded its efforts during the 1950s when it fought the deleterious effects of termination policy (government attempts to end federal ties to Indian communities and federal support of tribal governments), and continues to promote interests of tribal governments and to cultivate better public understanding of Indian and Native governments, people, and rights.

More than fifty tribes in twenty-seven states sent delegates to Denver, Colorado, in November 1944, to discuss the need for a national organization to protect recent gains made under the Indian New Deal. The delegates established the NCAI, which limited membership to persons of Indian ancestry, but allowed non-Indians to join without voting privileges. Learning from the SAI's mistakes, NCAI founders sought to build broad-based, nonpartisan support. NCAI founders planned vigorous lobbying campaigns aimed at protecting voting rights, Social Security benefits, and tribal land claims. As early as 1946, the NCAI admonished the federal government not to enact Indian policy without first soliciting input from the tribes affected. Lobbying by the NCAI and other American Indian interest groups spurred Congress to create the Indian Claims Commission in 1946.

During the height of termination activity during the 1950s, Joseph Garry, a World War II veteran and chairman of the Coeur d'Alene tribal council, led the NCAI's campaign to halt termination. The organization argued that Congress was acting unilaterally and that only tribes could sever ties with the federal government. Although the NCAI could not stop termination immediately, it slowed the process and ultimately convinced the government to accept the NCAI's position that termination could occur only with tribal consent.

By 1961 the Indian rights movement had swelled to include elements, such as the National Indian Youth Council, calling for more radical action than the NCAI typically employed. The NCAI renewed its lobbying efforts, focusing on securing benefits for Indians from Great Society legislation. The NCAI remained vital under Executive Director Vine DELORIA, Jr., who coined the expression "RED POWER" at the organization's 1966 convention. The organization also prompted Congress to pass the 1968 Indian Civil Rights Act, which required tribal consent before a state could extend its legal jurisdiction over a reservation and made provisions for returning reservations already under state authority to tribal control.

During the 1970s, the divide widened between the NCAI and more radical organizations such as the AMERICAN INDIAN MOVEMENT (AIM). When AIM protestors occupied Wounded Knee (South Dakota) in 1973 to protest excesses of the Pine Ridge Sioux Tribal Council under Richard Wilson, the NCAI defended Wilson and his administration as the duly elected tribal government and criticized AIM for violating tribal sovereignty. (See WOUNDED KNEE OCCUPATION.) Fragmentation within the Indian community contributed to NCAI influence waning during the remainder of the decade and into the 1980s as legal maneuvering surpassed legislative lobbying as a policy tool.

Nonetheless, the NCAI remains an active advocate for Indian issues and continues to provide an Indian voice to influence federal policy.

BIBLIOGRAPHY

Bee, Robert L. *The Politics of American Indian Policy*, 1982.

Bernstein, Alison R. *American Indians and World War II: Towards a New Era in Indian Affairs*. 1991.

Cowger, Thomas W. "'The Crossroads of Destiny': The NCAI's Landmark Struggle to Thwart Coercive Termination." *American Indian Culture and Research Journal* 20:4(1996): 121–144.

Hertzberg, Hazel. *The Search for an American Indian Identity: Modern Pan-Indian Movements*, 1971.

Rawls, James J. *Chief Red Fox Is Dead: A History of Native Americans Since 1945*. 1996.

Todd M. Kerstetter

National Congress of Spanish-Speaking People

See Congress of Spanish-Speaking People.

National Council of Negro Women

The National Council of Negro Women (NCNW) is a national coalition of black women's organizations that was founded by educator Mary McLeod BETHUNE in New York City on December 5, 1935. The NCNW has provided leadership and guidance to African-American women in their social and political lives. The founding meeting of representatives elected outstanding individuals such as Mary Church TERREL and Charlotte Hawkins Brown to leadership positions. After Bethune was unanimously voted president, her leadership enabled black women to become represented in public affairs at the national level. Bethune achieved this goal in part by establishing a headquarters in the nation's capital and employing an executive secretary.

Under Bethune's leadership, the council also became involved in international politics by supporting the founding of the United Nations. The NCNW supported "We Serve America" programs, launched the Harriet Tubman Liberty Ship, and established a successful journal, the *Aframerican Women's Journal*, which became *Women United* in 1949. The journal informed African-American women of major political issues that involved women. The NCNW also published *Telefact*, a newsletter written to inform members of the council and its affiliates of important issues and events relevant to legislation, international affairs, and economic development. Reflecting the intersections of race/ethnic, gender, and class interests, the council was actively with a diverse group of organizations, including the NATIONAL ASSOCIATION FOR THE ADVANCEMENT OF COLORED PEOPLE, National Council of Women, NATIONAL URBAN LEAGUE, national YMCA, LEAGUE OF

WOMEN VOTERS, National Council of Church Women, National Council of Jewish Women, and Council of Catholic Women, in order to gain knowledge of diverse ways to eliminate both racism and sexism as well as to "uplift the race."

After her retirement in 1949, Bethune was succeeded by Dorothy Boulding Ferebee, a physician from a family of leaders. Dr. Ferebee aimed to eliminate the segregation and discrimination against African Americans in health care, housing, education, and the ARMED FORCES. Within her "Nine Point Program," which asserted NCNW goals, Ferebee proposed that the council recommend qualified African Americans to government positions through voter registration campaigns. This would allow the passage of legislation to address lynching, the poll tax, and the status of black women. Under Dr. Ferebee's leadership, the council and other organizations fought to make more federal jobs available to African Americans. The NCNW was a force behind the founding of the FAIR EMPLOYMENT PRACTICES COMMITTEE.

The third president, Vivian Carter Mason, served a term of four years. Under Mason's leadership, the NCNW focused on school desegregation. Then, in 1957, the NCNW elected its fourth president, Dorothy I. HEIGHT, who developed a firm financial base through grants from foundations as well as a tax-exempt status in 1966. Height also constructed the Bethune Memorial Statue in Lincoln Park, Washington, D.C., in 1974. Today, the NCNW remains one of the oldest sociopolitical organizations founded and led by black women in the United States.

BIBLIOGRAPHY

Barnett, Bernice McNair. "Black Women's Collective Organizations: Their Struggles During the Doldrums." In *Feminist Organizations,* edited by Myra Marx Ferree and Patricia Yancey Martin. 1995.

Collier-Thomas, Bettye. "National Council of Negro Women." In *Black Women in America,* edited by Darlene Clark Hine. 1993.

Weisenfeld, Judith. "National Council of Negro Women." In *Encyclopedia of African-American Culture and History,* edited by Jack Salzman, David Lionel Smith, and Cornel West. 1996.

Shaunda Partida

National Education Association

The National Education Association (NEA) began as the National Teachers Association (NTA), founded in Philadelphia on August 26, 1857, by forty-three educators. The NTA enrolled members without racial restrictions, but women were not admitted until 1866.

In 1870 the National Association of School Superintendents and the American Normal School Association joined with the National Teachers Association to form the National Education Association (NEA). NEA's main purpose was to provide an annual convention for the discussion of ideas and to work in coordination with the state associations. The activities of the NEA soon broadened to include activism in securing federal legislation for schools and the establishment of a federal Department of Education.

After the PLESSY V. FERGUSON decision (1896) legalized the doctrine of separate but equal facilities for blacks and whites, blacks were barred from joining white state associations in the South. Blacks in various states throughout the nation formed their own local and state associations. In 1904, J. R. E. Lee of Tuskegee initiated the founding of the National Association of Colored Teachers (NACT) to give black teachers a national forum for discussing ideas and problems. So as not to exclude the white teachers in black schools, the name was changed to the National Association of Teachers in Colored Schools (NATCS) in 1907. Black educators fought for equal school funding, for the establishment and accreditation of black high schools in the South, and for national membership of black teachers in NATCS. To reflect this activism, NATCS became the American Teachers Association (ATA) in 1937.

Developments in the First Century

Though the NEA was conservative in its approach during its first century, 1857 to 1957, it was active in the concerns of black educators as early as the convention of 1884 at Madison, Wisconsin. The NEA supported the Morrill Act in 1862, which provided land grants to the states for founding colleges that provided both liberal and practical education, with emphasis on agriculture and the mechanical arts. In 1926 the vast inequities in school funding for black schools and colleges in the South, Maryland, and Oklahoma prompted the NEA to form a special committee with the NATCS. This committee, which became the Joint Committee of the NEA and the American Teachers Association, studied the problems of blacks in education, collected data on black health issues, and placed at least one black on the program of the General Session each year. In 1943, the Representative Assembly voted not to meet in a city that did not provide equal accommodations to blacks and other minorities.

NEA and the Civil Rights Movement

After the BROWN V. BOARD OF EDUCATION (1954) decision nullified the legality of separate schools for blacks and whites, the NEA expressed concern over integration. The organization did not commit itself to active support of school desegregation, however, until 1961. The greatest concern over integration was the fear of the loss of authority by black educators. Integration plans had to include minority representation on major committees and in holding offices. By 1970 all but two states had formed a single association open to all members without racial restrictions. As school desegregation occurred, the NEA worked to ensure the rights of black educators displaced by integration, providing money through the Du Shane Emergency Fund.

Concurrent with the unification of NEA affiliates, the black American Teachers Association (ATA) and the NEA merged in 1966. In 1968 Elizabeth Koontz became the first black president of the NEA. That same year, the NEA established the Center for Human Relations to coordinate all programs dealing with human relations and the rights of teachers. The NEA also became a partner with the Martin Luther King, Jr. Center for Social Change in Atlanta, Georgia. The 1973 NEA constitution provided guarantees for representation of minorities in the Representative Assembly, the Board of Directors, the Executive Committee, and all appointed committees. By 1979 all state affiliates had adopted affirmative action programs.

NEA Today

From a membership of 43 in 1857 to 703,829 at its centennial in 1957, the NEA today is the world's largest professional organization, with 2,000,800 members coming from fifty-three state affiliates and 12,000 local groups. It remains a voluntary association of teachers, administrators, and other educators associated with public schools, colleges and universities. The NEA also remains committed to advancing the cause of education and the welfare of its members.

BIBLIOGRAPHY

Dewing, Rolland. "The NEA and Minority Rights." *Journal of Negro Education.* 47, 4 (Fall 1978): 379–384.
Perry, Thelma D. *History of the American Teachers Association.* 1975.
Wesley, Edgar B. *NEA: The First Hundred Years: The Building of the Teaching Profession.* 1957.
West, Allan M. *The National Education Association: The Power Base for Education.* 1980.

Bertha H. Miller

National Indian Youth Council

In 1961 a national conference of Indians was held in Chicago to petition the administration of John F. KEN-NEDY to adopt a new Indian policy. Among those attending were young Indian college students who returned home disappointed that their elders were so timid in approaching the government. They determined that they could play a major role in policy formation; so in the summer of 1962 they met at Gallup, New Mexico, and created the National Indian Youth Council (NIYC). Among this group were Melvin Thom of Nevada, Herbert Blatchford of New Mexico, Clyde WARRIOR of Oklahoma, John Wincester of Michigan, and Bruce Wilkie and Hank Adams of Washington State.

Adopting Melvin Thom's slogan "For a Greater Indian America," they primarily emphasized instilling pride in being Indian and using skills developed in college to assist their people. Two basic ideologies emerged in the NIYC membership. Clyde Warrior hoped to articulate an Indian nationalism that would energize Indians of all ages. Hank Adams wanted to begin protests that would deal with immediate problems such as the fishing rights struggle in the Pacific Northwest.

The NIYC was not rigidly organized, and many activities were undertaken under its banner. In December 1964 celebrity-activists Marlon Brando and Dick Gregory, at the urging of Hank Adams, came to Washington State and participated in a "fish-in" that energized both the Indians and the state fish and game officers. The NIYC also conducted a vigorous protest at the Gallup Indian festival, where Indians provided entertainment but were otherwise not respected. The NIYC was the predecessor to the AMERICAN INDIAN MOVEMENT in encouraging Indians to speak for themselves.

During the Poor People's March in 1968 (part of the POOR PEOPLE'S CAMPAIGN) several NIYC members participated, but others refused to link Indian aspirations with African-American goals. Clyde Warrior died that summer, and the NIYC began to change in favor of more programmatic concerns. Through fund-raising and foundation grants it was able to support a central office under Gerald Wilkinson and soon began to play a major role on the national Indian organizational scene. Voter education and employment opportunities for Indians became well-developed parts of the NIYC activities. The NIYC cooperated with the SOUTHWEST VOTER EDUCATION PROJECT and dramatically increased Indian voting in ARIZONA and NEW MEXICO. Of the major Indian groups, only the NIYC was willing to link itself with non-Indian organizations and work for national reforms.

Recruitment of members for the NIYC became increasingly difficult in the late twentieth century because large numbers of Indians graduating from college did not want to become political. Also the programmatic thrust of the NIYC gave financial support that an impoverished college constituency could not provide. A core group of loyal supporters over the years has enabled NIYC to fulfill many of the organization's original goals. The NIYC is now located in Albuquerque, New Mexico, and is primarily involved in the problems of the Indians of that state.

BIBLIOGRAPHY
Steiner, Stan. *The New Indians.* 1968.

Vine Deloria, Jr.

National Lawyers Guild

Established in February 1937, at the height of NEW DEAL and Congress of Industrial Organizations (CIO) militancy, the National Lawyers Guild—as one of its founders noted on its fiftieth anniversary—was born in the struggle to create a pro-labor, antiracist alternative to the American Bar Association (ABA). Supported initially by prominent liberal politicians and New Deal government officials (Solicitor General and later SUPREME COURT Justice Robert Jackson was an early member), the Guild was largely organized by leftwing activists such as United Auto Workers (UAW) general counsel Maurice Sugar, civil liberties lawyer Carol Weiss King, and other radical lawyers who were either members or allies of the COMMUNIST PARTY USA (CPUSA), which served as both the leading force on the left and a facilitator and coordinator of progressive political action.

At its founding convention, the Guild committed itself to ROOSEVELT's Supreme Court reorganization plan, anti-lynching and anti–poll tax legislation, anti-censorship legislation, and reform of racist immigration laws. With an initial membership of five thousand, the Guild provided legal assistance to trade unionists, civil rights activists, and other groups of the center–left political coalition of the New Deal era. At the same time, it sought to provide practical assistance to young attorneys in supporting themselves and to African-American attorneys particularly, in finding ways to get office space in a segregated society.

The subject of attacks from conservative members of the media and the legal establishment from its beginning, the Guild consistently initiated legal challenges to accepted racist practices; and it opened its journal, the *Lawyer's Guild Review*, to the writings of W. E. B. DU BOIS and liberal NAACP counsel and future Supreme Court Justice Thurgood MARSHALL, when the American Bar Association journal was closed to them and other opponents of RACISM and SEGREGATION.

As the COLD WAR took shape, Guild lawyers, under the leadership of Executive Secretary Martin Popper, fought to revive and sustain New Deal legislation, defend labor, and battle the purges and blacklists of the period, challenging loyalty oaths and providing testimony against the McCarran Internal Security Act (1950), the MCCARRAN-WALTER IMMIGRATION ACT (1952), the Communist Control Act (1954), and other repressive legislation. When the EISENHOWER administration sought in 1953 to destroy the Guild by placing it on the Attorney General's List of Subversive Organizations (references to the Guild as "the legal arm of the Communist party" by Senator Joseph McCarthy and others became a 1950s Cold War mantra), the Guild challenged the concept on which the list was based and resisted the government's campaign step by step. (See MCCARTHYISM.) In a more liberal judicial atmosphere, created by the beginnings of the civil rights movement and the downfall and death of Joseph McCarthy, the administration finally withdrew its case in 1958. Like many blacklisted screenwriters in the period, Guild lawyers often represented their clients for very low fees; but when the cases reached appeals courts or the Supreme Court, they were often taken over by highly paid "respectable" attorneys.

Civil rights had been a central theme in Guild activity since its inception; and, in spite of relentless harassment by the FEDERAL BUREAU OF INVESTIGATION (FBI), it became the Guild's primary concentration in the 1960s. Building coalitions with ABA attorneys, Guild lawyers provided activist legal aid to the civil rights movement at Albany, Georgia; to the Mississippi FREEDOM SUMMER project; and to the MISSISSIPPI FREEDOM DEMOCRATIC PARTY. Guild lawyers also provided activist legal aid to the anti-war movement of the 1960s, and were in the vanguard of the defense of the BLACK PANTHER PARTY and the Chicago Eight. Although the "old left" was supposed to be dead in the 1960s, Guild members and allies such as Arthur Kinoy, Charles Garry, Mort Stavis, and William KUNSTLER became and remained role models for socially conscious lawyers in the United States.

In spite of decades of government campaigns to destroy it and media attempts to deny its achievements or even its continued existence, the National Lawyers Guild survived by keeping true to its founding principles. It has continued to renew itself through its assistance to the National Conference of Black Lawyers and in its attempts to provide legal assistance to the poor, as well as in working for civil rights and civil liberties legislation.

The principles that the Guild stood for and continues to represent were best summed up by African-American attorney and Guild activist Hayward Burns in 1984:

As we toil in the field together that day will come, when
the people come out of the fields and the factories, the
mines and the mills, the steel and glass towers, out of the
ghettoes, the barrios, the reservations . . . to the court—
the citadel of justice, and sit down in their rightful places,
and the doors will fling open before them. And they will
sit in a court of law that is also a court of justice.

BIBLIOGRAPHY

Auerbach, Gerald. *Unequal Justice: Lawyers and Social
Change in Modern America.* 1976.
Bailey, P. Roberts. "Progressive Lawyers: A History of the
National Lawyers Guild, 1936–1958." Ph.D. dissertation, Rutgers University, 1979.
Ginger, Ann Fagan, and Eugene M. Tobin, eds. *The National Lawyers Guild: From Roosevelt Through Reagan.*
1988.

Norman Markowitz

National Negro Congress

In 1933, activist John P. Davis approached Walter
WHITE, executive secretary of the NATIONAL ASSOCIATION FOR THE ADVANCEMENT OF COLORED PEOPLE
(NAACP) with a plan to form a federal watchdog
group representing black organizations across the
country. White assented and the Joint Committee for
National Recovery (JCNR) was established with Davis
at the helm. The JCNR's purpose was to ensure that
the federal government paid heed to the needs of
black organizations. Due to personality conflicts between Davis and White, however, the JCNR was short-
lived. But the JCNR's last organizational act led to the
establishment of one the largest black popular front
organizations, the National Negro Congress (NNC).

In 1935, Davis, with the help of political scientist
Ralph BUNCHE, organized a conference at Howard
University designed to examine the relationship between blacks and the NEW DEAL. The conferees presented a range of suggestions to improve the quality
of black life in the United States. Inspired to action,
postconference plans were drawn up for a national
body representing a broad coalition of black and white
labor, black religious groups, and civil rights and liberties organizations. A year later, the first meeting of
the NNC was called to order in Chicago, Illinois.

The NNC got off to a rousing start with over 800
delegates in attendance and with as many as 8,000 people appearing for the open evening sessions. A. Philip
RANDOLPH, the powerful head of the BROTHERHOOD
OF SLEEPING CAR PORTERS, was elected president. In
one of his first acts, Randolph declared that the future
of black labor and white labor—heretofore considered distinct and often antagonistic elements of the
American workforce—hinged upon mutual coopera-

tion and support. This declaration foreshadowed the
close relationship the civil rights movement leadership
would have with future progressive elements in labor.
Ironically, the policies that were instituted following
Randolph's call for a unified labor movement would
eventually lead to his resignation as NNC president
and contribute to the NNC's collapse.

At the local level, the NNC waged desegregation
battles, fought to increase the hiring of blacks in certain industries, and even campaigned to protect the
rights of black university students. Toward the end of
the 1930s and following Randolph's lead, the NNC at
the national level developed close ties to the Congress
of Industrial Organizations (CIO), the federation believed to be the best hope for black-white labor unity.
As the NNC increasingly relied on the CIO's financial
support the broad-based appeal of the NNC began to
fade for many of its constituents.

At the 1940 meeting of the NNC, Randolph resigned, claiming that the Communist Party (CP) had
infiltrated the Congress and had begun to use it as a
vehicle to enlist black support for the Nazi-Soviet pact.
Furthermore, despite his call for a unified labor movement, Randolph felt compelled to resign because he
never wanted blacks to cede control of their own organizations. This is precisely what he felt was happening with the NNC's relationship with the CIO and the
CP. With Randolph's resignation, the NNC was dramatically weakened and began to fade away.

But even before 1940 cracks had begun to appear
in the structure of the NNC. From the outset, black
conservatives expressed concern about the NNC's emphasis on workers' issues. Complicating matters for
the NNC organizers was the popular feeling among
black ministers that the Congress was too secular.
Clergy began to leave, having made clear their frustration that the delegates appeared more concerned with
economic and political matters than with ecclesiastical
issues. Finally, black professionals joined the ministers'
departure believing that the NNC's focus on labor issues disregarded the importance of entrepreneurship.

The NNC's early successes underline the appeal of
a national organization reflecting the needs and wants
of black Americans. The eventual collapse of the NNC
demonstrates how diverse the needs and wants of the
black community were and how difficult it was for any
single organization to represent black America.

BIBLIOGRAPHY

Griffler, Keith. *What Price Alliance?: Black Radicals Confront
White Labor, 1918–1938.* 1995.
Record, Wilson. *Race and Radicalism: The NAACP and the
Communist Party in Conflict.* 1964.
Wolters, Raymond. *Negroes and the Great Depression.* 1970.

Jonathan Scott Holloway

National Organization for Women

Organized in 1966, the National Organization for Women (NOW) developed into the premier women's rights organization in the United States. After being barred from introducing resolutions at a 1966 meeting of State Commissions on the Status of Women, a group of twenty-eight women, including Betty FRIEDAN and Pauli MURRAY, organized NOW, whose membership included both men and women. Friedan, author of *The Feminine Mystique* (1962), served as NOW's first president. The organizers saw NOW as doing for women what the NATIONAL ASSOCIATION FOR THE ADVANCEMENT OF COLORED PEOPLE (NAACP) had accomplished for African Americans.

Full equality for women was NOW's guiding principle. In practice the organization's aims included an end to discriminatory EMPLOYMENT and job advertising practices, as well as equal educational opportunities for women. In its first year NOW petitioned the federal government, including the EQUAL EMPLOYMENT OPPORTUNITY COMMISSION (EEOC), to comply with and enforce TITLE VII OF THE 1964 CIVIL RIGHTS ACT, which barred employment-related discrimination on the basis of race, color, religion, national origin, or sex. In 1967, NOW began campaigning for the EQUAL RIGHTS AMENDMENT and abortion rights. NOW also pushed for adequate child care, tax deductions for child care expenses, and paid maternity leave for working mothers. The NOW Legal Defense and Education Fund was incorporated in 1970, and has been the motivating power behind many of the women's rights cases brought before the SUPREME COURT. The organization added lesbian rights to its causes in 1971.

In 1968 members uncomfortable with the organization's commitment to abortion rights left NOW to form the Women's Equity Action League (WEAL). Since NOW primarily focused on sexual inequality in the public realm and not on gender roles in the private sphere, the group did not attract radical feminists (see FEMINISM). As a result, NOW's membership has been composed largely of professional women and men. NOW had approximately 300 members shortly after its founding; as of 1999, NOW has half a million members, with over 500 chapters throughout the United States.

From the beginning, NOW's tactics have involved traditional protest strategies such as boycotts, picketing, demonstrations, letter-writing campaigns, lobbying political representatives (and monitoring their votes), and use of the courts to force compliance with antidiscrimination legislation. Regional and state chapters of NOW implement policies set by the national organization, thereby ensuring a grass-roots component to the organization's structure.

Building on the liberalism of the 1960s and the nascent feminism developing among women in the civil rights movement, NOW quickly grew as an organization and counted many early successes. In 1967 President Lyndon JOHNSON signed an executive order barring the government and federal contractors from sex discrimination in hiring practices. In 1973 the Supreme Court decision in *Roe v. Wade* legalized abortion. However, the failure of state legislatures to ratify the Equal Rights Amendment as a constitutional amendment, the conservative social and political climate of the 1980s, and the growth of the right-to-life movement provided powerful challenges to NOW as it pursued its agendas. In the 1990s, NOW continues to fight for an equal rights amendment, economic and employment equality for women, reproductive rights, an end to violence against women (see VIOLENCE AGAINST WOMEN ACT OF 1994), and it promotes societal acceptance of diversities of race, gender, and sexual orientation.

Formed in 1966, the National Organization for Women (NOW) has lobbied, litigated, publicized, and demonstrated for social progress on gender issues. (AP/Wide World Photos)

BIBLIOGRAPHY

Carabillo, Toni, Judith Meuli, and June Bundy Csida. *Feminist Chronicles, 1953–1993.* 1993.

Davis, Flora. *Moving the Mountain: The Women's Movement in America Since 1960.* 1991.

Friedan, Betty. *It Changed My Life: Writings on the Women's Movement.* 1963; 1985 ed.

Gilbert, Jennifer. "Diversity, Difference and Power: The National Organization for Women and the Politics of Identity, 1966–1976." 1998.

National Organization for Women Records, 1966–1992. The Schlesinger Library, Radcliffe College. (NOW records at the Schlesinger Library are not the archives of the National Organization for Women, but are instead unprocessed NOW-related papers donated by former NOW leaders such as Betty Friedan. Access to the collection is restricted to researchers who obtain written permission from the NOW executive committee.)

Michelle A. Krowl

National Parks

Known especially for its large natural parks, which attract millions of visitors annually, the national park system also preserves numerous historical and archeological sites and interprets their significance to American history for visitors. The parks with their physical presence appeal to many visitors who otherwise avoid "history." Their original buildings and objects enhance understanding of our predecessors and their experiences. In earlier years most historical parks commemorated military and political history, but more recently, the National Park Service (NPS) has broadened its understanding of American history.

In 1955 "A Survey of the Public Concerning the National Parks" included this haunting quotation: "Well—we'd never plan to stay at one [a park] for overnight or [a] week because we wouldn't know if negroes [sic] could be allowed to stay in the cabins. I'd like to know if negroes [sic] can go to these places." In 1955, only George Washington Carver's birthplace in Missouri, the Lincoln Memorial, and Harpers Ferry in West Virginia preserved the history of American minorities or women or of civil rights struggles. Although its 1922 dedication had been segregated, Lincoln Memorial hosted Marian Anderson's 1939 Easter Sunday concert after the Daughters of the American Revolution refused her access to their concert hall. In 1963, the Rev. Dr. Martin Luther KING, JR., gave his "I Have a Dream" speech there. One speaker that August day was John Lewis, then head of the STUDENT NONVIOLENT COORDINATING COMMITTEE (SNCC). In 1987, Lewis became a congressman and member of the House Subcommittee on National Parks and Public Lands. There he helped enact legislation incorporating more African-American and civil rights historic sites into the now 378-unit NPS. Charles Pinckney's plantation site in South Carolina, Natchez, the Cane River Creole district in Louisiana, the Dayton Aviation Heritage site in Ohio, the Tuskegee Airmen National Historic Site in Alabama, the Nicodemus site in Kansas, and the New Orleans jazz district have all become parks, as has Manzanar, a World War II Japanese internment camp in California.

Some parks directly memorialize the civil rights movement and its roots. At the Old Courthouse at Jefferson National Expansion Memorial in St. Louis, Dred Scott sued for his freedom in 1846, resulting in the 1857 Supreme Court decision affirming slavery. The Boston African-American's Meetinghouse rang with abolitionists' denunciations of slavery; the Women's Rights' 1848 convention in Seneca Falls, New York, first called for gender equality. In 1859, abolitionist John BROWN raided Harpers Ferry's arsenal. Frederick DOUGLASS's home in Washington, D.C., shows this freed slave, orator, and civil rights pioneer fighting for blacks' and women's rights. The Dayton, Ohio, Aviation Heritage includes site black poet Paul Laurence Dunbar's home. The Mary McLeod Bethune Council House in Washington, D.C., the 1943–1965 headquarters of the NATIONAL COUNCIL OF NEGRO WOMEN, also houses the National Archives for Black Women's History. In Topeka, Kansas, the Monroe school site commemorates the BROWN V. BOARD OF EDUCATION, fight against educational segregation. In Atlanta, Georgia, Martin Luther King, Jr.'s birthplace, neighborhood, grave, and the Ebenezer Baptist Church are preserved; the recently designated Selma to Montgomery Trail in Alabama commemorates the 1965 civil rights march.

Other sites preserve and interpret various groups as they struggled for their rights: The Underground Railroad's preservation is being developed. Natchez, with both an antebellum mansion and the home of free black William Johnson has the interpretation of African Americans, slave and free, as a park purpose. The Cane River Creole National Historic Park preserves two antebellum plantations in Louisiana. Booker T. WASHINGTON's birthplace in Hardy, Virginia; the George Washington Carver National Monument in Diamond, Missouri; the Tuskegee Institute National Historic Site in Alabama with its educational heritage; and the Nicodemus National Historic Site in Kansas all tell of post–Civil War changes, as does the Maggie L. Walker National Historic Site in Richmond, Virginia, commemorating the African-American millionaire and first female bank president.

Other national parks and historic sites commemorate women's struggles for equality: Clara Barton, the American Red Cross's founder (in Glen Echo, Maryland); Eleanor ROOSEVELT, a fervent supporter of human rights (in Hyde Park, New York); and Alice PAUL, suffragist and author of the Equal Rights Amendment (the Sewall-Belmont House in Washington, D.C.).

Still other parks include such history almost inadvertently—plantations once worked by slaves including Robert E. Lee's Arlington House in Virginia; Hampton National Historic Site in Towson, Maryland; and a reconstruction of George Washington's birthplace east of Fredericksburg, Virginia. During the eighteenth century, the Virgin Islands' Christiansted on St. Croix had both an African slave-based sugar economy and a free black population. Fort Davis in Western Texas had African-American ("Buffalo") soldiers, as did many Civil War battlefields.

Parks also preserve and interpret Hispanic history, Native American history, Hawaiian history, First Amendment rights, and religious rights. Changing the name of one historic site from Custer Battlefield to Little Bighorn Battlefield, a civil rights issue for Native Americans, encountered fierce opposition in 1991. While the national park system is slowly becoming more diverse, interpreting that diversity—especially when as controversial as the history of slavery is—remains problematic, with guides at parks sometimes referring to slaves as "servants," obscuring their actual status.

National Park Service

The National Park Service as an organization has only slowly moved toward a culturally diverse workforce. The image of the National Park ranger often remains that of a white male in a Stetson hat. The first NPS civil rights director hired in 1971 to diversify the NPS workforce was then the only person of color among NPS senior management and the highest-ranking African American when most blacks worked in park service maintenance. Most minorities (and women) were kept in the lower paying jobs, with women serving as clerical workers and minority males as maintenance workers. By 1987, such employees had increased to 20 percent minorities, still mostly in clerical and maintenance positions. White women remained less than 25 percent of the workforce but increasingly held nonclerical positions. Five years later, the NPS had grown in total numbers of employees. Most groups—especially black females and Hispanic females—showed somewhat increased representation although black males' percentages decreased slightly. By 1997 women and minorities occupied all occupa-

tional categories and were better distributed throughout the professional and administrative ranks. Still, minority males remained concentrated in maintenance jobs and females in administrative positions. Recruitment and retention of minority and female employees, especially in isolated parks and with discriminatory attitudes still sometimes prevelant make increasing representation of all Americans in the NPS slow. In 1997, Robert G. Stanton became the first African-American director of the National Park Service. Today National Park Service regional directors include one African-American male, one Native-American male, one white female, and four white males—the same proportion as fifteen years ago. Current efforts to include more minorities and females as employees and visitors should eventually increase those numbers.

BIBLIOGRAPHY

Audience Research, Inc. "A Survey of the Public Concerning the National Parks." Conducted for the National Park Service, Department of the Interior. 1955.
Frank Faragasso, and Doug Stover, eds. *Cultural Resource Management: African-American History and Culture: A Remembering.* 1997.
Frank Faragasso, and Doug Stover, eds. *Cultural Resource Management: Slavery and Resistance.* 1998.
National Parks: Index 1997–1999. 1997.
National Park Service. *1987–1992 Workforce Composition Statistical Report.* 1993.
National Park Service. *Workforce Data as of September 30, 1997.* n.d.
National Park Service Website at www.nps.gov.
Official Park Guides for parks named, different dates; all published by NPS.
Sandrage, Scott A. "A Marble House Divided: The Lincoln Memorial, the Civil Rights Movement, and the Politics of Memory, 1939–1963." *Journal of American History* 80, 1 (1993): 135–167.
Savage, Beth L., ed. *African American Historic Places: National Register of Historic Places.* 1994.

Heather Huyck
Dianne Spriggs

National Rifle Association

The National Rifle Association (NRA) is the nation's leading "progun" lobby, dedicated to the RIGHT TO BEAR ARMS. The largest and best-financed special-interest group in the nation's capital, it is commonly recognized as the most powerful lobby in Washington. The NRA believes that any form of gun control will inexorably lead to the total prohibition of any private possession of firearms; therefore, it has challenged any and all legislation designed to circumscribe gun sales

The National Rifle Association, founded in 1871 to protect Second Amendment rights and to promote firearms skill and safety, has been successful in slowing federal efforts to limit the availability of guns and ammunition. Here, NRA mascot Eddie Eagle and executive vice president Wayne LaPierre are shown at a Washington, D.C., news conference. (AP/Wide World Photos)

and ownership, and seeks to preserve for Americans the right to own firearms. Formed in 1871, the NRA was originally a sporting organization intended to promote shooting proficiency, marksmanship, and safety with firearms. Throughout the 1960s and 1970s, the NRA shifted its focus to political action.

The NRA bases its claims on the Second Amendment to the U.S. Constitution, which reads: "A well regulated Militia, being necessary to the security of a free State, the right of the people to keep and bear Arms, shall not be infringed." The NRA insists that its stand is consistent with the expressed intentions of the Founding Fathers in safeguarding American freedom, and that any infringement of this safeguard is a threat to democracy itself. Gun-control groups maintain that the Second Amendment does not provide for the unrestricted possession of guns but only for the maintenance of a militia; and jurists would seem to agree, as the U.S. SUPREME COURT and a number of lower courts have never decided that the Second Amendment prohibits the restriction of certain firearms.

BIBLIOGRAPHY

Anderson, Jervis. *Guns in American Life.* 1984.

Davidson, Osha Gray. *Under Fire: The NRA and the Battle for Gun Control.* 1993.

Christopher Strain

National Student Association

Established in 1947 with covert U.S. government and Central Intelligence Agency (CIA) support, the National Student Association (NSA) came into existence as a response to Communist and other left forces' creation of the World Federation of Democratic Youth (WFDY) and the International Student Association (IUS)—organizations founded after WORLD WAR II to mobilize students on such issues as COLONIALISM, peace, and social EQUALITY.

Much controversy exists concerning CIA control of the NSA, particularly the involvement its most influential leader and early president (1950–1952), Allard Lowenstein, distinguished for his later civil rights, ANTI-APARTHEID, and anti–VIETNAM WAR activism. However, there is no doubt that the CIA controlled the NSA pursestrings in the 1950s and 1960s, thus destroying its independence and limiting the support it could give to civil rights activists and others engaged in struggles for domestic reform in the United States.

With CIA support, the NSA withdrew from the IUS and recruited through the NSA-connected Independent Research Service (led by former NSA vice president Paul Sigmund and Gloria STEINEM), sending delegations to world youth festivals at Vienna (1959) and Helsinki (1962) to challenge Communist and left influence. In so doing, the NSA often using

McCarthyite tactics to disrupt and discredit the festivals. The NSA played a role in the creation of the World Assembly of Youth (WAY), the CIA-funded counterpart to WFDY. Although there is a good deal of controversy on this point, some NSA representatives have admitted providing intelligence reports to the CIA on their international contacts.

Also, NSA officers often joined the CIA and then recruited students to work in the NSA. On civil rights and other domestic issues, the NSA supported positions of the liberal wing of the DEMOCRATIC PARTY, which, ironically, made it subject to attack from conservatives as left-wing, particularly from the conservative student organization Young Americans for Freedom (YAF) and conservative publisher and media personality William F. Buckley, Jr., in the early 1960s.

The radicalization of students in the 1960s—represented by the leadership of the STUDENT NONVIOLENT COORDINATING COMMITTEE in civil rights struggles and the growth of the STUDENTS FOR A DEMOCRATIC SOCIETY (SDS), involved in both campus and anti–Vietnam War issues—furthered divisions in the NSA, whose younger leadership included such figures as George McGovern campaign organizer Rick Stearns and anti–Vietnam War activist Sam Brown. In March 1967, an article in *Ramparts* magazine detailing CIA direction of the NSA's international activities devastated the organization, whose leadership repudiated all connections with the CIA and endorsed the "Dump Johnson" movement led by its former president Allard Lowenstein.

In 1982, after a long period of decline, the NSA joined with the National Student Lobby to form the United States Student Association, lobbying for student interests on such issues as student loans, scholarships, and tuition. Although Allard Lowenstein, Gloria Steinem, and others connected to the NSA's activities in the 1950s and 1960s went on to make major contributions to the struggle for civil rights, women's rights, and peace, the NSA–CIA connection did not help their reputations.

More important, the NSA's cold war international activities, reflexive anticommunist ideology, and CIA ties played a major role in preventing it from serving as the center of a progressive student movement in the 1960s at a time when student activism was at its all-time peak—even as the cold war priorities of the TRUMAN, KENNEDY, and JOHNSON administrations discredited and largely negated their liberal domestic programs.

BIBLIOGRAPHY

Allard K. Lowenstein Papers. Nicholas Murray Butler Library, New York, N.Y.

Chafe, William. *Never Stop Running: Allard Lowenstein and the Struggle to Save American Liberalism.* 1993.
Cummings, Richard. *The Pied Piper: Allard K. Lowenstein and the Liberal Dream.* 1985.
Kotek, Joel. *Students and the Cold War,* translated by Ralph Blumenau. 1996.

Norman Markowitz

National Urban League

An interracial group of elite blacks and whites established the National Urban League (NUL) in New York City in 1911. Concerned about the adjustment of black migrants new to northern and southern cities, the founders of the National League on Urban Conditions Among Negroes (its early name) initiated social work programs to address EMPLOYMENT discrimination, aid job placement, improve relationships with labor unions, and ameliorate the HOUSING and health conditions that blacks faced in urban areas. Although the national organization drew philanthropic support, a network of affiliates supported locally by community chests allowed the League to spread to eighteen cities by 1918. Professional social workers constituted the staff in each affiliate, and they played major roles as liaisons between blacks and industrial employers during the 1910s, 1920s, and beyond.

Developing resources and defining programs to support these activities became the responsibility of several national executive directors, among them George E. Haynes, Eugene Kinckle Jones, and Lester

National Urban League president John Jacobs speaking at a 1993 meeting. Originally formed to help migrant African Americans from the rural South to adjust to urban life in the North, the National Urban League pioneered social-service training for blacks. (AP/Wide World Photos)

B. Granger, who took office in 1941. Although Granger succeeded in increasing the national budget and the number of affiliates, he, unlike his predecessors, became more involved albeit reluctantly in civil rights activities. As militant black leaders and their grass-roots followers pressed federal officials and private employers to end employment discrimination, desegregate the ARMED FORCES, and pass civil rights legislation, Granger, pushed by younger local League executives, joined A. Philip RANDOLPH of the BROTHERHOOD OF SLEEPING CAR PORTERS and the NAACP's Walter Francis WHITE and his successor, Roy WILKINS, to articulate blacks' demands.

Whitney M. YOUNG, JR., executive director of the Omaha Urban League in the early 1950s, was one of the younger NUL officials who wanted Granger to identify the League with black activism. A World War II veteran who earned his social work degree on the G. I. Bill, Young, as industrial relations secretary of the St. Paul Urban League (from 1947 to 1950), learned that marching and picketing supplemented traditional League techniques. When he failed to convince employers to hire blacks or when his negotiations with biased realtors yielded few results, Young supported direct-action activities to achieve integrationist objectives. These beliefs and his experiences as an advisor to student activists from Atlanta University Center convinced NUL trustees to elect him Granger's successor in 1961.

During Young's ten-year term the League became closely identified with the civil rights movement. Young marched conspicuously in the 1963 MARCH ON WASHINGTON. In 1965 he walked with Martin Luther KING, JR., in the Selma-to-Montgomery March. He publicly pressed presidents John F. KENNEDY, Lyndon B. JOHNSON, and Richard M. NIXON to aid the civil rights cause. With urgency, he told corporate and foundation officials that because of riots in the inner cities massive funding was necessary for job training, housing rehabilitation, and business development. Even as he eschewed the term "BLACK POWER," he stressed the legitimate doubts of those blacks who questioned whether INTEGRATION was an achievable objective. Although Young channeled unprecedented funds from corporate, foundation, and federal sources to the NUL affiliates, he also encouraged local officials to redouble efforts in employment, housing, and education without neglecting protest methods whenever these promised better results.

BIBLIOGRAPHY

Dickerson, Dennis C. *Militant Mediator: Whitney M. Young, Jr.* 1998.
Moore, Jesse T., Jr. *A Search for Equality: The National Urban League, 1910–1961.* 1981.
Weiss, Nancy J. *The National Urban League, 1910–1940.* 1974.

Dennis C. Dickerson

National Welfare Rights Organization

During the 1960s, poor women came together together in a protest movement demanding "welfare rights." The protests were concentrated in the big Northern cities, and the protesters were mainly African Americans, although in some places they were Hispanics and in others whites. The women gathered in churches, community centers, antipoverty program offices, and homes, where they shared their experiences of poverty and government indifference. This was a time when thousands of families were migrating from the rural South and Puerto Rico to the big cities of the North, but deindustrialization in the cities meant a decrease in unskilled jobs at living wages. As a result, a huge reservoir was built of impoverished people, many of them in families headed by women. Few of these families got welfare benefits, partly because welfare so shamed people that few asked for it, and partly because welfare departments were skilled in stratagems of denial. However, the civil rights movement helped redefine the resulting poverty as the fault of the system, not of the poor, a fault that could be corrected by government action. By 1966, picketing and SIT-INS at welfare centers were spreading, fueled by the ideas that poor mothers deserved respect and that they deserved the income needed to raise their children, even a government-guaranteed income. Like the Southern civil rights struggle and the Northern riots, the protests by these women were an important expression of the post-WORLD WAR II black movement.

In 1967, many of these local groups came together to found the National Welfare Rights Organization (NWRO), led by George A. Wiley, who had recently resigned as associate national director of the CONGRESS OF RACIAL EQUALITY after losing out in a competition with Floyd McKISSICK to succeed James FARMER. Wiley became NWRO's first executive director, with Timothy Sampson as associate director. The top policy-making group, called the National Coordinating Committee of Welfare Rights Groups, was composed of one member from each state chapter. Johnnie Tillmon, a welfare rights leader from Watts, was elected chair, followed several years later by Beulah Sanders, a leader from New York City.

Federal community action programs often provided resources; many VISTAs (Volunteers in Service to America), for example, staffed welfare rights groups. NWRO leaders also worked closely with antipoverty legal services attorneys, who won stunning victories in the U.S. SUPREME COURT against residence laws (*Shapiro v. Thompson*), man-in-the-house rules (*King v. Smith*), employable mother rules (*Anderson v. Burson*), and other legal barriers that kept destitute families off the welfare rolls. At its peak in 1969, NWRO had 22,000 dues-paying members, and had sponsored hundreds of demonstrations. Afterwards, as urban rioting subsided and the civil rights movement lost its momentum, the number of local welfare rights groups fell sharply, and NWRO collapsed in 1973.

In retrospect, the welfare rights movement should be credited with two main achievements. First, it helped reduce poverty by making government benefits more available to women and children. The welfare rolls rose from 750,000 families in 1960 to more than three million in the early 1970s. Along with Food Stamps and Medicaid, many billions of dollars in welfare benefits and services were distributed to what Wiley called "the poorest of the poor."

The welfare rights movement also contributed to the pressures that led CONGRESS in 1972 to legislate the Supplemental Security Income program for the indigent elderly and disabled. Faced with rising complaints from mayors and governors about the growing costs of welfare, Congress had a choice of relieving local fiscal strains either by federalizing welfare or by federalizing the relief programs for the elderly and disabled. Congress chose the latter course, but the contribution of poor women in creating the political preconditions for this major antipoverty reform cannot be ignored.

BIBLIOGRAPHY

Hertz, Susan Handley. *The Welfare Mothers Movement: A Decade of Change for Poor Women?* 1981.

Kotz, Nick, and Mary Lynn Kotz. *A Passion for Equality: George Wiley and the Movement.* 1977.

Piven, Frances Fox, and Richard A. Cloward. *Regulating the Poor.* 1971.

Piven, Frances Fox, and Richard A. Cloward. *Poor People's Movements.* 1977.

West, Guida. *The National Welfare Rights Movement: Social Protest of Poor Women.* 1981.

Frances Fox Piven
Richard A. Cloward

National Woman's Party

The National Woman's Party (NWP) was formed in 1912 to pressure the national government to pass an amendment granting women suffrage (the right to vote). Originally known as the Congressional Union for Woman Suffrage, the organization began as a branch of the NATIONAL AMERICAN WOMAN SUFFRAGE ASSOCIATION (NAWSA). The group's leader, Alice PAUL, however, grew frustrated with NAWSA and led the Congressional Union out of that organization.

During the elections of 1914 and 1916, Paul and the Congressional Union attacked Democrats (who controlled Congress and the presidency) for failing to support suffrage. It was during the 1916 elections that the group took the name National Woman's Party and ran candidates for office. Never expecting to win in the elections, the NWP hoped its presence would demonstrate the strength of support for suffrage and force other candidates to address the issue.

The NWP next turned its attention to President Woodrow Wilson. In January 1917, NWP members began picketing the White House around the clock. Picketers were verbally and physically attacked; some were arrested on false charges. Despite these hard-

A group of suffragettes picket in front of the White House for the National Woman's Party in 1917. (Library of Congress)

ships, the picketing continued for eighteen months and helped wear down Wilson's resistance. In 1918, the president spoke out publicly in favor of a suffrage amendment. After months of debate Congress passed an amendment in 1919. On August 18, 1920, the NINE-TEENTH AMENDMENT was ratified, and women gained the right to vote. Many other organizations played a part in this victory, but the NWP was remarkable for its militancy and highly visible activities.

In 1923, the NWP drafted an amendment to the Constitution called the EQUAL RIGHTS AMENDMENT (ERA), designed to protect women's equality. The group campaigned for this idea for decades, and Congress finally passed the ERA in 1972. However, it was not ratified by the states. Even before the failure of the ERA, the NWP was losing importance as other organizations came to the forefront of the women's rights movement. Although the NWP continued its efforts for an ERA into the 1980s and 1990s, it was no longer a major voice in national affairs.

BIBLIOGRAPHY

Bernhard, Nancy E., and David McLean. "Alice Paul." In *American Decades, 1910–1919*, edited by Vincent Tompkins. 1996.
Gillmore, Inez Haynes. *The Story of Alice Paul and the National Woman's Party.* 1977.

John McCoy

Elijah Muhammad led the Nation of Islam for more than thirty years. Under his leadership, followers were encouraged to seek economic self-reliance and to rediscover their cultural identity. (CORBIS/Bettmann)

Nation of Islam

The Nation of Islam began in Detroit, Michigan in 1930, as the Allah Temple of Islam, a small black-nationalist Islamic movement founded by W. D. Fard, a Muslim missionary from the East, who preached a philosophy of political self-determination and racial separatism to the newly arrived black Southerners of the Great Migration. Fard believed that Western civilization would soon end in a race war, and he established an institutional framework—the Fruit of Islam, the Muslim Girls Training Corps, and the University of Islam—to separate black Muslims from white Christian America. Believed to be a victim of police brutality, Fard disappeared mysteriously in 1934 after he assigned leadership of his community to Elijah MUHAMMAD. Elijah Muhammad led the Nation of Islam until 1975, from its Chicago headquarters, and was the most important figure in the development of black nationalism and Islam among African Americans in the twentieth century. The members of the Nation of Islam believe that their ancestors are Asiatics, who were the original Muslims and the first inhab-itants of the earth, and they claim a divine identity for black Americans and for their founder, W. D. Fard, and prophetic status for Elijah Muhammad.

Building on the WORLD WAR I era black-nationalist legacies of Marcus GARVEY's UNIVERSAL NEGRO IMPROVEMENT ASSOCIATION and Noble Drew Ali's Moorish Science Temple of America, the goal of the Nation of Islam is to achieve racial justice for African Americans in their own nation or territory in the United States. This community plans to achieve its goal through a program that demands: the discipline of Islam; racial separatism; black economic and community development; equal opportunity and justice under the law; freedom for all Muslims in the federal prisons and for all black people on death row in U.S. prisons; an immediate end to racial violence and police brutality; exemption for African Americans from all taxation until racial justice is achieved; and equitable but racially separate educational institutions for all black Muslim children.

During WORLD WAR II, the Nation of Islam's membership decreased dramatically, as Elijah Muhammad and his son Herbert became involved politically with Satokata Takahashi, a Japanese national organizer among black Americans. Father and son were convicted of selective service violations (refusal to register for the draft) and were political prisoners in the federal penitentiary in Milan, Michigan from 1942 to 1946. In the 1950s and 1960s, as black Americans and Africans cracked the political power of white supremacy in the United States and abroad, Elijah Muhammad's institutional quest for economic power made the Nation of Islam the wealthiest black organization in American history. In that era, the Nation of Islam provided a community model and political inspiration for the BLACK POWER movement. MALCOLM X's phenomenal organizing efforts among young lower-class black men in Northern cities created powerful constituencies for the Nation of Islam across the United States; and the *Muhammad Speaks* newspaper, edited by a leftward-leaning staff, provided exemplary coverage of international news and anticolonial struggles in Asia and Africa. Elijah Muhammad's books, *Message to the Blackman in America* and *The Fall of America*, offered a powerful message of racial separatism, self-discipline, and black community development in the midst of the integrationist strategies and tactics of the civil rights movement. However, as the political tactics and strategies of the civil rights and black power movements became more sophisticated, Elijah Muhammad's economic agenda for his community produced a conservative vision of political activism, which was the deciding factor in Malcolm X's departure from the Nation of Islam in 1964.

In 1975, Elijah Muhammad died, and his son Warith Deen Muhammad inherited leadership of the Nation of Islam. The son made sweeping political and doctrinal changes to align his community with Sunni Islam. However, since 1978, Louis FARRAKHAN has led a revived Nation of Islam and published the *Final Call* newspaper. Farrakhan publicly endorsed the black presidential candidate, Rev. Jesse JACKSON, in 1984, and received $5 million for black American economic development from Libyan leader Muammar el-Qaddafi in 1985. His greatest political achievement was the organization of the MILLION MAN MARCH in 1995, which brought the healing spirit of Islam to more than one million black men who gathered in Washington D.C., and was the largest political gathering of African Americans in American history. Recognized as a gifted speaker, with a deep commitment to black community development, Farrakhan has been acknowledged as one of the most important political leaders in black America. Major factions of the Nation of Islam are led by John Muhammad in Highland Park, Michigan; Silas Muhammad in Atlanta, Georgia; and Emmanuel Muhammad in Baltimore, Maryland.

BIBLIOGRAPHY

Allen, Ernest, Jr. "Religions Heterodoxy and Nationalist Tradition: The Continuing Evolution of the Nation of Islam." *The Black Scholar* 26 (Fall–Winter 1996): 2–34.

Clegg, Claude Andrew, III. *An Original Man: The Life and Times of Elijah Muhammad.* 1997.

Essien-Udom, E. U. *Black Nationalism.* 1962.

Lincoln, C. Eric. *The Black Muslims in America,* rev. ed. 1994.

Malcolm X (with Alex Haley). *The Autobiography of Malcolm X.* 1965.

McCloud, Aminah Beverly. *African American Islam.* 1995.

Turner, Richard Brent. *Islam in the African-American Experience.* 1997.

Richard Brent Turner

Native Alaskan Civil Rights

American culture impacted Alaska Natives later than most other American native people. The United States did not acquire Alaska until 1867, and not until the twentieth century did appreciable numbers of nonnatives migrate to the region.

Of the major groups of Alaska Natives—Tlingit and Haida Indians, Athabaskan Indians, Aleuts, and Yupik- and Inupiaq-speaking Eskimos—only two, Aleuts and Tlingit Indians, were impacted significantly by the Russians, who lightly colonized Alaska after 1741. The Russians thoroughly subjugated the Aleut population, forcing the islanders into virtual servitude. In addition, virgin soil epidemics reduced the Aleuts from about twenty thousand to two thousand between 1741 and 1800.

The Tlingit Indians fared better than the Aleuts. A more sophisticated culture characterized by exogamous clan organization and a biotically abundant environment, the Tlingit early forced the Russians to become dependent upon them for food, and routinely threatened the Europeans with violence. Twenty-five years before the sale of Russian America, the government recognized the Tlingit as an "independent, settled" indigenous people entitled to protection of their lands and livelihood.

Because the U.S. CONGRESS suspended treaty-making in 1871, four years after the Alaska purchase, there were never treaties between the United States and Alaska Natives, all of whom were economically self-sufficient; neither were there traditional Indian reservations. Thus Alaska Natives enjoyed a distinct, more independent status than other American natives, which facilitated protection of their civil rights in the twentieth century. An aggressive people, many Tlingit welcomed American missionaries in the 1870s and embraced acculturation of American values.

Tlingit leaders educated in mission schools founded the first effective Native organization in the territory in 1912, the Alaska Native Brotherhood (ANB), which encouraged education and individual economic initiative. An Alaska Native Sisterhood (ANS) was founded three years later. By that time, Natives had begun to vote in territorial elections. In 1915 the ANB lobbied for a territorial Native citizenship act, which provided citizenship for specific Natives if they were endorsed by white residents.

The ANB became an effective representative of all Alaska Native rights in the 1920s and 1930s, helping to elect the first Alaska Native to the territorial legislature in 1924, Tlingit attorney William Lewis Paul, who worked successfully for Native widows' and orphans' benefits. Paul already had successfully defended Native voting rights.

In the 1940s, ANB and ANS leaders lobbied the territorial legislature for an antidiscrimination act. Elizabeth Peratrovich of Klawock provided leadership and inspiration leading to passage of the Alaska Equal Rights Act of 1945, banning discrimination. In the 1950s the ANB supported Alaska statehood.

In 1971, the U.S. Congress passed the ALASKA NATIVE CLAIMS SETTLEMENT ACT, establishing regional and village development corporations for all Alaska Natives, capitalized with $962.5 million; all Natives became corporate stockholders. The act confirmed Alaska Native title to 44 million acres of Alaska lands, and extinguished Native title to the remaining 330 million acres. The act identified 211 Alaska Native villages. In 1978, responding to Native demand, the state agreed to construct and fund high schools in all villages with more than fifteen eligible students. In 1980, Congress passed the Alaska Lands Act, which guaranteed Natives access to subsistence resources, a federal protection of Native needs and lifestyles contested by the state.

Today Alaska Natives enjoy full protection of their civil rights as Americans, though the administration of justice in Native villages is slow, and Natives are disproportionately represented as defendants in the state's criminal justice system.

BIBLIOGRAPHY

Arnold, Robert D. *Alaska Native Land Claims.* 1976.
Case, David S. *Alaska Natives and American Laws.* 1984.
Cole, Terrence M. "Jim Crow in Alaska: The Passage of the Equal Rights Act of 1945." *Western Historical Quarterly* 23 (November 1992): 428–44.
Haycox, Stephen. "Economic Development and Indian Land Rights in Modern Alaska: The 1947 Tongass Timber Act." *Western Historical Quarterly* 21 (February 1990): 20–46.
Haycox, Stephen. "William Paul, Sr., and the Alaska Voters' Literacy Act of 1925." *Alaska History* 2 (Winter 1986–87): 16–37.
Hinckley, Ted C. *John G. Brady: Missionary, Businessman, Judge and Governor, 1878–1918.* 1982.
Hinckley, Ted C. *The Canoe Rocks: Alaska's Tlingit and the EuroAmerican Frontier, 1800–1912.* 1996.
Mitchell, Donald Craig. *Sold American: The Story of Alaska Natives and Their Land.* 1997.

Stephen Haycox

Native American Graves Protection and Repatriation Act of 1990

The Native American Graves Protection and Repatriation Act of 1990 (NAGPRA) addresses an interrelated set of civil and cultural rights issues that stem from the early years of contact between Europeans and Native Americans and extend to the present day. The primary purpose of NAGPRA is to provide Native Americans and Native Hawaiians with legal protection for the graves and the remains of their ancestors. Most state and local governments long ago established legal protections for graves, graveyards, and human remains. For several reasons, Native American graves and human remains were generally exempted from such legal protection. Equally important, in a situation unlike that of any other group in America, the remains of hundreds of thousands of Native Americans reside in museums, universities, and federal agencies across the nation. In the vast majority of instances, these remains were acquired without the approval, or often even the knowledge, of the tribes or families with whom they were affiliated. This unique situation is the result, in the broadest sense, of the conflict between Europeans and Native Americans—a conflict that extended over several hundred years and across the entire nation.

From the seventeenth century through the late nineteenth century, Native Americans posed a serious impediment to European colonization and settlement. By the last quarter of the nineteenth century, the final days of armed conflict were occurring among the U.S. Army, U.S. citizens, and Native Americans in various parts of the West. Tribes in the remainder of the country had already been decimated by war and disease or placed on reservations (most often located far from their homelands). There was every indication that Native Americans would either become assimilated into the larger society or "disappear." That expectation, known as the "Vanishing Redman" theory, was widely accepted during the last part of the nineteenth century. In response to it, museums, universities, and federal agencies undertook a massive collection effort to "preserve" Native American culture before it disappeared. This effort included widespread disinterment of Native American graves for scientific study. Native American human remains were collected for other purposes as well. For many years, the Army decapitated the remains of Native American men, women, and children killed in battle for use in phrenology studies apparently aimed at "proving" the intellectual and cultural inferiority of Native peoples.

Most Native American cultures and religions have strong beliefs regarding the treatment of ancestors. Wholesale removal of remains from graves without permission of tribes or families and their placement in museums and other agencies caused great pain, anguish, and suffering among the vast majority of Native American people. These actions constituted a fundamental breach of personal, cultural, and tribal identity and a basic violation of religious beliefs. Native American efforts during the 1970s and 1980s to repatriate the remains of their ancestors from museums, universities, and federal agencies most often proved unsuccessful, in absence of the force of law.

In the late 1980s, Native Americans developed legislation and had it introduced to CONGRESS to address repatriation issues not only for human remains but also for cultural items. A long and difficult dialogue ensued, which included political confrontation between Native American people and museums, universities, and federal agencies. Eventually this dialogue resulted in a fundamental shift in longstanding values and principles in the national museum community regarding Native American rights. Compromise legislation was negotiated and passed in 1990 to provide for repatriation of human remains whose cultural affiliation could be established.

NAGPRA also provides for repatriation of certain cultural items, including sacred objects, objects of cultural patrimony, and unassociated funerary objects (objects that were originally part of a grave but were, at some point, separated from remains). The law establishes a process by which right of possession for such items may be determined. Finally, NAGPRA provides new protections for Native American graves and human remains on federal lands and prohibits trade in Native American human remains.

NAGPRA legislation marked a watershed in the relationship among Native Americans, museums, universities, scientific communities, and federal agencies. The legislation is complex, and elements of it remain contentious. However, on the whole, all parties affected by the legislation have helped implement it in good faith. The legislation has unquestionably helped to enhance the cultural, religious, and personal integrity of many Native Americans through repatriation of the remains of their ancestors or the repatriation of important cultural items. Through the dialogue between Native Americans and museums and related agencies that is required by the legislation, important

advances have been made in understanding and appreciating Native American art and culture. The legislation has also helped redress wrongs done in the past.

BIBLIOGRAPHY
Native American Graves Protection and Repatriation Act, *25 U.S.C. 3001 et seq.* [November 16, 1990] *U.S. House Report 101-877.* [October 15, 1990]

Dan L. Monroe

Native American Movement

The Native American Movement differed from other American civil rights movements because its main thrust often sought not integration into the dominant society, but rather preservation of separate, sovereign rights. Some might argue the Native American Movement dates to Opechancanough (Pamunkey, 1544?–1646), or Popé (Pueblo, 1630?–1690?), each of whom organized a pantribal resistance to European encroachment and fought to preserve native culture and autonomy. Others might date the movement to the last quarter of the nineteenth century when a variety of reform groups organized to improve the condition of Native Americans. Non-Indians dominated these groups, often broadly labeled "Friends of the Indian," and set agendas aimed at Americanizing Indians by eradicating all signs of Indianness. Only the National Indian Defense Association solicited Indian input and advocated self-determination. The Indian Rights Association, founded in 1882, sought to expose government malfeasance in administering Indian affairs, and intended to protect Indian rights by gaining U.S. citizenship for Indians and allotting tribal lands to individuals. As the twentieth century dawned, Chitto Harjo (Creek) led a pantribal movement in present Oklahoma to retain tribal customs, such as traditional tribal government and common land ownership, by resisting allotment.

The Native American Movement arguably began in 1911 with the SOCIETY OF AMERICAN INDIANS (SAI). Organizers modeled the SAI on the Indian Rights Association, but limited full membership to Indians. The SAI sought to address issues affecting a wide Indian constituency, including the nature of Indian relations to the BUREAU OF INDIAN AFFAIRS and the legality of peyote. Internal divisions, failure to cultivate widespread support among reservation communities, and difficulties raising funds contributed to the SAI's dissolution in the 1920s.

The NATIONAL CONGRESS OF AMERICAN INDIANS (NCAI) became the leading Indian rights group—some argue the most important Indian rights group in U.S. history—at its advent in 1944. The NCAI limited full membership to Indians. Non-Indians could join as associates without voting privileges. During its first two decades, the NCAI lobbied against federal termination policy (government attempts to end federal ties to Indian communities and federal support of tribal governments). The NCAI also endorsed the American Indian Chicago Conference in June 1961, a meeting of nearly five hundred Indians from ninety communities who wrote the "Declaration of Indian Purpose," a statement calling for the end of termination policy and advocating broad protection of Indian rights. More recently, the NCAI lobbied for Great Society benefits and it continues to advocate political causes and education.

Younger Indian leaders became disillusioned with the NCAI's conservative approach and criticized the NCAI for not defending American Indian culture. These younger activists formed the NATIONAL INDIAN YOUTH COUNCIL (NIYC) in 1961 to stir more aggressive political action and to promote cultural traditions as a source of pride and survival skills. The NIYC cooperated with the Makah tribal council to organize demonstrations to defend Indian fishing rights in the Pacific Northwest. In a series of "fish-ins" beginning in March 1964, Indians claiming treaty rights to fish the Quillayute River in WASHINGTON state began fishing without state fishing licenses, leading game wardens to arrest the fishers. The fishing protests led to a series of federal court cases from 1968 to 1979 in which the courts upheld fishing rights outlined in nineteenth-century treaties. Pressure from the NIYC also pushed the NCAI to become more active and to embrace "RED POWER," a phrase first used by Vine DELORIA, Jr., at the 1966 NCAI convention.

The generation gap in the movement expanded during the 1960s. Tribal leaders elected during the 1930s and 1940s generally distanced themselves from the African-American civil rights movement, viewing its own goals of maintaining tribal identities and special rights as unique. This generation tended to prefer working within established political channels. Meanwhile, younger American Indian activists participated in the civil rights movement and borrowed both tactics and rhetoric. The growing urban Indian population produced by the federal relocation program fostered this interaction and also contributed to more activism as urban Indians began to identify increasing numbers of pantribal issues.

In 1968 the movement expanded and took a militant turn with the formation of American Indians United, United Native Americans, and the most important and best-known Indian rights group, the AMERICAN INDIAN MOVEMENT (AIM). Its founders created AIM largely to fight problems of urban Indians. Indians in Minneapolis and St. Paul, for instance,

had difficulty finding work, lived in dilapidated housing, suffered from low incomes, and complained of police harassment and brutality. In a tactic probably inspired by the BLACK PANTHERS in California, members of the Twin Cities Indian community formed "Indian patrols" to monitor interactions between Indians and police. Anishinabe leaders, including George Mitchell, Mary Jane Wilson, and Dennis BANKS, organized the AIM in the summer of 1968 to protect urban Indians' rights, although it ultimately organized protests around the country, including on reservations. AIM supported and combined with Indians of All Tribes when the latter group occupied Alcatraz Island in November 1969. In 1970 AIM members occupied Mount Rushmore to call attention to Indian rights issues. In 1972 AIM and the NIYC participated in the "TRAIL OF BROKEN TREATIES," an automobile caravan that crossed the United States from the West Coast to Washington, D.C., to present to the BIA grievances and demands, including land restoration and renegotiation of all treaties. When government officials stalled, AIM occupied BIA headquarters.

AIM's best-known protest occurred in February 1973 at the Pine Ridge Reservation in SOUTH DAKOTA. Oglala Lakota traditionalists requested AIM's support in a dispute with the reservation government headed by Richard Wilson. Armed AIM members occupied the village of Wounded Knee to protest Wilson's authoritarian rule and to advocate indigenous sovereignty. (See WOUNDED KNEE OCCUPATION.) The U.S. government sent a heavily armed force to surround Wounded Knee, producing a siege from February 28 to May 7. The protest failed to return the Lakotas to a treaty relationship to the United States and to reinstate a tribal form of government, left two AIM members killed in firefights, and saw the U.S. government add AIM to the list of war protesters and civil rights activists considered enemies. Conflict between AIM and the government simmered until a 1975 shootout between FBI agents and AIM members on the Pine Ridge Reservation, which left two federal agents dead and AIM member Leonard Peltier imprisoned for life. AIM organized the Longest Walk in 1978, an event similar to the Trail of Broken Treaties and, perhaps, the group's last national protest. AIM continues to function at the local level.

The Native American Movement has fought for Indian rights for more than a century. Indian activism peaked during the 1960s and 1970s when it contributed to the NIXON administration adopting a policy of Indian self-determination and prompted Congress to return some tribal lands. The struggle for Indian rights continues in the judicial and political arenas, focusing on issues such as sovereignty, repatriation, and gaming.

Timeline

1911 Society of American Indians founded. First pantribal organization dedicated to addressing Indian issues. Internecine disagreements and narrow constituency rendered group ineffective, and it disbanded in the 1920s.

1934 Indian Reorganization Act adopted. Paved way for restructuring tribal governments based on written constitutions. Produced divisions within some tribes between those favoring the act and those preferring to retain traditional tribal governments.

1944 National Congress of American Indians founded. Emerged as the largest, most enduring, most reliable force for Indian input into federal policy making.

1961 Chicago Conference produced "Declaration of Indian Purpose"; National Indian Youth Council established.

1964 Fish-ins staged in Washington state with cooperation of Washington tribes and NIYC.

1968 American Indians United, United Native Americans, and American Indian Movement established.

1969 Alcatraz Island occupied by Indian people organized as Indians of All Tribes; occupation lasts until June 1971.

1970 Protesters occupy Fort Lawton in Seattle, Washington, Ellis Island in new York Harbor, and the *Mayflower II* and demonstrate at Plymouth Rock in Massachusetts.

1972 Trail of Broken Treaties organized by nine activist groups including AIM and NIYC. Caravans of protesters from Los Angeles, San Francisco, and Seattle converged at St. Paul, Minnesota, drafted grievances, and proceeded to Washington, D.C., where they occupied the Bureau of Indian Affairs building for five days in November.

1973 AIM leaders organize protest judicial system's handling of the Wesley Bad Heart Bull murder in Custer, South Dakota. On February 27, activists organized by AIM leaders occupy Wounded Knee, South Dakota, and hold the village until May 8.

1975 Two FBI agents killed in shootout with AIM members at Pine Ridge Reservation leading to the conviction of Leonard Peltier.

BIBLIOGRAPHY

Barringer, Sandra. "Indian Activism and the American Indian Movement: A Bibliographical Essay." *American Indian Culture and Research Journal* 21 (1997): 217–250.

Churchill, Ward, and Jim Vander Wall. *Agents of Repression: The FBI's Secret Wars Against the Black Panther Party and the American Indian Movement.* 1988.

Deloria, Vine, Jr. *Custer Died for Your Sins: An Indian Manifesto.* 1969.

Deloria, Vine, Jr. *Behind the Trail of Broken Treaties.* 1974.

Gibson, Arrell Morgan. *The American Indian, Prehistory to the Present.* 1980.

Matthiesson, Peter. *In the Spirit of Crazy Horse.* 1991.

Means, Russell. *Where White Men Fear to Tread: The Autobiography of Russell Means.* 1995.

Nabokov, Peter. *Native American Testimony: A Chronicle of Indian–White Relations from Prophecy to the Present, 1492–1992.* 1991.

Rawls, James J. *Chief Red Fox Is Dead: A History of Native Americans since 1945.* 1996.

Smith, Paul Chaat, and Robert Allen Warrior. *Like a Hurricane: The Indian Movement from Alcatraz to Wounded Knee.* 1996.

Todd M. Kerstetter

Native American Rights Fund

Created in 1970 with the support of the Ford Foundation, the Native American Rights Fund (NARF) supports a national Indian defense effort dedicated to protecting the survival and strengthening the sovereignty of the 557 federally recognized tribes and the 2 million Indian individuals living in the United States today. From the NARF main office in Boulder, Colorado, and branch offices in Anchorage, Alaska, and Washington, D.C., fifteen attorneys and their support staff represent Indian tribes and individuals in cases reflecting numerous issues in the field of Indian law and the five priorities developed by NARF's governing Board of Directors: preservation of tribal existence; protection of tribal natural resources; promotion of Native American human rights; accountability of governments to Native Americans; and development of Indian law.

Preservation of Tribal Existence

Activity in this area emphasizes continuity of tribal traditions, enforcement of treaty rights, and support for the rights of tribal governments to conduct and regulate their internal affairs. Specific work has focused on jurisdictional issues, federal restoration and recognition of tribal status, and economic development. Recent cases involve the integrity and jurisdiction of tribal courts, taxation authority of "Indian Country" tribes and communities, and tribal petitions and challenges regarding their federal acknowledgment.

Protection of Tribal Natural Resources

A sufficient and legally protected land and natural resource base is essential for the economic viability of tribes. Many Native American Rights Fund activities pertain to protecting the approximately 56 million acres of Indian-controlled land in the continental United States and the 44 million acres of land owned by Alaskan Natives. Recent cases concern compensation to the Alabama-Coushatta Tribes of Texas for 3.4 million acres of ancestral lands, illegally taken without federal approval between 1845 and 1954; the payment of annuities owed by the United States to the Northern Lakes Pottawatomi Nation of Canada; the securing of reserved water rights for the Nez Perce Tribe of Idaho; and on behalf of Norton Sound area Alaska Native villages, the assertion of legal priority for subsistence fishing over commercial fishing under federal law.

Promotion of Human Rights

Religious freedom is a Native American Rights Fund priority, and its resources are brought to bear in cases involving the repatriation of burial remains, the protection of sacred sites, and First Amendment rights of Native prisoners, members of the Native American Church, and other religious practitioners. Recent NARF legal actions have supported a National Park Service management plan for Devil's Tower in Wyoming, which asks that climbers voluntarily refrain from climbing Devil's Tower during the month of June and that state licenses for commercial climbers not be issued in that month.

Since its creation, the Native American Rights Fund has worked for tribal empowerment with regard to the education of Native children. Most public education programs circumvent tribal governments and maintain control over all major components of Indian education.

Through its Indian Education Legal Support Project, NARF works to tribalize education through confirmation of the unique sovereign rights of Indian tribes.

Accountability of Governments

The Native American Rights Fund holds federal and state governments accountable for appropriate enforcement of the laws and regulations governing Indian peoples. A landmark case in this area is *Cobell v. Babbitt* filed in 1996 on behalf of 500,000 Individual Indian Money (IIM) account holders. The suit charges the federal government with mismanagement and illegal conduct with regard to Indian trust accounts, representing billions of dollars. This case, when brought to trial, will be decided on principles of trust law that hold the United States responsible for the prudent management of money belonging to individual Indians and tribes.

The Development of Indian Law

Understanding that the careful and orderly development of Indian law is essential for the protection of Indian rights, the Native American Rights Fund supports the National Indian Law Library and the Indian Law Support Center. Serving both NARF attorneys and the general public, the National Indian Law Library processes nearly a thousand requests for information each year. Likewise, the Indian Law Support Center serves Indian communities and practitioners of Indian law across the United States by providing essential information and assistance throughout the year.

Throughout its history of work for the legal rights of Indian individuals and tribes, the Native American Rights Fund has been governed by a board of distinguished Indian leaders from across the country. Serving for a maximum of six years, individual members of the Board of Directors bring with them reputations for integrity, leadership, and respect from within Indian Country—qualities long associated with the most important Indian legal advocacy effort in the United States, the Native American Rights Fund.

BIBLIOGRAPHY

James, Marlise. *The People's Lawyers.* 1973.
La Potin, Armand, ed. *Native American Voluntary Organizations.* 1987.
Native American Rights Fund Annual Report. 1998.

Judith Antell

Native American Tribal Sovereignty

See Sovereignty, Native American Tribal.

Native Hawaiian Sovereignty Movement

The ongoing struggle for sovereignty and self-determination among descendants of Hawai'i's aboriginal settlers came to widespread national attention during the 1993 centennial observance of the overthrow of the sovereign Hawaiian monarchy by American businessmen, and subsequent annexation of the formerly independent kingdom to the United States in 1898. The case for sovereignty rests primarily on two premises: (1) illegality of the overthrow and subsequent annexation accomplished without plebescite; and (2) necessity for redress of social, political, and economic dispossession suffered by the majority of native Hawaiians.

The movement in the 1990s stemmed from political activism that emerged in the early 1970s. Protests against encroaching land development and misuse of natural resources brought attention to the plight of native Hawaiians, in turn engendering reexamination of the historical circumstances surrounding dispossession and the loss of sovereignty. That activism coincided with a renaissance of Hawaiian cultural practices and language.

Revisions to the state constitution in 1978 provided for the creation of the Office of Hawaiian Affairs (OHA). This state agency is charged with managing revenues generated by the so-called "ceded lands"— 1.431 million acres taken by the United States upon annexation, and handed over to state control in the Hawai'i Admissions Act of 1959. A second land trust consisting of 200,000 acres for homesteading was created by Congress in the Hawaiian Homes Act of 1920; breach of that trust was documented in the 1991 report *A Broken Trust* to the United States Commission on Civil Rights. Both land trusts are regarded as a potential land and economic base for a native Hawaiian nation.

Throughout the 1980s, groups advocating sovereignty and self-determination began to propose forms a sovereign government might take. These proposals fall largely into three basic configurations: (1) those that advocate complete independence from the United States; (2) those that advocate some form of a "nation within a nation" modeled on Native American nations; and (3) those that advocate self-determination within the existing political apparatus. The largest of these groups, Ka Lāhui Hawai'i, led by prominent activists Haunani-Kay Trask and Mililani Trask, claimed a membership of 14,000 in 1993; it has convened constitutional conventions, and published a Master Plan in 1995. In 1993, the People's International Tribunal was convened before a panel of international activists, to establish historical, moral, and legal bases for redress.

A Hawaiian Sovereignty Election Council (HSEC) was appointed by Governor John Waihe'e in 1993 to conduct a plebescite on the question, "Shall the Hawaiian people elect delegates to propose a native Hawaiian government?" HSEC sponsored educational workshops, held voter registration, and developed a timeline for a convention. A coalition of groups led by Ka Lāahui Hawai'i called for a boycott, on grounds that state funding of HSEC and the plebescite compromised impartiality. Hawaiians in 1996 voted 3–1 in favor of electing delegates. Although organizational work toward a convention has been carried forth by a successor group to HSEC called Hā Hawai'i, their work has been hampered by the statewide economic downturn.

BIBLIOGRAPHY

Dudley, Michael Kioni, and Keoni Kealoha Agard. *A Call for Hawaiian Sovereignty.* 1990.

Hawaii Advisory Committee to the United States Commission on Civil Rights. *A Broken Trust: The Hawaiian Homelands Program.* 1991.

Ka Lāhui Hawai'i. *The Sovereign Nation of Hawai'i: A Compilation of Materials for Educational Workshops on Ka Lahui Hawai'i.* 1993.

Kame'eleihiwa, Lilikala. *Native Lands and Foreign Desire.* 1992.

MacKenzie, Melody, ed. *Native Hawaiian Rights Handbook.* 1990.

Na Maka O Ka'Aina in association with Center for Hawaiian Studies, University of Hawai'i. *Act of War.* Video. 1993.

Nation of Hawai'i. http://www.hawaii-nation.com/.

Amy Ku'uleialoha Stillman

Nativism

Just a few years ago, the word "nativism" was languishing in relative linguistic obscurity. As recently as 1991, the word was rarely spoken or printed, except to refer to the anti-immigrant feeling of bygone eras: those of the KNOW-NOTHING PARTY of the mid-nineteenth century, for example, or the Chinese exclusion era at the turn of the century, or the so-called Red Scare of the post-WORLD WAR I era. (See CHINESE EXCLUSION ACTS.) The term, having first emerged to characterize the "antiforeign" parties of the mid-nineteenth century, had acquired an anachronistic ring; the kind of mob-driven, anti-foreign mentality the term evokes seemed to have little contemporary relevance.

Beginning in the 1990s, however, the word "nativism" made a dramatic comeback. Policy-makers, citizens' groups and the media began to employ the term with substantial frequency to characterize the current proponents of immigration restriction and the various policies they promote. Scholars also resurrected the word for contemporary usage.

The return of "nativism" to our political vocabulary occurred alongside the emergence of a virulent discourse of anti-immigrant hostility in this country the likes of which had not been seen for several decades. Americans had once again come to blame immigrants for a variety of the country's social ills; and dramatic restrictions on both the admission of prospective immigrants and the rights of those already here had been enacted by the mid-1990s. "Nativism," the word, became increasingly invoked by critics to both characterize and condemn these developments.

But are these developments accurately characterized as "nativist"? Determining whether particular social phenomena are, in fact, nativist is not a simple undertaking, in part because scholars differ substantially in their understandings of the term. A few analysts have defined "nativism" quite broadly to denote "strong attachment to a reference group to which one has, so to speak, 'been born.'" In this formulation, the racism of the KU KLUX KLAN represents a form of nativism, as did the anticommunism of the McCarthy era. Others have employed the term to refer to the adverse response of cultural majorities to "outsider" racial and ethnic groups; in this understanding, the dominant culture's treatment of American-born blacks or Jews are both exemplary forms of nativism.

Most analysts, however, more narrowly associate the term "nativism" with negative sentiment of various kinds toward foreigners—with "antiforeign" feeling. At times, the term is employed to refer to the expression of antipathy toward foreigners abroad; this use of the term suggests nationalist chauvinism or isolationism, sometimes with racial overtones. More commonly, however, "nativism" is associated with an exclusionary impulse directed toward the foreigner within; it suggests animosity or bias, in other words, toward *immigrants*, or toward aspiring immigrants. In historian John Higham's well-known formulation, nativism "should be defined as intense opposition to an internal minority on the ground of its foreign (i.e., 'un-American') connections."

Yet even assuming, as many scholars do, that nativism denotes negative attitudes or "hostility to foreigners," there remain important questions as to how to apply the term. For it is not always clear what sorts of policies and positions regarding foreigners qualify as hostile. Is it "hostile," for example, to curtail the numbers of immigrants admitted each year to this country, or to limit the public benefits noncitizens are entitled to enjoy? Obviously, nothing in this definition of nativism can help us to answer these questions.

There is, on the other hand, one particular form of "hostility to foreigners" that is consistently associated with nativism in both the scholarly literature and in colloquial usage: I refer to race- or ethnicity-based animus toward immigrants. According to one reference source, "[t]he nativist sentiment is one of ethnic prejudice, racism, and anti-immigration" (*Dictionary of American Immigration History*). Nativism as ethnonational bias against immigrants is unquestionably the most common understanding of the term today. In this usage, nativism is treated as closely analogous to RACISM; the suggestion is often that nativism is a species of racism, except that the objects of prejudice are foreigners or particular classes of foreigners rather than "native" minorities. But while this usage of the term is widespread, it is far from universal. Indeed, although certain core themes emerge in scholarly and colloquial discussions of nativism, conventional understandings of the term vary substantially. The result is that people are apt to disagree about whether a par-

ticular set of policies or attitudes can be properly designated as "nativist."

There is one aspect of nativism's meaning, however, about which nearly everyone concurs: that "nativism" is a term of intensely negative appraisal. The evaluative content of "nativism" is so strong, in fact, that historian John Higham—whose own work on historical American nativism did much to popularize the term—has more recently asserted that the word is of limited use to historians as an analytical concept because it is indelibly associated with "subjective irrationality" and "prejudice." In other words, Higham suggests, to call a thing "nativist" serves less to explain or describe it than to condemn it.

What Higham's remark suggests is that a core aspect of nativism's meaning resides in the "speech act" that the word performs (or that it can be used to perform). The effect of this speech act, almost invariably, is to register enormous social disapproval and disapprobation. It is a term of unmitigated political censure. This is why advocates for immigrants are eager to characterize the recent climate of immigration restrictionism in these terms. It is also why defenders of immigration restriction are so eager to avoid the charge. Some restrictionists furiously repudiate the designation: as they see it, calling anti-immigration views "nativist" (or "xenophobic" or "racist") is a form of "intimidation" by politically correct liberal zealots which serves to suppress real substantive debate. Many speak bitterly of the "motive assassination" and "liberal McCarthyite" assaults they have had to endure for airing their views, and urge restrictionists to smash the taboo against anti-immigration opinion that the threatened charge of "nativism" imposes by refusing to be silenced. Other restrictionists invoke the dangers of nativism themselves *on behalf* of their political project; as they tell it, nativism may not be upon us now, but it surely will be in the absence of stern and sober-minded reform (the theory being that Americans will take matters into their own hands if the government fails to get tough).

Despite the disagreement that may exist over precisely what nativism *is*, therefore, there appears to be virtually unanimity about what the charge of "nativism" does: To call a discourse or policy "native" represents an effort to disable it through social opprobrium. The word signals a zone of normative impropriety that most Americans—however restrictive their views on immigration—make every effort to avoid.

BIBLIOGRAPHY

Almendrala, Laarni C. "Proposition 187 Update: The Return of the Nativists," *Filipinas Magazine*. January 31, 1995.

Ball, Terrence, James Farr, and Russell L. Hanson, eds. *Political Innovation and Conceptual Change*. 1989.

Beck, Roy. "Challenging Immigration Fatalism." *The Social Contract*, Vol. II, No. 2. Winter 1991–1992.

Bennett, David H. *The Party of Fear: From Nativist Movements to the New Right in American History*. 1988.

Brimelow, Peter. "Time To Rethink Immigration?" *National Review*. June 22, 1992.

Cordasco, Francesco, ed. *Dictionary of American Immigration History*. 1990.

Davis, Ann. "Return of the Nativists," *National Law Journal*. June 19, 1995.

Dinnerstein, Leonard, Roger L. Nichols, and David M. Reimers. *Natives and Strangers: Blacks, Indians and Immigrants in America*, 2nd ed. 1990.

Graham, Otis L., Jr. "The Wind Has Shifted: A New Agenda for Immigration Reformers." *Social Contract*, Vol. II, No. 2. Winter 1991–1992.

Higham, John. "Another Look At Nativism." In *Send These To Me: Jews and Other Immigrants in Urban America*. 1975.

Higham, John. *Strangers in the Land: Patterns of American Nativism, 1860–1925*. 1970.

Karst, Kenneth L. "Paths to Belonging: The Constitution and Cultural Identity." *North Carolina Law Review*, Vol. 64. 1986.

Lipset, Seymour Martin, and Earl Raab. *The Politics of Unreason: Rightwing Extremism in America: 1790–1970*. 1970.

Perea, Juan, ed. *Immigrants Out! The New Nativism and the Anti-Immigrant Impulse in the United States*. 1997.

Sharry, Frank. "The Rise of Nativism in the United States and How to Respond to It." *National Immigration Forum*. Spring, 1994.

Smith, Rogers. "'The American Creed' and American Identity: The Limits of Liberal Citizenship In the United States," *Western Political Quarterly*, Vol. 41. 1988.

Linda Bosniak

Naturalization

Article I, Section 8, of the U.S. Constitution gives CONGRESS the power to "... establish a uniform rule of naturalization ..." Initially, this power was interpreted in a limited way to mean only that the national government had the authority to set national criteria for naturalization. The power to determine the rights of naturalized citizens was still viewed as being primarily within the legal purview of the states. In 1790, Congress passed the first federal naturalization law which made "free white persons" eligible for naturalization. From this time until the middle of the twentieth century, racial criteria served as one of the primary foundations of U.S. naturalization policy.

Conflict over states rights in the area of naturalization was central to the crisis leading up to the Civil War. When nonslave states began to naturalize free blacks, most southern states passed laws that indicated they would not recognize their CITIZENSHIP. This crisis over naturalization came to a head in the DRED SCOTT case of 1857 in which the SUPREME COURT ruled that free blacks could not become U.S. citizens. This decision was not challenged until after the Civil War when both the CIVIL RIGHTS ACT OF 1866 and the FOURTEENTH AMENDMENT, ratified in 1868, deemed that all persons born in the United States were both citizens of the United States and the state of their residence. However, states continued to retain significant discretion in determining the rights and privileges of citizens well into the twentieth century.

The United States continued to use explicit racial criteria in its naturalization policy after the Civil War. The naturalization law of 1870 provided that free whites or persons of African descent could apply for citizenship, but there was no political consensus on who could be classified as white. As a result, Congress passed more explicit racial restrictions as demonstrated by the 1882 CHINESE EXCLUSION ACT which made all Chinese immigrants ineligible for citizenship. Through the first half of the twentieth century, most individuals from East Asia who applied for naturalization were denied citizenship by the courts, as were many individuals from Central Asia and the Middle East.

In addition to discriminating on ethnic grounds, U.S. naturalization law has discriminated against women in a variety of ways. The naturalization law of 1855 stated that women automatically became citizens at the time of their husband's naturalization. Conversely, under a naturalization act in 1907, women who were American citizens automatically lost their citizenship if they married a foreign man. This restriction was short-lived, and in 1922 Congress gave married women citizenship that was not tied to that of their husbands.

A series of congressional and executive acts in the 1940s made a variety of new groups, including indigenous persons in U.S. territories, Chinese persons, Indians, and Filipinos eligible for naturalization. The Immigration and Nationality Act of 1952 stated that the right to naturalization shall not be denied because of race, sex, or marital status. This legislation remains the basic foundation for U.S. naturalization policy today and has made U.S. naturalization policy fairer and more conducive to the protection of civil rights for both ethnic minorities and women.

BIBLIOGRAPHY

Kettner, James H. *The Development of American Citizenship, 1608–1870*. 1978.

Schuck, Peter H., and Rogers M. Smith, *Citizenship Without Consent: Illegal Aliens in the American Polity*. 1985.

Exterior of the U.S. Immigration and Naturalization Service headquarters. Naturalization confers citizenship with all rights, privileges, and responsibilities available to the native-born, except for eligibility to become president of the United States. (UPI/CORBIS-Bettmann)

Smith, Rogers M. *Civic Ideals: Conflicting Visions of Citizenship in U.S. History.* 1997.

Smith, Rogers M. "'One United People': Second-Class Female Citizenship and the American Quest for Community." *Yale Journal of Law and the Humanities* 1 (1989): 229–293.

Ueda, Reed. "Naturalization and Citizenship." In *The Harvard Encyclopedia of American Ethnic Groups,* edited by S. Thernstrom. 1980.

Debra L. DeLaet

Nebraska

The state of Nebraska was born under racial controversy. First with conflicts between white settlers and Indians, and then with the specter of the U.S. Civil War and slavery. The area was first closed to white settlement by the Indian Intercourse Act in 1834. It was then opened to settlement by the Kansas–Nebraska Act of 1854, which established the territories of KANSAS and NEBRASKA. The 1854 act repealed the Missouri Compromise of 1820–1821, which had for over thirty years kept proslavery and antislavery forces at bay by dividing up new territories into slave and free areas along the 36° 30′ latitude.

While Kansas erupted almost immediately into violence over the slavery issue, Nebraska remained relatively peaceful due to its small number of immigrant slaveholders. The 1860 census, for example, listed fifteen slaves from a total black population of eighty-two.

The territorial legislature then abolished slavery in 1861. Nebraska entered the Union as the thirty-seventh state on March 1, 1867.

Nebraska was an ancestral home of the Oglala Sioux Indians as well as the Arapahoe, Cheyenne, Omaha, and Ponca tribes. The first twenty years of Nebraska's history as a state include many significant events and incidents in the conquering of these Plains Indians. Chief Crazy Horse, for example, famous for his involvement in the defeat of General George Armstrong Custer at the Little Big Horn, was captured and murdered at Fort Robinson in Nebraska.

More important to civil rights, however, is the story of Standing Bear, a Ponca chief. Standing Bear was forced to OKLAHOMA with his tribe as part of an Indian resettlement drive in 1876. Wishing to bury his dead son in the land of his ancestors, Standing Bear escaped the reservation and returned to Nebraska. He was captured, but two Omaha lawyers filed a writ of habeas corpus at the Omaha Federal Court. Judge Elmer S. Dundy ruled, "An Indian is a person within the meaning of the law," and Standing Bear was released.

African Americans have been present in Nebraska since the territory was opened for settlement, although in relatively lower numbers than in many states. Nebraska avoided the enactment of JIM CROW laws that were prevalent throughout the South. Discrimination and SEGREGATION were more personal than institutional until 1919, when Omaha experienced a race riot. Thereafter, school segregation was common. Public schools refused to hire blacks; the

University of Nebraska adopted a whites-only policy for student housing, athletic teams, and the health-related schools.

The NAACP and the NATIONAL URBAN LEAGUE established small offices in Lincoln and Omaha, but their successes were primarily limited to their involvement with government programs such as those offered under the New Deal (see NEW DEAL AND DEPRESSION). In the late 1940s, the Urban League's efforts led to the desegregation of public housing projects and to the opening of the Omaha Public School System to black teachers. Omaha experienced racial violence in the 1960s, with riots in 1966 and 1968. BLACK MUSLIM movement figure MALCOLM X was born Malcolm Little in Omaha on May 18, 1925. His father was a Baptist preacher involved in civil rights reform.

Women were granted the right to vote in Nebraska school-board elections in 1883, and in 1917 the Nebraska state legislature gave women the right to vote in U.S. presidential elections, three years before the passage of the NINETEENTH AMENDMENT granting all U.S. women with universal suffrage. The first women were elected to the Nebraska state legislature in 1924, and in 1987 Kay Orr was elected as the first female Republican governor in U.S. history. In response to President John F. KENNEDY's establishment of the federal Commission on the Status of Women task force, headed by former First Lady Eleanor ROOSEVELT, Nebraska's Governor Frank B. Morrison in 1961 established a state agency that eventually became known as the Nebraska Commission on the Status of Women. Headquartered in Lincoln, Nebraska, this agency continues to operate today on behalf of women's rights. In recent years, Nebraska was among thirty-five states that ratified the EQUAL RIGHTS AMENDMENT to the U.S. Constitution. Nebraska was also one of twenty-five states that successfully blocked passage of legislation prohibiting same-sex marriages (see GAY AND LESBIAN RIGHTS).

Census data for 1990 puts Nebraska's population at 1,578,395, with 3.6 percent black. The state had 12,344 Native Americans, about 5,500 Asians, and 37,000 residents of Hispanic ancestry.

BIBLIOGRAPHY

Federal Writers Project. *The Negroes of Nebraska.* 1940.

Mihelich, Dennis. The Formation of the Lincoln Urban League. *Nebraska History* 68 (1987): 63–73.

Nebraska Humanitarians website: http://www.visit-nebraska.org/reports/fam-human.html.

Nebraska Native Americans website: http://www.visit-nebraska.org/reports/fam-native.html.

Vogel, Philip E. "Nebraska." In *1998 Grolier Multimedia Encyclopedia.* 1998.

Michael Dawson

Nevada

When Nevada became a territory (in 1861) and a state (in 1864) many constitutional and statutory provisions relegated "Indians," "Negro" (or "colored") Americans, and "Chinese" Americans to positions inferior to those of whites. The term "white" was never defined legally, but members of these three specifically named groups were subject to criminal laws and taxes on an equal basis with whites, while denied the right to vote, hold office, serve on juries, attend public schools (unless separate schools for them were established—which happened once, for one school year), testify against whites in either civil or criminal cases (with the exception of the Chinese, who could testify against whites in civil cases), or marry whites.

Nevada was dominated overwhelmingly in its earliest years by the Union/Republican party, which repealed some of the testimony laws and began efforts to remove a state constitutional provision denying nonwhites the right to vote. However, the aftermath of a riot against the Chinese in Unionville in 1869 ended this mini-reconstruction and began a period of extensive additional discriminatory laws against the Chinese. Only one civil rights law—forbidding the state university to discriminate in admitting students on racial grounds—was passed during the nineteenth century.

Black Nevadans were few in number during the early decades but vigorously defended their rights. For example, the discriminatory school law was overturned by the state Supreme Court in 1872 after black parents in Carson City built a schoolhouse and sued when the school board refused to hire a teacher. But the denial of the right to vote to nonwhites did not end until passage of the FIFTEENTH AMENDMENT to the national Constitution. An effort in 1869 to defend the rights of the Chinese by federal legal action and by passage of a state law failed.

From the 1880s until the late 1950s new racially discriminatory laws were enacted occasionally and the old ones were not repealed. By the beginning of 1960 there was a widespread pattern of private discrimination against African Americans (and sometimes Indians and Hispanics) in public accommodations, employment, and housing. This pattern led to the designation of the state by some civil rights advocates as "the Mississippi of the West." However, the state did not have a pattern of racial segregation required by law and had not disfranchised citizens of color after 1870, so this name was somewhat inaccurate.

The modern civil rights movement began in the late 1950s. By 1971 there were state laws against private discrimination on racial grounds in public accommodations, employment, and housing. However, the state's Equal Rights Commission (established in 1961, before passage of these laws) has not enforced civil rights laws vigorously.

The modern effort was led in Nevada almost entirely by groups based in the black community, aided by a few courageous public officials, notably Democratic Governors Grant Sawyer (1959–1966) and Mike O'Callaghan (1971–1978). By the 1950s there was a large black population in southern Nevada and NATIONAL ASSOCIATION FOR THE ADVANCEMENT OF COLORED PEOPLE (NAACP) branches were active in Las Vegas, Reno, and Hawthorne, a small town with a black population of several hundred because of a federal facility there. In both north and south there was also scattered support from Jewish, Protestant, and Catholic religious leaders and a few white liberals.

Highlights of the modern civil rights movement include: in 1956 California labor leader Harry Bridges got a state judge to annul the miscegenation law, left over from territorial days; in 1960 the Las Vegas Branch of the NAACP (led by Dr. James B. McMillan) ended public accommodations discrimination by casinos/resort hotels in southern Nevada by threatening a march on the Las Vegas Strip, although northern casinos did not take such action until passage of the national CIVIL RIGHTS ACT in 1964; passage by the state legislature of a law against racial discrimination in public accommodations and employment in 1965 and a fair housing law in 1971; an NAACP-initiated federal suit in 1967 that desegregated public elementary schools in Las Vegas; another federal NAACP suit (still active) that resulted in a consent decree requiring southern casinos to concentrate on hiring black employees until their numbers reached the proportion of this group in the community; and a federal suit to end discrimination by a Las Vegas union and a state apprenticeship council.

There were never laws discriminating against Spanish-speaking Americans, although there has been private discrimination against members of this group. Hispanic numbers were low until the 1980s (although there had been high proportions of Hispanic railroad and other workers in southern Nevada from 1910 into the 1920s). Civil rights organizations in Hispanic communities were weak until the 1980s, except for an organization of Cuban Americans in southern Nevada active in the 1960s and 1970s.

Native Americans were in the 1860s subject to the same legal discrimination as other nonwhites and until the 1960s were discriminated against in actual practice, especially in the small counties. But Native Americans differ from all other Nevadans because they have a unique legal position that gives the federal government (and not the state of Nevada) almost exclusive jurisdiction over them, and because they were aborig-

inal owners of both land and water and have retained important self-governing powers and partial control over their resources. Until the 1930s, however, there were only three reservations, which provided a measure of protection of the land belonging to a minority of the state's Indian population.

The Nevada legislature passed statutes in violation of federal law to assert legal jurisdiction over Indians. On the other hand, the fact that most Nevada land has never been in private hands, combined with the temporary nature of the mining industry (Nevada's overwhelmingly important economic sector before the 1940s), allowed many Native Americans to live to a considerable extent as they had for thousands of years, until well into the twentieth century.

Native Americans experienced improvements in their situation during three periods. In 1916–1917 the federal government purchased land and established Indian "colonies," which had the legal status of reservations, in or near towns. During the Indian New Deal (from 1934 to about 1940), the Indian land base was expanded, largely through the creation of new reservations with agricultural potential, and Indian education was improved, with less emphasis on forced assimilation. And during the modern civil rights era, the Intertribal Council of Nevada (a coalition of the tribal governments of most reservations) and the Indian Affairs Commission (a state agency designed to advance their interests) gave Indians a stronger voice in the making of governmental decisions affecting them. Federal antipoverty and BUREAU OF INDIAN AFFAIRS programs of the 1960s and 1970s provided federal funds for tribal governments and federal subsidies for the establishment of numerous programs to be run by Indians themselves, from self-help housing through HEAD START to programs to improve Indian health.

Federal antipoverty programs after 1964 disproportionately aided African American and Native American groups, because these groups organized community action and other programs when offered the opportunity to do so, often before other groups. In this sense these programs were an extension of the civil rights revolution.

Many Nevadans claim that the state has always placed a high priority on individual freedom, pointing to the fact that legalized gambling is the basis of the modern Nevada economy and that legal prostitution exists in several small counties. But Nevada is behind most western and northern states in several civil liberties areas—for example, mere possession of marijuana is still a felony. The Nevada affiliate of the AMERICAN CIVIL LIBERTIES UNION was not organized until 1966, but since then has attempted to defend and enlarge civil liberties in the state.

Nevada was also slow to repeal nineteenth-century laws restricting the rights of women, although it has been for decades a community property state and it granted women the right to vote before adoption of the NINETEENTH AMENDMENT. The state legislature never ratified the national EQUAL RIGHTS AMENDMENT and the electorate voted against this amendment in an advisory vote in the 1970s. However, most state laws discriminating against women had been repealed by the 1990s.

The 1995 legislature repealed a statute criminalizing "the infamous crime against nature," but has not enacted laws to protect GAY AND LESBIAN RIGHTS.

BIBLIOGRAPHY

Coray, Michael S. "'Democracy' on the Frontier: A Case Study in Nevada Editorial Attitudes on the Issue of Non-White Equality." *Nevada Historical Society Quarterly* 21, 3 (1996): 189–202.

Crowley, Joseph N. "Race and Residence: The Politics of Open Housing in Nevada." In *Sagebrush and Neon: Studies in Nevada Politics*, rev. ed., edited by Eleanore Bushnell. 1976.

Earl, Philip I. "Nevada's Miscegenation Laws and the Marriage of Mr. and Mrs. Harry Bridges." *Nevada Historical Society Quarterly* 37, 1 (1994): 1–17.

McMillan, James B. *Fighting Back: A life in the Struggle for Civil Rights*. 1998.

Miranda, M. L. *A History of Hispanics in Southern Nevada*. 1997.

Rusco, Elmer R. *Good Time Coming? Black Nevadans in the 19th Century*. 1975.

Rusco, Elmer R., and Richard L. Siegel. "The ACLU in Nevada." *Justice in Nevada: Nevada Public Affairs Review* 2 (1990): 47–51.

Titus, A. Costandina. "Howard Cannon, the Senate, and Civil-Rights Legislation, 1959–1968." *Nevada Historical Society Quarterly* 33, 1 (1990): 13–29.

Elmer Rusco

New Africa, Republic of

See Republic of New Africa.

New Deal and Depression

The 1930s in America were times of economic distress. A period of great economic prosperity in the 1920s came to a screeching halt with the stock market crash of October 1929, and the overall economy crashed soon thereafter. From 1929 to 1932, approximately 11,000 banks failed, the Gross National Product fell at a rate of more than 10 percent annually, and farm prices fell by 53 percent. By 1935, unemployment exceeded 20 percent.

While the economic plunge hurt everyone, African Americans were hit harder than many, since their employment was predominately in agriculture and in the service sector. The drop in farm prices hurt blacks disproportionately, and those employed in the service sector were often displaced by whites and others moving down the social and employment ladder. For minorities, the unemployment rate may have been twice the national figure.

The election of President Franklin D. ROOSEVELT in 1932 raised the hopes of many, as he campaigned on a platform of government intervention to fix the economy. From 1933 to 1938, Roosevelt proposed and had enacted many innovative pieces of legislation he termed the "New Deal." The purposes of the New Deal were to stop and reverse the economic decline, put people back to work, and provide security for the elderly and those who could not provide for themselves.

Among Roosevelt's new programs were the Emergency Banking Act and the new Federal Deposit Insurance Corporation, which helped restore confidence in banks. The new Securities and Exchange Commission and its regulations helped stabilize the stock and securities markets. The Agricultural Adjustment Act established programs to stabilize and raise farm prices. The National Industrial Recovery Act established two programs: the Public Works Administration and the National Recovery Administration, designed to provide jobs, regulate business, and ensure fair competition. The Civilian Conservation Corps, Works Progress Administration, and National Youth Organization provided government employment. Other programs included a rural electrification program.

Programs under the National Labor Relations Act and the Fair Labor Standards Act were designed to establish fair employment standards, mandate maximum working hours, and minimum wages. Organized labor benefited greatly from these programs and laws, but the benefits were not proportionately available to African Americans and other minorities due to discriminatory practices within the labor unions and the exclusion of workers in the farm and service sectors from the effects of the laws.

Roosevelt did not pursue specific civil rights legislation, but he did much to break down color barriers within the federal government. He secured the appointment of many blacks to upper-level positions within the administration. One appointee, Mary McLeod BETHUNE, director of Negro affairs in the National Youth Organization, convened the upper-level appointees in an unofficial "Black Cabinet" in 1935. They met regularly to promote the interests of black Americans throughout the Roosevelt years.

Many of the laws enacted during the early days of the New Deal were hastily drafted and flawed. The United States Supreme Court declared several to be unconstitutional. Roosevelt made an attempt to pack the Supreme Court with more liberal judges to reverse these decisions, and when that effort failed, he turned to more traditional political efforts. Taxes were raised for the rich, and strict regulations were put in place under existing laws. By the end of the decade, however, unemployment was still over 17 percent.

One of the longer-lasting efforts of the New Deal was the Social Security Act of 1935. This created a system of old-age pensions, unemployment insurance, and welfare grants.

BIBLIOGRAPHY

Conkin, Paul K. "New Deal." *Microsoft Encarta Encyclopedia,* CD-ROM. 1994.

Kirby, John B. *A New Deal for Blacks.* 1978.

Lunardini, Christine. "Roosevelt's Black Cabinet." In *Encyclopedia of African-American Culture and History,* edited by Jack Salzman, David Lionel Smith, and Cornel West. 1996.

Pierce, Francis S. "Depression of the 1930s." *Grolier Multimedia Encyclopedia,* CD-ROM. 1998.

Sitkoff, Harvard. *A New Deal for Blacks.* 1978.

Weiss, Nancy J. *Farewell to the Party of Lincoln: Politics in the Age of FDR.* 1970.

Wolters, Raymond. *Negroes and the Great Depression.* 1970.

Michael Dawson

New Hampshire

From the time of the Revolutionary War, when twenty enslaved black men unsuccessfully petitioned the legislature for their freedom, New Hampshire has had a mixed record on civil rights. The state sent John P. Hale to the U.S. Senate in 1848, where he quickly introduced the first bill to abolish slavery, but also sent native son Franklin Pierce to the White House, where he signed the Fugitive Slave and Kansas–Nebraska Acts. Slavery, never widely practiced in New Hampshire, was never abolished under state law but it had effectively died out by the 1840s.

Subject to indignities of custom rather than law, New Hampshire's small black community began to organize for civil rights in the late 1950s, leading to the chartering of a branch of the NATIONAL ASSOCIATION FOR THE ADVANCEMENT OF COLORED PEOPLE (NAACP) in Portsmouth in 1958. A second branch was established in Manchester in 1964. In 1999, following a twenty-year struggle, New Hampshire became the fiftieth state to adopt a holiday named for Martin Luther KING, JR.

In 1965, following passage of the federal CIVIL RIGHTS ACT OF 1964, New Hampshire adopted a state human rights law and created a Human Rights Commission to eliminate discrimination in EMPLOYMENT, HOUSING, and public accommodations based on race, creed, or national origin. Over the years since, as social movements pressed for further protections, the statute was broadened to prohibit discrimination based on age and sex (1971), marital status and disability (1975), familial status (1992), and sexual orientation (1998). The Human Rights Commission, which is made up of volunteers appointed by the Governor, is authorized to investigate complaints, hold hearings, and levy fines or order payment of back wages.

The state created a Commission on the Status of Women in 1969, when similar bodies were being established in other states. The Commission pressed for a state equal rights amendment, which was adopted in the 1974 Constitutional Convention and ratified by voters later that year. The provision, which states that "Equality of rights under the law shall not be denied or abridged by this state on account of race, creed, color, sex or national origin," is now included in Article 2 of the Bill of Rights of the state constitution. Grassroots feminist organizing on issues such as domestic violence, women's health, and reproductive rights in the 1970s provided the grounding for the later establishment of statewide groups such as the Coalition Against Domestic and Sexual Violence, the New Hampshire Women's Lobby, and local chapters of the NATIONAL ORGANIZATION FOR WOMEN (NOW), and the National Abortion and Reproductive Rights Action League.

The AIDS crisis and legislation prohibiting homosexuals from adopting children or serving as foster parents prompted formation of the first statewide gay rights organization in 1985. Effective organizing over the next fourteen years led to the addition in 1998 of sexual orientation to the human rights statute, and to repeal of the adoption/foster care ban in 1999. The first Lesbian and Gay Pride March was held in Concord in 1987, and has been followed by annual marches in succeeding years.

Following a civil rights lawsuit filed by Jan Laaman, a prisoner, a federal court ordered improvements in conditions faced by inmates at the New Hampshire State Prison in 1977. The court order, followed by a consent decree that was in effect from 1978 to 1993, brought about improvements in health care, work opportunities, and educational and vocational programs for prisoners. Another lawsuit, filed by parents of residents at the Laconia State School, led in 1980 to court-ordered improvements and creation of a system of community care for people with development disabilities (see DISABILITY RIGHTS). The State School, where 1,200 children and adults were confined without adequate care, was shut down in 1991. It was the first such state school in the United States to be closed.

Founded in 1842 as the New Hampshire Asylum for the Insane, the institution that later became known as New Hampshire Hospital served as little more than a warehouse for as many as 2,700 patients with mental illness until 1984. After the asylum lost its accreditation in 1972 and gave it up again voluntarily in 1983, the State made a commitment to reform under pressure from legislators as well as the New Hampshire Alliance for the Mentally Ill, a parents' group.

The *Union Leader*, a Manchester-based daily newspaper that circulates statewide, was the primary nemesis of civil rights forces for the latter part of the twentieth century. Using editorials—often published on the front page—to bludgeon ideological opponents, the paper opposed the civil rights movement of the 1960s and in later years fought against gay rights, reproductive choice, and the Martin Luther King, Jr. holiday.

BIBLIOGRAPHY

Cunningham, Valerie, Mark Sammons, et al., eds. *Black Heritage Trail: A Resource Book.* 1996.

Arnold Alpert

New Jersey

New Jersey is, and always has been, deeply divided geographically, socially, and politically. Divisions between northern and southern regions, as well as tensions between more and less urbanized parts of the state, have had a pronounced effect on civil rights and race relations. The north–south division was most significant during the eighteenth and early nineteenth centuries. During this period, South Jersey, influenced by Philadelphia's Quaker abolitionists, tended to oppose slavery, whereas North Jersey, settled and dominated politically by planters from Barbados, tended to support the slave system. During the mid- and late-nineteenth century, the divisions between northern and southern parts of the state remained strong, but the ideological commitments of these parts began to change. South Jersey came to reflect the political and racial attitudes of border states, such as DELAWARE and MARYLAND, as North Jersey became more pro-Union and more racially tolerant. During the twentieth century, an urban–suburban divide replaced the north–south divide as the principal impediment to the struggle for racial justice in New Jersey. This divide also helped ignite the 1967 urban riots and has shaped New Jersey's civil rights policies in the aftermath of these riots.

Independence failed to bring freedom to most New Jersey slaves, whose numbers exceeded 12,000 (nearly 6 percent of the total population) at the close of the eighteenth century. The state's first constitution, adopted in 1776, established limited civil rights (including voting rights) for free blacks, but did not abolish slavery. In 1778, New Jersey's first governor, William Livingston (1723–1790), proposed abolition legislation but was rebuffed by the state assembly, in large part because of opposition by the state's northern counties, which experienced chronic shortages of free labor.

In 1804, New Jersey became the last northern state to abolish slavery, adopting the gradualist approach to EMANCIPATION recommended by the moderate New Jersey Society for Promoting the Abolition of Slavery. The abolition law also provided for compensation for slaveholders, who were permitted to exploit the labor of the ostensibly free children of their slaves while simultaneously receiving public subsidies for the maintenance of these children. New Jersey never passed a general emancipation act, and slavery endured in the state, in one form or another, until the passage of the THIRTEENTH AMENDMENT in December 1865.

Soon after the gradual abolition plan was adopted, the legal status of free blacks in New Jersey began to erode. In 1807, blacks were disenfranchised, although they had enjoyed the right to vote since the Revolution. They remained disenfranchised even after the ratification of the state's second constitution in 1844, which extended the franchise to poor whites but to neither blacks nor women. Petition campaigns and conventions organized by leaders of New Jersey's free blacks to protest disenfranchisement fell on deaf ears, in spite of passionate appeals to the principles of the Declaration of Independence and the consciences of whites. These campaigns and conventions were led by African-American clergymen and professionals, including Rev. Joshua Woodlin of Burlington County (chairman of the 1849 "Colored Convention" in Trenton) and Dr. John S. Rock of Salem (who was both a practicing physician and a prominent attorney). These leaders also organized resistance by New Jersey blacks to white supremacist colonization schemes during the mid-nineteenth century.

During the Civil War, many New Jersey whites—including Peace Democrats (the so-called Copperheads)—sympathized openly with the Confederacy, condemned the EMANCIPATION PROCLAMATION, worked to bar the migration of emancipated blacks to New Jersey, and opposed the enlistment of New Jersey blacks in the Union army. New Jersey also was the only northern state that, at least initially, failed to ratify the THIRTEENTH, FOURTEENTH, and FIFTEENTH AMENDMENTS to the U.S. Constitution. Although New

Jersey organized no black regiments during the war, nearly 2,900 New Jersey blacks enlisted in the Union army, most serving in the United States Colored Infantry (USCI) but a handful serving in cavalry regiments. At least 469 New Jersey blacks died during the war in the service of the Union.

Black men were not granted VOTING RIGHTS in New Jersey until 1870, after the passage of the Seventeenth Amendment to the U.S. Constitution. In spite of the activities of suffragist groups, women of all races gained the right to vote in New Jersey only after the NINETEENTH AMENDMENT was ratified in 1920. Women's suffrage suffered early setbacks in New Jersey, including the defeat in 1915 of a statewide suffrage referendum. Contrary to some views, this defeat was not due to the mobilization of immigrant votes by political bosses and liquor industry interests. Indeed, recent immigrants voted for and against women's suffrage in more or less equal proportion to the population as a whole.

During the later part of the nineteenth century, New Jersey blacks found themselves subjected increasingly to de facto segregation in public schools and public accommodations. These practices would be outlawed, at least officially, by the Civil Rights Act of 1884, which banned school SEGREGATION, guaranteed equal access to public accommodations, and ended employment discrimination based on race. However, compliance with the ban on discrimination was not widespread in many parts of the state, and New Jersey became known as "the Georgia of the North." The striking disparity in racial attitudes in New Jersey was reflected in the admissions policies of the state's colleges and universities. Whereas Paul ROBESON, the legendary black athlete, actor, and activist, graduated valedictorian from Rutgers College in 1919, Princeton University—a bastion of white Southern culture—did not begin to admit blacks until WORLD WAR II.

Drawn in large part by the need for industrial labor, many Southern blacks migrated to New Jersey during the early part of the twentieth century. The black population of the state grew from 89,760 in 1910 to 208,828 in 1930. Although tensions existed between these migrants and the poor European immigrants with whom they competed for jobs, there also were occasions for racial unity. For instance, attempts by the KU KLUX KLAN to recruit members in New Jersey met with angry resistance by both blacks and whites in cities such as Perth Amboy, where members of both races participated in anti-Klan rioting during the summer of 1923. Even so, between 1915 and 1944, New Jersey chapters of the Klan recruited approximately 60,000 new members, mainly in cities such as Newark, Camden, Trenton, Atlantic City, and New Brunswick. New Jersey trailed far behind states such as Indiana (ap-

proximately 240,000 new members) and Texas (approximately 190,000 new members).

The 1940s and 1950s witnessed a dramatic improvement of the legal rights of New Jersey blacks. In 1945, the New Jersey legislature passed the Act Against Discrimination, which banned racial discrimination in employment and established the Division Against Discrimination (in the Department of Education). In 1947, under the leadership of Republican Governor Alfred E. Driscoll, an outspoken supporter of civil rights, the new state constitution (Article I, paragraph 5) explicitly outlawed discrimination in public schools and in the state militia. Subsequently, this ban was extended to public accommodations (in 1949) and public housing (1954).

In spite of these encouraging developments, middle-class whites began to move from the cities to the suburbs, leaving New Jersey's major urban centers increasingly black and increasingly poor. White flight was accelerated by the availability, from the 1930s on, of subsidized Federal Housing Administration mortgages for many middle-class suburban homes. Between 1940 and 1960, large black ghettos emerged in cities such as Newark, Jersey City, Paterson, Elizabeth, Trenton, and Camden, even as the total population of these cities, and therefore their political clout, dropped dramatically. As city lines became color lines, and prospects for decent jobs, housing, and education declined for New Jersey blacks, urban aid, perhaps inevitably, became a racial issue.

Frustrated by the failure of the civil rights movement to translate its advances into political and economic power for African Americans, an increasingly militant and confrontational BLACK POWER movement, led by activists such as radical poet Imamu Amiri BARAKA (formerly known as LeRoi Jones), emerged in New Jersey's northern cities during the late 1960s. The frustrations of many New Jersey blacks exploded into violence in Newark on July 12, 1967, triggered by a graphic act of police brutality near a public housing development. Newark was engulfed by rioting, looting, and arson for five days. Governor Richard J. Hughes (Dem.) called in 500 members of the State Police and 1,000 National Guardsmen to reinforce 1,400 Newark police officers, who were ill-prepared to handle a civil disorder of this magnitude. Deliberate aggressiveness of the police and guardsmen, who were predominantly white, only aggravated racial tensions. Outbreaks of rioting also occurred that summer in Plainfield, New Brunswick, Jersey City, Englewood, and Elizabeth. In the wake of the 1967 riots, New Jersey blacks renewed their commitment to the Black Power movement, and in 1970 they elected Kenneth A. Gibson as the the first black mayor of Newark, New Jersey's largest city. However, the immediate response of state and federal officials focused on controlling the symptoms of urban unrest rather than on alleviating their underlying causes (i.e., severe economic deprivation, squalor and decay, and deeply rooted racial inequalities).

The recent history of civil rights in New Jersey has centered on a series of decisions by the state supreme court, which increasingly has assumed a policy-making role on issues such as equality in EDUCATION and the problem of residential segregation. However, at the close of the twentieth century, both of these issues remained unresolved.

In 1970, taxpayers and officials in New Jersey's low-income cities filed suit against the state, arguing that New Jersey's system of public school funding, which relied heavily on local school taxes, was discriminatory. New Jersey's poorer, urban school districts were predominantly black. In 1973, the state supreme court agreed, ruling in *Robinson v. Cahill* that this system violated the state constitution's promise of a "thorough and efficient education" for all children, regardless of race or income. When, in 1976, the state legislature rejected a proposal by Governor Brendan Byrne (Dem.) to fund urban school aid through a new state income tax, the state supreme court ordered all public schools closed until the legislators relented eight days later. In 1981, a new lawsuit, *Abbott v. Burke*, alleged continued disparities in school funding. Once again, the state supreme court assumed a policy-making role, ordering the legislature to provide more aid to poor school districts.

Municipalities in New Jersey had long used zoning ordinances to exercise broad authority over local land use, sometimes achieving de facto residential segregation by blocking the construction of low-income housing within their boundaries. In 1972, the local chapter of the NATIONAL ASSOCIATION FOR THE ADVANCEMENT OF COLORED PEOPLE (NAACP) sued Mount Laurel, a fairly affluent town in Burlington County, for discriminatory zoning policies. In 1975, *Mt. Laurel I*, the state supreme court's first ruling on the case, found for the plaintiffs, and declared the exclusionary zoning practices unconstitutional. However, this ruling did not issue clear mandates or enforcement mechanisms. In 1983, the court issued a second ruling, *Mt. Laurel II*, which required particular municipalities to revise their housing ordinances to accommodate low- and middle-income housing, and appointed three full-time superior court judges to oversee compliance with the decree.

BIBLIOGRAPHY

Bilby, Joseph G. *Forgotten Warriors: New Jersey's African American Soldiers in the Civil War.* 1993.

Calligaro, Leo. "The Negro's Legal Status in Pre-Civil War New Jersey." *New Jersey History* LXXXV (3 & 4) (Fall–Winter 1967): 167–180.

Fishman, George. *The African American Struggle for Freedom and Equality: The Development of a People's Identity, New Jersey, 1624–1850.* 1997.

Furer, Howard B. "The Perth Amboy Riots of 1923." *New Jersey History* LXXXVII (4) (Winter 1969): 211–232.

Gordon, Felice D. *After Winning: The Legacy of the New Jersey Suffragists, 1920–1947.* 1986.

Hagen, Lee, Larry A. Greene, Leonard Harris, and Clement Price. "New Jersey Afro-Americans: From Colonial Times to the Present." In *The New Jersey Ethnic Experience*, edited by Barbara Cunningham. 1977.

Hayden, Tom. *Rebellion in Newark: Official Violence and Ghetto Response.* 1967.

Jackson, Kenneth T. *The Ku Klux Klan in the City, 1915–1930.* 1967.

Jackson, Kenneth T., and Barbara B. Jackson. "The Black Experience in Newark: The Growth of the Ghetto, 1870–1970. In *New Jersey Since 1860: New Findings and Interpretations*, edited by William C. Wright. 1971.

Kirp, David L., John P. Dwyer, and Larry A. Rosenthal. *Our Town: Race, Housing, and the Soul of Suburbia.* 1995.

Mahoncy, Joseph F. "Woman Suffrage and the Urban Masses." *New Jersey History* LXXXVII (3) (Autumn 1969): 151–172.

Moss, Simeon F. "The Persistence of Slavery and Involuntary Servitude in a Free State." *Journal of Negro History* 35 (July 1950): 289–314.

Pingeon, Francis D. *Blacks in the Revolutionary Era.* 1975.

Pomper, Gerald, ed. *The Political State of New Jersey.* 1986.

Price, Clement A. *Freedom Not Far Distant: A Documentary History of Afro-Americans in New Jersey.* 1980.

Price, Clement A. "The Struggle to Desegregate Newark: Black Middle Class Militancy in New Jersey, 1932–1947." *New Jersey History* XCIX (3 & 4) (Fall–Winter 1981): 215–228.

Wright, Giles R. *Afro-Americans in New Jersey: A Short History.* 1988.

Wright, Marion T. *The Education of Negroes in New Jersey.* 1941.

Jason A. Scorza

New Mexico

Well before the first Europeans and Africans entered the region in the sixteenth century, New Mexico served as a crossroads of peoples and cultures. When the African Esteban and the Spaniard Cabeza de Vaca found their way to New Mexico in the 1530s, they encountered a vibrant mixture of Native American agriculturalists, traders, hunters, and nomads. After several unsuccessful attempts, the first permanent Spanish settlement was established in 1598 near Santa Fe.

Despite the severity of Spanish rule, including slavery and forced religious conversion, Pueblo peoples quickly learned to navigate the complicated Spanish bureaucracy. Throughout both the Spanish colonial period (1540–1821) and subsequent Mexican rule (1821–1846), Native Americans demanded political and civil rights, often successfully, through an array of petitions, letters of grievance, and written requests to government officials. In 1741, for instance, Isabel, an Indian slave, reacted to her master's opposition to her marriage to another Indian slave by writing a letter to the Spanish governor asking him to permit her marriage.

After U.S. annexation of much of the Southwest in 1848, Anglo-American newcomers to the region quickly set about establishing American political and economic rule, often through blatant land grabs and legal maneuverings. Still, the nineteenth and early twentieth centuries in New Mexico saw continued demands for equal justice and political representation by indigenous communities.

In northeastern New Mexico during the late nineteenth century, a loosely bound, racially mixed group of Chicano, Jicarilla Apache, African-American, and Anglo-American settlers struggled mightily against the Maxwell Land Grant Company and its desire to evict the settlers from the land. During the same period, the GORRAS BLANCAS (White Caps) of northern New Mexico executed raids and fence-cutting expeditions in response to Anglo attempts to monopolize the region's most profitable grazing land.

In spite of worsening poverty in the state during the Great Depression, demands for equal rights continued in the 1930s. At the University of New Mexico, for instance, Chicanos had long been denied equal access to social clubs and student societies. Unwilling to accept such marginalization, Chicano students helped introduce a state law in 1933 designed to prohibit secret fraternities and sororities. The law eventually failed to pass, but barely a month later the students, relying on the organization developed during the failed legislative attempt, successfully protested the racial slurs of a university professor.

New Mexico was also the site of several landmark events in the modern civil rights movement. In Albuquerque, repeated boycotts against stores denying service to African Americans led to the passage in 1952 of antidiscrimination ordinances, making Albuquerque one of the first U.S. cities to pass such laws in the twentieth century. Three years later, in 1955, the New Mexico Civil Rights Act prohibited discrimination in public places throughout the state. Earlier in the decade, Mexican-American miners and their wives led a major strike against a mining company in Silver City in southern New Mexico. That strike, against Empire Zinc Corporation, became the basis of the blacklisted

film *Salt of the Earth*, which provided one of the earliest statements of Chicana FEMINISM and activism.

During the 1960s, Chicano and Native American activism reached new heights. In 1966, protesting decades of land dispossession and loss of political rights, Reies López TIJERINA led Chicano protests in the Tierra Amarilla region of northern New Mexico. In one of the earliest and best known actions of the emergent CHICANO MOVEMENT, Tijerina and his followers occupied the Tierra Amarilla county courthouse and forced the governor of New Mexico to call out the National Guard. The period also witnessed the culmination of decades of bitter legal battles over the ownership of Blue Lake near Taos, when the lake and surrounding land were returned to the people of Taos Pueblo.

In the 1980s, New Mexico's enduring and complicated relationship with Latin America involved the state more deeply than ever in international human rights issues. Governor Toney Anaya declared New Mexico a Sanctuary State, offering a safe haven from deportation and likely execution to thousands of Central American refugees fleeing right-wing death squads in their home countries. In addition, in the last two decades of the twentieth century growing concern for the environment merged with social justice movements, leading to the founding of grassroots organizations such as Ganados del Valle and the Southwest Organizing Project. Such environmental justice groups have forced the larger environmental movement, including the radical Earth First! (founded in New Mexico in 1980), to take into account the uneven effect of environmental hazards on communities of color.

BIBLIOGRAPHY

Deutsch, Sarah. *No Separate Refuge: Culture, Class, and Gender on an Anglo-Hispanic Frontier in the American Southwest, 1880–1940.* 1987.

Fox, Steve. "From the Beat Generation to the Sanctuary Movement: Cold War Resistance Cultures in the American West." In *The Cold War American West, 1945–1989*, edited by Kevin J. Fernlund. 1998.

Gonzales, Phillip B. "Spanish Heritage and Ethnic Protest in New Mexico: The Anti-Fraternity Bill of 1933."*New Mexico Historical Review* 61 (1986): 281–299.

Gutiérrez, Ramón A. *When Jesus Came, the Corn Mothers Went Away: Marriage, Sexuality, and Power in Colonial New Mexico, 1500–1846.* 1991.

Montoya, María E. "Translating Property: The Maxwell Land Grant and the Conflict over Land in the American West, 1840–1920." Forthcoming.

Pulido, Laura. "Ecological Legitimacy and Cultural Essentialism: Hispano Grazing in the Southwest." In *The Struggle for Ecological Democracy: Environmental Justice*

Movements in the United States, edited by Daniel Faber. 1998.

Rosenbaum, Robert J. *Mexicano Resistance in the Southwest: The Sacred Right of Self-Preservation.* 1981.

Pablo R. Mitchell

Newspapers and Magazines

Before World War II, civil rights issues of blacks, women, gays, and other minority groups were often ignored or opposed by the mainstream press. This is probably because the press was almost exclusively the domain of white males. It wasn't until the last half of the twentieth century that newspapers and magazines became instrumental in the civil rights movement, bringing injustice, racism and bigotry issues to the forefront of American thought. News articles and photographs of peaceful black protesters being set upon by club-wielding police, often using tear gas and police dogs, helped frame the atmosphere of the civil rights movement in the 1950s and 1960s in the minds of many white Americans outside the South. It also helped bring a new level of awareness and pride to black Americans that the struggle for civil rights, though at times painful, had a momentum that could not be stopped. The print media's attention to civil rights issues expanded in the 1970s and 1980s to other groups, most notably women, Latinos, and gays and lesbians. In addition to coverage in mainstream media, many publications that cater to specific communities have sprung up in the past few decades. Examples include *Jet* and *Ebony* for blacks, *The Advocate* for gays, *El Diario* for Latinos and *Ms. Magazine* for women.

An estimated 4,000 black-owned newspapers have existed in American history, writes Charles A. Simmons, in *The African American Press: A History of News Coverage During National Crisis* (1998). The first black newspaper published in the United States, *Freedom's Journal,* was started in 1827 in New York City. The newspaper's publishers, Samuel Cornish and John B. Russwurm, founded it to counter the proslavery stance of another New York newspaper. In the next half-century, several dozen black newspapers sprang up in the Northeast, including *North Star* by abolitionist Frederick DOUGLASS, first published in 1847. In 1855, the first black paper west of the Mississippi River, *Mirror of the Times,* debuted in San Francisco. The 1880s saw a wave of new black newspapers, including the *Washington* (D.C.) *Bee, Philadelphia Tribune, Cleveland Gazette,* and *Indianapolis World.* Among the most notable black newspapers to champion civil rights issues was the *Boston Guardian,* which favored a more "radical" approach to black issues than the moderate philosophy of abolitionist Booker T. WASHINGTON. Another, the *New York Age,* advocated school integration in the 1940s. When the National Negro Newspaper Publishers Association began in 1940, more than 200 black newspapers and 120 black magazines existed. In 1956, the group changed its name to the National Newspaper Publishers Association and today represents about 150 black publishers. As of 1998, there were 214 black newspapers in the United States, including three major dailies: the *Chicago Defender, Atlanta Daily World,* and (Brooklyn) *Daily Challenge.* Magazines serving the black community include *Essence* and *Emerge.*

Newspaper and magazine coverage of the women's suffrage movement in the late 1800s early 1900s helped publicize the issue, even though a majority of newspaper coverage was negative. A notable and influential exception was famed editor Horace Greeley, who wholeheartedly endorsed voting rights for women. The next big wave of coverage came in the 1960s and 1970s with the modern "Women's Liberation" movement. One of the seminal newspaper articles on the movement, "The Second Feminist Wave," by Martha Weinman Lear, appeared in the *New York Times Magazine* (March 18, 1968). By 1971, there were more than 100 women's movement journals, newslet-

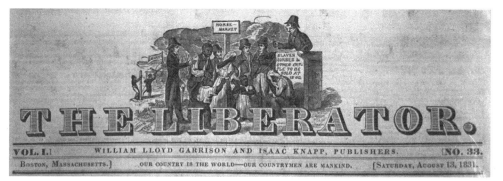

The Liberator *(1831–1865) gave voice to William Lloyd Garrison and Isaac Knapp's views against slavery and for women's rights.* (Library of Congress)

ters, and newspapers in the United States. *Ms. Magazine* began publishing in 1972, covering feminist civil rights issues, which other leading women's magazines of the time ignored or glossed over.

Until the 1970s, gay civil rights issues were rarely covered in mainstream media, except in the context of derision, dismissal, or denial. The gay and lesbian rights movement began in 1969 following a riot in New York City protesting police harassment of gay bar patrons. Within a few years, dozens of local gay newspapers sprouted in major cities. Often these publications were the only source of positive news for the gay community about gay issues. Among the most respected gay publications today are *The Advocate*, a biweekly newsmagazine, and *The Washington Blade*, a weekly newspaper, both started in 1967. A major criticism of many gay publications is their reliance on sex-oriented advertising.

Latinos have also suffered from stereotyping in newspaper and magazine coverage of civil rights issues. As a result, many Latinos have turned to Spanish-language publications for news of their community. New York City's *El Diario* is the oldest daily Spanish-language newspaper in the nation, founded in 1910. One of the largest Latino newspapers is the *El Nuevo Herald* in Miami, with a daily circulation of about 200,000. Magazines of note include *Hispanic* and *Vista*.

The epitome of revolutionary militancy, Huey Newton (right) was one of the best-known leaders of the Black Panther party in the 1960s. Newton was murdered in Oakland, California, in 1989. (AP/Wide World Photos)

BIBLIOGRAPHY

Alwood, Edward. *Straight News: Gays, Lesbians, and the News Media.* 1996.

Danky, James Phillip, ed. *African American Newspapers and Periodicals: A National Bibliography.* 1999.

Dickerson, James. *Dixie's Dirty Secret: The True Story of How the Government, the Media, and the Mob Conspired to Combat Integration and the Vietnam Antiwar Movement.* 1998.

Gabriel, John. *Whitewash: Racialized Politics and the Media.* 1998.

Reaves, Henry. "Thirty Years Ago in Benton County, Mississippi." *Skipping Stones*, Vol. 6 (Winter/Spring 1994): 20–21.

Senna, Carl. *The Black Press and the Struggle for Civil Rights: The African American Experience.* 1993.

Thompson, Julius E. *Percy Greene and the Jackson Advocate: The Life and Times of a Radical Conservative Black Newspaperman, 1897–1977.* 1994.

Waldron, Ann. *Hodding Carter: The Reconstruction of a Racist.* 1993.

Ken R. Wells

Newton, Huey

(1942–1989), political activist.

While student activists at Merritt Community College in Oakland, California in 1966, Huey Newton and Bobby SEALE created the BLACK PANTHER PARTY. The

party's ideas, influenced by MALCOLM X, were reflected in a ten-point program, which articulated demands around a number of the pressing issues facing African Americans. Many accounts attribute the program's development solely to Newton and Seale, but others suggest a more collective effort, which included the New York–based Black Panther Party.

Newton and Seale raised money by selling Mao Tsetung's *Red Book* and Franz Fanon's *The Wretched of the Earth* to purchase guns and print literature. The Black Panther Party initially monitored the activities of the Oakland police. As Newton was a prelaw student, he familiarized the party with California state laws, particularly regarding unconcealed weaponry and police conduct. They opened the first party office in January 1967.

As minister of defense, Newton became the primary symbol of the party's defiant image. As the party gained popularity in 1967 and chapters opened nationwide, Newton vaulted into global notoriety after a skirmish with police officer John Frey in October. Armed with a law book, motorist Newton claimed that Officer Frey was unjustified in stopping him on the road. An ensuing scuffle left Newton shot in the stomach and Officer Frey dead of a bullet wound, with Newton subsequently convicted of first-degree murder. A

Panther-led "Free Huey" campaign followed the incident, with a Huey National Defense Committee that raised funding in support of Newton's defense. This elevated the Black Panther Party's profile and facilitated its merger with the STUDENT NONVIOLENT COORDINATING COMMITTEE (SNCC).

Although imprisoned, Newton continued to provide leadership to the party. He influenced the party's survival programs, which provided basic necessities to the African-American community as a part of a lengthy revolutionary process. In January 1969, Newton ordered a purge in response to the numerous agent provacateurs (many from the FEDERAL BUREAU OF INVESTIGATION) within the ranks.

Having won an appeal, Newton was released from prison in August 1970. His ideas had become increasingly international during his incarceration. He eventually espoused a theory of "intercommunalism." In February 1971, Newton expelled Eldridge Cleaver and the entire international section, effectively formalizing the internally and externally influenced split in the Black Panther Party.

Into the 1970s, the Oakland-based party continued to impact local politics although much of the party had been diminished nationally by the FBI's COINTELPRO. In 1977, the party helped elect Oakland's first black mayor, Lionel Wilson.

Newton fled to Cuba during the 1970s, returning later in the decade. He earned a Ph.D. in philosophy in 1980 from the University of California, but he continued a long battle with drugs and criminal activity. He was fatally shot by a small-time drug dealer in 1989.

Born in Monroe, Louisiana on February 17, 1942, Newton was barely literate until the age of eighteen, when he taught himself to read. Yet he left a wealth of powerful writing to future generations, such as *To Die for the People* (1972), *Revolutionary Suicide* (1973), and his doctoral thesis, *War Against the Panthers: A Study of Repression in America* (1980).

BIBLIOGRAPHY
Maurrasse, David J. "Revolutionary Enough." Ph.D. dissertation, Northwestern University. 1996.
Newton, Huey P. *To Die for the People: The Writings of Huey P. Newton*. 1972.
Newton, Huey P. *Revolutionary Suicide*. 1973.
Seale, Bobby. *Seize the Time: The Story of the Black Panther Party and Huey Newton*. 1970.

David J. Maurrasse

New York

The history of civil rights in New York State has often been indistinguishable from that of the nation itself. Favored with a geographically advantageous location in the mid-Atlantic region, as well as a deep water port and major waterways, New York developed quickly as a commercial, financial, and manufacturing center. Slavery, first introduced to the Dutch colony of New Amsterdam in 1626, was abolished prospectively by the newly formed state legislature in 1799; under the terms of abolition, the last slaves in the state were freed on July 4, 1827. Although the legislature enacted universal white male suffrage in 1821, free blacks were still made subject to property qualifications, and did not receive the full franchise until the passage of the FIFTEENTH AMENDMENT to the U.S. Constitution in 1870.

Upstate New York was a hotbed of anti-slavery activity beginning in the 1830s, producing such well-known abolitionists as Frederick DOUGLASS, John Brown, and Harriet Tubman, and providing a series of crucial "stations" on the Underground Railroad to Canada and freedom. New York City, in contrast, with its commercial ties to Southern agriculture, and—by the late 1840s—its large population of Irish Catholics who feared black economic competition, was less sympathetic to the anti-slavery cause. In July 1863, white mobs protesting the institution of the draft in New York City lynched blacks, ransacked their homes, and burned the Colored Orphan Asylum in an orgy of violence that left over one hundred dead. The New York City DRAFT RIOTS remain the bloodiest civil disorder in national history.

After the Civil War, New York's black community remained relatively small. Barred from most skilled trades and labor unions, they worked on the margins, as liverymen, warehousemen, dockworkers, barbers, waiters, and domestics. Blacks began to move to New York City in greater numbers during the first two decades of the twentieth century, pushed by southern poverty, crop failures, and RACISM. The city's black population tripled between 1890 and 1910; by 1920, some 160,000 blacks lived in Harlem, which was rapidly becoming the economic, cultural, and social center of black New York. Greater numbers led to greater political assertiveness. The NATIONAL ASSOCIATION FOR THE ADVANCEMENT OF COLORED PEOPLE (NAACP), founded in 1910, made its national headquarters in New York City. W. E. B. DU BOIS became the organization's director of publicity and research, and edited its magazine, THE CRISIS. The NATIONAL URBAN LEAGUE was created in New York City in 1911 as a means to counter the effects of job discrimination among blacks.

It was Marcus GARVEY's UNIVERSAL NEGRO IMPROVEMENT ASSOCIATION (UNIA), however, that may have most influenced the average black New Yorker. Garvey, one of the many West Indian immigrants who came to New York City in the 1910s and 1920s, preached a doctrine of black cultural nationalism, economic self-determination, and African repatriation that, by the early 1920s, claimed four million members nationwide. Despite the relatively short life of his organization—Garvey was convicted of mail fraud and deported in 1926—the UNIA influenced black thinkers and activists, both in New York and nationally, for generations to come.

Another local impulse with national implications was the HARLEM RENAISSANCE, an outpouring of black literary, musical, and artistic expression that, during the 1920s, sought to use African themes to construct a uniquely African-American culture. Leaders of the Harlem Renaissance included writers James Weldon JOHNSON, Zora Neale Hurston, and Claude McKay, poets Langston HUGHES and Countee Cullen, and painter Aaron Douglas.

Black political activity continued during the Great Depression (see NEW DEAL AND DEPRESSION), a time when the black unemployment rate in New York reached 50 percent, double that of whites. The "Don't Buy Where You Can't Work" campaign, led by future Congressman Adam Clayton POWELL, Jr., and labor leader A. Philip RANDOLPH, succeeded in integrating the workforce at major white-owned businesses in Harlem. The outbreak of WORLD WAR II in Europe attracted a second wave of Southern black migration to New York, one that would not abate until the 1960s. Blacks faced discrimination in their attempts to obtain war-related employment, and Randolph began the MARCH ON WASHINGTON MOVEMENT in New York City in 1941 to pressure the federal government to adopt fair hiring practices. His efforts were partially rewarded when President Franklin ROOSEVELT signed an executive order prohibiting job bias in defense industries and creating a FAIR EMPLOYMENT PRACTICES COMMITTEE as an enforcement mechanism. Race relations in New York were tense during World War II, marked by a 1943 riot in Harlem, after the shooting of a black soldier by a white policeman, in which five blacks died and four hundred were injured.

In 1945, New York became the first state in the nation to establish a State Commission Against Discrimination. Two years later, Jackie ROBINSON of the Brooklyn Dodgers became the first black to play major league baseball in the twentieth century. Despite these legal and social advances, however, black New Yorkers suffered economically during the years after World War II with the disappearance of unskilled industrial jobs. New York City lost almost half of its supply of such jobs between 1945 and 1970, as the city's black population more than tripled. In addition, de facto residential segregation created isolated ghettos in New York City and upstate urban areas, breeding grounds for crime, drug addiction, alcoholism, low educational achievement, and family disintegration. Riots in New York City and Rochester during the summer of 1964 were expressions of the frustrations attendant to these conditions.

By the early 1960s, MALCOLM X of the NATION OF ISLAM had emerged as a major spokesman for disaffected blacks in New York's urban centers. Although Malcolm was unable to transform the Nation of Islam into a mass movement, his philosophy of black cultural pride, self-help, and separatism reached hundreds of thousands nationally, and his influence survived his 1965 assassination.

Much of the focus of the civil rights movement in New York during the 1960s centered around the issue of local control of public education in black neighborhoods. Resistance by whites to what became known as "community control" led to the racially divisive Ocean Hill–Brownsville crisis of 1968, which pitted white schoolteachers opposed to local control against New York City's black community. The racial tensions that surfaced during this crisis haunted the city for years afterward. Between 1975 and 1978, embittered whites supported municipal budget cuts and social service reductions that disproportionately impacted New York's black residents in the wake of a financial crisis in the city.

Racial tensions persisted through the 1970s and 1980s. In 1971, an uprising (the ATTICA REBELLION) of mostly black and Hispanic inmates at Attica State Correctional Facility near Buffalo provoked a furious response from white law enforcement officials, leaving thirty-nine dead. In 1986, and again in 1989, black youths who strayed into white New York City neighborhoods in Brooklyn and Queens died at the hands of whites. Largely as a result of the second of these incidents, David Dinkins was elected New York City's first black mayor in 1989 on a platform of racial healing. But even Dinkins's administration was not immune from the racially inspired violence that has been so much a part of New York's history. In 1991, the accidental killing of a black child by a Jewish motorist in the Crown Heights section of Brooklyn sparked four nights of violence, during which a Jewish rabbinical scholar was killed by black rioters.

By the 1990s, more persons of color lived in New York City than in any other single city in the United States. New York State had earned a reputation as a pioneer in the field of civil rights legislation. And more national civil rights organizations had been founded and headquartered in New York than in any other state. Despite this legacy, New Yorkers have continued to struggle for a racial peace that has seemed more elusive with each passing year.

The history of blacks and Hispanics in New York began to intersect after 1940, with the beginning of large-scale Puerto Rican migration to New York City.

Spurred by poverty and unemployment in Puerto Rico, the number of Puerto Ricans living in the city skyrocketed from 61,000 to over 800,000—about 10 percent of the city's population—between 1940 and 1970. Puerto Ricans, like blacks, suffered from racial discrimination and the effects of New York's deindustrializing economy. Among the organizations they formed to protect and expand their civil rights were Aspira, the Puerto Rican Legal Defense and Education Fund, and the more militant Young Lords Party, modeled after the Black Panther Party, which came to prominence in the 1960s. By the 1970s and 1980s, Puerto Ricans had been joined in New York City by immigrants from the Dominican Republic, Colombia, Mexico, Cuba, and other Latin American nations, making it a worldwide center of Latino culture and politics.

The national history of the women's rights movement in the United States is closely intertwined with that of women in New York State. The first Women's Rights Convention, organized by Elizabeth Cady Stanton and Susan B. Anthony, took place in Seneca Falls in 1848. In 1868, Stanton and Anthony formed the National Woman Suffrage Association to press the struggle for voting rights. By the early twentieth century, the women's labor movement in New York, notably the Women's Trade Union League (WTUL), had joined this struggle, and it achieved success on both state (1917) and national (1920) levels.

By the 1910s, women had entered New York's labor force in great numbers, and were beginning to demand rights as both workers and women. The Triangle Shirtwaist Company fire of 1911, in which 146 "sweatshop" women were killed, led to improvements in workplace safety conditions, as well as to the growth of labor unions such as the International Ladies' Garment Workers' Union (ILGWU). In 1916, Margaret Sanger began the national movement for reproductive rights when she opened a birth control clinic in Brooklyn. Sanger's crusade became a link to the rejuvenated women's movement of the 1960s in New York, which featured the publication of Betty Friedan's *The Feminine Mystique* (1963) and the founding of the National Organization for Women (1966). Feminist Congresswoman Bella Abzug and *Ms.* magazine editor Gloria Steinem helped lead the movement through the 1970s and beyond. As a center for white collar, professional, and activist women, New York continues to be on the cutting edge of American feminism.

New York has also been a major venue in the national struggle for gay rights. The modern gay rights movement began in New York City after a brutal 1969 police raid on the Stonewall Inn, a gathering place for homosexuals in Greenwich Village. The resulting Stonewall Riot led to the formation of two national gay rights organizations, the Lambda Legal Defense Fund and the National Gay Rights Task Force, which eventually helped secure the passage of New York's Gay Rights Bill and domestic partnership law. The AIDS epidemic swept through New York's gay population in the 1980s; by the early 1990s, over twenty thousand had fallen victim to it. In response, the Gay Men's Health Crisis (1981) and the more militant ACT-UP (1987) sought to mobilize individuals on the medical, legal, and political fronts. This effort continues today, facilitated by a growing number of gay elected officials who gained power in New York during the 1990s.

BIBLIOGRAPHY

Bernstein, Iver. *The New York City Draft Riots: Their Significance for American Society and Politics in the Age of the Civil War.* 1990.

Burrows, Edwin G., and Mike Wallace. *Gotham: A History of New York City to 1898.* 1999.

Chauncey, George. *Gay New York: Gender, Urban Culture, and the Makings of the Gay Male World, 1890–1940.* 1994.

Chesler, Ellen. *Woman of Valor: Margaret Sanger and the Birth Control Movement in America.* 1992.

Clark, Kenneth. *Dark Ghetto: Dilemmas of Social Power.* 1965.

DuBois, Ellen Carol. *Harriot Stanton Blatch and the Winning of Woman Suffrage.* 1997.

Gittell, Marilyn, and Maurice R. Berube, eds. *Confrontation at Ocean Hill–Brownsville.* 1969.

Greenberg, Cheryl L. *Or Does It Explode? Black Harlem in the Great Depression.* 1991

Haygood, Will. *King of the Cats: The Life and Times of Adam Clayton Powell, Jr.* 1993.

Huggins, Nathan Irvin. *Harlem Renaissance.* 1971.

Johnson, James Weldon. *Black Manhattan.* 1930.

Katz, William Loren. *Black Legacy: A History of New York's African-Americans.* 1997.

Korrol, Virginia Sanchez. *From Colonia to Community: The History of Puerto Ricans in New York City, 1917–1948.* 1983.

Lewis, Oscar. *La Vida: A Puerto Rican Family in the Culture of Poverty—New York and San Juan.* 1965.

Malcolm X (with Alex Haley). *The Autobiography of Malcolm X.* 1965.

Osofsky, Gilbert. *Harlem: The Making of a Ghetto, 1890–1930.* 1966.

Peiss, Kathy. *Cheap Amusements: Working Women and Leisure in Turn-of-the-Century New York.* 1986

Sleeper, Jim. *The Closest of Strangers: Liberalism and the Politics of Race in New York.* 1990.

Jerald E. Podair

Niagara Movement

W. E. B. Du Bois, William Monroe Trotter, and a group of nearly thirty African-American men gathered on the Canadian side of Niagara Falls in July 1905 to

Founding members of the Niagara Movement, the forerunner of the NAACP, 1905. (Schomburg Center for Research in Black Culture)

establish a movement dedicated to demanding and securing the full civil rights of black people. The Niagara movement issued a direct challenge to the power and dominance of Booker T. WASHINGTON and his accommodation of the racial status quo. Under the leadership of W. E. B. Du Bois, the Niagarites claimed for African Americans "every single right that belongs to a freeborn American, political, civil and social," and pledged that "until we get these rights we will never cease to protest and to assail the ears of America."

Ironically, the founding meeting of the group was held in Canada because of the racial restrictions of the hotels in Buffalo, where the meeting was originally scheduled to be held. The second annual meeting was held at the site of John Brown's raid in Harpers Ferry West Virginia. Here the members commemorated the 100th anniversary of John Brown's birth, and voted to include women in the organization. Three more meetings were held over the next three years; the largest was in Boston, which 800 attended.

The Niagara movement did not establish a strong organizational structure, and it suffered from tensions and rivalries. However, it laid the groundwork for the civil rights program that was carried forward by the interracial NATIONAL ASSOCIATION FOR THE ADVANCEMENT OF COLORED PEOPLE (NAACP), which Du Bois and other Niagara supporters helped to found in 1909. The Niagara movement disbanded in 1911.

BIBLIOGRAPHY

Lewis, Davis Levering. *W. E. B. Du Bois: Biography of a Race, 1868–1919.* 1993.
Meier, August, and Eliot Rudwick. "The Niagara Movement." *Journal of Negro History* (July 1957).

Patricia Sullivan

Nineteenth Amendment

The fight to secure a women's suffrage amendment to the United States Constitution was a long, sustained struggle. Four decades passed between January 10, 1878, when Senator A. A. Sargent of California proposed a slightly modified version of the FIFTEENTH AMENDMENT, and August 26, 1920, when Secretary of State Bainbridge Colby certified that, with TENNESSEE as the thirty-sixth state to ratify, the Nineteenth Amendment was the law of the land. The ranks of suffrage advocates included many leading figures in the history of women's rights: Elizabeth Cady STANTON, Susan B. ANTHONY, Lucy STONE, Julia Ward Howe, Carrie Chapman CATT, Ida B. WELLS-Barnett, and Alice PAUL.

Stanton was a moving force behind the Seneca Falls (NEW YORK) Convention of 1848. The persuasive efforts there of Stanton and the abolitionist leader Frederick DOUGLASS secured a small majority in support of a resolution declaring women's "sacred right to the elective franchise."

Two decades later, the alliance between advocates of racial and gender justice crumbled, as several feminists felt betrayed by CONGRESS's wording of Section 2 of the FOURTEENTH AMENDMENT, which included the Constitution's first explicit mention of the word "male." In 1869, Stanton and Anthony founded the National Woman Suffrage Association (NWSA), whose members campaigned against the Fifteenth Amendment and worked toward a new amendment that also guaranteed woman suffrage. Following adoption of the Fifteenth Amendment, the "Nationals," then engaged in a strategy called the "New Departure," asserted that their existing constitutional rights were being violated. Myra Bradwell, a Chicago feminist who was denied Illinois bar membership, argued that her privileges and immunities under the Fourteenth Amendment included practicing law. In *Bradwell v. Illinois* (1872), the United States SUPREME COURT disagreed.

In the 1872 national election, suffragists were arrested for attempting to vote; in federal court, they insisted unsuccessfully that their rights as citizens had

Women suffragists assembled on the steps of the Capitol, 1918. (Office of the Historian of the U.S. Senate)

been violated. In *Minor v. Happersett* (1875), the Supreme Court held "that the constitutions and laws of the several States which commit [suffrage] to men alone are not necessarily void."

Meanwhile, Stone, Ward, and their AMERICAN WOMAN SUFFRAGE ASSOCIATION (AWSA) focused on efforts to pass state amendments and legislation granting women "partial suffrage" (voting rights in selected elections); they insisted that woman suffrage was compatible with traditional American values. AWSA member Frances Willard was instrumental in enlisting the aid of the Women's Christian Temperance Union in the struggle for the vote.

In 1890, the retreat from radicalism continued when the two major suffragist organizations merged into the NATIONAL AMERICAN WOMAN SUFFRAGE ASSOCIATION (NAWSA), whose leadership included Anthony and Catt. NAWSA activists courted southerners by arguing that woman suffrage would enhance white political control. Nevertheless, the South remained a bastion of opposition. The West proved a more promising ground, as women gained the vote in WYOMING (1890), COLORADO (1893), IDAHO (1896), and UTAH (1896).

The Progressive Era witnessed a keen interest in suffrage, owing to labor leaders who saw the vote as a means to protect the growing number of women in the industrial work force, and social reformers who fought against political corruption. Members of

African-American organizations, such as Ida Wells-Barnett's Alpha Suffrage Club, joined the struggle, despite being shunned by white suffrage leaders. The opposition was active, too. Major business interests, particularly the liquor industry, united with anti-suffragist organizations, whose members included hundreds of thousands of women ("Antis").

The final push toward congressional endorsement reflected two distinct, though complementary, strategies. In 1916, Alice Paul and the NATIONAL WOMAN'S PARTY (NWP) organized women voters in western states in an effort to defeat President Woodrow Wilson and congressional Democrats. NWP protesters also engaged in hunger strikes, White House picketing, and acts of civil disobedience, garnering important media attention and public sympathy. More conservative NAWSA members were relentless in their efforts to keep personal pressure on politicians in the "Front Door Lobby."

By 1917, thirteen additional states had granted women the vote. During the Special War Session of the Sixty-fifth Congress that convened in April, suffrage supporters maneuvered through procedural barriers to bring the amendment to a vote. On September 24, 1917, the House as a whole voted itself a suffrage committee, bypassing the Judiciary Committee. On January 10, 1918, the amendment for the first time garnered the necessary two-thirds majority in the House. While in the Senate the amendment had been favorably reported out of committee by unanimous vote, the count came up two votes short in October, despite Wilson's vocal support. Republicans and Democrats could be found on both sides of the issue, and suffragists successfully targeted key opponents of the amendment in the fall congressional elections.

The die was now cast. During a special session in May, 1919, first the House (by a vote of 304 to 89, on May 21, 1919), then the Senate (66 to 30, on June 14, 1919) sent the Nineteenth Amendment to the states for ratification.

By early 1920, the roll of ratifying states stood at thirty-five. At Wilson's urging, Tennessee Governor Albert Roberts called a special legislative session to begin August 9. Under intense local and national pressure, on August 18, house members voted 49 to 47 in the affirmative. An immediate court challenge proved unsuccessful, and eight days later the national celebration began.

The struggle for women's rights was far from complete, as evidenced by the pervasive social, political, and legal discrimination women continued to experience. The Nineteenth Amendment did not provide sufficient constitutional protections outside the voting sphere, and in the latter decades of the twentieth century a new movement for women's rights sought new legal devices, including the EQUAL RIGHTS AMENDMENT, to secure those protections.

BIBLIOGRAPHY

Catt, Carrie Chapman, and Nettie Rogers Shuler. *Woman Suffrage and Politics.* 1926.

National American Woman Suffrage Association. *Victory: How Women Won It.* 1940.

Stanton, Elizabeth Cady, Susan B. Anthony, Matilda Joslyn Gage, and Ida H. Harper, eds. *History of Woman Suffrage.* 1881–1922.

Wheeler, Marjorie Spruill, ed. *One Woman, One Vote: Rediscovering the Woman Suffrage Movement.* 1995.

Michael Allan Wolf
Daniel A. Wolf

Nixon, Edgar Daniel ("E. D.")

(1899–1987), civil rights leader.

E. D. Nixon was one of the most influential African-American leaders in Alabama in the twentieth century and a key organizer of the MONTGOMERY BUS BOYCOTT of 1955–1956. As a Pullman car railroad porter from 1923 to 1964, he was influenced by, and became a staunch supporter of, union leader A. Philip RANDOLPH. Nixon had little formal education, but he was a large, powerful man with a booming voice, a char-

ismatic personality, and a fearless manner. In the 1940s, Nixon organized the Alabama Voters League and led a march of 750 men to the Montgomery county courthouse to attempt voter registration. In 1945 he was elected president of the Montgomery NAACP and, in 1947, he became president of the Alabama NAACP. In 1954, Nixon was the first black candidate in the twentieth century to seek elected office in Montgomery when he qualified to represent his precinct on the county Democratic executive committee. He was defeated but his candidacy raised the political aspirations of African Americans across Alabama.

In 1955, a political forum organized by his Progressive Democratic Association questioned white candidates for the Montgomery City Commission on current issues, including hiring and seating practices on the city bus line. This black political activity angered some local whites, but a candidate supported by Nixon was elected and, for the first time, a few black policemen were hired. A few months later, Nixon interviewed fifteen-year-old Claudette Colvin, who had been arrested for violating the city's segregated bus seating ordinance; but, believing she was not mature enough to withstand the pressure, Nixon decided against using Colvin for a test challenge. When Montgomery NAACP secretary Rosa PARKS was arrested on December 1, 1955, in a similar incident, Nixon rushed to the city jail to post her bond, putting up his home as security. Over the next few days, Nixon and other local leaders conferred with Parks and decided to use her as a test case.

Nixon was an organizer of, and became the treasurer of, the MONTGOMERY IMPROVEMENT ASSOCIATION (MIA), the organization formed to run the Bus Boycott; Martin Luther KING, JR., was elected its president. Meanwhile, tensions were high in Montgomery—Nixon's was one of several homes bombed during the boycott—and internally among the boycott organizers. Nixon angrily resigned as treasurer of the MIA, writing to King that he felt as if he were being "treated as a child." This was an example of Nixon's conflict with Montgomery's middle-class African-American community, centered around Alabama State College (now University), and represented his rivalry with football coach Rufus A. Lewis, which outlasted the boycott. As late as 1968, Nixon and Lewis ran on alternate slates of presidential electors pledged to Hubert HUMPHREY. Nixon's slate lost, effectively marking the end of his leadership role. Afterward he slipped into increasingly bitter obscurity before dying in 1987. In recent years, the value of his early contributions has been recognized and he is again revered for his courage and principles.

BIBLIOGRAPHY

Branch, Taylor. *Parting the Waters.* 1988.
Burns, Stewart, ed. *Daybreak of Freedom.* 1997.
Gray, Fred. *Bus Ride to Justice.* 1995.
Raines, Howell. *My Soul Is Rested.* 1977.
Sikora, Frank. *The Judge.* 1992.
Williams, Randall, ed. *The Children Coming On.* 1998.

E. D. Nixon Collection. Special Collections, Levi Watkins Learning Center and Library, Alabama State University, Montgomery.
E. D. Nixon Interviews. Civil Rights Radio Documentary Series, Southern Regional Council, Atlanta, GA.

Horace Randall Williams

Nixon, Richard Milhous

(1913–1994), U.S. president, 1969–1974.

Richard Milhous Nixon was the thirty-seventh president of the United States. As a CALIFORNIA congressman (1947–1953) his reputation was gained exposing the dangers of communism. From 1953 to 1961 Nixon served as vice-president. As the presiding officer of the Senate, his rulings favored the liberal attempts to limit the use of filibusters by lowering the cutoff vote from two-thirds to three-fifths. He ultimately cast the tie-breaking vote instituting that change.

His unsuccessful 1960 campaign for the presidency started with substantial support from civil rights leaders, but ended by alienating northern African Americans and southern whites. Nixon's 1966 return to active campaigning was followed in 1968 by his election as president. During this period he continued to support the SUPREME COURT's 1954 school desegregation decision (BROWN V. BOARD OF EDUCATION) and encouraged efforts to achieve full civil rights for all citi-

Richard Nixon taking the oath of office as president of the United States in Washington, D.C., January 1968. His wife, Pat, is at his side. (AP/Wide World Photos)

zens. However, to gain southern support and counter the appeal of George WALLACE a "southern" strategy evolved. If elected, Nixon promised to curtail enforcement of school desegregation, particularly the withholding of federal funds from school districts that failed to progress toward meaningful integration.

During his administration (January 20, 1969–August 9, 1974), the VIETNAM WAR and problems within the domestic economy captured most of the public's attention. However, there were important developments in the civil rights arena. The president unsuccessfully attempted to put two conservative southern judges—Clement Haynsworth and G. Harold Carswell—on the Supreme Court with the intent of creating a less activist court. In addition, through his Justice Department, Nixon actively opposed school busing. When in 1972 the Voting Rights Act (see VOTING RIGHTS ACT OF 1965) came up for renewal, the administration lobbied Congress for changes that liberals felt would weaken the 1965 act. The president's efforts to improve civil rights were primarily economic; he believed that equal employment opportunities provided the best route to racial equality. Nixon's 1969 executive order creating the Office of Minority Business Enterprise was intended to assist African Americans and other minorities in establishing businesses and expanding job opportunities. By 1971, substantial federal appropriations were assisting minority employers. Segregation in construction unions was common practice in 1969. In September of that year, the president instituted his version of the Philadelphia Plan, which required federal construction contractors to establish goals and timetables for hiring minority workers. This forced employers to establish hiring quotas and set-asides for minority subcontractors. This substantially changed the meaning of AFFIRMATIVE ACTION as the emphasis shifted from protecting the individual to granting privileges to certain disadvantaged groups. By fiscal 1973, the budget for civil rights enforcement was eight times greater than in fiscal 1969.

The women's movement received little encouragement from the Nixon administration. Few women received senior appointments. While Nixon did create the Presidential Task Force on Women's Rights and Responsibilities in 1969, its reports appear to have had only minor influence on the executive branch. Congressman Nixon had been an active supporter of the EQUAL RIGHTS AMENDMENT (ERA). As president, his support for the ERA was nominal and his contribution in gaining congressional approval minimal. His decisions regarding the needs of working mothers were usually determined by budgetary considerations, as evidenced by his veto of the Child Development Act.

BIBLIOGRAPHY

Ambrose, Stephen E. *Nixon: The Triumph of a Politician, 1962–1972.* 1989.

Hoff, Joan. *Nixon Reconsidered.* 1994.

Morris. Roger. *Richard Milhous Nixon: The Rise of an American Politician.* 1990.

Nixon, Richard Milhous. *The Memoirs of Richard Nixon.* 1978.

Parmet, Herbert S. *Richard Nixon and His America.* 1990.

Frank R. Martinie

North Carolina

Political scientist V. O. Key, Jr., in 1949 praised North Carolina for a balanced economy, a good government, and an enlightened outlook. A "progressive plutocracy," it enjoyed "a reputation for fair dealings with its Negro citizens." Although he ignored disfranchisement and segregation, boosters appropriated his views in creating a liberal image, portraying the Tar Heel State as the South's exception on race. This imagery is seen today, particularly in state civics textbooks. Suffice it to say that North Carolina's civic record reflects familiar southern racial and social trends.

Tar Heel inequality was prestatehood in origin. Patriarchy, servitude, slavery, and RACISM evolved in the Proprietary (1663–1729) and the Royal (1729–1776) colony. So did the benefits or burdens of Britons, Europeans, Indians, and Africans. The eight Lords Proprietors, who governed early on, were British, propertied, and loyal to the Anglican Church. They boasted vast lands from the King and the mastery of bond laborers. With the advice of an assembly elected by freeholders, they chose a governor and his council. Government, which excluded women and nonwhites, granted land, tax, and trade privileges to the wealthy. Land greed fueled the Tuscarora Indian War (1711–1713) and the Slave Code (1715, 1741), as elite oppression bred popular resistance. Declaring themselves Regulators in 1768, over seven thousand western yeomen refused to pay fees and poll taxes that benefited county officers and eastern aristocrats. Electing Regulator assemblymen to no avail, they seized offices at gunpoint and petitioned the royal governor for relief. But his militia killed scores of them at the Battle of Alamance (1771) and hanged the ringleaders. Hundreds of their survivors quit the colony, which was demanding independence on the same principle of taxation.

From statehood (the American Revolution) to RECONSTRUCTION race and class lines deepened. If the state constitution (1776) allowed free black taxpayers to vote or bondmen to be liberated for Continental army service, the legislature authorized execution of rebel slaves and, like the U.S. Constitution (1789), confirmed human bondage. Blacks (a third of the population) drew upon Afro-American culture, Revolutionary ideals of liberty, and church networks to forge an antislavery struggle. They enlisted white dissenters, among them Methodists and Quakers, as allies for manumission and abolition. Free blacks lost their franchise and permission to learn in the 1830s amid fear of servile insurrection, the rise of the common man, and Indians' removal to the American West. Many of the Cherokees escaped to the mountains and stayed. Racism made nonslaveholders (two-thirds of the white residents) defer to slavery and, despite strong Unionist sentiment, to secession. The Civil War brought a Union military victory, emancipation by the THIRTEENTH AMENDMENT (1865), and the Freedmen's Bureau (BUREAU OF REFUGEES, FREEDMEN, AND ABANDONED LANDS) to help the poor. State lawmakers enacted a BLACK CODE to control ex-slaves, but CONGRESS soon disallowed it and enfranchised freedmen, passing the FIFTEENTH AMENDMENT (1870) to guarantee their suffrage. Black Republicans attended the convention for a second state constitution (1868), which legalized black freedom and literacy. Twenty blacks were elected to the General Assembly, where they spoke for freedpeople and wage earners. Conservatives or Democrats, who defended the interests of planters and businessmen, were backed by a violent KU KLUX KLAN (KKK). Its terrorism underlay Democrats' capture of the state House and Senate in 1870. Thus congressional Reconstruction ended (sooner than in eight former Confederate States).

Law usually denied justice in the period from Redemption to the Great Depression. The "Black Second" Congressional District, the Republicans' bulwark in the east, sent four African Americans to Congress (1874–1901); the fourth won his term in 1898. Like these representatives, black state legislators championed learning (as in Colored Normal Schools), landlord–tenant fairness, and physical protection. Democrats summarily defeated these measures; expanded SEGREGATION, including Indian-only facilities; and deferred to big business. Aggrieved farmers bolted to the POPULIST PARTY in 1892 and joined the Populist–Republican or "fusion" alliance. Fusion reforms returned many African Americans and nonelite whites to office, yet the "equal, but separate" ruling in PLESSY V. FERGUSON (1896) and the cry of "Negro Domination" hardened Democrats. The white supremacy campaign of 1898 saw them sweep the elections and incite the bloody Wilmington riot. Soon these officials passed a Suffrage Amendment to disfranchise black and illiterate voters as well as laws to separate the races, anchoring a caste system that lasted until 1964. Segregation, belying its promoters, did not ensure tranquility. Black newspapers protested Democrats' defiance of the Constitution and Republicans' rush to be lily-white. Labor shortages hit rural areas during WORLD WAR I, as African Americans moved to the cities and to the North by the thousands. Job competition sparked devastating riots at Fayetteville and Winston-Salem in 1918. JIM CROW inflamed legislators in their rejection of the NINETEENTH AMENDMENT (1920) to enfranchise women. Following national ratification of the amendment, Buncombe County ex-suffragist Lillian E. Clement became the first female state legislator. Meantime, numerous North Carolinians sought to bend or break Jim Crow's rules. Among them were clubwomen, educators, ministers, suffragists, and working people.

Demands for democratic reform bridged the NEW DEAL (1933–1945) and BROWN V. BOARD OF EDUCATION (1954) eras. Representing the powerless, reformers (moderates, liberals, and radicals alike) put pressure on the government in Raleigh. Their broad agenda included equal schooling, legalization of Indian tribes, women's equity, prosecution for lynching and peonage, recognition of labor unions, and repeal of the poll tax. One forceful advocate was the NATIONAL ASSOCIATION FOR THE ADVANCEMENT OF COLORED PEOPLE (NAACP), whose branches grew from three in 1917 to eight-three, with twelve thousand members by 1955. In 1943 a North Carolina State Conference of NAACP Branches formed. Its president, Charlotte mortician Kelly M. Alexander, Sr., served bravely until 1985. NAACP branch litigation exposed group disparities. In *Hocutt v. Wilson* (1933) the North Carolina Superior Court approved a denial of admission to black applicant Thomas R. Hocutt by the School of Pharmacy at the University of North Carolina (UNC). Still, his case marked the beginning of "direct attack" on the *Plessy* doctrine. That strategy began to breach the walls of UNC in *McKissick v. Carmichael* (1951). Here the U.S. Court of Appeals for the FOURTH CIRCUIT ordered that Floyd B. McKISSICK, future executive director of the CONGRESS OF RACIAL EQUALITY (CORE), be admitted to the UNC School of Law. Branches also used direct-action strategies: an antilynching rally of 2,500 in Raleigh (1933); affirming the "Durham Manifesto," which denounced Jim Crow (1942); and backing a walkout by black Local 77 of the Congress of Industrial Organizations (CIO) from the R. J. Reynolds Tobacco Company in Winston-Salem (1943). After WORLD WAR II they sponsored a boycott of Lumberton's dilapidated black schools (1946); provided assistance along the route of CORE's first FREEDOM RIDE, a bus "Journey of Reconciliation," where four of the sixteen black and white riders were imprisoned (1947); and planned a March on Raleigh, although they canceled it after Governor W. Kerr Scott

pledged to rectify injustice (1949). Whereas urbanization and growing consciousness of freedom fed dissent, Dixiecrats blamed the PRESIDENT'S COMMITTEE ON CIVIL RIGHTS, black veterans (of World War II and the KOREAN WAR), and CIO organizers. This phobia abetted LYNCHINGS of blacks at Norlina and Coats, whippings in Columbus County, and hatred of the NAACP. At the SUPREME COURT's 1955 hearings on implementation, the state attorney general warned that there would be rampant rioting if *Brown* were enforced immediately.

Battles for first-class citizenship, however, expanded in the next decade. NAACP loyalists gathered petitions to enroll black children in white schools, even as racial bigots intimidated parents for signing them and pupils for enrolling. Then came an amendment to the state constitution called the Pearsall Plan (1956), named for Rocky Mount businessman Thomas J. Pearsall, whose committee designed it. It funded tuition grants for white children's private education and gave local districts complete authority over school operations. Using "freedom of choice," believed to be quieter than Virginia's "massive resistance," district officials delayed full compliance. Freedom of choice was outlawed in 1966. Black plaintiffs achieved firsts, enabling them to attend college as undergraduates at UNC (1955) and to occupy any seat on Duke Power Company buses (1956). Opponents such as the signers of the SOUTHERN MANIFESTO (1956) incited counter moves, such as a bill requiring the NAACP to certify its income and membership. State employees, consequently, often hid their memberships. In spite of passage of the CIVIL RIGHTS ACT OF 1957, authorities did not protect the state's freedom fighters. Whether workers, students, or others, they battled to achieve dignity by nonviolent means. In 1957, a few black youths, led by Douglas E. Moore, a Methodist minister and a follower of Martin Luther KING, JR., sat in the white section of a Durham ice cream parlor, and were arrested for trespassing. However, harassed Lumbee Indians near Maxton and Monroe blacks took up arms against the KKK in 1958 and 1959. Tired of Klan attacks on peaceful demonstrators, Monroe–Union County NAACP branch president Robert F. Williams, a former U.S. Marine, started a rifle club to defend the protestors. The national board temporarily dismissed him, citing that armed self-defense violated the NAACP's policy, but he stood pat. When violence disrupted Monroe's demonstrations in 1961, Williams fled to avoid arrest and left America for eight years. Even so, nonviolent protest energized the battle for liberation.

At the 1960 Greensboro SIT-INS or in the 1957 to 1964 Williamston Freedom Movement, citizens fought to end Jim Crow. Groups such as the SOUTHERN

CHRISTIAN LEADERSHIP CONFERENCE (SCLC) and the STUDENT NONVIOLENT COORDINATING COMMITTEE (SNCC), founded in May 1960 at Shaw University, facilitated mass marches, voter-registration drives, and interracial agreements. Activists (black, red, and white) experienced countless arrests, injuries, fines, imprisonment, and occasionally death. Yet they forced hesitant North Carolina into the tide of American democracy. CORE's 1963 offensive in Piedmont cities ignited the "Speaker Ban Law," which forbade any known Communists to speak at state-run colleges and universities. Simultaneously, Governor Terry Sanford established the Good Neighbor Council (GNC) to ease conflicts in desegregating public accommodations, employment practices, and electoral participation. He also launched the North Carolina Fund to fight illiteracy and poverty. By mandate of the CIVIL RIGHTS ACT OF 1964 and the VOTING RIGHTS ACT OF 1965, the state repealed Jim Crow regulations (except for marriage, tax records, and prisons). Some 155 of 173 school districts remained segregated; and seven in ten black state employees were janitors, maids, or messengers.

Post-1965 efforts to enforce civil rights show a pattern of progress and reaction, with new statutes limited by racist structures. An upgraded GNC developed equal-opportunity guidelines and named the North Carolina Department of Human Resources to implement them. A state Advisory Committee to the U.S. COMMISSION ON CIVIL RIGHTS acted as monitor. Members of the antipoverty, peace, feminist, and BLACK POWER movements demanded faster changes. Their radical demands, fueling protests in the wake of the VIETNAM WAR and King's assassination, also instigated a WHITE BACKLASH. Private or "segregated academies" multiplied after *Swann v. Charlotte-Mecklenburg County Board of Education* (1971), which permitted BUSING to desegregate schools. Antibusing candidate George C. WALLACE swept the state's 1972 presidential primary, while Republicans gained victories that fall, electing their first governor since 1896 (James E. Holshouser, Jr.) and a U.S. senator (Jesse Helms). Despite its support by North Carolina members of the NATIONAL ORGANIZATION FOR WOMEN and the American Association of University Women, legislators repeatedly rejected the 1972 Equal Rights Amendment banning sex discrimination. Intolerance undermined constitutional protections. Politically charged juries convicted the "Charlotte Three" and the "Wilmington Ten," including Rev. Benjamin Chavis, of arson and insurrection (1972), but acquitted African-American Joan Little of fatally stabbing the white jailer who she said had forced her to have sex with him (1974). Civil liberties advocates persevered, nevertheless. They got the 337-year sentences of the Three and the Ten commuted

and overturned by 1980. The not-guilty verdict for six Klansmen and neo-Nazis in the fatal shooting of five Communist Workers Party supporters at Greensboro (1979), let alone state opposition to a textile workers' union drive at J. P. Stevens Company in Roanoke Rapids, brought to mind old witch hunts. By 1997, the state was home to twenty-one hate organizations (compared to Mississippi's thirteen) that targeted social-justice activists, homosexuals, and people of color.

Because of vote-dilution schemes, black voting and officeholding have improved slowly. Nearly 25 percent of Tar Heel residents in 1981, African Americans claimed 255 or 5 percent of 5,037 elective positions. Helped by the canvassing of the VOTER EDUCATION PROJECT, blacks held twelve legislative seats in 1982. Years of NAACP suits culminated in redistricting, two majority-black congressional districts, and the election of black Democrats Eva M. Clayton and Melvin L. Watt to Congress (1992). However, under *Shaw v. Hunt* (1996), which upheld a Republican complaint of gerrymandering, the state redrew these districts in 1997.

Busing and rezoning have combined to advance school DESEGREGATION. Of 1,989 schools statewide, fifty-nine or 3 percent were totally black or white in 1983–1984. A unitary school system finally prevailed, albeit to incur "white flight" and de facto resegregation. The sixteen-institution UNC system has been slower to change. It resisted federal policies for affirmative action in admissions, faculty and staff hiring, and resource allocations to its five black institutions until 1981, when it signed a consent decree. Black enrollment on the eleven white campuses averaged 8 percent in 1985 and 10 percent by 1990. In 1990 moreover, the state reported 9 percent of blacks and 19 percent of whites with a bachelor's degree or higher, 12 percent of blacks and 24 percent of whites in managerial or professional occupations, and some 27 percent of blacks and 8 percent of whites living in poverty. Indeed, the community college system is more accessible to whites and minorities (black, Indian, Hispanic, and Asian) seeking post-secondary education than is the UNC system. Now, as participants in a "Centennial Symposium on the Wilmington Riot of 1898" pointed out, North Carolinians must remove all structural barriers to equality.

BIBLIOGRAPHY

Crow, Jeffrey J., Paul D. Escott, and Flora J. Hatley. *A History of African Americans in North Carolina.* 1992.

Douglas, Davison M. *Reading, Writing, and Race: The Desegregation of the Charlotte Schools.* 1995.

Franklin, John Hope. *The Free Negro in North Carolina 1790–1860.* 1971.

Gavins, Raymond. "The NAACP in North Carolina During the Age of Segregation." In *New Directions in Civil*

Rights Studies, edited by Armstead L. Robinson and Patricia Sullivan. 1991.

Jones, H. G. *North Carolina Illustrated, 1524–1984.* 1983.

Key, V. O., Jr. *Southern Politics in State and Nation.* 1949.

Logan, Frenise A. *The Negro in North Carolina, 1876–1894.* 1964.

Meier, August, and Elliott Rudwick. *CORE: A Study in the Civil Rights Movement, 1942–1968.* 1975.

Murray, Pauli, ed. *States' Laws on Race and Color.* [1950] 1997.

Myerson, Michael. *Nothing Could Be Finer.* 1978.

Prather, H. Leon, Sr. *We Have Taken a City: Wilmington Racial Massacre and Coup of 1898.* [1984] 1998.

Waynick, Capus M., John C. Brooks, and Elsie W. Pitts, eds. *North Carolina and the Negro.* 1964.

Raymond Gavins

North Dakota

North Dakota's most significant minority population consists of Native Americans, primarily Hidatsa, Mandan, Arikara, Chippewa, Dakota, and Lakota. Nearly half inhabit one of the state's four reservations, all of which were created prior to statehood. Accordingly, early civil rights issues—language, religion, occupation, education, landholding, voting, etc.—were dictated by specific treaties and the individuals charged with upholding them. More recent civil rights issues are mandated by the United States Constitution, federal legislation (the Allotment Act, Indian Reorganization Act, etc.), and tribal law.

Early federal involvement did not prevent legislators from abrogating the rights of Native Americans, however. Under a statute passed in 1895, no Indian could vote unless he had "adopted the habits of civilized life" and was not "subject to the authority of any Indian chief or council. . . ." The North Dakota Supreme Court overturned this measure in 1897.

While Native Americans were present long before European Americans, African Americans were not. Moreover, the first legislature (1862) attempted to ensure that no blacks took up residence. In his first annual message, Governor William Jayne urged that Dakota Territory remain the province of whites. The Territorial Council reflected this exclusionary attitude with a bill declaring: "No person of color, bond or free, shall reside upon the soil of Dakota Territory; and should any attempt to do so they must leave within twenty days or be jailed." The measure failed.

Although allowed residence in the Territory, blacks were initially denied the right to vote, sit on juries, and educate their children. They were also denied the right of interracial marriage. In 1868, the laws were repealed to comply with the forthcoming Fifteenth Amendment to the federal constitution. The misce-genation law remained in effect, albeit with little attempt at enforcement. Miscegenation laws were reintroduced in 1909 when the legislature resolved not only that blacks and whites could not marry, but also that they could not cohabit without benefit of marriage. North Dakota maintained this legislation until 1955.

Not all legislative activity was restrictively structured. Via legislation passed in 1883, women of the territory gained the right to vote for school officials. By this same act, women were allowed to hold school-related offices. The issue of broader suffrage for women was a matter of continual debate, yet little came of the issue until 1914. That year, by a margin of 9,000 votes, North Dakota men denied full suffrage to the state's women. In 1917, however, under the guidance of the Nonpartisan League, North Dakota women received immediate suffrage on local issues, and approval for a state constitutional amendment to be submitted to the people. However, before the lengthy process of amending the constitution could be completed, national women's suffrage was enacted.

Civil rights in the state are further mandated by the 1983 North Dakota Human Rights Act. Somewhat broader than its national counterpart, as well as more easily adjudicated, this legislation guarantees equal protection without regard to race, color, religion, sex, national origin, age, the presence of any mental or physical disability, and marital or public assistance status. Gays and lesbians are not protected under the North Dakota Human Rights Act. Indeed, a 1997 statute declared marriage was an institution reserved for heterosexuals.

BIBLIOGRAPHY

Crawford, Lewis F. *The History of North Dakota*, Vol. 1. 1931.

Newgard, Thomas P., William C. Sherman, and John Guerro. *African-Americans in North Dakota: Sources and Assessments.* 1994.

Roper, Stephanie Abbot. *African Americans in North Dakota, 1800–1940.* Master's thesis. University of North Dakota. 1993.

Schneider, Mary Jane. *North Dakota Indians: An Introduction.* 1986.

State Bar Association of North Dakota. *The North Human Rights Act and You.* 1985.

Kimberly K. Porter

Nullification

Nullification was a concept developed and championed by John C. Calhoun in the 1820s and 1830s to protect the "minority rights" of South Carolinians against what he regarded as the tyranny of the majority represented by the U.S. federal government, then headed by President Andrew Jackson. Calhoun proposed a process by which an individual state could resist the enforcement of a federal law within its borders that it considered to be unconstitutional (see CONSTITUTIONALISM). The law would then be nullified and thus inoperative in that state.

In 1828 the U.S. CONGRESS passed a tariff act designed more to protect certain Northern manufacturers and producers than to raise revenue. South Carolinians felt that their economy, based substantially on European trade, would be jeopardized by the act. The SOUTH CAROLINA state legislature then approved Calhoun's anonymously written *Exposition and Protest*, claiming the act to be unconstitutional because its purpose was protection rather than revenue; *Exposition and Protest* proposed nullification if Congress did not repeal the tariff act. In 1832, a new tariff act still failed to bring the necessary relief, and the state legislature moved to implement the nullification process.

A complex series of events followed, including Calhoun's resignation as Vice President of the United States and election to the U.S. Senate by the South Carolina legislature, and the nullification of the tariffs of 1828 and 1832 by a specially called convention in that state. There, too, a minority (called the Unionists) felt that the nullifiers who were in the majority were denying them their rights by requiring their acceptance of nullification. In the U.S. Congress, members debated a force bill sought by President Jackson to authorize federal military action, if necessary, to collect tariff duties within South Carolina. At the same time that this bill passed so did a compromise tariff proposed by Senator Henry Clay of Kentucky that provided for a gradual reduction in the tariff rates. In the end, South Carolina accepted the tariff compromise but nullified the now-meaningless Force Act so as to be able to claim a victory for the nullification process.

Clearly nullification had not worked as Calhoun had intended. He had insisted that a protective tariff could be made constitutional only with an amendment to the Constitution, and that even should that occur, the nullifying state could still secede from the Union rather than comply. Left without the support of other states, however, South Carolina instead meekly accepted the tariff compromise, all the while claiming a victory for minority rights. Equally significant, the minority Calhoun sought to protect was actually his state's slaveholders. While concerned with high tariff rates, South Carolina's slavery advocates wished also to set the precedent of nullifying a tariff bill and then being able to use the same process to nullify any future act of Congress that might challenge or indirectly threaten slavery. The compromise outcome allowed all sides to claim victory, but eventually nullification became a largely irrelevant issue—one which no state pushed for unilaterally again. In 1860 and 1861, when South Carolina seceded, to be followed by ten other slave states, it claimed no right of nullification in its defense of secession.

BIBLIOGRAPHY

Ellis, Richard E. *The Union at Risk: Jacksonian Democracy, States' Rights and the Nullification Crisis*. 1987.

Freehling, William W. *Prelude to Civil War: The Nullification Controversy in South Carolina, 1816–1836*. 1965.

Peterson, Merrill D. *Olive Branch and Sword: The Compromise of 1833*. 1982.

Sellers, Charles, ed. *Andrew Jackson, Nullification and the States-Rights Tradition*. 1963.

Wiltse, Charles M. *John C. Calhoun, Nullifier, 1829–1839*. 1949.

Frederick J. Blue

O

Oakes, Richard

(1942–1972), political activist.

Civil rights activist Richard Oakes was a founding member and first president of the Student Council of American Natives (SCAN), which was later renamed the Student Kouncil of Inter-Tribal Nations (SKINS). Oakes also played an important role in the activist organization Indians of All Tribes (IAT).

Oakes was born on the St. Regis Reservation in upstate New York and raised as a member of the Mohawk tribe. Little is known about his early life except that he left high school in his junior year and drifted into construction work. Oakes eventually resumed his formal education at Adirondack Community College and Syracuse University. His trade took him to California where he worked as an ironworker while attending San Francisco State College. Oakes married Annie Marufo, a Pomo woman from the Kashia people. Marufo was a single mother of five when they met, and Oakes willingly took on the responsibility of helping to raise her children.

Oakes soon became involved in campus politics after enrolling at San Francisco State. A group of Native American students there united to form the Student Council of American Natives (SCAN). As the first president of SCAN, Oakes was instrumental in the creation of a formal American Indian Studies Department at the school for the purposes of increasing awareness of Native American traditions and culture.

In order to draw public attention to the plight of Native American people across the United States, students from San Francisco State joined with members of a Bay Area group, Indians of All Tribes (IAT), to occupy Alcatraz Island, a former federal penitentiary in San Francisco Bay, on November 9, 1969 (see ALCATRAZ OCCUPATION). This symbolic occupation, which was planned and led by Oakes, lasted until June 11, 1971—becoming the longest occupation of a federal facility by Indian people. While the specific demands of the protesters were never met, this action had an indirect effect upon government policy with regard to Indian self-determination.

Leaders of the American Indian Movement hold a press conference on December 24, 1969, at Alcatraz Federal Penitentiary during their takeover in 1969–1970. Leaders speaking at the press conference include Richard Oakes (left), Earl Livermore, and Al Miller. (CORBIS/Bettmann)

In the fall of 1972, a Native American teenager got into an argument with a young white man. Oakes stopped the fight, but the white man's companion, 34-year-old Michael Morgan, fired a gun over Oakes's head. On September 20, 1972, Oakes was shot and killed by Morgan, who later claimed that Oakes had attacked him. Morgan was charged with manslaughter, but justified his actions on grounds of self-defense. He was acquitted at trial. Leaders of the American Indian Movement were outraged over the incident and the outcome of the trial. As a tribute to the fallen warrior, the 1972 TRAIL OF BROKEN TREATIES caravan to Washington, D.C., was organized. Oakes is considered by Native Americans to be a martyr in the cause of Indian rights.

BIBLIOGRAPHY

Johansen, Bruce E., and Donald A. Grinde, Jr. *Encyclopedia of Native American Biography.* 1997.
Notable Native Americans. 1995.
"The Student Kouncil of Inter-Tribal Nations, 25 Years Remembered," San Francisco State University website, http://thecity.sfsu.edu/mandell/skins.html (October 5, 1999).
"We Hold the Rock," National Park Service website, http://www.nps.gov/alcatraz/indian2.html (October 5, 1999).

Jennifer Mossman

Office of Federal Contract Compliance Programs

The Office of Federal Contract Compliance Programs (OFCCP), created by President Lyndon B. JOHNSON's Executive Order 11246 in 1965, is a little-known but muscular element in the federal government's effort to ensure equal EMPLOYMENT opportunity for minorities. After the landmark CIVIL RIGHTS ACT OF 1964, President Johnson issued his executive order, which expanded an order issued by President John F. KENNEDY in 1961 (11114), to prohibit discrimination based on RACE, RELIGION, or national origin by all employers who worked on projects related to federal contracts. The order created the OFCCP to supervise the government's enforcement of its nondiscrimination policy. In 1967, Johnson amended the order to cover discrimination based on sex, and subsequent legislation included workers with disabilities, VIETNAM-era veterans, and disabled veterans among the protected class.

The OFCCP, located in the Labor Department, was given responsibility to oversee nondiscrimination enforcement by the twenty-six agencies responsible for federal contracts. The office was given authority to cancel contracts or to bar violators from receiving federal contracts in the future, based on its own compliance reviews or on complaints filed in its regional offices. In addition to enforcing nondiscrimination, the OFCCP emerged as one of the offices most involved in the development of AFFIRMATIVE ACTION policies. In 1967, the OFCCP helped define affirmative action when it called for employers to develop specific numerical goals for minority employment and to reach those goals within a specific time frame. In the early 1970s, the OFCCP went further by developing specific goals for federal contracts in several cities, most notably Philadelphia, where the NIXON administration, through the OFCCP, declared contractors guilty of "underutilizing" minorities if the contractors did not employ roughly the same percentage of minority workers as was available in the local labor force.

Despite its significant power, the OFCCP generally has acted with restraint, and has preferred to rely on the voluntary cooperation of contractors rather than its ability to cancel contracts. From 1965 through September 1971 the OFCCP disbarred (banned from federal contracts) only one contractor, and prior to 1980 it attempted to disbar only twenty-seven (thirteen of those came during its most active period, 1977–1980). Its limited enforcement has resulted from insufficient funding and staffing, from the difficulty of setting specific goals for minority employment, and from a lack of support, and at times hostility, from presidential administrations. In particular, through the 1980s President Ronald REAGAN opposed the use of affirmative action and sought, unsuccessfully, to rewrite the office's regulations to exempt 75 percent of federal contractors from the office's jurisdiction.

The OFCCP receives mixed reviews from observers. Minority groups and affirmative action supporters find it difficult to assess its success in fighting employment discrimination, but the office was instrumental in defining affirmative action in federal policy. Since 1980 it has been at the center of congressional debates over affirmative action, even if it is less visible in the public eye than the EQUAL EMPLOYMENT OPPORTUNITY COMMISSION (EEOC), its high-profile but less powerful cousin in equal employment policy enforcement.

BIBLIOGRAPHY

Cohodas, Nadine. "Affirmative Action Assailed in Congress, Administration." *Congressional Quarterly Weekly Report* (Sept. 12, 1981): 1749–1753.
Detlefsen, Robert R. "Affirmative Action and Business Deregulation: On the Reagan Administration's Failure to Revise Executive Order No. 11246." In *Presidential Leadership and Civil Rights Policy,* edited by James W. Riddlesperger, Jr., and Donald W. Jackson. 1995.
Federal Regulatory Directory, 8th ed. 1997.

Graham, Hugh Davis. *The Civil Rights Era: Origins and Development of National Policy, 1960–1972.* 1990.

Pineda, Julian. "Policy Issues in Federal Contract Compliance: The Executive Order Program and Affirmative Action." Ph.D. dissertation, University of California, Santa Barbara. 1983.

Rodgers, Harrell R., Jr. "Fair Employment Laws for Minorities: An Evaluation of Federal Implementation." In *Implementation of Civil Rights Policy,* edited by Charles S. Bullock III and Charles M. Lamb. 1984.

Craig A. Kaplowitz

Oglala Sioux Civil Rights Organization

Most contemporary accounts portray OSCRO as an activist organization formed after Richard A. (Dick) Wilson narrowly defeated Gerald One Feather in an election for president of the tribe at the Pine Ridge Reservation in 1972. Charges of corruption and nepotism against Wilson's administration drew authority from the Indian Civil Rights Act of 1968, which purported to protect tribal members from abuse by reservation officials as well as infringements by state governments. With support from the BUREAU OF INDIAN AFFAIRS, Wilson founded the Guardians of the Oglala Nation (GOON) squad to suppress militant opposition and prevent assemblies. Opponents—many of whom lost their jobs after Wilson's election—used the remedy of impeachment provided in the tribal constitution. Federal officers guarded trial proceedings, at which Wilson appeared as both the accused and the presiding officer. His acquittal on February 22, 1973—which came as no surprise—evoked public condemnation from members of several organizations, including a traditional Council of Elders and the Oglala Land Owners Association.

Local observers have credited spokesmen for the latter with the founding of OSCRO. Included were traditionalists Gerald One Feather, Dick Little, Dave Long, Virgil Kills Strait, and Sievert Young Bear; mixed-blood artist/activist Hobart Keith; and, belatedly, Pedro Bissonette, with a distinguished mixed-blood heritage reaching back to the arrival in Sioux country of French trader Louis (Bijou) Bissonette in 1812.

After a meeting in Calico Hall near Oglala village, members of OSCRO and the Council of Elders extended an invitation that validated the intervention of activists from the AMERICAN INDIAN MOVEMENT (AIM). After Wilson refused to negotiate with Russell MEANS, members of OSCRO and AIM cooperated in protest, staging the WOUNDED KNEE OCCUPATION for seventy-one days. Soon after representatives of both organizations signed a truce, Bissonette was killed by officers during a pursuit allegedly intended to arrest

Alfred Pilsmore (left), an 84-year-old Oglala Sioux Indian, discusses Indian needs with Democratic presidential hopeful Robert F. Kennedy at the poverty-ridden Calico Indian Village on the Pine Ridge Indian Reservation in South Dakota on April 16, 1968. (AP/Wide World Photos)

him for previous crimes. Following his death, OSCRO faded into oblivion. For outsiders, only snippets of information from the Wounded Knee trial records commemorate its role in the most consequential Native American protest of the twentieth century.

In the Pine Ridge area, tribal members and non-Indians alike remember OSCRO for its role in defense of tribal rights to use natural resources on the reservation, coming at a critical time in the unique history of the Oglala Lakota Tribe. Sources listed below (see Bibliography) help to explain a division of members into (southern) "Bear People" and (northern) "Smoke People" after the killing of holy man Bull Bear in 1841. Some alleged that Red Cloud, the nephew of Old Smoke, was directly involved in the killing.

The split facilitated Red Cloud's rise to prominence as a defender of traditionalism against intrusions by whites or mixed bloods to the year 1904. Thereafter, for three decades, Jack and Charles Red Cloud helped to sustain a "Red Cloud party" that carried on under the name of Oglala Council, without federal recognition, in competition with an elected Oglala Business Council, which received federal recognition to represent the tribe. Red Cloud partisans delayed land allotment, prevented the lease of grasslands to outsiders until WORLD WAR I, and prevented any significant sale of "surplus" land except during the opening of Bennett County in 1910. They persisted in a defense of land ownership and use by tribal members until they won a slight majority in a new, federally recognized executive council elected according to terms of a Wheeler-Howard constitution, approved in 1935. Thereafter, Frank Wilson—half Oglala and half white from LaCreek in Bennett County, who represented nontraditionalists—marshaled influence based on infusions of New Deal monies in the 1930s to narrowly win the office of tribal president three times before Red Cloud party members produced a vote of seventeen councilmen in favor and only six against his impeachment, and removed him from the tribal presidency in 1941.

Political developments at Pine Ridge during the years 1964 through 1973 represented a continuation of this partisan competition. Dick Wilson built a political machine through access to federal funds available to him as head of the Oglala Sioux Housing Authority, which led to his narrow victory over Gerald One Feather in 1972, followed by the unsuccessful impeachment effort in February 1973. The ones who reacted to Wilson's acquittal by the formation of OSCRO were in the main the same persons who led the Oglala Land Owners Association, whose agenda differed little from that the Red Cloud party had professed since the turn of the century.

Although they failed to displace the Wilson administration at that time, a federal report for the year 1996 indicated an abiding consequence of their effort to preserve a place for tribal life. Members retained ownership and primary use of 1,772,716 of 3,155,200 acres contained by reservation boundaries established in 1889, or 56 percent, which exceeded the retention rate of any other tribe on the Great Plains except that of the Crow. Surely tribal members owe much to OSCRO and the Council of Elders, as well as to Red Cloud and his independent political party, for a historic defense of real estate equaled in the affairs of few tribal groups across the United States. For this as well as for an essential role in the occupation of Wounded Knee during 1973, OSCRO earned a place in the annals of both regional and national history.

BIBLIOGRAPHY

Biolsi, Thomas. *Organizing the Lakota.* 1992. General description of Oglala political history through the 1940s.
Feraca, Stephen E. "The Political Status of the Early Bands and Modern Communities of the Oglala Dakota." *Museum News* 27 (1 & 2) (Jan.–Feb. 1966): 26 pages. Pioneering study of nineteenth-century Oglala history based on research among elders.
Price, Catherine. *The Oglala People, 1841–1879.* 1996. Reliable study of nineteenth-century Oglala history based on library and archival sources.
Sayer, John William. *Ghost Dancing the Law: The Wounded Knee Trials.* 1997. Legal analysis that contains characteristic snippets of recognition for the role of OSCRO at Wounded Knee. 1973.

Herbert T. Hoover

Ohio

"So you're the little woman who made this big war," said President Abraham Lincoln to Harriet Beecher Stowe, as he leaned down to shake her hand on the White House lawn in 1862. Stowe's novel *Uncle Tom's Cabin* was first published in 1852 as a serial in a Cincinnati abolitionist newspaper. Stowe lived in Cincinnati for seventeen years. Her novel was based on accounts of slave escapes, along the Ohio River.

An examination of the history of civil rights in the state of Ohio reveals a mixed record of commitment to civil rights that has waxed and waned with the shifting sands of social thought, political ideology, and state budgetary pressures. At different points in time, Ohio has been a national trailblazer in guaranteeing civil rights and liberties, and at other times it has lagged behind in civil rights protections.

The Northwest Ordinance, enacted by Congress in 1787, established rules for the development of land northwest of the Ohio River, and Ohio was the first state to emerge. At the 1802 State Constitutional Convention, the vote against slavery carried by a considerable margin, but the vote on black franchise was split evenly. In February 1803, Ohio was legally admitted as the seventeenth state to join the Union. In 1804, Ohio enacted the first of its "Black Laws," which restricted the rights and movements of blacks (see BLACK CODES). Although these laws were not always enforced in northern Ohio, they remained on the books in Ohio until 1887. There were, indeed, differing attitudes about African Americans in the northern and southern parts of the state. From the 1820s to the 1840s, antislavery sentiment grew, however. The *Philanthropist*—the first abolitionist newspaper in the United States—and the *Genius of Universal Emancipation* were both small newspapers published by social reform–minded Quakers in Ohio. Colleges were established in the state with a strong antislavery philosophy, such as Franklin College, Oberlin College, and the Lane Seminary. Ohio also came to be known as the "trunk line" for the passage north to freedom for runaway slaves via the famous "Underground Railroad."

In 1854, the REPUBLICAN PARTY was formed, partly in opposition to extending slavery to the Western Territories. Among the well-known Ohio Republicans were Salmon P. Chase, who urged Lincoln forward toward an EMANCIPATION policy and was later appointed as chief justice of the U.S. SUPREME COURT; John Bingham, who was hailed by Justice Hugo BLACK as the "Madison of the FOURTEENTH AMENDMENT" and whose name is inseparably linked to the Equal Protection clause; and Edwin Stanton, secretary of war during the Civil War. Wilberforce College, which was purchased by the African Methodist Episcopal Church in the 1860s, became the first college in America established to serve black students. In 1848, state law established separate black schools in communities with twenty or more blacks of school age (see SEGREGATION). In 1859, the Ohio Supreme Court ruled that distinctly black children were not entitled to attend white schools.

In 1869, the state General Assembly ratified the FIFTEENTH AMENDMENT. Nevertheless, Ohio refused to amend the State Constitution to permit black suffrage (see VOTING RIGHTS), and the amendment's language was not added to the State Constitution until the twentieth century, although even then it had no practical effect on African Americans' voting rights. In 1884, Ohio passed a public accommodations law allowing blacks to use theaters and other public places. It also allowed blacks to become jurors. In 1887, Ohio's "Black Laws" were repealed. In 1896, the Ohio legislature passed an ANTI-LYNCHING law, the Smith Act, named after the legislation's sponsor Harry C. Smith,

a black state legislator and newspaper publisher from Cleveland.

In 1959, the Ohio Fair Employment Practices Law was enacted, which prohibited discrimination by reason of race, color, religion, national origin, or ancestry. The same year the Ohio Civil Rights Commission was established as the state agency responsible for enforcing antidiscrimination laws. The commission recommended new legislation that put teeth into antidiscrimination laws, and in ensuing years such legislation eliminated the most egregious practices. After the 1954 U.S. Supreme Court decision in BROWN V. BOARD OF EDUCATION, Ohio cities dealt with the problem of school segregation. All but a few school systems in Ohio were in compliance with the *Brown* decision thirty years after it was rendered.

In 1964, the U.S. Supreme Court ordered the reapportionment of the lower house of the Ohio legislature to give equal representation to the cities, based on a system of one person, one vote. As a result, in 1966 the General Assembly had twelve black members, or 9 percent of the membership of each house. In 1964, the Mississippi Summer Project was launched in Oxford, Ohio, at the Western College for Women (now part of Miami University); it was a training ground for a group of idealists who headed South to promote black voter registration. The nation was shocked that summer by the murder in MISSISSIPPI of three of those volunteers, James Chaney, Andrew Goodman, and Michael Schwerner (see the entry at CHANEY). In October 1965, Ohio enacted a law prohibiting discrimination in HOUSING. In 1976, laws

A group of people assembles before the A. Philip Randolph Institute's Voter Registration Headquarters in Cincinnati, Ohio. A voter registration "courtesy car" is parked out in front. (Public Domain)

prohibiting discrimination in credit were enacted, and in 1987 the 1965 housing discrimination law was amended and broadened.

In the 1830s came the beginnings of secondary-level education for girls in Ohio. Along with New York, Ohio led the nation in pre–Civil War efforts to secure WOMAN SUFFRAGE. In 1861, the General Assembly enacted laws permitting women to own real estate and to make contracts where husbands had deserted or neglected them, providing a court so authorized. In 1852, Ohio passed the nation's first law to protect women in the workplace. In 1872, Victoria Woodhull from Ohio was the first woman to run for president, representing the Equal Rights Party. Her running mate was Frederick DOUGLASS. In 1894, Ohio passed its first woman suffrage law giving women the right to run for school boards and vote in school-board elections. In the years 1887–1894, the legislature granted married women control over their own property, gave women the power to act as guardians, executors, or administrators, and allowed them to sue and be sued. By 1922 the first women were elected to the Ohio General Assembly. In 1923, the legislature voted to extend full civil rights to women of majority age. The same year the Ohio Constitution was amended to permit women to serve on juries. In 1973, the state enacted laws prohibiting discrimination by reason of sex.

In 1993, Cincinnati voters approved a city charter amendment requiring that no special class status be granted based upon sexual orientation. In 1998, in the case of *Equality Foundation of Greater Cincinnati v. Cincinnati*, the U.S. Supreme Court refused to hear a challenge to this law and let stand a lower federal appellate court ruling that upheld this amendment. Ohio is, however, currently attempting to prohibit same-sex marriage (see GAY AND LESBIAN RIGHTS).

Reformers and philanthropists in Ohio between the 1820s and the Civil War were often involved in a wide range of causes, such as women's rights, peace, missionary work, antislavery, and the rights of the handicapped, orphaned, insane, and criminal. Once this initial zeal faded, however, public apathy allowed conditions to deteriorate in the states institutions. Ohio struggled to keep its public charges in a healthy and humane environment. During the 1980s Ohio made significant strides in creating community-based rehabilitation and support options for people with severe psychiatric disabilities. In the 1990s Ohio revamped its extensive system of institutions for the mentally and emotionally stressed. National surveys ranked the state's care of its custodial patients well above the national average.

The Ohio Penitentiary, built in 1834, was a model prison in the nineteenth century. During the 1880s the legislature adopted a series of significant reforms, including improved job training, a parole system, and the establishment of reformatories for young offenders. Subsequently, however, prison conditions started to deteriorate. After bloody prison riots in 1952 and 1968, state officials made improvements to the state prison system. In 1897, Ohio had been an early convert to the electric chair, but lethal injection was authorized as an optional method of execution in July 1993.

Like much of the rest of America, Ohio became more racially and ethnically diverse in the late twentieth century. Before World War II, less than 5 percent of the state's population was African American. In the postwar years, thousands of Hispanics migrated to Ohio. Beginning in the 1970s, the number of Asians—largely from Vietnam, Korea, and India—began to migrate to Ohio's urban centers, many seeking professional and business positions. This has created new controversies such as whether Asian Indians should be included in minority set-aside programs. The Ohio Ethnic Intimidation Act was passed, and it is designed to prevent the violation of the rights of another by reason of race, color, religion, or national origin. In 1993–1994 it was found to be constitutional under both the Ohio and U.S. Constitutions.

BIBLIOGRAPHY

Annual Reports of the Ohio Civil Rights Commission. 1959 to present.

Estell, Kenneth, ed. *The African-American Almanac,* 6th ed. 1994.

Havighurst, Walter. *Ohio: A Bicentennial History.* 1976.

Knepper, George W. *Ohio and Its People,* 2nd ed. 1997.

McPherson, James M. *The Abolitionist Legacy: From Reconstruction to the NAACP.* 1975.

Vexler, Robert I., ed. *Chronology and Documentary Handbook of the State of Ohio.* 1978.

Jay P. Kesan

Oklahoma

Oklahoma is identified with both the South and the American Southwest. However, its social policies, especially those associated with race and gender, have resembled those of the states of the old Confederacy. At Oklahoma statehood in 1907, the founding fathers did not write antiblack provisions into the constitution, but they wasted little time in passing a segregation (JIM CROW) law at the first session of the new state legislature. During the next half century, Oklahoma enacted statutes that strictly separated blacks and whites in practically every area of social, public, and economic life.

Blacks waged a sustained fight in Oklahoma against legalized discrimination. Building on the efforts of prestatehood protest groups such as the AFRO-AMER-ICAN LEAGUE, African Americans of Oklahoma organized a chapter of the NATIONAL ASSOCIATION FOR THE ADVANCEMENT OF COLORED PEOPLE (NAACP) in 1913. Two years later, that group won the *Guinn* case (*Guinn v. United States*), which successfully overthrew the so-called "grandfather clause" that kept blacks from the polls. *Guinn* gave the youthful NAACP—organized nationally in 1909—its first major victory, and it became the first of five major cases that went to the United States SUPREME COURT from Oklahoma before the historic BROWN V. BOARD OF EDUCATION decision in 1954. During the era of the 1920s, some Oklahomans joined the KU KLUX KLAN to keep blacks from the polls through intimidation, but the Klan never gained the following or achieved the success it enjoyed in the Deep South.

Segregated schools, restricted public accommodations, and limited economic opportunity impeded black people's journey toward full equality in the pre-1960 era. Legal efforts, nevertheless, did bring about some notable gains in the field of education immediately prior to *Brown*. In 1948, Ada Lois Sipuel successfully sued the state for admission to the University of Oklahoma Law School, and in 1950, the United States Supreme Court declared in the *McLaurin* case (*McLaurin v. Oklahoma State Regents*) that educational institutions could not segregate black students within a university. For a number of years after *Brown*, most black undergraduates attended all-black Langston University, but by the 1970s the majority of African-American students studied at desegregated colleges in the state. Integration of higher education in Oklahoma helped to pave the way for relatively smooth desegregation of public schools, without the friction or outright violence witnessed in some Southern states. The courageous leadership of Oklahoma's governor, Raymond Gary, a politician from an area of Oklahoma known as "Little Dixie," played an important role in this peaceful process.

Access to public accommodations and greatly expanded economic opportunities for blacks came with the 1960s civil rights movement. With the passage of the CIVIL RIGHTS ACT OF 1964, the institution of race-based hiring goals (AFFIRMATIVE ACTION), and the VOTING RIGHTS ACT (CIVIL RIGHTS ACT OF 1965) Oklahoma began to move away from restrictive racial policies and social customs. Although the rhetoric of young blacks sometimes appeared more race conscious than that of their forebears, they turned increasingly to politics and the economic system to remedy their problems. Yet, at the end of the twentieth century, statistics on housing, education, health care, and economic conditions told of a need for greater

A group of six African-American students stand on the steps of a building on the campus of the University of Oklahoma on January 29, 1955. The students sought to break down the state's policy of racial segregation in education by enrolling at the university in Norman. (CORBIS/Bettmann)

progress among blacks if the state were to ever overcome the crippling legacy of a segregated past.

Indians lost their tribal sovereignty and became citizens of the state upon Oklahoma's entrance into the union. The Oklahoma legislature did not legally segregate Indians by law, but ingrained customs and a tangled web of sometimes confusing and contradictory federal and state laws made difficult their march toward civil treatment and civil rights. They often found themselves the victims of a double standard of justice, in a society that relegated them to a status that contributed significantly to their continuing poverty. The period after the 1960s saw Oklahoma Indians win more rights in court, but, as with blacks, the positive changes in the three decades after the sixties could not quickly erase the effects of years of discrimination.

Cultural heritage constituted an important part of the Indians' quest for civil rights. For most of them, cultural heritage meant a return to tribal customs and tribal rights, stripped from the them near the end of the ninetieth century and at Oklahoma statehood. In actuality, the movement to recapture those rights never disappeared but gained renewed force in the period of the late 1960s. The rebirth of Indian courts in particular marked an important step in the fight for self-determination and heritage. In the decade of the seventies, legal judgments that recognized Indian land claims, water, and other resource rights strengthened the emphasis on "Indianness." Agitation by Indian groups and recommendations by the Oklahoma Civil Rights Commission helped to highlight the demands for Indian rights in the state.

The movement of Oklahoma's women toward full equality also met with daunting challenges. The state's progressivism in the early twentieth century led to the ratification of the Nineteenth Amendment in 1919 and women's right to vote; the vagaries of Oklahoma politics enabled a woman, Alice Robertson, to win election to the United States Congress in 1920. Ironically, Robertson, had been an antisuffragette and during her tenure she did practically nothing to advance the cause of women in Oklahoma or the country generally. For most Oklahomans, custom still dictated that a woman's place was in the home. No dramatic expansion of women's rights came until women took a page from the black civil rights movement, until they raised consciousness and made their concerns politically paramount.

Socially and politically active women in Oklahoma addressed a number of specific issues related to gender discrimination; what they desired was represented by the phrase "an equal partnership with men." Economic opportunity and the right of reproductive choice (abortion rights) stood center stage in the fight for women's rights in the state. In 1973 the United States Supreme Court's struck down state laws that made abortion a crime in *Roe v Wade*. Yet, the Oklahoma legislature never repealed its anti-*Roe* statutes, despite protestations from the state Affiliate of the National Abortion and Reproductive League, the Religious Coalition for Reproductive Choice, and the National Organization of Women (NOW).

The struggle by women for ratification of the Equal Rights Amendment (ERA) in Oklahoma mirrored both the progressiveness and the continuing conservatism in the "Sooner" state. Backed by such powerful groups as NOW and the Religious Committee for ERA, women persuaded Oklahoma's legislative leadership to support ratification of ERA, a feat that took more than ten years. Anti-ERA forces led by the Moral Majority in Oklahoma, STOP ERA, and the Eagle Forum responded by pledging powerful resources against the measure. With the defeat of the amendment in January 1982 by a vote of 27–21, the Oklahoma senate sounded the death knell for ERA, although polls showed that if one excluded the undecided vote, a majority of Oklahomans favored the amendment. Although ERA experienced a narrow defeat, the vote on the measure and the public reaction to it measured the distance women in Oklahoma had traveled toward greater civil rights. It also outlined the challenges that still remained before "an equal partnership with men" was to become a reality.

During the final three decades of the twentieth century, the state also demonstrated greater tolerance for persons who practiced alternative lifestyles, especially those who had a sexual lifestyle different from that of most citizens, even though most Oklahomans repudiated homosexuality. The fight for full acceptance and recognition by law of gays and lesbians has remained difficult. Successful cases in state and federal courts, along with congressional antidiscrimination statutes, did assist in shattering the image of an Oklahoma totally immovable on the issue of homosexuality. Few people could have imagined in 1960, for example, that a Gay Pride march could take place in Bible-belt Oklahoma twenty years later without any notable friction or violence.

At the beginning of the twenty-first century, Oklahoma had traveled a great distance from the extreme social conservatism that had curtailed the enjoyment of civil rights for many groups at statehood. To be sure, a number of social and legal barriers have fallen, but long-ingrained customs and attitudes continue to conspire against the achievement of equality for some citizens.

BIBLIOGRAPHY

Cross, George L. *Blacks in White Colleges: Oklahoma's Landmark Cases*. 1975.

Edds, Margaret. *Free at Last: What Really Happened When Civil Rights Came to Southern Politics*. 1987.

Ellison, Ralph. *Going to the Territory*. 1986.

Franklin, Jimmie Lewis. *Journey Toward Hope: A History of Blacks in Oklahoma*. 1982.

Franklin, Jimmie Lewis. *Back to Birmingham: Richard Arrington, Jr., and His Times*. 1989.

Franklin, John Hope, and John Whittington Franklin, eds. *My Life and an Era: The Autobiography of Buck Colbert Franklin*. 1997.

Joyce, Davis D., ed. *"An Oklahoma I Had Never Seen Before": Alternative Views of Oklahoma History*. 1994.

Morgan, H. Wayne, ed. *Newcomers to a New Land*. 1980. (A ten-volume series on ethnic groups in Oklahoma published by the University of Oklahoma Press with separate titles by individual authors.)

Oklahoma Advisory Committee to the United States Commission on Civil Rights. *Indian Civil Rights Issues in Oklahoma*. 1974.

Oklahoma Advisory Committee to the United States Commission on Civil Rights. *Selected Administration of Justice Issues Affecting American Indians in Oklahoma*. 1989.

O'Reilly, Jane. "The Mysterious and True Story of the ERA in Oklahoma." *MS* 2 (1982): 240–49.

Reese, Linda Williams. *Women of Oklahoma, 1890–1920*. 1997.

Royster, Beatrice Horn. "Mayor Arrington: His Record and the Economic Future of Birmingham." *Black Business Network* 2 (1983): 2–4.

Strickland, Rennard. *The Indians in Oklahoma.* 1980.
Tate, Michael. "Red Power: Government Publications and the Rising Indian Activism of the 1970s." *Government Publications Review* 8A (1981): 499–518.

Jimmie Lewis Franklin

Oliphant v. Suquamish Indians (1978)

The SUPREME COURT's ruling in *Oliphant v. Suquamish Indians* (1978) significantly weakened Native Americans' control over activities on their own reservations. The case was brought by two white men who had been arrested by Suquamish tribal police for disturbing the peace, reckless driving, and resisting arrest during the tribe's annual Chief Seattle Days celebration. The men argued that Indian tribes had no criminal jurisdiction over non-Indians, even if the crimes were committed within reservation boundaries. The Supreme Court ultimately agreed.

Under traditional federal Indian law, tribal governments retained all inherent rights of government unless explicitly given away through treaty or taken away by federal legislation. The Supreme Court acknowledged this long-standing principle but enumerated another exception when examining Oliphant's case. Characterizing Indian tribes as domestic dependent nations, the Court ruled that the tribes could not exercise any authority inconsistent with their status, as such power challenged the sovereignty of the United States. Reiterating the doctrine that tribes were dependent entities, as opposed to wholly sovereign nations, the Court restricted tribal authority to internal affairs. As a result, the traditional principles of federal Indian law were actually subverted by the Court even as it conceded them.

The Supreme Court's ruling substantially eroded the axiom that tribal governments were sovereign within Indian country, and it raised a new set of questions. Since state police officers have no jurisdiction over reservations and tribal courts have no jurisdiction over non-Indians, who can stop non-Indians from committing crimes on Indian land?

See also AMERICAN INDIAN CIVIL RIGHTS ACT OF 1968; INDIAN SELF-DETERMINATION AND EDUCATION ASSISTANCE ACT OF 1975.

BIBLIOGRAPHY

Getches, David H., Charles F. Wilkinson, and Robert A. Williams. *Cases and Materials on Federal Indian Law.* 1993.
Grossman, Mark. *The ABC-CLIO Companion to the Native American Rights Movement.* 1996.

Rochelle C. Hayes

Olivares, Luis

(1934–1993), activist priest.

Monsignor Luis Olivares defied both church and state to provide sanctuary for the undocumented. He first answered the call to social activism in the 1970s, helping migrant farm workers protest their dangerous and degrading working conditions. Meeting UNITED FARM WORKERS founder César CHÁVEZ on the picket lines inspired the priest to continue fighting injustice. Olivares helped found the United Neighborhoods Organization (UNO), a grass-roots group that organized Latinos around issues of social justice. He also began speaking out against the working conditions of day laborers and supported immigrants' efforts at union organizing.

Upon becoming pastor at a Los Angeles Catholic church in 1981, Father Olivares started ministering to war refugees from Guatemala and El Salvador. He publicly condemned U.S. foreign policy in Central America, and when immigration authorities refused to grant the refugees political asylum, Olivares declared his church a sanctuary for anyone facing deportation. Federal officials of the Immigration and Naturalization Service (INS) began investigating the church; Olivares received death threats. Church leaders pressured him to comply with federal law. Olivares responded by expanding his offer of sanctuary to include all illegal immigrants and asking Americans to ignore a 1986 immigration act prohibiting the hiring of undocumented workers (see IMMIGRATION AND IMMIGRANTS). Throughout the controversy Olivares refused to back down, insisting that he was obliged to follow God's word.

Olivares became infected with HIV (AIDS) while on a visit to a refugee camp in El Salvador. He subsequently left his pastorship and concentrated his efforts on AIDS awareness, remaining an activist until he died of complications from the disease in 1993.

BIBLIOGRAPHY

Boyle, Father Gregory J., Father Luis Olivares, and Michael Kennedy. "Sanctuary for the Undocumented: Above the Law, but Faithful to a Higher Authority." *Los Angeles Times*, September 21, 1988.
Huebner, Albert L. "Priest Among the People." *Progressive*, December 1986.
Kenkelen, Bill. "L.A. Sanctuary Priests Openly Defy INS, Mahony." *National Catholic Reporter*, November 11, 1988.
Tobar, Hector. "Father Luis Olivares, Voice for the Poor, Dies of AIDS." *Los Angeles Times*, March 20, 1993.

Rochelle C. Hayes

Olympic Boycott (1968)

In 1968, the civil rights movement's impact extended to the Olympic Games in Mexico City, Mexico. The 1968 Olympics were targeted for a major boycott in order to address RACISM, racial injustice, and discrimination against American blacks in sports. While the boycott never materialized, the Mexico City Games are now remembered for the symbolic protest of Tommie Smith and John Carlos raising their black-gloved fists in a BLACK POWER salute during the 200-meter dash awards ceremony on October 16. Smith had broken an Olympic record in the event and received a gold medal, while Carlos received a bronze.

Harry Edwards, a sociology professor at San Jose State College, had founded the Olympic Committee for Human Rights in 1967 to generate support for the proposed Olympic boycott. Edwards' efforts had also

Extending gloved hands skyward in racial protest, U.S. athletes Tommie Smith (center) and John Carlos stare downward during the playing of the Star Spangled Banner after Smith received the gold and Carlos the bronze for the 200-meter run at the Olympics in Mexico City on October 16, 1968. (AP Photo/files)

coincided with similar plans by African nations that threatened to boycott the 1968 Olympics in protest of apartheid in South Africa and that country's and Rhodesia's participation in the Games. The Olympic Committee for Human Rights linked racism and discrimination in the United States to that faced by blacks in Africa and elsewhere. The six demands that prompted the Committee's boycott included barring the all-white teams from South Africa and Rhodesia and the hiring of more African-American coaches.

The International Olympic Committee, which organizes the Games, eventually reversed its decision and barred South Africa and Rhodesia from participating in the spring of 1968. This move significantly deflated the boycott effort being planned by Edwards and his Olympic Committee for Human Rights. Even though the Olympic boycott didn't happen, the obvious protest by athletes Smith and Carlos at the Mexico City Games successfully connected civil rights activism to blacks' experience in sports.

BIBLIOGRAPHY

Edwards, Harry. *The Revolt of the Black Athlete.* 1970.
Hartmann, Douglas. "The Politics of Race and Sport: Resistance and Domination in the 1968 African American Olympic Protest Movement." *Ethnic and Racial Studies* 19, no. 3 (July 1996): 548–566.
Moore, Kenny. "A Courageous Stand." *Sports Illustrated,* August 5, 1991.
Moore, Kenny. "The Eye of the Storm." *Sports Illustrated,* August 12, 1991.
Spivey, Donald. "Black Consciousness and Olympic Protest Movement." In *Sport in America,* edited by Donald Spivey. 1984.
Wiggens, David K. *Glory Bound.* 1997.

Joann D. Ball

Operation Breadbasket

Operation Breadbasket was a selective buying program established in 1962 in Atlanta, GEORGIA, by the SOUTHERN CHRISTIAN LEADERSHIP CONFERENCE (SCLC). The program's chief aim was the use of economic boycotts to pressure white employers to hire black workers (see EMPLOYMENT). The use of selective patronage and economic boycotts were not new protest tactics in black communities; earlier campaigns such as "Don't Buy Where You Can't Work" were used in northern cities to secure jobs for black workers in white-owned stores in the early 1920s. Moreover, the SCLC was founded *after* the success of the 1955 MONTGOMERY BUS BOYCOTT. Hence, as sociologist Gary Massoni states in "Perspectives on Operation Breadbasket," the selective-buying concept that Breadbasket employed worked well in the African-American community, for it drew on a successful strategy that combined community power, black equality, and a concern for economic issues.

Operation Breadbasket personnel initially consisted of a small group of black ministers brought together by the SCLC. Following a series of successes in Atlanta, the SCLC extended the program to its affiliate chapters throughout the South. Breadbasket moved north when the SCLC launched its first northern drive in Chicago in 1966, known as the CHICAGO FREEDOM MOVEMENT. The SCLC initially saw the implementation of Operation Breadbasket in Chicago as a means to recruit African-American ministers into the Chicago movement. Under the leadership of Jesse JACKSON—then a young divinity student and SCLC staff member—Breadbasket generated jobs for hundreds of black workers and became one of the Chicago Freedom Movement's most enduring legacies.

BIBLIOGRAPHY

Frady, Marshall. *Jesse: The Life and Pilgrimage of Jesse Jackson.* 1996.
Garrow, David J. *Bearing the Cross.* 1986.
Massoni, Gary. "Perspectives on Operation Breadbasket." In *Chicago 1966*, edited by David J. Garrow. 1989.
Ralph, James R. *Northern Protest.* 1993.

Lori G. Waite

Operation PUSH

See Rainbow/PUSH Coalition.

Oregon

In April 1999, Oregonians celebrating 140 years of statehood gathered in Salem to look back on their history of discrimination as well as their struggle to assure civil rights for all the state's citizens. The Oregon House and Senate both passed resolutions commemorating that struggle and its successes. The same month the University of Oregon hosted the third annual Northwest Regional Queer Conference, which addressed the climate in the state and region for GAY AND LESBIAN RIGHTS. Both gatherings reflected on discrimination in the past and the degree of progress made to assure full civil rights for all Oregon citizens. The conviction of a Korean-owned plant in Eugene for discriminating against women and African Americans around the time these two groups met made clear, however, that on the eve of the next millennium, the state still had a way to go.

The fight for civil rights may be said to have begun in 1804, when the arrival of York along with his master, William Clark, and the rest of the Lewis and Clark Expedition brought slavery to the future state of Oregon as well as American contact with the Native Americans there. When Oregon was officially made a territory of the United States in the 1840s, slavery was prohibited, but, despite the ban, some African Americans were held in slavery there. In 1853 a black couple successfully sued the state to free their five children (*Holmes v. Ford*). Oregonians made no further effort to legalize slavery, but they did demand an exclusion of free blacks. The year after the first ban on slavery was enacted, the provisional government of the territory voted to exclude blacks and did so again in 1849 after the first exclusion was repealed. This second exclusion law remained in effect until 1926. Although there is evidence of only one black man being forced out as a result of this law, its existence as well as one denying the vote to blacks and Indians undoubtedly discouraged free migration into the territory and, after 1859, into the state of Oregon.

Despite the law excluding them and a climate of racial discrimination, a growing number of African Americans settled in the state, especially on the coast around Portland. In 1867 schools in the city were legally segregated. Other nonwhites were also legally discriminated against. Hawaiians were denied the right to own land. The Oregon Anti-Chinese Association successfully advocated legislation denying Chinese the vote and allowing discrimination against Chinese in EMPLOYMENT. In the twentieth century an increase in discriminatory legislation followed an increase in the nonwhite population. The number of blacks in the state had risen with the coming of the railroad. In 1919 Portland added a residential segregation policy to its policy of segregating schools (see HOUSING). Miscegenation laws were passed to prohibit interracial marriage. Chinese and Japanese were somewhat freer to live where they chose in Portland but also confronted discrimination; "Whites Only" signs excluded them as well. Jews were generally included as white but faced enough subtle discrimination to form an antidefamation committee in 1906.

African Americans fought the violation of their political and other civil rights, especially through the state's chapter of the NATIONAL ASSOCIATION FOR THE ADVANCEMENT OF COLORED PEOPLE (NAACP); in 1926 the exclusion law was repealed and the following year the voting ban was lifted. Beatrice Canady was especially prominent in fighting remaining forms of discrimination against African Americans through her Portland paper, *The Advocate.* The influx of African Americans and other nonwhite groups seeking war-related jobs during WORLD WAR II resulted in renewed discrimination, however, especially in housing. Oregonians of Japanese ancestry confronted the most profound violation of civil rights during the war when they were forced, along with other Japanese Americans on the West Coast, into concentration camps and placed under curfews (see JAPANESE-AMERICAN INTERNMENT CASES).

The postwar years witnessed some improvement in the state's racial climate. In 1949 Oregon became one of the first states to pass a fair employment practice act (see FAIR EMPLOYMENT PRACTICES COMMITTEE). Four years later Oregon followed other West Coast states in banning discrimination in public accommodations. In 1969 gender was included as a category in the state's antidiscrimination law. Almost one hundred years earlier, Abigail Scott Duniway became the first woman to address the Oregon Legislature. Her leadership was important for victories such as a women's property act passed in 1878. Other forms of restrictive legislation, however, remained in force well into the twentieth century. In 1908 the U.S. SUPREME COURT, in *Muller v. Oregon*, upheld a state law limiting the workday for women to ten hours based on an assumption that public interest required the special protection of its future mothers. A liberal abortion law as well as laws forbidding such paternalistic practices as credit discrimination in the 1970s reveal a strikingly different climate for female civil rights a half-century later. Gays and lesbians were just beginning to fight for similar protection of their civil rights in that decade. In the 1990s they twice defeated efforts by the Oregon Citizen's Alliance to deny them basic civil rights.

BIBLIOGRAPHY

Dodds, Gordon B. *The American Northwest: A History of Oregon and Washington.* 1986.
Ho, Nelson C. *Portland's Chinatown: A History of an Urban Ethnic District.* 1978.
McLagan, Elizabeth. *A Peculiar Paradise: A History of Blacks in Oregon, 1788–1940.* 1980.
Taylor, Quintard. *In Search of the Racial Frontier: African-Americans in the American West, 1528–1990.* 1998.
Toll, William. *The Making of an Ethnic Middle Class: Portland Jewry Over Four Generations.* 1982.

Bess Beatty

Organization of Afro-American Unity

The Organization of Afro-American Unity (OAAU), a black nationalist organization and human rights group, was founded in Harlem, New York, on June 28, 1964. Led by MALCOLM X, a former member of Elijah MUHAMMAD'S NATION OF ISLAM, the OAAU was modeled after the Organization of African Unity and similarly designed to unite people of African descent across class, political, religious, and regional lines. It was also intended to be a secular counterpart to his Muslim Mosque, Inc., which Malcolm had organized shortly after leaving Muhammad's movement in March 1964 for those who followed him out of the Nation.

The program of the OAAU called for more indigenous control over the political systems, economic situations, and educational facilities of African-American communities. It advocated the organization of independent political clubs to educate black voters and elect African-American candidates to office. The membership of the OAAU was also encouraged to be entrepreneurial and to support and patronize black businesses. Rent strikes, aimed at improving housing conditions, were endorsed, as were the establishment of clinics to address drug addiction, black participation on local school boards, and a cultural revolution that would recognize the value of African-American artistic talent. There were some themes that carried over from Malcolm X's Nation of Islam past, such as his stress on self-defense, black pride, and economic self-help. However, most of the program of the OAAU was a synthesis of civil rights themes—electoral participation, boycotts, and enforcement of antidiscrimination laws—and a progressive black nationalism that emphasized African-American initiative, self-respect, and autonomy, along with the shared humanity of all people.

The primary constituency of the OAAU was the African-American community of New York City. The organization never attracted more than several hundred members, and these individuals were largely working-class people who had either followed Malcolm X out of the Nation of Islam or had been recently drawn to his more activist, but less racially chauvinistic, program and rhetoric. OAAU membership was restricted to African Americans, for it was believed that blacks had to first unite and work among themselves before inviting others into their affairs. However, unlike the Nation of Islam, the OAAU openly sought to align itself with integrated civil rights groups and was open to working alliances with progressive whites.

Unfortunately, the OAAU, due to several factors, never became a significant force in the African-American community. It was created in the midst of Malcolm X's conflict with his former mentor, Elijah Muhammad, who viewed the new organization as a direct challenge to his own. Scarce resources ensured that the OAAU would not grow rapidly, and surveillance and counterintelligence activities by the FEDERAL BUREAU OF INVESTIGATION (FBI) and other state agencies likely had the same effect. Additionally, Malcolm X, the person best able to organize and shore up the reputation of the new group, was abroad during much of 1964 in an attempt to internationalize the African-American freedom struggle and his own image as a viable leader and Sunni Muslim. Conceivably, the OAAU could have served as a bridge that would have linked Malcolm and his constituents to the ethos and agenda of the mainstream civil rights movement. However, his death on February 21, 1965, revealed the weaknesses of his nascent movement, which all but died with him.

BIBLIOGRAPHY
Breitman, George, ed. *By Any Means Necessary.* 1970.
Carson, Clayborne, et al. *Malcolm X: The FBI File.* 1991.
Clark, Steve, ed. *Malcolm X: February 1965, the Last Speeches.* 1992.
Clegg, Claude A., III. *An Original Man: The Life and Times of Elijah Muhammad.* 1997.
Goldman, Peter. *The Death and Life of Malcolm X.* 1976.
Lincoln, C. Eric. *The Black Muslims in America.* 1961.
Malcolm X (with Alex Haley). *The Autobiography of Malcolm X.* 1965.
Sales, William W., Jr. *From Civil Rights to Black Liberation: Malcolm X and the Organization of Afro-American Unity.* 1994.

Claude A. Clegg III

Organization of Chinese Americans

In response to the African American civil rights movement, a group of Chinese Americans realized the need for a national organization, with headquarters in Washington, D.C., that would be similar to other civil rights organizations. In 1971 Kung Lee Wang and others established the Chinese American Leadership Council, the predecessor to the ORGANIZATION OF CHINESE AMERICANS (OCA). In 1973 the inaugural OCA annual convention was held and Wang was elected as national president, serving until 1977.

This nonprofit, nonpartisan civic organization has the following goals: to promote the active participation of Chinese Americans and Asian Americans in civic affairs at all levels; to secure justice, equal treatment, and equal opportunity for Chinese and Asian Americans; to eliminate ignorance about and bigotry against Chinese and Asian Americans; to promote the cultural heritage of Chinese Americans; and to foster positive images of Chinese and Asian Americans. In the 1990s there were forty chapters with over four thousand members who were American citizens or permanent residents. There is also a branch in Hong Kong.

Among its many activities and accomplishments, the OCA played a major role in creating national awareness of the Vincent Chin hate crime; successfully lobbied to raise the Hong Kong immigration quota to ten thousand per year, beginning in 1979; persuaded the Pekin Illinois High School to change its nickname from "Pekin Chink" to "Pekin Dragon" in 1973–1974; contributed to the establishment of Asian Pacific American Heritage Week (in May) in 1979; and challenged the unfair Asian-American admission practices at several universities.

BIBLIOGRAPHY
Oral interview with Christine Chen. 1998.
Organization of Chinese Americans. Videotape. 1998.
Organization of Chinese Americans. *20th Annual National Convention Program.* 1998.

Sue Faun Chung

Ozawa v. United States (1922)

Prior to *Ozawa*, existing laws and legal precedents limited CITIZENSHIP to free white persons and persons of African descent but did not specifically exclude Japanese immigrants from NATURALIZATION. Ambiguity over whether free white persons included Japanese allowed many Japanese immigrants to declare their intention to become American citizens. Some even became citizens before the attorney general ordered federal courts to cease issuing naturalization papers to Japanese in 1906. The 1910 census counted over four hundred naturalized Japanese Americans.

When alien land laws made property rights contingent upon naturalization rights, the Pacific Coast Japanese Association Deliberative Council decided to support a test case to secure citizenship for Japanese immigrants. The organization thought Ozawa Takao was an ideal candidate to make a case for the naturalization of Japanese. Ozawa was an assimilated immigrant who had lived in America for twenty-eight years. He had attended American schools, married an American-educated woman, and spoke English with his children. Although Ozawa had satisfied all the criteria outlined in a 1906 act concerning naturalization, federal courts in California and Hawaii denied his citizenship petition.

The Supreme Court upheld the opinions of the lower courts, stating that Ozawa failed the racial requirements for naturalization. Apart from borderline cases which needed to be ruled upon individually, the court concluded that the legal reference to white persons was synonymous with Caucasians. Regardless of skin color, Ozawa was Mongolian rather than Caucasian and therefore did not qualify as a white person.

The decision that Japanese were unequivocally aliens ineligible for citizenship left Japanese immigrants politically marginalized while reinforcing alien land laws. The ruling also helped curtail Japanese immigration after the IMMIGRATION ACT OF 1924 denied entry to all aliens ineligible for citizenship.

BIBLIOGRAPHY
Chuman, Frank F. *The Bamboo People: The Law and Japanese-Americans.* 1976.
Ichioka, Yuji. "The Early Japanese Immigrant Quest for Citizenship: The Background of the 1922 Ozawa Case." *Amerasia Journal* 4 (1977): 1–22.

S. H. Tang

P-Q

Pacifism

In the seventeenth century, members of the traditional peace churches—Mennonites, Brethren, Quakers, and Amish—followed literally the New Testament injunction "Resist not Evil," and so were called nonresistants. The pacifism of their churches forbade support of state violence. Church members would not pay war taxes or pay to be exempted from the militia, and they would not perform alternative service. Intertwined with this pacifism was opposition to slavery. In the period of the Revolutionary War, the Society of Friends (Quakers) carried out an extensive campaign for the abolition of slavery. Friends were the first to recognize the injustice of the system and to respond in an organized fashion. By 1754, many Quakers were teaching that, apart from the violence by which slaves were obtained, slavery was wrong in itself as a violation of human rights.

By the early nineteenth century, churches not traditionally pacifist founded organizations to promote peace: The New York Peace Society, the Massachusetts Peace Society, and the American Peace Society. Secular arguments against violence began to emerge. By the time of the Civil War, pacifists practiced civil disobedience, tax refusal, public disturbances, boycotts, and direct actions such as sit-ins. The most effective pacifist organization in the nineteenth century was the New England Non-Resistance Society, headed by radical activist William Lloyd Garrison. Henry David Thoreau's celebrated essay "Civil Disobedience" was strongly influenced by Garrison's philosophy of Christian anarchism. Before the passage of the Fugitive Slave Act of 1850 when African-Americans began to arm themselves, Frederick DOUGLASS, allied with Garrison, practiced nonresistance for years. But the immature pacifist movement had not yet developed an effective, pragmatic practice of pacifism, and it fell apart during the Civil War.

With the advent of WORLD WAR I new organizations appeared: the Women's Peace Party (1914) and the People's Council of America (1917). The first organized opposition to the war came with the formation of the Anti-Enlistment League in response to the passage of the Conscription Law of 1917. Those who would not accept any service under military authority served harsh sentences in military prisons. As WORLD WAR II approached, pacifist groups such as the American Peace Mobilization opposed American entry into the war against Germany; but the German attack on Russia caused most peace groups to support U.S. entry into the war against the Nazis. Some organizations and individuals remained pacifist throughout the war, however. The *Catholic Worker*, with a circulation of over 100,000, sponsored the Association of Catholic Conscientious Objectors. But the antiwar effort began to crumble, leaving a small hardcore group of pacifists to oppose the war in isolation. The hardcore pacifist community was isolated in Civilian Public Service (CPS) camps and in prisons.

After World War II the Ban the Bomb movement was born. Physicist Albert Einstein, for example, urged resistance of all scientists to military research. A. J. Muste (1885–1967) emerged as a major figure in the pacifist community. Muste was active in the War Resisters League, and his adoption of nonviolent tactics

(From left to right) Communist theoretician Herbert Aptheker, SDS founder Tom Hayden, chairman of the Committee for Nonviolent Action A. J. Muste, and Yale history professor Staughton Lynd present their case at a public meeting at the Manhattan Center in New York City on January 16, 1966. Aptheker, Hayden, and Lynd had just returned from a peace mission to Hanoi, initiated as a result of what they perceived to be the failure of the U.S. government to negotiate with the Viet Cong and the North Vietnamese. (CORBIS/Bettmann)

influenced Martin Luther KING, JR., and early civil rights groups. Muste took a leading role during the VIETNAM WAR, organizing rallies, vigils, and marches to protest expanding U.S. involvement. Gradually a cadre of experienced nonviolent activists was being developed for whom nonviolence was a way of life. During the Vietnam War, many young people came to view the whole American society as part of a war culture, and huge numbers of them became radical pacifists. But in the 1970s the antiwar movement became badly fractured into violent and nonviolent factions. Pacifists made small nonviolent raids on Selective Service offices. When peace finally came in 1975, radical pacifism had passed from being an individual way of life to being a pragmatic mass political strategy. After the Vietnam War many radical pacifists returned to disarmament as the priority issue. The U.S. invasions of Granada and Panama in the 1980s, the Persian Gulf War of 1990, and the U.S.-led bombing of Serbia in 1999 provoked little public protest.

BIBLIOGRAPHY

Brock, Peter. *Twentieth Century Pacifism.* 1970.

Cooney, Robert, and Helen Michalowski. *The Power of the People: Active Nonviolence in the United States.* 1977.

Cortright, David. *Peace Works: The Citizen's Role in Ending the Cold War.* 1993.

Eric Cummins

Page Law (1875)

The Page Law (1875) restricted the entry of Chinese women immigrants into the United States, limited the growth of the Chinese American community, and helped to justify subsequent Chinese Exclusion legislation. Passed into law on March 3, 1875, "An Act Supplemental to Acts in Relation to Immigration"—sponsored by California congressman Horace Page, and commonly referred to as the Page Law—denied entry to contract or "cooly" laborers, criminals, and "women imported for the purposes of prostitution" from "China, Japan or any Oriental country." Where an earlier 1862 bill regulating the importation of Chinese contract labor penalized those transporting Chinese for "lewd and immoral purposes," the Page Law focused on Chinese women themselves, refusing entry to those who could not prove their moral character.

The Page Law was the first federal law to prevent women immigrants from entering the country on the explicit assumption that they may have been prostitutes; deportation of foreign-born prostitutes of any race would not become law until 1907. American officials who strictly enforced the law assumed that all Chinese women were prostitutes, and so effectively limited the immigration of all Chinese women to the United States. This resulted in a highly imbalanced ratio of males to females and, ironically, increased the demand for Chinese prostitutes. Arguments in favor of restricting the immigration of Chinese male laborers cited the apparent lack of families and the visibility of Chinese prostitutes as demonstrating the inability of the Chinese to assimilate into American society. Thus the Page Law itself constituted an essential part of the movement to exclude Chinese immigrants, and also contributed to the Chinese Exclusion legislation first enacted in 1882. (See CHINESE EXCLUSION ACTS; IMMIGRATION AND IMMIGRANTS.)

BIBLIOGRAPHY

"An Act Supplementary to the Acts in Relation to Immigration." Act of March 3, 1875. *United States Statutes at Large,* 477.

Chan, Sucheng. "The Exclusion of Chinese Women, 1870–1943." In *Entry Denied: Exclusion and the Chinese Community in America, 1882–1943.* 1991.

Espiritu, Yen Le. *Asian American Women and Men.* 1997.

Peffer, George Anthony. "Forbidden Families: Emigration Experiences of Chinese Women Under the Page Law, 1875–1882." *Journal of American Ethnic History*, 6 (1986): 28–46.

Peffer, George Anthony. *If They Don't Bring Their Women Here. Chinese Female Immigration Before Exclusion.* 1999.

Karen J. Leong

Pan-African Congresses

Six Pan-African Congresses were held between 1900 and 1945. These meetings brought together intellectuals and race leaders of the African Diaspora to discuss strategies for improving the conditions of Africans worldwide. The first congress was held July 23–25, 1900, in London. It grew out of the desire of diasporan Africans for freedom and progress, based on the collective vision of a dynamic Africa. This notion, better known as PAN-AFRICANISM, has animated many intellectuals and race leaders of the African Diaspora since the nineteenth century. The first conference was organized by Trinidadian lawyer Sylvester Williams and African Methodist Episcopal Bishop Alexander Walters. It petitioned Queen Victoria to grant autonomy to Great Britain's African and West Indian colonies within the British Empire. It also called for political and civil rights for African Americans. At the conference, W. E. B. Du Bois made his famous statement that the problem of the twentieth century would be that of the color line. Due to its participants' belief that European colonialism was a civilizing force in Africa, the first Pan-African Congress did not call for the complete overthrow of WHITE SUPREMACY and COLONIALISM.

The next Pan-African Congress took place February 17–21, 1919, in Paris. Du Bois and the Senegalese delegate to the French Chamber of Deputies, Blaise Diagne, organized the conference. Like its predecessor, it did not call for a complete end to European domination of Africa. The delegates viewed this as unattainable. Instead, they called for the ending of slavery and capital punishment in Africa, as well as land reform, improved education, and limited self-government.

The following three Pan-African Congresses—held in 1921 in London, in 1923 in Lisbon, and in 1927 in New York—had little impact despite their being presided over by W. E. B. Du Bois. During these years the most important and powerful proponent of Pan-Africanism was Marcus GARVEY, whose UNIVERSAL NEGRO IMPROVEMENT ASSOCIATION greatly overshadowed Du Bois's Pan-Africanist efforts.

The final and most important Pan-African Congress was held in Manchester, England, October 15–19, 1945. Although Du Bois, then 77, was revered as a presiding elder, the conference was dominated by continental Africans such as Kwame Nkrumah of the Gold Coast (later Ghana), Nnamdi Azikwe of Nigeria, Jomo Kenyatta of Kenya, and a host of other young African freedom fighters. This conference called, as it predecessors did not, for the complete liberation of Africa from European control as well as for the use of force to achieve this if peaceful negotiation did not work. The conference jump-started the African independence movement. Consequently, the late 1950s and 1960s saw most of the African continent gain its political freedom from Europe.

Since the sixth Pan-African Congress, there have been numerous gatherings and festivals of black intellectuals and artists from throughout the Diaspora. Along with the Pan-African Congresses of the first half of the twentieth century, these activities have fostered cooperation and unity among black race leaders throughout the African Diaspora.

BIBLIOGRAPHY
Abdul-Raheem, Tajudeen. *Pan Africanism: Politics, Economy, and Social Change in the Twenty-First Century.* 1996.
Geiss, Imanuel. *The Pan-African Movement: A History of Pan-Africanism in America, Europe, and Africa.* 1974.
Legum, Colin. *Pan-Africanism: A Short Political Guide.* 1962.
Lewis, David Levering. *W. E. B. Du Bois: Biography of a Race.* 1993.

Hayward Farrar

Pan-Africanism

Pan-Africanism is a global political movement with the primary goal of creating a unified, independent African continent free of colonial (i.e., non-African) ties—both economic and cultural. This transcontinental phenomenon has sought to unite African peoples from the Caribbean, Europe, and the Americas. The movement emerged because of the forced and massive dislocation of African people into the West and in response to the dehumanizing effects of deportation from their native lands, enslavement throughout the world, and the ultimate genocide of millions of African people. During the eighteenth and nineteenth centuries, African lands were colonized by European nations such as England, Germany, France, Portugal, and Belgium (see COLONIALISM). As a result, most of the natural mineral resources of the African continent were exported to industrialized European nations and did not benefit native African people. African people were widely dispersed—physically, psychologically, politically, and socially—and experienced a loss of freedom and dignity.

Some of the major philosophies of Pan-Africanism are as follows: (1) to create and maintain solidarity among persons of African descent; (2) to encourage persons of African descent to recognize Africa as their original homeland; (3) to instill a belief in a distinct African personality; (4) to strive for a united future Africa (at the same time not encouraging or indulging in unnecessary physical violence or vengeful acts against past oppressors); and (5) to build religious beliefs and understanding. In the early nineteenth century, many proponents of the movement called for the return of peoples of African descent to the African continent; this came to be called the "Back to Africa Movement" or the "Africa for the Africans Movement." The most famous of the early leaders of the modern Pan-Africanist movement were W. E. B. DU BOIS (the "Grand Old Man" of the movement) and Marcus GARVEY.

Du Bois organized and sponsored international PAN-AFRICAN CONGRESSES as early as 1900. Although he was a supporter of INTEGRATION of the races rather than their separation, Du Bois's stated purpose of these conferences was to protest the stealing of lands in the colonies, racial discrimination, and other issues of interest to blacks. From a 1923 separatist perspective, as reprinted in *The Philosophy and Opinions of Marcus Garvey: Or, Africa for the Africans*, Marcus Garvey described the movement as follows:

> The political re-adjustment of the world means this—that every race must find a home . . . [S]imultaneously Negroes (sic) are raising the cry of "Africa for the Africans," those at home and those abroad. It is a cry for political re-adjustment along natural lines, and this re-adjustment has come out of the war of 1914–18, because, we, as Negroes realize that if (with our knowledge and experience of western civilization) we allow the world to adjust itself politically without thought for ourselves, we would be lost to the world in another few decades.

Pan-Africanist views were supported and espoused by MALCOLM X in the 1960s. Alex Haley, in *The Autobiography of Malcolm X*, stated that Malcolm X "sought to refashion the broken strands between the American Negroes and African culture. He saw in this the road to a new sense of group identity, a self-conscious role in history, and above all a sense of man's own worth which he claimed the white man had destroyed in the Negro." Thus, in the United States, the Pan-Africanist movement of the 1960s and the 1970s continued to stress the need to strengthen both spiritual and political ties with the newly independent countries of the African continent.

Nearly a century after the first international Pan-African Conference, the seventh was held in Uganda in 1994. Its purpose was to continue the traditions and goals of the movement as previously established— namely, to serve as a counterforce to imperialism. In addition, present-day proponents of Pan-Africanism urge the resistance of the recolonization of Africa and its peoples in the next millennium.

BIBLIOGRAPHY

Abdul-Raheem, Tajudeen, ed. *Pan-Africanism.* 1996.
Garvey, Amy Jacques, ed. *The Philosophy and Opinions of Marcus Garvey: Or, Africa for the Africans.* [1923] 1986.
Grant, Joanne, ed. *Black Protest: History, Documents, and Analyses.* 1968.
Haley, Alex. *The Autobiography of Malcolm X.* 1964.
Legum, Colin. *Pan-Africanism: A Short Political Guide.* 1963.
Lemelle, Sid. *Pan-Africanism for Beginners.* 1992.
Marah, John K. *African People in the Global Village: An Introduction to Pan African Studies.* 1998.
Walker, David. *David Walker's Appeal, in Four Articles, Together with a Preamble to the Coloured Citizens of the World, but in Particular, and Very Expressly, to Those of the United States of America,* rev. ed. [1830] 1993.

Cynthia G. Hawkins-León

Pan-Indianism

See Pan-Tribalism.

Pantoja, Antonia

(1921–   ), Puerto Rican educator and community activist.

Antonia Pantoja was born into a working-class family in San Juan, Puerto Rico, in 1921. In 1944, she came to live in New York City, where she received her formal education while living and working in the Puerto Rican *barrio*. As a factory worker, Pantoja fought for workers' rights and aided unionization efforts (see UNIONS). She was also active in laying the foundations for a network of Puerto Rican social and cultural organizations. Through her work, Pantoja also played a leading role in devising solutions to many of the problems affecting the New York Puerto Rican community.

Pantoja viewed organizational bodies and strategies as vehicles for progressive social change and the promotion of civil rights for Puerto Rican diaspora communities. Among those in which she was most influential were the Puerto Rican Association for Community Affairs (1953), the Puerto Rican Forum (1958), ASPIRA (1961), and Boricua College (1970). In the 1980s she moved to California and helped organize the Graduate School for Community Development in San Diego. She followed up this achievement by being instrumental in the formation of an economic development corporation, Producir, in Puerto Rico.

Pantoja earned an undergraduate degree from Hunter College of the City University of New York. After teaching in New York City schools, she returned to college to earn masters and doctorate degrees in social work. She has been praised for her extraordinary achievements, especially for inspiring generations of Latino youth and for tirelessly dedicating her life's work to bringing educational and other opportunities to the Puerto Rican and other Latino communities. The sociologist Joseph Fitzpatrick referred to Antonio Pantoja as "the Puerto Rican community's inspiration and guiding spirit." In 1996, President Bill CLINTON awarded her the Presidential Medal of Freedom. (See also PUERTO RICAN MOVEMENT.)

BIBLIOGRAPHY

National League for Nursing. "Antonia Pantoja." In *Women of Hope: Latina Series.* 1999.

Perry, Wilhelmina. "Memories of a Life of Work: An Interview with Antonia Pantoja." *Harvard Educational Review* (Summer 1998).

Virginia Sánchez Korrol

Pan-Tribalism

In the second half of the twentieth century, many Native American leaders have turned to pan-tribalism as a necessary tactic and philosophy for their activism. This development seemed a natural response to the problems faced by Native Americans, for beyond the difficulties of individual tribes and nations, many challenges require united efforts. The roots of pan-tribalism may lie in the war alliances of the past, such as in King Philip's War (1675–1676), the Pontiac Rebellion (1763), and the War of 1812, when the Shawnee chief Tecumseh and his brother, the prophet Tenskwatawa, called upon all red men to unite against the expansionism of the U.S. government. A foreshadowing of pan-tribalism can also be seen in the Ghost Dance Religion, which was proclaimed by Wovoka, a Paiute mystic, and spread through the Western tribes, ending in the tragedy of the WOUNDED KNEE MASSACRE in 1890. In recent years the Native American Church (popularly known as the "Peyote Religion") has attempted to spread a pan-tribal spirituality.

In the twentieth century, a variety of organizations have been created to lobby Congress for favorable legislation, to pursue legal strategies in the courts, to court public opinion, and to improve economic, educational, and social conditions for Native Americans. In 1912 the SOCIETY OF AMERICAN INDIANS was established by Arthur C. Parker (Seneca), Charles Alexander EASTMAN (Santee Dakota), Charles E. Daganett (Peoria), and Carlos Montezuma (Apache), and in 1944 Indian employees of the BUREAU OF INDIAN AFFAIRS created the NATIONAL CONGRESS OF AMERICAN INDIANS. During the Franklin ROOSEVELT administration, Indian Commissioner John Collier proclaimed an "Indian New Deal" under the INDIAN REORGANIZATION ACT OF 1934 and the federal government encouraged several pan-Indian organizations.

In the wake of the civil rights movement of black Americans and in the context of the various protests of the 1960s and '70s, a RED POWER movement got under way. Clyde WARRIOR (Ponca) and Melvin Thom (Paiute) founded the NATIONAL INDIAN YOUTH COUNCIL in 1961. In 1968 the AMERICAN INDIAN MOVEMENT (AIM) was created by Russell MEANS (Sioux), Dennis BANKS, George Mitchell, and Clyde BELLECOURT (Chippewa/Ojibwa). In addition to lobbying, AIM favored more radical action, including SIT-INS, protest marches, occupations, and even (occasionally) violence. Two of AIM's most famous actions were the occupation of Alcatraz Island (1969) and the violent confrontation at Wounded Knee, South Dakota (1973). Many allied organizations came out of the American Indian Movement, such as the INTERNATIONAL INDIAN TREATY COUNCIL AND CONFERENCES and the WOMEN OF ALL RED NATIONS. The greatest support for pan-tribalism has come from within large American urban areas where Indian populations have been effectively divorced from their respective tribal traditions and have been amalgamated into Indian ghettos.

Independent of AIM and apart from radical politics, various economic, legislative, and social issues have demanded a pan-tribal response, and various organizations have been created to deal with specific areas of interest such as the NATIVE AMERICAN RIGHTS FUND (1970), the National Indian Educational Association (1970), National Tribal Chairmen's Association (1971), and the Council of Energy Resource Tribes (1976).

BIBLIOGRAPHY

Cornell, Steven. *The Return of the Native: American Indian Political Resurgence.* 1988.

Deloria, Vine, Jr., and Clifford M. Lytle. *The Nations Within: The Past and Future of American Indian Sovereignty.* 1984.

Hertzberg, Hazel W. *The Search for American Indian Identity: Modern Pan-Indian Movements.* 1971.

Patrick M. O'Neil

Parchman Farm

Parchman Farm, the fabled state penitentiary of MISSISSIPPI, is a sprawling twenty-thousand-acre plantation in the cotton-rich land of the Yazoo Delta. Its legend has come down from many sources: the work chants of the prisoners who have toiled there; the black country blues of ex-convicts such as Eddie "Son" House and Washington "Bukka" White; the writings of William Faulkner, Eudora Welty, Shelby Foote, and John Grisham. To generations of Southerners, Parchman is the quintessential penal farm, the closest thing to slavery that survived the Civil War.

Built on land acquired from the Parchman family, it opened in the early 1900s, following the abolition of convict leasing in Mississippi. Worked largely by black convicts, the prison had three objectives: punishment, profit, and racial control. In design, it resembled an antebellum plantation. The superintendent lived in splendor on the grounds. Each of the fifteen field camps was directed by a sergeant ("overseer"), who disciplined the convicts with a strap known as "Black Annie" and set down the daily routine. Under him was an assistant sergeant ("driver"), who worked the convicts in the fields, and a nightwatchman, who ran the barracks where they lived. The mass of convicts were known as "gunmen" because they toiled under the guns of selected inmates called "trusties." The gunmen spent twelve to sixteen hours each day in the fields. All around them was a "gun line," drawn in the dirt. If a convict crossed that line without permission, he would be shot. When a trusty killed or wounded a prisoner trying to escape, he was routinely pardoned by the governor.

Between 1900 and 1970, Parchman cotton produced huge revenues for the nation's poorest state. Change was inevitable, but it came slowly. In the 1960s, state officials used Parchman as a place to break the will of civil rights workers who came to Mississippi on the FREEDOM RIDES; but the move backfired, for it focused national attention on an institution that symbolized the racist brutality under attack. In the early 1970s, the federal courts stepped in, and prison reforms were mandated from the bench. Describing Parchman as "an offense to the conscience of civilized people," Judge William Keady desegregated the prison, closed the worst camps, and supervised the hiring of trained penologists and civilian guards. Today, with 6,500 inmates, Parchman is one of the largest penal institutions in the United States.

BIBLIOGRAPHY

Oshinsky, David M. *"Worse than Slavery": Parchman Farm and the Ordeal of Jim Crow Justice.* 1996.
Taylor, William B. *Brokered Justice: Race, Politics, and Mississippi Prisons, 1798–1992.* 1993.

David M. Oshinsky

Parker, John Johnston

(1885–1958), U.S. circuit judge.

Federal Judge John Johnston Parker was born in Monroe, NORTH CAROLINA, and educated at the University of North Carolina in Chapel Hill. Later, he practiced law, futilely pursued elective offices in North Carolina as a Republican, and prosecuted World War I profiteers. On March 21, 1930, President Herbert Hoover nominated forty-five-year-old Parker—judge of the United States Court of Appeals for the FOURTH CIRCUIT since 1925—as Associate Justice of the SUPREME COURT. The appointment precipitated protests by organized labor and the NATIONAL ASSOCIATION FOR THE ADVANCEMENT OF COLORED PEOPLE (NAACP). Labor assailed his well-supported judicial decision affirming a decree prohibiting unionization of West Virginia's bituminous coalfields. The NAACP targeted an element of Parker's New South progressive platform on which he ran as the GOP's 1920 gubernatorial candidate—his public statement disapproving black political participation and disavowing black support. Parker deemed such participation detrimental to harmonious race relations and to an issue-oriented campaign that avoided customary Democratic race-baiting. Notwithstanding a record of reaching out to black North Carolinians, his 1920 statement contributed to a personal transformation. Beset by the Association's initiative and by its unprecedented grassroots political mobilization, Parker's nomination suffered defeat in the Senate (39–41) on May 7, 1930, the NAACP's first major success in that filibuster-prone chamber.

Parker remained on the Fourth Circuit bench where he wrote opinions invalidating South Carolina's white primaries, applying a reason-based antidiscrimination principle to invalidate race-differentiated public school teachers' salaries as well as racially discriminatory railroad labor union practices and to forbid a South Carolina school board from imposing unequal public schools on black students. Parker's court complied with the Supreme Court's 1954 BROWN v. BOARD OF EDUCATION decision, construing it to hold that "the Constitution . . . does not require integration. It merely forbids discrimination." Application of this "Parker Principle" to public parks, golf courses, and local transportation, and his expressed hope that the spirit of Christian brotherhood might infuse race relations elicited denunciatory mail.

BIBLIOGRAPHY

Burris, William C. *Duty and the Law: Judge John J. Parker and the Constitution.* 1987.
Fish, Peter Graham. "Torchbearer for Pre-New Deal Southern Economic Development: Judge John J. Parker of the U. S. Court of Appeals for the Fourth

Circuit." In *An Uncertain Tradition: Constitutionalism and the History of the South,* edited by Kermit L. Hall and James W. Ely, Jr. 1989.

Goings, Kenneth W. *The NAACP Comes of Age.* 1990.

Peter Fish

Parks, Rosa Louise McCauley

(1913–   ), civil rights leader.

Rosa Parks is the civil rights activist whose defiance of JIM CROW segregation on a public bus in Montgomery, ALABAMA, sparked the MONTGOMERY BUS BOYCOTT, one of the first mass protests of the modern civil rights movement. On December 1, 1955, Parks's refusal to give up her seat and subsequent arrest engendered a boycott led by a young local minister, Rev. Martin Luther KING, JR. Following the national and international media attention and protracted court battle, the community-driven protest was ultimately successful, resulting in the desegregation of Montgomery's buses in December 1956. As an icon of the civil rights movement, Parks is often mistakenly characterized as a sim-

Rosa Parks smiles during a ceremony on Capitol Hill on June 15, 1999, at which she received a Congressional Gold Medal in honor of her role in the 1955 struggle to desegregate the public transportation system of Montgomery, Alabama. (CORBIS/Reuters Newmedia Inc.)

ple woman who chose not to stand because she had tired feet. However, Parks had been resistant to bus segregation laws prior to the boycott and was well known in the black community for her active role in the local chapter of the NATIONAL ASSOCIATION FOR THE ADVANCEMENT OF COLORED PEOPLE (NAACP). Parks was not only a catalyst for the boycott, but also a brave leader in the struggle against demeaning Jim Crow laws.

Born in Tuskegee, Alabama, to James and Leona McCauley, Parks was raised in rural Pine Level, Alabama, by her mother and grandparents. Parks received her earliest education in a one-room school where her mother was the teacher. As an adolescent, Parks moved to the city to attend the Montgomery Industrial School for girls. Although she did not finish high school, Parks's experiences at Industrial taught her the skills that would get her employment as an adult and the elegant manners that would later characterize her in the Montgomery community.

Rosa married Raymond Parks in 1932. The couple lived in Montgomery where Rosa worked as a nurse and seamstress and Raymond as a barber. In the early 1930s, Raymond Parks helped organize local support on behalf of the SCOTTSBORO CASE boys, nine teenagers falsely accused of raping two white women in Scottsboro, Alabama. Rosa and Raymond Parks shared an interest in racial politics and often discussed the difficulties of black life in the segregated South.

To challenge the limits of segregation, Rosa Parks joined the Montgomery chapter of the NAACP. Parks grew under the leadership of local NAACP president E. D. NIXON, an activist who was also a leading member of the BROTHERHOOD OF SLEEPING CAR PORTERS. Parks was elected chapter secretary in 1943, registered to vote in 1945 while working in voter-registration campaigns, led the chapter's Youth Council, and served as secretary of the state conference. Parks' participation in workshops at the HIGHLANDER FOLK SCHOOL in the fall of 1955 expanded her leadership skills and introduced her to a network of men and women activists from diverse communities throughout the South. Highlander, an egalitarian interracial institution founded in the 1930s as a training ground for union activists, became an important center for training civil rights activists.

Parks' act of resistance in the winter of 1955 was spontaneous, yet grounded in her personal knowledge of the wrongs of segregation and bolstered by her ties to community organizers in Montgomery and throughout the South. While Parks was riding home from work on a racially segregated bus, the driver asked Parks and three other black passengers to stand when the "For Whites Only" section of the bus filled. Only Rosa Parks refused. Parks's refusal to give up her seat was supported by local organizers such as E. D. Nixon and Jo Ann Robinson who led the local Women's Political Council. The groundswell of support from all sectors of black Montgomery despite the overwhelming possibility of white violence and harassment was groundbreaking. Throughout the year-long protest, Parks remained a leader in the boycott organization, the Montgomery Improvement Association, although she lost her job and there were numerous threats on her life. Parks was not the first black Southerner to resist the rules of segregation, but her actions when coupled with the collective protests of the community helped propel the South toward mass mobilization.

In the wake of the difficult boycott, Parks left Alabama and eventually settled with her husband in Detroit, Michigan. In 1965 Parks became a special assistant to Congressman John Conyers, Jr., who employed her for twenty-five years. In 1987 Parks founded the Rosa and Raymond Parks Institute for Self-Development. Parks has received numerous awards and honorary degrees, most notably the Congressional Gold Medal (1999) and the Martin Luther King, Jr. Award (1980).

Alice Paul on March 31, 1926, shortly after her appointment as an adviser to the Woman's Bureau of the U.S. Department of Labor. (CORBIS/Bettmann)

BIBLIOGRAPHY

Crawford, Vicki L., Jacqueline Anne Rouse, and Barbara Woods, eds. *Women in the Civil Rights Movement: Trailblazers and Torchbearers, 1941–1965.* 1990.

Friese, Kai. *Rosa Parks.* 1990.

Garrow, David, ed. *The Montgomery Bus Boycott and the Women Who Started It.* 1987.

Rosa Parks Oral History. *Black Women's Oral History Project.* Radcliffe College. 1978.

Blair L. Murphy

Paul, Alice

(1885–1977), suffragist and feminist.

Alice Paul imported the radical tactics of British suffragists into the American women's fight for the vote. Born into a wealthy Quaker family, Paul attended Swarthmore College and what became the Columbia University School of Social Work. Between 1907 and 1910, Paul worked at a settlement house in England and became involved with the suffrage fight there. A follower of radical suffragist Emmeline Pankhurst, Paul was arrested, imprisoned, and force-fed after a hunger strike. She began working with the National American Woman Suffrage Association (NAWSA) in 1912, after earning a Ph.D. in sociology from the University of Pennsylvania. Paul soon formed the Congressional Union, a subgroup within the NAWSA which lobbied for a federal amendment for women's suffrage. Expelled by the NAWSA for her militancy in 1914, Paul continued to lobby for a federal amendment and formed the National Woman's Party (NWP) in 1917. Paul's militant tactics included picketing the White House, as well as targeting Democrats for political defeat because of their inaction on women's issues. Imprisoned when they held up signs critical of the Wilson administration, NWP activists fought to be considered political prisoners. While more conservative suffrage leaders saw Paul as a dangerous menace who would alienate potential supporters, the NWP's militancy focused national attention on the issue of women's suffrage and helped legitimize the more traditional organizations like the NAWSA. After the suffrage fight, Paul continued her militant struggle for women's equality by introducing the Equal Rights Amendment to Congress in 1923. Although many women's organizations opposed the ERA on the grounds that it would undermine protective legislation for women, Paul spent the rest of her life trying to enact gender equality into American law.

BIBLIOGRAPHY

Ford, Linda. *Iron-Jawed Angels: The Suffrage Militancy of the National Woman's Party, 1912–1920.* 1991.

Lunardini, Christine A. *From Equal Suffrage to Equal Rights: Alice Paul and the National Woman's Party, 1910–1928.* 1986.

Renee Romano

Peace and Freedom Party

The Peace and Freedom Party is a CALIFORNIA-based political party "committed to democracy, ecology, feminism, and socialism," according to its most recently published platform. On civil rights issues, its platform commits it to "defend affirmative action," to "end discrimination based on race, sex, age, sexual orientation, or disability," and to "end environmental racism." In recent state elections it has opposed California ballot propositions that called for the reduction of benefits for illegal immigrants and for the end of AFFIRMATIVE ACTION programs as administered by state agencies and institutions of higher learning. It seeks to work "within the system" to promote social change.

The Peace and Freedom Party was established in 1967 in reaction to the VIETNAM WAR and racial unrest, and has run candidates for president, vice president, and many California statewide and local offices, since 1968. It made its best showing in a presidential election in 1968, when Black Panther Eldridge CLEAVER, and African-American comedian and activist Dick Gregory, each nominated for president by different party factions, won a total of about eighty-five thousand votes out of a total of about seventy-two million votes cast. Its best single vote-getter in a presidential

Black Panther leader Eldridge Cleaver, 1968 presidential candidate of the Peace and Freedom Party, stands next to bullet-riddled posters in the window of Black Panther headquarters in Oakland, California, on September 11, 1968. (AP/Wide World Photos)

election was its 1972 nominee, Dr. Benjamin Spock, the pediatrician and author, who won about sixty-one thousand votes, including fifty-five thousand cast in California. In 1996 its presidential nominee won about 22,500 votes out of over 100,000,000 cast. All of the 22,500 votes were cast in California.

The Peace and Freedom Party's candidates for senator from California have won an average of 1.85 percent of the vote since 1968, and its candidates for governor have won an average of 1 percent of the vote since 1970. The best showing by one of its candidates for statewide office was made by its 1978 candidate for State Controller, Elizabeth Cervantes Barron, who won 300,000 votes, or 4.6 percent of the total.

The Peace and Freedom Party has achieved its greatest electoral successes in local nonpartisan elections, where its members have won seats on city councils, school boards, special district boards, and local park and recreation boards.

In addition to contesting in elections, the Peace and Freedom Party has established food cooperatives, free health clinics, and community newspapers. It has helped organize labor union strikes and boycotts, demonstrations against nuclear power plants, nuclear tests, and militarism; and demonstrations supporting the rights of immigrants, gays and lesbians, and women seeking abortions. Its official newspaper is *The Partisan.*

The Peace and Freedom Party's formal organizational structure includes county central committees and a state central committee. California voters registered as members of the Peace and Freedom Party may be elected to its committees in California's primary election. The Party also allows citizens under eighteen years old, as well as aliens, to serve on its local or state committees if elected by the Party membership.

The Peace and Freedom Party holds conventions every two years to adopt the Party's platform and, in presidential election years, nominate its candidates for president and vice president. Candidates for Congress and state and local office are nominated in California's direct primary.

BIBLIOGRAPHY

Chester, Lewis, Godfrey Hodgson, and Bruce Page. *An American Melodrama: The Presidential Campaign of 1968.* 1969.

Farmighetti, Robert, ed. *The World Almanac and Book of Facts, 1997.* 1998.

Also used, and especially helpful, are the Internet web pages for the Peace and Freedom Party Central Committee, the Peace and Freedom Party's Alameda County and Sonoma County chapters, and *The Partisan.* Their locations are as follows:

Alameda County, California, Peace and Freedom Party: http://www.peaceandfreedom.org/index.html

The Partisan: http://www.geocities.com/CapitolHill/Lobby/3666/

Peace and Freedom Party California State Central Committee: http://www.come.to/peaceandfreedom

Sonoma County, California, Peace and Freedom Party: http://www.sonic.net/~emcfarla/pfpage.html

Malcolm Lee Cross

Peltier, Leonard James

(1944–), civil rights activist and Native American leader.

A prominent activist for the civil rights of native peoples, AMERICAN INDIAN MOVEMENT (AIM) leader, author, and humanitarian Leonard Peltier has been at the center of one of the most controversial federal legal cases in U.S. history, prompting an international outcry against his imprisonment since 1977. Amnesty International lists him as a U.S. political prisoner, and many regard him as the "Nelson Mandela of America."

Peltier was born September 12, 1944, in Grand Forks, NORTH DAKOTA, to Leo and Alvina Reabedeux, Ojibwa members of the Sioux nation. He grew up around copper mines and logging camps, where his parents worked as migrant laborers. Peltier left home in 1958, doing odd jobs until he reached Washington state, where he worked in the fishing industry. In the early 1960s he began his activist career through involvement in fishing rights conflicts, and in 1970 he

Leonard Peltier (center), the leader of the American Indian Movement, is escorted by guards across the yard at Okalla Prison in British Columbia, Canada, toward a helicopter waiting to take him to the United States, in accordance with a deportation order, on December 18, 1976. (CORBIS/Bettmann)

joined the American Indian Movement (AIM) as a fundraiser at the Pine Ridge, SOUTH DAKOTA branch. He was a principal organizer of the 1972 TRAIL OF BROKEN TREATIES, a protest march that began and ended in Milwaukee, WISCONSIN.

In 1973, AIM joined a coalition of native groups in the seventy-one-day WOUNDED KNEE OCCUPATION in South Dakota to protest authoritarian control by the tribal government, and to block the leasing of reservation lands to mining and timber companies. Though the standoff ended on May 9, 1973, harassment of protesters by tribal government authorities, the BUREAU OF INDIAN AFFAIRS, and the FEDERAL BUREAU OF INVESTIGATION (FBI) increased. Between 1973 and 1975, a "range war" raged, during which scores of AIM members and supporters were killed, and the movement as a whole was subjected to a relentless Counterintelligence Program (COINTELPRO). Mobilization against AIM and traditional native people was so intense that Sioux elders appealed to AIM nationally for protection. In 1975, Peltier assisted in creating an armed defense camp at the Harry Jumping Bull compound near Oglala on the Pine Ridge reservation.

On June 26, 1975, FBI agents Jack Coler and Ron Williams pursued AIM member Jimmy Eagle onto the Jumping Bull compound in an unmarked vehicle and engaged residents in a firefight that resulted in the deaths of Coler, Williams, and AIM member Joe Stuntz. A massive federal manhunt ended in the indictment and arrests of AIM members Dino Butler, Bob Robideau, Jimmy Eagle, and Leonard Peltier. Peltier was extradited from Alberta, Canada, by U.S. officials and brought to Fargo, North Dakota, to stand trial. Meanwhile, Butler and Robideau were acquitted by an Iowa jury on grounds of self-defense, and charges were dropped against Eagle. Eager for a conviction, the federal government vigorously prosecuted Peltier.

Though he was convicted and sentenced to two consecutive life sentences, the facts of Peltier's case and the slapdash handling of the prosecution by the government have resulted in widespread criticism from human rights organizations, foreign governments, legal advocates, judges, and other miscellaneous observers. Extradition affidavits were falsified, evidenced was tampered with or suppressed, testimony was coerced, and the trial was arbitrarily moved to the docket of a judge renowned for Indian convictions. In 1980, after failed appeals, the Leonard Peltier Defense Committee (LPDC) obtained twelve thousand pages of FBI documents through the Freedom of Information Act, though another six thousand pages were withheld for reasons of "national security" and later "lost." In 1986, even after the Eighth Circuit Court of Appeals found that the trial judge erred in his rulings, and that the government's prosecution of the case was faulty at best, Peltier's appeal was denied. Despite international protests, subsequent appeals for retrial or parole, in 1991, 1993, and 1996, were all denied. Nevertheless, Peltier continues to write about and be an advocate for human rights for indigenous peoples around the world.

BIBLIOGRAPHY

Matthiessen, Peter. *In the Spirit of Crazy Horse.* 1983.
Messerschmidt, Jim. *The Trial of Leonard Peltier.* 1983.
Peltier, Leonard. *Prison Writings: My Life Is My Sundance.* 1999.

Joseph Heathcott

Penn Center

Penn Center began as one of the first southern schools for newly free African Americans. Located on St. Helena Island, in Beaufort County, in the heart of SOUTH CAROLINA's Sea Islands, Penn School was founded in 1862 by Laura Towne and Ellen Murray, two white women sent by the Pennsylvania Freedmen's Aid Association. They were later joined by Charlotte Forten, the first black teacher to come to St. Helena. Their effort was part of the "Port Royal Experiment," which focused on teaching self-sufficiency to the African-American population during the transition from slavery to freedom. After the Civil War, Penn School specialized in more advanced education, including teacher training and political education and organizing.

In the early 1900s, the school operated as a normal, agricultural and industrial education institution. Penn School closed in 1948 and began operating as a local, national, and international resource center.

Prior to and during the 1960s, when integrated meetings were against the law, the Center played a pivotal role by hosting meetings for many civil rights groups, including the SOUTHERN CHRISTIAN LEADERSHIP CONFERENCE and the STUDENT NONVIOLENT COORDINATING COMMITTEE. Over the years, the Center has received financial help from Quakers, foundations, and many Penn alumni, some of whom have left their island but continue support of their old school.

Today, the History and Culture Program of the fifty-acre National Historic Landmark District maintains a substantial collection of materials on the Sea Islands and its people, conducts cultural and academic programs, and remains a catalyst for self-sufficiency for local people.

BIBLIOGRAPHY
Goodwine, Marquetta L. *Gullah/Geechee*, Vol.1: *The Serenity of St. Helena.* 1997.

Constance Curry

Pennsylvania

One of the political characteristics that set Pennsylvania apart from the other original American colonies was its emphasis on religious freedom, which attracted the Pennsylvania Dutch, primarily reformed Lutherans, to the region as well as other groups such as the Quakers, Amish, Mennonites, Dunkers, and Moravians, all or whose moral convictions played a role in shaping the colony's attitude toward slavery. Pennsylvania, though certainly not insulated from America's early climate of RACISM, was one of the more progressive of the original thirteen colonies in its attitude toward African Americans.

Slavery was not as prominent in Pennsylvania as it was in other states, in part, because Quakers could not morally reconcile the institution with their religion. The structure of Pennsylvania's economy also played a part in the colony's view of slavery because the absence of large plantations all but eliminated the need for indentured servitude or slavery. In retrospect it does not seem unusual that Pennsylvania was one of the first colonies to form an organized abolition movement, the Pennsylvania Abolition Society (1775). Still, the institution was practiced by many in Pennsylvania, including its celebrated founder, William Penn, who owned twelve slaves at one time.

The racial tension that developed in Pennsylvania was caused, in part, by competition for manual labor and craftsman work. In 1725 public officials in Pennsylvania adopted a BLACK CODE, which prevented free blacks from socializing with slaves. The measure was designed to preempt unified political activity within the black community. Nevertheless, many African Americans demonstrated loyalty during the Revolutionary War (1775–1776), which earned them some measure of acceptance in northern states. Toward the end of the eighteenth century, Pennsylvania passed a law whose aim was the gradual abolition of slavery. In addition, all free men were granted the right to vote in Pennsylvania in 1890.

In the early to mid nineteenth century, "slave catching," in which runaway slaves were seized and returned to their owners, was common in the United States. Pennsylvania was one of the first states to take exception to the activity by passing a "personal liberty" law in 1826 prohibiting slave catching. However, in 1842 a Maryland slave catcher challenged the law. In *Prigg v. Pennsylvania*, the U.S. SUPREME COURT struck down Pennsylvania's personal liberty law, ruling that states could not interfere with the apprehension of fugitive slaves. Not all Pennsylvanians were in favor of promoting civil rights for blacks. Indeed, the JIM CROW laws common in the South, which were designed to segregate blacks in schools, public transportation facilities, and parks were institutionalized in some regions of Pennsylvania. Before the Civil War, black communities tended to fare better in Pennsylvania in relation to other regions of the country, in part because of the latitude they were afforded in the areas of religious and educational institutions.

It was in Gettysburg, Pennsylvania, that Abraham Lincoln delivered his famous Gettysburg Address in November 1863, which honored those who gave their lives to protect the Union. During the Civil War blacks fought vigorously on the side of the Union, which elevated their social status. After the Civil War many blacks migrated from the South to Pennsylvania, where they were more likely to enjoy political and social equality. In 1881, long before the landmark 1954 Supreme Court decision in BROWN V. BOARD OF EDUCATION, the Pennsylvania legislature integrated Pennsylvania's schools. In 1882 the Pennsylvania Equal Rights Bill was passed, which prohibited discrimination against blacks in the use of public facilities. However, the same resistance to equality that plagued the United States was also rampant in Pennsylvania. JIM CROW laws were often formally and informally upheld at the local level until well into the twentieth century. In 1942 the Pennsylvania legislature prohibited discrimination against blacks in unions, which greatly improved access to higher-paying jobs. In 1961, through the efforts of Homer S. Brown, K. Leroy Irvis, and the NATIONAL ASSOCIATION FOR THE ADVANCEMENT OF COLORED PEOPLE (NAACP), a Pennsylvania law was passed prohibiting SEGREGATION in housing. Then, in 1966 the civil rights movement captured the nation's attention when the Supreme Court forced Girard College in Philadelphia to open its doors to African Americans.

The Constitution of the Commonwealth of Pennsylvania provides for the protection of civil rights for all residents of the state. Article I, section 26 of the Pennsylvania Constitution holds that "[n]either the Commonwealth nor any political subdivision thereof shall deny to any person the enjoyment of any civil right, nor discriminate against any person in the exercise of any civil right." Politically African Americans made significant strides in Pennsylvania during the latter half of the twentieth century. In 1983 W. Wilson Goode became Philadelphia's first black mayor and

Representative William Grey earned a leadership position in Congress in the late 1980s. Although Pennsylvania was certainly not insulated from the social injustices suffered by blacks, in many ways it paved the way beyond one of the most regrettable periods in American history.

The struggle for women's rights in Pennsylvania closely paralleled and was also intertwined with the civil rights struggle for African Americans. On December 9, 1833, Ester Moore founded the Philadelphia Female Anti-Slavery Society. Seven years later, in 1840, delegates convened in London, England, for the World's Anti-Slavery Convention. Female attendees were denied the right to seating on the convention floor. Among those delegates excluded was Sara Pugh, a Quaker teacher from Philadelphia who was attending the convention as a representative of the Philadelphia Female Anti-Slavery Society. Pugh, who shortly thereafter became president of the society, wrote a stern letter of protest on behalf of all the female attendees, which was addressed not only to the convention leadership but to the United States government, the press, and the world at large. On October 18, 1854, Philadelphia was the site of the Fifth National Women's Rights Convention.

Later in the nineteenth century, as the trade union movement flourished, another Pennsylvania woman, Mary Harris Jones, participated in a railroad strike in Pittsburgh, during which a roundhouse (a maintenance facility for locomotives) was burned to the ground. For her role in this and many other labor actions, particularly her organizing efforts among workers in the coalfields to the east of Pittsburgh, she became widely known as "Mother Jones."

On September 17, 1887, the Constitutional Centennial was celebrated in Philadelphia. During the celebration, Susan B. ANTHONY and other members of the National Woman Suffragist Association sent a protest document to U.S. President Grover Cleveland on behalf of women's rights and the need to amend the Constitution. It was not until 1915 that Pennsylvanians were presented with a measure granting women with the right to vote. This measure was defeated by the (male) citizens of Pennsylvania, only five years before the NINETEENTH AMENDMENT, granting women with the right to vote throughout the United States, was finally passed.

The mistreatment of blacks early in American history is paralleled only by the experiences of the American Indian. Several Native American tribes were forced off their land and driven westward onto reservations against their will upon the passage of the 1830 Indian Removal Act. Tribes such as the Choctaw from Mississippi and the Iroquois, which included the Mohawk, Oneida, Onondaga, Cayuga, and Seneca tribes who originated from the Great Lakes region, were driven westward and placed on reservations. These forced migrations were poorly organized and resulted in thousands of deaths due to starvation, disease, and exposure to the elements. The journey was figuratively referred to as the "trail of tears." Native Americans that settled in Pennsylvania received anomalous treatment. The Lenape Tribe, which settled near Allentown, Pennsylvania, peacefully coexisted with the native settlers of Pennsylvania for several years. The Lenape tribe, closely related to the Algonquins, traded fur with the settlers of Pennsylvania. Discriminatory acts against the Lanape in Pennsylvania were rare. The same cannot be said for the treatment of tribes from New York and others along Pennsylvania's eastern coast. The Indian Defense League was established in 1926 to protect Native Americans against discrimination.

BIBLIOGRAPHY
Blockson, Charles L. *African Americans in Pennsylvania.* 1994.
Greenwald, Maurine. "Women and Pennsylvania Working Class History." *Pennsylvania History* 63, no. 1 (Winter 1996): 5–16.
Wallace, Paul A. W. *Indians in Pennsylvania.* 1961.

Paul S. Kobel

Peonage

Debt peonage developed in the years immediately following the Civil War with the emergence of a sharecropping system. Once it was clear to freedmen that there would be no redistribution of land, no "forty acres and a mule," they accepted the sharecropping arrangement as preferable to a contract system, which worked them in gangs and thus reminded them too much of slavery. Planters preferred sharecropping because an acute lack of cash in the southern economy immediately following the war made it difficult to pay wages. As it turned out, planters gave up the control over the workforce that gang labor allowed in return for despotic control over the economic lives of their sharecroppers.

As some historians have concluded, sharecropping might have worked to the advantage of freedmen had it not been for a complex series of developments in the last three decades of the nineteenth century that led to peonage. A sharecropping family usually worked a twenty-five- to forty-acre farm, the size of the farm depending on the size of the family, and received one-half of the cotton and corn crops in return. A custom evolved whereby the landowner actually marketed the crops and gave the sharecroppers what they were "due." In addition, planters "furnished" sharecroppers with supplies during the year and charged their total bill against what their cotton crop brought in the market at the end of the year. Planters who did not themselves run commissaries developed arrangements with merchants. Interest rates charged at the commissaries or in mercantile establishments ranged from 50 to 70 percent.

Three other factors contributed to the emergence of debt peonage by mitigating any advantage the sharecropping system otherwise might have had for freedmen. First, disfranchisement, SEGREGATION, and the emergence of virulent RACISM by the end of the nineteenth century circumscribed alternative EMPLOYMENT opportunities, opportunities already seriously limited, and, perhaps even more important, established blacks as second-class citizens and made it dangerous for them to challenge the planters' calculations. In other words, if a sharecropper differed with the planter's accounting at the time of crop settlement, he could face life-threatening consequences. Second, southern legislatures and courts ruled that sharecroppers could not leave the employment of a planter while owing a debt. If they departed, the planter could use the law to force their return. In addition, in the rare instances when sharecroppers brought their difference with a planter before the law, the courts ruled that the planter owned the crop, and the sharecroppers had no legal standing in the courtroom. Finally, a custom developed whereby one planter could "buy" the debt of another planter's sharecropper. Although this action often was initiated by a sharecropper himself, who wanted a change, it kept him bound up in an exploitative system that smacked of another kind of slavery and essentially perpetuated the vicious cycle of debt.

Federal investigations into charges of peonage in the early twentieth century resulted in some convictions, but peonage was difficult to prove and problematic to prosecute in southern states. The custom persisted until its decline and virtual disappearance in the mid-1950s.

BIBLIOGRAPHY

Daniel, Pete. *Shadow of Slavery: Peonage in the South, 1901–1969.* 1972.

Mandle, Jay R. *The Roots of Black Poverty: The Southern Plantation Economy After the Civil War.* 1978.

Woodman, Harold D. *New South, New Law: The Legal Foundations of Credit and Labor Relations in the Postbellum Agricultural South.* 1995.

Jeannie M. Whayne

People United to Save Humanity

See Rainbow/PUSH Coalition.

Philanthropy and Foundations

In the United States, for much of the twentieth century to inquire about "civil rights" was to delve publicly and specifically into the the status of African Americans in American law, politics, and society. By the late 1960s, the accomplishments of the African-American civil rights movement had forced a broadening of what was meant by the phrase "civil rights." It was now acknowledged to embrace the rights of other ethnic groups, women, children, people with disabilities, gays, and lesbians.

The origins of philanthropic activity in civil rights extend at least as far back as the nineteenth century, when the abolitionist and WOMAN SUFFRAGE MOVEMENTS became important foci of philanthropic activism. From this tradition were born the African Methodist Episcopal (AME) Church, the Women's Christian Temperance Union, the NATIONAL ASSOCIATION FOR THE ADVANCEMENT OF COLORED PEOPLE (NAACP), the LEAGUE OF WOMEN VOTERS, the NATIONAL ASSOCIATION OF COLORED WOMEN, and the United Negro College Fund, to name just a few organizations for "social betterment."

The eventual support of the American philanthropic establishment for African-American civil rights in the twentieth century originated in its support for "Negro education" in the late nineteenth century. For example, the Carnegie Corporation had invested $1.7 million therein before commissioning Swedish economist Gunnar Myrdal to study American race relations in 1935. Myrdal's conclusions were published nine years later as a pioneering two-volume study titled *An American Dilemma.* Entering the public discourse as WORLD WAR II was coming to an end and just before the COLD WAR began, Myrdal's emphasis on resolving the contradiction between the nation's egalitarian creed and its practice of racial exclusion became a cornerstone in a new consensus on the need for racial reform.

The American Fund for Public Service, a small force in the philanthropic world if judged only by its $1 million endowment, also played an early role in the civil rights movement by donating $100,000 toward the establishment of the NAACP LEGAL DEFENSE AND EDUCATIONAL FUND in 1925. These funds financed the legal research that caused the NAACP to direct its litigation against SEGREGATION at public schools in the South. Although the Rosenwald Fund also supported the NAACP and allied groups, the most significant support for the African-American civil rights movement did not come until after WORLD WAR II.

The postwar history of the Ford Foundation provides an excellent sense of how civil rights became a major concern of the American philanthropic establishment. In 1950, the trustees of the Ford Foundation authorized a major effort to combat "racial barriers to equality of opportunity at all levels." Although the implementation of this priority was slowed by the "red scare" of the early 1950s, it was given new urgency in 1954 by the U.S. SUPREME COURT ruling in BROWN V. BOARD OF EDUCATION. For instance, the foundation financed the publication of several important monographs on racial issues, a commitment that has continued into the 1990s. In the late 1960s, the Ford Foundation extended its support beyond the NAACP Legal Defense and Educational Fund, to providing formative financial support to help establish similar funds for legal action on behalf of Native Americans, Mexican Americans, and Puerto Ricans.

The reemergence of a broad-based feminist movement in the middle 1960s also influenced the involvement of the Ford Foundation in civil rights and related issues. Following the precedent of its work in behalf of equality for African Americans, the foundation supported academic studies and legal actions attacking gender discrimination in the workplace and in higher education. In 1972, following its earlier support of ethnic studies programs and postgraduate fellowships for minority scholars, Ford also became a major force in establishing the field of women's studies as a discipline within the American academy.

In the field of children's advocacy, the Carnegie Corporation is the leading foundation of the post–World War II era. In the 1970s and 1980s the corporation was a consistent advocate for children's rights through its support of the CHILDREN'S DEFENSE FUND and the work of its own Carnegie Council on Children.

Despite at least thirty years of political mobilization by gays and lesbians, this category of legal activism is clearly well outside the philanthropic mainstream. If AIDS and AIDS-related giving is excluded, only 0.03 percent of charitable and foundation dollars go to all gay and lesbian causes. Although the Rockefeller Family Foundation has supported some gay rights advocacy, most of the philanthropic activity is being led by community-based foundations. Among the leading supporters of gay and lesbian rights are the Stonewall Foundation of New York City and the David Geffen Foundation of Los Angeles.

A decade after the enactment of the AMERICANS WITH DISABILITIES ACT (ADA) in 1990, disability rights also is still a marginal category for funders. Here too, the most important work is being done through community foundations, such as the San Francisco Foundation. Some advocacy, especially that surrounding ADA enforcement, is supported by government grants. Providing stable support for such programs, however, has grown more difficult as the public money allocated to them has diminished.

The investment of major American philanthropies and foundations in civil rights was set on its current course primarily in response to the African-American civil rights movement of the 1950s and 1960s. At the close of the twentieth century, whether the meaning of "civil rights" will be extended still further depends less on the actions of leading national givers than it does on the initiatives of smaller local and regional entities. Perhaps their initiatives will foster new priorities in the philanthropic community and in the larger American one as well.

BIBLIOGRAPHY

Carson, Emmett D. *Black Philanthropy and Self-Help in America.* 1993.

Disability Funding News. Silver Spring, Md.: CD Publications (monthly publication).*

Embree, Edwin R., and Julia Waxman. *Investment in People: The Story of the Julius Rosenwald Fund.* 1949.

Keppel, Ben. "Race, Poverty and the Symbolism of the Child." *Research Reports from the Rockefeller Archive Center* (Spring 1998):1–3.

King, Kenneth James. *Pan-Africanism in Education: A Study of Race Philanthropy in the Southern United States of America and East Africa.* 1971.

Lagemann, Ellen Condliffe. *The Politics of Knowledge: The Carnegie Corporation, Philanthropy and Public Policy.* 1989.

Magat, Richard. *The Ford Foundation at Work: Philanthropic Choices, Methods and Strategies.* 1979.

Odendahl, Teresa, and Michael O'Neill, eds. *Women and Power in the Nonprofit Sector.* 1994.

Shapiro, Joseph P. *No Pity: People with Disabilities Forging a New Civil Rights Movement.* 1993.

Sheftall, Beverly Guy. *Women's Studies: A Retrospective.* 1995.

Swanson, Gloria Garrett. *The American Fund for Public Service: Charles Garland and Radical Philanthropy, 1922–1941.* 1996.

Working Group on the Funding of Gay and Lesbian Issues. *Funders of Gay, Lesbian and Bisexual Programs: A Directory for Grant Seekers.* 1997; Addendum, 1999.

*Keppel's discussion of philanthropy and the disability rights movement is also drawn from his own experience as the grant writer for the Westside Center for Independent Living in Los Angeles, California, between 1993 and 1994. He also gratefully acknowledges the assistance of Mary Ann Jones, Executive Director of the Center; Kitty Cone, former grant writer for the Disability Rights Legal and Educational Fund; and Joan Leon, former Executive Director of World Institute for Disability, all of whom agreed to be interviewed for this essay.

Ben Keppel

Plessy v. Ferguson (1896)

The U.S. SUPREME COURT decision in *Plessy v. Ferguson* (1896) established the legality and constitutionality of separate-but-equal accommodations for blacks and whites. In other words, it validated JIM CROW forms of racial separation.

According to Charles A. Lofgren the press met the *Plessy* decision with apathy. Supreme Court historians of the early and mid-twentieth century ignored the decision or relegated it to footnotes on cases "involving rights of Negroes." Clearly, however, *Plessy* represented a backwards step in the attainment of the full rights of citizenship for black Americans and the end of progress until the advent of the modern civil rights movement.

Plessy was one of two test cases planned to challenge the constitutionality of an 1890 LOUISIANA state segregation statute. The statute required railroad companies to create "equal but separate accommodations for the white and colored races by providing two or more passenger coaches, or by dividing the passenger coaches by a partition." The statute, however, created an exception for "nurses attending children of the other race." In other words, black nurses caring for white children could ride in white-only coaches. The statute also provided for criminal sanctions against passengers and railroad officials who failed to comply with the law.

In 1890, African-American lawyers Louis Martinet and Rudolph Desdunes formed a citizens committee to plan and mount the challenge to the Jim Crow statute. The committee hired Albion Tourgee, a white attorney from New York and vocal proponent of racial equality, to serve as lead counsel and notified the railroad companies of their intentions to challenge the statute. Several companies viewed the provision of separate railroad cars as an economic burden.

The first test case challenged the statute on the grounds that it created an unconstitutional interference with interstate commerce. On February 24, 1892, Daniel Desdunes, an African American, boarded a train traveling between Louisiana and Alabama and sat in the white-only car. He was immediately arrested. The Louisiana Supreme Court held that the 1890 law was unconstitutional as applied to interstate travel.

On June 7, 1892, Homer Plessy boarded a train in New Orleans bound for Covington, Louisiana, to challenge the 1890 law as applied to in-state travel. He took a seat in the white-only car. He was arrested and charged with violating the Louisiana law. Albion Tourgee appealed the state court conviction to the United States Supreme Court.

Plessy challenged the statute under the FOUR-TEENTH AMENDMENT's privileges and immunities, due process, and equal protection clauses. Interestingly, Plessy's first claim was that because he was "seven eighths Caucasian," and not discernibly black, "he was entitled to every right, privilege and immunity secured to . . . the white race." The U.S. Supreme Court left this particular issue open for interpretation by the state court. Moreover, the Court held that enforced separation of the races as applied to internal commerce was a reasonable exercise of state power and did not abridge any clause of the Fourteenth Amendment. Plessy also challenged the segregation law on the grounds that it constituted a badge of slavery in violation of the THIRTEENTH AMENDMENT prohibition against slavery. The Supreme Court held that, "A statute which implies merely a legal distinction between the white and colored races—a distinction which must always exist so long as white men are distinguished from the other race by color—has no tendency to destroy the legal equality of the two races, or reestablish a state of involuntary servitude." The Court here legitimated the distinction between legal equality and socially acceptable segregation, which continued to justify the separate but equal doctrine in subsequent years.

The dissenting opinion, written by Justice John Marshall Harlan, called the Constitution "color-blind." Justice Harlan characterized the majority opinion as being as pernicious as the *Dred Scott v. Sandford* (1857) decision, which had denied the citizenship claims of free blacks. He argued that the Louisiana statute violated the personal liberty of every citizen and was "hostile to both the spirit and the letter of the Constitution of the United States."

BIBLIOGRAPHY

Aptheker, Herbert. *Afro-American History: The Modern Era.* 1971.

Foner, Eric. *Reconstruction: America's Unfinished Revolution 1863–1877.* 1988.

Henry, A'Lelia Robinson. *Perpetuating Inequality:* Plessy v. Ferguson *and the Dilemma of Black Access to Public and Higher Education.* 27 J. Law & Education 47 (1998).

Keith, Damon. *One Hundred Years After* Plessy v. Ferguson. 65 U. Cin. L. Rev. 853 (1997).

Lewis, David Levering. *W. E. B. Du Bois: Biography of a Race, 1868–1919.* 1993.

Lofgren, Charles A. *The* Plessy *Case: A Legal–Historical Interpretation.* 1987.

Plessy v. Ferguson. 163 U.S. 537; 16 S.Ct. 1138; 41 L. Ed. 256 (1896).

Wendy Brown-Scott

Political Parties

Long before the formation of political parties in the United States, race was a factor in the individual imagination, a force in the culture and society. RACE and RACISM permeated all facets of society by the time of the 1787 Constitutional Convention, when the Founding Fathers wrote a political compromise on these matters into the Constitution (see CONSTITUTIONALISM). Counting slaves as three-fifths of a person for purposes of congressional apportionment, the infamous "three-fifths" clause vividly exemplified the racism of that compromise. As James Madison of Virginia noted, this expedient was essential to get the Southern states to join the new government. However, this measure set into motion a continual problem for the very engines of democracy, the political parties. Their philosophical belief in equality notwithstanding, the Founding Fathers accepted slavery as consistent with American democracy and representative government. In the final analysis, the Constitutional Convention and its document, the U.S. Constitution, did not resolve the matter of CITIZENSHIP and CIVIL LIBERTIES for either the slaves or the free black population. Even the addition, later, of the Bill of Rights did not address the issue. Hence, as political parties evolved into mass-based organizations, the question of civil liberties remained unaddressed.

Some thirty or forty years later, political parties began to evolve from elite organizations into mass-based entities. By the Jacksonian era (1829–1837), the contradiction of regarding slaves as both human beings and as property became increasingly a hot issue, as a vocal minority of citizens agitated more and more against slavery. Slaves had no civil rights, while free "men and women of color" had virtually the same status. Before the Civil War, African Americans could vote only in five New England states. Of the two major parties, the Democrats were the first to make the transition to a mass-based organization. First known in the Jeffersonian era as the Republicans, then as the Democratic-Republicans, and finally as the Democrats (see DEMOCRATIC PARTY), they were the first to address the challenge of African-American civil rights and liberties.

The major civil rights issue of this era was the right to vote for free black men (see VOTING RIGHTS). The New York state legislature reduced the numbers eligible to vote by increasing the amount of property that free African Americans had to own in order to vote. Moreover, there were three statewide suffrage referenda in New York, in 1846, 1860, and 1869, on whether the state should extend to all free African Americans the unrestricted right to vote. Each time the Democratic Party ran successful year-long campaigns to defeat these referenda. In Pennsylvania, the state legislature denied voting rights to free African Americans in 1838, pleas and petitions from the African-American community there notwithstanding.

This occurred simultaneously with the extension of the franchise to nonpropertied whites. Legislatures in Tennessee and North Carolina stripped the right to vote from the free African-American population in 1834 and 1835, respectively. The fledgling Democratic Party mobilized the state electorate to pass these measures in order to expand the party's appeal to the rising white electorate.

The Democratic Party was thus a major force in the pre–Civil War era in denying voting rights to blacks. In this era, the Democratic Party led the drive to defeat more than fourteen statewide referenda on suffrage for free African Americans. In the East, Midwest, and West as well, the Democratic Party's opposition to universal suffrage for African Americans was unequivocal. Indeed, the party's position was anti-black civil rights on every measure, not just voting rights. The Dred Scott decision in 1857 (see DRED SCOTT V. SANDFORD) was the culmination of the trend to deny civil rights to free blacks. That decision emphatically stated that African-American slaves and free blacks had no rights under the Constitution. They were not citizens.

The Democratic Party's position was thus consistent; it vigorously opposed civil rights and political equality for African Americans. In the final analysis, the party backed the politics and policies of the Confederacy. And later, the Democratic Party would envision no civil rights or civil liberties for Native Americans, Mexican Americans, and other nonwhite minorities. As for the second of the two major parties, the REPUBLICAN PARTY, which formed in 1854, offered procivil rights rhetoric in the 1856 presidential election and platform promises to give free black men the vote and to free the slaves. Although the Republicans did not win in 1856, they did capture the White House in 1860 with Abraham Lincoln of Illinois as their standard bearer.

In the aftermath of Lincoln's assassination in 1865 as the Civil War was concluding, the Republican Party introduced and passed three amendments to the U.S. Constitution. The THIRTEENTH AMENDMENT abolished slavery, the FOURTEENTH AMENDMENT redefined citizenship to include blacks, whether former slaves or free, and the FIFTEENTH AMENDMENT provided black males with the right to vote. Hence, in post–Civil War America, the Republican Party, with the Democrats once again in opposition, laid the necessary legal foundation for the civil rights and liberties of both free and recently freed blacks. This extension of civil rights and liberties over the succeeding decades would lead to a split in the Democratic Party ranks, where its northern wing would abide by the law of the land and a grudging acceptance of these amendments. The southern wing of the party could disavow and repudiate these civil rights and liberties and would actively and forcefully work to nullify them in the South and to reverse them in the rest of the country.

In the period 1891–1901, the "Era of Disfranchisement," the Southern Democratic Party—with a host of state constitutional measures such as Grandfather Clauses (provisions excusing from suffrage tests those who have served in any war and their descendants and those who who were voters before January 1, 1867), the poll tax, the white primaries, the literacy test, the reading and interpretation test, a maintenance of poll tax receipts, White Supremacy Loyalty Oath, and extra-legal white violence (see LYNCHING)—negated the Fifteenth Amendment and purged the voter registration rolls of its new African-American citizens. With JIM CROW ordinances as well as PEONAGE and SEGREGATION laws—all sponsored and passed by Southern Democrats—the freedom and citizenship of American blacks was imperilled. African Americans in the South had effectively been reduced to second-class citizens. Southern Democrats had in effect returned the Constitution to its initial status, excluding people of color. Finally, when the Democrats captured the CONGRESS and the PRESIDENCY in 1912, Southern Democrats with the assistance of President Woodrow Wilson segregated the federal bureaucracy and put the federal government itself in opposition to the civil rights of the African American. Between 1913 and 1941, the Democratic Party used the federal bureaucracy to limit the civil rights and liberties of the African-American community.

In the midst of the context of the removal of African Americans' civil rights and liberties, the Republican Party pursued a "let-alone" policy toward the South. Although the party did sponsor supportive legislation like the "Enforcement Bill"—designed to guard African Americans' suffrage rights—none passed Congress, and the Democratic Party's dominance in this area continued. In the first half of the twentieth century, several Republican congressmen shifted from voting rights protection legislation to human rights protection legislation with their sponsorship of national anti-lynching legislation. Again, like the other protection bills, none passed. Each time the Democrats defeated the legislation. Hence, when the Democratic Party recaptured the national government in 1932, African Americans were still without substantive constitutionally based civil rights and liberties.

Initially, the F. D. R. administration (see Franklin ROOSEVELT) did little also. However, due to the protest of African-American civil rights leader A. Philip RANDOLPH, President Roosevelt issued Executive Order 8802, which banned discrimination in industries with federal contracts and created the FAIR EMPLOYMENT PRACTICE COMMITTEE (FEPC). His successor, President Harry TRUMAN, signed Executive Order 11063,

which banned racism in federal HOUSING. In fact, of all the civil rights-based executive orders, the substantial majority—eleven out of fourteen (1941–1965)—were signed by Democratic presidents. Following Roosevelt's and Truman's executive orders, Congress would pass the the CIVIL RIGHTS ACT OF 1957 and the CIVIL RIGHTS ACT OF 1960. This legislation, spearheaded and guided by Southern Democrat Lyndon B. JOHNSON of Texas, was the first such legislation to pass Congress in a century. The legislation also created both the U.S. Civil Rights Commission and a similar division in the Justice Department. A Republican president, Dwight D. EISENHOWER, signed the legislation into law.

Senator John F. KENNEDY, with Senator Johnson as his running mate, captured the White House in 1960. Early on, President Kennedy signed an executive order to ban discrimination in federal housing. In 1963, in the wake of a civil rights protest led by the Rev. Dr. Martin Luther KING, JR., the president sent to Congress the most far-reaching civil rights bill ever. His assassination later that year elevated Johnson to the presidency, and he used his well-honed legislative skills (he had been Senate Majority Leader) to get the CIVIL RIGHTS ACT OF 1964 passed. This was followed a year later by the VOTING RIGHTS ACT OF 1965 and, three years later, by the FAIR HOUSING ACT OF 1968. In the 1960s, as the Republican Party did in the 1860s, the Democratic Party re-integrated African Americans into the U.S. Constitution. These developments also strengthened the Thirteenth, Fourteenth and Fifteenth Amendments. In 1972, Augustus Hawkins, an African-American Democrat, promoted one of the last of the civil rights acts of the twentieth century; this Act created the EQUAL EMPLOYMENT OPPORTUNITY COMMISSION (EEOC) to monitor and ameliorate discrimination in employment.

As the century closes, Republican presidential administrations, starting with that of Ronald REAGAN, have sought a full-scale rollback of civil rights gains attained during the 1960s. Currently, at the state and congressional levels, the Republican Party has attacked AFFIRMATIVE ACTION and BUSING as remedies for racial discrimination and has launched throughout the country a near-comprehensive assault on Affirmative Action's education plans as well as social services and safety nets. The Democrats, particularly Southern Democrats—have now essentially realigned themselves with the Republican Party and shifted in line with the Republicans' assault on the rights of African-American and other minorities. Currently, the Democratic Party, in light of the Republican Party's success in manipulating racial politics, has also used code words and racial symbolism to exploit racial cleavages.

Overall, at the onset of the twenty-first century, neither party has used the past century to advance a progressive and bipartisan approach on race. Only in 1948 did the two parties approach bipartisanship—taking a similar approach in mild support for African Americans' civil rights. This short-lived bipartisanship, however, soon fell victim to an unprecedented four-way presidential race in 1948. Basically one party at a time has pushed civil rights for American blacks. Historically this partisan approach has left that party vulnerable to white opposition and electoral defeat; for example, using race in the 1980s and early 1990s, the Republicans exploited cleavages in the electorate and captured the White House and Congress, as a result. Even today, "playing the race card" is an effective tool too often used for partisan advantage.

BIBLIOGRAPHY

Gillette, William. *The Right to Vote: Politics and the Passage of the Fifteenth Amendment.* 1965.

King, Desmond. *Separate and Unequal: Black Americans and the U.S. Federal Government.* 1995.

Linden, Glenn. *Politics or Principle: Congressional Voting on Civil War Amendments and Pro-Negro Measures, 1838–1869.* 1976.

Morgan, Ruth. *The President and Civil Rights: Policy-Making by Executive Order.* 1970.

Porter, Kirk, ed. *National Party Platform, 1840–1972.* 1973.

Walton, Hanes, Jr. *When the Marching Stopped: The Politics of Civil Rights Regulatory Agencies.* 1988.

Hanes Walton, Jr.

Poll Tax

See National Committee to Abolish the Poll Tax.

Poole, Elijah

See Muhammad, Elijah

Poor People's Campaign

The Poor People's Campaign was a sustained multiracial effort to raise awareness of poverty in the United States. The Campaign grew out of Martin Luther KING, JR.'s, efforts to change the focus of the civil rights movement to the social and economic inequalities experienced by many Americans. With his colleagues in the SOUTHERN CHRISTIAN LEADERSHIP COUNCIL (SCLC), King began planning in 1967 a series of protests. He and other organizers rejected making specific legislative goals the point of the Campaign; rather the hope was to illustrate the meaning of poverty to Washington and to the nation. As such, the protest represented a

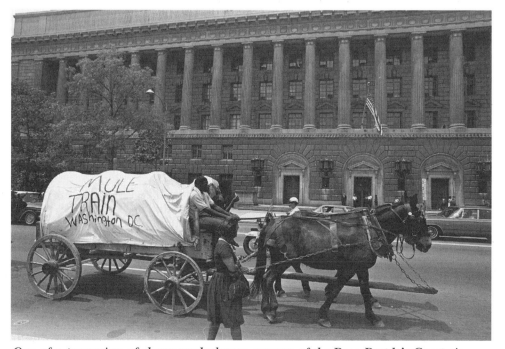

One of a procession of eleven mule-drawn wagons of the Poor People's Campaign makes its way across Pennsylvania Avenue on the way to the Southern Christian Leadership Conference headquarters in downtown Washington, D.C., on June 25, 1968. (AP/Wide World Photos)

direct criticism of President Lyndon B. JOHNSON'S WAR ON POVERTY and his Great Society programs.

Despite King's murder in April 1968, his aides decided to go ahead with the protest, but the logistics proved difficult. The plans called for poor people from across the United States to come to Washington, where they would build a shantytown on the Mall. From makeshift tents and plywood shelters, participants—around 20,000 over the course of the protests that began in May—spread across the capital. The diverse group of African Americans, Native Americans, whites, and Mexican Americans lobbied and non-violently disrupted Congress and federal agencies. Despite the criticism and disruptions, D.C. and federal authorities provided extensive support. In response to the disappointment of some participants, organizers eventually backed away from the sustained CIVIL DISOBEDIENCE that King had proposed. While the shantytown on the Mall was a striking symbol, weeks of rain, erratic supplies, squabbles, and even violence among the marchers soon proved discouraging. On June 24, 1968, after most participants had departed, police officers tear-gassed the remainder and tore down the remains of the shanties. To many, the Poor People's Campaign suggested the extreme difficulty of attacking economic inequality in the United States.

BIBLIOGRAPHY

Garrow, David J. *Bearing the Cross: Martin Luther King, Jr. and the Southern Christian Leadership Conference.* 1986.
Hampton, Henry, and Steve Fayer, eds. *Voices of Freedom: An Oral History of the Civil Rights Movements from the 1950s through the 1980s.* 1990.
Southern Christian Leadership Conference. *The Poor People's Campaign.* 1968.
Yglesias, José. "Dr. King's March on Washington, Part II." In *New York Times Magazine,* March 31, 1968.

Lucy G. Barber

Populist Party

The Populist movement of the 1890s voiced the grievances of millions against corporate domination of American society and sought far-reaching reorganization of the nation's political and economic systems. Its widest support found in the South and in the Great Plains states, Populism set itself forth as the champion of the productive classes, particularly the farmers, small business people, mine workers, and industrial labor. With its roots in the Farmers' Alliance and the Colored Farmers' Alliance of the late 1880s—two of the largest mass organizations in American history—the movement became institutionalized as the Populist (or People's) Party that in the 1890s elected members to the U.S. Senate and House of Representatives and

won control of numerous offices on the state level. A major feature of Populism was its effort to overcome the divisions fostered by RACISM, an effort requiring defense of black participation in the electoral process.

The famed leader of GEORGIA Populism, Tom Watson, argued that racism was a divide-and-conquer stratagem utilized by Wall Street interests to sustain their exploitative rule of the South. Watson was active in the fight to resist exclusion of black voters from the polls. The racial question came to the fore nowhere more sharply than in TEXAS, where blacks took part in Populist activities at all levels. Black delegates attended all party state conventions between 1891 and 1896, and several blacks served on the People's Party state executive committee. In such localities as Grimes County, Populist control of local politics resulted in black participation in law enforcement and in substantial improvement in salaries paid to black schoolteachers. The ARKANSAS People's Party wrote a platform that took a stand on behalf of the downtrodden, "regardless of race." As historian Lawrence C. Goodwyn suggests, there was an extended period in the post-RECONSTRUCTION South "when nascent forms of indigenous interracial activity struggled for life in at least parts of the old Confederacy." A campaign of terror was unleashed, however, against this black presence in politics, and in some counties white man's unions were organized that monopolized nomination of candidates for political office. Several black Populist leaders were in fact assassinated.

In NORTH CAROLINA a political alliance between whites and blacks was created in a fusion movement that brought together a predominantly white Populist organization and a predominantly black Republican Party. This alliance won control of state government and elected the black politician GEORGE H. WHITE to CONGRESS, where he served until 1901. Republican–Populist fusion posed a threat to the state's white supremacist Democrats and the corporations that saw racist politics as the safeguard of property, however, and a virulent white supremacist campaign was set in motion culminating in the election of 1898. North Carolina's Democrats and newspapers argued that government must be beholden to property owners and that numerical majorities would need to give way to the rich, who paid most of the taxes. The white supremacists defeated any would-be fusion state government and in Wilmington followed up their electoral victory with widespread violence against the interracial city administration that was still in office as well as a bloody assault aimed at the black community. The racists drove out Alex Manly, the black editor of the *Wilmington Record,* and destroyed the newspaper's printing plant. In the course of the violence dozens of blacks were murdered and hundreds of black citizens fled the city. Appeals for intervention by federal authorities went unanswered. On the state level the new Democratic administration disfranchised the black population. The events of 1898 were, in fact, a domestic counterpart of the racism that soon marked the emergence of the United States as a world colonial power.

Populism sought a political base among both white and black voters, but white Populists were often unable to conceive of unity on truly equal terms. In 1891 white farmers fought against a cotton pickers' strike called by the Colored Farmers' Alliance, and the People's Party held back from supporting federal intervention in the South on behalf of the citizenship rights of its blacks. White Populists opposed the Force Bill of 1890—proposed in Congress as protection for voting rights in the South—as an unwarranted intrusion upon STATES' RIGHTS. Despite its serious shortcomings on the racial question, the Populist Party contributed to exposing the connection between class domination and racism. The white and black masses of the South did share common interests, and white supremacy could only obscure that commonality of interests by violence and demagogic propaganda.

BIBLIOGRAPHY

Abramowitz, Jack. "Agrarian Reformers and the Negro Question." *Negro History Bulletin* XI (March 1974): 138–39.

Cecelski, David S., and Timothy B. Tyson. *Democracy Betrayed: The Wilmington Race Riot of 1898 and Its Legacy.* 1998.

Clanton, Gene. *Populism: The Humane Preference in America, 1890–1900.* 1991.

Edmonds, Helen. *The Negro and Fusion Politics in North Carolina, 1985–1901.* 1961.

Gaither, Gerald. *Blacks and the Populist Revolt: Blacks and Bigotry in the "New South."* 1977.

Goodwyn, Lawrence C. "Populist Dreams and Negro Rights: East Texas as a Case Study." *American Historical Review* LXXVI (December 1971): 1435–56.

Goodwyn, Lawrence C. *Democratic Promise: The Populist Movement in America.* 1976.

Saunders, Robert M. "The Southern Populists and the Negro, 1893–1895." *Journal of Negro History* LIV (Fall 1970): 339–56.

Shapiro, Herbert. "The Populists and the Negro: A Reconsideration." In *The Making of Black America*, 2 vols., edited by August Meier and Elliott M. Rudwick. 1969.

Woodward, C. Vann. *Tom Watson, Agrarian Rebel.* 1938.

Herbert Shapiro

Powell, Adam Clayton, Jr.

(1908–1972), clergyman, congressman.

Adam Clayton Powell, Jr., was born in New Haven, Connecticut, in November 1908. Soon after his birth, the Powell family moved to New York City, where his father assumed pastorship of Harlem's Abyssinian Baptist Church. The elder Powell would help to transform it into one of the largest congregations, black or white, in North America. After graduating from high school, Powell Jr. attended the City College of New York briefly, where he was a poor student. Undaunted, he then applied to Colgate University, was accepted, and graduated in 1930. Hoping to follow in his father's footsteps, he received a master's degree in theology from Columbia University in 1931.

Powell Jr. first came to the public's attention while serving as an assistant pastor and administrator at the Abyssinian Baptist Church. It was during this time that he rose to prominence as an organizer of public rallies and picketing that were intended to draw attention to the racist staffing policies and poor patient care at Harlem Hospital, efforts that would ultimately prove

Congressman Adam Clayton Powell, Jr., poses thoughtfully during a civil rights rally on the campus of the University of California at Berkeley in January 1968. (CORBIS/Ted Streshinsky)

to be successful. Beginning in 1932, he served as head of a network of relief programs funded by the church that provided food, clothing, and jobs to Harlem's indigents.

Building on the success of his campaign against Harlem Hospital, Powell expanded his efforts to include boycotts and public protests against property owners and businesses that either discriminated against blacks in hiring or otherwise took advantage of Harlem's residents. He made significant gains in these endeavors, forcing both retail stores and municipal agencies to hire more blacks and to begin to promote those few who were already in their employ. These public successes established an unshakable foundation of popular support for Powell that was to serve him well in the coming years.

Powell succeeded his father as church steward in 1936. Using the pulpit as a public forum, he was able to secure his election to the newly formed New York City Council. He also began to publish a weekly newspaper in 1941, *The People's Voice*, of which he was editor. In 1944, Powell was elected to the U.S. CONGRESS from the Twenty-Second (later Eighteenth) District. In 1946 he was re-elected, and was soon appointed to the House of Representatives' influential Education and Labor Committee.

Elected to Congress, Powell began to make waves almost immediately. He challenged the tradition that forbade black representatives from using Capitol facilities labeled as "Members Only." In open defiance, Powell took black constituents and staffers to dinner in the House restaurant, an act that earned him the immediate enmity of John E. Rankin of MISSISSIPPI, an unregenerate segregationist and bigot.

Powell introduced a host of civil rights legislation during his tenure, including measures intended to outlaw poll taxes, to eliminate all vestiges of SEGREGATION in the military, as well as anti-LYNCHING bills. He is best known for his repeated attempts to attach antidiscrimination riders to any programs that received federal funding. He would resort to this tactic so often that these riders would become referred to, collectively, as the "Powell Amendment."

In 1955 Powell attended the Bandung Conference for Asian and African Nations, a move that garnered him recognition and considerable acclaim both at home and abroad. On his return, he began to urge the U.S. government to take a firm stand against CoLONIALISM and provide assistance to the nonallied nations of the emerging Third World. In 1958, several aides of Powell's were implicated in a tax-evasion scam allegedly conducted under the auspices of the Abyssinian Church, but Powell managed to emerge unscathed, and was re-elected to Congress in 1958 and 1960.

In 1961, Powell was named chairman of the Committee on Labor and Education. Under his leadership, the Committee passed literally dozens of social welfare measures that created programs having to do with school lunches, loans for college and vocational training, grants to libraries, increases in minimum wage, standardized working hours, and training and rehabilitation programs for the deaf and blind. This body of legislation made up a considerable portion of the public social service achievements of both the KENNEDY and JOHNSON administrations.

The House Democratic Caucus stripped Powell of his committee chair in 1967 because of his refusal to pay a slander judgment rendered against him—a decision that led to the issuing of a warrant for his arrest in New York. The full House refused to seat him until the Judiciary Committee completed its investigation of him for "abuse of power" and misappropriation of public funds. He was stripped of his office, but was able to regain his seat via a special election held in April 1967. Re-elected in 1968, Powell was reinstated as a representative but was denied his seniority. Lacking any important committee appointments, and having lost most of his support in Harlem, he failed in his renomination bid in 1970. The following year, Powell resigned as head of the Abyssinian Baptist Church and retired to Miami, where he died in April 1972.

BIBLIOGRAPHY

Hamilton, Charles V. *Adam Clayton Powell, Jr.* 1991.
Haygood, Wil. *King of the Cats: The Life and Times of Adam Clayton Powell, Jr.* 1993.

Robert W. Nill

Prejudice

The word "prejudice," derived from the Latin word *praejudicium*, means previous judgment or a judgment made before the facts are examined. However, prejudgments, like misconceptions, are usually reversible when confronted with facts. Thus, the present definition of prejudice has evolved to include "an attitude with an emotional bias" (Wirth 1944:303) or "any unreasonable attitude that is unusually resistant to rational influence" (Rosnow 1972:53). Prejudice is an irrational suspicion that is immune to information. In popular speech, prejudice has come to refer to an attitude that involves the rejection of certain people based solely on their membership in a particular group (e.g., women) or based on certain identifying characteristics (e.g., skin color).

Prejudice operates at three levels: cognitive, emotional, and action. At the cognitive level, prejudiced individuals embrace certain beliefs about a group, such as their intellect; it is at this level that stereotypes develop. Stereotypes refer to oversimplified generalizations associated with any group. Although Americans have become increasingly reluctant to make generalizations about groups of people, there remains a strong tendency to assign certain attributes to different ethnic groups (NORC 1997). Such stereotypes are damaging because they deny the individual the right to be judged on the basis of merit; and minorities often internalize negative stereotypes about their own group, which can lead to feelings of insecurity and self-hatred.

The emotional level of prejudice involves feelings that the minority group arouses in individuals outside the group. For example, hostility is often felt by those who perceive minority groups to be a threat to their existing way of life. In parts of the world Jews have been the target of this kind of hostility, for centuries. Sociologists argue that slavery in the United States may have persisted long after it was economically viable simply because of the physical threat that large masses of freed Africans posed to white landowners. The 1992 Los Angeles riots and the violence between African and Cuban Americans in Miami in 1988 are other demonstrations of the way in which a sense of threat can erupt into racial/ethnic disturbances. Feelings of hostility often lead to discriminatory practices and perpetuate an existing system of ethnic stratification.

The action aspect of prejudice involves a predisposition to engage in particular types of behavior toward individuals or a group. This level of prejudice is, of course, closely related to discrimination, that is, actions taken against a minority group to restrict their access to valued societal rewards, such as adequate income and health care. There is a tendency for prejudicial attitudes to accompany discriminatory behavior. However, prejudice and discrimination do not always occur together. Some people make their behavior conform to the situations they find themselves in and may not express their prejudicial attitudes. Pressure from significant others, however, may cause relatively unprejudiced people to discriminate against particular individuals. Thus, situational factors determine the extent to which the action component of prejudice is expressed.

There are several explanations for ethnic prejudice. Three classes of theories of prejudice dominate the race and ethnic relations literature: psychological, social structural, and cultural. Psychologists and sociologists generally agree that prejudice is not an innate human characteristic, primarily because of historical evidence that people of different cultures do not all display antagonistic group relations. An important area of recent inquiry into the nature of prejudice emphasizes the many kinds of prejudice (Young-Bruehl 1998). Each kind may be caused by combinations of multiple factors and emerge under a different set of social conditions. No one explanation, then, is sufficient to explain the emergence and continuity of "the ancient weakness of prejudice" (Cooke 1966:12).

In some cases, prejudicial attitudes have psychological functions. For example, people with emotional or personality problems embrace prejudice to help them function from day to day. Some psychological processes involved in prejudiced attitudes are projection, scapegoating, and self-justification. Projection occurs when people see in others characteristics or feelings that they cannot admit that they have themselves. Scapegoating refers to individuals need to deal with frustration or the feelings of tension that result from failure to achieve a goal, by ascribing the failure to someone else. Self-justification occurs when people denigrate a person or group to justify their behavior toward the person or group. Psychological theories are apt to locate the origin of prejudice in the individual psyche or in individual personality development. Although prejudice appears to have functional qualities, it is actually a limiting process; the costs of being prejudiced may be emotional (e.g., living in fear of minorities) or financial (e.g., paying high costs to relocate to segregated neighborhoods).

Sociologists are likely to locate the origins of overt ethnic prejudice in intergroup competition for scarce resources in society. Prejudice is used as a rationalization for the exploitation and oppression of minorities. Thus, prejudice is a product of group interests that center around economic gain, social prestige, and political power. In 1981, for example, Vietnamese fishermen in Galveston Bay, Texas, encountered acts of intimidation by Caucasian fisherman and members of the Ku Klux Klan because they were perceived as challenging the economic dominance of the Caucasian fishermen. Chinese Americans were restricted to particular occupations in the nineteenth century primarily because Caucasian workers feared a surge of cheaper labor. Working women are heavily concentrated in poorer-paying gender-segregated jobs. Class theorists contend that capitalists or workers of the dominant group profit from prejudice.

Cultural theories of prejudice emphasize the role that society plays in teaching and rewarding prejudicial beliefs. Accordingly, prejudice is an outcome of socialization into a racist community or interacting in social situations where prejudicial attitudes are viewed as legitimate. People learn prejudice in the same way that they learn other aspects of the culture. Children begin to classify people on the basis of skin color and other cues between the ages of three and five and soon learn the stereotypes to associate with various groups.

Many parents (and teachers) do not make overtly racist statements, but prejudice is taught to children indirectly. Cultural theorists also look to the content of language for the roots of prejudice. In many societies around the world, the term "black" has negative connotations, whereas the term "white" has connotations of purity and cleanliness (Moore 1988). The very characteristics these colors connote are then assigned to individuals.

The United States was founded upon the values of equality and freedom. Because prejudice is often used to justify discrimination, this aspect of American life must be addressed in order to ensure full civil rights for all citizens. Public support for prejudiced statements has declined since the 1940s, perhaps because of exposure to the mass media, increased educational attainment which broadens people's perspectives, and increased equal-status contact between ethnic groups. Reducing prejudice will not eliminate minority group problems; until America eradicates all vestiges of ethnic stratification, ethnic prejudice may diminish, but it will not entirely disappear.

BIBLIOGRAPHY

Cooke, Paul P. *Civil Rights in the United States.* 1966.
Moore, Robert B. "Racial Stereotyping in the English Language." *Racism and Sexism: An Integrated Study.* (1988):269–279.
National Opinion Research Center (NORC). *General Social Surveys, 1972–1996: Cumulative Codebook.* 1997.
Rosnow, Ralph L. "Poultry and Prejudice." *Psychology Today* (Mar. 1972): 53.
Wirth, Louis. "Race and Public Policy." *Scientific Monthly* 58 (1944): 303.
Young-Bruehl, Elisabeth. *The Anatomy of Prejudices.* 1998.

Pamela Braboy Jackson

Presidency

Of the fifteen chief executives who served before Abraham Lincoln, nine owned slaves and four were "doughfaces" (that is, northern men with southern principles). Of the remaining two chief executives, John Adams spoke against slavery only in his private correspondence, and the other Adams, John Quincy, emerged as a civil rights champion only after leaving the White House. If Thomas Jefferson's timeless words in the Declaration of Independence ("all men are created equal") gave birth to the nation, the Founders who wrote the U.S. Constitution and created the office of the presidency saw no contradiction to including in their document nine separate protections for the South's peculiar institution. When they mandated that the president "shall take care that the laws be faithfully

President Harry S. Truman signs a bill in his White House office on July 1, 1948, declaring February 1 to be National Freedom Day, commemorating the passage of the Thirteenth Amendment to the U.S. Constitution banning slavery. Around him are some of the many African-American leaders gathered for the occasion. (Left to right): Harriet Lemons, J. E. Mitchell, Mary McLeod Bethune, E. C. Wright, C. Jernagin, and Elder Michaux. (CORBIS/Bettmann)

executed" (Art. II, Sec. 3), laws protecting slavery were perhaps foremost in their minds.

Not the first chief executive to realize that a house divided against itself cannot stand, Lincoln was the first to govern at a time when the North's people came to that realization. The EMANCIPATION PROCLAMATION (September 22, 1862) gave the Union's armies the noblest of causes and made inevitable the THIRTEENTH, FOURTEENTH, and FIFTEENTH AMENDMENTS to the Constitution that ended slavery forever and made Jefferson's words forever clear.

Of the twenty-six chief executives who served after Lincoln, the great majority proved more committed to preserving the contradiction between the nation's new ideal and the continuing reality of white over black. John Booth's shot at Ford's Theater elevated Andrew Johnson to the presidency, a determined foe of black voting rights. Ulysses S. Grant, fearless when in pursuit of the Army of Northern Virginia, proved such a timid commander-in-chief by the end of his tenure that he gave white supremacy free reign. After the Compromise of 1877 ended RECONSTRUCTION, every president from Rutherford B. Hayes to William McKinley sat equally still as the Ku Klux Klan rose across the South, LYNCHING became part of the mode of governance, and the SUPREME COURT legitimized the separate-but-equal doctrine in PLESSY V. FERGUSON (1896). The

Progressive Era (1900–1917) giants, Theodore Roosevelt and Woodrow Wilson, not only failed to challenge JIM CROW but incorporated it into their reformist impulse. In 1912, Bull Moose Theodore Roosevelt ran a self-described "lily white" campaign for the presidency. Five years later, while Wilson prepared to fight a war to make the world safe for democracy, federal workmen tacked up "White Only" and "Colored" signs over every federal toilet in Washington, D.C.

Beginning with Frankin D. ROOSEVELT's New Deal and World War II presidency (1933–1945), the movement to make the nation conform to its own democratic creed achieved a string of dramatic successes. On June 25, 1941, Executive Order 8802 prohibited discrimination in defense industries and established a FAIR EMPLOYMENT PRACTICE COMMITTEE. On July 26, 1948, Harry S. TRUMAN issued Executive Order 9981, abolishing segregation in the armed forces. Three years after the Supreme Court overturned separate-but-equal in BROWN V. BOARD OF EDUCATION (1954), Dwight D. EISENHOWER sent the 101st Airborne into Arkansas to enforce a federal court order to desegregate Little Rock Central High School.

Events before LITTLE ROCK (the MONTGOMERY BUS BOYCOTT) and after (the lunch-counter SIT-INS) brought the struggle for racial justice onto the nation's political stage by the time John F. KENNEDY took the oath of office. Forced to choose between the integrationists and the segregationists, Kennedy more often than not chose the movement—supporting integration of the University of Mississippi and the University of Alabama, and sending a civil rights bill to Congress. The next president, Lyndon B. JOHNSON, announced a war on poverty and pushed through Congress the most sweeping civil rights legislation since Reconstruction—the CIVIL RIGHTS ACT OF 1964 and the VOTING RIGHTS ACT OF 1965.

Thereafter, the nation entered a so-called period of "white backlash"—the result of major race riots in Watts (1965) (see WATTS RIOT) and Newark and Detroit (1967); the drain of a colonial war in Southeast Asia gone sour; and the contentious debate surrounding the welfare programs of the war on poverty in general and affirmative action strategies for enforcing the new civil rights legislation in particular. Republican Presidents Richard M. NIXON, Gerald FORD, Ronald REAGAN, and George BUSH all campaigned and governed against "racial preferences," "reverse discrimination," and other perceived excesses emanating from the movement's recent triumphs. Jimmy CARTER and Bill CLINTON, the two lone Democrats since Lyndon Johnson and both southerners like Johnson, trod gingerly on all racial matters.

While Clinton may know all of Martin Luther KING, JR.'s "I Have a Dream" speech by heart, he saw political advantage when campaigning against President Bush to play golf at a segregated Little Rock club with a television camera crew in tow. As president, Clinton's initial civil rights initiative had nothing to do with race (the abortive attempt to eliminate discrimination against homosexuals in the military). In the second term, he offered a qualified defense of affirmative action ("mend it, don't end it") and called for "a national dialogue on race" complete with a commission chaired by the eminent black historian John Hope FRANKLIN and a televised town hall meeting where the president roamed, microphone in hand, to ask citizens to share their personal experiences and feelings along the color line.

BIBLIOGRAPHY

Graham, Hugh Davis. The Civil Rights Era. 1990.
Hutchinson, Earl Ofari. Betrayed: A History of Presidential Failure to Protect Black Lives. 1996.
Logan, Rayford W. The Betrayal of the Negro: From Rutherford B. Hayes to Woodrow Wilson, rev. ed. 1965.
Morgan, Ruth P. The President and Civil Rights: Policy-Making by Executive Order. 1970.
O'Reilly, Kenneth. Nixon's Piano: Presidents and Racial Politics from Washington to Clinton. 1995.
Robinson, Donald L. Slavery in the Structure of American Politics, 1765–1820. 1971.
Sinkler, George. The Racial Attitudes of American Presidents: From Abraham Lincoln to Theodore Roosevelt. 1971.

Kenneth O'Reilly

Presidential Politics and Civil Rights

In the fifteenth month of his PRESIDENCY, Richard M. NIXON poked fun at the "southern strategy" that had brought him to the White House in the election of 1968 by playing a piano duet with Vice President Spiro T. Agnew at the Gridiron Club in Washington, D.C. The preliminary banter was strictly minstrel, with Agnew speaking in "darky" dialect. When the president began playing the favorite songs of Franklin D. ROOSEVELT and other predecessors, the vice-president drowned him out with a manic "Dixie" on his piano. Incredibly, the Gridiron audience of 500 capital luminaries roared with laughter at this equally incredible skit, stopping only when Nixon and Agnew ended with "God Bless America" and "Auld Lang Syne." Here, the Gridiron crew were suddenly solemn and on their feet, all singing along, all celebrating their nation.

Nixon was not the first candidate to exploit race as a tool to organize the votes necessary to carry a candidate to the Oval Office. The words themselves ("southern strategy") can be better understood as regionless code for white over black that dates back to the Founders and the presidency those great men created within the Constitution of the United States. Slavery and its attendant cash-crop economy had from the beginning made the South prone to vote as a bloc, a reality that led to specific constitutional protections for the peculiar institution and a disproportionate say in deciding who would be president. It should come as no surprise that nine of the fifteen commanders-in-chief and all five of the two-term presidents who served before Abraham Lincoln owned slaves.

For all the Civil War glory of ending slavery, that war's battlefields left certain things unchanged—particularly after the North abandoned Reconstruction with the Compromise of 1877. Both the reality of white over black and the white South's tendency to vote as a one-party bloc remained fixed. If the Republican party would dominate for some seventy years, the Democratic South remained poised to return to that familiar scenario of having a disproportionate say in electing the president.

The Great Depression's arrival in 1929 and Franklin D. Roosevelt's election in 1932 brought the Democratic party, and the white South back to life. Roosevelt's coalition, however, was always at odds. New Deal economic reforms offered black Americans hope enough to cause an exodus from the party of Lincoln to the party of Roosevelt. The white South, meanwhile, not only continued to vote Democratic but also to enforce Jim Crow by any means necessary. Roosevelt so feared alienating those voters that he remained silent even on Lynching. He had no civil rights program before A. Philip Randolph threatened, in the summer before Pearl Harbor, a massive all-black March on Washington to force an executive order creating a Fair Employment Practice Committee.

From the FDR years to the 1968 election, presidential politics revolved around Democratic party attempts to retain its hold on the white South and Republican attempts to exploit civil rights issues in order to crack the solid South. During Reconstruction, white southerners considered the GOP a black man's party. Republican strategy in this century's latter half stood that construct on its head. If the GOP could identify the Democrats as being inordinately pro-black, then race could be used to achieve a political revolution rivaling Roosevelt's own. When Harry S. Truman ran for election in 1948 he correctly calculated that the key to victory lay in holding together the liberal elements of the old Roosevelt coalition. To establish his liberal credentials, Truman desegregated the armed forces by executive order and sent civil rights legislation to Congress. While this enraged white southern elites and led to South Carolina Senator Strom Thurmond's candidacy on the Dixiecrat party ticket, Tru-

man also correctly calculated that the fresh memory of the Great Depression would preclude significant southern defection. But the Dixiecrats represented the first transitional step in the white South's move into the Republican bloc.

Republican strategy did not proceed smoothly. In 1957 Dwight D. Eisenhower, his hand forced by the Supreme Court decision Brown v. Board of Education (1954), sent troops into Arkansas to force state compliance with a federal court order to desegregate Little Rock Central High School. Acting in defense of federal order, Eisenhower said the decision to commit the 101st Airborne was the hardest of his presidency because it interfered with the effort to bring the white South over to the GOP. The first Republican candidate to make explicit racial appeals, Barry Goldwater, went down to monumental defeat in 1964 for reasons that had little to do with race. But Nixon knew that Goldwater's strategy (sans the warfare-state rhetoric) was sound, and was determined to use race during his next White House run. In 1960 he had ignored southern strategy entirely and lost narrowly to John F. Kennedy. Kennedy won in all southern states except Georgia and Florida.

Several things changed between 1960 and 1968. First, the civil rights movement's victories in Birmingham and Montgomery culminated in the death of legal segregation with passage of the Civil Rights Act of 1964 and the Voting Rights Act of 1965. Second, President Lyndon B. Johnson had pushed through Congress the welfare-state reforms necessary to implement his promised war on poverty. Rather than celebrate these triumphs, however, the movement turned leftward with "Black Power," "Off the Pig," and "Burn, Baby, Burn" rhetoric, and the nation's cities exploded. Watts (Los Angeles) in 1965 and Newark and Detroit in 1967 represented only the largest of hundreds of race riots. Finally, the presidential commission appointed to investigate the riots (the so-called Kerner Commission) identified white racism as the root cause.

Nixon's cause-and-effect relationship substituted the liberal excesses of John Kennedy's New Frontier and Lyndon Johnson's Great Society as the root cause of racial strife. Nixon also had to counter Alabama Governor George Wallace's third-party appeal for the racist vote. Everything from the fires in Detroit to the new affirmative action bureaucracies and court-ordered busing of school children made the white South ripe for revolt, and Nixon did not intend to lose those voters to Wallace. Race, to put this another way, was the ultimate wedge issue, a tool to pit black against white generally and the various segments of the old Roosevelt coalition against one another more specifically (for example, organized labor versus the organized civil rights community).

Southern strategy remained after Watergate. Republican Gerald FORD crusaded against busing. The next Republican, Ronald REAGAN, opened his 1980 campaign against Jimmy CARTER at the Neshoba, Mississippi, County Fair by telling the crowd that he was a states' righter. The Ku Klux Klansmen who murdered civil rights workers Michael Schwerner, James CHANEY, and Andrew Goodman in Neshoba sixteen years earlier had said they were states' righters, too. In 1988 George BUSH organized his GOP campaign around the great race taboo, the black man who raped a white woman. Democrat Bill CLINTON preempted a repeat of Bush's 1988 Willie Horton gambit in 1992 by baiting Jesse Jackson (the controversy involving singer Sister Souljah); posing with a black chain gang as backdrop for a crime control ad; golfing at a segregated Little Rock club; and presiding over the execution of a black man, Rickey Ray Rector, brain damaged enough to ask the men wielding the needle to save his last meal's dessert pie "for later."

In the White House, Bill Clinton has walked a tightrope along the color line. If, in the second term, he offered a mend-it–don't-end-it defense of affirmative action and a civil rights initiative intended to spark a national dialogue on race, it should be remembered that his calculus for countering Republican Southern strategy and winning office included that Arkansas executioner's search for a serviceable vein in Rickey Ray Rector's arm.

BIBLIOGRAPHY

Berman, William C. *The Politics of Civil Rights in the Truman Administration.* 1970.

Black, Earl, and Merle Black. *The Vital South: How Presidents Are Elected.* 1992.

Brauer, Carl M. *John F. Kennedy and the Second Reconstruction.* 1977.

Burk, Robert F. *The Eisenhower Administration and Black Civil Rights.* 1984.

Edsall, Thomas Byrne, and Mary D. Edsall. *Chain Reaction: The Impact of Race, Rights, and Taxes on American Politics.* 1991.

O'Reilly, Kenneth. *"Racial Matters": The FBI's Secret File on Black America, 1960–1972.* 1989.

O'Reilly, Kenneth. *Nixon's Piano: Presidents and Racial Politics from Washington to Clinton.* 1995.

Shull, Steven A. *A Kinder, Gentler Racism? The Reagan-Bush Civil Rights Legacy.* 1993.

Stern, Mark. *Calculating Visions: Kennedy, Johnson, and Civil Rights.* 1992.

Weiss, Nancy. *Farewell to the Party of Lincoln: Black Politics in the Age of FDR.* 1983.

Kenneth O'Reilly

President's Commission on the Status of Women

John F. KENNEDY appointed the President's Commission on the Status of Women (PCSW) in 1961 at the request of Esther Peterson, a labor lobbyist whom he had named director of the Women's Bureau. As there were 6.5 million married mothers in the labor force caring for children under the age of 18, Peterson intended the Commission to devise programs that would permit women to fulfill their roles both as mothers and as workers. In addition, Peterson hoped that the Commission would craft a compromise about constitutional equality that would break the stalemate over the EQUAL RIGHTS AMENDMENT that had existed since the National Woman's party proposed it in 1923.

Peterson recruited cabinet officers, members of Congress, the heads of prominent women's organizations, and business and labor leaders as members and induced Eleanor ROOSEVELT to serve as chair, her last public office. In its 1963 report, the Commission made proposals to enhance opportunity for women in private employment and in public employment (including the military), to expand the protection of federal and state labor laws, to increase access to education at all stages of life, to provide public support for child care services, to augment widows' benefits under Social Security, and to afford maternity benefits for women workers, among others. Its proposals for the elimination of selection by sex in the federal civil service and for equal pay legislation came to fruition before the conclusion of its term. It also endorsed constitutional equality for women through a carefully constructed legal challenge modeled on BROWN V. BOARD OF EDUCATION.

President Kennedy signed executive orders in November 1963 creating two continuing bodies at the federal level to monitor progress, which held annual meetings of the state commissions that were modeled after the PCSW. At the 1966 meeting of the state commissions, a group of women, acknowledging the constraints that limited governmental bodies, formed the NATIONAL ORGANIZATION FOR WOMEN, the first new feminist organization of the "second wave." Initially adopting much of the PCSW agenda as its own, the new feminist movement soon enunciated a more comprehensive and radical commitment to the elimination of social, economic, and political distinctions and hierarchies based upon sex.

BIBLIOGRAPHY

Chafe, William H. *The Paradox of Change: American Women in the 20th Century.* 1991.

Harrison, Cynthia. *On Account of Sex: The Politics of Women's Issues, 1945–1968.* 1988.

Gelb, Joyce, and Marian Lief Palley. *Women and Public Policies: Reassessing Gender Politics.* 1996.

Cynthia Harrison

President's Committee on Civil Rights

In December 1946, President Harry S. TRUMAN established by executive order the President's Committee on Civil Rights (PCCR). It issued a report the following year entitled *To Secure These Rights.* The report recommended a sweeping executive and legislative agenda, going further than Truman expected by advocating swift federal action to end segregation and violations of voting rights in the United States. Truman stunned some Democrats in following up the Commission's report by recommending an ambitious civil rights legislative agenda to CONGRESS in 1948 that included much that the PCCR supported, including the strengthening of the Justice Department, the abolition of the poll tax, further protections against lynchings, and an end to segregation in interstate transportation. While none of these recommendations were made law that year, Truman did follow through on recommendations to desegregate the armed forces. It was probably impossible to get some of the more ambitious proposals through Congress. Truman did not make it a top priority.

Truman was considered an unlikely president to take a special interest in civil rights—and he was the first one in the twentieth century to do so. He hailed from a border state and was not considered progressive in his days as a senator, but he is regarded as having a genuine interest in correcting some of the gross injustices in segregated American society. More important, there was strong political motivation. Republicans were threatening to take back the African-American vote, which they had enjoyed from the days following the Civil War up to the New Deal, with civil rights legislation of their own. (*See* NEW DEAL AND DEPRESSION.)

Truman's establishment of the PCCR and his liberal civil rights agenda were particularly noteworthy given the historical states' rights position of the Democratic party. While Franklin ROOSEVELT's New Deal laid the groundwork by challenging the foundation of states' rights, the Democratic party's commitment to civil rights could be said to have begun with the Truman administration and the issuance of *To Secure These Rights* by the PCCR.

BIBLIOGRAPHY

Grantham, Dewey W. *The Life and Death of the Solid South.* 1988.

Lamis, Alexander. *The Two-Party South.* 1988.

McCullough, David. *Truman.* 1992.

Milkis, Sidney M., and Michael Nelson. *The American Presidency: Origins and Development, 1776–1990.* 1990.

Wilhoit, Francis. *The Politics of Massive Resistance.* 1973.

Yarnell, Allen. *Democrats and Progressives.* 1974.

John Haskell

Prisoners

No notion of prisoner rights existed in nineteenth-century America. State ownership of the convict was complete. Those sentenced to prison lost all legal identity. Even after release, ex-felons had no right to vote, hold office, make contracts, own property, or compose a will. Those rights, and more, remained forfeited to the state. In the early twentieth century, certain rights were restored on parole, but only at the discretion of the parole board. This reduced civil status of prisoners was reaffirmed in state penal codes, in sections explicitly titled "Civil Death of Prisoners."

The U.S. SUPREME COURT concluded only in the 1970s that the Constitution applies also to prisoners. What has led to this change in legal status? A prisoner rights activism movement emerged in the late 1940s linked to the civil rights movement. Among the first prisoner rights activists was California's Caryl Chessman, a San Quentin prisoner whose jailhouse lawyering and manuscript smuggling led the way for prisoner First Amendment challenges; in the 1950s habeas corpus petitions of Black Muslim prisoners nationwide pressed for rights of freedom of religion, freedom of speech, access to law books, and freedom of *association.* Years of convict struggle inside and coalition building with reformers outside then forced the states to grant prisoners certain basic rights. In the late 1960s, prisoners won the right to inherit real estate and personal property; to correspond confidentially with attorneys, public officials, and journalists; to receive most books and printed material available to the free public; and to own their writing. A floodgate of previously censored communication then quickly opened between prisoners and the public. This launched a decade of investigation into inhumane conditions and physical abuse inside the prisons and a move toward scrupulous court oversight of prison practices. The Prison Movement produced an intelligentsia of prisoner readers and writers, including Eldridge CLEAVER and George JACKSON whose ideas drew wide support for the Movement among the free reading public.

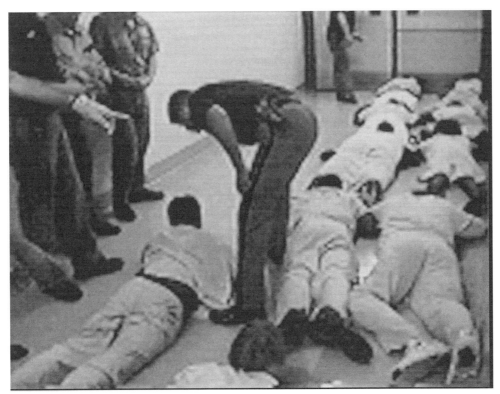

A videotaped image shows a prison guard urging a prisoner to crawl faster at the Brazoria County Detention Center in Clute, Texas, on September 18, 1996. The videotape, taken as a whole, strongly suggested that guards at the prison were guilty of abusive behavior toward the prisoners, and there were charges that the level of abuse often exceeded what was shown on the videotape. (AP/Wide World Photos)

Inside, the growth of secret political cell-study fired a radical convict activism that reached its zenith in the late-1960s to mid-1970s. Some prisoners organized unions; some engaged in revolutionary Marxist struggle. For a time, convict factions maintained links to activist groups in civil rights or revolutionary movements outside. The courts sometimes responded with reforms. In the late 1970s ex-prisoners were returned the right to vote after parole. Prison discipline was hard to maintain during these years. Attacks on guards increased, as did deadly assaults between opposing prisoner factions.

Most states soon found convict citizenship intolerable. Calls went out for special high-security prisons for revolutionary and other "troublemaker" convicts. By the mid- to late-1980s these "security housing units" came into use. Here prisoner activists—jailhouse lawyers, Muslims, unionists, gang members, revolutionaries—were housed in solitary cells where, among other rights, convict reading, writing, communication, and association were again severely limited.

This contraction of prisoner rights is reflected in the pattern of Supreme Court decisions of the 1980s and 1990s. A prisoner of the 1990s retains only the following rights:

1. *Speech and communication.* The right to uncensored mail from the outside, though a prisoner's own letters may be read, censored, or banned, especially when deemed a "security risk"; the right to write, though prisoner writing may be confiscated, censored, and its submission for publication outside or in the prison newspaper forbidden for "security reasons." Prisoners do not have a right to receive publications uncensored from the outside; in solitary confinement, prisoners may be lawfully denied reading and writing materials of any kind.

2. *Religion.* The right to free practice of religion, though the state is limited in its liability to provide resources for this practice.

3. An *Eighth Amendment right* to "the minimal civilized measure of life's necessities." This is usually taken to include freedom from physical beatings by guards. It does not extend to freedom from psychological torture. The Court acknowledges

an Eighth Amendment right to minimal medical care, though the state is under no obligation to give more than minimal care to prisoners with special needs.

Prisoners do not retain a right of association. Concerted prisoner political activity in the form of unions is expressly forbidden. Under the THIRTEENTH AMENDMENT, the Court has found that prisoners lack a constitutional right to a prison job; they also cannot refuse to work if asked. Convicts have no recognized right to be paid wages for their work, beyond a token wage if a state so chooses.

BIBLIOGRAPHY

Alexander, John K. *Render Them Submissive: Responses to Poverty in Philadelphia, 1760–1800.* 1980.
Cummins, Eric. *The Rise and Fall of California's Radical Prison Movement.* 1994.
Eriksson, Torsten. *The Reformers: An Historical Survey of Pioneer Experiments in the Treatment of Criminals.* 1976.
Mushlin, Michael, ed. *Rights of Prisoners.* 1993.
Robbins, Ira P., ed. *Prisoners and the Law.* 1985.
Rothman, David J. *The Discovery of the Asylum: Social Order and Disorder in the New Republic.* 1971.
Ruffin v. Commonwealth. 62 Va. (21 Gratt.) 790, 796 (1871).

Eric Cummins

Progressive Party presidential candidate Robert M. La Follette, the governor of Wisconsin. (CORBIS/Bettmann)

Progressive Party (1924)

On July 4, 1924, a convention in Cleveland called by the Conference for Progressive Political Action (CPPA) endorsed the candidacy for president of Wisconsin Senator Robert La Follette as a progressive independent. The CPPA, created in 1922, consisted of four major components: the Railroad Brotherhoods, politicized when government intervention ended their 1922 strike; the SOCIALIST PARTY, whose membership had declined steeply since 1912; the Committee of Forty-eight, representing the remains of Theodore Roosevelt's Progressive Party of 1912; and the radical agrarian parties in the states of the Upper Middle West and West, such as the Non-Partisan League (mobilized by the sharp drop in farm prices after the end of WORLD WAR I). At Cleveland a potpourri of reform organizations, including the NATIONAL ASSOCIATION FOR THE ADVANCEMENT OF COLORED PEOPLE (NAACP), were present, advocating every procedural and substantive reform since the Populist era (see POPULIST PARTY). The platform, and La Follette's ensuing campaign, stressed the danger of corporate monopolies. No effort was made to appeal to African-American voters, even though La Follette said he opposed discrimination based on class, race, or religion. While supported by W. E. B. DU BOIS and other NAACP leaders, La Follette refused to make any special appeal to black voters because he would not promise what he said he could not deliver if elected. In the election he won 16.5 percent of the popular vote but carried only Wisconsin (running second in eleven states). The CPPA disbanded early in 1925, ending any hope that La Follette's candidacy would lead to the formation of a permanent third party.

BIBLIOGRAPHY

La Follette, Belle Case, and Fola La Follette. *Robert M. La Follette,* Vol. II. 1953.
MacKay, Kenneth Campbell. *The Progressive Movement of 1924.* 1947.

James S. Chase

Progressive Party (1948)

Primarily because of President Harry S. TRUMAN's ardent cold war policies in 1947 and 1948, some members of the left wing of the DEMOCRATIC PARTY split off and formed the Progressive Party, nominating former vice president and one-time Secretary of Commerce Henry A. Wallace for president. While the Progressives were well known for their strong positions in favor of social reform, more progressive economic policies, and equal opportunity for African Americans, their most prominent position was their peace plank. They favored more cooperation with the Soviet Union and greater respect for the Soviets' sphere of influence.

The Progressives' impact on the election of 1948 turned out to be far less significant than was initially expected. Republicans remained unified behind their nominee, Thomas Dewey, but the Democrats suffered defections on the left with the Progressives and on the right with the candidacy of Strom THURMOND, who favored the states' right to run their own affairs, including the maintenance of racial segregation in the South and some border states. Thurmond charged that Truman and the regular Democrats were moving too far to the left on civil rights and on labor issues. This charge stole the thunder of the Progressives' attacks on Truman for not being liberal enough. In the end, Wallace garnered less than 3 percent of the vote in the general election. International affairs, which appeared to vindicate Truman's cold war policies, and tactical moves by Truman to shore up his left flank, including an ambitious civil rights agenda and the party's explicitly procivil rights plank at the national convention, had undermined the Progressives.

While the aim of the Progressives in 1948 was to move Truman to the left on economics, civil rights, and foreign policy, there is little reason to credit them with success. Truman remained a staunch cold warrior, he had pursued an ambitious redistributive economic policy called the Fair Deal before the Progressives formed, and his positions on civil rights were thought to be the result of political calculations concerning potential Republican strength among African-American voters in key states in the north and middle west. While some advisors to Truman were concerned about African-American defections to the Progressive party, the predominant concern was that black voters would return to their ancestral home, the party of Lincoln. Majorities of African Americans had only begun supporting Democrats in the 1930s because of the NEW DEAL programs of Franklin ROOSEVELT. However, next to nothing had been done by Roosevelt to secure basic civil rights. As a result, African-American voters were thought to be receptive to overtures from the GOP, especially since some Republican legislators were preparing to introduce civil rights legislation. Truman moved swiftly to desegregate the armed forces and introduce an ambitious civil rights agenda in the Congress designed to retain the allegiance of African-American voters in key states where they could hold sway, such as New York, Illinois, Pennsylvania, Ohio, and Michigan.

The Progressive Party was similar to the traditional Progressives from the turn of the century—representative of a left-leaning, good government, white middle class. While in favor of civil rights for African Americans, this was not a central priority, nor is the party typically credited with influencing Truman to any great extent.

BIBLIOGRAPHY

Berman, William C. *The Politics of Civil Rights in the Truman Administration.* 1970.
Markowitz, Norman D. *The Rise and Fall of the People's Century: Henry A. Wallace and American Liberalism, 1941–1948.* 1973.
Ross, Irwin. *The Loneliest Campaign: The Truman Victory of 1948.* 1968.
Sorauf, Frank J. *Party Politics in America,* 6th ed. 1988.
Sundquist, James L. *Dynamics of the Party System.* 1983.
Yarnell, Allen. *Democrats and Progressives.* 1974.

John Haskell

Project Head Start

See Head Start, Project.

Proposition 209

See California Civil Rights Initiative

PSP

See Movement for Independence—Puerto Rican Socialist Party

Public Opinion

When Alexis de Tocqueville, author of the nineteenth-century study, *Democracy in America,* reflected on American democracy and equality, he noted the importance of public opinion. A society with strong beliefs in equality, in contrast to one in which there is great inequality, values the opinions of the public. Tocqueville's insight provides a context within which public opinion in modern society can be understood. Believing in the collective wisdom of citizens, George Gallup, in the 1930s, developed the use of polling to determine public opinion. Since then, governmental decision makers have relied on public opinion polls. However, public opinion is more than a count of citizens. It can emerge from small groups taken seriously by those in power.

There is public opinion that includes all Americans or the members of a large group of them, such as blacks, whites, northerners or southerners, or the members of a smaller group whose opinions are perceived to be of value. Public opinion becomes an expression of the culture, which can be shaped by RADIO, TELEVISION, and NEWSPAPERS or by interpersonal communication. What does the public think about an issue? Today, researchers use polls, surveys, interviews, and a content analysis of the media to determine public opinion. These different measurement techniques help us understand the collective sentiment about an event or issue.

What is the relationship between public opinion and civil rights? During the first half of the twentieth century, America was mostly a racially segregated society. Stark opinion differences between white Americans and black Americans reflected that SEGREGATION. The mainstream press largely ignored the southern violence directed against blacks. The black press, including the *Chicago Defender* and the *Pittsburgh Courier*, became an important source of information to northern and southern blacks. LYNCHING was publicized, along with the ANTI-LYNCHING CAMPAIGN of the NATIONAL ASSOCIATION FOR THE ADVANCEMENT OF COLORED PEOPLE (NAACP). During the 1930s and 1940s, black radio, together with black newspapers, enhanced communication in the black community, where the white media were absent. Black media encouraged southern blacks to move North. More important, the black media began to act as catalysts for the civil rights movement. This period of history was described by Swedish social scientist Gunnar Myrdal in AN AMERICAN DILEMMA as a conflict between the values of freedom and equality and white PREJUDICE directed against blacks. This conflict becomes the major theme in media reporting of civil rights. American public opinion and civil rights are set in the framework of the conflict between American values and prejudice. This is the American dilemma.

DESEGREGATION court cases dealing with education in SOUTH CAROLINA, DELAWARE, VIRGINIA, the District of Columbia, and KANSAS were gaining news coverage in the mainstream press. Soon what would become famous as the BROWN V. BOARD OF EDUCATION Supreme Court decision became front page news. Aldon Morris, in *The Origins of the Civil Rights Movement*, notes the results of a Gallup poll on July 10, 1954, finding that Americans outside the South overwhelmingly approved of the Court's 1954 decision. This begins an increase in support for school desegregation. The southern reaction, however, was one of shock and dismay. White public opinion in the North differed from white public opinion in the South.

William Brink and Louis Harris, in *The Negro Revolution in America*, reported that, in 1963, 71 percent of whites nationwide approved of Dwight EISENHOWER's use of federal troops to integrate a public high school in Little Rock, ARKANSAS. In contrast, only 44 percent of white Southerners agreed. Sixty-five percent approved of Kennedy's use of troops in the integration of the University of Mississippi. Among southern whites, 37 percent backed this federal action. Clearly, nationwide white public opinion in the mid-1960s supported federal action to achieve civil rights.

Expanded newspaper coverage of desegregation coincided with the increasing popularity of television. Media coverage of the 1955–1956 MONTGOMERY BUS BOYCOTT portrayed segregation on city buses in the context of a social movement. Although two years earlier in Baton Rouge, LOUISIANA, a citywide boycott had led to the desegregation of that city's buses, it received little coverage beyond local newspapers. National public opinion was being shaped by media coverage of Montgomery. Emerging as spokesman for the boycott was Rev. Martin Luther KING, JR. He would become a popular civil rights leader around whom the national media, especially television, would frame the civil rights movement. King was able to focus national attention on specific civil rights issues, including voter registration, employment, fair housing, and education.

Television played a critical role in the civil rights movement. Live coverage of violence committed by the police in Birmingham, ALABAMA, in 1963 shocked the nation as police dogs and fire hoses were turned on black children. The *New York Times* headlines of May 13, 1963, read "U.S. Sends Troops Into Alabama After Riots Sweep Birmingham; Kennedy Alerts State's Guard." The American public was witness to the serious gap between equality and prejudice. Publicity of southern violence led to anger among Northern blacks.

The American dilemma was further dramatized at the 1964 Democratic National Convention held in Atlantic City, NEW JERSEY; live television captured Fannie Lou HAMER, a black woman, appealing to be seated representing the MISSISSIPPI FREEDOM DEMOCRATIC PARTY. The all-white regular Mississippi delegation refused to seat any blacks. One year later, the local police and political authorities in Selma, Alabama, were shown taunting and insulting black marchers. For the first time, ABC television interrupted a prime time movie to show a news flash of the violence in Selma. Resulting northern outrage contributed to the passage of the VOTING RIGHTS ACT OF 1965.

The effect of civil rights victories on the black community was one of rising expectations. National press coverage helped shape public opinion in favor of desegregation and against racist elements in the South. Nightly television news programs covering public protests contributed to the changing public view of segregation. This change is described in *Racial Attitudes in America* by Howard Schuman et al. who found that, in 1942, only 32 percent of the public favored integrated schools. By 1956, however, the number was up to 50 percent. By 1982, 90 percent of the national public approved of racially integrated schools. Historically, the blatant contradiction between the American creed and prejudice and discrimination against blacks strongly affected public opinion. Attainment of the goals of the civil rights movement was hastened significantly by media coverage—first by the black press and then by the national media; this coverage, in turn, affected public opinion. Clearly, public opinion helped determine the direction of public policy. Changing national public opinion in support of the southern civil rights movement led to its social, political, and legal gains. Embedded in American culture, public opinion remains a critical component of civil rights and public policy.

Today, civil rights issues have become more complex. Laws banning discrimination extend to many groups, including women, gays, lesbians, and the disabled. More than ever, with increasing available information, public opinion will play an even greater role in civil rights and resulting public policy.

BIBLIOGRAPHY

The Black Press: Soldiers Without Swords. Film. Stanley Nelson, director. 1998.

Brink, William, and Louis Harris. *The Negro Revolution in America.* 1964.

Brink, William, and Louis Harris. *Black and White.* 1967.

Eyes on the Prize. Film. Henry Hampton, director. 1986.

Chong, Dennis. "How People Think, Reason, and Feel about Rights and Liberties." *American Journal of Political Science* 37 (1992): 867–899.

Glynn, Carroll J., Susan Herbst, Garrett J. O'Keefe, and Robert Y. Shapiro. *Public Opinion.* 1999.

Key, V. O., Jr., *Public Opinion and American Democracy.* 1961.

Schuman, Howard, Charolette Steeh, and Lawrence Bobo. *Racial Attitudes in America.* 1985.

Raymond D'Angelo

Puerto Rican Legal Defense and Education Fund

Inspired by the NATIONAL ASSOCIATION FOR THE ADVANCEMENT OF COLORED PEOPLE (NAACP) and MEXICAN AMERICAN LEGAL DEFENSE funds, the Puerto Rican Legal Defense and Education Fund, Inc. (PRLDEF) was founded in 1972. Based in New York City, PRLDEF has this mission: (1) to provide high-quality legal representation on behalf of the Puerto Rican community to secure the fair and equal protection of the law and of the civil rights of Puerto Ricans; and (2) to promote legal education and information among Puerto Ricans in order to increase the number of Puerto Rican lawyers serving the community and make Puerto Ricans aware of their legal rights. Headed by a president and general counsel, the organization has two main components: the Legal Division and the Education Division.

Utilizing litigation as a tool to remedy inequality, the Legal Division has initiated numerous class action lawsuits addressing a variety of civil rights issues in New York, and in several other states with significant Puerto Rican populations. The case that the organization is most often identified with is *Aspira of New York v. the N.Y.C. Board of Education,* one of its first lawsuits, which concerned the language rights of students in the public school system. This lawsuit resulted in a settlement by consent decree.

The Education Division has promoted the development of public interest–oriented Puerto Rican lawyers by providing a variety of services to prelaw college students, law students, and attorneys. These services include law school entrance examination preparatory courses, counseling, scholarships, internship opportunities, and civil rights training.

As with many other public interest organizations, fund-raising has been a major ongoing concern for PRLDEF. Provision of sufficient staff to carry out the organization's basic mission, not to mention program development, has at times been problematic because of a lack of reliable funding. Also troublesome was the lack of stable leadership that plagued the organization from its inception until 1993, with a constant succession of persons occupying the president and general counsel position.

Although adequate funding continues to be an issue, the 1993 appointment of Juan Figueroa, a former Connecticut legislator, as president and general counsel appears to have resolved PRLDEF's leadership crisis. Figueroa, who has continued to lead PRLDEF, has identified the organization's litigation priorities as: EDUCATION rights, HOUSING rights, VOTING RIGHTS, EMPLOYMENT rights, Latina rights, and the administration of criminal justice. The stability secured by Figueroa's tenure and the recent merger of PRLDEF and the Institute for Puerto Rican Policy, a maverick research organization noted for its innovative advocacy work, promises to provide the long-term vision and creativity required for PRLDEF's evolution into a mature civil rights organization.

These changes are fortuitous. As a result of the changing demographics of the communities PRLDEF has traditionally served, the constituency impacted by its work is no longer primarily Puerto Rican but is a very diverse group of Latinos. Among PRLDEF's challenges are to ensure that its mission remains relevant in meeting the needs of these newcomers and to maintain a credible leadership role as a representative of their interests.

BIBLIOGRAPHY

"Centro Archives: Puerto Rican Legal Defense and Education Fund, Inc. 1972–1990." Center for Puerto Rican Studies, City University of New York. This is a summary of a collection of records including annual reports, board minutes, correspondence, memoranda, and staff attorney case files of the organization from 1972 to 1990.

William Ho-Gonzalez

Puerto Rican Liberation

The movement for liberation spans the entire course of Puerto Rican history since the conquest of the island by Spain in 1493. The indigenous Taino population manifested resistance in many forms against the invaders and the cruel system of forced labor imposed upon them in the colonized society. Although the Tainos were decimated within decades, the liberationist, anticolonial process continued in subsequent centuries in the long-term struggle for national sovereignty from Spanish rule and for an end to the slave system. The movement gained strength in the nineteenth century with the consolidation of an autonomist and separatist struggle and growing pressure for

Supporters of independence for Puerto Rico march on July 25, 1998, in Guanica, Puerto Rico, where one hundred years before the United States invasion landed. The sign the demonstrators are carrying reads, in translation, "Long live free Puerto Rico." (AP/ Wide World Photos)

the abolition of slavery. In 1868 a free republic was declared in the mountain town of Lares, and though quickly suppressed by the Spanish authorities, the "*Grito de Lares*" ("Cry of Lares") has continued to resonate in the Puerto Rican drive for national self-determination to the present day. The strategic unity of the separatist and abolitionist struggles is exemplified in the figure of Dr. Ramón Emeterio BETANCES (1827–1898), the acclaimed national leader who, himself a mulatto, waged a lifelong battle for Puerto Rican liberation on both major fronts.

Puerto Rican liberation took a new course in the twentieth century, after the country fell under U.S. occupation as a result of the Spanish-American War in 1898. Freedom from U.S. colonial rule became the central issue on the national agenda, gaining greatest intensity in the actions of the Nationalist Party, under the leadership of Pedro ALBIZU CAMPOS (1891–1965), during the 1930s and 1940s. The decreeing of U.S. citizenship for Puerto Ricans in 1917 and the establishment of commonwealth status at mid-century further solidified the so-called "permanent association" between the two countries, as did the ascendancy of the statehood party during the late 1960s. As the twenty-first century begins although plebiscites indicate an electoral preference for both statehood and autonomy, patriotic sentiment runs high, and the movement for national independence continues unabated.

The migration of Puerto Ricans to the United States, while extending back to the late nineteenth century, reached massive proportions in the post–World War II period, exceeding a million during the 1960s. The duration and size of this presence, along with the social and racial discrimination faced by the emigrant communities, drew the struggle for Puerto Rican liberation into a direct relation to the greater movement for justice and civil rights. Puerto Ricans in New York City and other urban centers have long lived and worked alongside African Americans, suffering with them as second-class citizens the hardships wrought of social prejudice, and readily joining in the struggle against RACISM and for civil rights. Puerto Rican civil rights activism was most visible in the struggle for school DESEGREGATION and community control in Ocean Hill–Brownsville (Brooklyn) in the 1960s and in the efforts of the Young Lords Party during the BLACK POWER movement of the late 1960s and early 1970s. The example of Arturo Alfonso Schomburg (1874–1938), the black Puerto Rican bibliophile and collector who made the intellectual cause of the African diaspora his own, shines over all efforts to unify Puerto Ricans with the history and legacy of the civil rights movement. The famed Schomburg Center for Research in Black Culture in Harlem stands as a testament to his central contribution to BLACK STUDIES and the HARLEM RENAISSANCE.

Increasingly since the 1980 Census introduced the category "Hispanic," Puerto Ricans in the United States have been officially classified as Hispanics or Latinos. The second-largest national group among Latinos after the Mexican Americans, Puerto Ricans have long stood in the forefront of the struggle for language, cultural, and immigrant rights, starting with their solidarity with Cubans in the late-nineteenth century struggle against Spanish colonialism. Because of their status as U.S. citizens and their direct juridical and political incorporation into U.S. affairs, Puerto Ricans on the island also figure as part of the civil rights struggle, and have been duly vocal on such issues as AFFIRMATIVE ACTION and bilingual education.

Puerto Rican liberation promises to play a key role in the civil rights movement in the years ahead. Their close ties and identification with African Americans place Puerto Ricans in a strategic position to link the black and Latino movements at a time when the two largest minority populations are typically counterposed in the public mind as mutually competitive and potentially conflictive. Among Latinos, Puerto Ricans are the nationality whose experience demonstrates most dramatically the racism, stigmatization, and social injustice confronting the entire group, and gives the lie to any facile projections of Hispanic assimilation. Finally, as regards movements for social change on a national and international scale, the struggle for the liberation of Puerto Rico and its colonial diaspora emphasize the need to understand the goals and strategies of civil rights in their integral relation to pressing issues of foreign policy and national sovereignty. Though it has often been ignored in the past, addressing the persistent colonial status of Puerto Rico belongs squarely on the agenda of the U.S. civil rights movement.

BIBLIOGRAPHY

Back, Adine. *Up South in New York: The 1950s School Desegregation Struggles.* 1997.

Jennings, James. *Puerto Rican Politics in Urban America.* 1984.

Lewis, Gordon K. *Puerto Rico: Freedom and Power in the Caribbean.* 1964.

Seda Bonilla, Eduardo. *Derechos cíviles en la cultura puertorriqueña.* 1963.

Torres, Andrés, and José E. Velázquez. *The Puerto Rican Movement: Voices from the Diaspora.* 1998.

Juan Flores

Puerto Rican Movement

The Puerto Rican movement can be understood as a reinvigoration of the struggle for Puerto Rico's self-determination and independence that began in the 1960s. It is part of a continuum in an effort that started in earnest in the 1860s with the work of physician, abolitionist, and separatist, Dr. Ramón Emeterio BETANCES. In the early through the mid-twentieth century, the struggle was led by lawyer, Nationalist, and independence activist, Dr. Pedro ALBIZU CAMPOS. As in the past, the movement unfolded both on the island and in the States. A slogan that characterized the rejuvenated effort was "¡Despierta Boricua! ¡Defiende lo tuyo!" ("Wake up, Puerto Rican! Defend what is yours!").

An important difference that characterized the later movement was the large number of participants and the variety of participating organizations, a reflection of the size of the Puerto Rican community in the New York metropolitan area. Concurrently, there was a merger of Puerto Rican nationalist sentiments and concerns with issues of inequality and racism in the United States. Most groups promoted a radical transformation of U.S. society, seeing this as part of their mission. There were also a number of collaborative efforts, as groups would put aside ideological differences to work on common goals. One such joint effort was instrumental in securing the 1979 release of five Nationalists who had been incarcerated since the early 1950s. Together, several groups also demonstrated for the release of several other activists such as Eduardo Pancho Cruz, Carlos Feliciano, and Martín Sostre, who had been jailed for proindependence actions. The groups also joined forces to demonstrate on behalf of Puerto Rican independence before the United Nations, at the annual Puerto Rican Day Parade, or on other occasions. The movement has been referred to as a radical struggle that continued through the 1970s and 1980s and persists to this day in a less conspicuous and less organized manner than its earlier form.

Unlike prior independence struggles, the movement has not had a single major leader. In Puerto Rico, the principal leaders included lawyers Juan Mari Brás, who led the Puerto Rican Socialist Party in the 1970s, and Rubén Berríos Martínez of the Puerto Rican Independence Party. Writer Juan Antonio Corretjer, a former Nationalist Party leader, led the Liga Socialista in the 1960s and 1970s. In the States several organizations were important, including the Young Lords Party (YLP) and the Puerto Rican Socialist Party (PSP—U.S. branch), El Comité (later known as Movimiento de Izquierda Nacional Puertorriqueño, MINP), and the PUERTO RICAN STUDENT UNION (PRSU), also known as Unión Estudiantil Boricua. The Fuerzas Armadas de Liberación Nacional (FALN) captured the attention of national and international media because it was associated with several acts of terrorism, but its list of members, other than Guillermo William Morales, was not public knowledge.

Fifteen alleged members of the FALN remain incarcerated in U.S. jails.

The Puerto Rican movement in the United States was part of an overall social movement that characterized American culture during the 1960s and beyond. It was tied to the civil rights and black liberation movements, women's and gay rights struggles, and the efforts of Native Americans and Chicanos. The movement was also tied to international struggles for self-determination such as those of Vietnam and Cuba. There were five principal organizations (discussed below), plus some smaller groups.

The Youngs Lords Party, which evolved into the Puerto Rican Revolutionary Workers Organization, is often cited as the catalyst for the Puerto Rican movement. There are several reasons for its prominence, including youthful exuberance, innovative direct action, and the ability to capture the attention of the mass media—all despite its lacking a real tie to the liberation movement based in Puerto Rico. The Lords are remembered for their great outburst of pride and courage.

Originating in Chicago, the Young Lords were primarily comprised of street youth although most of the leadership consisted of college-educated young people. The group succeeded in establishing multiple chapters in New York City, followed by chapters in other Eastern cities. Eventually they started chapters in Puerto Rico. As a militant action-oriented organization, the Lords launched a series of actions dubbed "offensives," which included efforts to improve street cleaning in East Harlem, the takeover of the detoxification unit at Lincoln Hospital in the Bronx, and the takeover of a church in East Harlem to establish community-based program when the church was not normally in use. *Ofensiva Rompecadenas* (the Offensive to Break Chains) marked their move to Puerto Rico in the hope of integrating themselves in the independence struggle. While in Puerto Rico, they also participated in efforts to organize tenants and impoverished homeowners in Puerto Rico's shanty towns.

The Young Lords leadership consisted of many young women and men, including several who would eventually occupy positions in the media. Others would become teachers, lawyers, and community organizers. Some of the more important leaders of the Lords included Mickey Meléndez, Richie Pérez, Juan González, Denise Oliver, Gloria Fontañez, Luis Garden, Pablo GUZMAN, Iris Morales, and Felipe Luciano.

The MOVEMENT FOR INDEPENDENCE, or Movimiento Pro Independencia (MPI), which in 1971 became the Puerto Rican Socialist Party (PSP), was to grow into the largest organization in the movement. MPI was founded in Puerto Rico in 1959, and in the 1960s chapters were started in U.S. cities with large

Puerto Rican communities. In the 1970s, when MPI converted to the PSP, an aggressive organizing strategy in the United States was a top priority. Although based in Puerto Rico, PSP integrated itself into U.S.-based community struggles for economic and social justice.

The formula that linked U.S. community struggles with independence for Puerto Rico in the PSP was consistent with that of other movement groups. The PSP was unique in that it was an extension of a leading organization on the island; consequently, it appealed to many young Puerto Ricans, who were hungry for such a direct link. Up to the late 1970s, the U.S. section of the PSP exhibited an impressive capacity for building chapters throughout the diaspora, which extended as far as California. Throughout this period, it had to contend with a fundamental conflict, as it guarded a delicate relationship that supported both Puerto Rican independence and organizing for radical change in the United States. PSP leaders in the United States occupied positions in education and community agencies. Among the many leaders were Digna Sánchez, José Velásquez, José Antonio Irizarry, Olga Sanabria, José La Luz, Edwin Vargas, and Andrés Torres.

The third largest group and most important student contingent was the PUERTO RICAN STUDENT UNION (PRSU) (Unión Estudiantil Boricua). Its members were generally full-time students enrolled in many campuses throughout the northeast, especially New York City. The Union also established community offices, first in the South Bronx, later in Brooklyn, and finally in East Harlem. This was done to have students serve the community, which they did in several arenas, such as organizing tenants and providing drug-abuse counseling.

Together with the Young Lords, PRSU organized the first national conference of Puerto Rican students, in 1970 at Columbia University. In 1971, the Union also participated in the organization of the first national conference on Puerto Rican studies, held in November at Princeton University. PRSU became a force in the U.S. student movement for building solidarity for Puerto Rican independence. Within the academy, the Union promoted a culturally appropriate curriculum along with admissions and retention services for Puerto Ricans and other Latinos. PRSU contributed to both the creation and the defense of Puerto Rican studies, and its members were critical in the founding of the Center for Puerto Rican Studies of the City University of New York, the first and most comprehensive research institution devoted to the field.

Most members of the PRSU came from chapters that they established, at Bronx Community College, Brooklyn College, City College of New York, Columbia University, Lehman College, and New York City Community College. Other chapters existed in area high schools, and many other PRSU members attended colleges where chapters did not exist. The leadership of the Union consisted of students who would later become teachers, college professors, lawyers, doctors, and community and labor organizers. Among the many leaders were Hildamar Ortíz, Elena Román, Peggy Martínez, Clara Palermo, Mirna Martínez, Carlos Aponte, William Nieves, Diego Pabón, Anthony Román, Emilio González, Héctor Villafañe, José Cruz, José Berríos, Félix Cortéz, Carlos Sanabria, Pedro Pedraza, and Félix Flores.

El Comité, which in 1975 became Movimiento de Izquierda Nacional Puertorriqueño (MINP), was originally organized on the West Side of Manhattan, in New York City, around 1970. Initially, it was a militant community-based organization that sought to combat construction programs designed to replace low-income housing available to the working class. It quickly evolved into a revolutionary cadre organization with links to other Latino struggles, but maintained a focus on issues pertaining to the Puerto Rican community and the independence of Puerto Rico. The work of El Comité spread to other locations, including Boston, and was largely responsible for reenergizing the campaign to free the five Nationalist prisoners.

Much like the other movement organizations, El Comité was a multi-issue organization offering a comprehensive program for the community while maintaining a presence in the universities. This organization was also involved in the formation of the Latin Women's Collective, a predecessor to contemporary Latina women's organizations. El Comité published *Unidad Latina*, in which it addressed a wide variety of issues that had an impact on the local communities while relating those issues to international developments.

Many leaders of El Comité continue as community activists, and as in the other organizations, some have become professionals in a variety of fields. The primary organizers were Federíco Lora, Esperanza Martell, Américo Badillo, Frank Vergara, Manny Ortíz, Julio Pabón, Nancy Miranda, Max Colón, Iris Vergara, Orlando Colón, Noel Colón, María Collado, and Lourdes García.

The Movement for National Liberation, or Movimiento de Liberacíon Nacional (MLN), was a mass organization that developed in 1977, several years after the earlier dominant groups were started. Like the original Young Lords, it was organized in Chicago and was oriented more toward nationalism than Marxism. According to historian Andrés Torres, the group accepted armed struggle as a method of achieving self-determination and independence for Puerto Rico. From its inception, the MLN organized public support for the clandestine Armed Forces of National Liberation (FALN). As a result, several of its members were arrested and imprisoned for refusing to cooperate with grand jury investigations in Chicago and New York. Despite the continual persecution, MLN organizers managed to establish programs in day care and social services. By the late 1980s, the MLN had chapters in New York, Philadelphia, Hartford, Boston, and San Francisco. Like other groups, the MLN sought to organize a community base for its political beliefs by providing for the day-to-day needs of local residents.

In addition to the groups outlined, the Puerto Rican movement also included smaller groups that also organized for self-determination. Resistencia Puertorriqueña and Casa Betances were two such entities. Groups that were organized by non–Puerto Ricans also participated in the fight for sovereignty of the island, one such group being the Puerto Rico Solidarity Committee (PRSC). Also, numerous independent student organizations existed in public and private U.S. universities where there were sizable Puerto Rican enrollments. They worked for self-determination of the island in conjunction with community and civil rights objectives.

BIBLIOGRAPHY

Rodríguez-Morazzani, Roberto. "Puerto Rican Political Generations in New York: Pioneros, Young Turks, and Radicals." *Centro Bulletin*, Center for Puerto Rican Studies, IV (1) (1992):96–116.
Torres, Andrés, and José Velázquez, eds. *The Puerto Rican Movement: Voices of the Diaspora.* 1998.

Basilio Serrano

Puerto Rican Socialist Party

See Movement for Independence—Puerto Rican Socialist Party.

Puerto Rican Student Union

Also known as Unión Estudiantil Boricua in Spanish, the Puerto Rican Student Union (PRSU) was founded in the fall of 1969 in New York City by university students. An aggressive, nationalist, and leftist organization, the Union brought together hundreds of students of the City University and private colleges in New York City and students in nearby locations. PRSU boasted solid roots and a fervent following among the first generation of Boricua (Puerto Rican) youth to seek higher education en masse. Throughout its years of activity, the PRSU was to receive notice on several occasions in the New York and Puerto Rico press; but it was among the student population that the group won respect and admiration for its uncompromising commitment to promoting self-esteem and opening the doors of opportunity for Puerto Ricans.

The Union came into existence following the footsteps of other smaller and more fragmented groups of Puerto Rican students who were involved in the struggles for free, open university education and ethnic studies programs. PRSU's militancy emulated and was comparable to that of the STUDENT NONVIOLENT COORDINATING COMMITTEE (SNCC) and the STUDENTS FOR A DEMOCRATIC SOCIETY (SDS). The Union was unique in that it was based in the community and operated from storefronts in the tenements of the Bronx, Brooklyn, and Manhattan in addition to several college campuses. The major chapters of the PRSU were located at the City College of New York (CCNY), Columbia University, Bronx Community College, New York City Community College, and Brooklyn College. Small contingents also existed in Lehman College and Hunter College, and activists were found in numerous college campuses as far away (from New York City) as Princeton and Yale universities. Two high school chapters also existed, at Monroe High School in the Bronx and another at the High School of Art and Design in Manhattan.

The Union was involved in a variety of activities, ranging from those on the university level to the campaign to limit U.S. military use of Puerto Rico. Its goals were liberationist and proempowerment at the university and community levels and in Puerto Rico. At the university level, PRSU sought to implement and develop the departments of Puerto Rican studies while also supporting efforts for African-American and Asian-American studies. The Union also sought to secure "open admissions" and to expand the college recruitment of Puerto Rican and other Latino university youth. Union members played an important role in the development of the City University–wide Center for Puerto Rican Studies, which is still the largest research center of its kind in the United States. The Union was instrumental in defending the existence and the expansion of the first Bilingual College Program, which was started at Bronx Community College and later moved to Lehman College. The Union was also supportive of struggles on various other college campuses in the United States and Puerto Rico, including California. A strong working relationship existed between the PRSU and the Federación Universitaria Pro Independencia (FUPI) of the University of Puerto Rico. PRSU also collaborated with numerous Puerto Rican organizations that actively sought the independence of Puerto Rico, including El COMITÉ, Movimiento Pro Independencia (MPI; MOVEMENT FOR INDEPENDENCE, later the Puerto Rican Socialist Party), and the Young Lords Party (YLP).

On the community level, the Union members were active in the struggle for improved low-rent housing. They organized rent strikes and were active with the "squatters movement" and the "urban brigade," which sought to rehabilitate housing in the Columbia University area and the South Bronx. The PRSU also organized a detoxification program for drug addicts who were affiliated with the community work in the Bronx.

The Union was instrumental in organizing defense committees on behalf of imprisoned activists. Committees to free or defend activists Eduardo Pancho Cruz, Carlos Feliciano, and others were organized or integrated by PRSU members.

In Puerto Rico, the Union was most active in the campaign to end the military use of Culebra, an off-shore island-municipality of about 800 people. Culebra was used by the U.S. Navy and other invited navies for bombing practice of air-to-surface and water-to-shore bombs. The Union, together with FUPI activists, set up camp sites on Culebra and from those sites participated in efforts to disrupt the bombing practice. The Union help rid the island of the bombing, which was both dangerous and disruptive to the economic development of that impovershed Puerto Rican island. Unfortunately, some, if not all, the military operations were moved to the neighboring island-municipality of Vieques.

Also in Puerto Rico, the Union joined forces with the Young Lords Party. Union activists moved in with the Lords in their Santurce headquarters and joined them in their efforts to fight the forced removal of poor homeowners. In an effort to rid San Juan of perceived "urban eyesores," the prostatehood government sought to demolish homes that were built along a canal in the heart of San Juan. The Lords and Union members sought to educate and organize the residents of that neighborhood in order to ensure that they would be properly compensated if they chose to vacate their homes. The Union also integrated itself into the overall work of the Lords, thereby ensuring that the economic costs of operating in Puerto Rico were met.

The Union leaders changed throughout its eight-year history. The original organizers included William Nieves, Hildamar Ortíz, Diego Pabón, Yvonne Domínguez, Anthony Román, Peggy Martínez, and Carlos Aponte. Later, other leaders included Emilio González, Héctor Villafañe, José Cruz, Josée Berríos, Elena Román, Rubén Díaz, Carlos Sanabria, Pedro Pedraza, José Pérez, and Elba Saavedra. Once they graduated, many PRSU activist became lawyers, others teachers and professors, and still others medical workers.

BIBLIOGRAPHY

Pérez, Richie. "Unión Estudiantil Boricua—Puerto Rican Student Union in Palante." New York, Latin Revolutionary News Service 3, no. 3 (1971): 6–7.

Rodríguez-Morazzani, Roberto. "Puerto Rican Political Generations in New York: Pioneros, Young Turks, and Radicals." *Centro Bulletin*, New York, Center for Puerto Rican Studies, Hunter College, vol. IV, no. 1 (1992).

Serrano, Basilio. "Rifle, Cañón y Escopeta: A Chronicle of the Puerto Rican Student Union." In *The Puerto Rican Movement: Voices From the Diaspora*, edited by Andrés Torres and José Velázquez. 1998.

Basilio Serrano

PUSH

See Rainbow/PUSH Coalition.

Quakers

See Pacifism.

R

Race

Take a typical American college class roll. What will the class be like? Instinctively the teacher sets about grouping and differentiating. First names include Wen, Kareem, Abena, Tanuja, Brandon, Jessica, Isaiah, Joseph, Maria; among last names are Brodsky and Ayanian. The most obvious differences are sex. Certain ethnic possibilities come to mind: Chinese, Arabic, African, Indian, Irish, Jewish, Russian, Armenian. Once the class meets, other identifications are possible. Joseph and Kareem both turn out to be African American, the latter presumably Black Muslim. As expected Tanuja looks Indian, and Wen Chinese, while Maria (who has about the same coloring as Tanuja) has a Hispanic accent. Brandon, Jessica, Ayanian, and Isaiah, on the other hand, all have about the same coloring and accents; only their names suggest different national origins. Abena is indeed of African origin, and so is her father (but not her mother); she is no darker than Joseph or Kareem. As the roll call continues, mind, eyes, and brain move back and forth: gender, ethnicity, race.

Although ethnic and racial associations are helpful in mapping and remembering a class, the reason these particular students have the color, hair, eyes, or other so-called racial characteristics is not because they belong to this or that race, but because they have inherited a set of genes from their parents—who inherited from their parents, from theirs, ad infinitum. If the class were composed entirely of Indians, Irish, or African Americans, the students would still have substantial color differences. Indeed, we now know that each

human being has a unique genetic program (DNA), which can be used to identify that person definitively, for example, in a court of law. So where does race come in?

The standard dictionary definition is the same as Charles Darwin's in *Origin of Species* (1859): "a group of persons, animals, or plants, connected by common descent or origin." Although members of the human "race" have been sizing each other up racially since time out of mind, attempts at precise classification began surprisingly late, the landmark being the writings of Count Gobineau, also in the mid-nineteenth century. Such outlines have varied enormously. Typically they have had a biological basis: readily apparent physical attributes such as color, hair, or stature. The simpler a conceptual scheme, the better; it is easier to remember and manipulate. Most of them have featured a few broad groupings. 'Three' has been a favorite number (Caucasian/white, Mongoloid/yellow, Negroid/black). The trouble is that the world's peoples have many more colors than that. Carleton Coon's standard work of the 1960s, *The Living Races of Man* (1965) had five: Caucasoid, Mongoloid, Australoid (Australian aborigines and Melanesians), Congoids (black Africans), and Capoids (the so-called Hottentots and Bushmen, now commonly called Khoisans). Still not enough colors. The 1998 printing of the fifteenth edition of the *Encyclopaedia Britannica* had nine population groupings, the basis of which was not so much biology as geography: European, Asiatic, African, Indian, American Indian, Australian, Polynesian, Micronesian, and Melanesian. As Thomas Kuhn argued, in *The Structure of Scientific Revolutions* (1962), as conceptual schemes become increasingly complicated, whatever they may gain in strict accuracy, they lose in convenience and explanatory power. Sure enough, the current *Britannica On-Line* has quietly dropped the article on "Race," folding the subject into a larger piece on "Human Evolution."

It is still early on in the development of the science of human genetics, to which we look hopefully for breakthroughs on such major killers as cancer and Alzheimer's Disease, and macro studies of population groupings have by no means abated. Just as the Greek conception of the stationary, spherical Earth remains useful in such practical endeavors as surveying or navigation, centuries after being discarded in favor of the Copernican concept of a world in motion, so physicians dealing with such diseases as hypertension, prostate cancer, or heart disease (all of which seem to have a markedly higher incidence among African Americans) continue to employ racial categories for the simple reason that they work. There are in fact dominant gene pools, concentrated in peoples who have lived and intermarried for long periods in comparative isolation. Certain blood types predominate in South Asia or China; the sickle-cell trait and anemia associated with resistance to malaria mainly but not entirely affect Africans and African Americans. As long ago as 1950, in the aftermath of the Holocaust of WORLD WAR II, the famous UNESCO statement on race declared its utter lack of utility outside biology. Some anatomists hold it has no validity there either. The controversy surrounding the book by Richard Herrnstein and Charles Murray, *The Bell Curve: Intelligence and Class Structure in American Life* (1994), which argued that African Americans are on average mentally inferior, confirms that the long debate is far from over. The *Britannica On-Line* editors are, however, following a pronounced trend among historians and social scientists, who have come to regard race not so much as a reality as a model.

Like nations, races are what Benedict Anderson has aptly called "imagined communities." They are ideas, constructs, historical phenomena, made in history by historical forces. They acquire meaning and reality only in relation to Others: no race without consciousness of race, no CLASS without class-consciousness, no love without lovers. Where only one race exists, as in pre-Columbian America or most parts of Africa before the nineteenth century, race is not a factor. Above all, race is a reflection of power, of the relationship between dominant and subordinate groups in history. Race thinking grew up, first in association with the African slave trade, second in association with European imperialism. As these and many other examples attest, the Holocaust against Jews during World War II being the most flagrant example, race has often been

employed in order to dehumanize a people, to justify discrimination, dispossession, or genocide. If race works, it also kills. As the African-American philosopher Alain Locke put it in the 1920s, much false race theory is therefore quite authentic race history.

Although physical anthropologists have long objected that such groupings have no biological reality, mixing up racial with other kinds of "imagined communities" also has a long history. Nationalities or proto-nationalities, such as the Irish, Scots, or Welsh, have all been called races, as have the language group to which they belong, the Celts. Winston Churchill referred to the British (or was it the English?) as the Island Race. Black Africans, whom Coon called Congoids, have been divided into language groupings (Nilotic and Bantu) that have sometimes been termed races; so have language groups in Europe, for example, Germans and Slavs. Although South Asians have sometimes been classified as a race, within India a racial distinction is often made between Dravidians (early inhabitants, dark-skinned, concentrated in the South) and Aryans (lighter-skinned migrants and invaders from Central Asia, concentrated in the North). The language of race (as well as of nationality) was also used to differentiate South Asian religious communities, themselves somewhat artificially constructed, Hindu and Muslim. Jews, a religion, have also been called both nation and race. The language of race has even been mixed up with that of class, as well as that of gender.

Just as a teacher moves half-consciously, back and forth, from gender to nationality to race, searching for associations and categories that help to arrange and remember a class of students, so human beings have been sizing one another up for centuries. The idea of race has helped cause literally millions of casualties. Of the making of races there is no end.

BIBLIOGRAPHY

Banton, Michael. *Racial Theories.* 1987.
Kevles, Daniel. *In the Name of Eugenics.* 1985.
Montagu, Ashley. *Statement on Race.* 1951.

John W. Cell

Racial Disturbances Against Asian Americans

Racial disturbances targeting Asian Americans resulted from the volatile combination of racist NATIVISM and economic depression. Frequently blaming immigrants for their economic misfortune, perpetrators used violence and coercion to vent their frustration and to expel Asian Americans. For three nights in 1877, mobs destroyed and looted Chinese laundries throughout San Francisco's neighborhoods. The public disorder led city officials to enact licensing laws to undermine Chinese-owned laundries. An 1885 disturbance in Rock Springs, WYOMING, began when Chinese workers at a coal mining company declined to join a strike for higher wages. An organized throng soon came together to destroy the Chinese presence. Assailants fired at unarmed Chinese immigrants and burned down their dwellings. The massacre left twenty-eight Chinese dead and fifteen wounded.

Racial incidents persisted in the twentieth century. Mobs threatened Japanese, Filipino, Asian-Indian, and Korean farm workers with physical harm. In 1930, a mob as large as four hundred beat up dozens of Filipinos in a dance club near Watsonville, CALIFORNIA. Respectable organizations such as the Native Sons of the Golden West publicly criticized these disturbances, but they too believed the Asian immigrant presence to be a danger and did nothing to prevent these events from occurring.

Since World War II, violent acts against Asian Americans were perpetrated by individuals rather than large groups. Anti-Japanese attitudes led to twenty-five documented incidents from January 10 through March 7 of 1945, the first year interned Japanese Americans could return to the West Coast. In California, vandals burned the home of Joe Takeda and fired gunshots at the residents as they rushed outside to fight the fire. Determined to isolate and to terrorize the Takedas, the arsonists even severed telephone lines, thereby ensuring that assistance would not come too soon.

One dramatic incident of individual violence was the 1982 murder of Vincent Chinn in Detroit, MICHIGAN. After blaming Japanese for layoffs at automobile plants, two white men chased Chinn for twenty minutes before bludgeoning him with a baseball bat. Although Chinn died four days later, each attacker received probation and paid $3,780 in fine and fees. A few years later, the United States Civil Rights Commission reported that violence against Asian Americans was a national problem.

BIBLIOGRAPHY

Chan, Sucheng. *Asian Americans: An Interpretive History.* 1991.

McClain, Charles J., and Laurene Wu McClain. "The Chinese Contribution to the Development of American Law." In *Entry Denied: Exclusion and the Chinese Community in America, 1882–1943*, edited by Sucheng Chan. 1991.

Takaki, Ronald. *Strangers from a Different Shore: A History of Asian Americans.* 1989.

Taylor, Sandra C. *Jewel of the Desert: Japanese American Internment at Topaz.* 1993.

S. H. Tang

Racial Disturbances Against Blacks

When blacks have attempted to assert their civil rights in the United States, they often have encountered racial violence. Putting aside the violence perpetrated as a part of the institution of slavery, one can distinguish four phases of this type of violence, which parallel key shifts in African-American history.

The first phase accompanied the emancipation of slaves in the northern United States after the American Revolution. The emergence of a free African-American population created problems for racist white Americans: what rights should be extended to blacks? Efforts by African Americans to assert their right to freedom of religion by establishing their own churches often met with mob incursions, derision, and sometimes open violence. By the 1830s and 1840s a wide variety of black institutions became the subject of mob violence as African Americans joined the chorus of abolitionists while attempting to create a civic life of their own. Often these riots took the form of crowds of whites attacking and destroying black churches, educational institutions, and homes. Not infrequently such attacks led to bloodshed, as white mobs brutally beat blacks who came into their hands. Blacks sometimes fought back, increasing the casualties on both sides.

The second phase occurred during the aftermath of the Civil War and accompanied the great EMANCIPATION that took place in the South. During RECONSTRUCTION southern blacks asserted their political and civil rights forcefully. They marched to the polls, elected local, state and national officials, and proclaimed their equality with whites. White southerners found this development unacceptable, and many resorted to violence unmatched either before or since in American history. We do not know how many blacks were killed by groups such as the KU KLUX KLAN. News and body counts were hidden from the outside world. But in Camilla, GEORGIA, a political pogrom in 1871 left over thirty dead; in Opelousas, LOUISIANA, as many as two hundred died in 1868; and in Colfax, Louisiana at least 105 blacks were killed in 1873, many of them by summary execution after they had surrendered to whites striving to deny them political rights. Incidents like these, although with fewer casualties, occurred hundreds of other times. If every body could be counted, as many as twenty thousand African Americans might be found to have been killed during Reconstruction. Lynch law ruled after 1877 (the end of Reconstruction) in the South, and by the beginning of the twentieth century was extended to the North. Such LYNCHING added thousands of dead in a reign of terror intended to stifle any effort to assert black civil rights.

The third phase accompanied the great MIGRATION and urbanization of blacks in the first part of the twentieth century. As African Americans streamed out of the rural South and to the industrial North, they found new opportunities. Often some civil rights were extended to them. However, they also ran into increasing hostility as they competed for the right to a coveted job or a home in a desirable neighborhood. The result was an explosion of race riots in which whites invaded black areas, beating and killing the residents. The best known of these disturbances erupted in East St. Louis in 1917, Chicago in 1919, and Tulsa in 1921.

It is against this backdrop that the modern civil rights movement emerged in the 1950s and 1960s. There was no guarantee that those African Americans who participated in the MONTGOMERY BUS BOYCOTT, attended Little Rock's Central High School, sat down at JIM CROW lunch counters, or joined FREEDOM RIDES and freedom marches would not face the same type of violence that had occurred earlier in the century. However, mobs in the mid-twentieth century seldom lynched anyone; nor did they come armed to the teeth prepared to massacre their opponents. Instead they hurled bricks and rocks, shouted obscenities, and sometimes even struck their opponents with their fists. Open mob violence soon shriveled in the glare of the television camera and under the power of the national state, but violence against blacks who were asserting their civil rights did not totally disappear. Some whites turned to lethal crimes of anonymity, as bombings and murders led to casualties among those who supported civil rights.

The history of the battle for civil rights for African Americans goes back to the earliest days of the American republic and the creation of a large free black population. Between that time and the middle of the twentieth century, whatever gains there were in civil rights came at a tremendous cost. Those who fought for civil rights more recently took their lives into their hands. Some paid dearly, but they also had far greater and more permanent success than those who went before them.

BIBLIOGRAPHY

Gilje, Paul A. *Rioting in America.* 1996.
Rable, George C. *But There Was No Peace: The Role of Violence in the Politics of Reconstruction.* 1984.
Shapiro, Herbert. *White Violence and Black Response: From Reconstruction to Montgomery.* 1988.
Williamson, Joel. *The Crucible of Race: Black–White Relations in the American South since Emancipation.* 1984.

Paul A. Gilje

Racial Disturbances Against Latinos

Like other peoples of color in the United States, Latinos have been the targets of violent attacks simply because of their race or ethnicity. For example, as early as 1849, when thousands flooded into CALIFORNIA in search of gold, a drunken mob attacked a Chilean community in San Francisco, killing one woman and raping two others. Hangings and beatings persisted throughout the century as European-American populations moved west into former Mexican lands and various ethnic groups encountered one another.

Outbreaks of violence also characterized the twentieth century, especially in times of crisis. In June 1943, when wartime patriotism depicted nonwhites as a threat to security, young Mexicans came under attack for their style of dress during the so-called ZOOT-SUIT RIOTS. Asserting pride in their culture and, more specifically, their generation, the zoot-suiters stood out by wearing their own uniforms and speaking a mixed form of Spanish and English known as *caló*. The local press, however, depicted these displays as unpatriotic and reflective of a juvenile crime element. Servicemen who had never seen Mexicans before and learned of them from the local newspapers did not develop good opinions. Accordingly, some viewed them as a foreign enemy on the domestic front and, armed with clubs and loaded into taxi cabs, groups of servicemen descended upon the zoot-suiter night spots on June 3. For ten days they beat and stripped the youths, sometimes shaving their distinct "ducktail" haircuts. The disturbances lasted until Navy officials declared downtown Los Angeles off limits to their men.

Violent as they were, these attacks and others reminded Latinos that the United States could be a land of oppression as easily as a land of opportunity. Events like the servicemen's riots of 1943 continue to play a role in organizing Latinos to demand social equality and improve the treatment of their communities.

BIBLIOGRAPHY

Acuña, Rodolfo F. *Occupied America: A History of Chicanos.* 1988.
Mazón, Mauricio. *The Zoot-Suit Riots: The Psychology of Symbolic Annihilation.* 1984.
McWilliams, Carey. *North from Mexico: The Spanish-Speaking People of the United States.* 1948.

Tomás F. Sandoval, Jr.

Racial Disturbances Against Native Americans

As European colonies first took hold on North America's East Coast in the early seventeenth century and for some time thereafter, the Native American population greatly outnumbered colonists. The first treaties negotiated by the colonists were to secure their safety from a position of inferior strength. However, as colonists' numbers swelled and introduced diseases began to take their toll on the indigenous populations, the balance of power shifted. By the 1830s racially inspired Jacksonian Indian-removal policies began to escalate the forceful expulsion of Indians from their lands.

Much of the history of U.S.–Indian relations is marked by the naked use of power to take lands away from Native Americans and to force resistant Indian groups onto reservations. Hostile actions ranged from the use of superiorly armed U.S. forces to condoned acts of barbarism by individual frontiersmen. Examples include the 1830s Trail of Tears involving forced deportations of Southeastern Indians to OKLAHOMA 800 miles away. Many died from exposure to winter blizzards, epidemics, and starvation. The Navajo of the Southwest similarly endured forced relocation in the 1864 Long Walk. Another example followed the discovery of gold in CALIFORNIA in 1849. Whites implemented an extermination policy to clear remaining Native Americans from prospective gold fields and settlements.

Once on reservations, Native Americans were not safe from hostilities. In northeastern OREGON, the Nez Perce Reservation was unilaterally reduced by Congress to make way for encroaching settlers. In 1877, U.S. military units chased resistant Nez Perce bands for 1,000 miles while engaging in numerous skirmishes until their capture near the Canadian border in eastern MONTANA.

The end of the nineteenth century marked the low point of the American Indian population. Native populations dramatically rebounded, however, throughout the twentieth century. Still, racial actions would occur, such as the 1973 siege of Indian activists by U.S. agents at Wounded Knee in South Dakota (see WOUNDED KNEE OCCUPATION), later condemned by the U.S. COMMISSION ON CIVIL RIGHTS.

BIBLIOGRAPHY

Cadwalader, Sandra L., and Vine Deloria, Jr. *The Aggressions of Civilization: Federal Indian Policy Since the 1880s.* 1984.

Washburn, Wilcomb E., ed. *Handbook of North American Indians: History of Indian-White Relations*, Vol. 4. 1988.

Wooster, Rober. *The Military and United States Indian Policy, 1865–1903.* 1995.

Richard C. Hanes

Racism

Racism is the belief that human beings are divided into several clearly identifiable groups called RACES and that all members of a race share certain fundamental, biologically hereditary characteristics with one another that they do not share with members of any other race. Ideologies based on racism and race usually assume the superiority of one group over another. Racism is a modern concept that assigns human beings to discrete categories such as Negroid, Caucasoid, and Mongoloid; but since WORLD WAR II, race has been rejected as not having a biological basis. Racism also is associated with attitudes and practices of a once dominant group toward a previously designated inferior group. In its different forms, racism is not invariably fixed on appearance or pigmentation. People with the same physical appearance often suffer from racism based on religious caste and actual or imagined ancestry; the untouchables in India and the Catholics of Northern Ireland belong to the same racial groups as their oppressors. The Hutus and Tutsis in Rwanda and Burundi differ little in appearance; however, each tribe has repeatedly instituted genocidal campaigns against the other, based chiefly on ancestry.

The ancient Hebrews and the classical Greeks developed a concept of racism to explain the ascendancy of their people in comparison to others whom they viewed as different and inferior in particular ways. In the Old Testament, the Hebrews saw themselves as superior to other people because they worshipped one God, Jehovah. The Hebrews did not claim that other people were biologically inferior, but believed that their covenant with God gave them a right to conquer alien people and to possess their land. The Greeks tried to explain their differences with other people by arguing that their barren soil and rough terrain compelled them to become independent and more intelligent than everyone else. Greek racism did not presuppose the innate inferiority of other people; Greek superiority was held to be circumstantial. These ideas laid the foundation for a thoroughgoing system of attributing to ethnic groups certain inferior traits and for a rationale for the repression and enslavement of human beings.

Modern racism originated in seventeenth-century British America. Virginia settlers had discovered the importance of tobacco in the boom of the 1620s, and the planter class at first largely depended on white indentured servants; but the use of these servants posed many dangers and inconveniences, as in time they were set free, became armed, and demanded land for themselves. At one point in 1676, disgruntled former indentured servants and their children overwhelmed the colonial government in Jamestown, Virginia, and burned the town down. This "dangerous" class was sequentially replaced with Africans in the late seventeenth century. The Africans arrived as indentured servants, but in little more than a generation their status evolved into one of slavery. African slavery in its nascent form was a simple practicality devoid of a formalized system of racial justification.

Thomas Jefferson, in *A Summary View of the Rights of British America* (1774), attempted to explain to the French *philosophes* the reasons for slavery in America. Although Jefferson opposed slavery and believed that it was an affront to natural law, the practice could be understood on the basis of the "inferiority" of African people. Because Africans were inferior, Jefferson reasoned that the planters could not offer them liberty or citizenship; to do so would harm American society. He presented an inventory of the inferior traits of Africans. Their inferiority was reflected in an "immovable veil of black," which covered their passions and repulsed whites. African men, Jefferson reflected, recognized the superior beauty of white women to that their own women by their preference for white women. Africans never produced poetry; they did not understand geometry. Jefferson's views would resonate throughout the next two centuries as justification for slavery and for the establishment, after EMANCIPATION, of theories of WHITE SUPREMACY.

Black Americans were emancipated as a by-product of the Civil War (see EMANCIPATION PROCLAMATION). Their emancipation did not abolish the inferior status assigned to former black slaves or to free blacks in the South and the North. The vast majority of white Americans believed them that blacks were innately inferior. The REPUBLICAN PARTY, for many reasons, implemented a program of equal rights and black male suffrage in the South that had important effects on blacks in the North. Radical RECONSTRUCTION was brief. The "redeemers" eventually established JIM CROW style SEGREGATION and disfranchised the freedmen. The gentry had been troubled about the growing coalition between the freedmen and Whigs (southern whites who had supported the Union during the Civil War), for such collaboration imperiled the economic and political status of the white elites. With the dominance of Booker T. WASHINGTON's accommodationism, which condoned social segregation and touted self-help and economic development among blacks, effective black advocacy of equality was crushed until the early 1900s.

At the beginning of the twentieth century, northern blacks were gaining political power along with immigrants. The political reality in northern cities was an acceptance of the principle of power sharing among ethnic groups. In this environment, blacks gained political and economic opportunities. Some prospered sufficiently to constitute a middle class with the ambition and skills needed to strive for civic equality. The new political terrain gave blacks electoral clout in municipal, state, and national elections. WORLD WAR II gave blacks further opportunities for better jobs and leverage against racism. By 1948 the DEMOCRATIC PARTY had split over civil rights for blacks; and with the start of the COLD WAR, racism was a liability to the West in its competition with the Communists for the "hearts and minds" of Asians and Africans. A number of SUPREME COURT decisions from the 1930s to the 1950s demolished Jim Crow segregation. The CIVIL RIGHTS ACT OF 1964 and the VOTING RIGHTS ACT OF 1965 established equality and the vote for all blacks as the law of the land.

The civil rights revolution did not defeat racism; it demonstrated that racism was not immutable—it could be changed by the law and by external circumstances. It was the promise of America, embedded in its Declaration of Independence and the Constitution, that allowed blacks to achieve—in law at least—racial equality.

BIBLIOGRAPHY

Fredrickson, George F. *The Comparative Imagination: On the History of Racism, Nationalism, and Social Movements.* 1997.

Genovese, Eugene D. *The Slaveholders' Dilemma: Freedom and Progress in Southern Conservative Thought: 1820–1860.* 1994.

Miller, John C. *The Wolf by the Ears: Thomas Jefferson and Slavery.* 1977.

Peden, William, ed. *Notes on the State of Virginia.* 1982.

Claude Hargrove

Radicalism

"Radicalism" in the United States owes its origin to the "Radical Reformation" of 16th- and 17th-century Europe and the mixture of civil rebellions and millenarian movements going back in human memory to earliest times. Indeed, much of American radicalism reflects the belief in a Golden Age before hierarchies, and contains an Old Testament–style rebuke of existing authorities as evil usurpers.

Indian rebellions against European colonizers, notably "King Philip's War" in 1675, might be taken alongside the transplanting of Pietist colonies (like the Ephrata colony, established west of Philadelphia in 1733) as the precursors of political radicalism. The many volumes of Ephratan hymns, a veritable poetry of collective life and apocalyptic anticipation, are arguably the first published texts of American radicalism. But Thomas Paine's antimonarchical *Common*

Sense (1776) is the first widely read document and the first with direct bearing upon the fate of the incipient nation. The revolution that it inspired was radical in effect only for white colonists; slaves and Indians would have fared better had national consolidation and territorial expansion been halted.

Paine's life nevertheless characterized the fate of radicalism in another important way. His attack on wrongful colonial authority and the need for free elections gained him the enmity of ungrateful American conservatives, forcing him from postrevolutionary public life. His return from political activity in Europe later found him shunned even by old friends like Thomas Jefferson for his unabashed atheism and his concern for the increasing divide of wealth and poverty in the new republic.

The burden of radicalism had already passed on to the direct action of Daniel Shays's followers, whose rebellion in Massachusetts in 1786 sought to redress economic privilege. Fifteen citizens were sentenced to death (two were actually hung), a small figure compared to the victims of racial pogroms directed at real and potential uprisings by nonwhites. Hundreds of followers of Tecumseh and The Prophet were slaughtered in 1811, thousands more to come in the process of seizing Indian lands. The continuing casualties of slavery included Gabriel Prosser in 1800, Denmark Veysey in 1822, and Nat Turner in 1831, who led slave rebellions, all crushed. Black fugitives had joined with surviving Indian peoples in many locations, together defending communities for several decades in the Seminole Wars, which were fought to several brutal conclusions by future president Andrew Jackson, among others. In matters of race as of civil insurrection against wealth, ruthlessness was the standard treatment for radicals.

Radicalism nevertheless found new outlets in the twin sites of the early labor movement and the perfectionist social movements of the 1830 to the 1850s. Urging shorter hours, free public schools, and free land in the West, early workers' movements also made educational points articulated best by intellectuals George Henry Evans and Frances Wright: that racism, like class exploitation, wounded all hopes for freedom. The contrary vision of a "white republic" in which class would remain fluid as race would stand as absolute marked the corruption of labor movements by politicians and a succession of blue collar demagogues.

The great reform movements of the mid-nineteenth century—woman's rights, abolitionism, and spiritualism—began from a different standpoint. Social class as such concerned them less than the vision of universal citizenship and multidimensional improvement. Meeting in Seneca Falls in 1848, the first woman's rights convention declared a revolutionary

principal afoot. Half the human race would hereafter speak rather than accept silently the indignities and handicaps of submission. Closely linked with this movement through outstanding personalities and ordinary footsoldiers of reform, abolitionists like William Lloyd Garrison and Frederick DOUGLASS declared the human right to expropriate wrongful "property." Spiritualism, an often misunderstood link between the movements and a larger population of sympathizers, grew from a rejection of patriarchal Calvinism and a belief in the oneness of human spirit with surrounding nature.

The outbreak of Civil War eclipsed every movement but war itself—and EMANCIPATION. Abolitionists as well as the radical Women's National Loyal League demanded that President Abraham Lincoln set out emancipation as the war's goal. As Lincoln responded with the EMANCIPATION PROCLAMATION, what W. E. B. DU BOIS called the largest "general strike" in history soon followed: African Americans abandoning "their" plantations and opening the way for Union victory. Disappointment followed. Republican "Radicals," never as trustworthy as the abolitionists and organized women had hoped, laid out a vision of a postwar South in which their party could rule by crushing the slavocracy. But they did not offer freed slaves the means to reorganize the new southern society themselves, and in the end (by 1876) the "radicals" had abandoned African Americans to what Du Bois called "a new capitalism and a new enslavement of labor," a model for imperial expansion across the planet.

In this great saga, real radicals had several more hands to play. The first American followers of Karl Marx, mostly German immigrants, set out plans for a radicalized labor movement with (as many hoped) a special place for racial egalitarianism. Intermittently, for the next half-century, African Americans, Mexican Americans and Asian Americans would find that thin section of socialists and labor radicals ready to take on race issues with special urgency. The American-born members of the International Workingmen's Association (organized in the United States 1866–1873), led by Victoria Woodhull, embraced Marxism along with antiracism, woman suffrage, free love, and spiritualism, putting up a ticket of herself and Frederick Douglass for president and vice-president in 1872. This movement was swept away in postwar conservative reaction, arose in different form following the national railroad strike in 1877, and re-emerged in the labor and populist movements of the 1880s to the 1890s.

The KNIGHTS OF LABOR, more reformers than unionists, nevertheless briefly mobilized a half-million working people during the middle of the 1880s, including thousands of women, Mexican Americans, and African Americans (Asian Americans were excluded). Their hope to halt the advance of capitalism and create the guidelines for industrial democracy was foiled by industrial barons, aided by political authorities, the press—and by the new and determinedly exclusionary American Federation of Labor. Repeatedly thereafter, unions formed on less exclusionary lines were swept aside, well into the twentieth century.

Populism (its constituent movements known as the Farmers Alliance) revived multiracial radicalism in other forms. Great cooperative institutions in the South and challenges to the two-party system in South and West seemed to shake the profit system. A Colored Farmers Alliance in the South swept in tens of thousands of African Americans, and African-American voters threatened to tip the balance toward populism in Louisiana and elsewhere. LYNCHINGS, voter fraud, and generalized terrorism met these challenges, and a section of populism (led by Tom Watson, erstwhile courageous support of black rights) itself turned to racism. Brave socialist efforts to halt the Spanish-American war and the American slaughter of Filipino nationalists were made in vain. A large and influential SOCIALIST PARTY, founded and led after the turn of the century by Eugene V. Debs, created a constituency of working people only to be crushed by the repression of President Woodrow Wilson's government after 1917. The emerging modern liberalism and conservatism, well into the 1940s, assumed racial boundaries as proper, and their leaders with but few exceptions cooperated in punishing egalitarian movements. World wars, fought under the banners of emancipation, subtly aimed at reapportioning regions of economic influence. Genuinely radical movements struggled against overwhelming odds to change the agenda.

Intellectuals like W. E. B. Du Bois, labor activists such as A. Philip RANDOLPH, and advanced figures within such labor movements as the Industrial Workers of the World (IWW) proposed drastic changes in society's racial orientation as well as its economic-political character. But a thorough emphasis on racial egalitarianism did not emerge until the 1920s, when a defeated American Left looked abroad to forces shaking the colonial world.

Communists, too closely tied to Russian leadership but heroic in their own local circumstances, struggled to build an antiracist movement. In part, they succeeded amazingly—at least until the COLD WAR—in building unions devoted (if only abstractly in racial and often gender terms) to egalitarianism and industrial democracy. They also spurred a radical interracial culture, from films to cabaret music to literature, which flourished through the middle of the 1940s.

The cold war chilled radicalism, as liberals joined with conservatives to detach social justice and the re-

distribution of wealth from a welfare state program. Civil rights radicalism, never quite crushed as labor radicalism had been, revived only by direct action, from the MONTGOMERY BUS BOYCOTT to the lunch-counter sit-ins to the appearance of BLACK POWER during the 1960s, with leaders stretching from Martin Luther KING, JR., and MALCOLM X to Stokely CARMICHAEL. The antiwar movement, environmentalism, feminism, Indian, Chicano, Asian and still later, the gay movements, all added new dimensions to radical claims. A municipal reform movement brought African-American figures with long records of radical alliances to power locally during the 1970s and the 1980s. But by the 1980s, the recuperative power of capitalism had overwhelmed resistance in most quarters. Radicalism again consisted, as it had during other low periods, largely of support for revolutionary movements abroad, from Africa to Central America; and these movements too were almost uniformly defeated, or in the end domesticated and their radical plans set aside.

By the close of the century, radicalism was dispersed and institutionally weak. But new immigrant populations (most notably, from the Dominican Republic and Haiti) showed signs of a radical sentiment urgently needed to reawaken movements damped down by defeat and disappointment.

BIBLIOGRAPHY

Brecher, Jeremy, *Strike!* 1998.

Buhle, Mari Jo. *Women and American Socialism.* 1981.

Buhle, Mari Jo, Paul Buhle, and Dan Georgakas, eds. *Encyclopedia of the American Left.* 1998.

Buhle, Mari Jo, Paul Buhle, and Harvey J. Kaye, *The American Radical.* 1995.

Buhle, Paul. *Marxism in the United States.* 1991.

Buhle, Paul, and Edmund Sullivan. *Images of American Radicalism.* 1998.

Du Bois, W. E. B. *Black Reconstruction in America, 1860–1880.* 1935.

Duberman, Martin. *Paul Robeson.* 1988.

Filippell, Ronald L., ed. *Labor Conflict in the United States: An Encyclopedia.* 1990.

Flacks, Richard. *Making History: The American Left and the American Mind.* 1988.

Kelley, Robin D. G. *Hammer and Hoe: Alabama Communists During the Great Depression.* 1990.

Messer-Kruse, Timothy, *The Yankee International: Marxism and the American Reform Tradition, 1848–1876.* 1998.

Whitman, Alden, ed. *American Reformers: An H. W. Wilson Biographical Dictionary.* 1985.

Paul Buhle

Radical Republicans

Radical Republicans were a faction of the REPUBLICAN PARTY in the Civil War era. From the party's origins in the mid-1850s until the waning of RECONSTRUCTION in the 1870s, a group of Republicans in CONGRESS adopted policies on slavery, the South, and race that were more principled and more extreme than the majority of the party. At a time of crisis in the nation's history when events were moving very rapidly, the Republican Party's radical wing was always in the vanguard of change. Constantly raising the stakes, the radicals kept up the pressure on the party's congressional leadership as well as on the Republican administrations headed by Presidents Abraham Lincoln, Andrew Johnson, and Ulysses Grant.

Although the specifics of the radicals' policies were always changing, the essence of their RADICALISM was constant, namely, that they took a firm and uncompromising stance toward slavery and race in advance of the rest of the Republican Party. In the 1850s, radicals like Salmon P. Chase of OHIO and John P. Hale of NEW HAMPSHIRE pushed for an aggressive approach to slavery that would challenge the institution through passage of legislation aimed, not just at restricting its expansion, but at challenging its legitimacy throughout the nation and threatening its existence in the southern states. While most Republicans hedged, the radicals insisted that slavery was utterly incompatible with the Constitution and laws of the United States. Naturally, the radicals were confrontational and intransigent toward the southern slaveholders and secessionists and more likely than other Republicans to base their opposition to slavery on principle and morality. Although few publicly advocated the immediate and unconditional abolition of slavery (the position taken by the abolitionists themselves), the radicals' objective was nevertheless to free the slaves as soon as possible but within the limits of the political and constitutional order.

When war broke out, some radicals like Charles SUMNER and Horace Greeley were willing to let the South go, but most endorsed the use of military force to put down the rebellion. As a group, the radicals were the most earnest in pressing for a vigorous prosecution of the war. To this end, they established the Joint Committee on the Conduct of the War as an instrument for keeping pressure on the Lincoln administration. Radicals also demanded confiscation measures more punitive than the rest of the party, urging in particular that property in slaves be included. The emancipation of the slaves and their enlistment in the Union armed forces was another demand of the radicals and, by late 1862, it had become accepted by the President. As they organized to develop and enforce a more aggressive prosecution of the war, the radicals became an identifiable and cohesive bloc within the party and the term, "Radical Republican," with "radical" usually capitalized, began to emerge, suggesting

that the radicals were close to becoming a party within the party, not just a loose grouping or faction.

By war's end, the radicals organized to oppose Lincoln's conciliatory approach to the reorganization and readmission of the former Confederate states. In their Wade-Davis bill, they prescribed alternative and more rigid terms and claimed that Congress, not the President, should control post-war southern policy. When Andrew Johnson seized the initiative in 1865 and implemented a plan they considered too lenient and forgiving, the radicals opposed him vehemently. Led by Thaddeus STEVENS in the House and Charles Sumner in the Senate, they tried to establish new Republican-controlled governments in the South based on universal suffrage, with former Confederates disfranchised and banned from officeholding. Unavailing, however, were their efforts to confiscate Confederate land and to hold the southern states under federal military supervision until they changed their political attitudes and priorities and also treated the former slaves decently and respected their newly acquired rights as citizens. Meanwhile, the radicals' attempts to extend the suffrage to blacks outside the South ran into opposition in those states such as Ohio and INDIANA where constitutional amendments were defeated by popular vote in the late 1860s.

Reconstruction soon ran into difficulties in the South as the radicals had feared would happen because its provisions were insufficiently forceful and tough. Struggling to sustain the federal presence, they urged stricter supervision of voting rights by means of the Enforcement Acts passed in 1870–1871 and were instrumental in getting Congress to pass a new Civil Rights Act in 1875 (see CIVIL RIGHTS ACT OF 1875). This measure was more comprehensive than the earlier CIVIL RIGHTS ACT OF 1866 that was limited to legal rights and so did not guarantee African Americans access to public accommodations. But, like Reconstruction itself, the radicals had begun to lose steam. Their momentum, considerably damaged by their failure to remove President Andrew Johnson from office in 1868, was ebbing, as was their cohesion. In 1872, some gravitated to the liberal Republican movement, while others who were more attached to the Republican Party as an institution of reform backed Ulysses Grant's reelection.

Radicalism's decline was explicable by more fundamental developments, however. The issues of slavery, sectionalism, and war that had precipitated, and then forged, Republican radicalism were now being replaced by trade and finance, labor and capital, and industrialization and urbanization as the central issues of American public life. On these matters, radical Republicans did not agree, nor should they have been expected to. After all, their great achievement of formulating and insisting on a thoroughgoing approach to slavery and equal rights and their forceful prosecution of the war and the reconstruction of the South had already been accomplished, even though the final outcome was less than they had hoped.

BIBLIOGRAPHY

Benedict, Michael Les. *A Compromise of Principle: Congressional Republicans and Reconstruction, 1863–1869.* 1974.

Foner, Eric. *Free Soil, Free Labor, Free Men: The Ideology of the Republican Party Before the Civil War.* 1971.

Trefousse, Hans L. *The Radical Republicans: Lincoln's Vanguard for Racial Justice.* 1969.

Michael Perman

Radio

Although radio has been part of American life since the 1920s, African Americans did not play a significant role in the medium until the 1960s. The impact radio has had on civil rights is minimal when compared to newspapers, magazines and television. At times, radio may have hurt the civil rights movement by portraying blacks in a stereotypical and subservient way and ignoring black issues. This was particularly true in the 1940s and 1950s, with black characters such as Amos and Andy, and Rochester, the ever-loyal servant on the "Jack Benny Show." Prior to WORLD WAR II, there were few black performers, deejays or announcers on radio. The first major radio network series dealing exclusively with black contributions to American society, "Freedom's People," debuted in 1941 on NBC's Red network. It featured music, dramatic presentations, and interviews of prominent blacks to advance the message of racial equality. (See also FREEDOM'S PEOPLE.) In the 1950s, radio began covering civil rights demonstrations. Much of the dialogue and information on the issues came from black deejays. Atlanta's WERD became the first black-owned radio station in America in 1950, followed two years later by KCKA in Kansas City. In 1953, Leonard Evans of Chicago launched the National Negro Network of 40 stations from Miami to Los Angeles. Its broadcasts featured news, sports, entertainment, and public service shows.

The 1960s ushered in a new era in civil rights, with limited radio coverage of peaceful protests by supporters of Dr. Martin Luther KING, JR., and more militant actions by African groups such as the BLACK PANTHER PARTY. Radio stations broadcast many of King's speeches, including his landmark "I Have a Dream" speech. Black radio had its critics during this time, many from the African American community. During the Detroit race riot of 1966, the city's black-owned WCHB completely ignored the event. A year later when the Watts area of Los Angeles erupted in rioting, black station KGFJ's coverage consisted mostly of official announcements from police. The Smithsonian Institute produced a 13-part series titled "Black Radio: Telling It Like It Was," in 1996 for public radio stations. It looked at black radio from the 1920s to the 1990s, emphasizing radio's involvement in the civil rights movement.

Today, many African American leaders are concerned that the government deregulation of radio in 1996 will have an adverse effect on black stations. In a 1997 report, the Civil Rights Forum on Communications Policy in Washington, D.C., found only 203 black-owned radio stations in the U.S., down from 229 in 1995. It predicted more losses over the next few years and concluded, "The ability of black people to control the flow of news programming entering their community will be significantly undermined."

Gay and lesbian issues were rarely, if ever, discussed on radio before the 1960s. That changed in 1962 when WBAI-FM in New York broadcast a 96-minute program featuring nine young gay men who openly and frankly discussed their homosexuality. In the late 1990s, there were 80 gay-oriented radio programs across the country, many of which are broadcast over the Internet. Among them were Chicago-based "LesBiGay," "This Way Out," and an Internet radio show for gay teens, "CoolBeans."

BIBLIOGRAPHY

Barlow, William. "Radio." In *Encylopedia of African-American Culture and History,* edited by Jack Salzman, David Lionel Smith, and Cornel West. 1996.

Barlow, William. *Voice Over: The Making of Black Radio.* 1999.

Savage, Todd. "Radio Active." *The Advocate* (September 14, 1999): 80.

Tyson, Timothy B. *Radio Free Dixie: Robert F. Williams and the Roots of Black Power.* 1999.

Ken R. Wells

Rainbow/PUSH Coalition

The Rainbow/PUSH Coalition is a non-profit organization based in Chicago, ILLINOIS. It was formed in 1996 from the merger of Operation PUSH, founded in 1971, and the National Rainbow Coalition, founded in 1986. Both organizations were founded by the Reverend Jesse L. JACKSON.

People United to Save Humanity (Operation PUSH) was formed after Jackson resigned from the SOUTHERN CHRISTIAN LEADERSHIP CONFERENCE (SCLC) in the early 1970s. In the late 1960s Jackson, then a young divinity student, headed the Chicago chapter of OPERATION BREADBASKET, a selective buying program that SCLC had established in 1962. After the assassination of Dr. Martin Luther KING, JR., in 1968, the new leaders of the SCLC found it difficult to maintain the organization's momentum. The Chicago chapter of Operation Breadbasket continued to fare well however. In 1970 for example, under Jackson's leadership, the Chicago chapter of Operation Breadbasket hosted the first Black EXPO, a convention enabling black businesses to gather together and exchange information. The Black EXPO convention was an enormous success that generated national attention for Jackson. But Jackson's ambitious leadership style and increasing popularity clashed with the sagging leadership of the SCLC. Increasing tensions between the young, charismatic Jackson and SCLC leaders led to Jackson's departure from the SCLC and the founding of a new organization called Operation PUSH.

Jackson founded Operation PUSH in 1971. The new organization was originally called People United to Save Humanity, but the word "save" was later dropped in favor of the more modest-sounding "serve." Jackson took many of the programs he had initiated while working with Operation Breadbasket to his new organization. Hence, as Marshall Frady writes in *Jesse: The Life and Pilgrimage of Jesse Jackson*, Operation PUSH turned out to be mostly a reconstitution of Breadbasket's program of economic militancy widened into a more general social ministry.

Headquartered on Chicago's Southside, Operation PUSH evolved into an organization that is not easily defined. It consisted of black Chicagoans from all walks of life—e.g., entertainers, business people, and Jackson devotees who followed him after his departure from the SCLC. The famous Saturday morning meetings, formerly associated with Operation Breadbasket, quickly became a PUSH staple. Due to Jackson's ministerial training in the black church and his oratorical style, the PUSH Saturday morning meetings, complete with band, gospel choir, and a large congregation, became increasingly popular in Chicago. Despite the resemblance to a black church revival, as Frady points out, Operation PUSH was not quite a church but "more a curious montage of assorted ad-hoc social initiations with churchly inflections."

Although the goals of Operation PUSH—the acquisition of better jobs, quality education and health care for African Americans—were similar to those of Operation Breadbasket, many PUSH initiatives were sharply criticized as helping only the black middle class. In light of such criticism Jackson initiated a new program in the late 1970s that focused exclusively on the concerns of disaffected black youth. Jackson called his new program EXCEL, short for EXCELLENCE. It was through the PUSH–EXCEL program that Jackson popularized the refrain "I am somebody."

In 1984 along with his first presidential campaign, Jackson organized the Rainbow Coalition to serve as the political arm of his growing sociopolitical movement. A constituency of the "voiceless and downtrodden" became the foundation for what Jackson termed a "Rainbow Coalition" of Americans—the poor, minorities, residents of rural areas, struggling farmers, feminists, gays and lesbians, and others who historically, according to Jackson, had lacked representation. Jackson had offered himself as an alternative to the mainstream DEMOCRATIC PARTY. In 1986, the organization became the National Rainbow Coalition. Jackson began to devote more of his time to his political activities and the National Rainbow Coalition. In 1989 he gave up the leadership of PUSH. By 1991, PUSH was in severe financial and organizational crisis. Jackson's personal involvement was apparently crucial to PUSH's survival.

In September 1996, Operation PUSH and the National Rainbow Coalition merged to form the Rainbow/PUSH Coalition. Jackson is the organization's president and CEO. The combined operation continues to work with African-American and other minority interests to secure business equality and economic freedom. It also pursues political interests that are compatible with its overall goals, such as its (unsuccessful) efforts to defeat California's Proposition 209, which opposed affirmative action programs.

BIBLIOGRAPHY

Frady, Marshall. *Jesse: The Life and Pilgrimage of Jesse Jackson.* 1996.
House, Ernest R. *Jesse Jackson and the Politics of Charisma: The Rise and Fall of the PUSH/Excel Program.* 1988.
Wilkinson, Brenda. *Jesse Jackson Still Fighting for the Dream.* 1990.

Lori G. Waite

RAM

See Revolutionary Action Movement

Randolph, Asa Philip

(1889–1979), civil rights and labor leader.

A. Philip Randolph was born on April 15, 1889, in Crescent City, Florida, to the Reverend James William Randolph and Elizabeth Robinson Randolph. His father ministered to domestic servants and unskilled workers. Both parents were the children of former slaves.

A. Philip Randolph, president of the Brotherhood of Sleeping Car Porters, served as President Harry S. Truman's civil rights adviser. Randolph was instrumental in persuading Truman to desegregate the armed forces. (© Archive Photos)

Randolph's family moved to Jacksonville, Florida, in 1891, where he attended the Cookman Institute, which was one of the first high schools for blacks. After high school, due to economic problems, he was unable to further his education and had to settle for a series of menial jobs. In 1914, WORLD WAR I broke out in Europe, though the United States did not become directly involved in the conflict until three years later. The Great War, as it was know then, caused large numbers of Europeans to cross the Atlantic to New York City, in search of a better life (see IMMIGRATION AND IMMIGRANTS). At the same time, black southerners came northward to New York, lured by similar hopes of a better life. These two simultaneous migratory flows became known as the Great Migrations (see MIGRATION). Among the black southerners coming to New York was A. Philip Randolph. He came to New York initially to pursue an acting career but instead decided to attend New York's City College on the out-skirts of Harlem, where he studied economics and politics, and was exposed to the beginnings of what soon became known as the HARLEM RENAISSANCE.

As a student at City College, Randolph was exposed to socialist groups then active on campus and subsequently joined the SOCIALIST PARTY, eventually running on the Socialist Party ticket in 1920 as a candidate for New York State comptroller. As the United States moved to enter the war in Europe, Randolph expressed his views about the participation of the workers of the world in this war, stating that it was not their concern. He suggested to blacks that they should not honor the draft but should seek to fight racial injustice and to bring about racial reforms in labor and industry, the armed services, public schools, and government, and should become active in political arenas at home. He became acquainted with the socialist journalist Chandler Owen, and together they edited the *Messenger,* a monthly Socialist Party magazine, from 1917 until 1923. Meanwhile, in Russia, the czarist regime was overthrown and eventually replaced by a Marxist government whose social ideals seemed to echo some of the causes that Randolph had come to espouse. (Randolph never became a communist, however, preferring instead a resolutely democratic form of unionist socialism.)

During his editorship of the *Messenger,* Randolph was scrutinized by the Department of Justice because of the newly rising "red scare" and because of his pronounced opposition to national leadership and organizations that he claimed were not in touch with the realities of the masses. Randolph and Owen continued to make a stand for unionism among black workers. The editorial offices of the *Messenger* were raided several times by the authorities during the early 1920s.

In 1925, Randolph organized the BROTHERHOOD OF SLEEPING CAR PORTERS in Harlem to fight against the Pullman Company for better wages and hours. He worked for and achieved the recognition of this union by the American Federation of Labor (AFL), which subsequently granted an international charter giving it equal status with other unions. Later, the AFL merged with the Congress of Industrial Organization (CIO), becoming the AFL-CIO. Randolph was eventually named a vice president of the AFL-CIO in 1955. After the departure of Randolph and Owen, the *Messenger,* now much more unionist than socialist, continued as the official organ, or journal, of the Brotherhood of Sleeping Car Porters. The Brotherhood and Randolph had became predominant powers among "Negro" workers by the end of the 1930s. As Randolph became more involved in the union movement, he withdrew from membership in the Socialist Party, which he came to feel was out of touch with the needs and desires of black American workers.

Internationally in later years, Randolph was a hero and spokesperson for the emerging black man's struggle in Africa, as Tom Mboya, General Secretary of the Kenya Federation of Labour in Nairobi, Kenya, suggested in *The Challenge of Nationhood: A Collection of Speeches and Writings by Tom Mboya* (1970). Randolph had worked around the world, in particular assisting Maida Springer, Special Representative of the AFL-CIO, and Tom Mboya with the union organization of Kenyan women workers in the 1950s. Nationally his record is equally impressive as a leader and activist and fighter for racial justice.

Randolph was a forerunner in the achievement of many African-American milestones. He led the first March on Washington in 1941 (see MARCH ON WASHINGTON MOVEMENT), for the right of blacks to work and to fight in WORLD WAR II. This brought immediate action from President Franklin D. ROOSEVELT in the form of Executive Order 8802 and subsequently from President Harry TRUMAN in 1947, in the form of Executive Order 9981. These orders respectively banned the exclusion of blacks from employment in defense-related factories and banned SEGREGATION in the ARMED FORCES. The greatest and most remembered organizational feat by Randolph was his leadership of the MARCH ON WASHINGTON on August 28, 1963. This later march focused on jobs and freedom. However, for Randolph the 1963 march was the apex of his career as he brought together many great Americans in a nonviolent protest at the Washington Monument as the Reverend Dr. Martin Luther KING, JR., delivered his "I Have a Dream" speech. This was a great moment in history for Randolph, who had the vision to believe that blacks and whites could come together in harmony and brotherhood.

Randolph's integrity, commitment, courage, actively innovative leadership, and organizational skills in the fight for freedom and racial justice made him a significant contributor to the civil rights movement.

BIBLIOGRAPHY

Bond, Julian, and Andrew Lewis. *Gonna Sit at the Welcome Table*, 2nd ed. 1995.

James, Dante J. *For Jobs and Freedom* (video recording). 1996.

Mboya, Tom. *The Challenge of Nationhood: A Collection of Speeches and Writings by Tom Mboya.* 1970.

Pfeffer, Paula F. *A. Philip Randolph, Pioneer of the Civil Rights Movement.* 1990.

Quarles, Benjamin. "A. Philip Randolph: Labor Leader At Large." In *Black Leaders of the Twentieth Century.* 1982.

Williams, Juan. "In Search of A. Philip Randolph: For Jobs and Freedom." Article is posted at the PBS Website:http//:www.pbs.org./weta/apr/aprbio.html. 1998.

Dorothy A. Smith-Akubue

Rapier, James T.

(1837–1883), Alabama black leader and congressman.

Politician, public servant, and an early advocate of civil rights, James Thomas Rapier was an important leader at both state and national levels during RECONSTRUCTION.

Born into an accomplished free black family in Florence, ALABAMA, Rapier attended school in Nashville, Tennessee. He then drifted for a couple of years—gambling, drinking, and earning a living by working on riverboats—before resuming his education in Ontario, Canada. While there, he underwent a religious conversion and gained experience as a teacher. In 1864 he returned to the South, determined to help African Americans on the verge of freedom.

In Alabama, Rapier's activities were diverse. He organized a state affiliate of the National Negro Labor Union and served as director of a freedmen's savings bank. He created and edited the first black-owned newspaper in the state (1872), dedicated to the REPUBLICAN PARTY and equal rights. His influence within the state party was significant, and he received two public statewide appointments, first as a tax assessor and later as Collector of Internal Revenue. At the same time, he enjoyed commercial success as a cotton planter, engaging in enlightened management practices toward his black tenants. He was also generous in his support of black churches and schools.

His public service, however, was disrupted by unfounded charges of corruption and incompetence. Similarly, his efforts on behalf of the Republican Party, as both candidate and campaigner, were frequently marred by intimidation, outright violence, and electoral fraud on the part of his opponents. Yet, as a U.S. congressman from Alabama (1872–1874), Rapier sought legislation to improve the prospects and livelihoods of all southerners. Furthermore, in championing equal rights for blacks, he was careful to avoid fomenting racial hostilities. Given the often deadly political atmosphere in the South, he never pressed the issue of social equality between blacks and whites.

Both in CONGRESS and as a prominent figure at many black conventions, Rapier demonstrated a broad commitment to civil rights, seeking protection for agricultural laborers and federal programs to provide land and schools for the freedmen. He regularly called for the enforcement of both the FOURTEENTH

AMENDMENT and the FIFTEENTH AMENDMENT, and in debates preceding the CIVIL RIGHTS ACT OF 1875 he insisted that any compromise regarding full rights for African Americans would be tantamount to an admission of inferiority. In his final years, however, Rapier began to despair of white commitment to guaranteeing opportunities for black men and women or their physical safety. Increasingly, he diverted his energies toward investigating black emigration from the South, and he made several trips to KANSAS with a view to establishing new communities there.

Like that of such contemporaries as John Roy LYNCH of Mississippi and Josiah T. Walls of Florida, Rapier's leadership was long depicted as inept and self-seeking. More recently, historians have provided fresh interpretations by recognizing the biases of white sources, and by demonstrating that the careers of Rapier and others were constantly hampered by the stigma of race.

Rapier, who never married, died of tuberculosis at age forty-five.

BIBLIOGRAPHY

Schweninger, Loren. *James T. Rapier and Reconstruction.* 1978.
Schweninger, Loren. "James T. Rapier of Alabama and the Noble Cause of Reconstruction." In *Southern Black Leaders of the Reconstruction Era,* edited by Howard N. Rabinowitz. 1982.

Andrew M. Kaye

Raza Unida Party, La

During the period of 1970 through 1982, a political party arose in the communities of the Southwest and Midwest that served to further the cause of civil rights for Mexican Americans. Named the La Raza Unida Party, or El Partido de la Raza Unida in Spanish, it would field candidates in TEXAS, CALIFORNIA, NEW MEXICO, and even Washington, D.C., and find limited success. Within its ranks it united a diverse group of Chicano activists whose philosophy ranged from Marxism to separatism to moderate liberalism, but whose commitment to civil rights was firm.

La Raza Unida Party or RUP, as it came to be known, began almost simultaneously in two very different places. In Texas it was an offshoot of the Mexican American Youth Organization (MAYO), an activist group best known for its school walkouts (see MEXICAN-AMERICAN STUDENT ORGANIZATIONS). In COLORADO it grew from CRUSADE FOR JUSTICE, a radical working-class civil rights organization that focused on internal community-building. The two organizations would come together in 1969 at the Chicano

Youth Liberation Conference held in March 1969 in Denver, Colorado. There, Rodolfo "Corky" GONZALES, leader of the Crusade, would call for the formation of a Chicano political party. The Texas contingent would be the first to establish an official party, and they would choose to make it more electorally focused and slightly moderate in platform.

The RUP officially began in Crystal City, Texas, a predominantly Mexican-American agricultural community. In the spring and fall of 1969, high school students there had led a walkout of the public schools, protesting discrimination, poor facilities, a dead-end curriculum, and racist teachers. After winning most of their demands, the students, their parents, and their MAYO supporters organized the RUP. Masterminding both MAYO and RUP was José Angel GUTIÉRREZ, a Crystal City native with a degree in political science. In their first election in the spring of 1970, the party swept the majority of the school board and city council positions. By 1976, it held most of the county offices too, women making up almost half of the elected officials. The party's platform called for multilingual and multicultural educational programs from preschool to college (see MULTICULTURAL); equalized funding for all school districts; free early childhood education; and the establishment of private Chicano colleges and universities. The platform also called for lowering the voting age to eighteen; breaking up monopolies; fair distribution of wealth; passage of the EQUAL RIGHTS AMENDMENT; and the abolishment of capital punishment.

Through its efforts, the VOTING RIGHTS ACT of 1965 would now be applied to Mexican Americans; bilingual education would be greatly expanded; and single-member districts would become the norm in many communities throughout the Southwest.

From Crystal City the party spread throughout Texas and the Southwest. Its impact promoted the recruitment of more Mexican Americans to the traditional U.S. parties and the inclusion of many of their issues in the platform of the DEMOCRATIC PARTY. The RUP also attracted many Mexican Americans to the political process, leading to the multiplication of Mexican-American officeholders. By 1982, the RUP would succumb to external pressures from the mainstream political parties and the government as well as to internal divisions over issues of ideology and leadership.

BIBLIOGRAPHY

García, Ignacio M. *United We Win: The Rise and Fall of La Raza Unida Party.* 1989.
García, Ignacio M. *Chicanismo: The Forging of a Militant Ethos Among Mexican Americans.* 1997.
Múñoz, Carlos, Jr. *Youth, Identity, Power: The Chicano Movement.* 1989.

Navarro, Armando. *Mexican American Youth Organization Avant-Garde of the Chicano Movement in Texas.* 1995.

Navarro, Armando. *The Cristal Experiment: A Chicano Struggle for Community Control.* 1998.

Schockley, John Staples. *Chicano Revolt in a Texas Town.* 1974.

Ignacio M. García

Reagan, Ronald W.

(1911–), U.S. president, 1981–1989.

When Ronald Reagan became president, the civil rights movement had reached a point where legal distinctions between the races had already been outlawed, but discrimination against minority groups in society remained a problem. Reagan, however, did not believe that government policy should deal with minority groups as a whole; rather the problem in civil rights was one of individual-based discrimination that should be addressed one case at a time. Reagan wished to limit the involvement of the national government in civil rights policy and in some cases to roll back commitments that had already been made in civil rights. Changes in policy were made in the areas of EMPLOYMENT, VOTING RIGHTS and representation, EDUCATION, and HOUSING discrimination.

In the area of employment, the Reagan administration cut the budgets and staff for the EQUAL EMPLOYMENT OPPORTUNITY COMMISSION and the OFFICE OF FEDERAL CONTRACT COMPLIANCE and lessened the enforcement of claims about "pattern or practice discrimination." Instead, the administration pursued cases only where there were "identifiable victims." The Civil Rights Division of the Department of Justice, led by William Bradford Reynolds, attacked the concept of AFFIRMATIVE ACTION and helped to roll back its enforcement.

Reagan opposed the extension of the VOTING RIGHTS ACT OF 1965, which was due to expire in 1982. Ironically, when it became obvious that there was a groundswell of support for its extension, the president claimed credit for congressional passage. Enforcement of the Voting Rights Act declined during the Reagan years, and the administration in some cases argued that the responsibility for proving discrimination fell on the plaintiffs rather than the states, a misreading of the law.

In education, Reagan pursued a policy of retrenchment in the enforcement of SCHOOL DESEGREGATION plans. He favored the use of voluntary programs of desegregation rather than mandatory programs, and only then when de jure patterns of segregation existed. This marked a distinct step back from previous law.

President Ronald Reagan meeting with Native American leader Wilma Pearl Mankiller and other Cherokee representatives. (UPI/CORBIS/Bettmann)

Housing enforcement by the federal government had always been weak, but under the Reagan administration it declined from previous enforcement standards. Budgets supporting federal housing research were cut, and the rate of fair housing litigation under the Reagan administration declined by more than one-half from that of the preceding years.

President Reagan thus represented a change in focus, opposing the use of the federal government for the enforcement of civil rights laws that applied to social groups, preferring to deal instead with individual discrimination. This approach marked a distinct change from the patterns of the previous twenty-five years, and began a new era of defining civil rights in a narrower way.

BIBLIOGRAPHY

Amaker, Norman C. *Civil Rights and the Reagan Administration.* 1988.
Detlefsen, Robert R. *Civil Rights Under Reagan.* 1991.
Reagan, Ronald. *An American Life.* 1990.
Riddlesperger, James W., Jr., and Donald W. Jackson. *Presidential Leadership and Civil Rights Policy.* 1995.
Stewart, Joseph, Jr. "Between 'Yes' and 'But': Presidents and the Politics of Civil Rights Policy-Making." In *The Presidency Reconsidered,* edited by Richard W. Waterman.

James W. Riddlesperger, Jr.

Reconstruction

Before the Civil War ended in 1865, northern political leaders began the process of reconstructing the Union. The period in American history known as Reconstruction is generally dated from 1863, when President Abraham Lincoln and Republican congressmen first proposed plans for restoring seceded states, to 1877, when removal of the last Union troops from the South signaled that southern states were again fully equal in the Union. Up until his death in April 1865 Lincoln had hoped that the process would be rapid and relatively simple, whereas a growing number of Republican congressmen, known as Radicals, demanded a more thoroughgoing transformation of the South. By 1865 the North was in general agreement that the South at the very least must give up slavery. Lincoln's EMANCIPATION PROCLAMATION, issued during the war, signaled the end of legal bondage in the United States; the THIRTEENTH AMENDMENT, ratified in 1865, abolished it completely. With this amendment the federal government guaranteed all Americans the most basic civil right of freedom from slavery.

Whether the civil rights of African Americans would extend beyond freedom was one of the most intensely debated questions in the decade after the war ended. The widespread practice in northern states of discriminating against blacks precluded a simple mandate to the South that freed people must be assured full equality. Events in the South, however, invigorated the emerging concept of a federal guarantee of full civil rights for all citizens.

Because Andrew Johnson, the Southern Democrat from Tennessee who became president when Lincoln was assassinated, allowed the South considerable discretion over its own affairs in the first months after the war, southerners were able to pass BLACK CODES that severely restricted the civil rights of freed people. Once the RADICAL REPUBLICANS (see also Thaddeus STEVENS; Charles SUMNER) took control of Reconstruction they nullified the Johnson-sponsored state governments that tolerated discrimination and racial violence and began the process of transforming the South by guaranteeing black rights. The first major effort to protect Southern African Americans was the creation of the Freedmen's Bureau (the BUREAU OF REFUGEES, FREEDMEN, AND ABANDONED LANDS), which was authorized to punish those responsible for denying blacks those "civil rights belonging to white persons." This legislation established the concept, still alien to most Americans, that African Americans were citizens entitled not just to some rights but to equal civil rights with whites. The CIVIL RIGHTS ACT OF 1866, which, like the Freedmen's Bureau, was passed by overriding Johnson's veto, was a further effort to legalize the right of the federal government to intervene when civil rights were violated. Although intended to aid the transition of blacks to lives as free citizens, the concept implied the right of federal intervention in other civil rights cases.

Radical Republicans recognized that a congressional act was a precarious base for assuring the right of federal intervention in civil rights cases. Accordingly, they determined to protect their assertion of federal power with a constitutional amendment. The FOURTEENTH AMENDMENT, ratified in 1868, is the fundamental guarantee of federal protection of civil rights. The amendment defined citizens of both the states and anyone born in the United States or naturalized there; therefore, whatever the intent of white southerners might be, black southerners were their equals as citizens. The amendment denied any state the right to deny "the privileges or immunities" of citizens or deprive "any person of life, liberty, or property, without due process of law" or to deny "equal protection of the laws." This amendment revolutionized the concept of citizenship and entitlement to civil rights already assured by the United States; civil rights had been nationalized. Political implications in the amendment eroded the long-held distinction between civil and political rights. Two years later, the FIF-TEENTH AMENDMENT further expanded federal power by denying states the right to deprive anyone the vote based on "race, color or previous condition of servitude." A year later, passage of the KU KLUX KLAN ACT made private violation of civil and political rights a crime. This amendment and law marked the high point of federal protection of black political and civil rights. Two years later, the Freedmen's Bureau ceased operation in the South, signaling a retreat from a Reconstruction based on black equality. During the Grant administration Congress did pass the CIVIL RIGHTS ACT OF 1875, which prohibited discrimination in all public accommodations, in places of entertainment, on public transportation, and on juries. The law was only loosely enforced, however, and in 1883 the SUPREME COURT declared most of its provisions to be unconstitutional.

This was six years after the Compromise of 1877 had settled the disputed presidential election of 1876 by requiring the victorious Republican administration of Rutherford B. Hayes to remove the last federal troops from the South in exchange for being given the presidency. Despite guarantees written into the Constitution, a resurgent South effectively denied Southern blacks' civil and political rights. Increasingly through the remainder of the nineteenth century, the Fourteenth Amendment protected the rights of corporations—defined as persons—more than the rights it was designed to protect. Well into the twentieth century, blacks and other groups in all parts of the United States were routinely denied fundamental civil rights. The Reconstruction years, however, had provided them with the tools to fight back. The Fourteenth Amendment was the cornerstone of a strong civil rights movement, which surfaced almost a century after the amendment was enacted.

BIBLIOGRAPHY

Belz, Herman. *Emancipation and Equal Rights: Politics and Constitutionalism in the Civil Rights Era.* 1978.

Foner, Eric. *Reconstruction America's Unfinished Revolution, 1863–1877.* 1988.

Hyman, Harold M. *A More Perfect Union: The Impact of the Civil War and Reconstruction on the Constitution.* 1973.

Kaczorowski, Robert. *The Politics of Judicial Interpretation: The Federal Courts, Department of Justice and Civil Rights, 1866–1876.* 1985.

Nelson, William E. *The Fourteenth Amendment: From Political Principle to Judicial Doctrine.* 1988.

Nieman, Donald. *To Set the Law in Motion: The Freedmen's Bureau and the Legal Rights of Blacks, 1865–1868.* 1979.

Bess Beatty

Reconstruction Amendments

See Fifteenth Amendment; Fourteenth Amendment

Redemption

"Redemption" refers to the period in which Southern Democrats regained control of their state governments from RADICAL REPUBLICANS beginning in the early 1870s. Although federal troops left the South in 1877 and Republican political influence had all but disappeared, the process of Redemption continued until 1910, when the last southern state accomplished total disfranchisement of its black population. Redemption not only included the wresting of political control away from Republicans in the South but also involved expanding the scope of state government and greatly reducing the political and economic rights of African Americans. The latter was a process that continued for many decades.

Conservative southern electorates had begun to vote out radical officeholders as early as 1869, but Southern Democratic leaders achieved total political control of their states by 1877 in part because of the controversy surrounding the presidential election of 1876. In an election that required 185 electoral votes to elect a president, Democratic candidate Samuel J. Tilden fell one electoral vote short in his race against Republican candidate Rutherford B. Hayes. Hayes received 166 votes. Republicans in CONGRESS, however, questioned the legitimacy of an additional nineteen votes for the DEMOCRATIC PARTY in LOUISIANA, FLORIDA, and SOUTH CAROLINA. In exchange for those nineteen votes—which would ensure Hayes a presidential victory—the REPUBLICAN PARTY promised Southern Democrats a number of concessions. These included the appointment of a southerner to Hayes's presidential cabinet, more federal aid for internal improvements including support of the Texas and Pacific Railroad, and, most important, the removal of the last federal troops in the South. While Republicans did not honor all of the details of this compromise after southerners agreed to the inauguration of Hayes, it did leave the South completely in the hands of the Redeemers, who immediately established a regime of repression.

Those Democrats who "redeemed" their states in the post–Civil War South constituted an uneasy political coalition of Confederate army veterans, prewar slave-owning Democrats, old Whigs who typically favored industrial growth, and remaining conservative Republicans who had shifted their political alliance. While some dissension did exist within the party, particularly when it came to deciding the economic future of the South, the Democrats were united in one important goal: to revoke the gains African Americans had made during RECONSTRUCTION and reestablish WHITE SUPREMACY in the South.

In their quest for political control and white supremacy, Democrats resorted to a number of stratagems including intimidation, violence, electoral fraud, and complex legislation. Often they bypassed popular elections and simply appointed favored individuals to public office. While some factions in the state Democratic parties sought to manipulate the black vote to their advantage, all Democratic coalitions ultimately sought to disfranchise the entire African-American population in the South. The FIFTEENTH AMENDMENT, one of the great pieces of Reconstruction legislation, prohibited states from discriminating against potential voters because of their RACE or previous condition of servitude, but Southern Democrats devised ways around this. Most states adopted poll taxes that often had to be paid well in advance of elections. A voter might have to preserve the tax receipt and show evidence of payment to the registrar and to the election official at the ballot box. Taxes were not only high but cumulative. Since payment of the tax was optional, complicated, and financially oppressive, it worked well to limit black suffrage.

Eight states in the South also added amendments to their constitutions that stated that all qualified voters had to be able to read a passage of the United States Constitution or provide a reasonable interpretation of it before the registrar. Given the high rate of illiteracy in the South, the "understanding clause" disfranchised a significant part of the population—both black and white. If a potential voter were required to interpret the meaning of the Constitution, it was solely up to the registrar to determine whether or not he had satisfactorily answered the questions posed to him. After 1895, South Carolina, LOUISIANA, ALABAMA, and Georgia passed laws substituting the ownership of taxable property for literacy in determining voter registration. Regardless of the criteria for voter eligibility, the standards of literacy and high monetary value of the taxable property one was required to possess were beyond the means of most blacks, who worked largely as sharecroppers and tenant farmers and had very little education.

Many of the strategies the Democrats devised as methods to circumvent the Fifteenth Amendment frequently had the result of disfranchising a substantial portion of the poor white population. Some states, like Louisiana, sought to provide loopholes for underprivileged whites. The most common loophole was the "grandfather clause," which exempted from literacy and property tests those individuals who had been entitled to vote on January 1, 1867, together with their

sons and grandsons. VIRGINIA, Alabama, and Georgia borrowed the concept and applied it to war veterans and their future descendants. The inheritance of the right to vote based on one's forefather's voting status completely excluded all former slaves and merely served as one more way to disfranchise the black population. Efforts on the part of Democrats to reform the electoral system to include a greater portion of the poor white population came too little and too late. The exclusion of poor whites from the electorate only deepened class resentment and fueled growing agrarian unrest. This unrest culminated in the creation of the POPULIST PARTY, which challenged the political hegemony of the Democratic Party in the South.

Democratic political control in the South ultimately meant social and economic control too. Democrats reduced taxes and cut funds to many public service agencies. Support for public EDUCATION was minimal at best, and what little money was available largely aided white children. JIM CROW laws called for the SEGREGATION of the races in all public spaces. African Americans accused of crimes were rarely given fair trials and, if convicted, they might be lynched (see LYNCHING) or sent to prison to work on chain gangs. The negation of political and civil rights hampered economic mobility and ensured that most blacks would be tied to the land as sharecroppers, working for former slaveowners in a state of perpetual debt. Redemption ushered in a long period of repression in the South.

BIBLIOGRAPHY

Ayers, Edward. *The Promise of the New South: Life After Reconstruction 1877–1906*. 1995.
Grantham, Dewey. *The Life and Death of the Solid South: A Political History*. 1988.
Kousser, J. Morgan. *The Shaping of Southern Politics: Suffrage Restriction and the Establishment of the One-Party South, 1880–1910*. 1974.
McMillen, Neil R. *Dark Journey: Black Mississippians in the Age of Jim Crow*. 1989.
Perman, Michael. *The Road to Redemption: Southern Politics, 1869–1879*. 1984.
Woodward, C. Vann. *Origins of the New South, 1877–1913*. 1951.
Woodward, C. Vann. *The Strange Career of Jim Crow*. 1955.

Natalie J. Ring

Red Power

Following World War II, the U.S. government adopted tribal termination and urban relocation policies aimed at forcing American Indian assimilation into mainstream white society. Subjected to RACISM in the cities and facing a decline in social services on reservations, Indian radicalism began to emerge by the mid-1960s. A seventeen-month Indian occupation of abandoned federal penitentiary facilities on Alcatraz Island in San Francisco Bay, beginning in 1969, brought the Red Power movement to the nation's attention (see ALCATRAZ OCCUPATION). Inspired by the African-American civil rights movement, Indian activism involving widespread protest and confrontation was prevalent for the next decade. An occupation of BUREAU OF INDIAN AFFAIRS (BIA) offices in Washington, D.C., and a siege at Wounded Knee in the early 1970s further dramatized the plight of American Indians (see TRAIL OF BROKEN TREATIES; WOUNDED KNEE OCCUPATION).

The AMERICAN INDIAN MOVEMENT (AIM), founded in 1968, became the principal organization in the movement. Its goals were to combat job and housing discrimination, to alleviate Indian poverty, and to reassert treaty rights.

The resulting heightened awareness of Indian issues contributed to the emerging era of Indian self-determination in the 1970s, which continued to the end of the twentieth century. Passage of the INDIAN SELF-DETERMINATION AND EDUCATION ASSISTANCE ACT OF 1975 opened new funding avenues for tribal economic development and began shifting responsibility for administering hitherto federal Indian social service programs from the BIA to individual tribes. Significant court decisions exercising tribal rights and interests were won. The last major event associated with Red Power was a peaceful 1978 march into Washington, D.C., by several hundred American Indians to dramatize past dislocations of Indian peoples from their homelands.

BIBLIOGRAPHY
Josephy, Alvin M., Jr., and Joane Nagel, eds. *Red Power: The American Indians' Fight for Freedom.* 1999.
Stern, Kenneth S. *Loud Hawk: The United States Versus the American Indian Movement.* 1994.

Richard C. Hanes

Red Summers of 1917–1921

When James Weldon JOHNSON, the African-American poet, composer, and NATIONAL ASSOCIATION FOR THE ADVANCEMENT OF COLORED PEOPLE (NAACP) secretary, spoke of the "Red Summer" of 1919, he captured the essence of the race riots that bloodied the streets of twenty-five cities and towns in the six-month period from April to October 1919. The Red Summer witnessed more race riots than any year up to 1943 and,

later, the 1960s. The best known of these riots erupted in Chicago, where thirty-eight people (twenty-three blacks and fifteen whites) were killed in a racial war, set off by competition between blacks and whites for housing, jobs and unions, political power, schools, and parks and beaches. The death toll from the 1919 riots was staggering: in addition to the thirty-eight dead in Chicago, seven were killed in Knoxville, TENNESSEE; six in Washington, D.C.; and four in Longview, TEXAS. The bloodiest riot of 1919 erupted in rural Phillips County, ARKANSAS, where as many as 120 blacks were slaughtered by whites for having the audacity to organize a sharecroppers' union.

Race riots in the early twentieth century were not unique to the Red Summer of 1919. Indeed, 1919 stood at the midpoint of the five deadliest years of race rioting in American history; from 1917 to 1921, more people died from this kind of bloodshed than before or since. Most of these horrific riots resulted from white resistance to blacks' efforts to improve their lives through migrating out of the South, seeking better-paying jobs, and organizing for civil rights. In 1917, in East St. Louis, ILLINOIS, some fifty people, including nearly forty blacks, were killed; that same year, in Houston, Texas, seventeen whites were shot to death by black soldiers. Racial rioting and slaughter persisted after 1919, particularly in 1920 in FLORIDA, where a resurgent KU KLUX KLAN killed at least forty African Americans who tried to vote.

The very worst riot of the bloody 1917 to 1921 era disgraced Tulsa, OKLAHOMA. In 1921, Tulsa's blacks were establishing a thriving business community and demanding equal rights. Ignited by an alleged rape of a white girl by a black youth, the city exploded in late May. White mobs armed with clubs, cans of gasoline and torches, rifles, and even machine guns hunted down and killed black men and women. In Tulsa's flourishing black district, block after block of businesses and homes were burned to the ground. The grisly death toll probably exceeded two hundred. The pursuit of a better life including both civil rights and economic opportunity—a laudable goal, and American to the core—was an especially hazardous undertaking for African Americans during this five-year period of race riots.

BIBLIOGRAPHY
Ellsworth, Scott. *Death in a Promised Land: The Tulsa Race Riot of 1921.* 1982.
Rudwick, Elliott. *Race Riot at East St. Louis, July 2, 1917.* 1964.
Tuttle, William M., Jr. *Race Riot: Chicago in the Red Summer of 1919.* 1970.

William M. Tuttle, Jr.

Reeb, James Joseph

(1927–1965), civil rights activist and martyr.

Reverend James Reeb, a Unitarian minister and social worker, was one of several northern white clergymen who responded to Martin Luther KING, JR.'s call to join the 1965 Selma-to-Montgomery March, a crucial campaign of the civil rights struggle of the 1960s.

Reeb, born in Wichita, Kansas, went to high school in Casper, Wyoming, and considered Casper his home. After graduating from St. Olaf's (Lutheran) College in Minnesota, Reeb attended Princeton Theological Seminary in preparation for the Presbyterian ministry, but his humanitarian interests led him to social work. While serving as a hospital chaplain and a YMCA youth director in Philadelphia, Reeb converted to Unitarianism with its emphasis on individual religious experience rather than commitment to a creedal faith. After several years copastoring the Unitarian All Souls Church in Washington, D.C., Reeb accepted the position as project director of a community development program in a Boston ghetto.

On March 7, 1965, while living in Roxbury, Massachusetts, Reeb saw televised reports of "Bloody Sunday," in which civil rights protesters confronted mounted police using tear gas and wielding clubs at the Edmund Pettus Bridge in Selma. The next day Reverend Reeb caught a plane to Alabama to join the protest. On the evening of March 9, as they walked to a church meeting in Selma several unknown white assailants attacked Reeb and two other Unitarian ministers. Reeb's death, two days after a fatal blow to his head, sparked national sympathy for King's efforts to register southern black voters, and led thousands to join the protesters. Galvanized by substantial white support for the Selma campaign, and the public perception that Reeb died a martyr's death for the cause, CONGRESS passed the VOTING RIGHTS ACT OF 1965.

BIBLIOGRAPHY

Howlett, Duncan. *No Greater Love: The James Reeb Story.* 1966.

Sitkoff, Harvard. *The Struggle for Black Equality, 1954–1980.* 1981.

Weisbort, Robert, *Freedom Bound: A History of America's Civil Rights Movement.* 1990.

Cynthia Taylor

Rehabilitation Act of 1973

The original intent of the legislation that became the Rehabilitation Act of 1973 was simply to expand an existing vocational rehabilitation program and to include a provision for independent living assistance for persons who were so significantly disabled that they were not considered employable. The final version of this bill changed prior practices by assigning the highest priority for rehabilitation services to the most significantly disabled clients, but independent living centers were not funded until 1978.

The most important feature of this act was Section 504, the first federal legislation to prohibit discrimination on the basis of disability. Although a similar measure had been introduced in 1972 by Senator Hubert HUMPHREY and Representative Charles Vanik as an amendment to the CIVIL RIGHTS ACT OF 1964, the principal impetus for Section 504 came from several Senate staff members who copied the provisions of Title VI of the Civil Rights Act of 1964 and Title IX of the Education Amendments of 1972. Section 504 stated: "No otherwise qualified handicapped individual . . . shall, solely by reason of his handicap, be excluded from participation in, be denied the benefits of, or be subjected to discrimination under any program or activity receiving Federal financial assistance." Two other provisions dealt with architectural accessibility and federal employment, as well as an AFFIRMATIVE ACTION program for disabled workers. After the bill had twice been vetoed by President Richard NIXON, the legislation including these sections was finally enacted in 1973 without any real discussion of their possible meaning.

The lack of extensive political debate about the principle of forbidding discrimination on the basis of disability seemed to impede effective implementation of these provisions. The administrative regulations for Section 504 were not signed until April 28, 1977 (see REHABILITATION ACT PROTEST AND TAKEOVER OF 1977). The first major SUPREME COURT interpretation of this section, in 1979 (*Southeastern Community College v. Davis*), significantly curtailed its breadth. Moreover, a 1978 survey revealed that 90 percent of federally assisted employers were not in compliance with the provisions of Section 503. Many of the concepts developed in the implementation of Section 504, however, subsequently became the basis for similar provisions in the AMERICANS WITH DISABILITIES ACT OF 1990.

BIBLIOGRAPHY

Berkowitz, Edward D. *Disabled Policy: America's Programs for the Handicapped.* 1987.

Percy, Stephen L. *Disability, Civil Rights, and Public Policy: The Politics of Implementation.* 1989.

Scotch, Richard K. *From Good Will to Civil Rights: Transforming Federal Disability Policy.* 1984.

Tucker, Bonnie P. "Section 504 of the Rehabilitation Act after Ten Years of Enforcement: The Past and the Future." *University of Illinois Law Review* (Summer 1989): 845–921.

Harlan Hahn

Rehabilitation Act Protest and Takeover of 1977

After CONGRESS had adopted Section 504 of the RE-HABILITATION ACT OF 1973, almost without discussion, the Department of Health, Education, and Welfare (HEW) was designated as the lead agency to issue administrative regulations to implement this ban against discrimination on the basis of disability. As government lawyers and disability activists became aware of the implications of this prohibition, HEW officials tried to delay signing draft regulations, and disabled citizens sought to exert increased pressure on them through litigation and other tactics.

On April 5, 1977, after Joseph Califano, Jr., had become secretary of HEW under President Jimmy CARTER, disabled protestors occupied HEW buildings in San Francisco, Washington, D.C., and elsewhere. When they stayed in offices overnight, an attempt to starve them out failed, as members of the BLACK PANTHER PARTY and other groups distributed food. Meanwhile, Califano even became worried about the headlines that could result if his pet dog bit a group of disabled demonstrators in front of his house, as it too became a protest site. The signing of the regulation on April 28, 1977, with Califano's support, marked the beginning of the modern disability rights movement.

BIBLIOGRAPHY

Califano, Joseph A., Jr. *Governing America: An Insider's Report from the White House and the Cabinet.* 1981.
Johnson, Roberta Ann. "Mobilizing the Disabled." In *Waves of Protest: Social Movements Since the Sixties,* edited by Jo Freeman and Victoria Johnson. 1999.
Scotch, Richard K. *From Good Will to Civil Rights: Transforming Federal Disability Policy.* 1984.
Shaw, Randy. *The Activist's Handbook: A Primer for the 1990s and Beyond.* 1996.

Harlan Hahn

Rehnquist, William Hubbs

(1924–   ), Chief Justice of the United States.

In 1986, President Ronald Reagan appointed William H. ("Bill") Rehnquist Chief Justice of the United States. Born in Wisconsin, Rehnquist graduated from Stanford Law School in 1952, and accepted a one-year U.S. SUPREME COURT clerkship with Justice Robert H. Jackson. Following this, he spent many years in private

U.S. Supreme Court Chief Justice William Rehnquist is a judicial conservative. Originally appointed to the Court by Richard Nixon, Rehnquist was appointed as chief justice by Ronald Reagan. (Reuters/Gary Hershorn/Archive Photos)

practice in Phoenix, Arizona, and enjoyed a brief stint as an assistant attorney general in the NIXON administration. In 1972, he was named an associate justice of the Supreme Court.

Both of his nominations, in 1972 and 1986, were strongly opposed by civil rights interest groups, who questioned and challenged the constitutional philosophy he articulated as a law clerk during the BROWN V. BOARD OF EDUCATION decisions. Also questioned were his interpretation of the FOURTEENTH AMENDMENT, his political activities surrounding DESEGREGATION and voting registration, and the biases revealed in memos written on the EQUAL RIGHTS AMENDMENT while he was in the Nixon administration. More important, civil rights activists have consistently been concerned with many specific opinions he has written while on the Supreme Court. His political and legal philosophy honors the state government over the federal and the power of the government over the rights of the individual, and demonstrates a consistent belief in the limits and constraints of the federal judiciary. As chief justice, he has led a majority that has restricted the coverage of the equal protection clause of the Fourteenth Amendment and has limited many constitutional protections provided for women, the accused and convicted, people of color, and other political minorities.

BIBLIOGRAPHY

Brown v. Board of Education, 347 U.S. 483 (1954); 349 U.S. 294 (1955).

Davis, Sue. "Justice Rehnquist's Equal Protection Clause: An Interim Analysis." *Nebraska Law Review* 63 (1984): 288–313.

Davis, Sue. *Justice Rehnquist and the Constitution.* 1989.

Rehnquist, William H. "The Notion of a Living Constitution." *Texas Law Review* 54 (1976): 693.

Rehnquist, William H. *The Supreme Court: How It Was, How It Is.* 1987.

Rehnquist, William H. *All the Laws but One: Civil Liberties in Wartime.* 1998.

Rehnquist, William H., and Clyde Adams Phillips. *Grand Inquests: The Historic Impeachments of Justice Samuel Chase and President Andrew Johnson.* 1999.

Savage, David G. *Turning Rights: The Making of the Rehnquist Court.* 1992.

Tucker, David F. B. *The Rehnquist Court and Civil Rights.* 1995.

United States Congress. Senate. Nomination of William H. Rehnquist to be Chief Justice of the United States. 99th Congress, 2d Sess. July 29, 30, 31, and August 1, 1986.

Michelle Donaldson Deardorff

Religion and Civil Rights

Whereas economic and political contingencies ultimately decided the direction of civil rights, religion

Many prominent African-American religious leaders were also active in the civil rights movement. Shown here are Ralph Abernathy, Fred Shuttlesworth, and Martin Luther King, Jr. (AP/Wide World Photos)

was the vital catalyst that gave the movement moral authority and created the appearance of unity. Members of religious organizations, clerical and lay, were in the forefront of movement demonstrations, and any place or venue the Reverend Dr. Martin Luther KING, JR., appeared was certain to produce media coverage and the impression of a unified church actively engaged in the struggle. The religious emphasis in the civil rights movement changed over time. In the earliest years of the modern struggle, between the late 1920s and the early 1950s, both white and black religious activists of the period were generally drawn from those liberal communities shaped by the "social gospel" movement. Between 1955 and about 1965, the most active years of the struggle, the religious energy of the previous period was harnessed by King to the folk tradition of the southern BLACK CHURCH. Then, beginning in about 1964–1965, the movement was driven by a new political force—nationalistic, secular, urban, and more northern—that challenged the primacy of the religious emphasis and often overwhelmed it.

The earliest attempts to end southern SEGREGATION, apart from the work of the NATIONAL ASSOCIATION FOR THE ADVANCEMENT OF COLORED PEOPLE (NAACP), began in the 1920s through the efforts of an interracial core of activists who had ties to religious or spiritual groups. One of the earliest organizations to send agents to the South was the FELLOWSHIP OF RECONCILIATION (FOR), a pacifist group with no specific religious affiliation but influenced by Quakerism and religious liberalism. The first traveling FOR secretary, between 1923 and 1928, was George Collins, who was replaced by the end of the decade by Howard Kester. Other organizations soon followed FOR into the field: the Federal Council of Churches, the Fellowship of Southern Churchmen, and the AMERICAN FRIENDS SERVICE COMMITTEE. During the decade of the thirties, FOR's multifaceted approach to the segregation issue gained it important new members in the black community, including A. Philip RANDOLPH, James Weldon JOHNSON, Howard Thurman, Benjamin Elijah MAYS, and Will ALEXANDER. By the time A. J. Muste became executive director of FOR in 1941, the organization had added Gandhian activism to its interest in race relations and war resistance. Two young African-American activists, James FARMER, a Methodist, and Bayard RUSTIN, a Quaker, joined the staff of FOR shortly thereafter, and over the next two decades, their work and the organization they represented were frequently intertwined with the activities of the best-known black activist of the time, A. Philip Randolph. Randolph's MARCH ON WASHINGTON MOVEMENT, intended only for black participants, existed in counterpoint to the interracial policies of FOR and what

Reverend Jesse Jackson visits a construction site in Oklahoma City, Oklahoma, 1995. (AP/Wide World Photos)

would become the CONGRESS OF RACIAL EQUALITY (CORE).

The Congress of Racial Equality, which dates from a founding memorandum written by Farmer in 1942, was concerned that it not be identified as a religious body—a problem that some CORE founders had with FOR—yet it became difficult for it to resist the spiritual inclinations of its earliest participants. Farmer himself was a seminary graduate, a pacifist, and the son of a clergyman; his reforming zeal had been fired by the Methodist Youth Movement, a breeding ground for social activists. Through the efforts of Farmer, George Houser—a graduate of Union Theological Seminary, and others with assorted ties to religious communities, the FOR cell at the University of Chicago was transformed into what would become the nucleus for CORE. CORE was designed to be a grass-roots civil rights organization, with a central core of activists who would be trained in Gandhian techniques of nonviolence in order to engage in direct challenges to segregation. The first test of its Gandhian strategy came when members "used their bodies" to protest segregation at the White City roller rink in Chicago, although Farmer regarded the subsequent challenge to Jack Spratt's restaurant in the city as "the first organized civil rights SIT-IN in American history," because it achieved its goal while the White City incident did not. Many of the practices adopted by CORE—nonviolence, satyagraha (practiced by GANDHI), church-based meetings, seminary-trained leadership, and moral witnessing—could readily have identified the

organization as a form of social gospel activism, despite its claims to being a secular group. The most notable action project of CORE in the 1940s was its partnership with FOR on a "Journey of Reconciliation," a prototype for the FREEDOM RIDES of the 1960s. The chief planners for the interracial trip through the upper South to challenge JIM CROW were Bayard Rustin and George Houser. For his effort, Rustin was ultimately sentenced to thirty days on a chain gang in North Carolina.

Against the background of the steady legal challenges advanced by the NAACP, a new, obviously church-based attack on segregation appeared in the 1950s: in Baton Rouge, LOUISIANA, in 1953, and in Montgomery, Alabama, in 1955. In Baton Rouge, the grass-roots movement against the segregation policies of the local bus company was led by the Reverend T. J. Jemison, who depended on black church congregations and their resources to support a boycott of the bus line. The movement's efforts produced a limited victory and a model for later protests. In 1954, school segregation was dealt a symbolic blow by the SUPREME COURT decision BROWN V. BOARD OF EDUCATION. Then in 1955, following the arrest of Rosa PARKS, the historically notable bus boycott began in Montgomery, bringing its leader, Martin Luther King, Jr., to national attention and laying the basis for the MONTGOMERY IMPROVEMENT ASSOCIATION (MIA). Especially in Montgomery, what historian Lerone Bennett has called black church culture played a formative role in the movement's success. Ministers led the boycott, relied on churches and their facilities for resources, and depended on church members to maintain the energy for the boycott. The MUSIC of the southern black church, its preaching tradition, its theological emphasis, and its ability to mobilize members were central to the success of the boycott and of the organizations that subsequently grew out of it—first the MIA and then the SOUTHERN CHRISTIAN LEADERSHIP CONFERENCE (SCLC).

Writer Aldon Morris has called the SCLC the "decentralized arm of the black church," and although it was not always visible in civil rights confrontations, it provided both the ideological strength and the organizational unity that were so vital to the struggle. King had been persuaded to adopt Gandhian strategies of nonviolent direct action, reportedly by adherents of the FOR–CORE experience, Bayard Rustin and the Reverend Glenn Smiley. King grafted Gandhian spirituality onto social gospel activism and combined them with the black church folk tradition. SCLC was led by clergymen, both at the national level and the local. And, like MIA, it depended for its support on local black congregations and the tradition of spirituality they sustained. King, seminary-trained and the holder of a doctorate in theology, was the powerful head of SCLC. Theologian James Cone believed that there was a unique emphasis in the sermons of black clergymen, particularly evident during these years, that he identified as a black theology of liberation. Spiritual enthusiasm and the sermons of black preachers helped keep support for the movement high, despite often major setbacks, as in Albany, GEORGIA, in 1961, when SCLC was unable to create a united front with the STUDENT NONVIOLENT COORDINATING COMMITTEE (SNCC) to root out entrenched segregation. The movement had entered a new phase with the emergence of SNCC in 1960. SNCC had been born of student-led sit-ins, mainly at lunch counters and restaurants, and had no obvious connection with the black church. Yet the young people in SNCC had been brought up in the church, admired King, and, though seemingly separated from the SCLC, had learned their activism from church-related organizations such as the Nashville Christian Leadership Council and the black college community. Although SCLC and SNCC frequently operated along different tracks, both owed a debt to the black church tradition.

The highwater mark of the civil rights movement, as well as King's church-based leadership of it, was achieved with the MARCH ON WASHINGTON in 1963. After that, the political ground shifted. Black power advocates and black nationalists garnered the media attention previously focused on King, and the political objectives changed to voter registration, EMPLOYMENT, and HOUSING, and away from nonviolent direct action. The black church, however, continued to be a voice on all these matters in the local community. The passing of a national focus on civil rights after 1972 returned the vision of the black church to the local issues that had previously drawn its attention. The increase in a black middle class reduced both black church growth and enthusiasm for the sort of radical activism of the past. Numerous scholars have recently called for another generation of church-based leaders—and the restoration of the church-based community—to address the complex problems of black urban areas.

BIBLIOGRAPHY

Branch, Taylor. *Parting the Waters: America in the King Years.* 1988.
CORE papers on microfilm.
Farmer, James. *Lay Bare the Heart: An Autobiography of the Civil Rights Movement.* 1985.
FOR records are part of the Swarthmore College Peace Collection.
Kapur, Sudarshan. *Raising Up a Prophet: The African-American Encounter with Gandhi.* 1992.
Morris, Aldon. *The Origins of the Civil Rights Movement.* 1984.
Robinson, Armstead L., and Patricia Sullivan, eds. *New Directions in Civil Rights Studies.* 1991.
Robinson, JoAnn O. *Abraham Went Out: A Biography of A. J. Muste.* 1981.

Carol V. R. George

Religious Freedom Restoration Act

Enacted in response to the SUPREME COURT's 1990 decision in *Employment Division v. Smith*, the Religious Freedom Restoration Act of 1993 (RFRA) was an extraordinary attempt by CONGRESS to protect the rights of religious minorities and, indeed, of all religious believers.

Prior to *Smith*, the Supreme Court had interpreted the Free Exercise Clause of the First Amendment to provide significant protection for religiously motivated conduct. For example, the Court had ruled that states could not deny unemployment compensation to Sabbatarians who refused Saturday employment, nor could they punish Amish parents who refused to send their children to high school. Although the Court's constitutional doctrine was complex and multifaceted, it generally required strict judicial scrutiny when a law had the effect of substantially burdening a religious practice. If the government could not demonstrate that the burden was justified by a "compelling" interest, an exemption from the law was constitutionally required.

In *Smith*, the Supreme Court adopted a dramatically different approach. Asked by members of the Native American Church to recognize a drug-law exemption for the sacramental use of peyote, the Court not only refused to do so, but it also declined to apply the strict judicial scrutiny that its precedents appeared to require. Marking a fundamental shift in doctrine, the Court declared that generally applicable laws ordinarily do not require special constitutional scrutiny and therefore do not require religious exemptions. *Smith* essentially reduced the Free Exercise Clause to a prohibition on laws that discriminate against religion. Nondiscriminatory laws that burden religious practices, by contrast, would no longer be subject to serious constitutional scrutiny.

The Court's decision was controversial, and it triggered a political reaction that defied the logic of conventional ideological divisions. Supported by a diverse array of religious and secular organizations, Congress was virtually unanimous in concluding that the Supreme Court's new doctrine gave inadequate protection to religious freedom. Remarkably, Congress also concluded that it had the power to overturn the Court's interpretation of the Free Exercise Clause and to impose its own interpretation on the states. Thus, in its enactment of RFRA, Congress expressly repudiated *Smith* and attempted to "restore" the Court's preexisting doctrine, declaring that "Government shall not substantially burden a person's exercise of religion even if the burden results from a rule of general applicability," unless the burden "is in furtherance of a compelling governmental interest."

The constitutionality of RFRA was suspect from the beginning; and when the question reached the Supreme Court in the 1997 case of *City of Boerne v. Flores*, the Court invalidated RFRA, at least as applied to state and local laws, thereby reinstating the restrictive approach of *Smith*. In a decision with potential implications for other forms of civil rights legislation, the Court ruled that Congress, by substituting its own interpretation of the Constitution for that of the Court, had exceeded its FOURTEENTH AMENDMENT power to "enforce" the Bill of Rights.

In response to *Boerne*, some states have adopted or are considering state-law legislation implementing RFRA-like standards, and new legislation also has been introduced in Congress.

BIBLIOGRAPHY

Laycock, Douglas, and Oliver S. Thomas. "Interpreting the Religious Freedom Restoration Act." *Texas Law Review* 73 (1994): 209–245.
Symposium. "The Religious Freedom Restoration Act." *Montana Law Review* 56 (1995): 1–306.
Symposium. "Reflections on *City of Boerne v. Flores*." *William and Mary Law Review* 39 (1998): 597–960.
Symposium. "Requiem for Religious Freedom?" *University of Arkansas at Little Rock Law Journal* 20 (1998): 555–812.

Daniel O. Conkle

Reparations

During the 1970s, a number of Japanese Americans began expressing the need to seek compensation for the wrongs done to their people during World War II. The JAPANESE AMERICAN CITIZENS LEAGUE (JACL) passed resolutions making reparations an issue of concern, and in 1974 created its National Redress Committee. This campaign for reparations, also commonly known as the redress movement, came together at a time when Japanese Americans began openly reflecting on the impact of wartime internment on their lives. Some participated in "Day of Remembrance" pilgrimages to relocation centers and demonstrated for redress.

In 1978, the redress committee published a statement calling for monetary reparations. It argued that because West Germany paid restitution to Jews, the United States should compensate Japanese Americans for their unlawful persecution. At the biennial JACL convention that same year, the redress committee recommended that the JACL ask for $25,000 for each individual or heir who suffered through the internment experience. It also called for a $100 million trust fund to be managed by a Japanese American Foundation for the benefit of the nation's Japanese-American communities. The JACL national council unanimously adopted the redress committee's proposal and elected Clifford Uyeda, the chairman of the redress committee, to be their new national president.

The call for reparations received criticism from many members of the Japanese-American community. Some Japanese Americans claimed that no amount of money could compensate for the suffering they had endured, while others simply wanted to let the past rest. California Senator S. I. Hayakawa even described relocation as a blessing in disguise because it forced Japanese Americans out of their ethnic enclaves.

Vocal opposition, both within and outside the Japanese-American community, led the redress committee to question whether seeking legislation directly aimed at reparations was prudent. Taking the advice of Japanese-American legislators, professional lobbyists, and civil rights advocates, the JACL instead voted to ask for a congressional commission to officially establish that an injustice had occurred.

The change in strategy incensed some redress activists and led to the formation of two additional redress efforts, the National Council for Japanese American Redress and the National Coalition for Redress/Reparations. After failing to pass its own redress bill, the NCJAR tried to fight for reparations through the courts. William Hohri, the leader of the NCJAR, filed a $27 billion class action suit against the United States. Meanwhile, the NCRR employed grassroots tactics such as letter-writing drives and public rallies. The

NCRR's main contribution to the reparations movement was its mobilization of Japanese-American communities behind the cause.

Created in 1980, the Commission on Wartime Relocation and Internment of Civilians began holding public hearings throughout the country. As they told their stories before the commission, Issei and Nisei (Japanese immigrants and their American-born descendants) shared their experience with the American public for the first time. After listening to over 750 witnesses, the majority of whom were former internees, the commission concluded that an injustice had been committed. Its 1983 report entitled *Personal Justice Denied* stated that military conditions did not necessitate the evacuation and detention of Japanese Americans.

The commission suggested five remedies to right the wrong committed against Japanese Americans during the war. Among its recommendations was a national apology from Congress and the President, a foundation to fund research and educational activities, and an appropriation of $1.5 billion for the foundation and for reparations to those who were relocated. Each of the 60,000 survivors was to receive a one-time compensation of $20,000. Among the commission members, only California Congressman Dan Lundgren, who thought reparations would set a dangerous precedent to be followed by other minorities, objected to the recommendation for individual payments.

Partially due to the REAGAN administration's opposition to monetary compensation, five years passed before both houses of Congress passed a redress bill in August 1988. On August 10, 1988, President Ronald Reagan signed the CIVIL LIBERTIES ACT OF 1988. A year later, the House of Representatives appropriated $50 million for reparations in the 1990 fiscal year. Although the Senate tried to push the appropriation to the following fiscal year, Japanese Americans, many of them World War II veterans, lobbied Senator Daniel Inouye of Hawaii to fight for the redress appropriations. Both houses ultimately agreed to fund the reparations as an entitlement program.

On October 9, 1990, the first redress payments went out to the oldest living former internees. In addition to monetary compensation, the successful campaign for reparations informed the American public of the injustices experienced by Japanese Americans. To some extent, these political activities also brought together different generations and alleviated internal generational splits inside the Japanese-American community.

BIBLIOGRAPHY

Chan, Sucheng. *Asian Americans: An Interpretive History.* 1991.

Daniels, Roger. *Asian America: Chinese and Japanese in the United States since 1850.* 1988.

Daniels, Roger, Sandra C. Taylor, and Harry H. L. Kitano, eds. *Japanese Americans: From Relocation to Redress.* 1991.

Hatamiya, Leslie T. *Righting a Wrong: Japanese Americans and the Passage of the Civil Liberties Act of 1988.* 1993.

Hohri, William Minoru. *Repairing America: An Account of the Movement for Japanese-American Redress.* 1988.

S. H. Tang

Republicanism

Republicanism is a concept that refers to a set of political beliefs and values shared by an array of social groups and classes in American history. It is regarded as the opposite of liberalism and has been employed by historians to explain an ideology, or world view, that de-emphasizes material self-interest and stresses collective prosperity and the good of the commonwealth. The use of this term to illustrate the existence of an anticapitalist tradition in the United States has steadily gained popularity since the 1980s and has also generated a protracted debate about the value of the concept in interpreting the past.

Scholars first used the concept of republicanism to explain the nature of the political ideology that drove the American Revolution. Bernard Bailyn's *The Ideological Origins of the American Revolution* (1967), Gordon Wood's *The Creation of the American Republic,* and J. G. A. Pocock's *The Machiavellian Moment* (1975) all set the frame of the debate. Collectively these books argued that American revolutionary rhetoric drew on classical republican notions of society rooted in traditional English political thought. Classical republicanism included emphasis on virtue, aversion to the pursuit of private wealth, distaste for luxury, fear of corruption, celebration of independence, and devotion to the common good. These historians disagreed with Louis Hartz's *The Liberal Tradition in America* (1955), which argued that early American political ideology was liberal in nature: individualistic, ambitious, and capitalistic.

Republicanism, introduced as a concept for understanding the political traditions of the United States, ultimately evolved into a tool for explaining the ideology of various socially disadvantaged groups. The idea of an anticapitalist tradition in the American past helped labor historians explain what motivated working-class uprisings in the nineteenth century. "Labor republicanism" drew on the symbols and language of the Revolution and informed a class consciousness intent on challenging the hegemony of the elite during the industrialization of America. In the 1830s, working artisans spoke of virtue and luxury and the threat of capital acquisitiveness. In the late nineteenth century, the KNIGHTS OF LABOR spoke in similar terms. Others saw evidence of a "republican producer ideology" in the lives of yeomen farmers in the South. Southerners' fear of burgeoning commerce in the North was reflected in the desire to maintain independent control over one's land. Southerners lived in an agrarian world dominated by communal relations, a system of barter rather than cash exchange, and a limited connection to the larger market. The republican ethos in the South, which stood in opposition to the aggressive capitalism of the North, provided one more reason why the South was historically a distinctive region.

The values of republicanism also influenced the lives of women. During the American Revolution, women contributed to the political world by raising patriotic sons. Mothers had a duty to instill morality and civic virtue in their children. A mother's commitment to her family was a commitment to the state. The language of "Republican Motherhood" provided the justification for women's political behavior both in the home and in the public arena. It altered the female domain, drew women into the public political realm, and encouraged citizens to begin to think of women as political creatures.

While republicanism has been helpful in defining alternative political and social traditions in the United States, some critics contend that its application to the working class, the agrarian class, and women has expanded the use of the term so considerably that it has lost its original meaning. These critics question whether the political theory of classical republicanism during the Revolutionary era bears any relationship to the language and actions of individuals a century later. The growing elasticity of the term has given some cause for worry that republicanism has outlived its usefulness. This flexibility has also drawn attention to a deeper problem inherent in the use of the concept to explain the actions of ordinary men and women. Was republicanism merely a vocabulary or a collection of traditional symbols that could be identified in the discourse of politicians, activists, and common people, or was it an all-encompassing ideology with the power to influence the behavior of historical actors? In other words, did language or theory alone drive the course of history, or did the actual life experiences of individuals shape their actions and belief systems? At the very least, it can be argued that the concept of republicanism has expanded our understanding of the past by providing an explanation for an alternative world view to liberal capitalism that previous historians had either ignored or had been unable to account for.

BIBLIOGRAPHY

Appleby, Joyce. "Republicanism and Ideology." *American Quarterly* 37 (Fall 1985).

Appleby, Joyce. *Liberalism and Republicanism in the Historical Imagination.* 1992.

Fink, Leon. "The New Labor History and the Powers of Historical Pessimism: Consensus, Hegemony, and the Case of the Knights of Labor." *Journal of American History* 75 (June 1988).

Hahn, Steven. *The Roots of Southern Populism: Yeomen Farmers and the Transformation of the Georgia Upcountry, 1850–1890.* 1985.

Kerber, Linda. *Women of the Republic: Intellect and Ideology in Revolutionary America.* 1980.

Rodgers, Daniel T. "Republicanism: The Career of a Concept." *Journal of American History* 79 (June 1992).

Shalhope, Robert E. "Toward a Republican Synthesis: The Emergence of an Understanding of Republicanism in American Historiography." *William and Mary Quarterly* 29 (January 1972).

Wilentz, Sean. *Chants Democratic: New York City and the Rise of the American Working Class, 1788–1850.* 1986.

Natalie J. Ring

Republican Party

The United States' Republican Party formed in the 1850s as a response to the regional divisions and fence-straddling of the Democrats and Whigs on the slavery issue. The Republicans attracted antislavery Whigs, some antislavery Democrats, and others concerned about the continuation of the enslavement of African Americans in the South and border states and the extension of the practice to the territories. The party also distinguished itself from the Democrats by favoring federal government action to ensure economic development, particularly development that was favorable to business and banking interests.

Abraham Lincoln was the first Republican president, elected in 1860. Lincoln led the Union during the Civil War in its successful effort to suppress the rebellious southern states and end slavery. The assassination of Lincoln at the end of the war emboldened the more radical elements of the party in the CONGRESS—the so-called RADICAL REPUBLICANS. These Republicans impeached President Andrew Johnson (Lincoln's successor, who planned a sympathetic response to the southern insurrection), hobbling the presidency, and then imposed martial law on the South during the RECONSTRUCTION period (1865–1877). In addition, they zealously sought to guarantee the civil rights of freedmen in the region. During Reconstruction, northern generals, carpetbaggers, and newly freedmen ruled the southern states at the expense of the pre–Civil War elite in the region, many of whom had owned slaves.

A compromise to settle the contentious election of 1876 led to the withdrawal of Union occupation of the region (i.e., the end of Reconstruction). Republicans retained an interest in guaranteeing African Americans VOTING RIGHTS and other rights, as their power in national politics depended on the election of some southern representatives—black or white—to the Congress. The Republican Party in the southern states became known as the "black and tans," referring to its support base of freedmen and poor white farmers who had never benefited from the practice of slavery. By the 1890s, the zealous generation of Radical Republicans, who had been most interested in securing the rights of blacks, had for the most part died or left politics. In addition, other national trends that favored Republicans enabled the party to secure control of the U.S. Congress and PRESIDENCY without southern support. As a result, Republicans lost interest in fighting what appeared to be a losing battle to guarantee African Americans' voting rights; and the Southern Democrats regained a total grip on power in the states that had comprised the Confederacy. These Democrats' principle objective was to implement a rigid system of SEGREGATION, which they succeeded in doing by denying blacks and some poor whites the right to vote.

Despite its failure to follow through on the promise of securing basic civil rights for blacks, the Republican Party—the party of Lincoln—was regarded through the early decades of the twentieth century as the party more sympathetic to the plight of African Americans. The progressive wing of the party (as well as the splinter PROGRESSIVE PARTY, which was formed largely from disgruntled Republicans) listed civil rights for blacks as one of its goals. Yet there were other agenda items that were of higher priority, and the fight for voting and civil rights was never undertaken in earnest by the party.

The Great Depression in the 1930s led to the dwindling of African-American support for the Republican Party. While the southern wing of the DEMOCRATIC PARTY remained staunchly segregationist, New Yorker Franklin D. ROOSEVELT (first elected president in 1932) provided relief and jobs for the poor, who were disproportionately black, and this won the allegiance of a majority of African-American voters for the Democratic Party by the election of 1936.

As late as the 1950s it was still an open question as to which party, if either, would take the lead in the civil rights fight. Democrats pursued economic policies that many African Americans supported, but many Republicans, particularly those in the Northeast, were sympathetic to the plight of African Americans in the South and were among those who were most enthusiastically supportive of civil rights legislation in the 1950s. Republican Vice President Richard M. NIXON managed to garner the support of many in the civil rights establishment and about 30 to 35 percent of

the black voters in his unsuccessful bid for the presidency in 1960. But the Californian Nixon (despite being politically moderate himself) symbolized a gradual movement of the party away from its more moderate roots in the Middle West and Northeast to the West, where Republicans tended to be more conservative and less interested than eastern Republicans in seeing the federal government intervene in the economy, civil rights, or almost anything else. When the Republicans nominated arch-conservative Barry Goldwater of Arizona for president in 1964, the contrast between the parties was the sharpest it had been in decades. Goldwater was against federal intervention in state affairs—which was an extremely popular position among whites in the South who did not like the Democrats' gradual movement in the direction of civil rights during the administration of John F. KENNEDY (1961–1963). Kennedy's successor, Lyndon B. JOHNSON, immediately pushed hard for civil rights legislation.

The 1964 presidential campaign pitted Goldwater against Johnson; it proved to be a watershed in the history of the American political parties. The Democratic candidate committed himself to the civil rights of African Americans, and made it a top priority; the Republican (while no racist himself) objected to federal intervention to achieve these ends. African Americans deserted the Republican Party in droves and Johnson won in a landslide. While the civil rights and voting rights legislation pushed through by Johnson in the 1960s proved widely popular and gained bipartisan support in the Congress, many Americans felt that some of the subsequent goals of the civil rights movement went too far. School BUSING for INTEGRATION, AFFIRMATIVE ACTION, and welfare payments to single mothers in the big cities became the hot button issues of the 1970s and 1980s. Republicans successfully capitalized on the concerns of a broad segment of middle- and working-class whites by taking tough, conservative stances on these issues. This so-called "social issue conservatism," a new emphasis for the party, earned it dominance in presidential politics for a generation. Richard M. Nixon (elected in 1968 and 1972), Ronald REAGAN (1980 and 1984), and George BUSH (1988) were all swept into office, usually by huge margins, in part because of their conservative positions on these racially charged issues.

Today, the Republican Party struggles with internal divisions regarding social issues, including those involving race questions. One segment of the party stresses the social-issue conservatism that was so successful politically for them in the 1970s and 1980s, while another faction invokes the name of Lincoln and takes a more moderate stance, with the hope of attracting more minority voters.

BIBLIOGRAPHY

Black, Earl, and Merle Black. *Politics and Society in the South.* 1987.

Sorauf, Frank J., and Paul Allan Beck. *Party Politics in America.* 1992.

Sundquist, James L. *Dynamics of the Party System.* 1983.

Tindall, George Brown. *Disruption of the Solid South.* 1972.

John Haskell

Republic of New Africa

In March 1968, black nationalists Robert F. WILLIAMS, Richard Henry (Imari Abubakari Obadele), and Milton Henry (Gaidi Obadele) convened a meeting in Detroit, Michigan, attended by hundreds of black militants. Those present eventually called for the independence of the Afro-American community from the United States, which was declared to be a repressive, racist regime.

The Republic of New Africa movement hoped to create an autonomous black republic extending throughout certain of the states of the American South—ALABAMA, GEORGIA, LOUISIANA, MISSISSIPPI, and SOUTH CAROLINA—assisted by reparations of at least $400 billion dollars demanded from the U.S. government for centuries of slavery and racist oppression that blacks had endured within the United States.

The new nation to be created by the Republic of New Africa movement was to be governed by the principles of *ujamaa*—the Swahili word for "communitarianism"—and it received support from COMMUNIST PARTY leader Angela DAVIS and other important radical political figures.

The movement did not renounce violence, however, as it claimed the right of self-defense and the right to use violence to obtain its ends if more moderate means failed. At a 1969 conference held by the movement at the New Bethel Baptist Church in Detroit, violence erupted between police, who besieged the building, and the conference participants, who resisted. A police officer was killed, and four conference participants were wounded. This led to the trial of three movement members for murder, and their acquittal.

A 1971 police raid on the movement's regional headquarters in Jackson, Mississippi resulted in the death of a police officer as well as the trial and conviction of eleven movement members, including the acting president, Imari Obadele. Although the influence of the movement declined in the late 1970s and 1980s, it remained active into the 1990s and the new century. It moved its national headquarters from Detroit to Washington, D.C. in 1985. During the 1990s, it continued to organize at the local level in black neighborhoods of major American cities, maintaining a membership roughly estimated at between five thousand and ten thousand.

BIBLIOGRAPHY

Lumumba, Chokwe. "Short History of the U.S. War on the Republic of New Africa." *Black Scholar* 12 (January–February 1981): 72–81.

Obadele, Imari. *Revolution and Nation-Building: Strategy for Building the Black Nation in America.* 1970.

Patrick M. O'Neil

Revels, Hiram Rhodes

(1827–1901), clergyman, U.S. senator, and educator.

Born a free person of color and of mixed blood in Fayetteville, Cumberland County, North Carolina, Hiram Rhodes Revels was educated in a school run by a free black woman. As a student, he attended a Quaker seminary in Indiana, Drake County Seminary in Ohio, and Knox College in Illinois. Ordained a minister in the African Methodist Episcopal Church in Baltimore, he later traveled to various congregations, preaching and lecturing in Illinois, Indiana, Ohio, Missouri, Tennessee, Kentucky and Kansas. At the outbreak of the Civil War, Revels organized two black regiments in Maryland. He later migrated to MISSISSIPPI to serve as a chaplain of a regiment in 1864.

During RECONSTRUCTION, Revels's religious and educational experiences aided his rise to leadership positions: He was elected a city alderman (Natchez, Mississippi, in 1868), a member of the state senate of Mississippi (1869), and upon the readmission of Mississippi to the Union was elected—as a Republican—to the United States Senate, serving from February 22, 1870, to March 3, 1871. In 1873, he would serve as Secretary of State *ad interim* of Mississippi. It was, however, his service as the first African American elected to the U.S. Congress that has given him a firm place in history. His legacy to black Mississippians and to Americans as a whole remains a mixed one, according to biographer Julius E. Thompson. Even in the area of civil rights he was a conservative. As a U.S. Senator, Revels voted for the readmission of TEXAS under a Republican government, NATURALIZATION to be extended to blacks, and for the enforcement of the FIFTEENTH AMENDMENT. As he left the Senate in 1871, he favored DESEGREGATION of public schools. Other issues Revels spoke for included enforcement of federal elections laws, construction of levees along the Mississippi River, eradication of franking privileges, and prohibition of land grants and right-of-way to the

Hiram Revels was elected to the U.S. Senate from North Carolina during the Reconstruction era in 1871. He was the first African American to be elected to the Senate. (U.S. Senate Historical Office)

New Orleans and Northeastern Railroad. His efforts to get a black man, Michael Howard, nominated and appointed to West Point in 1870 were unsuccessful; he also spoke for the employment of black mechanics in the U.S. Navy Yard and for the United States' effort to annex the Dominican Republic.

A conciliatory man, Revels, according to Thompson, never demanded complete equality and full civil rights for blacks. After serving in national office, he returned to Mississippi and was appointed to the presidency of Alcorn University, serving from 1871 to 1873, then again from 1876 to 1882. His years there were often turbulent; he was often caught between black demands for a more aggressive leader and whites' resistance to him. His efforts to seek whites' approval led to his refusing in 1875 to testify before a U.S. Senate committee investigating charges of murder and intimidation relating to the election of Democrats in Mississippi.

Revels later became active in the growth of Rust College after moving to Holly Springs, Mississippi, and he also became a district superintendent in the African Methodist Episcopal Church. He died on January 16, 1901, in Aberdeen, Mississippi.

BIBLIOGRAPHY

Libby, Billy W. "Senator Hiram Revels of Mississippi Takes His Seat, January–February, 1870." *Journal of Mississippi History* 37: 381–394.

Thompson, Julius E. *Hiram R. Revels, 1827–1901: A Biography.* 1982.

Thompson, Julius E. "Hiram Rhodes Revels, 1827–1901: A Reappraisal." *Journal of Negro History* 79: 297–303.

Charles Vincent

Revolutionary Action Movement

The Revolutionary Action Movement (RAM) was a predecessor organization of what became known as the BLACK POWER movement. Formed in 1963, RAM posed an early radical challenge to the principal civil rights organizations, although it remained a small and secretive group among mainly college-educated activists. RAM called for armed self-defense of the black community, and placed black civil rights within the context of a larger struggle for "revolutionary nationalism."

For inspiration, RAM looked to Robert F. WILLIAMS, the organization's honorary chairman. Born in 1925 in Monroe, NORTH CAROLINA, Williams was a veteran of the army and marines, and had become acquainted with left-wing politics as a factory worker in Detroit and New York. In 1956, Williams returned to Monroe, where he gained national attention as president of the local branch of the NATIONAL ASSOCIATION FOR THE ADVANCEMENT OF COLORED PEOPLE (NAACP). Although Williams shared the civil rights goal of INTEGRATION, he defiantly broke with the NAACP, Martin Luther KING, JR., and the civil rights establishment over the question of nonviolence. In the face of terror perpetrated by white supremacists, Williams stood for armed self-defense, and he organized rifle clubs among his largely working-class following. In 1961, the police and the FEDERAL BUREAU OF INVESTIGATION (FBI) accused Williams of kidnapping two KU KLUX KLAN (KKK) members in the midst of a black protest. Williams contended that he had only protected the KKKers from retribution by angry blacks, but expecting no justice in North Carolina he fled to Cuba and later to China. In exile, Williams continued to publish his newsletter, *The Crusader,* which espoused a mixture of nationalist and Marxist ideas about American blacks, urging a war of self-defense and liberation from imperialism.

Williams's work and his booklet *Negroes with Guns* (1962) caught the attention of many SNCC, CORE, and other young civil rights activists disillusioned with the strategy of relying on nonviolence and on the goodwill of the Kennedy–Johnson administration. Small circles of such militants formed RAM chapters in Atlanta, Detroit, New York, Oakland, Philadelphia, and other cities. RAM positioned itself "somewhere between the NATION OF ISLAM and SNCC," adopting a nationalist analysis of African Americans as constituting an internal colony, while also supporting the goals of civil rights within American society. Max Stanford, RAM leader and former student organizer from Harlem, articulated a "revolutionary nationalism" that envisioned pan-African identity (see PAN-AFRICANISM) and a black nation built upon the socially radical ideas of Che Guevara and Mao Zedong.

Testifying before a House subcommittee in 1967, FBI director J. Edgar Hoover warned of the dangerous links between Stokely CARMICHAEL of SNCC and Stanford of RAM, the field chairman of "a highly secret all Negro, Marxist-Leninist, Chinese Communist–oriented organization which advocates guerrilla warfare to obtain its goals." In fact, although Carmichael and Stanford had known each other in Harlem, and although RAM's strident nationalism influenced SNCC's Atlanta office, RAM remained on the periphery of SNCC and the civil rights movement. Nor did RAM survive to play a part in the full explosion of the Black Power movement. Never more than a small, semi-secret network, lacking internal cohesion, and under intense FBI scrutiny, RAM members suffered a series of arrests. Most spectacularly, in 1967 sixteen RAM members were arrested for conspiracy to murder Roy WILKINS of the NAACP and Whitney YOUNG of the NATIONAL URBAN LEAGUE. When RAM folded in 1968, former RAM members such as Bobby SEALE in Oakland and General Baker in Detroit had already moved on to other radical nationalist or Black Power projects—including what was to become the BLACK PANTHER PARTY and the League of Revolutionary Black Workers.

BIBLIOGRAPHY

Carlisle, Rodney. *The Roots of Black Nationalism.* 1975.

Carson, Clayborne. *In Struggle: SNCC and the Black Awakening of the 1960s.* 1981.

Cohen, Robert Carl. *Black Crusader: A Biography of Robert Franklin Williams.* 1972.

Meier, August, and Elliot Rudwick. "Black Violence in the 20th Century: A Study in Rhetoric and Retaliation." In *The History of Violence in America: Historical and Comparative Perspectives, A Report Submitted to the National Commission on the Causes and Prevention of Violence,* edited by Hugh Davis Graham and Ted Robert Gurr. 1969.

Pearson, Hugh. *The Shadow of the Panther: Huey Newton and the Price of Black Power in America.* 1994.

Williams, Robert F. *Negroes with Guns.* 1998.

Charles Postel

Rhode Island

The history of blacks in Rhode Island starts in 1649, when the first slaves arrived in the colony. The first civil rights legislation passed in Providence in 1652, requiring that all "indentured servants" be freed after ten years' service. The law was enforced for whites but not for blacks. The colony banned the importation of slaves in 1774 but did not ban slavery per se until ten years later, when it freed all children born of slaves and shortly thereafter banned the ownership of slaves in the state outright—it was the first state to do so. When the U.S. CONGRESS first met in 1790, the Rhode Island delegation submitted a proposal to ban slavery throughout the United States, but Congress refused to adopt the measure.

In 1780 Newport Gardner, a former slave whose African name had been Occramar Marycoo, became the first president of the Free African Union Society in Newport. The society advocated a movement of "back to Africa" many years in advance of Marcus GARVEY and his followers. Some years after the society's founding, in 1826, Gardner actually returned to his African homeland, bringing along his sons and some members of his church.

Because of the presence of a sizable free-thinking Quaker, Congregationalist, and Episcopalian population, Rhode Islanders early on had been relatively liberal toward the black population. But toward the end of the eighteenth century, hatred of blacks by Rhode Island whites began to increase substantially, culminating eventually in riots by whites, who in 1831 destroyed portions of the black neighborhoods of Hard Scrabble and Snowtown in Providence. Black men lost the right to vote in 1822 and did not regain it until a new state constitution was adopted in 1842. In 1824 the first black church to be incorporated in the United States was founded in Newport. Newport was also the birthplace of the African Union Society, an early civic self-help organization for African Americans.

After restoration of the right to vote for blacks in 1842, civil rights progress for blacks continued as Rhode Island banned racial segregation in schools in 1866, lifted a ban on interracial marriages in 1881, and barred discrimination in public accommodations in 1885. The turn of the twentieth century saw further progress, including a 1917 march in Providence protesting racial violence in the South. Civil rights issues took center stage following the landmark CIVIL RIGHTS ACT OF 1964. Soon after its passage, Rhode Island banned HOUSING discrimination and Providence began desegregating its mostly black schools through busing, with little of the rancor that accompanied such measures in allegedly liberal neighboring MASSACHUSETTS.

Rhode Island state law bans discrimination against women. The state was among the first to ratify the federal EQUAL RIGHTS AMENDMENT to the U.S. Constitution in 1972. The state enacted a law in 1995 banning discrimination in housing, public accommodations, employment, real estate transactions, and credit privileges based upon sexual orientation (see GAY AND LESBIAN RIGHTS). Rhode Island has refrained from joining in efforts that have been gaining momentum in some other states to pass legislation condemning or prohibiting same-sex marriages.

The major tribe of Native Americans in Rhode Island, the Narragansetts, had been confined to a reservation in the aftermath of the Great Swamp Massacre of 1675, when many white settlers were killed. Over the next hundred years the tribal population diminished as some members moved out of the colony and white settlers began to take lands from them, a practice called "land grabbing." To halt this practice, a treaty was signed in 1790 between the tribe and the state of Rhode Island, but it was not adequately enforced. Subsequently, the Rhode Island Narragansett population became so minute that the state assembly officially declared the tribe to be "abolished" in 1884. In the aftermath of World War II, however, widely dispersed Narragansetts began to reenter their traditional homelands, holding town meetings in the historic New England tradition of those who had displaced them. These meetings served to galvanize Native American consciousness in the state until in 1975 a group of Narragansetts filed a land claim suit against the state of Rhode Island, accusing it of failing to abide with provisions of the 1790 treaty. In August 1983, the U.S. government finally moved to void the 1884 abolishment and to restore full recognition of the Narragansetts as a legitimate tribal group eligible for federal funding.

BIBLIOGRAPHY

Bartlett, Irving H. *From Slave to Citizen: The Story of the Negro in Rhode Island.* 1954.

Coughtry, Jay. *Creative Survival: The Providence Black Community in the Nineteenth Century.* 1984.

Morales, Jorge. "11-Year Itch (Rhode Island's Gay Rights Law)." *The Advocate* (June 27, 1995): 26–27.

Ken R. Wells

Richardson, Gloria

(1922–   ), lawyer and activist.

Gloria Richardson has been a lifelong advocate for the poor and disadvantaged. Richardson was born May 6, 1922, to Mabel Pauline St. Clair Hayes and John Edwards Hayes, who raised their daughter in an elite family. Their circumstances enabled Gloria to attend Frederick Douglass High School and Howard University Law School. After she completed her law degree, married and had a daughter, Richardson's interest in the civil rights movement flourished in the 1960s.

Richardson became very active in changing local politics in Cambridge, MARYLAND. In 1962, she became co-chair of the Cambridge Nonviolent Action Committee (CNAC), which used protest tactics similar to those of the STUDENT NONVIOLENT COORDINATING COMMITTEE (SNCC), which was based in the South. In 1963, she confronted the Cambridge City Council and demanded that programs in support of full INTEGRATION of African Americans be implemented throughout the community. Her activism led her to many arrests, including the "Penny Trials," which fined protesters a penny. However, after being released from jail, Richardson organized more pickets and demanded equal employment opportunities (see EQUAL OPPORTUNITY), the elimination of police brutality, the construction of low-income HOUSING, and VOTING RIGHTS for African Americans in Cambridge.

Between July 1963 and August 1964, racial conflict erupted and intensified in Cambridge. In response, Richardson wrote letters of appeal for a peaceful resolution and met with local and national government officials. However, in spite of her efforts as a leader in the Northern civil rights struggle, critics accused her of provoking some of the racial violence in Cambridge, Maryland. Richardson left Cambridge in 1964 and began working in the New York City Department of Aging.

BIBLIOGRAPHY

Barnett, Bernice McNair. *Sisters in Struggle: Invisible Black Women Leaders of the Civil Rights Movement, 1940–1975.* Forthcoming.

Giddings, Paula. *When and Where I Enter: The Impact of Black Women on Race and Sex in America.* 1984.

Thompson, Kathleen. "Gloria Richardson." In *Black Women in America,* edited by Darlene Clark Hine. 1993.

Shaunda Partida

Right to Bear Arms

A controversial freedom, the right of U.S. citizens to keep firearms, derives from the Second Amendment to the U.S. Constitution, which reads, "A well regulated Militia, being necessary to the security of a free State, the right of the people to keep and bear Arms, shall not be infringed." For many Americans, individual ownership of guns is a birthright; for many others, it is a threat to personal and public safety. The former contend that the right of individuals to bear arms is guaranteed by the Constitution; the latter claim that the Second Amendment applies only to the necessity of maintaining a militia to guard against usurpations by the federal government. Accordingly, debate over gun control has centered around the intention of the framers of the Constitution.

The Second Amendment has come before the SU-PREME COURT in a series of cases, including *United States v. Cruikshank* (1876), *Presser v. Illinois* (1886), *Miller v. Texas* (1894), and *United States v. Miller* (1939). Lower federal courts have made more than three dozen rulings. In none of these decisions have the courts ruled that the Constitution guarantees the right of any citizen to own any gun; in other words, the courts have decreed that guns are subject to regulation. Despite these rulings, many Americans continue to believe that they have an unrestricted right to possess firearms. (See STATES' RIGHTS.)

The question of gun ownership is a question belonging not only to history and constitutional law but also to political theory. As an extension of self-defense doctrine, the right to bear arms may be regarded as a human or natural right, which exists in people in a state of nature, apart from government; but, as an outgrowth of American constitutional law, the right to bear arms resembles instead a civil right, intended to protect individuals against individuals. In the first instance, it is a negatively democratic right, ensuring freedom from restrictions; in the latter, it is a positively democratic right, subject to regulation for the public good. It represents a conflict of individual and communal rights.

Major gun control legislation includes the Gun Control Act of 1968, passed after the assassinations of President John F. KENNEDY, Senator Robert KENNEDY, and Rev. Dr. Martin Luther KING, JR., and the 1993 Brady Handgun Violence Prevention Act, or Brady Bill, requiring a waiting period for handgun buyers. Handguns are either outlawed or restricted to such a degree that their ownership is extremely rare in most European countries and Canada. No such prohibition exists on the national level in the United States. Flashpoints for the debate over gun control include the Bernard Goetz case, in which a vigilante shot four unarmed youths on a New York subway on December 22, 1984, and the shooting deaths of twelve students and one teacher at the hands of two schoolmates at Columbine High School in Littleton, Colorado, on April 20, 1999, as well as other school shootings. As the number of children using guns has continued to rise at an alarming rate, the ongoing debate, still unresolved, has intensified, as have efforts to enact further gun control legislation.

BIBLIOGRAPHY

Anderson, Jervis. *Guns in American Life.* 1984.
Carter, Gregg Lee. *The Gun Control Movement.* 1997.
Kates, Don B., Jr., and Gary Kleck. *The Great American Gun Debate: Essays on Firearms and Violence.* 1997.
Long, Robert Emmet, ed. *Gun Control.* 1989.
Weir, William. *A Well Regulated Militia: The Battle Over Gun Control.* 1997.

Christopher Strain

Rives, Richard T.

(1895–1982), federal judge.

Richard Rives was born in the ALABAMA Black Belt in 1895. His family had lost its money and plantation in the Civil War, and his mother remained an unreconstructed Rebel. His father, however, thought that blacks should be given equal opportunities. "Perhaps it was a good thing the Yankees won the Civil War," he said. Richard Rives later admitted that in his youth, he "just accepted it as a way of life that blacks shouldn't vote, that they were to be treated almost as a different species of people from the whites."

Rives attended Tulane University for a year before studying law in a Montgomery law office; he passed the bar at the age of 19 and started a politically tinged trial practice. Rives was one of a handful of lawyers in Alabama who represented convict miners, prisoners who were leased to companies as laborers. At the same time he advised the Montgomery Board of Registrars and the local American Legion branch how to exclude blacks from voting. He attended a few meetings of the KU KLUX KLAN in the 1920s, but never joined. "I'm not really pure on this question of bigotry," Rives admitted late in life, "but I think my own experience is some indication that people change their views as they go along." Rives served as president of both the Montgomery and Alabama bar associations, and politicians courted him for his support. He managed the 1932 Senate reelection campaign of Hugo L. BLACK and Bibb Graves's 1942 campaign for a third term as governor. When Graves died before the primary, Rives declined an offer to be the Democratic candidate and, therefore, governor.

In the 1930s Rives proposed to the Alabama legislature a constitutional amendment to allow anyone with a sixth-grade education to vote. His frequent discussion of racial issues with his Harvard-educated son after World War II deeply influenced him. In 1946 Rives spoke around Alabama against a proposed amendment to the state constitution requiring that local registrars certify that all prospective voters "understand and interpret" any provision of the United States Constitution. "The chains we forge to shackle qualified Negroes," he declared, " . . . would not only breed resistance in the Negro, but, far worse, would rub a moral cancer on the character of the white man." A federal court quoted Rives's remarks in declaring the amendment unconstitutional.

In 1951 Rives was appointed to the United States Court of Appeals for the FIFTH CIRCUIT. He joined with Judges John Minor WISDOM, Elbert P. TUTTLE, and John Robert BROWN to enforce the SUPREME COURT's decision in BROWN V. BOARD OF EDUCATION. They "made as much of an imprint on American society and American law as any four judges below the Supreme Court have ever done on any court . . . ," observed Burke Marshall, assistant attorney general in the administration of John F. KENNEDY. "If it hadn't been for judges like that on the Fifth Circuit, I think Brown would have failed in the end."

In the aftermath of the MONTGOMERY BUS BOYCOTT, Rives wrote the opinion in *Browder v. Gayle* (1956) that declared unconstitutional those state statutes and city ordinances that required SEGREGATION in public transportation. The "separate but equal" doctrine had no remaining validity in any area of public law, he stated. Rives's opinions touched every area of race relations law, from DESEGREGATION and public accommodations to voting rights, jury selection, and the right to petition government for the redress of grievances. He was particularly concerned about how decisions could be enforced. Rives correctly predicted that Montgomery would close its parks rather than allow blacks to use them. He was the "prime mover" behind the court's dismissing further criminal contempt-of-court proceedings against Mississippi governor Ross Barnett in 1965 after Barnett openly disregarded court orders to enroll James MEREDITH at the University of Mississippi. "We just had a bear by the tail," Rives said. "A trial would accomplish nothing. It was better to let him go."

For his views Rives was castigated, but he was an unusually patient man who saw good in nearly everybody and never lost faith in the ability of the average Southerner to adjust his views as he had. Years later, when asked if the ostracism hurt, he said, "No indeed! I knew what they were missing if they didn't want my company." In 1960, after serving as a chief judge for a year, Rives suddenly resigned because he thought Judge Elbert Tuttle had an opportunity to be appointed to the Supreme Court if Richard NIXON was elected president. Justice Hugo Black called Rives a cross between "a lion and a lamb," and wrote, "He ranks as one of our greatest judges."

BIBLIOGRAPHY

Bass, Jack. *Unlikely Heroes.* 1981.
Black, Hugo L., Jr. "Richard Taylor Rives, 1895–1982." *Alabama Lawyer* 44 (Jan. 1983): 59.
Read, Frank T., and Lucy S. McGough. *Let Them Be Judged.* 1978.

Roger K. Newman

Roberts, Edward V.

(1939–1995), activist for the rights of the disabled; director, California Department of Rehabilitation, 1975–1982.

Edward Roberts is often referred to as the "father of the Independent Living Movement." He contracted polio in 1953 at age 14, became paralyzed from the neck down, and thereafter relied on a respirator. Doctors told his parents he would never finish school, marry, or hold a job. Roberts at first viewed himself as a "helpless cripple," but after almost two years of hospitalization he returned home and began attending high school by telephone and then in person. When, despite his good grades, he was denied a diploma for not having taken driver's education or physical education, his mother, a one-time labor organizer, fought the decision and won.

In 1962, after two years of community college, Roberts applied to the University of California, Berkeley. When the California Department of Rehabilitation declared him "infeasible" for employment and refused to fund his further schooling, supporters generated negative newspaper coverage that compelled a reversal of the ruling. However, the library, cafeterias, and many classrooms were inaccessible or reachable only by very circuitous routes. Dormitory floors were not strong enough to hold his eight-hundred-pound iron lung. The student infirmary at last agreed that he could reside there. Needing help with dressing and eating, he enlisted some friends, but usually hired aides paid by the state in-home support services program.

A dozen other physically disabled students joined Roberts in the infirmary in the mid-1960s and became a budding activist group nicknamed "The Rolling Quads." Observing and participating in campus politics, they applied the strategies and ideologies of the minority students' and women's movements to their own situation. Roberts drew upon both movements' calls for personal and collective self-determination and feminists' repudiation of the notion that "anatomy is destiny." In 1968 the Department of Rehabilitation agreed to fund the residential program, but when the counselor in charge sought to expel two students for having low grades and threatened others for advancing through school to slowly, the group organized a protest that drew campus and news media attention. The counselor was reassigned.

At this point the students began to discuss how to get control of their lives as consumers of services rather than clients. One reason many were making slow progress toward graduation was that the off-campus community was almost completely inaccessible to them. In 1969 they successfully lobbied the City of Berkeley to begin installing sidewalk curb cuts. In fall 1970 a Department of Health, Education and Welfare grant enabled them to open the University of California's Physically Disabled Students' Program (PDSP). PDSP hired disabled counselors to find wheelchair-accessible off-campus apartments and to compile a list of potential personal aides. Its wheelchair workshop, run by wheelchair riders, offered round-the-clock repairs and innovative designs. Its advocacy department assisted students with the bureaucratic tangles of government benefit and service programs. Geared to physically disabled students and staffed by wheelchair riders, PDSP soon received requests from blind students. It expanded the personal assistance list to include readers. Roberts, who was studying community organizing, recognized that a broader constituency would facilitate collective political power.

In spring, 1972 to serve the parallel needs of disabled nonstudents, the leaders of the movement established the Center for Independent Living a few blocks from campus. Roberts served as its director for one year, 1974–1975. In 1975 newly elected governor Jerry Brown appointed him Department of Rehabilitation director. Roberts promoted independent living, not just paid employment. By securing federal funding for ten California centers patterned after the Berkeley Center for Independent Living, he helped launch a movement that would transform the rehabilitation system nationwide. In 1983 he cofounded a think tank, the World Institute on Disability, in Oakland. In 1985 he received a MacArthur Fellowship.

Crisscrossing the United States and the globe and brimming with self-assurance, Roberts introduced countless numbers of disabled people to concepts of independent living and disability rights. He redefined "disability" as a social, rather than a medical, problem, as an issue of civil rights and equal access, not medical treatment. Rejecting diagnostic categories, he came to espouse a cross-disability political movement. Most important, he demanded self-determination. Independent living meant not physical self-sufficiency, but individual choice—free from professional control and girded by appropriate support services (personal assistance, accessible housing, and transportation), and as a right that would ensure community integration. Self-determination also meant the collective empowerment of disabled people to run the programs that affected their lives. "If we have learned one thing from the civil rights movement in the United States," declared Roberts, "it's that when others speak for you, you lose."

Roberts died of a stroke on March 14, 1995.

BIBLIOGRAPHY
Shapiro, Joseph. *No Pity: People with Disability Forging a New Civil Rights Movement.* 1993.

Paul K. Longmore

Robeson, Paul

(1898–1976), singer and actor.

When Paul Robeson led a march of several thousand to the nation's capital on September 24, 1946, the action, called the American Crusade to End Lynching, was but a new chapter in the long history of black Americans' struggle for equal rights. On that occasion, Robeson, then the most famous African American, was spokesman for a delegation that confronted President Harry S. Truman in the White House with a demand that he support federal anti-lynching legislation (see Anti-Lynching Campaign). Truman, a Democrat, refused.

Paul Robeson in a 1925 picture taken at Madame St. George's studio in London. (AP/Wide World Photos)

By a remarkable coincidence, on April 9, 1898, the date of Robeson's birth in Princeton, New Jersey, the Negro weekly *Cleveland Gazette* reported that Ida B. WELLS-Barnet, a black crusader against lynching, had visited the White House to urge that President William McKinley take action to stop those horrible crimes then rampant throughout the racist post-RECONSTRUCTION South. McKinley, a Republican, refused.

In the half-century between those two White House encounters, however, a notable change had taken place in the black community. Reflecting a new militancy that had developed during World War II, Robeson shocked Truman by remarking that if the government would not protect black citizens from mob violence, then his people would have to defend themselves.

When Paul Robeson emerged in the 1940s as a major forerunner of the civil rights upsurge in the 1960s, it was yet another development in his multifaceted career as athlete, scholar, actor, and concert singer. The son of a fugitive-slave father and a mother from a family of abolitionists, Robeson resolved from childhood to achieve what his community saw as its highest goal: "to be a credit to the race." Second-class citizenship, enforced by the ruling ideology of white supremacy, could be overcome, he believed, by individual effort.

In both mind and body, Robeson was uniquely equipped to become an exemplar of excellence. Entering Rutgers College at age seventeen as its sole African-American student, he became the legendary "Robeson of Rutgers"—All-American football star . . . hero in baseball, basketball, and track . . . champion orator for four years . . . prize-winning scholar and valedictorian of the Class of 1919. A graduate of Columbia Law School in 1922, Robeson was encouraged by his wife, Eslanda Cardozo Goode, to accept the offer of playwright Eugene O'Neill to become an actor in several of his plays. After his debut as a performing artist, Robeson, who was gifted with a bass-baritone voice of unusual richness, went on to become an international concert singer while continuing to play leading roles on the stage and in film.

Like many other African-American performers before and after World War I, Robeson found greater opportunity in Europe than at home, where blacks were denied equal rights in the arts as in all other areas of life. In the decade before the outbreak of World War II, Robeson made his home in London and was lionized as one of Britain's foremost performers. In that capital of the world's greatest empire, Robeson's life was drastically changed. First, as he would say, was his discovery there of Africa—meeting African students and workers and studying African languages. His interest in the outlook for oppressed people of

color led him to visit the Soviet Union in 1934, where he was impressed by the progress being made by non-white ethnic groups that had been oppressed in the former Czarist empire. He would become a Marxist.

Appalled by the rise of fascism in Europe, and considering the Hitler regime to be a KU KLUX KLAN in power, Robeson decided to devote his life to the fight against fascism as well as for colonial liberation. In London he gave support to revolutionaries like Jawaharlal Nehru and Jomo Kenyatta, who, after imprisonment and struggle, became heads of state, respectively, of India and Kenya.

Following his return to America at the outbreak of World War II, Robeson was active as cofounder and chairman of the Council on African Affairs (CAA), with W. E. B. DU BOIS and W. Alphaeus Hunton as his principal partners. Until it was suppressed by the U.S. government as an alleged subversive organization in 1955, the CAA was the only American organization supporting the liberation movements in the African colonies and South Africa.

Beginning in 1949, Robeson was made one of the main targets of the anti-communist witch hunts that became known as McCARTHYISM, but his militancy never wavered. On June 12, 1956, when he was summoned to appear before the HOUSE UN-AMERICAN ACTIVITIES COMMITTEE (HUAC) and was asked why he did not stay in Russia, he replied: "Because my father was a slave, and my people died to build this country, and I'm going to stay here and have a part of it just like you. And no fascist-minded people will drive me from it. Is that clear?" Despite the total ban on his activities, Robeson's book *Here I Stand* was independently published in 1958. In part autobiographical, the book summarizes his views on the fight for equal rights for black Americans, and presents his outlook on national and world affairs.

Ill health did not permit Paul Robeson to take an active part in the civil rights movement of the 1960s, but in a 1964 press statement he said he was heartened "to see the active and often heroic part that leading Negro artists—singers, actors, writers, comedians, musicians—are playing today in the freedom struggle." His statement concluded: "There is more—much more—that needs to be done before we can reach our goals. But if we cannot yet sing, 'Thank God Almighty, we're free at last,' we surely can all sing together, 'Thank God Almighty, we're *moving*!' " (Full text is in *Here I Stand*, 1971 edition.)

Robeson died on January 23, 1976. His epitaph was words from an anti-fascist speech he made in London's Albert Hall in 1937: "The artist must elect to fight for freedom or slavery. I have made my choice. I had no alternative."

BIBLIOGRAPHY

Brown, Lloyd L. *The Young Paul Robeson: "On My Journey Now."* 1997.
Duberman, Martin Bauml. *Paul Robeson.* 1988.
Editors of *Freedomways. Paul Robeson: The Great Forerunner.* 1978.
Foner, Philip S. *Paul Robeson Speaks.* 1978.
Robeson, Paul. *Here I Stand.* 1958.
Schlosser, Anatol I. "Paul Robeson: His Career in the Theatre, in Motion Pictures and on the Concert Stage." Dissertation, New York University. 1970.
Seton, Marie. *Paul Robeson.* 1958.
Stewart, Jeffrey C. *Paul Robeson: Artist and Citizen.* 1998.
Stuckey, Sterling. *Slave Culture: Nationalist Theory and the Foundations of Black America.* 1987.
Von Eschen, Penny M. *Race Against Empire: Black Americans and Anticolonialism, 1937–1957.* 1997.

Lloyd L. Brown

Robinson, Bernice

(1914–1994), educator.

On John's Island, near Charleston, SOUTH CAROLINA, in January 1957 a very nervous Bernice Robinson took charge of her first adult literacy class. An established NAACP activist, she had said that she would help with a Highlander extension program on the Sea Islands after visiting the folk school in 1956 (see HIGHLANDER FOLK SCHOOL). Her cousin, Septima CLARK, and Myles HORTON of Highlander had asked her to teach. She may have been a beautician by training, but Horton insisted that the fact that the people already knew and trusted Robinson was more important than was formal teacher training. In fact, Horton believed that accredited teachers would be less successful because they would tend to apply their schoolroom routines to adults.

The impetus for the adult class had come from a local leader, Esau Jenkins, who recognized that illiteracy rendered the islanders vulnerable to economic and political exploitation. He visited Highlander with Clark in 1955 and was keen to boost black voter registration. The adult classes, later called CITIZENSHIP SCHOOLS, were a key part of Highlander's efforts to further Jenkins's plans. With the white primary outlawed, South Carolina authorities had strengthened the literacy test for voter registration (see VOTING RIGHTS). Robinson's students would ultimately be obliged to read a section of the state constitution out loud to a white registrar and complete a registration form correctly. Through classes two nights a week during the three slack months of the farm year, Robinson enabled them to do this—and more.

Crucially, she asked her students what they wanted to learn. At a time of accelerating out-migration, many longed to be able to read the letters their children sent home and to reply. With few department or other stores accessible, others wanted to know how to complete a mail-order form, and several men asked for math instruction to ensure they were not cheated at the Charleston market. Some students wanted to learn to write their own names. Robinson's teaching strengthened the students' self-respect. They no longer had to rely on others to read their personal mail; they could buy new clothes by catalog; they were less likely to be taken advantage of in business; and the pride they felt in their own signatures was reflected in the bonds they felt with Robinson, each other, Jenkins, and Highlander. This gave them the courage to register to vote and the urge to vote as a bloc.

Demand for Citizenship Schools spread along the Carolina islands so that soon there were too many classes for Robinson and Clark to teach. By 1961, when the program was transferred from Highlander to the SOUTHERN CHRISTIAN LEADERSHIP CONFERENCE (SCLC), Robinson had become a teacher trainer. While Clark transferred to SCLC, Robinson stayed with Highlander during the difficult time following the forced closure of its Monteagle site and its reestablishment in Knoxville, Tennessee. She was frequently on the road, providing guidance for the growing number of civil rights activists involved in the VOTER EDUCATION PROJECT, notably in MISSISSIPPI in 1963. She subsequently teamed up again with Mrs. Clark on the SCLC's Citizenship School program, revising its curricula to include HEAD START proposals, Planned Parenthood, and other initiatives that addressed the concerns of local communities. During the 1970s she, like Clark, returned to Charleston and briefly—and unsuccessfully—pursued elected office. She died there in 1994.

BIBLIOGRAPHY

Clark, Septima, with Cynthia Brown. *Ready from Within: Septima Clark and the Civil Rights Movement.* 1986.
Oldendorf, Sandra B. "The South Carolina Sea Island Citizenship Schools, 1957–1961." In *Women in the Civil Rights Movement,* edited by Vicki Crawford, Jacqueline A. Rouse, and Barbara Woods. 1993.

Peter J. Ling

Robinson, Jack ("Jackie") Roosevelt

(1919–1972), baseball player and civil rights advocate.

In 1947, Jackie Robinson was the first African American to play major-league baseball after the sport was

Jackie Robinson at the Brooklyn Dodgers spring training camp in Vero Beach, Florida, in March 1956, his last season as a major-league baseball player. (AP/Wide World Photos)

segregated in 1889. The grandson of a slave, Robinson ushered in a multicultural era in professional sport and American life. His on-field action backed up his social statement. The career-long Brooklyn Dodger was elected to the Baseball Hall of Fame in 1962.

Robinson first gained fame as a multi-sport athlete at the University of California at Los Angeles. Drafted into the Army in 1943, he quickly began his civil rights protests, fighting his race-based rejection from officer candidate school. Successful, the second lieutenant was later court-martialed for not sitting in the back of a segregated army bus in TEXAS; acquitted, he was honorably discharged. After the military, Robinson played baseball for the Negro Leagues' Kansas City Monarchs. In 1945, Dodger general manager Branch Rickey—balancing benevolence with box-office considerations—signed the infielder to a minor-league contract. Two years later, Robinson was in the big leagues. Subject to spikings, beatings, death threats, and a regular verbal barrage by fans and players alike, Robinson refused to retaliate, and this, coupled with his refusal to quit, earned him the respect of both blacks and whites. While Robinson was not the best African-American ballplayer in the late 1940s, Rickey selected him based on his strength of character and his nonviolent attitude.

Retiring in 1957, Robinson continued his activism and fund-raising for the NATIONAL ASSOCIATION FOR THE ADVANCEMENT OF COLORED PEOPLE (NAACP). Though he generated political controversy as a some-time supporter of the Republican Party in the 1960s, Robinson's legacy as a civil rights pioneer is not debatable.

BIBLIOGRAPHY

Falkner, David. *Great Time Coming: The Life of Jackie Robinson from Baseball to Birmingham.* 1995.
Robinson, Jackie. *I Never Had It Made.* 1972.
Tygiel, Jules. *Baseball's Great Experiment: Jackie Robinson and His Legacy.* 1983.

Gregory L. Parker

Robinson, Randall

(1941–   ), human rights activist.

Randall Robinson, champion of human rights in Africa and the Caribbean, was born in Richmond, Virginia, the son of two teachers. After attending Norfolk State College and serving in the U.S. Army, Robinson received a B.A. from Virginia Union College in 1967, and went on to receive a law degree from Harvard University in 1970. During this period, Robinson's opposition to the VIETNAM WAR led him to question American policy toward COLONIALISM in Africa. During the early 1970s, Robinson worked as a lawyer and community activist in Boston, and organized protests of U.S. firms doing business with colonial governments in Africa.

Randall Robinson (right) shakes the hand of South African leader Nelson Mandela. (AP/Wide World Photos)

In 1975, Robinson became a congressional foreign affairs aide. Two years later, with support from the CONGRESSIONAL BLACK CAUCUS, he founded TRANS-AFRICA, a congressional lobbying group for Africa and the Caribbean. His primary task during the following years was to lobby for government action against South Africa's apartheid system. In 1984, Robinson organized the Free South Africa Movement, and launched a dramatic series of sit-ins at the South African embassy in Washington, D.C. Robinson's efforts resulted in the imposition of serious economic sanctions against South Africa in 1986 and the eventual victory there of majority rule.

During the 1990s, Robinson was an influential critic of human rights abuses in Africa, notably by military regimes in Ethiopia and Nigeria. Also, in 1994, he staged a successful twenty-seven–day hunger strike against the Clinton administration's policy of refusing asylum to Haitian refugees, and he helped persuade Clinton to end military rule in Haiti by threatening invasion.

BIBLIOGRAPHY

Lincoln Institute. *TransAfrica: A Lobby of the Left.* 1985.
Robinson, Randall. *Defending the Spirit: A Black Life in America.* 1998.

Greg Robinson

Robinson, Ruby Doris Smith

(1942–1967), civil rights activist.

Ruby Doris Smith Robinson held crucial leadership positions in the STUDENT NONVIOLENT COORDINATING COMMITTEE (SNCC). As a fearless activist in the field, an administrative assistant to the executive secretary, and finally as the executive secretary and most powerful female officer, she significantly influenced SNCC's development during the early and mid-1960s.

Ruby Doris Smith was born and grew up in Summerhill, a black neighborhood in Atlanta, GEORGIA. She attended Spelman College, and it was during her college years that she dedicated her life to the Civil Rights Movement. Her initial involvement was in the SIT-INS and economic boycotts directed by the Atlanta Student Movement during 1960. Smith's civil rights activities increased as the movement gathered momentum in the following years; 1961 proved to be a watershed year for her. In February, she joined an SNCC delegation that went to Rock Hill, SOUTH CAROLINA, to protest SEGREGATION and the (previous) jailing of demonstrators. As a result of this protest, she served a thirty-day jail sentence and gained a reputation within the movement for determination, courage, and absolute dedication to the cause of freedom. Shortly after her release from prison, Smith joined the

SNCC-led second wave of Freedom Riders in Birmingham, ALABAMA, and experienced violence in Montgomery, arrest in Jackson, and incarceration in Mississippi's infamous PARCHMAN Penitentiary. In July, she participated in SNCC's initial project in McComb, Mississippi, before returning to Spelman for the fall semester.

After participating in the ALBANY MOVEMENT in 1962, Smith began assisting James FORMAN, SNCC's new executive secretary, in the organization's Atlanta office. Her administrative skills became critical as SNCC expanded its membership and projects, and her colleagues consistently credit her with keeping the always chaotic main office running as efficiently as possible. She became famous within SNCC for possessing a unique ability to see through any attempts to use organizational resources for personal reasons, while at the same time doing everything possible to assist field staff in their always difficult and often dangerous assignments. In addition to her administrative duties, she also participated fully in the frequently intense internal debates that focused on topics such as the goals and policies of FREEDOM SUMMER, the roles of white and black women within SNCC, and the evaluation of white participation in the organization. In 1964, she toured Guinea with a SNCC delegation which, collectively, was moved by the growing independence movement in Africa and its implications for the freedom struggle in the United States, and in 1966 she was elected executive secretary in the midst of SNCC's movement toward a more militant orientation that was increasingly identified with BLACK POWER.

In the midst of her hectic administrative responsibilities, Smith married Clifford Robinson in 1963, and the couple had a son, Kenneth Toure, in 1965. After a characteristically heroic struggle to balance activism, marriage, motherhood, and deteriorating health, Ruby Doris Smith Robinson succumbed to cancer in October 1967.

BIBLIOGRAPHY

Fleming, Cynthia Griggs. *Soon We Will Not Cry: The Liberation of Ruby Doris Smith Robinson.* 1998.

Stephen C. Messer

Roosevelt, Eleanor

(1884–1962), first lady, writer, human rights activist.

Anna Eleanor Roosevelt was born into wealth and society, the daughter of Anna Hall and Elliott Roosevelt and the niece of Republican President Theodore Roosevelt. When she married her distant cousin, Franklin Delano ROOSEVELT, who also became president, her

First Lady Eleanor Roosevelt meets with Japanese Americans in Tacoma, Washington, on December 14, 1941, one week after the Japanese attack on Pearl Harbor. (CORBIS/*Seattle Post-Intelligencer* Collection)

place in history was already assured, but she attained a larger historical significance in her own right as a champion of liberal political causes and human rights.

Eleanor was raised by her maternal grandmother and attended a boarding school in England. Her experience at the boarding school allowed her to eradicate an intense, innate shyness and paved the way for her subsequent career. She was a social worker prior to marrying Franklin Roosevelt in 1905 at the age of twenty-one. They had six children, one of whom died in infancy, but her husband was not involved with his home and children to the highest degree. After Eleanor discovered his long-term affair with her social secretary, Lucy Page Mercer, she resolved more than ever to maintain a career and an identity of her own.

In 1918 Eleanor became active in the LEAGUE FOR WOMEN VOTERS and the Women's Trade Union League. She became vitally involved in her husband's political career in 1921, when he was first stricken with poliomyelitis, becoming active in DEMOCRATIC PARTY politics on his behalf and on her own. She encouraged him not to abandon his political career because of his new disability and was instrumental in convincing him to seek (and win) the New York governorship in 1928. After he was elected president in 1932, she continued her political activism and was a highly influential

member of his administration, even though she did not hold either elective or appointive office.

Eleanor championed the causes of women, racial equality, and the unemployed. During the presidential years (1933–1945), she wrote a nationally syndicated daily newspaper column, "My Day," and had her own radio program, which served to complement and enhance the impact of her husband's "Fireside Chat" broadcasts. As an example of her work for the unemployed, she worked to bring a small-scale manufacturing project to an impoverished coal-mining town in West Virginia. She was a supporter of the National Youth Administration, which provided employment for youths, and of the American Youth Congress.

A life-long advocacy of Eleanor's was racial equality. She was neither shy nor reticent nor inclined to compromise in her advocacy and was willing to make well-publicized statements that did not fail to make some of those in positions of power feel uncomfortable. In 1939 she resigned her membership in the Daughters of the American Revolution in protest over its denial of access to Constitution Hall by African-American singer Marian Anderson. Eleanor was also an active supporter of efforts to repeal the poll tax (see VOTING RIGHTS). The intensity of her advocacy was such that she came to the attention of FEDERAL BUREAU OF IN-

VESTIGATION director J. Edgar Hoover, who maintained a file on Eleanor along with many other individuals and organizations regarded as being aligned with or at least partially supportive of "communist and subversive causes." The FBI never directly interrogated or harassed her, however. In 1943 she became involved in the efforts of black women to break the SEGREGATION barriers in the Armed Forces Nurse Corps. Her meeting with activist Mabel K. Staupers brought great public attention to these efforts.

After the death of her husband in 1945, Eleanor Roosevelt was appointed in 1947 by President Harry TRUMAN as one of the first delegates to the newly formed United Nations, where she chaired the commission that drafted the Universal Declaration of Human Rights. She often stated in later years that she regarded this assignment as the greatest achievement of her career. In chairing the commission, she sought to ensure that the needs and aspirations of the common men and women of the world were ably and amply represented. At the United Nations, she also championed the admission of Jews to Palestine and the creation of the state of Israel.

In 1948 she returned to the domestic political arena by joining with other prominent liberal Democrats to found the AMERICANS FOR DEMOCRATIC ACTION (ADA), and in 1949 she helped found a nonpartisan, political group, the National Committee for an Effective Congress. She attended the 1960 Democratic National Convention, which nominated John F. KENNEDY for president, and was greeted with a standing ovation. Her autobiography was published in 1961. Her last public task was to serve as chair of the PRESIDENT'S COMMISSION ON THE STATUS OF WOMEN, but she died on November 7, 1962, before the commission could publish its report.

BIBLIOGRAPHY

Hine, Darlene Clark. "Nursing." In *Encyclopedia of African-American Culture and History*, edited by Jack Salzman, David Lionel Smith, and Cornel West. 1996.

Kearney, James. *Anna Eleanor Roosevelt: The Evolution of a Reformer.* 1968.

O'Reilly, Kenneth. "Federal Bureau of Investigation." In *Encyclopedia of African-American Culture and History*, edited by Jack Salzman, David Lionel Smith, and Cornel West. 1996.

Roosevelt, Eleanor. *Autobiography of Eleanor Roosevelt.* 1961.

Scharf, Lois. *Eleanor Roosevelt: First Lady of American Liberalism.* 1987.

Sigler, Jay A., ed. "The United Nations." In *Civil Rights in America: 1500 to the Present.* 1998.

Michael Dawson

Roosevelt, Franklin Delano

(1882–1945), U.S. president, 1933–1945.

President of the United States from 1933 until 1945, Franklin D. Roosevelt has been studied more than any other holder of that office except for Abraham Lincoln; but he was by temperament and design so secretive that his views on racial issues—as on many other matters—remain hidden. Although there is broad agreement that the years of his presidency were a watershed in the struggle for civil rights, Roosevelt's personal role was, at the most generous interpretation, ambiguous.

Given Roosevelt's privileged upbringing, his lack of sensitivity to the plight of black Americans was not surprising. Nor was his service during the Wilson years as Assistant Secretary of the Navy under the staunchly segregationist Josephus Daniels calculated to lead him to question prevailing racial attitudes. And the keystone of his fence-building activities within the DEMOCRATIC PARTY during the 1920s was to forge close ties with Southern leaders—ties that proved crucial to his winning the 1932 Democratic presidential nomination.

Two variables appear to have largely shaped the treatment of blacks by NEW DEAL agencies. One was the extent of centralized control from Washington, D.C., blacks typically faring the worse the more local autonomy was allowed. The second was the attitude and commitments of the agency head. The two leading early New Deal recovery programs—the Agricultural Adjustment Administration (AAA) and the National Recovery Administration—impacted African Americans adversely. State administration of relief under the Federal Emergency Relief Administration allowed rampant discrimination against blacks. The Civilian Conservation Corps segregated its enrollees. The Tennessee Valley Authority offered no challenge to Southern racial mores. On the other hand, the Public Works Administration under Secretary of Interior Harold ICKES, the National Youth Administration under Aubrey Williams, the Farm Security Administration under C. B. ("Beanie") Baldwin, and, to a lesser extent, the Works Progress Administration under Harry Hopkins treated blacks fairly.

To the extent that racial issues became a matter for presidential decision making, Roosevelt's response appears to have been determined primarily by a calculus of political gain and loss. On the one side, there was pressure from a nucleus of racial liberals within the administration—the most influential of whom were FDR's wife, Eleanor, and Interior Secretary, Ickes—backed by the growing importance of the black vote, which by 1936 had become a significant part of the

President Franklin D. Roosevelt sits at his desk in his White House office. (Library of Congress)

New Deal coalition in northern urban centers. On the other side was the influence of the Southern congressional delegation—many of whom chaired key committees thanks to the seniority system—whose support was critical for the adoption of administration measures.

Given the power imbalance between the two sides, the first side's successes were primarily symbolic (such as the assembling of the "Black Cabinet" under the aegis of Mary McLeod BETHUNE to advise on racial matters), while the second side won on matters of substance (such as the "purge" in February 1935 of those members of the AAA who wished to protect tenants and sharecroppers). Even when Roosevelt felt compelled to come out publicly in favor of such measures as the federal ANTI-LYNCHING legislation sponsored by the NATIONAL ASSOCIATION FOR THE ADVANCEMENT OF COLORED PEOPLE or the repeal of the poll tax pushed by the SOUTHERN CONFERENCE FOR HUMAN WELFARE, his support failed to go beyond lip service. Probably his single most important contribution to civil rights was indirect: his pushing through the 1936 Democratic National Convention repeal of the two-thirds rule governing presidential nominations, thereby breaking the South's veto power.

The coming of World War II altered the power balance, at least to an extent, in favor of civil rights. The most dramatic example was when alarm over the threatened march on Washington organized by A. Philip RANDOLPH, the head of the BROTHERHOOD OF SLEEPING CAR PORTERS, forced FDR to issue on June 25, 1941, Executive Order 8802 barring racial discrim-

ination by defense contractors and establishing a temporary FAIR EMPLOYMENT PRACTICES COMMITTEE. And though Roosevelt personally continued to shy away from frontally challenging Southern white sensibilities, the struggle against Nazism impelled wartime propaganda to embrace the ideal of racial equality under the slogan "Americans All."

BIBLIOGRAPHY

Badger, Anthony. *The New Deal: The Depression Years, 1933–40.* 1989.

Freidel, Frank. *Franklin D. Roosevelt: A Rendezvous with Destiny.* 1990.

Jeffries, John W. *Wartime America: The World War II Home Front.* 1996.

Kirby, John B. *Black Americans in the Roosevelt Era: Liberalism and Race.* 1980.

Sitkoff, Harvard. *A New Deal for Blacks: The Emergence of Civil Rights as a National Issue,* Volume I: *The Depression Decade.* 1978.

John Braeman

Rosenwald, Julius

(1862–1932), retail executive and philanthropist.

Rosenwald, chairman of the board of Sears, Roebuck from 1908 until his death, devoted most of the last quarter-century of his life to philanthropy, primarily aiding African Americans.

In 1911, he read a passage from Booker T. WASHINGTON's autobiography *Up from Slavery,* including this

Julius Rosenwald. (Library of Congress)

sentence: "The actual sight of a first-class house that a Negro has built is ten times more potent than pages of discussion about a house he ought to build, or perhaps could build."

In May 1911, Rosenwald and Washington met in Chicago's Blackstone Hotel and agreed to work on two projects. The first involved the creation of YMCAs for African Americans, where Rosenwald would donate $25,000 if other parties would contribute $75,000. This plan inspired major philanthropic activity among blacks. In Chicago, 10,000 African Americans contributed $67,000 toward the YMCA; in Washington, D.C., 4,500 blacks contributed $27,000. Many of the contributors were former slaves who donated their life savings. "The organizing of the colored people in the gathering of subscriptions," Washington wrote in 1914, "the inspiration that comes from labor in common for the common good—all this is in itself a character-building process, and has a far-reaching influence upon the churches and other religious organizations throughout the country."

A second plan involved the construction of schools throughout the South. Here Rosenwald agreed to donate $25,000 to each school if other organizations would contribute $75,000. African Americans also had to contribute to each school; Rosenwald would not agree to a donation unless his money was matched by some contributions from blacks, as Rosenwald was a believer in Andrew Carnegie's philosophy of using philanthropy to inspire self-sufficiency.

When Rosenwald died in 1932, he had contributed $4.4 million of the $62 million he donated to philanthropy to building 5,357 schools in the South for African Americans. His contributions were matched by $18.1 million in government funds, $1.2 million from foundations, and $4.7 million from African Americans. After Rosenwald's death, the Julius Rosenwald Fund continued the school-building program in a limited way. The Rosenwald Fund also created a series of fellowships, modeled after the Guggenheim Fellowships, that gave grants to African-American novelists, poets, playwrights, historians, and sociologists. These fellowships continued until the Rosenwald Fund's liquidation in 1948.

Rosenwald's daughter, Edith Rosenwald Stern (1895–1980) and her husband, Edgar Stern, Sr. (1885–1959), also continued the Rosenwald tradition of aiding African Americans, chiefly through substantial contributions to Dillard University, a historically black institution in New Orleans.

BIBLIOGRAPHY

Boorstin, Daniel. "Transforming the Charitable Spirit: From Conscience to Community." In *The Julius Rosenwald Centennial.* 1963.

Embree, Edwin R., and Julia Waxman. *Investment in People: The Story of the Julius Rosenwald Fund.* 1949.

Werner, M. R. *Julius Rosenwald: The Life of a Practical Humanitarian.* 1939.

Wooster, Martin Morse. *Should Foundations Live Forever? The Problem of Perpetuity.* 1998.

Martin Morse Wooster

Russell, Richard Brevard, Jr.

(1897–1971), U.S. senator.

Richard Russell, a leading opponent of civil rights in the U.S. Senate, was born in Winder, GEORGIA, son of a state supreme court justice. After obtaining a law degree from the University of Georgia in 1918 and serving in the Georgia Legislature, Russell was elected governor of Georgia in 1931. The following year, he won a special election to fill the unexpired term of U.S. Senator William Harris. Russell was elected to a full term in 1936, and reelected five times.

Although he generally supported NEW DEAL reforms during his early years in the Senate, Russell consistently opposed civil rights efforts. In 1937, he headed a southern filibuster to defeat an anti-lynching bill. In 1944 and 1945, Russell managed the effort to withdraw funding from the wartime Fair Employment Practices Committee. After World War II, he became a leading conservative. In 1948, Russell led a group of twenty-one southern legislators pledged to filibuster against any civil rights bills in CONGRESS, and he ran as a southern alternative to President Harry TRUMAN at that year's Democratic Convention, though he did not join the DIXIECRAT revolt. In 1949, Russell introduced legislation to encourage black "relocation" in the North, and he continued to champion such relocation during the 1950s and 1960s. Meanwhile, he used his position as chair of the Senate Armed Services Committee to oppose civil rights legislation, and in 1957 and 1964 he led filibusters against civil rights bills. He also denounced civil rights protesters as lawbreakers. Russell died in office in 1971, two years after becoming president pro tempore of the Senate.

BIBLIOGRAPHY

Mann, Robert. *The Walls of Jericho: Lyndon Johnson, Hubert Humphrey, Richard Russell, and the Struggle for Civil Rights.* 1996.
"Richard Russell." *Current Biography.* March 1949.

Greg Robinson

Bayard Rustin. (Library of Congress)

Rustin, Bayard

(1912–1987), civil rights and peace activist.

Bayard Rustin played a crucial though largely behind-the-scenes role in both the civil rights and peace movements from the 1950s until his death in 1987, being most active during the period when he worked with Martin Luther KING, JR.

Born in West Chester, Pennsylvania, in March 1912, Rustin was both an academic and athletic standout in the West Chester schools. Upon his graduation, he attended Wilberforce University and Cheyney State Teachers College before settling in New York City in 1937, where he attended City College. There he acted as an organizer for the school's Young Communist League. Eventually becoming dissatisfied with the COMMUNIST PARTY, he transferred his allegiance to the SOCIALIST PARTY and the WAR RESISTERS LEAGUE, an action that led to his arrest and imprisonment for violation of the Selective Service Act. After serving for twenty-eight months, Rustin was paroled; and he left the United States to work abroad for the FELLOWSHIP OF RECONCILIATION (FOR). He spent several years in India and Africa, where he witnessed up close the nonviolent aspects of the Indian and Ghanaian independence movements. Soon after Rustin returned to the United States, he was arrested again, this time for public indecency. This incident marked the first time that

his homosexuality had become a matter of public record, and it resulted in his dismissal from the FOR staff. Despite the damage done to his professional standing by this episode, his career as a crusader for social justice was far from over.

In 1956, Rustin was approached by the author Lillian SMITH on behalf of Martin Luther King, Jr., who hoped that Rustin could provide some advice on how to apply Mahatma GANDHI's principles of CIVIL DISOBEDIENCE and nonviolence to the MONTGOMERY BUS BOYCOTT. Recognizing the opportunity, Rustin traveled to Montgomery to assist King in crafting a strategy that could be applied anywhere in the South; and it was from these meetings that the SOUTHERN CHRISTIAN LEADERSHIP CONFERENCE (SCLC) would emerge. Rustin was also instrumental in organizing the 1957 Prayer Pilgrimage to Washington, D.C., a pair of Youth Marches for Integrated Schools held in 1958 and 1959. As the civil rights movement grew during the 1960s, so too did Rustin's role within it. Perhaps his greatest achievement was in organizing the August 1963 MARCH ON WASHINGTON for Freedom, during which King gave his famous "I Have A Dream" speech. Rustin is credited by most as being the man most responsible for carrying the march through to fruition, no mean feat considering that there were at least a quarter of a million people present, representing a bewildering array of political and social groups.

With the passage of the CIVIL RIGHTS ACT OF 1964 and the VOTING RIGHTS ACT OF 1965, Rustin concluded that the worst of the struggle was over and that his talents would best be served if he turned his attention away from the type of grassroots organizing that he had been doing to focus instead on forging a coalition for social change, encompassing minority groups, secular organizations, political liberals, and the radical element of trade unions. Unfortunately, the growing polarization in the United States over the VIETNAM WAR, between those on the political fringe and those in the mainstream, would doom this attempt.

The deaths of both King and Robert KENNEDY, combined with growth of the BLACK POWER movement, helped to fragment the political program that Rustin and others had labored to build. Although he was never without influence among social reformers, Rustin would never enjoy the degree of power and prestige that he held as a member of King's inner circle. Still he was unwavering in his devotion to demo-cratic principles and peaceful change. He spent the last decade of his life as a delegate for the human rights group Freedom House, serving as an election monitor and a human rights observer in numerous trouble spots, including Chile, El Salvador, Grenada, Haiti, and Zimbabwe. It was while stationed in Haiti that Rustin first fell ill, and he never recovered, passing away on August 24, 1987. Although he was never the most visible figure in the civil rights movement, Rustin's role in the struggle was nearly as important as that played by the men and women who took center stage.

BIBLIOGRAPHY

Anderson, Jervis. *Bayard Rustin: Troubles I've Seen, A Biography.* 1997.
Haskins, James. *Bayard Rustin: Behind the Scenes of the Civil Rights Movement.* 1997.
Levine, Daniel. *Bayard Rustin and the Civil Rights Movement.* 2000.

Robert W. Nill

S

Salt of the Earth Strike

On October 17, 1950, Mexican-American zinc miners, members of the International Union of Mine, Mill and Smelter Workers, from Empire Zinc Corporation in Hanover, New Mexico, called a work stoppage. Thus began a fifteen-month strike that later inspired the classic film *Salt of the Earth*. Their demands were for parity in paid holidays with other miners, pay for transit to work, compensation for time spent underground, and elimination of the no-strike clause in their contract. The company responded through violent repressive tactics, culminating in a court injunction that prohibited the workers from picketing. This act nearly brought the strike to a halt.

The wives of the workers, who had organized themselves as part of a ladies auxiliary to the UNION, offered an alternative to the court injunction's limitations. As the court injunction only prohibited the mine workers from picketing, they offered themselves as substitutes to carry on the duties of the picket line. After much heated debate, the union accepted this as the only available option. The involvement of women at the forefront of the struggle raised questions around strictly defined gender roles and machismo, leading to a raising of consciousness among both men and women on gender issues. This struggle therefore addressed RACE, CLASS, and gender concerns. The strike finally came to an end on January 24, 1952. Although the workers gained a substantial wage increase along with significant fringe benefits, the union suffered great financial losses in fines, and the strike leaders received prison sentences.

BIBLIOGRAPHY

Griswold Del Castillo, Richard, and Arnoldo de Leon. *North to Aztlan: A History of Mexican Americans in the United States.* 1996.

Silverton Rosenfelt, Deborah. "Commentary." In *Salt of the Earth,* edited by Michael Wilson and Deborah Silverton Rosenfelt. 1978.

Elizabeth Garcia

Sam, Alfred Charles

(ca. 1870–?), black nationalist, entrepreneur, pan-Africanist.

Chief of the Akim tribe of Africa's Gold Coast, Alfred Charles Sam devised the first large-scale "back to Africa" movement, a plan to transport and colonize African Americans from Oklahoma and Kansas to the coastal West African country of Liberia. With the establishment of the Akim Trading Company in 1911, Sam expedited his pan-Africanist vision and sold shares of the company for twenty-five dollars. From 1913 to 1914, his emigration movement galvanized many African Americans living on the Great Plains of the United States. Thanks to Sam's enigmatic appeal and the revenue he received from the selling of company stock, Sam purchased a large ship, the *Liberia*. The feat invigorated the hearts and minds of thousands of Midwestern African Americans and also drew the attention—and the suspicion—of national and international authorities.

On June 19, 1914, the *Liberia* docked at the Galveston, Texas, harbor carrying Sam and his chief lieutenants, whose mission was to take representatives from Sam's numerous followers, who had congregated at camps in and around Galveston, back to Africa. By August 21, the ship had set sail for Africa, but not without harassment from the British Navy. On January 13, 1915, the *Liberia*, along with a select group of African-American colonists, reached the port of Saltpond, in Liberia. To their dismay, however, the black colonists found that life in the small African nation seemed to be far rougher than they had been led to believe. This, combined with the flagrantly inconsistent promises made to them by Sam, forced many of the colonists to return to the United States, heart-broken and disillusioned. Thus as quickly as the fame of Alfred Charles Sam rose, so did it fade. Sam was dismissed as a fraud and religious fanatic by 1917. Even so, the cursory treatment by history of Sam's contributions to the black freedom struggle did not destroy his vision, for his efforts spawned the future, more successful movement led by pan-Africanist and black nationalist Marcus GARVEY (see also PAN-AFRICANISM), who founded the UNIVERSAL NEGRO IMPROVEMENT ASSOCIATION (UNIA), which emphasized the need for both black American economic empowerment in the United States and for migration to Africa.

BIBLIOGRAPHY

Bittle, William E., and Gilbert Geis. "Alfred Charles Sam and an African Return: A Case Study in Negro Despair." *Phylon* 23 (1962): 178–94.

Bittle, William E., and Gilbert Geis. *The Longest Way Home.* 1964.

Geiss, Imanuel. *The Pan-African Movement.* 1974.

Lewallen, Kenneth A. "Chief Alfred C. Sam: Black Nationalist on the Great Plains." *Journal of the West* 16 (1977): 49–56.

Donny C. Barnett

Santa Clara Pueblo v. Martinez (1978)

On May 15, 1978, the United States Supreme Court decided the case of *Santa Clara Pueblo v. Martinez*. The case emphasized the difficult issues and questions raised by the American Indian Civil Rights Act, which was signed into law ten years earlier after years of congressional investigations examining the denial of rights to individual Native Americans by tribal, state, and federal governments. The act afforded residents of reservations the same civil liberties and protections in relation to tribal authorities that citizens under federal and state jurisdictions enjoyed. The Pueblo tribe, among others, did not support the legislation, arguing that it would be an unnecessary federal intrusion into tribal customs and governments. As Justice Thurgood MARSHALL wrote in his opinion for the Supreme

Indians of the Santa Clara Pueblo in New Mexico making pottery. (H.T. Correy/National Archives and Records Administration)

Court, the *Martinez* case asked the Court to decide "whether a federal court may pass on the validity of an Indian tribe's ordinance denying membership to the children of certain female tribal members."

The Santa Clara Pueblo, which had been in existence for over 600 years, passed an ordinance in 1939 which permitted tribal membership to children of male members who married outside the tribe, but denied membership to children of female members who married outside the tribe. Julia Martinez, a full-blooded Pueblo, married a Navajo in 1941. The couple's daughter was denied membership into the Pueblo tribe, which excluded her from voting in elections, holding secular office, or retaining rights of inheritance. Martinez sought federal relief under the AMERICAN CIVIL RIGHTS ACT OF 1968. The Court held that federal courts do not have the authority to provide such relief based on the language of the legislation, which indicates that federal courts may only scrutinize tribal ordinances in the context of habeas corpus. Any other review by the federal courts, according to the Supreme Court, would be a violation of tribal sovereignty.

BIBLIOGRAPHY
Champagne, Duane, ed. *Chronology of Native North American History.* 1994, pp. 353, 417.
Santa Clara Pueblo v. Martinez. 436 U.S. 49 (1978)

Matthew May

Savio, Mario Robert

(1943–1996), civil rights activist, student protest leader, teacher.

Born on Manhattan's Lower East Side, the son of Joseph Savio, a Sicilian immigrant and sheet-metal worker, and Dora Berrette, Mario Savio grew up in Queens. In his early youth, Mario was heavily influenced by the Catholic Church, but during his teen years he came to perceive Catholicism in a negative light. As he made friends with Jewish teens in his Queens neighborhood, he gradually came to feel that Jewish culture displayed "much more respect for critical thinking than there was in Catholic culture." In 1961 he graduated as valedictorian, first in his high school class of more than 1,200 students. He began his higher education at Manhattan College, a Catholic institution in the Bronx, but after a year, he transferred to Queens College and then to the University of California at Berkeley (UCB) in fall 1963.

Before arriving at Berkeley, Savio had an already well-developed political conscience. He had attended meetings of the Catholic Worker movement but limited his involvement because he found the organization too narrowly Catholic. In summer 1963 he was an antipoverty project construction worker in Mexico. After reading David Horowitz's book *Student,* a vivid account of UCB campus political activists, he decided to transfer to Berkeley that fall.

Berkeley turned out to be an exciting, stimulating place for Savio. The activist cause that attracted him most was civil rights. He was among 115 students arrested in a March 1964 SIT-IN protesting racially discriminatory practices at the Sheraton Palace Hotel in San Francisco, a protest which ended triumphantly when the hotel agreed to sign a nondiscrimination agreement.

While in jail, Savio heard about the Mississippi Summer Project, and in the summer of 1964 he went to MISSISSIPPI and joined the FREEDOM SUMMER crusade. He became involved in the voter registration drive and taught in the FREEDOM SCHOOLS. He experienced racist violence and bigotry firsthand and was shocked by the murder of three fellow Freedom Summer volunteers—James Chaney, Andrew Goodman, and Michael Schwerner (see the biographical entry at James CHANEY).

Upon returning to Berkeley in the fall of 1964, Savio was determined to increase student involvement in the civil rights movement. When UCB officials sought to impose new restrictions upon student political activity by banning political advocacy and fund-raising from the Bancroft-Telegraph Avenue strip where it had been centered, Savio and his fellow student civil rights movement veterans quickly deployed sit-in tactics against the Berkeley administration at the dean's office on September 30. On October 1, police, on orders of Berkeley campus administrators, sought to arrest Jack Weinberg, a former UCB graduate student-activist for defying the ban against political advocacy on campus. Students prevented the arrest by staging a massive sit-in around a police car on Sproul Plaza. Savio gave a speech from atop the police car, which brought him to the attention of media nationwide as the leading voice of the new FREE SPEECH MOVEMENT (FSM).

After the police car incident, Savio's most memorable moments in the FSM came during two pivotal confrontations: the Sproul Hall sit-in of December 2, 1964, which was the largest on-campus act of civil disobedience to that point in American history, and the Greek Theatre convocation of December 7. Savio's speech at the Sproul Hall sit-in came to symbolize the essence of the student radicalism of the mid-1960s. The Sproul sit-in ended in mass arrests, after which the FSM launched an effective campus-wide student strike. The UCB administration then staged a convocation at Berkeley's Greek Theatre on December 7 to promote its compromise position. At the conclusion of the program, a defiant Savio, previously denied the right to speak there, walked onto the rostrum to speak. Police responded by physically dragging him from the platform, shocking and angering thousands of assembled students and faculty. In response to this fiasco, Berkeley's Academic Senate ended the crisis on December 8 by backing the FSM's demand for new campus rules that would not regulate the content of speech on campus.

Because of his role in the Sproul sit-in, Savio received a four-month jail sentence. His new media celebrity haunted him, as it conflicted with his egalitarian belief in grassroots movements composed of political equals rather than of charismatic leaders and followers. Subsequently, he shunned the political limelight and resigned from the FSM leadership in spring 1965. After spending a year abroad, Savio applied for readmission to UCB, but the nervous Berkeley administration sought an excuse to bar his readmission and found one after he returned to campus, spoke at a rally, and gave out leaflets in defiance of a campus regulation against nonstudent leafleters.

Savio was also active for a time in the ANTI-WAR MOVEMENT. In spring 1965 he spoke at Berkeley's mass teach-in against the VIETNAM WAR, and he was arrested in a sit-in against Navy recruiters at Berkeley in 1966. He ran for the California State Senate in 1968 on the PEACE AND FREEDOM PARTY ticket, but by the end of the 1960s, he had dropped out of active political life and left academia.

Savio returned to the campus world and to political activism decades later. He attended San Francisco State University and received his bachelor's degree in physics in 1984 and his master's in physics in 1985. In these same years, he spoke out against the Reagan administration's funding of the Contra War in Nicaragua and supported the Berkeley student movement's drive to divest university funds from businesses tied to the apartheid regime in South Africa (see ANTI-APARTHEID MOVEMENT). While teaching mathematics and philosophy at various California colleges, he spoke out publicly against Proposition 187, a California voter initiative designed to deny benefits to illegal immigrants (see IMMIGRATION AND IMMIGRANTS), and against Proposition 209, which sought to repeal AFFIRMATIVE ACTION (see CALIFORNIA CIVIL RIGHTS INITIATIVE). Just prior to his death in 1996, he helped students at Sonoma State mount a successful campaign against unilateral fee hikes that would have made higher education there less accessible to poorer students.

BIBLIOGRAPHY

Savio, Mario, and Nadav Savio. *In Defense of Affirmative Action: The Case Against Proposition 209.* 1995.

Robert Cohen

SCEF

See Southern Conference Educational Fund

School Desegregation

On May 17, 1954, the United States Supreme Court ruled unanimously in *Brown v. Board of Education of Topeka, Kansas,* that it was unlawful to segregate school children by race (see BROWN V. BOARD OF EDUCATION), thus overturning the "separate but equal" doctrine that had been established fifty-eight years earlier in PLESSY V. FERGUSON (1896). The Civil War, fought in the middle of the previous century, had resulted in emancipation for black slaves, but nearly one hundred years later African Americans still had not achieved full racial equality. "Separate but equal" had been the guiding principle for race relations in the entire nation, especially in the states of the former Confeder-

acy, and it became clear almost immediately after the Supreme Court's 1954 decision that integrated public schools was an idea that the vast majority of Southern whites were not prepared to accept. While African Americans were jubilant over the *Brown* decision, they also understood that actual implementation of the Supreme Court's order would be infinitely more difficult to achieve, and few expected that schools which had been segregated for decades would suddenly become desegregated overnight. While some school districts outside the South did comply quickly, Southern politicians and local leaders defied the Court's ruling. By 1956 the Southern states were waging a campaign of "MASSIVE RESISTANCE" to school desegregation, and were promising to resort to whatever means were necessary to maintain segregated schools, even if it meant shutting them down. Over the next few years one Southern state after another passed a series of laws aimed at defeating *Brown.* By the early 1960s, however, the South had largely abandoned "massive resistance" in favor of other schemes that, while less confrontational, were equally effective at keeping blacks and whites in separate schools.

One of the early tactics used by Southern school districts was the Pupil Placement Boards. Created by the state legislatures, these boards operated to maintain segregation by assigning students to schools that the board considered to be in the "best interest" of the child, which almost always meant assigning black children to black schools and white children to white schools. To give the appearance of being nonracist, a board would occasionally assign a black student to a white school, but would never assign a white student to a black school. When the NATIONAL ASSOCIATION FOR THE ADVANCEMENT OF COLORED PEOPLE (NAACP) effectively challenged these placement boards in the mid-1960s, local school districts adopted "freedom of choice" plans. Despite the egalitarian-sounding phrase, freedom of choice was, for all intents and purposes, a cruel hoax that perpetuated segregation. In theory, black and white students were free to choose which school they would attend; in practice, their choice was often complicated by a variety of factors, not the least of which was centuries of deeply ingrained racial prejudice (see RACISM). White children would not voluntarily attend black schools, nor would very many black children voluntarily choose white schools—where they knew they would not be welcomed. The lack of transportation could also hamper their choice. Decades of residential SEGREGATION (both *de jure* and *de facto*) had inevitably led to separate schools, and because many localities did not provide free public school transportation, black children wishing to attend white schools often had to travel at their own expense. Furthermore, while the *students* were

Fifteen-year-old Dorothy Counts, the first black student to attend Harding High School in Charlotte, North Carolina, is chided and harassed by students on her way home from school on September 5, 1957. She is escorted by Dr. Edwin Tompkins, a family friend. (AP/Wide World Photos)

theoretically free to attend the school of their choice, teachers and staff usually were not, which meant that the schools were still racially identifiable in terms of personnel. For these reasons and more, freedom of choice was bound to fail. By 1968, more than 90 percent of the black children in the South attended schools that were predominantly black, despite several years of "free" choice.

In its first major school desegregation ruling since *Brown*, the U.S. Supreme Court ruled in *Green v. New Kent County* (1968) that ineffective freedom of choice plans could not be tolerated so long as the schools remained segregated. In *Alexander v. Holmes* (1969) the Court declared that school districts should move to desegregate "at once." In *Swann v. Charlotte-Mecklenburg* (1971) the Court unanimously approved the use of BUSING as a means of achieving desegregation, acknowledging for the first time the extent to which residential segregation had hampered efforts to integrate the schools. The *Swann* ruling—often referred to as "the busing decision"—set off a furor across the country and also ignited a national debate over the lengths that the federal judiciary should go in order to achieve a racial balance in the public schools. In a phenomenon known as "white flight," angry whites fled the cities in droves, many opting for private academies or lily-white suburban school dis-

tricts rather than allow their children to be bused into inner-city schools that were becoming increasingly African American or Hispanic. When the busing crisis erupted in Boston, Massachusetts, it became apparent that segregation and racial prejudice were not just a Southern phenomenon. In one of its last major rulings in support of school desegregation, the Court held in *Keyes v. Denver School District No. I* (1973) that schools in the North and West, like those in the South, were responsible for policies that resulted in racial segregation in the public school system. This case also recognized Hispanics' rights to desegregation as well as African Americans.

The liberal consensus that had shaped the Supreme Court for the previous twenty years ended in 1974 over the issue of metropolitan consolidation. To prevent whites from seeking refuge in white suburban school systems, some federal judges began to merge city and county schools into one consolidated system. In a five-to-four decision, the Court ruled in *Milliken v. Bradley* that a federal judge exceeded his authority in merging Detroit's predominantly black public schools with those of the surrounding white suburbs. The *Milliken* decision signaled the Court's retreat from school desegregation, and sent a clear message to white parents that they would no longer be forced to send their children to school with blacks or Hispanics. The liberal idealism of the Kennedy–Johnson years had given way to the conservative backlash of the Nixon era; four of the five Supreme Court justices voting in the *Milliken* majority were Nixon appointees.

For millions of schoolchildren across the nation, school desegregation has become a fleeting memory. Today, many of the nation's public schools have quietly resegregated, and now that the political pendulum has swung to the right, school desegregation is no longer considered a national priority. Current support for private school vouchers is growing among whites (and an increasing number of blacks), which threatens to erode further the support for public education. Since the resegregation of the 1970s, many African-American parents have become more concerned with the quality of education than with the racial composition of the school. While opinion polls continue to show that most Americans of all races support the concept of school desegregation, working to achieve that goal over the years has been a different matter. As we begin the new millennium, that reality remains elusive.

BIBLIOGRAPHY

Bass, Jack. *Unlikely Heroes: The Dramatic Story of the Southern Judges of the Fifth Circuit Who Translated the Supreme Court's Brown Decision into a Revolution for Equality.* 1981.

Douglas, Davison M. *Reading, Writing & Race: The Desegregation of the Charlotte Schools.* 1995.

Formisano, Ronald P. *Boston Against Busing: Race, Class, and Ethnicity in the 1960s and 1970s.* 1991.

Kluger, Richard. *Simple Justice: The History of Brown v. Board of Education and Black America's Struggle for Equality.* 1975.

Lukas, J. Anthony. *Common Ground: A Turbulent Decade in the Lives of Three American Families.* 1985.

Martin, Waldo E., Jr. *Brown v. Board of Education: A Brief History with Documents.* 1998.

Orfield, Gary. *Must We Bus? Segregated Schools and National Policy.* 1978.

Orfield, Gary, and Susan Eaton, and The Harvard Project on School Desegregation. *Dismantling Desegregation: The Quiet Reversal of Brown v. Board of Education.* 1996.

Pratt, Robert A. *The Color of Their Skin: Education and Race in Richmond, Virginia, 1954–89.* 1992.

Pride, Richard, and J. David Woodard. *The Burden of Busing: The Politics of Desegregation in Nashville, Tennessee.* 1985.

Schwartz, Bernard. *Swann's Way: The School Busing Case and the Supreme Court.* 1986.

Wilkinson, J. Harvie. *From Brown to Bakke: The Supreme Court and School Integration: 1954–1978.* 1979.

Robert A. Pratt

Schwerner, Michael

See the entry at CHANEY, James

SCLC

See Southern Christian Leadership Conference

Scott, Dred

See Dred Scott v. Sandford

Scottsboro Case

In Scottsboro, Alabama, in March 1931, nine black teenagers were accused of raping two white women on a freight train. Four trials took just four days. Eight of the nine black teenagers were convicted and sentenced to death. The Communist Party of the United States called the trials "legal lynchings," and announced its intention to fight in the courts and in the streets to free the "Scottsboro Boys." After fending off a challenge from the NATIONAL ASSOCIATION FOR THE ADVANCEMENT OF COLORED PEOPLE (NAACP) for control of the case, the Communist Party appealed to the Alabama Supreme Court, which upheld the convictions. But in *Powell v. Alabama* (1932), the U.S. SUPREME COURT ordered new trials, on the grounds that the defendants had been denied counsel in violation of the rights guaranteed under the equal protection clause of the FOURTEENTH AMENDMENT. The first retrial was held in April 1933. Despite a powerful defense and the recantation of one of the alleged victims, defendant Haywood Patterson was again convicted and sentenced to death. Two months later, the trial judge granted a defense motion for a new trial on the grounds that the guilty verdict contradicted the evidence. The prosecution pushed ahead, and in late 1933, Patterson and Clarence Norris were tried before a new judge, quickly convicted, and sentenced to death. In *Norris v. Alabama* (1935), the U.S. Supreme Court reversed those convictions on the grounds that black people had been excluded from juries.

There were eleven trials in all. The defendants were spared the electric chair, but they each spent between six and nineteen years in jail for a crime they did not commit. Scottsboro brought the horrors of JIM CROW justice to the attention of people all over the world, and it enouraged many white Americans to join black Americans in their long struggle for freedom and equality.

BIBLIOGRAPHY

Carter, Dan T. *Scottsboro: A Tragedy of the American South.* 1969.

Goodman, James. *Stories of Scottsboro.* 1994.

James Goodman

Left to right: Scottsboro Deputy Sheriff Charles McComb, New York defense attorney Samuel Leibowitz, and seven of the defendants in the Scottsboro case at the Scottsboro, Alabama, jailhouse on May 1, 1935. (AP/Wide World Photos)

Seale, Bobby

(1936–   ), cofounder of the Black Panther Party.

Bobby Seale was raised in Texas and Oakland, California. After high school and service in the Air Force, he attended Merritt Community College in Oakland, where, inspired by the victories of the civil rights movement in the South, he successfully led the struggle for a BLACK STUDIES curriculum. Then, working as the youth program director at the North Oakland War on Poverty Center in October 1966, Seale founded the BLACK PANTHER PARTY along with Huey P. NEWTON. The party organized armed patrols to curb police brutality. When the California state legislature introduced a bill outlawing these activities in May 1967, Seale led an armed protest at the capitol in Sacramento, announcing the Black Panther Party to the world. The party's objectives were reflected in its ten-point platform, which emphasized freedom, full employment, and equality of opportunity for African Americans.

In August 1968, Seale spoke at the Democratic National Convention in Chicago, and with seven prominent members of the white left, was arrested for inciting riot. In trial, he was bound and gagged by the judge for asserting his right to defend himself. All charges were eventually dropped and Seale became an icon of resistance to American injustice. A year later, he was arrested on charges of conspiracy to murder an FBI informant (see FEDERAL BUREAU OF INVESTIGATION). The trial in New Haven in 1970 and 1971 attracted nationwide attention as the entire student body of Yale University voted to strike and shut down the school. The National Guard attempted to quell the protest with bayonets and tanks, and Yale's president, Kingman Brewster, announced: "I am skeptical of the ability of black revolutionaries to achieve a fair trial anywhere in the United States" (*Newsweek*, May 4, 1970).

In April 1973, Seale ran for mayor of Oakland, forcing a runoff election with the white Republican incumbent. He registered tens of thousands of new voters and laid foundation for the election of Oakland's first black mayor, Lionel Wilson, in 1977—breaking a one-hundred-year cycle of white Republican Party rule.

BIBLIOGRAPHY

Seale, Bobby. *Seize the Time: The Story of the Black Panther Party and Huey P. Newton.* 1970. Reprint 1991.
Seale, Bobby. *A Lonely Rage: The Autobiography of Bobby Seale.* 1978.

Joshua Bloom

Second Amendment to the U.S. Constitution

See Right to Bear Arms

Second Amenia Conference

See Amenia Conferences

Second World War

See World War II

Segregation

Jim Crow segregation, nationally sanctioned by the 1896 SUPREME COURT decision PLESSY V. FERGUSON, was the legal and extra-legal code separating black Southerners from white Southerners and deeming all blacks worthy of second-class citizenship. The *Plessy* case, as a historical benchmark for JIM CROW legislation, ruled that "separate but equal" accommodations for black and white passengers on intrastate trains did not violate the constitutional rights of African Americans. *Plessy* set the precedent for all Jim Crow laws; as long as equal facilities were provided for blacks, racial separation could legally be enforced. Until the BROWN V. BOARD OF EDUCATION's decision in 1954 proved that

separate was inherently unequal, racial segregation was the law of the land.

Scholars have debated the origins of segregation. At the center of the debate is the "Woodward Thesis," advocated by the eminent historian of Southern history, C. Vann WOODWARD. In his groundbreaking text *The Strange Career of Jim Crow*, first published in 1957, Woodward argued that segregation was an explicit choice made by Southern whites and endorsed by conservative blacks at the turn of the twentieth century. Woodward argued against the notion that segregation was a continuation of older forms of race-based social systems, but instead posited that conservative Southerners, white populists, and the erosion of the influence of Northern white racial moderates, caused the shift toward segregation laws. Opponents of the Woodward thesis, such as historian Howard Rabinowitz, present evidence that de facto Jim Crow customs were an established part of the Southern, urban, post–Civil War landscape. Rabinowitz argued that the passage of Jim Crow laws at the close of the nineteenth century merely transformed widely propagated customs into law. But beyond the debate over the origins of segregation, the passage of segregation laws in the 1890s limited the possibilities for black Southerners at the turn of the century.

Segregation had its roots in Northern cities before the EMANCIPATION, but Jim Crow law eventually became closely intertwined with Southern life. From the 1890s to the 1960s, Jim Crow law crosscut the Southern landscape with many formal rules that lim-

A black man enters a movie theater in Belzoni, Mississippi, by the "colored" entrance in October 1930. (Library of Congress)

Four African-American boys seated at row desks in an all-black school in Missouri, ca. 1930. (CORBIS/ Bettmann)

ited the societal possibilities of black life. The first battles over the most conspicuous forms of Jim Crow began with the public affronts that black Southerners received at public accommodations and on public transportation. Intrastate and interstate travel throughout the South was segregated and provided black Southerners with unequal and inadequate facilities. Even bus and train stations were divided by race, with separate entrances and waiting rooms for black patrons. Blacks were barred from white hotels and restaurants, so black travelers had to make careful plans for food and lodging. In addition to not being welcome at privately owned public facilities, African Americans were also barred from white public parks, pools, and beaches throughout the South. These constant reminders of blacks' status made public facilities the object of public and hidden black resistance.

Blacks of all classes and backgrounds were barred not only from the white sections of buses and trains but also from HOUSING designated for whites only. Tax-paying Southern blacks were provided with inferior schools, few public facilities, and insufficient roads, electricity, and sewage in black communities. Conditions at most black schools throughout the Jim Crow South were substandard; from secondhand, outdated textbooks to inadequate facilities, most black schoolchildren received second-class treatment. Black housing and land ownership were often restricted by both legal and extra-legal means. In Southern towns blacks were often railroaded into marginal neighborhoods where the conditions of the streets and sewage were substandard. In more rural areas, blacks' attempts to own land and small businesses were often undercut by unfair lending practices or by threats of

violence. However, black neighborhoods often provided needed community cohesion in the face of white hostility.

Segregation also politically marginalized black citizens. Disfranchisement was the norm in most communities for African Americans; thus most blacks were not represented at the polls and received unfair treatment in courts with all-white voter registration–based jury trials. But segregation also took on extra-legal dimensions. Informal racial mores also allowed many white citizens to call African Americans by pet names such as "boy," "Uncle," or "Auntie," never as "Mr." or "Mrs.," "Sir" or "Ma'am." The implied etiquette of Jim Crow even forced black pedestrians to step off the sidewalk and into the gutter when whites wanted the right-of-way and made black men look at the ground rather than gaze directly into the face of any white woman. In all, segregation sanctioned an unwritten code of extreme white domination that served to destabilize the tenuous hold black Americans had on CITIZENSHIP.

Segregation also constricted the economic possibilities for black workers (see EMPLOYMENT). Often whites discouraged independence or entrepreneurial spirit, preferring that blacks be limited to working for others. Often black workers held the dirtiest, most dangerous, and least desirable positions because these jobs were designated as appropriate for them. Newly opened plants and mills in the South often excluded blacks entirely or segregated workers within plant facilities. Even the better opportunities open to blacks at federal shipyards and army bases were often racially divided, with the better jobs reserved for white workers. Black professionals who provided services to black customers, mostly in more urban communities, often did much better than blacks who were forced to work outside the African-American community.

This is not to assert, however, that Jim Crow was an exclusively regional phenomenon. Segregated housing and schooling were often the norms in Northern states as well. Segregation within the federal government—encouraged first by Theodore Roosevelt and institutionalized by Woodrow Wilson in the 1910s—was not dismantled until the 1940s. Despite Franklin D. ROOSEVELT's somewhat progressive approach to racial politics, he sent segregated troops to Europe during WORLD WAR II. Only pressure from black activists at home resulted in FDR's Executive Order 8802, which increased black employment opportunities in defense plants yet failed to address segregation within the military (see ARMED FORCES). The activism of black soldiers after both world wars put pressure on the government's claims that it was an advanced and equitable nation. America's armed forces were not desegregated until Harry S. TRUMAN issued an executive

order barring discrimination in July 1948 (see President's Committee on Civil Rights).

Through collective boycotts at the turn of the century, to both hidden and public acts of defiance
throughout the twentieth century, African Americans
continuously challenged the limits of legal segregation. The National Association for the Advancement of Colored People (NAACP), an integrated
coalition of activists founded in 1909, agitated almost
continuously against the injustice of the "separate but
equal" doctrine. As both a national body and as local
chapters that emerged throughout the South, the
NAACP served as a consistent force of opposition to
the inherent inequality of segregation. The NAACP
was not the only organization to challenge segregation
law; countless black unions, civic leagues, voter organizations, and black nationalist groups throughout the
United States protested the injustices of Jim Crow legislation. And despite the all-encompassing nature of
Southern segregation, black life did exist beyond the
bounds of Jim Crow. From the turn of the twentieth
century to the birth of the modern civil rights movement, African Americans, using both hidden and public forms of subversion, resisted the rules that made
them second-class citizens. Countering the restrictive
limits of the Jim Crow South, black people sustained
vital lives and established autonomous institutions outside the white-dominated public sphere. These activities, however, have not mitigated the fact that segregation was a very real dividing line that did place a
lesser value on black life and did attempt to demean
black people on a daily basis.

BIBLIOGRAPHY

Cell, John W. *The Highest Stage of White Supremacy: The Origins of Segregation in South Africa and the American South.*
1982.

Johnson, Charles S. *Patterns of Negro Segregation.* 1943.

Litwack, Leon F. *Trouble in Mind: Black Southerners in the
Age of Jim Crow.* 1998.

Rabinowitz, Howard N. *Race Relations in the Urban South,
1865–1890.* 1978.

Woodward, C. Vann. *The Strange Career of Jim Crow.* 1957.

Blair L. Murphy

Sellers, Cleveland "Cleve"

(1944–), Black Power advocate and SNCC
program director.

Sellers advocated Black Power as Program Director
of the Student Nonviolent Coordinating Committee (SNCC) and was charged by the government
of South Carolina with being the major instigator of
the Orangeburg Massacre in 1968.

Growing up in Denmark, South Carolina, Sellers
became an active civil rights proponent through the
influence of Rev. Henry Grant, Rector of St. Philips
Episcopal Church at Voorhees College. In 1962, Sellers left Denmark to attend Howard University, where
he became deeply involved in SNCC and its evolution
into a major civil rights organization. After experiencing the brutality of white resistance during Freedom
Summer, as well as the failure of the Mississippi Freedom Democratic Party at the 1964 Democratic National Convention, Sellers joined a group of SNCC
members who pushed for tighter internal organization and open advocacy of Black Power. Exhausted by
the resulting tensions within SNCC and growing external opposition to Black Power, Sellers enrolled at
South Carolina State College in Orangeburg in 1967.

In February 1968, Sellers was wounded by police
gunfire as he attempted to flee a campus demonstration against a segregated bowling alley. Although he
did not plan the rally and was not physically present
until its bloody and deadly conclusion (which left
three dead and thirty wounded), he was convicted for
inciting the incident and sentenced to prison. After
his release from prison, Sellers completed his bachelor's, master's, and doctoral degrees. South Carolina
pardoned him for his conviction in 1993. He lives in
Denmark, S.C., and teaches African American History
at the University of South Carolina.

BIBLIOGRAPHY

Marsh, Charles. "Cleveland Sellers and the River of No
Return." In *God's Long Summer: Stories of Faith and Civil
Rights.* 1997.

Sellers, Cleveland, with Robert Terrell. *The River of No
Return: The Autobiography of a Black Militant and the Life
and Death of SNCC.* 1973.

Stephen C. Messer

Senior Rights

Rising birthrate trends after World War II, coupled
with increasing life expectancy, contributed to a rapidly growing aged population in the United States toward the end of the twentieth century. Correspond-
ingly, laws recognizing senior rights grew in
socio-political importance. Historically, U.S. common
law did not distinguish senior citizens as a separate
group. As with other age groups, competency factors
normally prevailed. However, national social programs
have expanded a set of special rights recognizing the
unique needs and limitations of the elderly. Because
aging is clearly an individual process, the definition of
"senior" must be culturally derived. The age 65, first
identified by Social Security as the age to fully qualify

Roslyn Wolf of Queens, N.Y., holds a life preserver that says "Save Medicare" while watching the House vote on passage of new Medicare legislation on October 19, 1995. (AP/Wide World Photos)

for pensions, is commonly accepted as the threshold when mental alertness, health, physical endurance, strength and flexibility, and the senses generally decline.

Three of the more visible rights accorded seniors are rights to retirement income, access to medical care, and protection from workplace discrimination. However, public discourse over senior rights has grown to span a broad spectrum of issues including: private pension benefits; application of legal tort rules; punishment and continued imprisonment of elderly offenders; the influence of senile dementia on legal capacity and responsibility; medical decisions at the end of life; shielding the elderly from bankruptcy; the legal rights of grandparents; medical experimentation on demented patients; and rights of persons confined to nursing care against their will but without court orders. New special accommodation accorded seniors was exemplified by the 1995 Housing for Older Persons Act, which exempted senior housing from certain FAIR HOUSING ACT requirements. The Act granted the right of seniors to live in communities specially catering to their needs and excluding other segments of society.

Social Security—officially known as Old Age, Survivors and Disability Insurance—was born as part of the NEW DEAL in the 1930s to combat poverty among the elderly during the Depression era. Though not without critics, the elderly's right to an income into retirement continued to enjoy a broad-based support through the later twentieth century. Intense demands for reform by the end of the century were largely driven by concerns over the program's long-term financial viability. The recognized right to a retirement income was eventually extended to private employer pension plans by passage of the 1974 Employees Retirement Income Security Act; a Supplemental Security Income program provides additional cash for particularly needy seniors. Prior to 1965, most seniors had no health insurance. To address this dire situation in the face of rapidly rising medical costs, Congress passed the Social Security Amendments of 1965, introducing Medicare, a federally subsidized acute care health insurance for those 65 years and older. By the 1990s, all but 3 percent of seniors enjoyed the right to participate in Medicare. The courts have upheld that competent elderly adults also have the right to refuse life-sustaining medical treatment.

In part an outgrowth of the African-American civil rights movement, AGE DISCRIMINATION, or ageism, grew in public concern. Efforts to include ageism prohibitions in the CIVIL RIGHTS ACT OF 1964 failed, but Congress did mandate a study on the subject. The resulting 1965 report noted widespread ageism based on inaccurate stereotypes and outlined the numerous problems aging citizens faced in retaining employment. In response, Congress passed the Age Discrimination in Employment Act (ADEA) of 1967, banning discrimination by employers against employees or job applicants over 40 years of age. Later amendments to the sweeping piece of legislation eliminated the mandatory retirement age. A key exception in ADEA to the prohibition against workplace age discrimination is the Bona Fide Occupational Qualification (BFOQ) provision, by which age limitations may be demonstrated as reasonably necessary by an employer for business operation. Quickly becoming the focus of key court cases involving ADEA, the courts upheld the appropriateness of BFOQ in such cases as *Western Air Lines, Inc. v. Criswell* (1985).

As the American population grows older, rights for those with declining mental capacities, such as dementia, have risen in prominence. Not only do seniors have a right to court-appointed guardianship to protect their personal interests, but advocates argue that senior wards also have a right through adequate safeguards to be protected from abuse of the guardianship system. To protect these existing rights and fight for the recognition of others, numerous organizations have grown through the years. The most visible and one of the more powerful lobbying groups in Washington, D.C., is the AMERICAN ASSOCIATION OF RETIRED PERSONS (AARP). A newly recognized branch of law, known as elder law, emerged associated with formation of the National Academy of Elder Law Attorneys and publication of the *Elder Law Journal.*

BIBLIOGRAPHY

American Association of Retired Persons. Website: http://www.aarp.org.

American Bar Association. *Legal Guide for Older Americans: The Law Every American over Fifty Needs to Know.* 1998.

Frolik, Lawrence A., ed. *Aging and the Law: An Interdisciplinary Reader.* 1999.

Millman, Linda J. *Legal Issues and Older Adults.* 1992.

National Senior Citizens Law Center. *Representing Older Persons: An Advocate's Manual.* 1990.

Posner, Richard A. *Aging and Old Age.* 1995.

Strauss, Peter J., Robert Wolf, and Dana Shilling. *Aging and the Law.* 1990.

Richard C. Hanes

Servicemen's Riots of 1943

See Zoot-Suit Riots

Sexism

The civil rights movement helped fuel social consciousness of sexism. As is true of other minority groups, women have historically been victims of cultural stereotyping. Up until the twentieth century women were often viewed as the property of their husbands or other male consorts. In light of this, women's rights were blatantly overlooked in the law, and it was not until the 1960s that women began to successfully fight against sexual discrimination and harassment, using the very laws that had previously neglected them.

During the 1960s increasing numbers of young women, rejecting traditional women's roles, were entering jobs in factory and office, but on average they earned only 57 percent of male wages. Women were further shortchanged by labor laws passed at the turn of the century that prevented women from working overtime; moreover women were frequently required to work the lowest-paying, most menial jobs. Female activists sought to change conditions in the workplace by appealing to the courts under the equal protection clause of the FOURTEENTH AMENDMENT. In 1963, the Equal Pay Act (EPA) became an amendment to the Fair Labor Standards Act of 1938 and served to raise society's consciousness of sexual discrimination as a legitimate issue for all women. The 1963 victory worked to level the playing field of the workplace. Representative Katherine St. George (R-N.Y.) perfected the compromise language of the EPA to read "equal pay for equal work," which aided in the bill's acceptance. The bill was also successful because it specifically prohibited men's wages from being lowered. Instead, the bill made sure that women would be paid the exact amount as men for comparable jobs.

The EPA enabled women to become more visible in society and guaranteed them protection under the law. Prior to this amendment, a woman's autonomy was in no way protected; her job could be taken away without notice; she could be paid less for performing the same job that others performed; she could be refused a job for no reason. By 1964 newfound protection came to women in the form of the inclusion of discrimination based on sex to TITLE VII OF THE 1964 CIVIL RIGHTS ACT. The inclusion protected women from all the injustices that could occur when they interviewed or were hired for a job, such as an employer's refusal to hire based on sex, discrimination in discharge, discrimination in training programs, and sexually stereotyped advertisements relating to employment. In other words, the CIVIL RIGHTS ACT OF 1964 prohibited any form of discrimination in the workplace based on a person's sex. However, the federal agency established to enforce this law, the Equal Employment Opportunity Commission (EEOC), failed to act on behalf of women for most of the 1960s. But by 1973, under a new set of administrators, the EEOC had filed 147 suits, and occupational barriers against women began to fall. Congress passed a series of laws reinforcing this ban on sex discrimination; women even succeeded in gaining a tax deduction for child-care in families where both parents worked. Another law, the Pregnancy Discrimination Act (PDA), was passed in 1978 to protect women's rights in the workplace; it prohibited discrimination against women based on pregnancy, childbirth, or related medical conditions. As pregnancy is a condition unique to women, it was not previously protected under a traditional short-term disability insurance program. The PDA was a reaction to the *General Electric Co. v. Gilbert* case, where an employer refused to grant pregnancy disability benefits under the company's otherwise all-inclusive benefits program, and the court found that the pregnancy was not covered under Title VII. The PDA serves to reinforce women's job security and protect their benefits during pregnancy or if related health problems arise during one.

Soon after the passage of Title VII of the Civil Rights Act of 1964, AFFIRMATIVE ACTION policies were adopted by employers and these were quickly used by women to gain jobs as well as economic equality. Almost immediately, however, there was significant public backlash when white males were passed over for women and minorities, and plaintiffs filed "reverse discrimination" suits. In most cases, the courts agreed with the plaintiffs, and at present the number of affirmative action programs has greatly decreased.

Women's battle for respect in the workplace has proven to be ongoing. A 1980 study of federal employees found that 42 percent of women claimed to be victims of sexual harassment in the workplace. The key elements in deciding a sexual harassment case in court, as defined by the EEOC, are the conditions of whether the sexual advancements are unwelcome and if they contribute to creating a hostile work environment. A hostile environment is a place where the alleged victim is unable to successfully perform a job because he or she suffers physical or psychological harm in the workplace. In *Meritor Savings Bank v. Vinson*, the U.S. Supreme Court upheld the concept of a hostile work environment as actionable under the Civil Rights Act of 1964. A romantic relationship in the workplace is one that can be consensual, but often such intimacies may instead be relationships based on power and intimidation with a superior making sexual advances toward an inferior. In the *Meritor* case, Mechelle Vinson agreed to have sex with her male supervisor out of fear of losing her job, which contributed to a hostile work environment.

In 1991, the controversial Clarence Thomas and Anita Hill hearings helped raise awareness of sexual harassment in the workplace. During Supreme Court justice Clarence Thomas's Senate confirmation hearings, Anita Hill accused Thomas of sexual harassment while under his employ from 1981 to 1983. The nationally televised hearings were watched by a large audience, which demonstrated the nerve the subject struck in the United States. The media attention generated by these hearings not only made women across the nation more aware of sexual harassment, but also spurred women's groups to demand further changes in the workplace. Many employers, realizing their potential liability from sexual harassment claims, have tried to prevent the occurrence of sexual harassment altogether by publishing employee handbooks based on the EEOC definition of it and establishing an "open door" policy, which creates a supportive and nonthreatening environment for the alleged victim to seek help. Some companies even conduct informal employee surveys, inspect the workplace for objectionable material, and train supervisors to recognize sexual harassment.

BIBLIOGRAPHY

Brock, David. *The Real Anita Hill.* New York. 1993.
Morrison, Toni, ed. *Race-ing Justice, Engendering Power.* New York. 1992.
Siegler, Jay A. *Civil Rights in America: 1500 to the Present.* Detroit, MI: Gale Research. 1988.
Toobin, Jeffrey. "The Burden of Clarence Thomas." *New Yorker* (Sept. 27, 1993): 38–51.

Christy Wood

Shaw v. Reno (1993)

In *Shaw v. Reno* (1993), the United States SUPREME COURT reviewed a North Carolina congressional redistricting scheme to determine whether two of its congressional districts, CD 1 and CD 12, constituted racial gerrymanders contrary to the Equal Protection Clause of the FOURTEENTH AMENDMENT.

Shaw was significant for a number of reasons. First, it created a new constitutional cause of action. Prior to *Shaw*, plaintiffs could raise two types of voting rights claims: (1) claims that they were being deprived of their right to vote; and (2) claims that their votes were being diluted by being submerged beneath the votes of the statistical or white majority. These two types of voting rights actions were exercised, predominantly, by minority plaintiffs, vote dilution claims being reserved exclusively to minorities. In *Shaw*, a third type of voting rights claim was created, one which provided a constitutional right to a colorblind electoral process. This action was available to plaintiffs of any race.

By creating a constitutional right to a colorblind electoral process, allowing plaintiffs to raise equal protection challenges against states that had separated voters into electoral districts on the basis of race, the Court had arguably created a cause of action antithetical to its vote dilution jurisprudence.

Prior to *Shaw*, the remedy of choice for advocates of affirmative action in voting rights was the creation of majority-minority districts (MMDs), districts in which roughly 65 percent of the voting-age population was comprised of a minority. MMDs promoted the election of minority preferred candidates by creating an electoral mass in a district sufficient to ensure that minority votes would not be outweighed by nonminority votes. North Carolina's CD 1 and CD 12 were MMDs.

Many advocates of affirmative action in voting rights believe that MMDs are essential to providing for effective representation of minorities in state and federal elections. Without the creation of such districts, minorities will not get elected to office in numbers sufficiently representative of their numbers in the electorate.

MMDs pose a significant constitutional problem, however, since they require states to take race into account in drafting electoral district boundaries. In *Shaw*, the plaintiffs had challenged CD 1 and CD 12, both bizarrely shaped, particularly the latter, on grounds the districts were so irregular they could only be understood as an attempt to segregate racial groups for the purposes of voting. The Supreme Court agreed with the plaintiffs but left ambiguous whether the *Shaw* ruling only applied to bizarre-shaped districts. In *Miller v. Johnson* (1995), the Court clarified that the *Shaw* ruling was not limited to bizarre-shaped districts but applied any time race could be established as the predominant factor in the drafting of an electoral district.

Perhaps the most significant implication of *Shaw*, then, was that it may have spelled the end to affirmative action in voting rights. Specifically, would it be possible, following *Shaw* and *Miller*, to create MMDs without using race as a predominant factor in the creation of such districts, thus running afoul of the equal protection requirements of the Constitution? The answer to this question will likely have to await the next round of congressional redistricting.

BIBLIOGRAPHY

Bierstein, Andrea. "Millennium Approaches: The Future of the Voting Rights Act After *Shaw, De Grandy,* and *Holder. Hastings L. J.* 46 (1995): 1457.

Guinier, Lani. *The Tyranny of the Majority: Fundamental Fairness in Representative Democracy.* 1994.

Miller v. Johnson, S.Ct. 2475 (1995).

Peacock, Anthony A., ed. *Affirmative Action and Representation: Shaw v. Reno and the Future of Voting Rights.* 1997.

Pildes, Richard H., and Richard G. Niemi. "Expressive Harms, 'Bizarre District,' and Voting Rights: Evaluating Election-District Appearances After *Shaw v. Reno.*" *Michigan L. Rev.* 92 (1993): 483.

Shaw v. Reno, 509 U.S. 630 (1993) (*Shaw I*).

Shaw v. Hunt, 517 U.S. 899 (1996) (*Shaw II*).

"Symposium: The Voting Rights Act After *Shaw v. Reno.*" *PS: Political Science and Politics* 28 (March 1995) 1: 24.

Thernstrom, Abigail M. *Whose Votes Count? Affirmative Action and Minority Voting Rights.* 1987.

Anthony A. Peacock

Shuttlesworth, Fred L.

(1922–   ), civil rights leader.

The Rev. Fred Shuttlesworth, a legendary figure in the civil rights movement, was born in Montgomery County, Alabama. After pursuing theological studies at Selma University, Shuttlesworth was named pastor of Birmingham Bethel Baptist Church in 1953. He immediately became active in the ALABAMA activities of the NATIONAL ASSOCIATION FOR THE ADVANCEMENT OF COLORED PEOPLE (NAACP). When the state outlawed the NAACP in 1956, Shuttlesworth founded the ALABAMA CHRISTIAN MOVEMENT FOR HUMAN RIGHTS (ACMHR), which he affiliated with Rev. Martin Luther

KING JR.'s SOUTHERN CHRISTIAN LEADERSHIP CONFERENCE (SCLC). Shuttlesworth led ACMHR in protests on behalf of VOTING RIGHTS and school DESEGREGATION. He persisted even after his home was destroyed by a bomb set by members of the KU KLUX KLAN on Christmas night in 1956, and he was beaten when he attempted to enroll his children in an all-white school in 1957. State authorities also harassed Shuttlesworth. In 1961, his car was impounded by Alabama authorities to help satisfy a judgment for libel against SCLC trumped up by state authorities in court. The same year, he was forced to serve a jail term for violating a bus segregation ordinance, though the law was found unconstitutional.

In 1963, Shuttlesworth persuaded King to make Birmingham the center of civil rights protest, and he led nonviolent marchers through downtown areas. The violent police reaction they experienced led to landmark federal legislation on civil rights. Shuttlesworth also headed SCLC protests in St. Augustine, Florida, in 1964, and Selma, Alabama, in 1965. He continued civil rights organizing in later years. In 1995, he gained widespread attention when he led a demonstration at the home of African-American Supreme Court Justice Clarence Thomas.

BIBLIOGRAPHY

Branch, Taylor. *Parting the Waters: America in the King Years, 1954–1963.* 1988.

Manis, Andrew Michael. *A Fire You Can't Put Out: The Civil Rights Life of Birmingham's Reverend Fred Shuttlesworth.* 1999.

Greg Robinson

Simkins, Mary Modjeska Monteith

(1899–1992), civil rights activist.

Modjeska Simkins was the eldest of eight children born to Henry Clarence Monteith and Rachel Evelyn Hull Monteith of Columbia, South Carolina. She was named for her aunt Mary and for a Polish actress, Helena Modjeska. She attended Benedict College's school from first grade through the completion of high school and remained there until she finished college in 1921. She pursued further study at Morehouse College (summer school), Columbia University, Eastern Michigan University, and the University of Michigan, Ann Arbor. Benedict College awarded her the Doctor of Laws degree in 1990.

Her first full-time job was a teaching position in the teacher-training division of Benedict College; shortly thereafter, she found employment as a teacher at the Booker T. Washington School in Columbia. After she married Andrew Whitfield Simkins in December 1929, she was not permitted to return to teaching because married women could not be employed in the public schools. Through her family's contacts, she landed a position as Director of Negro Work for the South Carolina Tuberculosis Association in 1931. She remained there until 1942, when her contract was not renewed as a result of her political activities for the cause of civil rights for black Americans. In the mid-1950s, after a long stint of full-time volunteerism, she began working at the Victory Savings Bank—the only black-owned bank in South Carolina—where several of her family members held key positions. She was a teller and a branch manager at Victory Savings, and she served on its board of directors for many years.

Throughout her long years of public service, Simkins was active in more than fifty progressive and reform organizations. She was a founding member of the South Carolina Conference of the NATIONAL ASSOCIATION FOR THE ADVANCEMENT OF COLORED PEOPLE (NAACP), the SOUTHERN REGIONAL COUNCIL, the SOUTHERN CONFERENCE FOR HUMAN WELFARE, and the Richland County Citizens Committee, as well as the Southern Organizing Committee, which she served for more than fifty years.

In 1942, Simkins was elected state secretary of the South Carolina Conference of the NAACP, a position she maintained until 1957. During this period, major projects undertaken by the organization were lawsuits on behalf of black citizens, and Mrs. Simkins was in the forefront of this activity. In 1951 the South Carolina Conference filed *Briggs v. Elliott* as a full attack on segregation in Columbia's public schools. Simkins was a major motivating power behind the lawsuit. Much of the groundwork for the court case was done in her home at her dining room table. *Briggs* became one of the desegregation suits collectively heard by the Supreme Court in 1954 as BROWN V. BOARD OF EDUCATION.

After 1957, Simkins's projects in South Carolina were channeled mainly through the Richland County Citizens Committee (RCCC), an offshoot of the South Carolina Citizens Committee and which had been organized by members of the South Carolina NAACP in 1944. A major success of the organization was the improvement of living conditions for black mental health patients at South Carolina's state-supported hospital. As public relations director of the RCCC, Simkins sponsored a weekly program on WOIC radio station. Her slogan for these programs was "I woke up this morning with my mind set on freedom."

Throughout her long career, Mrs. Simkins sought to foster the development of real competition among political parties. In her youth, she worked with the REPUBLICAN PARTY and, for a short time in 1947, the National Progressive Party (see PROGRESSIVE PARTY

[1948]). Later she shifted her allegiance to the DEMOCRATIC PARTY. She also supported two third-party movements in South Carolina: those of the Progressive Democratic Party (1940s) and the United Citizens Party (1970s). She was given the title of "Honorary Lifetime President" of the United Citizens Party. Simkins left an indelible imprint on the lives she touched, and she made major contributions to the struggle for full democracy for all American citizens.

BIBLIOGRAPHY
Aba-Mecha, Barbara Woods. *Black Woman Activist in Twentieth Century South Carolina: Modjeska Monteith Simkins.* 1978.
Beardsley, Edward H. *A History of Neglect: Health Care for Blacks and Mill Workers in the Twentieth-Century South.* 1987.
Reed, Linda. *Simple Decency and Common Sense: The Southern Conference Movement, 1938–1963.* 1991.

Barbara A. Woods

Singleton, Benjamin ("Pap")

(c. 1809–1892), promoter of black migration.

Born into slavery in Nashville, Tennessee, Benjamin "Pap" Singleton became a central figure in the massive migration of poor Southern blacks to KANSAS with the onset of REDEMPTION in the 1870s. Confronted with escalating violence and disfranchisement, and fearing re-enslavement, multitudes of rural African Americans, called EXODUSTERS, fled the old Confederate states in a quest for freedom and self-sufficiency as homesteaders in the West. While this exodus was largely unplanned, spontaneous, and without formal leadership, Singleton's work as a land promoter and founder of several black colonies in KANSAS was instrumental in spurring the migration, which reached its apex in 1879. Believing that he was directed by God to lead blacks out of the South, Singleton began traveling throughout Kentucky, Tennessee, and Mississippi in 1873, advertising resettlement through his Edgefield Real Estate and Homestead Association. The best known of the association's settlements were the Cherokee Colony (1875) in southeastern Kansas and the Singleton Colony (1878) near Topeka.

In contrast to the integrationist vision of equality and civil rights held by black REPUBLICAN PARTY leaders, Singleton believed that only segregated communities could ensure black freedom. As with many freedpeople, land ownership was central to Singleton's understanding of freedom as it signaled relief from white surveillance and coerced labor. His work was a response to the failure of the federal and state governments to protect the civil rights of African Americans in the South. Ultimately, he would promote black MI-GRATION out of the United States altogether, forming the United Trans-Atlantic Society in 1885.

BIBLIOGRAPHY

Athearn, Robert. *In Search of Canaan: Black Migration to Kansas, 1879–1880.* 1978.

Bontemps, Arna, and Jack Conroy. *They Seek a City.* 1945. Reprint, 1966. Reprint, 1997.

Garvin, Roy. "Benjamin or 'Pap' Singleton and His Followers." *Journal of Negro History* 33 (1948): 7–23.

Painter, Nell Irvin. *Exodusters: Black Migration to Kansas After Reconstruction.* 1976. With new introduction, 1986.

Micki McElya

Sit-Ins

The student sit-in movement of the early 1960s galvanized the civil rights movement and provided a new tactic for mass action. On February 1, 1960, four black freshmen from North Carolina A&T went to the Woolworth's store in Greensboro, sat down at the whites-only lunch counter and demanded service. Although this was not the first use of the sit-in in the South, in this case the store manager did not call in the police to have the students arrested, nor were they served. The four remained at the counter until the store closed and came back the next day with reinforcements. Soon black students occupied every seat at the lunch counter, effectively shutting down the business until they finally (six months later) were served.

This sit-in commanded widespread national attention and galvanized a student-led movement throughout the South. Within a week, black students had initiated sit-ins in Durham and Winston-Salem, North Carolina. Soon they spread to Nashville, Tallahassee, Montgomery, and Atlanta. Within two months, sit-ins had taken place in 125 cities in nine states. The students not only came up with a new strategy to protest at sites that excluded blacks, a powerful tool when boycotting was not an obvious option, but also provided momentum for a movement that had seemed to stall after its victory in the MONTGOMERY BUS BOYCOTT in 1956.

Sit-ins sent the message that young blacks were not content with the status quo in the South and that they were willing to organize in their own communities for change. In protesting against the demeaning forms of SEGREGATION that affected them in their everyday lives, they attacked the whole JIM CROW system with its stigma of black inferiority. But the sit-in movement surprised observers, who wondered what had led black college students, a group generally regarded as conformist and conservative, to embrace protest. Some saw the target of the sit-ins, the right to eat at lunch counters with whites, as an expression of the young blacks' assimilationist and middle-class orientation. Indeed, the young protesters were careful to express their support for American values and political insti-

A sit-in is held at the Toddle House Coffee Shop in Atlanta, Georgia, in 1963.
(Danny Lyons/Magnum Photos, Inc.)

tutions and to present a positive image of blacks. Inspired by advocates of nonviolence such as James LAWSON and Martin Luther KING, JR., black students who organized sit-ins followed a strict code of protest. They dressed well, were nonviolent, and refused to counterattack even when provoked by white violence. A handout developed by the Nashville students summarized their code: "Do show yourself friendly on the counter at all times. Do sit straight and always face the counter. Don't strike back, or curse back if attacked. . . . " Many students were attacked, as white demonstrators spat on them, threw food at them, and beat them. Police often used tear gas to clear out local stores and had the students arrested. By August 1961, nearly 70,000 blacks and sympathetic whites had participated in sit-ins. Some 3,600 had been jailed. Soon sit-ins would spread beyond lunch counters to target other segregated public spaces, such as libraries, movie theaters, and beaches, where students held "swim-ins," "wade-ins," and "read-ins."

The sit-in movement succeeded in ending segregation at lunch counters in many places in the South, especially in the border states. Over eighty cities, including Nashville and San Antonio, opened their facilities to blacks as a result of the sit-ins. Chain stores proved particularly vulnerable to the tactic. The Greensboro Woolworth's, the site of the first sit-in, agreed to serve blacks within six months. By the end of 1961, the entire Woolworth chain had changed its policy to serve blacks.

But the sit-in movement was even more important for the organization it inspired. In April 1960, two months after sit-ins erupted across the South, Ella BAKER, the executive director of the SOUTHERN CHRISTIAN LEADERSHIP CONFERENCE (SCLC), invited the leaders of the student movement to one of its meetings. There the students decided to form a new organization, the STUDENT NONVIOLENT COORDINATING COMMITTEE (SNCC), which would be independent of older civil rights organizations such as the SCLC. In the ensuing years, SNCC would develop new theories of group-centered leadership that would challenge the charismatic leadership model of Martin Luther King, Jr., and the SCLC. The new group continued direct action through sit-ins and other protests but also began a campaign of voter registration. Moving into communities in the Deep South, most notably in the Mississippi Delta, SNCC field workers did the slow and dangerous work of fostering local leadership and building grassroots momentum for civil rights. Over time SNCC became one of the most militant and radical of all the civil rights organizations. What began as a fight for a cup of coffee led to the development of a new political consciousness among many young blacks.

BIBLIOGRAPHY
Bond, Julian, and Andrew Lewis, eds. *Gonna Sit at the Welcome Table.* 1995.
Carson, Clay. *In Struggle: SNCC and the Black Awakening of the 1960s.* 1981.
Chafe, William. *Civilities and Civil Rights: Greensboro, North Carolina, and the Black Struggle for Freedom.* 1981.
Raines, Howell, ed. *My Soul Is Rested: Movement Days in the Deep South Remembered.* 1977.

Renee Romano

Sleeping Car Porters

See Brotherhood of Sleeping Car Porters

Smith, Howard Worth

(1883–1976), congressman.

Howard W. Smith, a self-described "reactionary" and opponent of civil rights, was born in Broad Run, Virginia. After attending Law School at the University of Virginia and serving as a lawyer and state judge, Smith was elected to the U.S. House of Representatives from Virginia in 1932. He soon became a notorious opponent of NEW DEAL welfare and labor legislation, which he considered unconstitutional. He also organized segregationist opposition to civil rights legislation, and opposed all attempts to ban poll taxes and LYNCHING. Smith was also an outspoken advocate of NATIVISM. In 1939, he introduced a bill to deport any alien who "advised a change" in the American form of government or engaged in domestic political activity. Although these provisions were later deleted, the Smith Act, passed in 1940, provided for registration and fingerprinting of all aliens and made it a federal crime to advocate the violent overthrow of the U.S. government.

In 1954, Smith became chairman of the House Rules Committee. During the following years, he repeatedly used his powers to block or delay civil rights bills and was notorious for making quorum calls, scheduling hearings, and adding amendments in order to wear down opposition. In 1957, Smith concealed himself for ten days in order to delay Rules Committee consideration of a civil rights act. Ironically, Smith introduced the amendment banning gender discrimination in employment to the CIVIL RIGHTS ACT OF 1964 in hopes of defeating the Act, but its passage helped spark the modern Women's Rights Movement (see WOMEN AND CIVIL RIGHTS STRUGGLES). Smith retired after being defeated in a congressional primary in 1966.

BIBLIOGRAPHY

Dierenfield, Bruce J. *Keeper of the Rules: Congressman Howard W. Smith of Virginia.* 1987.

Smith, Howard Worth. *Our Paternal Hearth.* 1976.

Greg Robinson

Smith, Lillian

(1897–1966), novelist, civil rights advocate.

Lillian Smith used the written word to distinguish herself as a literary activist who became one of the most vociferous critics of racial SEGREGATION among white Southern liberals. Best known for her *Strange Fruit* (1944), a best-selling novel about the psychological damage wrought by segregation, Smith wrote numerous other books and countless articles condemning racial injustice over the course of four decades. *Strange Fruit*'s publication marked the beginning of Smith's career as a nationally known figure in an emerging civil rights movement. But long before the work's publication, and long after, Smith employed her gifts as a writer to indict the racial status quo.

Smith was born in Jasper, Florida, and lived the greatest part of her life in small communities in the Deep South. The seventh of nine children, she grew up in a respected, prosperous family where she learned the values that many Southern children of her day received from their parents: the importance of religion; the virtues of democracy; and the rituals of racial segregation. Smith often wrote of the painful segregation she experienced growing up: her parents' RACISM forced upon her a separation from the black people she came to love during the early years of her childhood. Other experiences deepened that pain. A well-trained musician who attended the Peabody Conservatory in Baltimore, Smith left the United States in 1922 to teach music at a Methodist Mission school in China, where she watched missionaries demean the very people they meant to convert.

When she returned to the United States in 1925, Smith became a director of the Laurel Falls Camp for Girls, a camp her father had founded nearly a decade earlier in Clinton, Georgia. Smith remained director of the camp until 1948, but other passions demanded her attention. She began to read extensively about children, psychology, and racism, and she began to write fiction that explored many of her intellectual interests and concerns. In 1935, Smith founded the *North Georgia Review*. The journal quickly gave her a public forum to articulate a critique of JIM CROW that grew increasingly militant over time.

In 1938, she began work on *Strange Fruit*, a book that served both as fiction and as a psychological study of WHITE SUPREMACY. Though her main characters were an interracial couple, Smith seemed more interested in the white people who inhabited fictional Maxwell, Georgia. The author's attention to the details of Southern life took her reader past the facades that masked the evils of segregation and plumbed the depths of racial anxiety. Smith's other works, most notably *Killers of the Dream* (1949), addressed similar themes from a more autobiographical perspective. Her work shook readers nationwide, including Eleanor ROOSEVELT and J. Waites WARING, both longtime, powerful civil rights advocates.

Smith never limited her activism to the printed page. In 1946, she joined the advisory committee of the CONGRESS OF RACIAL EQUALITY (CORE). She also befriended members of the STUDENT NONVIOLENT COORDINATING COMMITTEE (SNCC). When both organizations began to advocate violence, however, Smith balked. She resigned from CORE in 1966 and criticized SNCC. That same year, she died after a long struggle with cancer, still fiercely loyal to the principles of racial justice and nonviolence that drove her in the years before there was a concrete movement.

Author Lillian Smith. (Library of Congress)

BIBLIOGRAPHY

Lillian Smith Papers, Southern History Collection. University of North Carolina at Chapel Hill.

Miller, Kathleen. "Out of the Chrysalis: Lillian Smith and the Transformation of the South." Ph.D. Dissertation, Emory University. 1984.
Obituary, *New York Times*, September 22, 1966.
Sosna, Morton. *In Search of the Silent South: Southern Liberals and the Race Issue.* 1977.

Matt Gladue

Smith v. Allwright (1944)

The 1944 U.S. SUPREME COURT ruling *Smith v. Allwright* (321 U.S. 649), which overturned the "white primary," is considered by many civil rights scholars to be the foundation of the modern civil rights movement. The white primary was a device frequently used by Southern states to deny voting rights to their African-American citizens. It involved the establishment of primary elections, from which black voters were barred, to select the candidates of a party (normally the Democratic Party) for the general election. Since most Southern states were then predominantly one-party regimes, nomination by the party was tantamount to election, and blacks were effectively disfranchised.

The NATIONAL ASSOCIATION FOR THE ADVANCEMENT OF COLORED PEOPLE (NAACP) brought a succession of court challenges to the white primary under the FIFTEENTH AMENDMENT. In *Nixon v. Herndon* (1927), the Supreme Court unanimously overturned a Texas statute that barred blacks from voting in primaries. The Texas legislature then altered the law to allow the parties' executive committees to discriminate. In *Nixon v. Condon* (1932), the Court narrowly overturned that statute as well, since it constituted state action. Shortly after that ruling, the Texas Democratic Convention adopted a resolution making blacks ineligible to vote in primary elections. This time, the NAACP challenge was unsuccessful. In *Grovey v. Townshend* (1935), the Court unanimously ruled that a political party was a private organization, and such private discrimination was not covered by the Fifteenth Amendment.

After *Grovey*, African Americans remained excluded from primary elections for several years. However, when the Supreme Court ruled in an unrelated case, *Classic v. United States* (1941), that primaries were an integral part of the general election process, NAACP Counsel Thurgood MARSHALL began planning a new challenge to the white primary. With Dr. Lonnie Smith, a Houston dentist, agreeing to serve as plaintiff, Marshall brought suit in the Texas state courts in November 1941, charging that Smith had been illegally prevented from voting in the 1940 Texas primary elections. When the Texas court, as anticipated, ruled against Smith, the NAACP appealed to the U.S. Supreme Court. On April 3, 1944, the Supreme Court struck down the white primary by an 8-to-1 vote. Justice Stanley Reed's majority opinion, which relied heavily on *Classic*, found that the place of the primary in the state electoral process was so central that a denial of equality constituted state action. In contrast, Justice Owen Roberts's lone dissent criticized the Court for overturning the previous unanimous decision in *Grovey*.

Smith v. Allwright was an important civil rights victory; it symbolized the power of blacks to challenge discrimination through the courts. However, the ruling did not immediately lead to mass black voting in the South. A few states—notably South Carolina—attempted unsuccessfully to evade the ruling by amending or repealing their laws concerning the primary election, in order to make it a fully "private" process. Other states resorted to discriminatory registration procedures such as literacy tests, or to intimidation to prevent blacks from voting. While Southern black registration slowly increased, it remained below average until after passage of the VOTING RIGHTS ACT OF 1965.

BIBLIOGRAPHY
Hine, Darlene Clark. *Black Victory: The Rise and Fall of the White Primary in Texas.* 1979.
Kluger, Richard. *Simple Justice.* 1976.
Sitkoff, Harvard. *The Struggle for Black Equality.* 1979.
Tushnet, Mark V. *Making Civil Rights Law: Thurgood Marshall and the Supreme Court, 1936–1961.* 1994.

Greg Robinson

SNCC

See Student Nonviolent Coordinating Committee

Socialist Party

Although not formally organized in the United States until 1901, the Socialist Party merged several existing organizations committed to replacing capitalism with a cooperative commonwealth system. It encompassed diverse, and frequently conflicting, ethnic, class, occupational, and regional constituencies advocating a variety of methods, from class warfare to ameliorative reforms designed to improve the daily life of workers, to realize this end. The party achieved its greatest electoral success in the United States prior to WORLD WAR I. In 1912, the party's perennial presidential candidate, Eugene V. Debs, won 6 percent of the popular vote. Although individual Socialists were prominent in the drive for racial equality (e.g., as founders of the NAACP, in 1910), the party initially did not take a stand in favor of civil rights or otherwise appeal specifically to African Americans. Racial discrimination was seen as part of the larger problem of capitalist exploitation even though Debs personally disapproved of drawing a color line in party and union activities.

The party's membership and popular support declined in the 1920s but revived in 1932 as a result of the Depression only to drop precipitously in 1936, preempted by the New Deal on the right and the Communists on the left. It was never a serious factor thereafter in national elections although it continued to exert a considerable moral influence through its respected six-time (1928–1948) presidential candidate, Norman Thomas. The 1928 platform endorsed a federal anti-lynching bill. By 1936 the party called for economic, political, and legal equality for African Americans, and subsequently it became increasingly explicit in endorsing a civil rights agenda. Thomas was not among the major civil rights leaders but served as an advisor to those who were. After 1956 the party no longer nominated a national ticket, and in 1972 it ceased to be a party but became an interest group, styling itself "Social Democrats, U.S.A."

BIBLIOGRAPHY

Harrington, Michael. "The Socialist Party." In *History of U.S. Political Parties*, vol. III, edited by Arthur M. Schlesinger, Jr. 1973.

Shannon, David A. *The Socialist Party of America.* 1955.

James S. Chase

Social Science

Broadly defined, "social science" encompasses a range of academic disciplines: political science, sociology, economics, anthropology, and psychology to name just a few. Although one can discern connections between these fields and much older fields of inquiry, the modern notion of the social sciences began to develop only over the course of the last one hundred years. At the same time that these fields were maturing, the United States was undergoing extensive structural changes in its economy, the demographics of its population, and its role in the international scene. At the end of the nineteenth century, the United States was becoming an industrially based economy, massive waves of immigrant populations were complicating social relationships in American cities, and the age of U.S. imperialism had begun with victory in the Spanish-American War of 1898. Ethnic and racial populations were deeply involved or implicated in all of these changes.

Because racial and ethnic minorities played such important roles in factories, cities, and international affairs, social scientists turned their attention to the quality and texture of their life. Furthermore, because these populations were so often denied the fruits of American democracy, much social science scholarship also took on the role of proposing solutions that would lead to a more just world where all populations could enjoy their full civil rights and liberties.

Some of the earliest and most influential scholarship in this area came from the Department of Sociology at the University of Chicago and the Department of Anthropology at Columbia University, where Robert Park and Franz Boas were pioneers in their respective disciplines. Park made famous the race relations cycle that claimed people of different races would first come into contact, then conflict, and then adjust. Put more simply, this cycle suggested that, given time, blacks would assimilate into the American mainstream. Although dated by today's standards, Park's ideas were heralded at the time for the way in which they offered solutions to so-called black social disorganization. Boas trained generations of scholars to examine populations' cultural differences in their own terms. Boas's ideas on cultural relativism taught people to respect the vitality and survival strategies of other cultures even when they do not seem functional by "normal" standards. Boas's ideas laid the foundation for the establishment of such disciplines as African and African-American studies.

Building on the social and political implications of Park's, Boas's, and other academics' scholarship, civil rights and liberties organizations such as the National Association for the Advancement of Colored People (NAACP) worked closely with social science experts to prove that black Americans deserved access to full citizenship. To cite just a few examples, E. Franklin Frazier's, Horace Cayton's, and St. Clair Drake's ethnographic and sociological work detailed the terrible effects of housing and employment discrimination. The analyses of Ralph Bunche and Doxey Wilkerson illuminated the ways in which blacks were denied fair access to the electoral system. Most famously, Kenneth and Mamie Clark's findings from their psychological testing of black students were used to support the plaintiffs' case in Brown v. Board of Education, the 1954 Supreme Court case that successfully challenged Segregation in public education. The Clarks' work, known as the "Doll Studies," examined the psychological damage racial segregation in education had upon young black students.

The relationship between social science and civil rights public policy was made clear on other important occasions and in shifting fashion. In the mid-1930s, W. E. B. Du Bois, a prominent black intellectual-activist, argued that justice for blacks would only come via black cultural and economic nationalism. A decade later, Gunnar MYRDAL's *An American Dilemma*, a massive research project examining the systemic degradation of black life, was published. This text advanced the idea that black salvation would come via racial INTEGRATION and an honest investment by all citizens in the "American Creed," the ideal that life, liberty, and justice were open to and for all Americans.

Just as Du Bois was famous for his ardent belief in social science as a cure-all for racial injustice, *An American Dilemma* became famous for the way in which it helped develop a faith in the value of the social science race relations expert. In the 1960s, philanthropic foundations and the federal government increasingly looked to these race relations experts for answers as the nation struggled to come to grips with the legacies of racial discrimination, social fragmentation, and poverty. Social scientists' views, particularly on topics such as welfare and housing, were held in high esteem after the CIVIL RIGHTS ACT OF 1964 and the VOTING RIGHTS ACT OF 1965 failed to stem the tide of racial antagonisms and despair that characterized the post–civil rights movement.

BIBLIOGRAPHY

Boas, Franz. *Race, Language, and Culture.* 1940.
Clark, Kenneth. *Dark Ghetto: Dilemmas of Social Power.* 1965.
Du Bois, W. E. B. *The Souls of Black Folk.* 1903.
Du Bois, W. E. B. *Black Reconstruction: An Essay Toward a History of the Part Which Black Folk Played in the Attempt to Reconstruct Democracy in American, 1860–1880.* 1935.
Frazier, E. Franklin. *The Negro Family in Chicago.* 1932.
Herskovits, Melville. *The Myth of the Negro Past.* 1941.
Myrdal, Gunnar. *An American Dilemma: The Negro Problem and Modern Democracy.* 1944.
Park, Robert. *Race and Culture Contacts.* 1934.

Jonathan Scott Holloway

Society of American Indians

The fact that the first official meeting of the American Indian Association, soon renamed the Society of American Indians (SIA), was held on Columbus Day in 1911 was particularly meaningful, given that the goals of the organization both promoted and challenged colonial cultural values. These dual goals—on the one hand, to assimilate American Indians into mainstream culture and, on the other, to promote their rights as indigenous peoples—were understandable given the historical period and the personal experiences of the organization's founding members, individuals who were among the best educated and most professionally successful American Indians of that time. Having received turn-of-the-century assimilationist education and religious instruction, these early SAI leaders—including Rosa LaFlesche, Carlos Montezuma, Charles EASTMAN, and Sherman Coolidge, the Society's first president—supported the Americanization of Indians through hard work, moral correctness, and social contribution. A future for Indian peoples would be found in the virtues of mainstream American life and through accommodation to the dominant society. Though different from one another in many ways, including tribal membership, religious affiliation, and extent of assimilation, these young native SAI leaders shared Progressive Era beliefs in the abilities of American Indian people and, given education and opportunity, their potential to advance.

Although similar in philosophy and goals to other early-twentieth-century Indian reform groups, the SAI was distinct in its requirement that only American Indians could become voting members, with non-Indians restricted to associate membership. In this regard, the SAI is noteworthy as being the first national Indian reform organization governed exclusively by Indians themselves.

This Indian leadership agreed not only on the Society's twin goals of assimilation and self-determination for native peoples but also on the two principal endeavors to be undertaken in support of these goals: the publication of an educational journal intended to enlighten the general public about the aspirations and abilities of American Indian peoples and an annual Society convention. Published from 1913 to the early 1920s, the Society's *Quarterly Journal* emulated scholarly publications of the time and was distributed widely, not only to Society members but to a more general readership. Annual meetings were convened mostly in the Midwest and the East in the early years of the Society, perhaps in conjunction with the organization's Washington, D.C., headquarters. Later on these meetings were held more frequently in Western states, with some thought to increasing membership from that region.

Annual conventions were heralded as forums where members from around the country, Indian and non-Indian alike, could come and participate, expressing various points of view on a range of matters such as education, health, and the pressing need for reservation reform. By the time of WORLD WAR I, the Society was discussing other, more internally divisive topics: American Indian citizenship; American Indian use of peyote; and the proper role of the BUREAU OF INDIAN AFFAIRS. By 1917, conflict within the Society over these matters had grown considerably, contributing to cancellation of the annual meeting. The final SAI conference was held in the fall of 1923, and by the mid-1920s Society membership had significantly eroded from its 1913 peak of 619 persons. The group's initial energy and focus had so greatly diminished that the Society of American Indians could not continue to exist.

In spite of its problems, the SAI played a key role in early twentieth-century Indian activism. This first national intertribal Indian reform organization in America gave testimony to the strength and the intelligence of persons defining themselves in relation to the complex circumstances and conditions of their lives.

BIBLIOGRAPHY

Hertzberg, Hazel W. *The Search for an American Indian Identity: Modern Pan-Indian Movements.* 1971.

Iverson, Peter. *Carlos Montezuma and the Changing World of American Indians.* 1982.

Johnson, David L., and Raymond Wilson. "Gertrude Simmons Bonnin, 1876–1938: 'Americanize the First American,'" *American Indian Quarterly* (Winter 1988): 27–40.

McNickle, D'Arcy. *Native American Tribalism: Indian Survivals and Renewals.* 1973.

Welch, Deborah. "Zitkala-Sa: An American Indian Leader, 1876–1938." Ph.D. dissertation, University of Wyoming, 1985.

Wilson, Raymond. *Ohiyesa: Charles Eastman, Santee Sioux.* 1983.

Judith Antell

South Carolina

Perhaps no state better exemplifies the tumultuous, difficult, and perplexing history of race relations in the United States than South Carolina. Through much of its history, there has been a black majority in South Carolina. Notwithstanding, the state was the first to secede from the Union before the Civil War, it quickly and systematically overturned the significant political and social gains made for African Americans during RECONSTRUCTION, and it was the first state to challenge the constitutionality of the VOTING RIGHTS ACT OF 1965. RACISM and exclusion from the political process have been hindrances for African Americans in South Carolina throughout its history. In the midst of this struggle, however, African Americans have made important and progressive contributions to South Carolina's history, and they continue to influence its direction.

Persons of African descent first arrived in South Carolina as slaves of the Spanish during Spain's early attempts to settle parts of North America. In 1526 these slaves rebelled against their captors and remained these when the Spanish deserted their settlement. Following Spain's exit, the African-American population slowly grew until by roughly 1708, it constituted a majority of the people in South Carolina.

The entry of white settlers into the region and the diminishment of the Native American population, provided whites with a majority from around 1748 until 1820, when the South Carolina census indicated that African Americans were again the majority—but the overwhelming number of that majority were slaves of the settlers. Unlike the Native Americans, these slaves were mostly immune to malaria. They were skilled in herding livestock and in planting, and had acquired extensive knowledge of botanical lore, thus proving very useful for white landowners during the rice boom of the 1730s and with the growing predominance of cotton production in South Carolina and in the South as a whole.

Despite their proficiency in these and other areas, they remained slaves, an unacceptable condition that stirred passion for freedom. Many resisted the trappings of their forced labor by being purposefully insolent, working inefficiently, pretending to be incompetent, and privately mocking their white owners. Casual resistance turned into armed conflict in the 1739 Stono Rebellion, in which many of the slaves participated. This insurrection was, however, brutally repressed. In 1822, freeman Denmark Vesey organized a slave rebellion in South Carolina, and many other revolts occurred on a smaller scale in the state.

As determined as some slaves were in attempting to escape their bondage, most white citizens of South Carolina defended the institution of slavery at the political level just as fiercely. Representatives from South Carolina were vociferous advocates for the rights of slaveholders during the formulation and ratification of the United States Constitution, and U.S. Senator John C. Calhoun was an ardent and influential opponent of anti-slavery legislation throughout his career. The forcefulness of white South Carolinians' determination to see that slavery remain under the jurisdiction of the individual states was evident when South Carolina became the first state to secede from the Union upon the election of Abraham Lincoln to the presidency in 1860. The next year, the first shot of the Civil War was fired by the Confederacy at Fort Sumter, South Carolina, and the bloody battle commenced.

Following the Union victory in the Civil War, the United States government began its RECONSTRUCTION program in an attempt to shape a new South. Many believed that the policies of Reconstruction would work well in South Carolina, where blacks made up a majority of the population, and initially this was the case. African-American males voted Republican and formed majorities in both houses of the South Carolina legislature; eight were elected to the U.S. House of Representatives, and still more held offices throughout the state and local government. No Southern state had more African Americans serving in government during Reconstruction than South Carolina. It seemed that African Americans would finally realize the promises of democracy.

Many white South Carolinians had other ideas. Vigilante organizations such as the KU KLUX KLAN expressed their bitterness at the sudden turn of events in violent fashion. During the Reconstruction era in South Carolina, eight Republican legislators (black and white) were murdered. The use of terrorism and the fear it caused created a situation in which African Americans became reluctant to vote in areas where their choices might have tipped the balance toward candidates more friendly to them. In 1876, Wade Hampton, a Democrat, was elected governor. Hampton's administration began the trend toward Democratic administrations favoring white rule, and a new state constitution completely disfranchised African Americans in 1896. Democratic governors such as "Pitchfork" Ben Tillman (elected in 1890), Cole Blease, and "Cotton" Ed Smith (in the 1940s) campaigned and won by capitalizing on the bigotry of white voters, and managed to codify SEGREGATION laws that took away voting and other civil rights from African Americans. By 1940, segregation and discrimination were facts of life in South Carolina.

In 1942, a small group of activists formed the South Carolina Negro Citizens' Committee in order to protest the all-white primary and encourage voter registration among black South Carolinians. This effort is said to mark the beginning of the modern civil rights movement in the United States. In the late 1940s and early 1950s, CITIZENSHIP SCHOOLS were founded to instruct citizens in obtaining voting rights and overcoming discrimination and JIM CROW laws. The SOUTHERN CHRISTIAN LEADERSHIP CONFERENCE (SCLC), led by the Reverend Dr. Martin Luther KING, JR., took over the administration of the citizenship schools in the 1960s. These schools and their efforts became significant factors in the civil rights movement. However, South Carolina was still governed and represented by the forces of segregation and the Old South.

Democrat Strom THURMOND governed South Carolina in the late 1940s. Thurmond became the strongest voice of a group of Southern Democrats who called themselves DIXIECRATS and who adamantly opposed the strongly pro–civil rights plank of the national Democratic Party platform for the 1948 election year. Thurmond even ran as a third-party candidate for the presidency, but lost to Harry S. TRUMAN. In spite of that loss, South Carolina's office holders continued to defend segregationist policies and participated against the NAACP in arguments before the Supreme Court during the landmark BROWN V. BOARD OF EDUCATION case in the early 1950s. Increasingly,

however, public sentiment around the nation would galvanize Congress and these policies would soon be outlawed.

As the cause of civil rights marched on, South Carolina was forced to officially recognize the rights of all of its citizens to vote and freely participate in elections, thanks to the Voting Rights Act of 1965. This allowed for a substantial increase in voter registration among African Americans, and gagged the bigoted rhetoric white politicians had used for years in their speeches and policies. Black voters in South Carolina utilized their newfound clout to help elect candidates who supported the goals of the civil rights movement, and more black political leaders have gained statewide and local office. In 1992, African-American James Clyburn was elected to represent his district in the U.S. House of Representatives.

BIBLIOGRAPHY

Bethel, Elizabeth Raul. *Promiseland: A Century of Life in a Negro Community.* 1981.
Davis, Marianna. *The History of Blacks in South Carolina.* 1979.

Matthew May

South Carolina Progressive Democratic Party

In 1944, white SOUTH CAROLINA Democrats in the state legislature defied SMITH V. ALLWRIGHT and vowed continued exclusion of African-American voters from the primary. This recalcitrance inspired black South Carolinians to pursue their right to vote even more ardently. That spring of 1944, African Americans, led by journalist John McCray and activist Osceola E. McKaine, formed a statewide protest organization, taking members from the "Fourth Term for Roosevelt" clubs. The new Progressive Democratic Party (PDP) had chapters in every South Carolina county. The state leadership of the NATIONAL ASSOCIATION FOR THE ADVANCEMENT OF COLORED PEOPLE (NAACP) supported the PDP, and the PDP in effect became the political or voting wing of the South Carolina NAACP. This group challenged, albeit unsuccessfully, the seating of South Carolina's all-white delegation at the 1944 Democratic National Convention in Chicago. The national DEMOCRATIC PARTY's credentials committee disqualified the PDP on a technicality: the PDP had not followed the Democratic Party rules requiring precinct and county meetings before selecting delegates or forming a party.

After the unprecedented challenge of the black delegation to the national Democratic Party, the PDP held a convention in South Carolina and sponsored

African-American activist Osceola McKaine as a candidate for the U.S. Senate against regular Democrat Olin Johnston. McKaine campaigned in almost every county, and the party welcomed money and support from whites both within and outside the state. According to the official voting records of South Carolina, McKaine received only 3,214 votes, but fraud and intimidation, easily documented by the PDP, were rampant. NAACP Legal Counsel Thurgood MARSHALL submitted affidavits and a brief to the U.S. Justice Department asking for criminal action against South Carolina election officials. The PDP also contested the seating of Olin Johnston in the U.S. Senate because of unfair election practices. Neither the Senate nor the Justice Department responded. The PDP's main objective, however, was always VOTING RIGHTS. The PDP worked from the precinct level to build an organization concentrated on voter registration. The Progressive Democrats and the NAACP had mounted a registration drive that increased the number of black voters on the rolls from 1,500 to 50,000 between 1940 and 1946. Despite KU KLUX KLAN marches and cross burnings, despite the fraud and intimidation of the 1946 election, 35,000 African-American voters went to the polls in the 1948 primary.

BIBLIOGRAPHY

Burton, Orville Vernon, et al. "South Carolina." In *The Quiet Revolution: The Impact of the Voting Rights Act in the South, 1965–1990*, edited by Chandler Davidson and Bernard Grofman. 1994.

Richards, Miles S. "Osceola E. McKaine and the Struggle for Black Civil Rights, 1917–1946." Ph.D. dissertation, University of South Carolina, 1994.

Sullivan, Patricia. *Days of Hope: Race and Democracy in the New Deal Era.* 1996.

Orville Vernon Burton

South Dakota

The history of civil rights in South Dakota is tied closely to the history of Native Americans, women, and certain immigrant groups. Each of these had to fight for its rights against a dominant society that either failed to perceive injustice or consciously sought to perpetuate it.

Before statehood was achieved in 1889, the central conflict pitted Native Americans, who had inhabited the area for thousands of years, against an increasingly numerous populace of white settlers. Treaty after treaty between the two sides left a trail of broken promises. Not only was the Indians' land taken away from them, but they were also denied citizenship and the vote and had their culture stripped from them.

Citizenship and its privileges were finally acquired by all Indians in 1924.

South Dakota had one of the largest immigrant populations of any state. Most of these groups were relatively easily assimilated. The most conspicuous exceptions were several Anabaptist sects, including Hutterites and Mennonites. The former, especially, suffered persecution during WORLD WAR I, when pacifists were jailed, physically assaulted, and deprived of their property. German-Americans, in general, had their right of free speech limited during the war.

The constitution writers at the time of statehood set up a special election on whether to grant women voting privileges, but the proposition failed. Seven more referendums were required before final victory was achieved for woman suffrage in 1918, two years before ratification of the NINETEENTH AMENDMENT. During the 1960s, women accelerated their efforts to achieve full equality. The most conspicuous advance was the creation by the state legislature in 1968 of a Commission on Human Relations (later renamed the Human Rights Division), which investigated alleged violations of Title VII of the CIVIL RIGHTS ACT OF 1964 and other infringements of civil liberties. Significant improvements occurred later for women, blacks, Native Americans, foreign students, and other minorities.

BIBLIOGRAPHY

Griffith, T. D. et al. *South Dakota.* 2nd ed. 1998.
Norris, Kathleen. *Dakota: A Spiritual Geography.* 1993.

John E. Miller

Southern Christian Leadership Conference

In 1957 a group of young Southern ministers formed an organization in Atlanta, Georgia, which they initially called the Southern Negro Leaders Conference on Transportation and Nonviolent Integration. These ministers believed that the BLACK CHURCH should play an important role in the civil rights movement and that a regional organization was needed to coordinate efforts and serve as a forum of ideas. Rather than accept individuals as members, the new group would be a coalition of local civil rights organizations, civic leagues, and churches. The group's name was soon changed to the Southern Christian Leadership Conference (SCLC). The Rev. Dr. Martin Luther KING, JR., was the leader and most well-known member of the new organization. King was already one of the nation's most famous civil rights activists due to his role in the MONTGOMERY BUS BOYCOTT (see also ALABAMA) and his presence in SCLC lent the organization immediate prominence. King would head the SCLC until his as-

Joseph E. Lowery speaking on behalf of the Southern Christian Leadership Conference in 1988. (AP/Wide World Photos)

sassination in 1968, and for many Americans the SCLC was "his" organization.

The SCLC decided early on that its focus would be on VOTING RIGHTS and that its methods would be entirely nonviolent. In its early years the group had little money or personnel with which to pursue its goals, but in 1961 the SCLC became involved in protests taking place in the city of Albany, Georgia. King made several visits to support the ALBANY MOVEMENT, but the SCLC failed to help it significantly. By 1963, the SCLC was ready to mount a major protest of its own. Birmingham, Alabama, was chosen as the site of the protest in the hopes of exposing the violent RACISM of its white politicians and police (see BIRMINGHAM CAMPAIGN). The massive but nonviolent protest was met with fire hoses and attack dogs. This brutal spectacle was televised, resulting in unprecedented support from white Northerners for the civil rights movement. The SCLC and other civil rights organizations then carried out the 1963 MARCH ON WASHINGTON, where King gave his famous "I Have a Dream" speech. Together, these actions played a major role in securing the passage of the CIVIL RIGHTS ACT OF 1964. The years 1964 and 1965 saw the SCLC at the height of its success, symbolized by King receiving the Nobel Peace Prize in 1964.

In 1965 the SCLC decided to capitalize on its recent victories by staging a protest against restrictions on the right of African Americans to vote. The protest—in Selma, Alabama—was once again met with violent resistance as police arrested and beat protestors. Tele-

vision audiences were aghast, and their response contributed to the passage of the VOTING RIGHTS ACT OF 1965 later that year.

King firmly believed that the SCLC had to address the poverty, poor HOUSING, and lack of job or educational opportunities faced by many African Americans. After the passage of the Voting Rights Act, the SCLC began moving in this new direction. Early efforts included the Chicago Campaign of 1966, followed by efforts in Cleveland and Louisville in 1967. However, the organization found it impossible to gain national attention and support as it had in the past and won only a few minor victories. Undeterred by these failures or by growing dissension within the SCLC, King insisted that an anti-poverty protest for people of all races be organized. This POOR PEOPLE'S CAMPAIGN was to take place in Washington, D.C., in April 1968, but when King was assassinated on April 4, the SCLC was thrown into great confusion. Although the organization did carry out the Poor People's Campaign under the leadership of Rev. Ralph D. ABERNATHY, the protest failed to win support from the general public. There was also muffled opposition from the Johnson administration, as a result of the growing association of the SCLC with the ANTI-WAR MOVEMENT.

Following the Poor People's Campaign, the SCLC went into decline. Divisions within the civil rights movement were only made worse by the death of King, and no organization suffered more from these problems than the SCLC. It gradually returned to its original focus on nonviolent social protest and voting rights for African Americans in the South. Today, largely out of the public eye, the SCLC continues to organize, educate, and register voters in the southern United States.

BIBLIOGRAPHY

Garrow, David J. *Bearing the Cross: Martin Luther King, Jr., and the Southern Christian Leadership Conference.* 1986.

Garrow, David J. "Southern Christian Leadership Conference." In the *Encyclopedia of African-American Culture and History,* edited by Jack Salzman, David Lionel Smith, and Cornel West. 1996.

Peake, Thomas R. *Keeping the Dream Alive: A History of the Southern Christian Leadership Conference from King to the Nineteen-Eighties.* 1987.

John F. McCoy

Southern Conference Educational Fund

The Southern Conference Educational Fund (SCEF) began in 1946 as an offshoot of the SOUTHERN CONFERENCE FOR HUMAN WELFARE (SCHW). The parent organization initiated SCEF solely to provide a tax-exempt status for SCHW. Many SCHW members and influential leaders remained active with SCEF when the earlier organization died. These included, among others, Eleanor ROOSEVELT, Walter Francis WHITE of the NATIONAL ASSOCIATION FOR THE ADVANCEMENT OF COLORED PEOPLE (NAACP), Mary McLeod BETHUNE of Bethune-Cookman College, and Charlotte Hawkins Brown, founder and president of the Palmer Memorial Institute in NORTH CAROLINA. SCEF addressed the single issue of racial equality between 1946 and the organization's decline in the 1970s. It dedicated its monthly publication, *Southern Patriot*, to an educational campaign aiming to raise white Southerners' moral consciousness on the wastefulness of the JIM CROW society.

In making its case against Jim Crow schools, SCEF made arguments similar to those that attorneys presented before the Supreme Court in the case of *Brown v. the Board of Education of Topeka, Kansas* in the early 1950s (see BROWN V. BOARD OF EDUCATION). SCEF pointed out that segregation was so oppressive that were physical parity ever to be achieved, such as equal facilities, true equality would still not exist. The value of a law degree, for example, relied in part upon the value it had in the greater society. Essentially, the society at large tended to regard less highly a degree from a small, separate institution than a one from a large state university with a long legal tradition and thousands of distinguished alumni.

SCEF worked closely with other civil rights organizations, particularly the NAACP. SCEF members Clifford and Virginia DURR of Montgomery, ALABAMA, assisted with the law case of Rosa PARKS that sparked the MONTGOMERY BUS BOYCOTT in 1955 and 1956. SCEF supported L. C. and Daisy BATES in the Little Rock, ARKANSAS, school integration crises between 1957 and 1959. In the 1960s, SCEF bailed civil rights workers out of jail in several places in the South.

The struggles of SCHW and SCEF are summarized in what historian Linda Reed has termed the "Southern Conference Movement," so identified because of the sustained efforts related to issues of race and gender equality. The movement is important because the participants' struggle for a just society reached beyond their involvement with SCHW and SCEF. It sought the input of all Southerners, black or white, rich or poor, male or female. A great number of blacks and women became influential Southern Conference Movement leaders. If individual black leaders can be referred to as "race" leaders in that they placed race above other struggles for a just society, Southern Conference Movement leaders—black *and* white—may be labeled "human" leaders in that they wanted all persons to share in an equal system.

BIBLIOGRAPHY
Barnard, Hollinger F. *Outside the Magic Circle: The Autobiography of Virginia Foster Durr.* 1985.
Dunbar, Anthony P. *Against the Grain: Southern Radicals and Prophets, 1929–1959.* 1981.
Reed, Linda. *Simple Decency and Common Sense: The Southern Conference Movement, 1938–1963.* 1991.
Salmond, John. *A Southern Rebel: The Life and Times of Aubrey Willis Williams, 1890–1965.* 1983.

Linda Reed

Southern Conference for Human Welfare

In the 1930s when most Americans suffered economic and psychological hardships related to the Great Depression, many Southerners held symposia, forums, and conferences to discuss the impact of the economy on their lives and how they could work more closely together on issues specific to the Southern economy. Southerners still sought to fulfill the prophecy of nineteenth-century New South spokesmen who had envisioned a region as industrialized as the North. However, while the South had risen to a new level of industrialization, it had not realized its greatest potential and lagged behind other sectors of the country.

In November 1938 a number of black and white liberals founded the Southern Conference for Human Welfare (SCHW) to address economic backwardness in the South. SCHW broke with the notion that blacks were to blame for Southern poverty; the interracial organization now uniquely set out to address the concerns of organized labor along with political and social equality for blacks. SCHW members linked economics with unsatisfactory racial situations, and Southern white opponents immediately saw an impending threat to their way of life; they steadily spoke out against SCHW's interracial meetings and its program for equality.

The establishment of SCHW connected with the poor Southern economy in that the group helped to spur President FRANKLIN D. ROOSEVELT to create the National Emergency Council (NEC). Roosevelt then asked the Council to conduct a fact-finding survey of the South. The NEC's *Report on Economic Conditions of the South*, made public in August 1938, named the South as economic problem number one. The *Report* in fact brought together a number of Southerners from various backgrounds who remained dedicated to the efforts of SCHW, some for only a few years but several for the greater portion of their lives. Of upper-middle-class origins, Lucy Randolph MASON had worked directly with the NEC in its formulation of the *Report*. She, and others who had not already known one another, came together for the first time during the period of SCHW's founding. All of them had shown outstanding leadership ability in their local communities, many even on the national level. A significant characteristic of those who joined SCHW is that they and all others who became members of SCHW opposed racial discrimination and economic oppression and stood for racial equality. Until its demise in the fall of 1948, Mason and others, such as ELEANOR ROOSEVELT, remained supportive of SCHW.

BIBLIOGRAPHY

Barnard, Hollinger F. *Outside the Magic Circle: The Autobiography of Virginia Foster Durr.* 1985.
Dunbar, Anthony P. *Against the Grain: Southern Radicals and Prophets, 1929–1959.* 1981.
Reed, Linda. *Simple Decency and Common Sense: The Southern Conference Movement, 1938–1963.* 1991.
Salmond, John. *A Southern Rebel: The Life and Times of Aubrey Willis Williams, 1890–1965.* 1983.

Linda Reed

Southern Manifesto

On May 17, 1954, the United States SUPREME COURT issued its ruling in BROWN V. BOARD OF EDUCATION, and the event had a calamitous effect on the American South. In it, the newly appointed Chief Justice, Earl WARREN, overturned the 1896 PLESSY V. FERGUSON Supreme Court decision that had governed race relations for decades, convincing his colleagues on the high court to adhere to the language that "in the field of public education the doctrine of 'separate but equal' [should have] no place." The *Brown* decision meant that allowing school systems intentionally to draw attendance boundaries that perpetuated racial SEGREGATION was unconstitutional because it violated the FOURTEENTH AMENDMENT. As every school in the South was segregated by law, the court was calling for a drastic change in the way that children were to be educated.

Having laid down the basis for this revolution in the social framework of K–12 education, the high court seemed to back away from the consequences. The remedial portion of its ruling, *Brown II*, issued in 1955, stated that the DESEGREGATION of schools must proceed "with all deliberate speed." This vague and ambiguous language, a concession to the more conservative justices so that the verdict would be unanimous, did little to deter Southern resistance to INTEGRATION. Throughout the South many whites opposed any attempt at it, sometimes with violence. State and local politicians either stood aside or, in many cases, led the resistance themselves.

It was in this atmosphere that in March 1956 one hundred Southern congressmen issued what became known as the Southern Manifesto. They decried the *Brown* decision as "judicial encroachment" and charged that the high court was "creating chaos and confusion" and "destroying the amicable relations between the white and Negro races" that had grown up in the ninety years since the Civil War. They also charged that with the *Brown* decision the judicial branch was making new law, instead of overseeing the application of existing law as it should (*New York Times*, March 12, 1956). They then went on to praise those who opposed integration with "any lawful means," and pledged to reverse the *Brown* decision and prevent its enforcement to the best of their abilities.

This Manifesto, signed by eighty-one members of the House of Representatives and by nineteen senators (only three Southern senators refused to sign the document: Lyndon JOHNSON, Albert Gore, and Estes Kefauver), emboldened those who were committed to resist integration. The support of so many powerful men, who had publicly stated that the *Brown* decision was illegal and implied that it would eventually be reversed, lent legitimacy to their cause. They now knew they could count on substantial support in Congress for their activities.

BIBLIOGRAPHY

Bartley, Numan. *The Rise of Massive Resistance: Race and Politics in the South During the 1950s.* 1969.
Branch, Taylor. *Parting the Waters: America in the King Years, 1954–1963.* 1988.
Kluger, Richard. *Simple Justice.* 1975.
McMillen, Neil. *The Citizens' Council: Organized Resistance to the Second Reconstruction, 1954–1964.* 1964.
Patterson, James T. *Grand Expectations: The United States, 1945–1974.* 1996.
Schwarz, Bernard. *Inside the Warren Court.* 1983.
Sitkoff, Harvard. *The Struggle for Black Equality, 1954–1980.* 1981.
Woodward, C. Vann. *The Strange Career of Jim Crow*, 3rd ed. 1966.

R. David Riddle

Southern Negro Youth Congress

The Southern Negro Youth Congress (SNYC) was organized in Richmond, Virginia, in February 1937. Between its formation in 1937 and its demise in 1949, the SNYC played a critical role in the struggle of black Americans for full citizenship. By 1939 the organization established a headquarters in Birmingham, Alabama, from which it coordinated a sustained challenge to the segregation system across the South.

The organization's initial membership drew from the 1930s student movement, the Communist Party, and the Congress of Industrial Organizations (CIO). (See COMMUNIST PARTY USA.) Early leaders included Edward Strong, William Richardson, Louis Burnham, and James E. JACKSON, JR., although from its inception, women played key roles in the organization by the early 1940s women assumed formal leadership positions. Dorothy Burnham, Sallye Davis, Augusta Jackson Strong, and Esther Cooper JACKSON, who served as the SNYC's executive secretary during the 1940s, provided the organization with a foundation and dynamic leadership.

The SNYC's connection with the Communist Party provided links to an international arena of striving and to a cadre of aggressive grassroots organizers. The SNYC was, however, firmly rooted in the institutional and intellectual life of black communities across the South. Its members and constituencies came to the organization from the black Baptist church, the NATIONAL ASSOCIATION FOR THE ADVANCEMENT OF COLORED PEOPLE (NAACP), women's clubs, and fraternal and benevolent associations. Members of the SNYC worked hard to build coalitions, drawing on organizations, institutions, and individuals across lines of class, gender, and generation. They also reached out to white Southerners who were committed to racial and economic justice.

During its twelve-year existence the SNYC organized eight Youth Legislatures in cities like Richmond, VA, Birmingham, AL, Chattanooga, TN, and Columbia, SC. The Youth Legislatures were laboratories of the SNYC's vision of life and the quest for racial justice. The meetings brought together individuals and organizations active in the fight for justice in the South and the nation. Local advisory boards were formed and included older leaders from respective host cities. Federal government officials, national labor leaders, and icons of the black quest for freedom, such as W. E. B. DU BOIS and Paul ROBESON, gave speeches. Legislature participants broke into small working groups that hammered out plans of action and drew up resolutions for federal legislation. SNYC leaders used the Legislatures as organizing tools. The Legislatures invigorated local campaigns and helped garner support for the SNYC's agenda of political and economic transformation. They also provided important venues for connecting local battles to broader international ones.

In 1940 the House Un-American Activities Committee listed the SNYC as a Communist Party front and agent of foreign powers. The Federal Bureau of Investigation placed the organization and its leaders under surveillance over the next twelve years. Although the SNYC's affiliation with the Communist Party did little to hamper its support in black communities through the WORLD WAR II years, by 1947, with the advent of the cold war, the organization encountered increased opposition along many fronts. In 1948 the Internal Revenue Service withdrew its tax-exempt status. Liberal organizations stopped providing financial and public support. Its final Youth Legislature, held in Birmingham, was smashed by local vigilantes and the city's chief of police, Eugene "Bull" Connor. By 1949 the organization ceased operations and its members were forced to pursue new avenues of struggle. The SNYC left, however, a lasting imprint on the black battle for freedom, the extent of which has yet to be fully revealed.

BIBLIOGRAPHY

Jackson, Esther Cooper, and James E. Jackson, Jr. Interview with Peter F. Lau. 1997.
Kelley, Robin D. G. Hammer and Hoe: Alabama Communists during the Great Depression. 1990.
Papers of the Southern Negro Youth Congress. Moorland-Spingarn Library, Howard University, Washington, D.C.
Richards, Johnnetta. The Southern Negro Youth Congress: A History. Ph. D. dissertation, University of Cincinnati. 1987.
Sullivan, Patricia. Days of Hope: Race and Democracy in the New Deal Era. 1996.

Peter F. Lau

Southern Poverty Law Center

A major nonprofit organization dedicated to enforcing civil rights law in America, the Southern Poverty Law Center is also renowned for its efforts in tracking and challenging racist hate groups, and for developing antiracist curricula for schools.

Founded by Morris DEES and Joseph Levin in 1971, the Montgomery-based Center began taking cases that extended the civil rights legal victories of the 1950s and 1960s, with a focus on implementing the CIVIL RIGHTS ACT OF 1964 and the VOTING RIGHTS ACT OF 1965. Civil rights activist Julian BOND served as the Center's first president, assembling a staff of lawyers and researchers funded mainly through donations.

The Center has won major victories and established legal precedents in cases of prison reform, DESEGREGATION of recreation facilities, state legislature reappointments, sex discrimination, and hate crimes. The Center brought the first civil suit against the KU KLUX KLAN in Decatur, ALABAMA, in 1979, which established the accountability of hate groups for the violent behavior of their members. Subsequent legal challenges bankrupted the United Klans of America and the White Aryan Resistance.

In 1981, the Center created a division called Klan-watch to monitor hate groups; its bimonthly newsletter *Intelligence Report* is now standard reading for law enforcement agencies and antiracist organizations nationwide. The Center's offices were burned by the Klan in 1983, and staff frequently endure death threats.

The Center took a more public turn in 1989 when it commissioned Maya Lin, who earlier designed the Vietnam Memorial, to design the CIVIL RIGHTS MEMORIAL at its Montgomery headquarters. By 1992, the Center had moved into curricular development with its "Teaching Tolerance," a portfolio of materials to assist schools in promoting diversity, and *Teaching Tolerance* magazine, which reaches 300,000 teachers. The Center also has created a civil rights movement curriculum for high schools, the video for which won a 1995 Academy Award for Best Short Documentary.

BIBLIOGRAPHY

Dees, Morris. *Hate on Trial.* 1993.

Dees, Morris. *Gathering Storm: America's Militia Threat.* 1996.

Joseph Heathcott

Southern Regional Council

Founded in 1919 by Southern white moderates as the COMMISSION ON INTERRACIAL COOPERATION, the Southern Regional Council (SRC) is a biracial race relations organization. Inspired by Howard B. Odum and based in Atlanta, Georgia, the SRC has supported the goals of better race relations, economic development, social welfare, and civil rights. Historically, its mission has been to promote racial justice, protect black citizens' democratic rights, and broaden their civic participation in the life of the South.

Initially composed mainly of white Southerners who wanted to address the problem of race riots, LYNCHINGS, and other conflicts in the South, the SRC has grown over the decades to include many African-American members. Early leaders of the organization were white sociologist Howard B. Odum (president) and the black educator Guy Johnson (executive secretary). Lillian SMITH, a white writer, was an active member of the SRC, which gives an annual book award in her name to honor authors who tell true stories about the South and its race relations.

The SRC has distinguished itself from other race relations organizations by its nonpartisan and non-profit status, its politically moderate civil rights agenda, and its research and information dissemination tactics. It has often been criticized by black civil rights organizations, such as the CONGRESS OF RACIAL EQUALITY (CORE) and the STUDENT NONVIOLENT COORDINATING COMMITTEE (SNCC), and more radical white race relations organizations, such as the SOUTHERN CONFERENCE EDUCATIONAL FUND (SCEF), because it firmly maintained a nonmilitant stance on race relations and opposed "active demonstrating" and direct protest tactics.

In its early years, the SRC strategically focused on black voting rights, anti-lynching, anti-race riots, fair HOUSING, and EQUAL EMPLOYMENT OPPORTUNITY. Through background reports and analytical research, it was successful in promoting public education to end the all-white primary in the 1940s (see VOTING RIGHTS), establishing state human relations councils to prevent school closings in the 1950s, and founding the VOTER EDUCATION PROJECT in the 1960s and 1970s. During the 1980s and 1990s, the SRC continued to gather extensive information and fund research, but it also implemented other effective methods of social change, such as organizing voter registration awareness and prison reform. Recently, the SRC launched the Partnership for Interracial Unity, the Fair Representation in Voting Rights, and other programs to advance equal opportunity for all people in the South.

BIBLIOGRAPHY

Reed, Linda. *Simple Decency and Common Sense: The Southern Conference Movement, 1938–1963.* 1991.

Southern Changes. 1995–1998. (*Southern Changes,* the SRC's quarterly journal, is a forum of ideas and opinions on issues and events in the American South.)

Donny C. Barnett

Southern Strategy

In the period of the civil rights movement, the term "Southern strategy" refers to the attempt to attract conservative whites to the REPUBLICAN PARTY through a refusal to support the demands of the movement. Political scientist Joseph A. Aistrup attributes the first formulation of the Southern strategy to Barry GOLDWATER's Republican presidential campaign in 1964. Seeing little opportunity for Republicans to win the African-American vote in the near future, Goldwater concluded that the Republicans should concentrate on winning the traditionally Democratic votes of conservative Southern whites.

Goldwater lost the election, but he succeeded in turning the Republican Party in a more conservative direction. During the next four years, the party would prune its liberal Nelson Rockefeller wing and attempt to harvest the votes that George Wallace was stripping from the DEMOCRATIC PARTY in both the South and the North.

Although Goldwater began the process, Richard NIXON is generally credited as the main architect of the Southern strategy, which he used successfully in the 1968 presidential campaign. A pragmatic and conservative politician, Nixon could not help but notice the success of George WALLACE in exploiting the "backlash" of whites in both the North and South to the civil rights campaigns over open housing and desegregated schools. At the Republican National Convention in Miami, Nixon won the support of conservative Southern delegates by promising a "go-slow approach on civil rights," specifically pledging opposition to open housing and court-ordered school busing in the South. Nixon's campaign rhetoric delicately avoided outright racism while echoing many of the "code words" of George Wallace—support for "law and order" and opposition to "forced busing." This helped him win the Southern white vote, and with it the election.

Once Nixon was elected, the Southern strategy continued to be a part of his public policy, thanks in part to conservative advisers. Harry S. Dent and Kevin Phillips, two of Nixon's conservative advisors, were instrumental in hammering out policy on the basis of the Southern strategy. Dent, a Southerner, used the term to describe public policies that would pit white and black voters against one another.

Political scientist and lawyer Kevin Phillips published *The Emerging Republican Majority* in 1969. This exhaustive analysis of changes in regional voting patterns called attention to the political realignment that began to surface in the late 1960s. Though he denied that the study should be read as a strategy paper for the GOP, many saw it as a validation for the Southern strategy. Phillips found that in 1968 upwards of 85 percent of Southern white votes went either to George Wallace or Richard Nixon. To Phillips this defection of traditionally secure Democratic votes represented a national political realignment. On the basis of these observations, he forecasted good times for the Republican Party. He predicted a new "cycle of American politics," in which a majority Republican Party would draw strength from the "Heartland, South, and California" and would overwhelm the Democratic Party strongholds in the Northeast, the Pacific Northwest, and among African-American voters. Although Phillips denied it, his analysis implied that the Republicans could ignore the African-American vote as underregistered or already captured by the Democrats. This was a view that invited the Republican Party to drift into a kind of complicit relationship with the white conservative "backlash" against the politics of reform.

BIBLIOGRAPHY

Aistrup, Joseph A. *The Southern Strategy Revisited: Republican Top-Down Advancement in the South.* 1996.

Edsall, Thomas Byrne, and Mary D. Edsall. *Chain Reaction: The Impact of Race, Rights, and Taxes on American Politics.* 1992.

Evans, Rowland, Jr., and Robert D. Novak. *Nixon in the White House.* 1971.

O'Reilly, Kenneth. *Nixon's Piano: Presidents and Racial Politics from Washington to Clinton.* 1995.

Phillips, Kevin P. *The Emerging Republican Majority.* 1969.

Radosh, Ronald. *Divided They Fell: The Demise of the Democratic Party, 1964–1996.* 1996.

Rieder, Jonathan. "The Rise of the Silent Majority" in Fraser, Steve and Gary Gerstle, eds. *The Rise and Fall of the New Deal Order, 1930–1980.* 1989, pp. 243–268.

Wills, Garry. *Nixon Agonistes.* 1970.

R. David Riddle

Southern Student Organizing Committee

The Southern Student Organizing Committee (SSOC) was a Nashville-based organization of white Southerners, primarily college students, which promoted black equality and other progressive causes across the South from its founding in 1964 until its demise in 1969. SSOC's roots were in the black-led STUDENT NONVIOLENT COORDINATING COMMITTEE (SNCC), as the group was created by the forty-five young people who attended a meeting of white civil rights supporters jointly organized by white SNCC staff members Sam Shirah and Ed Hamlett and activist white students in Nashville.

Initially, SSOC worked to build support for black equality among working-class whites, participated in civil rights campaigns in black communities, and helped organize desegregation protests at many of the region's predominantly white colleges and universities. By 1966, though, issues such as the VIETNAM WAR and university reform competed with civil rights for attention in the group. Moreover, SNCC's turn toward racial separatism, culminating in the rise of BLACK POWER, encouraged SSOC to work exclusively with Southern whites. These developments created serious internal problems for SSOC because they revealed that the activists disagreed over precisely which whites and which issues should be the focus of their work. While some advocated that SSOC try to draw white students into the civil rights and antiwar movements, many others believed that SSOC should work exclusively in white communities on issues of interest to the residents, such as municipal services and unemployment. These differences contributed to SSOC's factionalization and helped to precipitate its collapse in June 1969.

BIBLIOGRAPHY

Joye, Harlon E. "Dixie's New Left." *Trans-action* 7:11 (September 1970), pp. 50–56, 62.

Michel, Gregg L. *"We'll Take Our Stand". The Southern Student Organizing Committee and the Radicalization of White Southern Students, 1964–1969*. Ph.D. dissertation, University of Virginia. 1998.

Gregg L. Michel

Southern Tenant Farmers' Union

Labor organizer H. L. Mitchell liked to claim that the Southern Tenant Farmers' Union (STFU) was "a mass movement, something like the civil rights movement thirty years later." Galvanized by Norman Thomas's 1934 visit to northeast Arkansas, local SOCIALIST PARTY members Mitchell and Clay East brought together black and white tenants and sharecroppers to form the STFU. Initially determined to claim for sharecroppers their government payments under the Agriculture Adjustment Act's crop reduction program, the organization quickly grew into an interracial social movement that challenged the power wielded by large landholders over indebted sharecroppers, tenants, and small farmers, both black and white, in the rural South. Led by a coalition of Socialists, radical Christians, and African-American preachers (who made up half of the union's executive board), and supported by the national office of the NATIONAL ASSOCIATION FOR THE ADVANCEMENT OF COLORED PEOPLE (NAACP), by 1936 the organization enrolled 25,000 members, two-thirds of them black, in Arkansas, Missouri, Oklahoma, and Texas.

The STFU organized the men and women who bore the brunt of the collapse of the cotton economy during the 1930s. In addition to leading a strike of Arkansas cotton pickers in 1936, the union sought to break the dependency engendered by the crop-lien system, which kept sharecroppers and tenants perpetually in debt to their landlords.

The STFU's most significant achievement, the creation of an interracial union movement in the segregated rural South, made it vulnerable to violent repression by planters and their allies. However, interracialism created internal tensions as well, as not all white tenants proved ready to abandon racial privilege, and not all black sharecroppers easily placed their trust in whites, some of whom had helped suppress earlier attempts at black farm union organization. Mitchell insisted that in the STFU "there are no 'niggers' and no poor white trash . . . , only Union

men," but some segregated locals persisted. Nevertheless, where blacks and whites worked and lived in close proximity, they joined the same organization. Ultimately, in bringing the "disinherited" of both races together, the STFU sought to radically change the entire Southern economic and political structure, of which RACISM was an integral part.

The STFU prefigured aspects of the civil rights movement in several other ways as well. First, it drew on the latent political activism of the black church, which breathed life into the "union gospel," providing it with the community standing and stirring oratory of local preachers such as E. B. McKinney and playing union songs set to gospel music by the union's unofficial bard, John Handcox. Second, the union's leadership, if not always its constituency, embraced nonviolence on both tactical and philosophical grounds. Finally, in order to defend against repression and publicize the sharecroppers' plight, the STFU recruited privileged advocates from churches, universities, and political organizations far beyond the confines of the rural South.

Despite rapid expansion and early success, by the end of the decade the STFU faded away; but the union's original vision of an interracial movement of the poor set an important precedent for the wave of change that swept the South during the 1960s, much as Mitchell claimed.

BIBLIOGRAPHY

Blackside Productions. "Mean Things Happenin'," episode five of the PBS series "The Great Depression."

Dunbar, Anthony P. *Against the Grain: Southern Radicals and Prophets, 1929–1959.* 1981.

Grubbs, Donald H. *Cry from the Cotton: The Southern Tenant Farmers' Union and the New Deal.* 1971.

Kester, Howard. *Revolt Among the Sharecroppers*, introduction by Alex Lichtenstein. 1997 [1936].

Mitchell, H. L. *Mean Things Happening in This Land: The Life and Times of H. L. Mitchell, Co-founder of the Southern Tenant Farmers' Union.* 1979.

Southern Tenant Farmers' Union Papers. Southern Historical Collection, University of North Carolina, Chapel Hill, N.C.

Thomas, Norman. *The Plight of the Share-cropper.* 1934.

Thrasher, Sue, and Leah Wise, "The Southern Tenant Farmers' Union" (interviews with former members). *Southern Exposure* 1 (Winter 1974): 5–32. Reprinted in *Working Lives: the Southern Exposure History of Labor in the South*, edited by Marc S. Miller. 1980.

Whayne, Jeannie M. *A New Plantation South: Land, Labor, and Federal Favor in Twentieth-Century Arkansas.* 1996.

Wolters, Raymond. *Negroes and the Great Depression: The Problem of Economic Recovery.* 1970.

Alex Lichtenstein

Southwest Voter Registration Education Project

The Southwest Voter Registration Education Project (SVREP) is a nonpartisan, nonprofit, tax-exempt organization that developed as part of the spreading campaign for equal VOTING RIGHTS and increased political participation that followed the U.S. VOTING RIGHTS ACT OF 1965. William C. "Willie" VELÁSQUEZ began the undertaking while working as assistant director of field organizing and fund-raising for the national council of La RAZA UNIDA (self-described as "el partido politico de los Chicanos" or "the Chicanos' political party"). The voter registration project emerged from a national convention of the party in El Paso, Texas, in 1972.

SVREP became an independent entity in 1974, focused on empowering Hispanic Americans generally and Mexican Americans particularly, along with Native Americans and other minorities, through a three-step process of (1) educating people about the democratic process, (2) registering eligible voters, and (3) turning out the vote. When SVREP began, Velásquez ran it from the La Raza Headquarters in Washington, D.C. With Velásquez as executive director, SVREP mounted more than a thousand education and registration campaigns in hundreds of cities and on Native American reservations.

SVREP has focused on five southwestern states—Arizona, California, Colorado, New Mexico, and Texas—which in the mid-1970s contained sixty-one of every one hundred Hispanic citizens in the United States; but SVREP has extended its reach with programs in Idaho, Kansas, Montana, Ohio, Oklahoma, South Dakota, Utah, and Wyoming.

In 1998, SVREP claimed 2.1 million Latino registered voters in California alone and another nearly 1.8 million in Texas—significant increases from its early numbers. In 1972 the entire United States counted about 2.5 million registered Hispanic voters, whereas by 1988 the number reached 4.6 million, an 84 percent increase. SVREP expected California alone to have 2.7 million Latino registered voters for the presidential election in 2000.

Between the presidential elections of 1976 and 1988, SVREP saw the number of Hispanic votes cast in its five-state focus area increase by about 60 percent, from one million to 1.6 million. In the 1996 presidential election, Latinos in the focus area cast 1.97 million votes.

SVREP's understanding of the importance of information gathering and dissemination in matters of public policy, and of voter participation, gave rise in 1984 to the Southwest Voter Research Institute (SVRI), in San Antonio, established to ascertain, analyze, and announce the interests and positions of the Latino electorate. To honor its deceased founder, SVRI was renamed in 1997 the William C. Velásquez Institute (WCVI).

SVREP has also pushed in the courts to protect minority voting rights, particularly from dilution. Under its own name and through its SVRI/WCVI research complement, SVREP has helped win about a hundred voting rights cases. Examples of its casework are *League of United Latin American Citizens, Council No. 4386 v. Midland Independent School District*, 812 F.2d 1494 (5th Cir. 1987); *Common Cause of California v. Board of Supervisors of Los Angeles County* (49 Cal. 3d 432 1987); *Sanchez v. King*, 550 F. Supp. 13 (D. N.M. 1982); and *Seamon v. Upham*, 536 F. Supp. 931 (E.D. TX 1982).

BIBLIOGRAPHY

De la Garza, Rodolfo O., Robert R. Brischetto, with David Vaughan. *The Mexican American Electorate, Information Sources and Policy Orientations*. 1983.

Hernandez, Andrew. *The Southwest Voter Registration Education Project Legacy: La Esperanza del Futuro—15th Anniversary SVREP 1974–1989*. 1989.

Puente, Maria. "Hispanics Prove Pivotal," *USA Today*, November 4, 1998, 4A.

William C. Velásquez Institute Archives. WCVI, San Antonio, Tex.

Thomas J. Davis

Sovereignty, Native American Tribal

In the eighteenth century, the United States inherited the centuries-old European international policy of treating the New World's indigenous groups as sovereign (independent) political entities. The 1784 U.S. Constitution explicitly recognized tribal sovereignty and one of the first federal laws, the Indian Trade and Intercourse Act of 1790, defined U.S.–Indian relations for the following two centuries. In *Worcester v. Georgia* (1832), the Supreme Court described tribes as "domestic dependent nations," meaning Native Americans held the right to occupy their lands and exercise their inherent powers essentially free of state controls, subject only to the ultimate (plenary) authority of the federal government. The United States, responsible for Indian health and welfare through a unique trust relationship, could unilaterally terminate specific rights, but only when benefiting Indian peoples.

Despite the seemingly favorable U.S. policies, the legal rights of Indian individuals were neither a major concern of the federal government nor the courts throughout much of the nineteenth century. Tribal relations were largely guided by treaties rather than common law and legal dealings with individuals were essentially avoided. The U.S. government applied a system for policing and punishment that operated beyond the reach of the courts. Indian agents with ready access to the military exercised broad authority, detaining thousands of individuals for a wide range of alleged actions through the years.

By the 1870s Indian issues rose in the national eye as Western settlement expanded and social reformer's shifted attention from slavery. Demands for action gathered momentum. An 1879 federal court ruling in *United States ex rel. Standing Bear v. Crook* asserted that Indians off-reservation are "persons" having due process and equal protection under the Fourteenth Amendment. The army thus held no broad authority to detain Indians without full civilian due process protections. However, Indians' precise legal standing remained poorly defined.

In 1884 the Supreme Court ruled that the Fourteenth Amendment of the U.S. Constitution did not automatically grant citizenship to Indians. Consequently, U.S. citizenship had to be gained by receiving a land allotment under the 1887 DAWES SEVERALTY ACT, through treaties, marriage to non-Indian citizens, or military service. Congress, with the 1924 Indian Citizenship Act, finally granted citizenship to all Indians born in the United States, but the act did not provide constitutional protections from their own tribal governments. In some cases tribal members could therefore be subjected to harsher legal penalties from their governments than non-Indians in the larger society since constitutional protection did not apply. The act also made Indians citizens of the states they resided in, though not subject to state jurisdiction while on Indian lands. Though able to vote and hold state office, they are not subject to state law on Indian lands.

Influenced by the African-American civil rights movement, a series of Congressional hearings in the 1960s focused on the lack of consistent civil rights protections offered by tribal governments. As a result, Congress passed the Indian Civil Rights Act (ICRA) of 1968 that imposed protections of free speech, free exercise of religion, due process and equal protection of laws on tribal governments. Not extended was the right to a jury in civil cases, free legal counsel for indigents, search and seizure protections, and the First Amendment prohibition on government establishment of religion.

Respecting tribal sovereignty, interpretation of ICRA is left to the tribes and tribal courts, not federal courts. Federal courts could only review tribal court decisions in criminal cases involving writs of habeas corpus. Other issues such as gender discrimination in tribal ordinances cannot be challenged under federal law. By the late twentieth century, tribal court systems grew as many tribes gained greater economic and political power. However, uniform application of tribal court jurisdiction was minimal due to the broad diversity of tribal legal systems. Besides those patterned after Western society models, some tribes retained traditional indigenous systems and others no system at all.

Other legal distinctions also developed. Title VII of the 1964 Civil Rights Act explicitly exempted Indian hiring preferences from its due process protections in some instances. The 1974 Court ruling, *Morton v. Mancari*, affirmed that American Indians can be treated differently from other U.S. citizens by the federal government despite anti-discrimination laws. Tribes are political not racial groups on occasions when the U.S. government bases its actions on the long-standing legal responsibilities to protect Indian interests and promote tribal sovereignty. If the Indian preference laws were only designed to help Indians as individuals, they then could be determined racist.

The resulting branch of U.S. law, commonly termed Indian Law, is an aberration in the U.S. legal system with tribal governments and their peoples possessing a unique legal status. Members of federally recognized tribes hold three citizenships, receiving certain benefits and protections from the federal, state, and tribal governments. With civil rights protections differing from other citizens, determining who is Indian has important legal consequences. Constituting a political rather than racial matter, tribal members may derive membership from birth or marriage and may have substantial non-Indian ancestry. Conversely, a person of total Indian ancestry who has never established a relationship with a tribe may not enjoy Indian legal status. Each of the over 500 recognized tribes in the United States is responsible to determine membership as an exercise of their individual sovereignty. In general, an Indian is anyone with some degree of indigenous ancestry, considered a member of an Indian community, and promoting themselves as Indian.

BIBLIOGRAPHY

Cohen, Felix S. *Felix S. Cohen's Handbook of Federal Indian Law.* 1971.

Getches, David H., Charles F. Wilkinson, and Robert A. Williams, Jr. *Cases and Materials on Federal Indian Law,* 3rd edition. 1993.

Harring, Sidney L. *Crow Dog's Case: American Indian Sovereignty, Tribal Law, and United States Law in the Nineteenth Century.* 1994.

Washburn, Wilcomb E., ed. *Handbook of North American Indians: History of Indian-White Relations,* Vol. 4. 1988.

Wilkins, David E. *American Indian Sovereignty and the U.S. Supreme Court: The Masking of Justice.* 1997.

Wilkinson, Charles F. *American Indians, Time, and the Law: Native Societies in a Modern Constitutional Democracy.* 1987.

Williams, David C. "The Borders of the Equal Protection Clause: Indians as Peoples." *U.C.L.A. Law Review,* 38 (1991): 759–870.

Richard C. Hanes

Sports

During the nineteenth and twentieth centuries, American sports have served as a cultural arena in which individuals and communities that differ by race, ethnicity, class, gender, and physical ability have contested for power—that is, for the right to define themselves and negotiate for full participation in American life.

Many first-generation immigrant males from Europe were uninterested in American sports, remaining attached to their own imported physical cultures. Immigrant sportsmen, who had used institutionalized sport to legitimize nationalist sentiments in their native countries, adapted their homeland athletic organizations to fit the American experience. German *Turner* and Czech *Sokol* leagues—ethnic fraternities promoting noncompetitive gymnastic exercises—doubled as political pressure groups that asserted the immigrant's right to cultural independence, agitated for improved working-class conditions, and rallied against such ethno-political restrictions as Sunday blue laws and prohibition.

The second generation preferred participating in American sports to demonstrate they were not "greenhorns" and to promote individual and community esteem. The Irish, Italians, Poles, and Jews became prominent in sports that fit their socioeconomic status. Boxing, in particular, provided a forum for individual achievement on a national scale. Although branded an activity fit only for the lower classes, the sport's practitioners served as public symbols that both confirmed a particular ethnic group's toughness and ingenuity and combated popular stereotypes.

Sport spectatorship also served to unite disparate groups. The common identification with a "home" team created a public conception of home rooted in geography, not social difference. The turn-of-the-century baseball stadium was a public space where uprooted Americans—both native-born and new immigrant—shared common hopes and experiences, allowing the ties of masculinity and male sociability to span class and ethnic chasms.

African Americans used sports to foster a sense of community in developing urban neighborhoods and as a forum for racial assertiveness. The white sporting establishment excluded black athletes through a "gentlemen's agreement" among baseball owners, "anticolored" unions in horseracing, and by "drawing the

Jesse Owens sprinting at the 1936 Summer Olympics in Berlin. (AP/Wide World Photos)

Wilma Rudolph at the conclusion of a relay race at the 1960 Summer Olympics in Rome. (AP/Wide World Photos)

color line" in professional prizefighting. SEGREGATION, which implied inequality, reinforced ideas of "race" and racial difference. Interracial competition, in turn, symbolized equality of opportunity and full participation in American society.

The boxing ring and the runner's track served as high-profile arenas for challenges to the racial status quo, with notions of "colored" inferiority disproved with every black victory. African-American athletes had to negotiate their inclusion into white-controlled sports cautiously. Black athletic successes in times of virulent racism hardened white intolerance for interracial sport. Yet under different circumstances black sporting heroes formed cultural bridges between their community and white America. The extraordinary accomplishments of the boxer Joe Louis and the sprinter Jesse Owens against a backdrop of 1930s fascist intolerance, and the gold-medal performances of track star Wilma Rudolph during the height of 1960s COLD WAR competitiveness, prompted whites to applaud black accomplishments in the name of American nationalism.

The integration of baseball stands as one of the most powerful episodes in modern race relations and black Americans' attempts to assert their right to occupy public space. Challenged by the black press and emboldened by an emerging post–WORLD WAR II racial liberalism, Branch Rickey signed Jackie ROBINSON to the Brooklyn Dodgers in 1945, at last desegregating the "national pastime." Robinson's influence testifies to the power of an individual to alter popular beliefs. Though a proud and combative man, he consistently "turned the other cheek" when confronted with verbal and physical assaults, greatly impressing Americans of all colors with his composure and dignity. The successful integration of baseball anticipated the strategies of the future civil rights movement, as a small number of brave black men and women, assisted by sympathetic whites, risked violent confrontation and idealized racial integration.

Persistent racial prejudice transformed many black athletes from stoic pioneers into militant protesters who sought to use their popularity and access to the media to change society. Muhammad ALI, in particular, represented the proud black athlete in revolt against a nation that refused to grant him full civil liberties. His assertion of individual pride ("I am the greatest"), outspokenness against racial inequality, and refusal to serve in the Vietnam War emboldened the liberal-minded of all races and ethnicities. Inspired by Ali, and urged into the spotlight by more radical elements of the community, black collegiate athletes during the 1960s collectively protested against bans on interracial dating, segregated student housing, and hostile racial climates. Sprinters Tommie Smith and John Carlos brought the rebellious black athlete's protest against the chimera of racial equality to international television when they raised black-gloved fists high in the air on the victory podium during the 1968 Olympics.

So entrenched was the idea of sports as a male preserve that the absence of women in the 1960s protests, and their underparticipation in organized athletics in general, barely registered notice. The accomplishments of twentieth-century female athletes have engendered public ambivalence. The early century feats of the multitalented Babe Didrikson, for example, were viewed as incontrovertible proof of female ability by some and as a deviant transgression of true womanhood by others. American women still must fight to overcome a sporting ideology that often equates female athletic excellence with mannishness and the surrender of "femininity." Because some women's contests are shorter in duration or confined to smaller spaces than men's, women also confront sporting patterns that suggest female "frailty" and sexual inequality. Through both daily participation in sports and remarkable athletic achievements, female athletes have forcefully challenged cultural stereotypes of masculine skill and feminine weakness and asserted their right to define sport and womanhood on their own terms.

Paralleling the drive for equal rights in other areas, women's demands for equal athletic opportunity emerged as a major theme in post–World War II American sport. The efforts of tennis star Billie Jean King to create an independent women's tennis tour and equalize prize money was consistent with the broader attempts of women to gain control over their own bodies. With the passage of Title IX of the Education Amendments (1972), the federal government established that girls and boys have the same right to participate in school athletics. Though Title IX generated more funds for women's sports, many scholars and activists describe the results as disappointing. For example, some university athletic directors employ a notion of equality based on capitalist, and not democratic, values, arguing that women's sports are not as profitable as men's and should not be equivalently funded.

As the demands for equal access to sports—that most public of public spheres—demonstrate, ideas of rights and entitlement are dynamic and hotly contested. Not merely games, sports reflect ideological and social divisions and serve as a popular and accessible arena within which Americans make claims and negotiate their differences.

BIBLIOGRAPHY

Cahn, Susan. *Coming on Strong: Gender and Sexuality in Twentieth-Century Women's Sport.* 1994.

Levine, Peter. *Ellis Island to Ebbets Field: Sport and the American Jewish Experience.* 1992.

Mangan, J. A., and Roberta Park, eds. *From "Fair Sex" to Feminism: Sport and the Socialization of Women in the Industrial and Post-industrial Eras.* 1987.

Riess, Steven A. *City Games: The Evolution of American Urban Society and the Rise of Sports.* 1989.

Roberts, Randy. *Papa Jack: Jack Johnson and the Era of White Hopes.* 1983.

Ruck, Rob. *Sandlot Seasons: Sport in Black Pittsburgh.* 1987.

Sammons, Jeffrey T. *Beyond the Ring: The Role of Boxing in American Society.* 1988.

Tygiel, Jules. *Baseball's Great Experiment: Jackie Robinson and His Legacy.* Expanded ed. 1997.

Vertinsky, Patricia, and Gwendolyn Captain. "More Myth than History: American Culture and Representations of the Black Female's Athletic Ability." *Journal of Sport History* 25 (1998): 532–561.

Wiggins, David K. *Glory Bound: Black Athletes in a White America.* 1997.

Matthew Andrews

Stanton, Elizabeth Cady

(1815–1902), nineteenth-century women's rights advocate.

Elizabeth Cady Stanton was born in Johnstown, New York, an intellectually precocious girl who studied Greek and liked to read in her father's law office. She attended Emma Willard's Female Seminary, and in 1840 married abolitionist Henry Stanton. Although involved in the crusade against slavery, Stanton was always more interested in fighting the discrimination she faced as a woman. She protested the sexism she encountered in the abolitionist movement, and in 1848 helped organize the first woman's rights convention in the United States, in Seneca Falls, New York. Although busy with her seven young children, Stanton became an important writer and speaker for the cause of women's rights, agitating not only for suffrage, but also for reform of discriminatory divorce and property laws. During the Civil War, Stanton laid aside the issue of suffrage to focus on aiding the Union.

Women suffragettes Elizabeth Cady Stanton (left) and Susan B. Anthony. (Library of Congress)

Expecting some reward after the war, she was bitterly disappointed by the FOURTEENTH and FIFTEENTH AMENDMENTS, which inserted the word "male" into the Constitution and explicitly enfranchised only black men. Splitting with many female abolitionists, who insisted that civil rights for the freed slaves must come first, Stanton lobbied against the use of increasingly racist and nativist (see NATIVISON) language in the Fourteenth and Fifteenth Amendments. In 1869, Stanton helped organize the NATIONAL WOMAN SUFFRAGE ASSOCIATION (NAWSA), which sought a federal amendment granting women the right to vote. Opponents of Stanton formed the *American Woman Suffrage Association* to work for women's suffrage on the state level. The two groups merged in 1890, and Stanton was elected president of the new National American Woman Suffrage Association. Stanton soon resigned, in part because of her frustration at NAWSA's exclusive focus on the issue of suffrage. She spent her last years criticizing organized religion for degrading women.

BIBLIOGRAPHY

Banner, Lois. *Elizabeth Cady Stanton: A Radical for Woman's Rights.* 1980.
Griffith, Elisabeth. *In Her Own Right: The Life of Elizabeth Cady Stanton.* 1984.
Lutz, Alma. *Created Equal: A Biography of Elizabeth Cady Stanton.* 1974.

Renee Romano

States' Rights

The term "states' rights" refers to the powers the states have to govern themselves. By dividing power between the states and the national authority, the federal system of the United States practically invites quarrels over which powers belong to the states and which to the national government. Such controversies have been a constant throughout American history and reflect ambiguities written into the U.S. CONSTITUTION.

The most dramatic assertions of states' rights in American history have come when Southern and Northern states have resisted national power in issues involving slavery and race. The concept of states' rights is closely associated with the South because it has so often been linked to racism and slavery there. Southern states insisted that the regulation of their slaves amounted to a states' right. However, Northern states also asserted their rights on such matters. Several Northern states enacted "personal liberty laws" in response to congressional efforts to help white Southerners retrieve runaway slaves. In 1854, Massachusetts, for example, virtually nullified the 1850 federal fugitive slave law by forbidding sheriffs, militia soldiers, lawyers, or other state officers from acting on behalf of slave catchers. The state insisted, contrary to federal law, that alleged fugitives from justice had due process rights, the authors of these personal liberty laws claiming a state right to protect their residents from obnoxious federal laws. The powers the states have to govern themselves are often called police powers, meaning the power to protect the health of their citizens and maintain order. At the end of the nineteenth century, the states used police power to justify the laws they enacted segregating their citizens according to race. SEGREGATION laws, the states claimed, were necessary to maintain good order.

For much of the first century of American history, states had exercised their police powers without dissent from the federal government. The Civil War and its aftermath led CONGRESS to challenge state powers with new federal laws. The CIVIL RIGHTS ACT OF 1866, for example, defined citizenship for the first time and stated the rights American citizens enjoyed. Every right Congress claimed for American citizens came at the expense of the powers states held over their citizens. Adoption of the FOURTEENTH AMENDMENT in 1868 allowed the federal courts to supervise states' police powers. The Fourteenth Amendment defined citizenship, required the states to treat their citizens equally, and forbade the states from interfering with citizens' due process rights or their privileges or immunities. Never again would states enjoy sole or exclusive powers over their citizens. The federal courts began to look more closely at state laws passed on the basis of their police powers. The police power, the U.S. SUPREME COURT insisted, had to genuinely benefit everyone, not merely some segment of the population. In several cases the Supreme Court knocked down state laws designed to protect workers' health. At the same time, the Court accepted the states' theory that segregation promoted good order. Even when the Court upheld such discriminatory laws, the justices claimed they did so because the laws truly benefited the whole population.

In the nineteenth century, the Supreme Court guarded states' rights, only to reduce them through much of the twentieth. The Court preserved states' rights in the *Slaughterhouse Cases* (1873) and proclaimed the states "indestructible" in *Texas v. White* (1868). In the Great DEPRESSION, Congress posed new challenges to states' rights. In the 1930s, President Franklin D. ROOSEVELT persuaded Congress to pass a series of laws collectively known as the NEW DEAL. Many of these laws asserted new powers for the federal government at the expense of the states. As Roosevelt remained in office for twelve years, he chose every member of the Supreme Court before his death. The

Roosevelt Court, as it is called, believed modern society required a strong federal government. Before Roosevelt came to office, the states had several virtually unchallenged powers over economic matters; by the time of Roosevelt's death in 1945, federal agencies routinely regulated manufacturing and many other economic issues once left to the states.

Despite these dramatic changes, the job of protecting citizens' civil rights remained a state right. African Americans emerged from the horrors of post–Civil War racial violence and the LYNCHING era understanding that they must look to the federal government for protection, not the states. States' rights offered few protections for minority groups. Civil rights organizations campaigned to end school SEGREGATION in federal courts more than in state courts. When the Supreme Court declared the segregation of public schools unconstitutional in 1954, its decision shattered the once-exclusive powers states had exercised over their schools.

The states' rights doctrine suffered a blow when white supremacists used it to resist DESEGREGATION. Southern congressional delegations relied on states' rights arguments to resist civil rights legislation in 1964 and 1965, convincing many Americans that states' rights was no more than a cover for violent racism. In court, Southern states offered states' rights to justify their resistance to desegregation, which led the Supreme Court to render sharper decisions in *Katzenbach v. McClung* (1964) and *Heart of Atlanta Motel v. United States* (1964) than it might have done otherwise. The *McClung* decision, for example, involved a small Birmingham, Alabama, restaurant with no customers from outside the state. Determined to smite segregation, the justices ruled that the hamburgers McClung served came from out of state and thus justified federal regulation. After *Katzenbach v. McClung* states had hardly any rights with which to exclusively regulate local commerce.

In recent years the Supreme Court has been more attentive to the rights of states. In *United States v. Lopez* (1995), the Court declared unconstitutional a federal law against carrying guns into public schools, insisting that states should police the schools. In *Printz v. United States* (1997), the Court ruled that Congress could not "commandeer" state employees to run background checks on purchasers of guns. The justices based this last decision on the Tenth Amendment, a part of the Constitution ignored for most of its history. At the end of the twentieth century, the Supreme Court, because of its conservative makeup, has revived states' rights.

BIBLIOGRAPHY

Belknap, Michal R. *Federal Law and Southern Order: Racial Violence and Constitutional Conflict in the Post-Brown South.* 1987.

Benedict, Michael Les. "Sovereign Nation of Sovereign States: Federalism Through the Civil War Era." In *A Bicentennial Collection of Essays,* edited by Mary A. Hepburn. 1988.

Urofsky, Melvin I. *A March of Liberty: A Constitutional History of the United States.* 1988.

Zimmerman, Joseph F. *Contemporary American Federalism.* 1992.

Christopher Waldrep

Steinem, Gloria

(1934–   ), feminist writer and editor.

A partisan of but not a participant in the U.S. civil rights movements of the 1950s and 1960s, Gloria Steinem is best known for her tireless work for feminism. She has been a symbol of and for the women's movement.

Feminist author Gloria Steinem answers questions after giving a speech at Saint Barnabas Hospital in West Orange, New Jersey. (Laurence Agron/Archive Photos)

She was born into a white, lower-middle-class family on March 25, 1934, in Toledo, Ohio, to a Jewish father and a non-Jewish mother. Her paternal grandmother, Pauline Perlmutter Steinem, had been an Ohio suffragist. Steinem had a difficult childhood; her parents divorced, and for years she cared for her mother, who suffered from a lingering illness. Steinem attended Smith College, graduating magna cum laude in 1956. She studied briefly in India, returning to direct the Independent Research Service in Cambridge, Massachusetts, an organization connected to the NATIONAL STUDENT ASSOCIATION. She moved to New York City in 1960 to become a journalist, and there became involved in the radical politics of the 1960s, including the left wing of the DEMOCRATIC PARTY. She chose not to go South to help with voter registration. "I didn't go and I've regretted it."

Before her involvement in the women's liberation movement, Steinem marched with the Women's Strike for Peace against the VIETNAM WAR and worked closely with Dolores HUERTA of the UNITED FARM WORKERS; she brought members of the NATIONAL WELFARE RIGHTS ORGANIZATION to a Democratic Policy Council meeting. In 1969, she attended a speak-out on abortion, organized by Redstockings, a New York–based radical women's liberation organization, which motivated her to full participation in the women's movement. Feminism became the bedrock of her life.

Speaking across the country, she traveled with a number of African-American women: Dorothy Pittman, a radical child care activist; Florynce Kennedy, a radical feminist lawyer and activist; Margaret Sloan, a civil rights activist; and Jane Galvin-Lewis, from the NATIONAL COUNCIL OF NEGRO WOMEN. With Bella ABZUG, Shirley CHISHOLM, and Betty FRIEDAN, she founded the National Women's Political Caucus, to encourage women to run for political office. She helped organize the Women's Action Alliance, to mobilize people of color and the poor to fight against social and political discrimination.

In 1972, with others, Steinem founded *Ms.*, the first mass-market feminist magazine. Its first printing, three hundred thousand copies, sold out within eight days. During Steinem's first fifteen years with *Ms.*, the magazine took up every feminist issue, including abortion rights, sexuality, economic justice, marriage, the family, and the culture. The word "Ms.," a title of courtesy that does not indicate a woman's marital status, became part of the national lexicon. In 1987, advertisers' demands to control copy forced the sale of the magazine; and in 1990, a new *Ms.* was published, this time without advertising; Steinem served as a consulting editor.

Steinem lobbied state legislators for passage of the EQUAL RIGHTS AMENDMENT, and attended the founding meetings of the Coalition of Labor Union Women and of Women Against Pornography. In 1977, she served as a commissioner appointed by President Jimmy CARTER to the National Committee of the Observance of International Women's Year. In 1983, she published *Outrageous Acts and Everyday Rebellions*, a collection of her essays and articles. She also wrote *Marilyn: Norma Jean*, with George Barris, in 1988. Her 1992 semi-autobiography, *Revolution from Within: A Book of Self Esteem*, was criticized by many in the women's movement for her emphasis on pop psychology and for focusing too much on the individual and too little on CLASS and RACE.

BIBLIOGRAPHY

Daffron, Carolyn. *Gloria Steinem*. 1987.
Heilbrun, Carolyn G. *The Education of a Woman: The Life of Gloria Steinem*. 1995.
Henry, Sondra. *One Woman's Power: A Biography of Gloria Steinem*. 1987.
Hoff, Mark. *Gloria Steinem: The Women's Movement*. 1991.
Steinem, Gloria. *Outrageous Acts and Everyday Rebellions*. 1983.
Steinem, Gloria. *Revolution from Within: A Book of Self Esteem*. 1992.

Barbara Winslow

Stevens, Thaddeus

(1792–1868), Congressman.

Stevens was a leading Republican member of the House of Representatives during the Civil War and RECONSTRUCTION and advocate of emancipation and civil rights.

Born in Vermont and a graduate of Dartmouth College, Stevens moved to southeastern Pennsylvania where he became an iron-maker, attorney, and politician. After two terms in Congress as a Whig (1849–1853), he returned to the House in 1858 and served as a Republican until his death. Always the subject of bitter controversy, he advocated emancipation and civil rights in a way which left little room for compromise. As a young man residing near the Maryland border he defended countless fugitive slaves, usually for no fee. In 1860, he opposed all concessions to southern states threatening secession. During the Civil War, he urged President Abraham LINCOLN to move more quickly to emancipation and was publicly critical of the slow pace the President pursued. Urging confiscation of the slaveowners' lands and their distribution to freedmen, he successfully persuaded Congress to approve equal pay for black soldiers with their white counterparts.

During Reconstruction, he was the leading House member of the Joint Committee on Reconstruction

Pennsylvanian Thaddeus Stevens, a leader of the Radical Republicans in the U.S. House of Representatives in the post–Civil War era. (Library of Congress)

and successfully urged the House to repass the civil rights and freedmen's bureau bills over Andrew Johnson's vetoes in 1866. He was among the chief architects of the FOURTEENTH AMENDMENT and thus helped lay the foundation for the civil rights revolution of the twentieth century. Forced to compromise on many occasions, he called for measures which became part of the FIFTEENTH AMENDMENT granting black suffrage after his death. Far ahead of his time in regard to interracial democracy, he helped point the way to later equality.

BIBLIOGRAPHY

Brodie, Fawn M. *Thaddeus Stevens, Scourge of the South.* 1959.

Current, Richard N. *Old Thad Stevens: A Story of Ambition.* 1942.

Palmer, Beverly, and Holly Ochoa, eds. *The Selected Papers of Thaddeus Stevens.* 2 vols. 1997–1998.

Trefousse, Hans L. *Thaddeus Stevens: Nineteenth-Century Egalitarian.* 1997.

Frederick J. Blue

Stone, Lucy

(1818–1893), women's movement founder.

Lucy Stone was a well-known women's rights leader and skilled public speaker of the nineteenth century. Born on August 13, 1818, in West Brookfield, Massachusetts, Stone, along with her eight siblings, helped her parents operate their farm and make shoes. Her father did not endorse her academic ambitions, but nonetheless lent her money to help her pay for her studies at Mount Holyoke Seminary and Oberlin College. At the latter institution she became the first woman to speak publicly, and, upon her graduation in 1847, the first female college graduate from her home state of Massachusetts. Stone became known for her radical views, and, with fellow student Antoinette Brown (Blackwell), worked aggressively for women's rights at the Oberlin school. Following her college years, Stone lectured on women's issues and on abolition. The Worcester (Massachusetts) convention on women's rights in 1850, the first such convention with a national scope, was in part orchestrated by Lucy Stone.

Stone married Henry Brown Blackwell (brother of the first female doctor in the United States, Elizabeth

Lucy Stone, founder of the American Woman Suffrage Association, was the first woman to be arrested for civil disobedience in U.S. history. (Library of Congress)

Blackwell) in 1855, but kept her maiden name. (Women who followed this practice were subsequently nicknamed "Lucy Stoners.") The year after her marriage, she presided over the Seventh National Women's Rights Convention, but soon interrupted her political activism to care for her infant daughter Alice. In 1858 Stone became the first woman arrested for an act of CIVIL DISOBEDIENCE in the United States, when she chose to protest the disenfranchisement of women by refusing to pay property taxes on her new home in Orange, New Jersey. Throughout the 1860s she continued her reform activities with a variety of organizations supporting the rights of women and of African Americans.

Stone rose to greater prominence within the women's movement when she organized opposition to Elizabeth Cady STANTON and Susan B. ANTHONY within the suffragist movement. More militant feminists like Stanton and Anthony objected to the exclusion of women from the proposed FIFTEENTH AMENDMENT, which sought to altogether prohibit the disfranchisement of African-American men (who had been merely "disfavored" by the FOURTEENTH AMENDMENT). Stanton and Anthony refused to support the Fifteenth Amendment in its existing form, and furthermore embraced progressive social reforms such as the issue of divorce. In response to Stanton and Anthony's formation of the National Woman Suffrage Association, Stone and others formed the AMERICAN WOMAN SUFFRAGE ASSOCIATION (AWSA) in November 1869. AWSA worked for the ratification of the Fifteenth Amendment, and viewed NWSA as racist for its failure to do the same. The two competing organizations became the principal factions in the women's rights movement.

Stone founded and edited AWSA's popular feminist periodical, *Woman's Journal*. Upon the merger of the American Woman Suffrage Association with the National Woman Suffrage Association in 1890, Stone maintained a leading role in the new organization, the NATIONAL AMERICAN WOMAN SUFFRAGE ASSOCIATION. She died in Boston in 1893.

BIBLIOGRAPHY

Blackwell, Alice Stone. *Lucy Stone: Pioneer of Woman's Rights.* 1971.
Frost-Knappman, Elizabeth, with Sarah Kurian. *The ABC-Clio Companion to Women's Progress in America.* 1994.
Kerr, Andrea Moore. *Lucy Stone: Speaking Out for Equality.* 1992.
Wheeler, Leslie. *Loving Warriors: Selected Letters of Lucy Stone and Henry B. Blackwell.* 1981.

Sarah Kurian

Stonewall Riot

An altercation between patrons of a New York City bar and police officers sparked what has come to be remembered as the symbolic beginning of the modern gay movement. On June 27, 1969, police began what could have been a routine raid on the Stonewall Inn, a bar on Christopher Street in Greenwich Village reputed to be Mafia-owned. When some of those being arrested resisted, other patrons outside began to throw bottles, bricks, and coins at the officers, who retreated into the bar. In reaction, the growing crowd tried to break down the door and set the building on fire. The police called for reinforcements, and soon over four hundred police arrived on the scene. For several hours, the city's highly trained Tactical Patrol Force battled about two thousand men and women who threw objects, burned trash cans, chanted insults, and formed jeering Rockettes-style chorus lines. The next night another large confrontation occurred at the site.

Though gay men and lesbians had first begun organizing for political and social change in the United States in the early 1950s, most of the Stonewall rioters came from a different segment of the population than the early organizers. Most of the earlier "homophile" activists had been white and middle class; in contrast, many of those who fought back at the Stonewall Inn were working-class people of African-American or Hispanic origin. In addition, since wearing insufficient amounts of gender-appropriate clothing was grounds for arrest during a bar raid, drag queens and butch lesbians initiated the first confrontations with police.

The fight almost immediately developed political implications. A homophile activist who happened upon the conflict alerted the local press, and he and others began chants of "Gay Power" that echoed through the crowd. The next day, "Gay Power" graffiti appeared on the site. Within weeks, a number of homosexual men and women formed the Gay Liberation Front (GLF); and as word of the riot spread, other liberation-oriented groups formed across the country.

In contrast to the earlier homophile movement, gay and lesbian activism after Stonewall employed more confrontational tactics and mobilized a younger, more radical base. Reflecting the influence of other radical movements of that decade, including the BLACK POWER movement and the STUDENT MOVEMENT, they called for a revolution in social institutions and a liberation from oppression. Inspired by calls for "Black Pride," these activists called for "Gay Pride." Women, previously on the margins of homophile organizations, joined gay liberation, and some, reacting to male chauvinism in gay groups and anti-lesbian sentiment among feminists, formed a separate lesbian liberation movement, which has often been allied with the movement for gay liberation.

The Stonewall riot is remembered not only as the beginning of a shift in political strategy but as a marker for a change in consciousness among gay men and lesbians. Across the United States and in other parts of the world, annual celebrations and parades are held in late June on or around the anniversary of the riot.

BIBLIOGRAPHY

D'Emilio, John. *Sexual Politics, Sexual Communities: The Making of a Homosexual Minority in the United States, 1940–1970.* 1983.

Duberman, Martin. *Stonewall.* 1993.

Jay, Karla, and Allen Young, eds. *Out of the Closets: Voices of Gay Liberation,* 2nd ed., 1992.

Teal, Donn. *The Gay Militants: How Gay Liberation Began in America, 1969–1971.* 2nd ed., 1995.

Pippa Holloway

Student Movements

American students never stood more highly than they did during the late 1950s and 1960s—the era of the civil rights movement. Despite their youth and inexperience, they were greatly relied upon to serve as the foot soldiers in the war against poverty and social injustice. If there was a fountainhead of student involvement in the civil rights struggle, it was probably the Nashville Student Movement. A select group of students from Fisk University, Tennessee State University, the American Baptist Theological Seminary, the Meharry Medical College, and Vanderbilt University attended workshops in Nashville, Tennessee, on "nonviolent direct action" that were conducted by the Reverend James LAWSON. Besides being a minister, a faculty member at the Vanderbilt University Divinity School, and a lecturer for the FELLOWSHIP OF REC-ONCILIATION (FOR) out of Chicago, Lawson was also an exponent of nonviolence. He had studied the Gandhian concepts of "ahimsa" and "satyagraha" (see Mohandas GANDHI) as well as the principles of Christian direct action as espoused by Dr. Martin Luther KING, JR. Reverend Lawson seemed to be in search of a cause that would allow him to apply his learning. Toward this end, he offered a series of workshops on the Fisk University campus, where he attracted a group of stalwarts who were highly committed to the cause of civil rights. This group included Diane NASH, John LEWIS, Bernard Lafayette, James Bevel, Marion Barry, and a host of others.

The SIT-IN that was executed on February 1, 1960, by Franklin McCain, Joseph McNeil, David Richmond, and Ezell Blair, Jr., all of North Carolina A&T College

at Greensboro was by no means the first. Several other sit-ins had been carried out in a number of cities across the country but failed to garner as much publicity. The Nashville Student Movement was in the process of finalizing plans for a sit-in when the Greensboro protest occurred. When the Greensboro demonstration received national attention, the Lawson group accelerated efforts to launch similar protests. Within two months, their actions were paralleled by civil rights activists in fifty-four cities and nine states.

The Lawson group launched sit-ins against the segregated lunch counters in six department stores in Nashville (see SEGREGATION). Lawson made sure that their training imbued them with the determination and patience necessary to handle a wide array of circumstances. As a consequence, the students were able to withstand fierce physical abuse as well as suffer repeated arrests, but ultimately all of the targeted lunch counters were opened to black customers. The efforts of the Nashville Student Movement were widely publicized and were refocused onto other segregated facilities in the Tennessee capital. When Ella BAKER, executive secretary of the SOUTHERN CHRISTIAN LEADERSHIP CONFERENCE (SCLC), wanted to harness some of the energies of student protesters, she made sure that members of the Nashville movement were contacted. She invited them and many other students who were involved in sit-ins across the South to meet in Raleigh, North Carolina, April 15–16, 1960, to create an organization that would "coordinate" such protest activities. Out of this would come the STUDENT NONVIOLENT COORDINATING COMMITTEE (SNCC).

In May 1961 the CONGRESS OF RACIAL EQUALITY (CORE) sponsored a FREEDOM RIDE to test the enforcement of the *Boynton v. Virginia* Supreme Court decision. That ruling had been handed down on December 5, 1960, and prohibited racial discrimination in all facilities connected to interstate travel. On May 4, 1961, James FARMER, along with thirteen other Freedom Riders, set out on a trip through the Deep South. With them was John Lewis of the Nashville Student Movement. There were so many outrages—mob attacks, firebombings, and even arrests—that plagued this trip that Farmer considered terminating it. When the Nashville movement offered encouragement, fresh riders, and even some money to the project, Farmer agreed to allow them to join the Freedom Ride in Birmingham, Alabama—which they did.

The problems with mobs continued on the trip to Montgomery, Alabama. When racists assailed the group at the bus terminal as well as during a subsequent mass meeting at the First Baptist Church, it took federal intervention to help the Freedom Riders get going again. The ride ended in Jackson, Mississippi, where the protesters were tried and convicted of violating the state's laws about race-mixing in bus travel. The Freedom Riders were fined $200 and were sentenced to sixty days at the infamous Parchman prison (see PARCHMAN FARM). By this time, however, Americans had gotten involved in the rides; they were of different ages, races, genders, and philosophies, but they were all determined to help knock down the barriers to interstate travel. The Freedom Rides continued throughout the summer of 1961.

Students also played a leading role in voter registration efforts (see VOTING RIGHTS), which soon engaged the attention of all the major civil rights organizations. Beginning in August 1961, SNCC dispatched former Harlem, New York, schoolteacher Robert P. MOSES to McComb, Mississippi. His assignment was to help the local branch of the NATIONAL ASSOCIATION FOR THE ADVANCEMENT OF COLORED PEOPLE (NAACP) to educate, inspire, and help register blacks in the rural areas of the state. Few blacks in Mississippi voted. Moses was soon joined by other young activists, including much of SNCC's staff and a growing number of young whites. Among these workers were James Chaney, Andrew Goodman, and Michael Schwerner, who were later murdered (see the entry at CHANEY). Local people were killed as well. Despite the violence and intimidation, a growing number of blacks were enfranchised in the state. The blacks of MISSISSIPPI became so encouraged that they even formed their own political party, the MISSISSIPPI FREEDOM DEMOCRATIC PARTY (MFDP). Emboldened, the MFDP challenged the seating of the regular Mississippi delegation to the DEMOCRATIC PARTY's national convention of 1964. The MFDP lost the challenge and its candidates failed to win any offices, but they at least gained a new confidence in themselves, they gained exposure to a nationwide television audience, and they enjoyed a very real opportunity to participate in the American political system.

The daring of Bob Moses to walk the dirt roads of Mississippi to talk to seemingly insignificant black farmers and sharecroppers soon began to pay off. Groups like the COUNCIL OF FEDERATED ORGANIZATIONS (COFO) and the VOTER EDUCATION PROJECT were developed to facilitate efforts like those Moses pioneered. Now similar actions spilled over into other states—e.g., the Lowndes County Project in Alabama. A young student from Howard University named Stokely CARMICHAEL proved his ability to get things done; he used his organizing skills to register black voters and to encourage blacks to run for office, and he helped to create a new political party in the state—the BLACK PANTHER PARTY.

Another Nashville civil rights organization, the SOUTHERN STUDENT ORGANIZING COMMITTEE (SSOC), was organized in 1964. The SSOC was made-

up primarily of white college students. It was involved in efforts to promote black equality and subsequently become involved in the ANTI-WAR MOVEMENT as well. The organization disbanded in 1969, as a result of factional disputes regarding the scope of its activities.

When discussing the contributions of America's students to the civil rights movement, their participation in freedom marches must not be forgotten. They made up a large number of the actual marchers. They also seemed to want new experiences and an expansion of their learning. Moreover, unlike working adults, they did not have jobs or professional standing that they feared would be endangered by their participation in activities not sanctioned by the Southern power structure. Students also served as march organizers and leaders. They would bring out the youthful participants in cities all across America. Moreover, they would explain in full detail to the marchers exactly what was expected of them.

This was one of the reasons why SNCC was so important in the civil rights movement. SNCC had courageous and charismatic young people who were able to influence other American youths. James FORMAN, Stokely Carmichael, John Lewis, James Bevel, and others had a gift for mobilizing large numbers of people, both young and old. Problems came only when some of these organizers became suspect of the older, more established civil rights leaders. SNCC people were cynical about middle-class values and life-styles. Although they worked with all the well-established civil rights groups—NAACP, SCLC, CORE, and the NATIONAL URBAN LEAGUE—they continued to harbor some doubts about older Americans.

Although Lewis was more trusting of the older generation, both Forman and Carmichael eventually felt that the student organizers were being used. The older leaders, they believed, would meet, plot strategy, and even make private deals with the white establishment while leaving their younger counterparts uninformed—or out of the loop. This happened during the 1965 Selma to Montgomery March, held in support of political rights and social justice for blacks in ALABAMA. The student organizers had been hard-pressed by the authorities and it was difficult to keep the marchers peaceful and hopeful. Then, at the last minute, Dr. King failed to confront a police barricade on the outskirts of Selma. Instead, after speaking with an official outside, he turned the march around. Forman and other student organizers felt betrayed and did not try to conceal their anger from the press. This showing stimulated controversy about divisiveness within the movement, thereby undermining confidence in its effectiveness.

The abandonment of the doctrine of nonviolence by the more impatient members of the civil rights movement soon followed. Leaders like Forman and Carmichael began leading SNCC in a more militant direction. They saw nonviolence merely as a tool to be used or discarded when the situation demanded. They simply could not believe that individuals like John Lewis were wedded to nonviolence as a way of life; a growing number of people in SNCC shared this opinion. Consequently, in the spring of 1966, Lewis was forced out as chairman of SNCC and was replaced by Carmichael. Another divisive issue within SNCC had to do with the participation of whites. Whites had served the organization well in all phases of its activities: sit-ins, freedom rides, voter registration, marches, etc. At one point SNCC even relied on a white student organization, the STUDENTS FOR A DEMOCRATIC SOCIETY (SDS), to do much of its fund-raising.

In the early days of their reform, SNCC and the SDS shared similar views. Both opposed racism, violence, poverty, unbridled capitalism, imperialism, and other forms of social injustice. They also shared a distrust for "establishment" people with middle-class values. As these two groups matured, SNCC became radical over the issue of RACE, while SDS became radical over the issue of personal liberties (the use of drugs) and the VIETNAM WAR. They eventually came to have different priorities and were unwilling to compromise. In the end, impatient activists in both organizations moved toward a new RADICALISM that cost them in both membership and financial contributions. SNCC, with its new cry for BLACK POWER, was drawn toward the controversial Black Panther movement (see BLACK PANTHER PARTY), and ended up merging itself out of existence. SDS also became more radical and splintered into new factional groups, some of which, like the Weather Underground, came to advocate terrorist activities.

Among the 1960s campus revolts, one of the largest and most significant took place on the campus of the University of California at Berkeley. In the fall of 1964 a twenty-one-year-old philosophy major, Mario SAVIO, captured the national spotlight as the eloquent spokesman for the Berkeley Free Speech Movement (FSM). Despite his young age, Savio was already a veteran of the San Francisco Bay Area civil rights movement and had participated in FREEDOM SUMMER, the SNCC-sponsored voter registration drive in Mississippi. The Berkeley revolt served as a model for campus rebels across the United States as they protested war, CENSORSHIP, and racism during the 1960s, bringing to the burgeoning protest against the Vietnam War many tactics that had earlier been used and were continuing to be used by those involved in the civil rights struggle.

BIBLIOGRAPHY

Blum, John Morton. *Years of Discord—American Politics and Society.* 1991.
Davis, Townsend. *Weary Feet, Rested Heart.* 1998.
Faircloth, Adam. *To Redeem the Soul of America.* 1987.
Farmer, James. *Lay Bare the Heart: An Autobiography of the Civil Rights Movement.* 1998.
Forman, James. *The Making of Black Revolutionaries.* 1985.
Garrow, David. *Bearing the Cross.* 1986.
Gitlin, Todd. *The Sixties—Years of Hope, Days of Rage.* 1987.
Lewis, John. *Walking with the Wind—A Memoir of the Movement.* 1998.
Stoper, Emily. *The Student Nonviolent Coordinating Committee.* 1968.

A. D. Simmons

Student Nonviolent Coordinating Committee

One of the five major black civil rights organizations advocating nonviolent direct protest action during the 1960s, the Student Nonviolent Coordinating Committee (SNCC) was founded in 1960 at historically black Shaw University in Raleigh, North Carolina. SNCC's establishment followed the widespread and successful student SIN-INS initiated in 1960 by four black college students, who sat down at a racially segregated lunch counter in a Greensboro, North Carolina, department store and were refused service because of their race. This event sparked a wave of student sit-ins, out of which SNCC was born and would evolve for almost a decade.

SNCC began as an organization led by college students striving to achieve civil rights through the use of nonviolent, direct-action protest tactics. With the guidance of Ella BAKER, an exemplary organizer, adviser, and mentor, SNCC developed a group-centered, participatory-democratic, grassroots leadership structure. Although Baker and other SNCC organizers had been affiliated with the NATIONAL ASSOCIATION FOR THE ADVANCEMENT OF COLORED PEOPLE (NAACP), the SOUTHERN CHRISTIAN LEADERSHIP CONFERENCE (SCLC), and the CONGRESS OF RACIAL EQUALITY (CORE), SNCC was an autonomous organization with its national office in Atlanta, Georgia. SNCC's membership base was drawn from black and white colleges throughout the United States. In the early phase, Jane Stembridge, Connie Curry, Casey HAYDEN, and Bob Zellner were among the white students who held important SNCC positions. Black student leaders, including Marion Barry, Diane NASH, John LEWIS, Julian BOND, Praithia Hall, Bernice Reagon, and Ruby Doris Smith ROBINSON, typically had been trained in NAACP youth branches and student government associations at Fisk University and other black colleges. Frustrated by what appeared to be ineffective, accommodationist, and legalistic tactics of the NAACP and SCLC, SNCC activists envisioned the possibility of immediate social change.

SNCC field workers were daring "shock troopers" and let it be known that they were impatient with the slow pace of change as they initiated aggressive FREE- DOM RIDES in interstate transportation, as well as voter registration and EDUCATION campaigns; lived inside local rural communities in MISSISSIPPI, ALABAMA, GEORGIA, and other Black Belt states; and were subjected to the abuses of white segregationists, such as beatings, unlawful arrest, and even LYNCHING. These dedicated students would create a state of agitation and urgency unmatched by the efforts of other more established, older, and bureaucratic organizations. With its decentralized structure, SNCC was more open than other groups to bringing masses of black citizens into the civil rights movement.

In 1964, Fannie Lou HAMER and Victoria GRAY co- founded the Mississippi Freedom Democratic Party (MFDP), an independent black political party estab- lished as a result of disfranchisement and virtual ex- clusion of African Americans from the state of Missis- sippi's white-controlled Democratic Party. The idea of the MFDP was developed and implemented by Robert Parris MOSES, a SNCC leader from Massachusetts, James FORMAN, executive secretary of SNCC, and other SNCC activists who organized voter registration campaigns in Mississippi during FREEDOM SUMMER 1964, when over a thousand black and white college students from around the country came to Mississippi to join Hamer, Gray, Unita Blackwell, and other local people in the struggle for voting and other rights. Freedom Summer activists lived, worked, and even died with black Mississippians in rural, isolated, and impoverished black communities throughout the state. Bob Moses and other SNCC activists as well as the COUNCIL OF FEDERERATED ORGANIZATIONS (COFO) used FREEDOM SCHOOLS as organizing tools for implementation of massive voter education and registration on which MFDP was based.

In 1966, the focus of SNCC changed. Following the bloody 1965 Selma voting rights marches, in which black children, women, and men were beaten (and some killed), SNCC moved away from its early empha- sis on nonviolence and Southern community organiz- ing to a philosophy of BLACK POWER, which was artic- ulated by SNCC leaders Stokely CARMICHAEL and H. Rap BROWN. The heightened militancy of SNCC eventually resulted in its highly publicized vote to ex- clude all whites from important positions. As its "Black Power!" rhetoric spread throughout urban ghettos, SNCC became increasingly separatist and nationalist.

Along with contradictions involving gender stratifica- tion inside SNCC, this shift created much divisiveness and conflict, which weakened its support from within and engendered counterattacks from without, espe- cially from the FEDERAL BUREAU OF INVESTIGATION. Older black organizations considered such aggressive black militancy to be counterproductive. Nevertheless, SNCC's calls for black unity, pride, and socioeconomic power brought the civil rights movement closer to serving the needs of the masses of poor blacks.

BIBLIOGRAPHY

Barnett, Bernice McNair. "A Structural Analysis of Lead- ership: Martin Luther King, Jr., and the Civil Rights Movement," Ph.D. dissertation, University of Georgia, 1989.

Carson, Clayborne. *In Struggle: SNCC and the Black Awak- ening of the 1960s.* 1981.

Dittmer, John. *Local People.* 1994.

McAdam, Doug. *Freedom Summer.* 1988.

Morris, Aldon. *The Origins of the Civil Rights Movement.* 1984.

Moses, Robert Parris. Interview with Bernice McNair Bar- nett. 1994.

Payne, Charles. *I've Got the Light of Freedom: The Organizing Tradition in Mississippi.* 1995.

Zinn, Howard. *SNCC: The New Abolitionists.* 1965.

Bernice McNair Barnett

Students for a Democratic Society

Students for a Democratic Society (SDS) was reorgan- ized in 1960 from the student affiliate of the League for Industrial Democracy (LID), an Old Left organi- zation from which SDS separated in 1965. Inspired by civil rights activities taking place in the South, many members hoped to develop SDS as a Northern coun- terpart to the STUDENT NONVIOLENT COORDINATING COMMITTEE (SNCC), but the early SDS focused more on philosophical debates rather than direct action, and used educational programs, publications, and conferences in an attempt to achieve reform.

SDS operated its headquarters first in New York, then in Chicago, after 1965, and sponsored chapters on college campuses around the country. As the num- bers of chapters grew, however, the loose bureaucratic structure of the organization hindered cooperation between the national office and individual chapters, often leaving SDS groups to act locally without direc- tion.

For SDS's national convention in 1962, Tom Hay- den drafted "The Port Huron Statement," which not only highlighted the SDS philosophy but also served as an important manifesto for the New Left. The dec- laration addressed a range of issues, but the "values"

Tom Hayden, the bearded founder of the Students for a Democratic Society, in the midst of a news conference in front of the federal building in San Francisco, California, on March 21, 1969. On the left, Hayden's attorney Charles Garry answers a local television reporter's question. (AP/Wide World Photos)

section held the deepest resonance for youth alienated by the culture of the COLD WAR era. The statement also advanced the idea of "participatory democracy," which, although never firmly defined, generally held that individuals should be able to participate in making decisions that affected their lives, thereby supplementing existing representative democracy.

In 1963, SDS attempted to translate philosophy into practice by organizing programs such as the Economic Research and Action Project (ERAP), which was dropped as a national project in 1965 but lingered in a couple of communities until 1967. ERAP failed to achieve its goal of uniting and mobilizing the urban poor, but ERAP members tested participatory democracy in communal living arrangements and scored limited community victories in Cleveland, Ohio, and Newark, New Jersey.

Beginning in 1965, SDS addressed the ANTI-WAR MOVEMENT by sponsoring the first large-scale demonstrations against the VIETNAM WAR, advocating draft resistance, and encouraging anti-war protest on college campuses. SDS members at the University of Chicago protested draft tactics by taking over the university administration building in 1966, while students at Columbia University responded similarly in 1968 by occupying buildings on campus in which they established "communes" and demanded an end to war-related research at the university.

As its ranks increased, the ideological composition of SDS changed as well. Membership figures rose from approximately 4,000 members in 1965 to over 30,000 by 1968. Many new SDS members favored aggressive action and "resistance" tactics over intellectual debate

and the traditional protest strategies employed by the "old guard." Women also expressed increasing dissatisfaction with the dominance of males in SDS leadership roles. By the late 1960s, SDS had become a collection of rival factions, including the Revolutionary Youth Movement (RYM), the Maoist Progressive Labor Party (PL), which advocated support of a working-class movement, and the militant Weatherman (named after a Bob Dylan lyric), which hoped to unite classes and races in revolution. A leadership struggle between the PL and Weatherman groups in 1969 signaled the collapse of SDS as a unified organization. Small, ineffective fragments of former SDS factions continued into the 1970s before dissolving completely.

BIBLIOGRAPHY

Hayden, Tom. *Reunion: A Memoir.* 1988.
Heath, Louis, ed. *Vandals in the Bomb Factory: The History and Literature of the Students for a Democratic Society.* 1976.
Miller, James. *"Democracy Is in the Streets": From Port Huron to the Siege of Chicago.* 1987.
Sale, Kirkpatrick. *SDS.* 1973.
Unger, Irwin. *The Movement: A History of the American New Left, 1959–1972.* 1974; reprinted 1988.

Students for a Democratic Society. Papers, 1958–1970. The State Historical Society of Wisconsin. SDS papers are also available on microfilm. This collection, which is described in *Students for a Democratic Society Papers, 1958–1970: A Guide to the Microfilm Edition of the Original Records in the State Historical Society of Wisconsin* (1977) by Jack T. Ericson, contains records of and publications by SDS, as well as extensive correspondence among SDS members and other individuals and organizations active in the New Left movement of the 1960s.

Michelle A. Krowl

Suffrage

See Voting Rights

Sumner, Charles

(1811–1874), congressman.

Charles Sumner was a leading Republican member of the Senate during the Civil War and RECONSTRUCTION and advocate of emancipation and civil rights.

Born in Boston and a graduate of Harvard University and Harvard Law School, Sumner quickly became involved in politics and reform. A member of the faction known as the Conscience Whigs, he led the challenge to conservative textile manufacturers, charging them with an unholy alliance with slaveholding cotton planters of the South. He helped found the Free Soil party in 1848 and was elected to the United States Senate in 1851.

Charles Sumner of Massachusetts, a leader of the Reconstruction-era Radical Republicans in the U.S. Senate. (© Archive Photos)

Sumner spent the remainder of his life in the Senate leading the Republican attack on slavery and its proponents. In 1856, he was rewarded for his vehement speech against the Kansas-Nebraska Act by being caned into bloody unconsciousness by Democratic Representative Preston Brooks of South Carolina. Upon recovery, he again led the opponents of slavery.

During the Civil War, Sumner worked with others in urging President Abraham LINCOLN to adopt emancipation as a war goal as well as equal rights for those freed. His Reconstruction record included his being architect of the terms of the South's reentry into the Union, advocate of civil rights for the freedmen, chair of the Senate Foreign Relations Committee, and opponent of Presidents Andrew Johnson and Ulysses S. Grant on both civil rights and foreign policy. After his death, Congress enacted the CIVIL RIGHTS ACT OF 1875 which included some of the provisions he had fought for. It was an act that was far ahead of its time. Sumner's commitment to civil rights brought the nation closer to the egalitarian goals of the twentieth century.

BIBLIOGRAPHY

Blue, Frederick J. *Charles Sumner and the Conscience of the North.* 1994.

Donald, David. *Charles Sumner and the Coming of the Civil War.* 1960.

Donald, David. *Charles Sumner and the Rights of Man.* 1970.

Palmer, Beverly, ed. *The Selected Letters of Charles Sumner.* 2 vols. 1990.

Frederick J. Blue

Supreme Court

The Supreme Court stands at the top of the nation's judicial system. Its justices are appointed for life terms by the president, with the Senate's agreement. Combining life tenure with a political method of appointment is thought to ensure that the justices can interpret the Constitution without shifting as the prevailing political winds shift, while guaranteeing that the justices will in the long run not get too far out of line with what the American people want. The Supreme Court's actions in the field of civil rights confirm that the justices rarely depart for long from what a sustained consensus among Congress and the presidency on issues as central as civil rights are to the American political system.

Before the Civil War, the Supreme Court was a reasonably consistent supporter of the STATES' RIGHTS view of the Constitution, which effectively protected slavery. Responding to demands from politicians, the Supreme Court thought it could definitively resolve the constitutional controversies over slavery in DRED SCOTT V. SANDFORD (1857), but the Court's holding that Congress lacked power to regulate slavery in the territories actually exacerbated the nation's divisions by fueling the Republican Party's growth.

After Reconstruction, some Supreme Court decisions were consistent with a modern civil rights vision, as in its holding that states could not exclude African Americans from juries (*Strauder v. West Virginia*, 1880). When Reconstruction ended, the Court's decisions interpreting the Constitution and civil rights statutes restrictively were in line with the exhaustion of the civil rights impulse in Congress and the presidency. The Court's 1883 decision invalidating a federal statute mandating equality in public accommodations foreshadowed its refusal to overturn a Louisiana statute requiring segregation in railroads (PLESSY V. FERGUSON, 1896).

Plessy was consistent with the general course of public policy during a period that African-American historian Rayford Logan called the "nadir" of race relations. Over the next few decades, the Court made a few gestures in the direction of civil rights, invalidating

A line of people wait in the early morning outside the U.S. Supreme Court on October 6, 1997, the first day of the Court's new term. (AP/Wide World Photos)

a Louisville ordinance requiring segregated housing (*Buchanan v. Warley*, 1917) and an Oklahoma law that effectively barred African Americans from voting (*Quinn v. Oklahoma*, 1915). These decisions represented a modest commitment to civil rights, but they were equally influenced by the Court's individualist *laissez faire* philosophy and in any event had almost no practical effects.

Transformed by President Franklin D. ROOSEVELT's appointments, the Court developed a general theory of constitutional interpretation that authorized it to act when "discrete and insular minorities" faced prejudice in legislatures which prevented them from protecting their interests through ordinary political processes. This theory was designed to protect African Americans. Notably, however, African Americans had by then become an important constituency in the Roosevelt Democratic Party, and the Court's decisions in the 1940s and 1950s supporting civil rights repre-

sented the views of an important segment of the New Deal coalition.

BROWN V. BOARD OF EDUCATION (1954) invalidated school segregation, the practice at the core of the Southern system of race relations. Intensely controversial in the South, the decision nonetheless had substantial support in the North. Internationally minded elites also supported *Brown*, because they found segregation an embarrassment in the on-going ideological competition with the Soviet Union for the allegiance of recently independent nations in Africa and Asia.

The Supreme Court under Earl WARREN continued to support civil rights. It interpreted the Constitution to invalidate many laws that promoted race discrimination directly and obstructed efforts to interfere with the civil rights movement's protest activities in decisions based on unclear and sometimes inconsistent interpretations of the First Amendment's free speech guarantee. When the civil rights movement gained enough political power to achieve its goals through legislation, the Court upheld the new statutes and interpreted them generously.

As support for civil rights eroded after the late 1960s, the Court briefly continued on its earlier path. Its decisions generally endorsing BUSING as a remedy for school segregation were highly controversial. President Richard NIXON's four appointees, and then those of presidents Ronald REAGAN and George BUSH, gradually brought the Court back into line with public views. In the late 1980s the Court issued a series of decisions sharply narrowing the scope of civil rights statutes, which were so at odds with prevailing public opinion that Congress overturned them. In the early 1990s the Court severely restricted AFFIRMATIVE ACTION programs.

Often thought of as distinctively valuable because of its independence from political influences, the Supreme Court has only occasionally, and never for long, been at odds with the political branches, as its actions in civil rights cases show.

BIBLIOGRAPHY

Abraham, Henry J. and Barbara A. Perry. *Freedom and the Court: Civil Rights and Liberties in the United States.* 1998.

Harrison, Maureen, and Steve Gilbert, editors. *Civil Rights Decisions of the Supreme Court: 19th Century.* 1994.

Harrison, Maureen, and Steve Gilbert, editors. *Civil Rights Decisions of the Supreme Court: 20th Century.* 1994.

Wiecek, William M. *Liberty under Law: The Supreme Court in American Life.* 1988.

Mark Tushnet

T

Talmadge, Eugene

(1884–1946), Georgia governor.

From his first election for agricultural commissioner in 1926, to his final campaign for governor in 1946, Eugene Talmadge, descended from a family of large landowners, won elections by relying on a mix of racism and agrarian populism. His populist stance included attacks on government spending at both state and national levels. He declared martial law in 1931 in order to eliminate reckless spending by the state highway department. Beginning in 1934, he championed STATES' RIGHTS against what he considered to be federal interventions under the NEW DEAL, and even considered running for president against Franklin D. ROOSEVELT in 1936. He served as governor of Georgia from 1933 to 1937 and from 1941 to 1943.

Although racist statements were always part of his populist rhetoric, Talmadge did not make race a central issue in his campaigns until the 1940s. He began to denounce the New Deal, not only for its consolidation of power at the national level, but also for its effects on the status of Southern blacks. Equating the New Deal with RECONSTRUCTION, he assailed federal recovery programs that enabled blacks to earn higher wages than poor white farmers. Running for reelection, Talmadge continued to make race a central issue in 1942, as he attacked the University of Georgia's College of Education for its alleged promotion of racial equality. He lost that election to a progressive opponent, Attorney General Ellis G. Arnall. Academic freedom was a central issue of the campaign, as Talmadge had earlier established dominance over the Board of Regents, ultimately causing ten state-supported colleges to lose accreditation, as well as the law and medical schools. In his final gubernatorial campaign, in 1946, Talmadge opposed the right of blacks to vote in primaries and to sit in the front of buses that passed through Georgia. He died soon after winning the 1946 election, but Talmadge had a lasting impact on Southern politics well into the 1960s, as many politicians continued to oppose national policies by adopting his mix of populism and racism.

BIBLIOGRAPHY

Anderson, William. *Wild Man from Sugar Creek: The Political Career of Eugene Talmadge.* 1975.

Bartley, Numan V. *The Creation of Modern Georgia.* 1990.

Coleman, Kenneth, ed. *A History of Georgia.* 1977.

Logue, Calvin M. *Eugene Talmadge: Rhetoric and Response.* 1989.

Tindall, George. *The Emergence of the New South, 1913–1945.* 1967.

S. Karthick Ramakrishnan

Television

Broadcast television is a national communications medium because signals transmitted from one location can be relayed to other locations across the country simultaneously. The medium is regulated by the Federal Communications Commission (FCC), which dictates that broadcasters serve the public interest or their licenses may be reallocated or revoked. During

719

the height of 1950s civil rights activism, this standard was tested when WLBT's (Jackson, Mississippi) license was successfully challenged by a group of citizens who had documented the station's failure to serve its predominantly African-American audience.

Considering television's national public service ethic, it was hoped and expected by many that, when it became available to Americans in 1946, the appearance of blacks in programming would help equalize African-American status in postwar American life. Yet early network television programming adopted historically biased depictions of race that had been common to film, vaudeville, and radio before it: from *Amos n' Andy*'s (CBS, 1951–1953) minstrelsy, to *The Jack Benny Show*'s (CBS, 1950–1964) comic foil, Rochester, to *Beulah*'s (ABC, 1950–1953) faithful "mammy" character.

From the late 1950s through the 1960s, three TV sites in particular began to challenge such stereotypical portrayals. *The Nat King Cole Show* (NBC, 1956–1957), which featured the shared interaction of white and black performers on the same stage, was successful with a widespread audience, though it filled only a fifteen-minute time slot. Televised sporting events also displayed the shared interaction, on equal terms, of white and black America on the playing field. And, finally, throughout the 1960s each of the three major networks (ABC, CBS, NBC) expanded its nightly news reports and started documentary series or specials that tackled pressing social issues, including civil rights.

By the late 1960s, sitcoms and action-adventure series that demonstrated African Americans' adherence to the middle-class American Dream—and that presumed INTEGRATION to be the norm—found a home in prime time. Most famous among these were *Julia* (NBC, 1968–1971) and *I, Spy* (NBC, 1965–1968). Simultaneous to the rise of the BLACK PANTHER PARTY and to the increased public prominence of separatist rights leaders such as Stokely CARMICHAEL and MALCOLM X—each of whom was portrayed on television as a threat to mainstream America (e.g., CBS, 1965, *CBS Reports: Watts, Riot or Revolt?*; ABC, 1968, *Newark: The Anatomy of a Riot*; or CBS, 1974, *Four Portraits in Black*)—assimilationist rights initiatives for inclusion within the American system became increasingly palatable to the American polity and were presented as such to the American TV audience.

As the 1970s began, the networks' share of the expanding, well-educated, urban, socially activist youth audience was shrinking. In this climate, networks were willing to give ethnically, racially, and economically diverse variety series and sitcoms a chance. The resulting programs, created largely by independent producers such as Norman Lear, included *The Flip Wilson Show* (NBC, 1970–1974); *Good Times* (CBS, 1974–1979); and *The Jeffersons* (1975–1985). In the late 1970s, *Roots*

(ABC, January 23–30, 1977) and *Roots: The Next Generations* (ABC, February 18–February 25, 1979) literally invented the miniseries form and captured the unprecedented attention of the entire viewing nation while focusing on slavery—an American institution typically suppressed from public discussion.

In the 1980s, *The Cosby Show* (NBC, 1984–1992) came to be both praised and critiqued as the epitome of post–civil rights era representations of race. The show was the first predominantly black-cast sitcom to portray an affluent, intact, African-American nuclear family. *Cosby*'s enormous mainstream popularity reinvigorated debates over authenticity in TV portrayals of African-American life and culture. Why, for example, did programs such as *Frank's Place* (CBS, 1987–88), *South Central* (Fox, 1994), or *Under One Roof* (CBS, 1995)—each of which overtly addressed the social problems, continuing racial discrimination, and class-struggles that *The Cosby Show* avoided—die quickly during the same era in which *Cosby* was so beloved? By the mid-1980s television had changed. From 1987 on, the Fox network challenged the classic three networks as it targeted an urban, youthful, black and Latino audience with fast-paced programs featuring diverse casts such as *In Living Color* (Fox, 1990–1994), *Roc* (Fox, 1991–1994), and *Martin* (Fox, 1992–1997). The networks continue to have their dominance challenged with the emergence of UPN, the WB, and PAX-TV. Cable TV also became an everyday presence in many American homes by the early 1980s. Cable promised to offer programming for populations that were typically underrepresented in over-air broadcasting. Black Entertainment Television (BET) was founded in 1980 by Robert L. Johnson with the explicit goal of providing black-focused entertainment. In addition to commercial cable and broadcast networks, public television, educational television stations, and local public access TV stations offer alternative routes for the dissemination of information regarding race and rights within the American landscape.

As a new century begins, means of communication that use the television monitor independent of broadcast, satellite, or cable programming (e.g., video games, VCRs, WebTV, etc.) will likely alter this landscape much further. Whether these new technologies succeed in helping to realize full participation in American polity for all U.S. citizens will likely alter the historic perception of television's fulfillment of its early promise, as well as the lasting import of its continuing, conflicted struggles.

BIBLIOGRAPHY

Bodroghkozy, Aniko. "Is This What You Mean by Color TV?" In *Private Screenings: Television and the Female Consumer*, edited by Lynn Spigel and Denise Mann. 1992.

Classen, Steve. "Southern Discomforts: The Racial Struggle over Popular TV." In *The Revolution Wasn't Televised: Sixties TV and Social Conflict.* 1997.

Cripps, Thomas. *"Amos n' Andy* and the Debate over American Racial Integration." In *American History/ American Television: Interpreting the Video Past,* edited by John E. O'Connor. 1983.

Curtin, Michael. *Redeeming the Wasteland: Television Documentary and Cold War Politics.* 1995.

Gray, Herman. *Watching Race: Television and the Struggle for "Blackness."* 1995.

Lipsitz, George. "The Meaning of Memory: Family, Class, and Ethnicity in Early Network Television Programs." In *Private Screenings: Television and the Female Consumer,* edited by Lynn Spigel and Denise Mann. 1992.

MacDonald, J. Fred. *Blacks and White TV: African Americans in Television Since 1948.* 1992.

Victoria E. Johnson

Tenayuca, Emma

(1917–   ), labor activist.

Emma Tenayuca was a leading activist during the Depression era on behalf of improved working conditions for Mexican Americans and other minority peoples in TEXAS. Born on December 21, 1917, Tenayuca had become an activist by the time she was fourteen years old. In 1931, she helped organize a march of unemployed workers at the state capitol in Austin. At the age of seventeen, she joined the workers of the Finck Cigar Company in their walkout and was briefly jailed as a result. Soon after the cigar strike, Tenayuca helped to establish the San Antonio chapter of the International Ladies' Garment Workers Union (ILGWU), in addition to working for the communist Workers Alliance.

Throughout the 1930s, Tenayuca pushed for improved working conditions for Mexican-American pecan shellers. The movement came to a head in 1938, when two thousand pecan shellers went on strike because of a 15 percent wage cut. Union officials eventually replaced Tenayuca as strike leader because of strong public reaction to her communist affiliation, but the strikers named her their honorary leader and eventually won a minimum wage in March 1938. Tenayuca ended her association with the COMMUNIST PARTY USA following the signing of the Nazi-Soviet pact shortly before WORLD WAR II. Despite this decision, the HOUSE UN-AMERICAN ACTIVITIES COMMITTEE blacklisted her. Unable to find work in San Antonio, Tenayuca moved to San Francisco, California, where she received a degree in liberal arts. In the 1960s, she returned to Texas, where she taught elementary school until her retirement in 1982.

BIBLIOGRAPHY

Meier, Matt S. ed. *Notable Latino Americans.* 1997.

Palmisano, J. *Notable Hispanic American Women,* Book 1. 1993.

Aaron Oppliger

Tennessee

Tennessee's history of civil rights extends from pioneering efforts of liberation to rabid acts of suppression, and reflects the state's geographic and demographic differences.

The U.S. Supreme Court avoided a confrontation with President Andrew Jackson by deciding that it had no jurisdiction in the suit the Cherokee nation brought to assert treaty rights. After three decades of egregious treaty violations and relocations in contiguous areas of Tennessee, Georgia, and the Carolinas, the United States government in 1838 forcibly removed 13,000 Cherokees from their lands, detained them in stockades, and then marched them through Tennessee on the "trail of tears" to the Oklahoma Territory.

The Civil War and RECONSTRUCTION divided Tennessee between a Unionist Republican East and a secessionist Democratic West. In its brief Reconstruction period, 1867 to 1869, a Republican Tennessee government ratified the FOURTEENTH AMENDMENT—and thereby avoided military Reconstruction. However, Republican power in Tennessee proved ephemeral. Power was restored to a Democratic government that rescinded some civil rights and instituted early forms of legal racial segregation. The earliest expression of the KU KLUX KLAN provided the armed terror that ushered in this political change.

African Americans and a few white allies resisted the retreat from the democratic reforms of 1865–1869. In 1884, for example, Ida B. WELLS, refused to move from the first-class coach to the separate and inferior accommodation reserved for African Americans and thereby tested emerging JIM CROW laws. The Tennessee Supreme Court found "that her persistence was not in good faith to obtain a comfortable seat for a short ride." Wells's case showed that as all three branches of the federal government retreated from the defense of civil rights, state and local officials stepped forward to keep people like Wells in the places to which white-supremacist policies assigned them (see WHITE SUPREMACY).

The Tennessee legislature flickered with hope for civil rights in the 1880s. The Democrats split into factions and Republicans won statewide and local elected offices with a bloc of the remaining African-American voters. Limited efforts to stem the ebbing tide of civil rights brought more political terror, however. After their success in the 1888 elections, the Democrats immediately passed voting legislation that disfranchised African-American men and reduced Republican strength to make Tennessee part of the "Solid South" until the VOTING RIGHTS ACT OF 1965.

With hope in government eroded, African Americans in Tennessee continued their efforts for civil rights when and where they could. Fisk University in Nashville provided W. E. B. DU BOIS a "great assembly of youth and intelligence." Ida B. Wells continued her resistance from her Memphis-based newspaper, *Free Speech.* After a riot and LYNCHING in 1891 in Memphis, Wells left the city on a crusade against lynchings and mob violence. Nothing expressed racial subordination as completely as the lack of punishment of whites for lynching African Americans. From 1889 to 1899, eighty-nine African Americans were lynched in Tennessee. Du Bois and Wells both contributed to the formation in 1909 of the NATIONAL ASSOCIATION FOR THE ADVANCEMENT OF COLORED PEOPLE (NAACP), which took up the crusade against lynching.

The drama of subordinated civil rights and resistance to it appeared on many stages. The Tennessee Centennial celebration of 1897 included a Negro Building where the apostle of accommodation, the ed-

ucator BOOKER T. WASHINGTON, spread the Creed of Tuskegee—loyalty to the political and economic system of the time and to the white people who controlled it. He challenged African Americans to show their moral superiority by suffering wrongdoing patiently and using the limited opportunities afforded them well.

Several years earlier, Tennessee coal miners, predominantly white, had impatiently expressed an interracial bond with convict laborers, who were predominant black. In 1891 the Tennessee Coal, Iron and Railway Company used convict labor to displace coal miners in East Tennessee and to erode the floor of the miners' wages. The appalling conditions of convict labor surpassed the cruelties of slave labor, and the mortality and morbidity in the coal mines measured the full depravity of the system. From July until November, thousands of miners organized armed militias that freed 458 convict laborers from their stockades or en route to the mines. The state militia crushed the miners' "convict war," however, with unspecified casualties and more than 500 arrests in the winter of 1892. By the time of the Tennessee Centennial and Washington's oration, the state had opened up Brushy Fork state prison, operated its own deadly mine with convict

(Third from left) Martin Luther King, Jr., stands on the balcony of the Lorraine Motel in Memphis, Tennessee, on April 3, 1968, the day before King was assassinated. On the left are Hosea Williams and Jesse Jackson. On the right is Ralph Abernathy. (AP/Wide World Photos)

labor, and provided African Americans yet another test of their moral capacity for patience and suffering.

The role of women in this insurrection and in other efforts for civil rights of both whites and blacks goes undocumented, as is the case so often. Tennessee women gained national attention in their successful effort to win ratification for the *Nineteenth Amendment,* establishing suffrage for women, from the state legislature. Less noticed was the leadership of a few women and the actions of many that led to a general strike in the Southern textile industry, including East Tennessee, in 1929.

Just prior to the NEW DEAL, the brightest spot of political participation by African Americans in Tennessee in the 1920s had the tarnish of deep-seated political corruption and machine politics. Edward "Boss" Crump, elected mayor of Memphis in 1909, dispensed patronage to African Americans, provided more public services to them than previously, and did nothing to disfranchise African-American voters. Instead, he organized them. His ability to deliver a solid bloc of votes—white and black—meant control of the Democratic primaries and hence of statewide elections. National election victories for Democrats came from the soiled South of white supremacy and racial subordination. Federal programs, such as the Tennessee Valley Authority (TVA) and the Farm Security Administration, provided new sources of benefits and new standards of equal pay, as well as in its schooling, and encouraged land ownership. Democratic segregationists, such as Crump, fought the two projects for those reasons.

Events made clear that it would take more than the New Deal to change local race relations in Tennessee. In 1940 Elbert Williams, a charter member of the fledgling NAACP branch in Brownsville was lynched and seven other local NAACP leaders were literally expelled from Haywood County by white mobs, which included a sheriff, because the blacks had inquired about voting. After World War II, however, the climate of civil rights was changing nationally and statewide. Boss Crump's dominance of the Democratic Party became undone in part because of changes in the civil rights planks in the national party's platform in 1948 that led him to bolt the party and support STATES' RIGHTS candidates.

Events in Tennessee were precursors of the "second Reconstruction" of the civil rights movement, as they had foreshadowed the first Reconstruction. Voter registration drives began in Haywood and Fayette counties in 1959 that tested the will of the federal government to enforce the CIVIL RIGHTS ACT OF 1957. Newly registered voters were moved off the land they worked and out of the homes they rented. The merchant-leaders of the African Americans' registration efforts

were boycotted by suppliers of everything from soft drinks to gasoline. John DOAR, new to the civil rights division of the Justice Department, acted within a lame-duck Republican administration to renew a century-old precedent of direct federal involvement in local civil rights conflicts that the KENNEDY administration would continue.

At the same time, sit-in demonstrations to integrate the segregated lunch counters of Nashville's downtown department stores in a 1960 protest provided profound new leadership for the civil rights movement that would move federal officials further and faster than they wanted to go. The student leaders from Nashville—Marion Barry, James Bevel, James Lawson, Bernard Lafayette, John LEWIS, and Diane NASH—with others, formed the STUDENT NONVIOLENT COORDINATING COMMITTEE (SNCC). Nash, the leader of the Nashville group, led the first modern civil rights mass demonstration, a silent march of more than a thousand participants, and politely but firmly gained an early and official concession. Mayor Ben West agreed that the lunch counters of Nashville should be integrated. Lewis and Nash would play key roles in the FREEDOM RIDES, FREEDOM SUMMER, and the Selma march as well.

The history of civil rights in Tennessee after the VOTING RIGHTS ACT OF 1965 parallels the mixed experience of success and continued shortcoming of other Southern states. Barriers to registration were removed and African American candidates were elected to public office—but not without problems and the violation of law. A three-judge federal court in 1992 found that Tennessee had violated the Voting Rights Act in redistricting the state senate districts. In reaching its decision, the court found evidence of racial-bloc voting, lingering effects of past racial discrimination, and evidence of official discrimination after 1965.

In the 1970s the Tennessee legislature passed the EQUAL RIGHTS AMENDMENT, and then rescinded its actions. Women made progress on other fronts, however. Just as African Americans protested unpunished violence towards them, women organized to have domestic violence and rape recognized and treated as violent crimes. The Tennessee Task Force Against Domestic Violence successfully raised state funds to support shelters and provided police departments with training in handling cases of domestic violence. Similarly, groups of persons with disabilities, with the assistance of the federal AMERICANS WITH DISABILITIES ACT OF 1990, have organized locally and statewide to achieve the same access to public places and transportation to which race had posed barriers earlier. Despite inadequate funding, groups have emerged to defend the rights of PRISONERS. Similarly, groups have given attention to new labor issues. The Tennessee Industrial Renewal Network (TIRN) has worked to protect the rights of workers against plant closings and replacement by temporary workers. The TIRN has also turned attention to the international dimensions of workers' rights and grievances by conducting exchanges of workers in East Tennessee and in Mexico.

This most recent work on civil rights in Tennessee highlights the role of the Highlander Research and Education Center (HREC). Founded in 1932 as the HIGHLANDER FOLK SCHOOL it serves as a safe haven where people can talk freely about their lives and build solidarity. It has hosted the old and the young of the civil rights movement—including Rosa PARKS and early members of SNCC—and has propagated the spirit of the anthem of the movement, "*We Shall Overcome.*" This work, as well as HREC's current work on the environment, the rights of gay men and lesbians, and economic justice, suggests the importance of halfway houses or free spaces where people can come together; find people like themselves; and have the tools and networks with which to address their problems in local struggles of liberation. Highlander's work expresses the lesson expressed by Ida B. Wells that the civil rights of groups undermined by racism, sexism, and other forms of prejudice and discrimination have common links and economic underpinnings.

BIBLIOGRAPHY

Alexander, Thomas B. *Political Reconstruction in Tennessee.* 1950.

Cartwright, Joseph H. *The Triumph of Jim Crow.* 1976.

Couto, Richard A. *Lifting the Veil: A Political History of Struggles for Emancipation.* 1993.

Couto, Richard A. "Race Relations and Tennessee Centennials." *Tennessee Historical Quarterly: Tennessee Between the Wars, 1860–1920* 55 (1996):144–59.

Duster, Alfreda M., and Ida B. Wells. *Crusade for Justice: The Autobiography of Ida B. Wells.* 1970.

Goings, Kenneth W., and Gerald L. Smith. "Duty of the Hour: African-American Communities in Memphis, Tennessee, 1862–1923. In *Tennessee Historical Quarterly: Tennessee Between the Wars, 1860–1920* 55 (1996): 130–43.

Halberstam, David. *The Children.* 1998.

Hamburger, Robert. *Our Portion of Hell.* 1973.

Jahoda, Gloria, *The Trail of Tears: The Story of the Indian Removal, 1813–1850.* Rev. ed. 1995.

Lamon, Lester C. *Blacks in Tennessee, 1791–1970.* 1981.

Lewis, Ronald L. *Black Coal Miners in America: Race, Class, and Community Conflict 1780–1980.* 1987.

Rural West Tennessee African-American Affairs Council et al. v. Ned McWherter et al. 836 F. Supp. 453 (W.T. Dist.). 1933.

Taylor, Alrutheus. *The Negro in Tennessee, 1865–1880.* 1947.

United States v. Harris. U.S. Reports 106 (Boston: Little, Brown, 1883).

Wolfe, Margaret Ripley. "The Feminine Dimension in the Volunteer State." In *Tennessee Historical Quarterly: Tennessee Between the Wars, 1860–1920* 55 (1996): 112–29.

Richard A. Couto

Terrell, Mary Eliza Church

(1863–1954), activist.

Born into the African-American elite of Memphis, Tennessee, on September 23, 1863, Mary Church Terrell emerged as one of the leading twentieth-century civil rights activists. For more than sixty-six years, she was an ardent champion of racial and gender equality.

She spent her early years in Memphis, a city convulsed by violent and bitter racism. Her parents, Robert Reed Church and Louisa Ayers, attempted to protect her from discrimination. However, her inevitable experiences in a racist environment made her resolve to excel academically to prove the abilities of African Americans, especially women. She graduated from Oberlin College in 1884 with honors and taught for a

Portrait of Mary Church Terrell. (Prints and Photographs Division, Library of Congress)

few years at the M Street High School in Washington, D. C. While at the high school, she met her future husband, Robert H. Terrell, who later became a federal judge upon the recommendation of Booker T. WASHINGTON.

From 1896 to 1949, Terrell used various strategies to fight for racial and gender equality. She became the founder and first president of the NATIONAL ASSOCIATION OF COLORED WOMEN (NACW). Symbolizing unity among women, this self-help organization offered sisterly support for its members and created programs that addressed racial problems through the elevation of African-American women. Terrell wrote numerous articles and delivered several speeches on LYNCHING, the peonage system, educational inequity, chain gangs, and the disenfranchisement of African Americans. In her writings, she also sought to further racial understanding by educating white people about the realities of African-American life.

During the last decades of her life, Terrell became a militant activist, working assiduously to bring a definitive end to discrimination in the United States, particularly in the nation's capital. For three years, she led a struggle to reinstate 1872 and 1873 laws that "required all eating-place proprietors to serve any respectable, well-behaved person regardless of color, or face a $1,000 fine and forfeiture of their license." These laws had disappeared by the 1890s when the District of Columbia code was rewritten.

Prodded by the desire to deal discrimination a deadly blow, Mary Church Terrell, at age seventy-seven, used direct action tactics such as picketing and boycotting to attack segregated eating facilities. On February 28, 1950, Terrell, dressed in an attire that included hat and gloves, and accompanied by two African-American and one white collaborator, entered Thompson Restaurant, one of several nearby public eating establishments. The proprietor, John Thompson, refused to serve the African-American members of the interracial party. Immediately Terrell and her cohorts filed affidavits. The case of *District of Columbia v. John Thompson* became a national symbol against segregation in the United States, attacking one of the remnants of the nineteenth-century JIM CROW system in Washington, D. C.—segregated public eating places.

Throughout the three-year struggle, Terrell and her cohorts targeted other segregated facilities. Finally, on June 8, 1953, the court ruled that segregated eating facilities in Washington, D. C., were unconstitutional. Terrell lived to see the U. S. Supreme Court mandate the desegregation of public schools in BROWN V. BOARD OF EDUCATION. Two months later, on July 24, 1954, this valiant civil rights fighter died.

BIBLIOGRAPHY

Jones, Beverly W. *Quest for Equality: The Life and Writings of Mary Church Terrell, 1863–1954.* 1990.

Beverly W. Jones

Test Bias

Every day in modern society personnel decision makers choose among candidates who seek entry into employment positions and academic programs. These decisions are based, wholly or partially, on scores these candidates receive on standardized (multiple-choice) examinations, even though evidence exists that such tests are culturally biased against certain ethnic groups, primarily African Americans and Latinos and, in some cases, gender biased against all women. This entry examines the impact of the continued use of standardized examinations to decide the allocation of highly sought-after opportunities.

The argument in favor of the use of standardized examinations is, assuming there is a statistical relationship between how well candidates perform on these tests and how well they perform in the employment position or academic program, that a personnel decision based on these tests improves the quality of the decision—even if the test is culturally biased. Furthermore, educational institutions increasingly are using standardized examinations to assess student performance. In the context of employment, companies may use standardized examinations if the employer can show that business reasons necessitate the use of such tests. Although there is not universal agreement that standardized examinations are unfair to white women or African Americans and Latinos, organizations that administer these examinations acknowledge that test bias exists. However, representatives of the organizations attribute the difference in performance of African Americans and Latinos of both sexes and of white women to the lack of exposure that members of these groups have had to some of the cultural situations being tested on the examinations.

The validity of the assumption that there is a relationship between performance on standardized examinations and performance in the employment position or academic program should be researched in terms of each specific test, although the assumption is usually unquestioned. If the results of the research indicate that the test is biased, a better test should designed. Some standardized examination administrators have taken steps to reduce the cultural bias of their tests by hiring people of diverse ethnic backgrounds to create new versions of the tests. However, this does not address the basic underlying assumption in using standardized examinations: that these examinations can objectively measure and predict an individual's ability to perform in a given employment position or academic program. It is probably impossible to create a test that does not reflect the cultural experiences of the testers. Although this may not invalidate the use of the test—as in the case where these cultural experiences are important to the predicted performance—that is not what most people think when they consider what standardized test scores mean. Considering that organizations use standardized examinations to determine who will be able to avail themselves of the most sought-after employment opportunities and academic programs, there is a fairness rationale against using these types of examinations—unless they accurately predict what they purport to predict. In the years prior to the passage of the CIVIL RIGHTS ACTS of 1957, 1960, and 1964, various literacy and general-comprehension tests had been used to prevent African American from voting. There is a danger that standardized testing may have a similar effect, even if unintended, by unfairly denying members of certain ethnic groups access to various employment and educational opportunities. There is indeed a need to counter or mitigate the effect of such test bias.

In order to minimize the effect of test bias, some users of standardized examinations apply different cut-off scores to members of differing ethnic groups. Although opponents of AFFIRMATIVE ACTION have legally challenged this practice, there is a statistically valid basis for the practice, in addition to a fairness rationale. A test score is a valid tool with which to make personnel decisions only if a particular examination predicts performance equally for both sexes and all ethnic groups. Where the examination predicts performance more accurately for different groups, then using different test scores that reflect this difference is statistically valid. Arguably, even if the examination predicts performance equally for members of different ethnic groups, there are nonetheless societal values—including a need for diversity and the remediation of societal discrimination—that justify this practice.

BIBLIOGRAPHY

Green III, Preston C. "Can Title VI Prevent Law Schools from Adopting Admissions Practices That Discriminate Against African-Americans." In *Southern University Law Review* 24 (1997).
Hacker, Andrew. *Two Nations Black and White, Separate, Hostile and Unequal.* 1995.
Hawkins, B. Denise. "A Multiple-Choice Mushroom: Schools, Colleges Rely More Than Ever on Standardized Tests." In *Black Issues in Higher Education* 8 (Feb. 9, 1995).
Hunt, Earl. "When Should We Shoot the Messenger? Issues Involving Cognitive Testing, Public Policy, and the Law." *Psychology, Public Policy and Law.* 2 (September/December 1996).
Kane, Thomas J. "Racial and Ethnic Preferences in College Admissions." In *Ohio State Law Journal* 59 (1988).
Kennedy Manzo, Kathleen. "SAT "Recentering": Percentiles and Rankings Will Not Change." In *Black Issues in Higher Education* 18 (Jun. 30, 1994).
Malamud, Deborah C. "Affirmative Action, Diversity, and the Black Middle Class." In *University of Colorado Law Review* 68 (1997).
Selmi, Michael. "Testing for Equality: Merit, Efficiency, and the Affirmative Action Debate." In *University of California Los Angeles Law Review* 42 (1995).

Pamela Edwards

Texas

Race relations in twentieth-century Texas are direct products of the turbulence of the nineteenth century which witnessed the end of black slavery as a result of a bloody and costly American Civil War and the failure of RECONSTRUCTION to alter significantly the social, political, and economic position of Southern blacks. During the nineteenth century, the few pieces of legislation that attempted to provide civil rights to blacks were systematically undermined and rendered ineffective by several landmark decisions of the SUPREME COURT—the most notable being PLESSY V. FERGUSON (1896). This process of subjugation began even before the Reconstruction era ended with the Compromise of 1877 when the federal government officially withdrew its regularly army soldiers from the South and left enforcement of black rights in the hands of Southern state governments. Although Southern officials pledged to uphold the constitutional rights of blacks as defined by the FOURTEENTH and FIFTEENTH AMENDMENTS, the Supreme Court made it relatively easy for Southern states to establish a segregated society without essentially violating their promise to protect blacks. The Court decisions concerning the nature, intent, and scope of the Reconstruction amendments and the constitutionality of the enforcement and civil rights laws, contributed not only to black disenfranchisement and the process of relegating them to second-class citizenship, but also served as a catalyst for the civil rights movement in Texas.

Beginning in 1878, whites in the black belt counties of Texas organized associations, unions, and clubs with the express purpose of ousting blacks from local, county, and state politics. These organizations used violence and a number of schemes to prevent blacks from voting, and their actions were aided and abetted by elected government officials. This behavior on the part of white Texans reached its peak between 1895 and 1923. Every state legislature that convened during that period amended the primary election law with the intention of maintaining its purity—its whiteness. The 1923 legislature was very specific in its language when it enacted a white Democratic primary statute. The law proclaimed that only white persons belonging to the Democratic party were eligible to participate in its primary elections. Texas, then, became the only ex-confederate state that explicitly discriminated against its black and Mexican-American citizens on the basis of color.

The white primary was the most powerful of the subterfuges used to render blacks politically impotent. The full meaning of the white primary cannot be grasped unless one realizes that Texas was a one-party state from 1870 to 1980, and winning in the Democratic primary was tantamount to winning in the general election. Even if blacks were literate, paid poll taxes, or owned property, they could not change the color of their skin. Thus, they could never, as long as the white primary stood, take part in the most essential element of the electoral process. Blacks were aware of this dilemma, but they were equally cognizant of the fact that overthrowing the white primary would prove to be very complicated, time-consuming, and costly, necessitating carefully unified and sustained efforts by blacks and their white allies. A twenty-three-year struggle to accomplish this goal would place black Texans at the vanguard of the modern civil rights struggle.

It is important to note that black Texans never acquiesced in disfranchisement, nor completely relinquished their tenacious grip on the ballot. Each attempt to wrest the ballot from their hands met with individual and group opposition. Black leaders frequently debated with each other and struggled for methods and solutions for retrieving the vote. Although locked out of participation in the Democratic primaries during the 1920s, 1930s, and part of the 1940s, black Texans were nevertheless politically active. Black newspapers reported political developments. Social, religious, economic, and political clubs and organizations all paid attention to the struggle for political and civil rights. Black leaders urged payment of poll taxes and participation in the general elections. The large middle-class population in Houston, Dallas, and San Antonio was also a positive factor. In fact, Houston had the largest number of black professionals of any city of its size, making it psychological and economically predisposed for the social movement that was gripping the state. It is well to note that the single most important factor responsible for political activism among black Texans from 1920 to 1944 was the fight against the white Democratic primary.

Thus, when Houston City Democratic Executive Committee adopted a white primary resolution in 1921 barring blacks from the forthcoming election, the black leadership of the city reacted swiftly. They asked the court, via *Love v. Griffin* (1928), for an injunction to restrain the said committee from taking such action. Failing in this effort, they took the case all the way to the SUPREME COURT, which held that the issue in the *Love* case was moot because the election for which the injunction was sought was over.

Love v. Griffin was instructive for blacks throughout the state. If they were going to overthrow the white primary, they would have to elicit the support, resource, and expertise of the NATIONAL ASSOCIATION FOR THE ADVANCEMENT OF COLORED PEOPLE (NAACP). So, starting in 1924 with the NAACP as their modus operandi, black Texans embarked upon a series of court cases to overturn this discriminatory law. The first two, *Nixon v. Herndon* (1927) and *Nixon v. Condon* (1932), involved an El Paso dentist, Lawrence D. Nixon, who sought unsuccessfully to register to vote in the Democratic primary. In each case the court ruled in Nixon's favor, but each time stopped short of declaring the white primary unconstitutional. Disappointed with the NAACP's handling of the above cases, and with the organization's disinclination to involve black attorneys from Texas, black Houstonians took their own case, *Grovey v. Townsend*, to the Supreme Court in 1935. While this case suffered the same defeat as the previous ones, it impacted upon the civil rights movement in Texas in several ways: (1) it forged a greater unity between black Texans and the national office of the NAACP; (2) it brought more militant, younger blacks to the movement; and (3) it led to the establishment of the Texas State Conference of (NAACP) Branches, a statewide organization charged with directing the state's civil rights movement. Established in 1938, the Texas State Conference planned and initiated lawsuits against racial discrimination in the areas of voting rights, jury service, employment, housing, and public accommodations. The Texas State Conference also played a major role in helping to equalize black teachers' salary with their white counterparts in Dallas and Houston in 1943.

After the establishment of the Texas State Conference of Branches, blacks prepared, via *Hasgett v. Werner* (1941), for the final assault on the white primary. While litigation in *Hasgett* was underway, the Supreme Court issued a ruling in *Classic v. United States* (1941) and stipulated that a voter's right extended to primary elections. Elated over this decision, the NAACP decided to drop Hasgett in favor of a new case that would reflect the latest finding of the court. In April 1942, Thurgood MARSHALL, special counsel for the NAACP, presented the argument for the new case,

Smith v. Allwright, to the Supreme Court. Two years later on April 3, 1944, the high court declared the white primary unconstitutional.

The *Smith v. Allwright* decision had a profound impact on civil rights, voting rights, and race relations in the South, especially in Texas. Black Texans saw this decision both as a second emancipation and as a tool for dismantling the apartheid system of this country. No sooner was this decision rendered when the black leadership turned their attention to Jim Crow in higher education. In 1946, Heman Marion Sweatt, a Houston native, became the plaintiff in a test case to integrate the University of Texas Law School. Upon being denied admission, Sweatt filed a lawsuit (*Sweatt v. Painter*) against the University of Texas. After hearing the case in 1951, the Supreme Court ordered the

Heman Marion Sweatt registers for classes at the University of Texas School of Law in Austin, 1950. Sweatt was admitted to the law school pursuant to the U.S. Supreme Court's decision in Sweatt v. Painter, *a case that is often said to have paved the way for* Brown v. Board of Education. *(From the UT Student Publications, Inc., Phtographs, ca. 1895–1985 [CN00323B], The Center for American History, The University of Texas at Austin. Used with permission.)*

University to admit Sweatt. The Court held that Sweatt's rights had been violated even though the state of Texas had established Texas State University for Negroes with a law school to accommodate Sweatt in 1947.

The struggle to desegregate the University of Texas resulted not only in a favorable Supreme Court decision to admit blacks to graduate and professional schools in the state, but it also set precedent for Brown v. the Board of Education. In the *Sweatt* case the Court *implied* that the doctrine of "separate but equal" was unconstitutional. In *Brown*, it stated explicitly that "separate but equal" was unconstitutional. Viewing *Brown* as a pathway to equality and a boost to the civil rights movement, black activists became all the more determined to change the status quo. From 1955 to 1966, they launched a steady campaign to integrate public schools and to gain access to better jobs and public facilities. Although support for change grew steady among African Americans, success in the modern civil rights movement was not won easily. White segregationists mounted an organized, well-financed campaign to forestall public school integration. Consequently, it took more than a decade of legal battles, civil rights protests, and tragically violent confrontations before the majority of Texas schools were integrated.

From 1960 to 1970, each battle for civil rights required hard work, commitment, and constant pressure (boycotts, protests, demonstrations) on public officials. Sometimes it also required physically testing the law as many students joined the sit-in demonstrations across the state and country. Led by Progressive Youth Associations and friends of the Student Non-violent Coordinating Committee (SNCC), students in Texas along with other blacks engaged in a wave of Sit-Ins that effectively desegregated many eating facilities and bolstered the Civil Rights Act of 1964, which legally assured gains in public accommodation—in hotels, restaurants, swimming pools, and golf courses.

Much of the civil rights activities between 1970 and 1998 focused on consolidating the gains of previous decades. For example, it would be difficult to exaggerate the political significance of the overthrow of the white primary. In 1940, only 30,000 blacks were registered voters. By 1948, this number more than tripled to 100,000. In 1964, black voter registration reached 345,000, 57 percent of the black voting-age population. This number increased even more when the Voting Rights Act of 1965 struck down the poll tax as a voting requirement. Moreover, court mandated reapportionment in 1966 allowed blacks to send the first three members of their race to the Texas legislature since Reconstruction—Curtis Graves and

Joseph Lockridge to the House and Barbara JORDAN to the Senate. Between 1972 and 1974, black attorneys, working along with Mexican Americans, led a campaign against at-large-member districts. The SUPREME COURT concurrence in single-member districts enabled African Americans to win a number of legislative seats in major urban areas. Today, thirty-five blacks sit in the Texas legislature compared to fifteen in 1985. Single-member districts also affected school board and city council seats. Statewide, blacks on city councils jumped from 59 to 135 between 1970 and 1998. Black elected officials increased from 45 in 1971 to 472 by 1992. Among African-American office holders in 1982 were three small-town mayors. In 1998 two of the state's largest cities, Houston and Dallas, had black mayors.

Hispanics, Asians, and other minorities also benefited from the civil rights movement. In 1929, Mexican Americans and other peoples of Latin American descent organized the LEAGUE OF UNITED LATIN AMERICAN CITIZENS (LULAC) to help fight discrimination and to push for full social, political, economic, and educational rights for the above group. Playing a similar role to the NAACP, LULAC helped to politicize its members before and after *Smith v. Allwright*. The election of Raymond L. Zeller as mayor of El Paso in 1957 bears out this point. Because of LULAC, Hispanic leaders, and a bill sponsored by Barbara Jordan in 1976 to extend the voting right bill to Texas and other western states in order to prevent discrimination based on language barriers, Hispanics now hold a number of elected offices throughout the state.

Despite the above gains by minorities in the state of Texas, it would be premature to write the epitaph of the civil rights movement. Unfinished agendas abound. There are still pressing economic issues relating to employment, housing, and services. The issue of AFFIRMATIVE ACTION is still considered a divisive factor in many cities although the city of Houston defeated an effort to repeal affirmative-action measures. (See also HOPWOOD V. STATE OF TEXAS.) Hate groups, such as the KU KLUX KLAN, are still visible in many locales. The most notorious hate crime of the twentieth century occurred in Jasper, Texas, on June 7, 1998 when a black man, James Byrd, was beaten and dragged to his death behind a pickup truck on a rural road by three white men, who reportedly had ties with white supremacist groups. There is no gainsaying that the problem of race remains in Texas. But by the same token, no one can deny that the civil rights movement in Texas changed the political landscape of this state.

BIBLIOGRAPHY

Barr, Alwyn. *Black Texans: A History of Negroes in Texas, 1528–1996.* 1997.

Barr, Alwyn, and Robert Calvert, editors. *Black Texans for Their Times.* 1981.

Beeth, Howard, and Cary Wintz. *Black Dixie: Afro-Texan History and Culture in Houston.* 1992.

Davidson, Chandler. *Biracial Politics: Conflict and Coalition in Metropolitan South.* 1972.

Hine, Darlene Clark. *Black Victory: The Rise and Fall of the White Primary in Texas.* 1979.

Ladino, Robyn Duff. *Desegregating Texas Schools: Eisenhower, Shivers and the Crisis at Mansfield High.* 1996.

Pitre, Merline. *Through Many Dangers, Toils and Snares: The Black Leadership in Texas 1868–1900.* 1997.

Smallwood, James M. *The Struggle for Equality of Blacks in Texas.* 1983.

Winegarten, Ruthe. *Black Texas Women: 150 Years of Trial and Triumph.* 1995.

Merline Pitre

Thind, United States v. (1923)

During the early part of the twentieth century, some federal courts granted citizenship to Asian Indians, who successfully argued that they were Caucasians and therefore "free white persons" eligible for citizenship. In 1920, Bhagat Singh Thind, a resident since 1913 and a World War I army veteran, used the argument to gain citizenship from a federal court in Oregon. The Bureau of Naturalization hoped to bring an end to the naturalization of Asian Indians by appealing the case to the Supreme Court.

A few months before it was to decide on *United States v. Bhagat Singh Thind*, the Supreme Court concluded in *Ozawa v. United States* that the reference to free white persons in the naturalization law was synonymous with Caucasians. This legal outcome seemed to enhance Thind's position.

Although Thind had the support of judicial precedent and anthropological evidence, the high court decided unanimously against him. It rejected the use of scientific arguments to interpret the racial requirements for naturalization. Because "free white persons" were words of common speech, the common-speech understanding of the law applied. Even though they were often "legally" Caucasians, Asian Indians were not white people in the eyes of the common man and the framers of the 1790 naturalization law. According to this standard, physical characteristics defined who was white, and "white persons" was a more narrow legal category than Caucasian racial origin. The court also cited the 1917 Immigration Law, which had excluded Asian Indians from immigration, as evidence that Congress did not want Asian Indians to become citizens.

After the ruling, federal authorities were able to revoke the citizenship of seventy-five naturalized Asian

Indians. Government officials also began escheat proceedings (proceedings to transfer land holdings back to the government because of the absence of legal heirs to those holdings) since Asian Indians, as aliens ineligible for citizenship, became subject to alien land laws.

BIBLIOGRAPHY
Haney-Lopez, Ian. *White by Law: The Legal Construction of Race.* 1996.
Jensen, Joan M. *Passage from India: Asian Indian Immigrants in North America.* 1988.

S. H. Tang

Third World Student Strikes

During 1968–1969, African-American, Asian-American, Chicano, and Native-American students at San Francisco State College (SFSC) and the University of California at Berkeley (UCB) organized coalitions on each campus known as the Third World Liberation Front (TWLF). Each TWLF led student strikes demanding the establishment of Third World Colleges with comprehensive Asian-American, African-American, Chicano, and Native-American Studies programs. The significance of these strikes was twofold: first, minority students were able to unite in solidarity against institutional RACISM, and second, the strikes won concessions in the formation of ETHNIC STUDIES programs that have remained in the forefront of academic change.

The concept of a "Third World" provided a unifying factor for the TWLF student activists. The term identified parallel colonial and racial experiences of minorities throughout U.S. history. Examples of common racial oppression included: genocide of the native Indians, the enslavement of Africans, the forced relocation of Chicanos in the Southwest, and the passage of Asian immigration exclusion legislation. This past was linked with the history of Western colonization in the Third World countries of Asia, Africa, and Latin America. Contemporary international movements for independence and self-determination in those locales were viewed as related to the demands of U.S. Third World minorities for political power. These international movements provided legitimacy and inspiration for the students.

Strike tactics involved informational picketing (during which leaflets were passed out to onlookers), blocking of campus entrances, mass rallies, and teach-ins. Popular support was often met with repression in the form of police arrests, tear gas, and a variety of campus disciplinary actions. Mutual-assistance pacts between area police departments enabled the rapid formation of riot squads dispatched from throughout the San Francisco Bay area. During the fall and spring semesters of 1968–1969, hundreds of students were arrested in the strike at SFSC, including more than 450 on one sweep alone. Similarly, over 155 students were arrested during the UCB strike, which lasted the entire winter quarter of 1969. In the last two weeks of the dispute, the UCB campus witnessed the stationing of National Guard troops to maintain martial law.

The establishment of Ethnic Studies programs has been one of the chief legacies of the strikes. These programs have expanded nationally in over 250 universities, colleges, and high schools. Both UCB and SFSU provide undergraduate and graduate degree programs in Ethnic Studies. Another important legacy of the strikes was the establishment of closer working relationships between students and the community. The post–TWLF era witnessed large numbers of students becoming involved in community-based organizing efforts. Student support for the International Hotel anti-eviction movement (see INTERNATIONAL HOTEL EPISODE), the ALCATRAZ OCCUPATION by Native Indians, BLACK PANTHER PARTY defense activities, and the UNITED FARMWORKERS strike were all outgrowths of this legacy.

BIBLIOGRAPHY
Blauner, Robert. *Racial Oppression in America.* 1972.
Munoz, Carlos. *Youth, Identity, Power: The Chicano Movement.* 1989.
Nee, Victor G., and Brett de Bary Nee. *Longtime Californ': A Documentary Study of an American Chinatown.* 1972.
Omatsu, Glenn. "The 'Four Prisons' and the Movements of Liberation: Asian American Activism from the 1960s to the 1990s." In *The State of Asian America: Activism and Resistance in the 1990s,* edited by Karin Aguilar-San Juan. 1994.
Research Organizing Cooperative. *Strike at Frisco State! The Story Behind It.* 1969.
Umemoto, Karen. "On Strike! San Francisco State College Strike, 1968–69: The Role of Asian American Students." *Amerasia Journal* 15, no. 1 (1989): 3–41.

Harvey Dong

Thirteenth Amendment

The Thirteenth Amendment to the Constitution, ratified on December 6, 1865, abolished slavery in the United States. "Neither slavery nor involuntary servitude, except as a punishment for crime whereof the party shall have been duly convicted," Section One of the amendment reads, "shall exist within the United States, or any place subject to their jurisdiction." Section Two gives to Congress the "power to enforce this article by appropriate legislation."

The Civil War hastened the demise of slavery and paved the way for the Thirteenth Amendment. Lacking opposition from Southern representatives who had left to serve the Confederacy, the Republican-dominated Congress took preliminary steps toward emancipation. In 1862, they abolished slavery in the District of Columbia, prohibited slavery in the territories, repealed the Fugitive Slave Act of 1850, and authorized the liberation of rebels' slaves upon their escape to Union lines or seizure by the federal army. In September 1862, President Abraham Lincoln issued an emancipation proclamation, which announced the end of slavery in those areas of the United States still in rebellion on January 1, 1863. (This included neither the slaveholding border states still in the Union, nor those areas of the South occupied by federal forces.) Lincoln's proclamation inspired many slaves to leave their masters and join the Union army, and valiant service by black soldiers later that year helped sway Northern public opinion in favor of abolition.

By 1864, Congress stood poised to abolish slavery outright. Because many doubted its ability to emancipate by statute, Congress took up a number of proposed abolition amendments. In the Senate, lawmakers rejected Charles SUMNER's attempt to include the phrase "all persons are equal before the law" in an amendment and instead settled upon compromise language patterned after the Northwest Ordinance of 1787. On the other hand, Sumner's proposed enforcement clause, a potential source of national power, was included in the final draft of the Thirteenth Amendment. After brief debate, the Senate passed the measure, but the House, where Democrats retained greater strength, failed to adopt by the necessary two-thirds margin. Opposition stemmed mainly from fears of alienating border state unionists and expanding national power at the expense of state sovereignty.

Republican success in the 1864 Congressional elections provided the push necessary for passage. With Union victory imminent, many Democrats abandoned their party's official opposition and either supported the amendment or abstained from voting. On January 31, 1865, the House passed the Senate's abolition amendment, and the Confederacy's defeat and President Andrew Johnson's endorsement helped bring about ratification by the end of 1865. All of the former states of the Confederacy, with the exception of Mississippi, approved the Thirteenth Amendment, although most did so only because Congress required ratification for complete readmission into the Union. (Mississippi finally ratified in 1995.)

The meaning and scope of the new amendment were unclear. Some Republicans believed it conferred civil rights upon freedpersons, while other supporters believed they had voted only to abolish involuntary servitude. In any event, after ratification Southern state governments imposed restrictions upon the economic opportunity and social behavior of the newly freed slaves. These "BLACK CODES" included vagrancy, contract, and apprenticeship laws to control black labor, as well as laws prohibiting racial intermarriage. Some of the harshest codes regulated blacks' right of assembly and forbade whites from supplying blacks with firearms or liquor. Such restrictions prompted many Congressional Republicans to advocate a FOURTEENTH AMENDMENT to guarantee civil rights.

Until recently, the Supreme Court's interpretation of the Thirteenth Amendment weakened its potential as a bulwark of civil rights. Although the Court stated in the *Civil Rights Cases* (1883) that Section Two of the amendment gave Congress the power to outlaw "badges and incidents" of slavery, the Court simultaneously held that the amendment gave Congress no power to ban racial discrimination in public accommodations. This interpretation of the amendment held for more than a hundred years, until the Court overturned the ruling in *Jones v. Mayer* (1986), a housing discrimination case. Here the justices broadly interpreted Congress's power to eliminate "badges of slavery" by prohibiting private acts of racial discrimination in contractual and property relationships. Despite the controversial nature of the *Jones* decision, the Thirteenth Amendment now holds a significant place in modern civil rights law.

BIBLIOGRAPHY

Kyvig, David E. *Explicit and Authentic Acts: Amending the U.S. Constitution, 1776–1995.* 1996.

Maltz, Earl M. *Civil Rights, the Constitution, and Congress, 1863–1869.* 1990.

ten Broek, Jacobus. *Equal Under Law.* 1965.

Wiecek, William M., and Harold M. Hyman. *Equal Justice Under Law: Constitutional Development, 1835–1875.* 1982.

Timothy S. Huebner

Thomas, Robert K.

(1925–1991), Cherokee nationalist, anthropologist, philosopher, teacher.

Raised traditionally in eastern Oklahoma, Robert K. Thomas studied under "action anthropologist" Sol Tax at the University of Chicago. This background led him to become a seminal figure in forging the peculiar blend of activism and academics known as "applied anthropology."

Thomas was instrumental in organizing the 1961 "Chicago Conference," considered decisive in launching the unprecedented wave of American Indian activism sweeping the United States over the next two decades. From 1963 to 1967, while directing the Carnegie Cross-Cultural Education Project in Oklahoma, he followed up with a series of summer workshops at the University of Colorado to devise strategies to address problems confronting Indians.

These sessions had such impact that Thomas was asked to replicate them in Canada from 1966 to 1971. In 1971, he also played a pivotal role in founding the Indian Ecumenical Conference, devoted to reforming the policies of Christian churches vis-à-vis native peoples. His efforts are widely viewed as keys to the assertion of aboriginal rights and proliferation of First Nations postsecondary institutions throughout Canada.

It was during this period of intense activism that Thomas did his most influential theoretical work, applying the concept of "internal colonialism" to the situation of native peoples in contemporary North America. His ideas have had a profound effect on the thinking of groups such as the AMERICAN INDIAN MOVEMENT and the INTERNATIONAL INDIAN TREATY COUNCIL.

After 1981, Thomas worked with Sioux scholar Vine DELORIA, Jr., and others at the University of Arizona to develop the first graduate program in American Indian Studies, meanwhile devoting more and more of his time to fulfilling his role as a much revered Cherokee elder, wherein he was respectfully known as "Uncle Bob."

BIBLIOGRAPHY

Pavlick, Steve, ed. *A Good Cherokee. A Good Anthropologist: Papers in Honor of Robert K. Thomas.* 1998.

Steiner, Stan. *The New Indians.* 1968.

Thomas, Robert K. "Colonialism: Classic and Internal." *New University Thought* 4, no. 4 (1967): 44–53; subsequently included in *The Way: An Anthology of American Indian Literature,* edited by Shirley Hill Whitt and Stan Steiner. 1972.

Thomas, Robert K. *Getting to the Heart of the Matter: Collected Letters and Papers.* 1990.

Ward Churchill

Thurmond, James Strom

(1902–   ), senator.

Strom Thurmond, a leading Senate opponent of civil rights, was born in Edgeville, South Carolina. After serving as city and county attorney, state senator,

An exhausted but tenacious Senator Strom Thurmond exits the Senate floor on August 1, 1957, at the conclusion of his record twenty-four-hour, eighteen-minute filibuster against a civil rights bill. (AP/Wide World Photos)

South Carolina circuit judge, and World War II army pilot, Thurmond was elected governor of South Carolina as a member of the DEMOCRATIC PARTY in 1946. As governor, he supported funding for black education, but he denounced the Fair Employment Practices Commission and criticized black voting in state primaries.

In July 1948, after the adoption of a civil rights plank at the Democratic Convention led Southern delegates to form the breakaway States' Rights Party (the DIXIECRATS), Thurmond ran as the Party's presidential candidate, although he insisted that his opposition to civil rights was based on states' rights rather than racism. Thurmond won thirty-nine electoral votes, all in the South.

In 1954, Thurmond won a special election to the U.S. Senate as a write-in candidate and began the first of eight full terms. He quickly assumed leadership of Southern opposition to civil rights legislation. In 1956, he helped draft the SOUTHERN MANIFESTO denouncing school integration. In 1957, Thurmond filibustered for a record twenty-four and one-half hours against a civil rights bill. In 1963, he denounced the MARCH ON WASHINGTON as Communist-influenced. In September 1964, after he fought vainly to defeat the CIVIL RIGHTS ACT OF 1964, he switched to the REPUBLICAN PARTY.

After 1965, under pressure from black voters, Thurmond shifted toward greater support for civil rights, and he was notable as the first Southern senator to hire a black aide. In 1997, Thurmond became the longest-serving and oldest senator in history.

BIBLIOGRAPHY

Bass, Jack, and Marilyn W. Thompson. *Ol' Strom: An Unauthorized Biography of Strom Thurmond.* 1998.

Cohodas, Nadine. *Strom Thurmond and the Politics of Southern Change.* 1993.

Greg Robinson

Tijerina, Reies López

(1926–   ), land rights activist.

In 1967, Reies López Tijerina was catapulted into national headlines after he led an armed raid against a courthouse in northern New Mexico. Successfully defending himself against state charges of assault and kidnapping stemming from the incident, Tijerina cemented his status as a Chicano movement hero and spokesman. Using political theater and fiery oratory, Tijerina focused attention on the 1848 Treaty of Guadalupe–Hidalgo, which had guaranteed the property rights of Mexican citizens living in the new American Southwest after the Mexican-American War.

Tijerina's early history revealed a crusading spirit. Born near Falls City, Texas, to a family who followed the migrant trail, Tijerina became a convert to Pentecostalism as a teenager. He spent two years studying to become a minister at an Assemblies of God bible college in Texas before leaving the school in 1946 to travel the Southwestern United States as a revivalist preacher. In 1955, having broken with the denomination over doctrinal matters, Tijerina and some followers attempted to launch a utopian community in the Arizona desert. That experiment failed and Tijerina arrived in New Mexico in 1957.

In New Mexico, he infused the nearly moribund land-grant struggle with great energy. Tijerina accused Anglo-Americans of not just robbing the land but also of threatening the culture of the state's Spanish-speaking residents. He traveled to Spanish and Mexican archives and concluded that his crusade was buttressed by centuries of colonial law as well as the 1848 treaty. In the wake of the courthouse raid, moreover, Tijerina declared he was ready to die for his cause. In 1963, the first meeting of the Alianza Federal de Mercedes Reales (Federal Alliance of Royal Land Grants), an organization Tijerina founded, attracted thirty-seven people. By 1967, the Alianza was claiming membership in the thousands and several hundred attended that year's convention in Albuquerque.

Tijerina's main goal was to see land-grant claims adjudicated by U.S. or international courts. His method was to seek publicity. In 1966, Tijerina and his followers took over a portion of Kit Carson National Forest (New Mexico) and declared 500,000 acres a sovereign republic. Aliancistas then arrested two forest rangers for trespassing and being a public nuisance. In 1967, Tijerina's group intended to conduct a citizens' arrest of the local district attorney who, Tijerina argued, violated protesters' constitutional rights by disrupting Alianza meetings. The plan was abandoned when Aliancistas started shooting at the Tierra Amarilla courthouse instead. In 1968, Tijerina headed the Southwest contingent of the Poor People's Campaign to Washington, D.C. There, in solidarity with Native Americans, he tried to force a meeting with U.S. Supreme Court justices. That same year, Tijerina ran for New Mexico governor on the People's Constitutional Party ticket. The state Supreme Court, however, ruled Tijerina ineligible because of a prior felony conviction—he had interfered with a U.S. forest service officer.

Ultimately, Tijerina spent two years in federal prison on assault convictions stemming from his participation in the 1966 occupation of the National Forest. Released in 1971, Tijerina was barred under the terms of his five-year parole from holding office in the Alianza. When Tijerina resumed the presidency of the organization in 1976, neither he nor the organization commanded the same attention as before although he continued to study the land-grant question.

BIBLIOGRAPHY

Bustos, Rudy Val. *Like a Mighty Rushing Wind: The Religious Impulse in the Life and Writing of Reies López Tijerina.* Ph.D. dissertation, University of California, Berkeley. 1991.

Gardner, Richard. *Grito! Reies Tijerina and the New Mexican Land Grant War of 1967.* 1970.

Hammerback, John C., Richard J. Jensen, and José Angel Gutiérrez. *A War of Words: Chicano Protest in the 1960s and 1970s.* 1985.

Nabokov, Peter. *Tijerina and the Courthouse Raid.* 1969.

Tijerina, Reies López. *Mi lucha por mi tierra.*

Lorena Oropeza

Till, Emmett, Lynching of

Emmett Louis Till was born near Chicago on July 25, 1941, and was murdered in the Mississippi Delta on August 28, 1955, making him the best-known young victim of racial violence in U.S. history.

Visiting relatives shortly before he would have become an eighth grader, Till entered a store in Money, in Leflore County, and as a prank behaved suggestively

Emmett Till in Chicago, Illinois, not long before he was lynched and murdered in August 1955 in the woods near Greenwood, Mississippi, at the age of fourteen. (CORBIS/Bettmann)

toward Carolyn Bryant, the twenty-one-year-old wife of the absent owner. Because of the breach of racial etiquette, Roy Bryant and his half-brother, J. W. Milam, both armed, soon thereafter abducted Till from the home of his relatives, pistol-whipped him, murdered him, and then dumped the corpse into the Tallahatchie River. Bryant and Milam were prosecuted about a month later; but, despite forthright testimony by the victim's mother, Mamie Till, a jury of twelve white men acquitted them. The verdict was widely condemned in the press outside the South and beyond the United States. A guileless victim who was only fourteen years old, a pair of champions of racial supremacy and white womanhood who walked free—these elements of the case would haunt novelists like James Baldwin and Toni Morrison (both of whom wrote plays about Till), troubadour Bob Dylan (who wrote a song), and poet Gwendolyn Brooks (who contributed a ballad). Such brutality revealed the precarious conditions blacks faced—especially in the rural South—as did no other episode, and the intolerable anachronism of such violence helped to inspire the civil rights movement in the early 1960s.

BIBLIOGRAPHY

Huie, William Bradford. *Wolf Whistle.* 1959.

Whitfield, Stephen J. *A Death in the Delta.* 1988.

Stephen J. Whitfield

Title VII of the 1964 Civil Rights Act

Title VII of the CIVIL RIGHTS ACT OF 1964 prohibited discrimination in hiring and promotion by trade unions and most private businesses on the basis of RACE, color, religion, national origin, or sex. It created the five-member EQUAL EMPLOYMENT OPPORTUNITY COMMISSION (EEOC) to investigate charges of discriminatory employment practices and to resolve any complaints through mediation.

The provisions barring employment discrimination were among the most controversial of President John F. KENNEDY's 1963 omnibus civil rights bill. EMPLOYMENT discrimination had been a contested political issue since 1946, when CONGRESS killed President Franklin D. ROOSEVELT's FAIR EMPLOYMENT PRACTICE COMMITTEE (FEPC), an agency created during WORLD WAR II to investigate charges of racial discrimination in defense industries. Kennedy, convinced that a bill containing provisions about employment discrimination could not pass, did not include a national FEPC in the bill he proposed in June 1963. But lobbyists for civil rights organizations, who had long wanted an FEPC for private businesses, and those for organized labor, who thought that they needed a federal law to stop discrimination on the part of union locals, convinced the House Judiciary Subcommittee to add a title about employment discrimination to the bill.

The proposed Title VII generated a great deal of congressional debate. Republicans were wary of any expanded federal regulatory authority over private employers, and they sought to limit the power and scope of the EEOC; Southern Democrats charged that the proposed bill would mandate preferential hiring and treatment of blacks. As a result, Title VII supporters agreed to a variety of amendments limiting the regulatory power of the EEOC. Senator Everett Dirksen (R-Illinois) amended the title to include language making clear that it only covered intentional discrimination, and that it did not allow the use of preferential treatment or racial quotas to undo past discrimination. The federal EEOC, unlike many state FEPCs, would have no "cease and desist" authority; it could not order an offending business to change its practices. The EEOC also was not allowed to file cases in federal courts although the title did allow the U.S. attorney general to file suit when a pattern of employment discrimination was believed to exist. (In 1972, the EEOC was given power to file its own cases in federal court.) The EEOC thus lacked most enforcement powers in its inception; it instead had to resolve individual grievances through mediation and conciliation.

The most important amendment to Title VII, however, was proposed by Representative Howard Smith (D-Virginia), who suggested that the bill should also outlaw job discrimination on the basis of sex. Although it was originally thought this amendment would hurt the bill and lessen its chance of passing, it was championed by female members of the House of Representatives, and became law.

Despite these limitations, Title VII was one of the most influential and consequential sections of the Civil Rights Act of 1964. Although Title VII specifically forbade the use of "racial quotas" and did not require employers to achieve racial balance in their workforce through preferential hiring, the EEOC quickly moved beyond its original mandate of responding to individual complaints to determining patterns of discrimination and investigating entire industries. By the 1970s, the EEOC had negotiated settlements with corporate giants such as AT&T, General Electric, and General Motors, which agreed to hire greater numbers of women and minorities. Historian Hugh Graham has argued that in the process of implementing the federal prohibition on employment discrimination, the EEOC began to demand not just an absence of discrimination but a positive change in employers' workforces, requiring preferential treatment on the grounds of race or sex in order to compensate for the results of past discrimination. Title VII served as one

of the foundations for AFFIRMATIVE ACTION requirements, in hiring; but Title VII cases, especially those involving individual complaints rather than a pattern of discrimination, have proved difficult to win in the courts because they place a burden on the employee, who must prove discriminatory treatment.

Title VII has had a significant impact on hiring practices in the United States and on the composition of the workforce. Although the EEOC did not initially take seriously its mandate to outlaw sex discrimination, women's groups such as the NATIONAL ORGANIZATION FOR WOMEN (NOW) pushed the EEOC to treat sex discrimination the same as racial discrimination. Today, women of all races are among the principal beneficiaries of Title VII. A study of the economic consequences of equal employment practices from 1963 to 1972 found that although the share of income earned by white men declined, their loss was redistributed less to nonwhite men than to nonwhite women (whose share of income increased by half) and to white women (whose share of income doubled).

BIBLIOGRAPHY

Brooks, Roy L. *Rethinking the American Race Problem.* 1990.
Burstein, Paul. *Discrimination, Job and Politics.* 1985.
Faludi, Susan. *Backlash: The Undeclared War Against American Women.* 1991.
Graham, Hugh. *The Civil Rights Era.* 1990.
Loevy, Robert D. *To End All Segregation: The Politics of the Passage of the Civil Rights Act of 1964.* 1990.
Loevy, Robert D., ed. *The Civil Rights Act of 1964.* 1997.
Whalen, Charles, and Barbara Whalen. *The Longest Debate: A Legislative History of the 1964 Civil Rights Act.* 1985.

Renee Romano

Toure, Kwame

See Carmichael, Stokely.

Trail of Broken Treaties

Greeted by a cold rain on the first day of November 1972, the first vehicles of the "Trail of Broken Treaties" caravan arrived in Washington, D.C. Originating on the West Coast, the caravan was comprised of several hundred American Indians who had traveled across the country and converged on the city to carry out a week-long schedule of ceremonies, meetings, and peaceful protests. Hoping to capitalize on election-week media coverage, the Trail of Broken Treaties brought a list of twenty points for presentation to federal officials. While the Twenty Points document had been constructed by the Trail's leaders less than two weeks before the group's arrival in Washington, the ideas it contained were old and represented traditional views held throughout Indian Country.

An attempt to reestablish a sovereign government-to-government relationship between Native-American tribes and the United States, the Twenty Points called for the restoration of treaty activity between federal and tribal governments (see TREATY RIGHTS), the reinforcement and recognition of existing treaties, the creation of a commission to review treaty commitments and violations, mandatory relief against treaty-rights violations, judicial recognition of the Indian right to interpret treaties, and removal of any state control over Native-American lands and resources. With regard to both its forceful assertion of SOVEREIGNTY for Indian people and the specificity of its demands, the Twenty Points was one of the most important documents ever presented to the national government by a Native-American people. Any possibility for its serious consideration was quickly lost, however, in the confusion that overtook the Trail of Broken Treaties gathering.

Expecting to find decent accommodations, hot showers, and food when they arrived in Washington, road-weary Indians from throughout the United States found instead that they had no assigned places to stay, little or no provisions, and no real acknowledgment from federal officials. Advance preparations had fallen through and hundreds of them found themselves stranded in an unfamiliar city. On the morning of November 3, not more than twenty-four hours after the first members of the group entered the city, the Trail of Broken Treaties determined its final destination: the BUREAU OF INDIAN AFFAIRS building on Constitution Avenue. Having nowhere else to go, caravan participants sought shelter in "their" building while Trail leaders met with federal officials to address what was quickly becoming a logistical nightmare. Before any plans could be carried out, however, a confrontation between police and Native Americans erupted in the lobby of the Bureau. Within minutes the police were pushed out onto the street and the building was barricaded from within. The Bureau of Indian Affairs was officially "occupied" and would remain so for the next week.

Original Trail organizers had planned orderly, peaceful demonstrations, not the forceful occupation of government property that had now occurred. Nonetheless, events were in motion and the group's energies were necessarily directed away from vigils, discussions, and presentations and directed instead toward strategies for the temporary possession and eventual relinquishment of Bureau headquarters. Several days of negotiations between Trail organizers and White House representatives resulted in terms of surrender, including the creation of a government

task force to study the Trail's concerns and proposals, a formal White House response to each of the Twenty Points, amnesty for Bureau occupiers, and financial assistance to help them get home. On November 8, one week after the takeover began, the final Native Americans left the building.

The occupation of the Bureau of Indian Affairs—that resented controller of generations of native people—made great symbolic sense. The actual reasons for the takeover were far less politically strategic than practical, however. Hundreds of tired, confused, and frustrated Indians needed a place to stay and the Bureau building was seen as a source of relief. The takeover of the Bureau of Indian Affairs might have been interpreted by some as a bold and noble act of political resistance. However, damage to the building and its contents, and the destruction and removal of important tribal documents, as well as those pertaining to individual Native Americans, resulted in notable negative press and public opinion. The predominant force behind the Trail of Broken Treaties and the occupation of the Bureau, the AMERICAN INDIAN MOVEMENT (AIM), had now secured in the American imagination its reputation as a militant organization capable of violence.

While its organizational disarray and responsibility for the destruction of material property—much of which pertained to the histories and futures of Indian peoples themselves—compromised the Trail of Broken Treaties in the minds of many, Indians and non-Indians alike, an evenhanded evaluation of this event must consider its importance in bringing together in common cause hundreds of Native Americans from around the country. The Trail marked the first time in American history that a massive intertribal coalition, made up of Indians of all ages, all occupations, reservation-based and urban, brought its collective grievances directly to the White House. The Twenty Points called for a genuine change of federal policy: a new institutional structure designed to facilitate Native Americans' progress. Both the caravan and the document reminded everyone of the long history of independence and resistance shared by Indian peoples across the United States.

BIBLIOGRAPHY

Akwesasne Notes. *BIA, I'm Not Your Indian Any More: Trail of Broken Treaties.* 1973.

Deloria, Vine, Jr. *Behind the Trail of Broken Treaties: An Indian Declaration of Independence.* 1985.

Johnson, Troy R. "Roots of Contemporary Native American Activism." *American Indian Culture and Research Journal* 20, no. 2 (1996): 127–154.

Smith, Paul Choat, and Robert Allen Warrior. *Like a Hurricane*. 1996.

Judith Antell

TransAfrica

TransAfrica, an organization founded in 1977, is an advocate for the rights of persons of African descent. Based on concepts of PAN-AFRICANISM, internationalism, and mobilization of blacks within the greater diaspora, in pursuit of its goals TransAfrica assesses U.S. and foreign government policy and legislation to determine its legitimacy.

Today TransAfrica boasts over twenty thousand members and a separate educational institution, TransAfrica Forum, which provides foreign service training for minorities, publishes a quarterly journal of opinion, and hosts lectures on a variety of relevant topics. TransAfrica's membership roster includes a number of public figures, among them Mary Frances BERRY, Danny Glover, Camille Cosby, Maya Angelou, and Jesse JACKSON. The high-profile membership list brings mainstream exposure and attracts financial support.

One of its first campaigns was in protest of South African apartheid; TransAfrica successfully influenced CONGRESS to pass the Anti-Apartheid Act of 1986, which led to U.S. economic sanctions against South Africa. TransAfrica's strategy included political protests and economic boycotts. It is estimated that TransAfrica's efforts led to a loss of $10 billion by South African businesses; and Nelson Mandela's release from prison and South Africa's democratic elections of 1994 represented a major victory for the organization. Although TransAfrica's Free South Africa movement greatly increased public awareness of the organization, its President Randall ROBINSON argued that members of the media place too much emphasis on TransAfrica's work in South Africa, to the neglect of other projects. He wanted to emphasize the diversity within TransAfrica's advocacy work.

One of TransAfrica's victories in the 1990s involved Haiti. Its efforts received widespread media attention after Randall Robinson began a lengthy hunger strike in an attempt to change American policy toward Haiti. Robinson demanded that exiled former Haitian President Jean Bertrand Aristide be returned to power, and that Haitian refugees be treated as equals to their Cuban counterparts. As a result, President William CLINTON reformed his policy toward the Haitian government, so that treatment of Haitian refugees improved, and President Aristide was reinstated.

A major campaign that TransAfrica has been pursuing focuses on the Caribbean banana trade. In brief, the European Union (EU) favored receiving banana imports from former colonies, with the result that an American-owned company, Chiquita, complained to and was supported in its position by the World Trade Organization (WTO), in protest of the EU policy. In a 1999 press release, Robinson attacked the U.S. government's use of economic hegemony and likened the trade negotiations to those in 1954, involving Guatemala and the United Fruit Company (UFCO). Ironically, Chiquita is the UFCO renamed.

Over the course of its existence, TransAfrica has attracted both critics and allies. One major area of contention was TransAfrica's very public stance against the former ruler of Nigeria, Sani Abacha. Despite the fact that the Abacha regime was a dictatorship, many critics argued that TransAfrica had supported other controversial leaders and organizations. Other critics argued that TransAfrica should not publicly oppose black leadership. TransAfrica responded by saying that no government, no matter the race of its leader, should commit large-scale atrocities. Moreover, on March 13, 1995, TransAfrica issued a public letter calling for the cessation of the Abacha regime, democratic elections, and return to civilian rule. In spite of some criticism, TransAfrica has continued to receive substantial contributions from numerous corporations and benefactors such as Coca-Cola and Adolph Coors, as well as the Ford and Carnegie foundations.

During the last quarter century, TransAfrica has grown steadily in scope, membership, and public

Randall Robinson speaks at a press conference in Washington, D.C., on January 9, 1986. (CORBIS/Bettmann)

exposure. Although reactions to its campaigns vary considerably, TransAfrica has proved its value among Washington lobbyists.

BIBLIOGRAPHY

Beinart, Peter. "Tough Love." *New Republic* 209 (6) (1993): 15.

"Conversations with Randall Robinson." *Journal of International Affairs*. 46 (1) (1992):145.

Jones, Joyce, and Eric Smith. "Will New bill Help Africa or Exploit It?" *Black Enterprise* 29 (1998):2.

Marriot, Michel and Lucy Shackelford. "Brother Against Brother," *Newsweek*, p. 47, May 22, 1995.

Ogletree, Charles, and Randall Robinson. "The Banana War's Missing Link—Campaign Funding," *Christian Science Monitor*, p. 11, March 31, 1999.

Robinson, Randall. *Defending the Spirit: A Black Life in America*. 1998.

Robinson, Randall, and Ralph Nader. "A Forced March to Congress' Tune," *Los Angeles Times*, Washington Edition, p. A11, March 11, 1998.

Donna Patterson

Treaty Rights

In U.S. law, the rights held by individual persons come from a wide variety of sources. Some basic rights are guaranteed by the U.S. Constitution or by the constitutions of the various states within the federal union. Others are derived from statute law on either the federal or state levels; still other rights may rest on the common law or even on treaties.

Foreign diplomats generally enjoy so-called diplomatic immunity from arrest and prosecution on the basis of international treaties that reinforce and define ancient customary rights. The Treaty of Paris (1783), by which Britain recognized the independence of the United States, gave British and American citizens reciprocal claims to property seized in the Revolutionary War. Subsequently, in virtually all treaties of annexation, the United States guaranteed to residents of newly acquired territory equal rights with U.S. citizens.

Quite literally thousands of treaties grant, limit, and define special rights for foreign nationals in U.S. jurisdictions. Rights and obligations under tax statutes; duties to serve in, and exemptions from, military service; the right to consultation with diplomatic personnel following arrest; and the like are all prescribed in specific treaties with individual nations. Certain key human rights for aliens are protected by the U.S. Constitution, of course, rather than by treaty grant—for example, aliens facing death, imprisonment, fine, or loss of property are entitled to legal counsel, trial by jury, compulsory power to summon witnesses, the right against compulsory self-incrimination, freedom from cruel and unusual punishment, and so forth, as provided by the Fourth, Fifth, Sixth, Seventh, Eighth, and Fourteenth Amendments.

The horrifying events of WORLD WAR II—especially the Holocaust and the general disregard for the rights of citizens by their own governments—produced a new regime in international law following that conflict. The Charter of the United Nations (1945) set down certain general principles of human rights, and these were expanded on and made more specific by the Universal Declaration of Human Rights (1948). The Genocide Convention provides certain protections for citizens of, and aliens within, signatory countries as well.

In U.S. law, the chief limitation on treaty rights is created by the inherent limitations of treaty law itself within the constitutional structure. Although Article Six makes treaties "the supreme law of the land," treaties may not contradict the U.S. Constitution, and their relation to federal statute remains ambiguous. Unless provisions of a treaty are of such a nature and are expressed in such language as to be self-executing, they do not override statutory law until Congress enacts enabling legislation implementing the terms of the treaty.

In addition, although the self-executing provisions of a duly ratified treaty will invalidate any federal law or any state constitutional or statutory provisions to the contrary, a federal statute appropriately enacted subsequent to the ratification of a treaty invalidates any provision of the treaty contradictory to it—as the courts have expressed it, "the last act of the sovereign will prevail."

In addition to the limitations on treaty rights, in general, persons within the jurisdiction of the U.S. courts have no recourse to appeal to supranational bodies from the decisions of the U.S. judiciary. This contrasts with the situation within the European Union (EU), where the rights of national citizens, EU nationals resident in other EU territory, or resident non-EU aliens can appeal from the domestic courts of any member nation to the EU courts for final judicial determination of rights.

In regard to treaty rights within U.S. law, however, it has been primarily American Indians and their tribal organizations that have enjoyed the widest range of such rights. In 1871, Congress ended the practice of making treaties with the Indian tribes, but numerous treaties predate the abandonment of the treaty process and still have the force of law. The Indian nations were not recognized as truly sovereign entities in U.S. law, however, for they were, as the Supreme Court held, "dependent, domestic sovereignties."

As limited sovereignties, Indian tribes have been granted various degrees of self-government by treaties, acts of Congress, and administrative regulations of the Department of the Interior and the Bureau of Indian Affairs. Treaties have also provided immunities from various sorts of federal, state, and local taxation on Indians or their reservations. Similarly, courts have upheld certain hunting, fishing, and gathering rights enjoyed by tribal members within the various states.

The grant of land to Indian tribes by treaty and later dispossessions from these lands by subsequent treaties or by acts of Congress have been one of the most poignant aspects of Indian history. Despite the role of treaty rights for Indians, most native American rights arise from the direct application of constitutional rights to the Indians or their indirect application through the 1924 congressional grant of U.S. citizenship to Indians. In addition, congressional enactments against discrimination have general application to Indians within U.S. society.

Finally, in *Talton v. Mayes* (1896) and in subsequent decisions, such as *United States v. Wheeler* (1978), the U.S. Supreme Court has held that tribal governments are not automatically constrained by the U.S. Constitution. Over the years, some tribal members have complained of the undemocratic and abusive behavior of tribal leaders. In 1968, therefore, Congress passed the Indian Civil Rights Act, which applied various constitutional safeguards, both procedural and substantive, to the actions of tribal governments.

(See also AMERICAN INDIAN CITIZENSHIP ACT OF 1924; AMERICAN INDIAN CIVIL RIGHTS ACT OF 1968.)

BIBLIOGRAPHY

Corwin, Edward S. *National Supremacy: Treaty Power vs. State Power.* 1965.
Deloria, Vine, Jr., and Clifford M. Lytle. *American Indians, American Justice.* 1983.
Jacobs, F. G., ed. *European Law and the Individual.* 1976.
Pevar, Stephen L. *The Rights of Indians and Tribes: The Basic ACLU Guide to Indian and Tribal Rights,* 2d ed. 1992.
Sohn, Louis B., and Thomas Buergenthal. *International Protection of Human Rights.* 1973.

Patrick M. O'Neil

Trotter, William Monroe

(1872–1934), editor and radical civil rights leader.

William Monroe Trotter was born in Boston, Massachusetts, attended Harvard, was the first African American to be elected to Phi Beta Kappa, and was the founding editor of the *Boston Guardian.*

Trotter used the *Guardian* skillfully to promote his radical views on civil rights and to champion a number of political causes, especially his persistent attack on the black leader Booker T. WASHINGTON as the na-

tion's chief hurdle to racial equality. Trotter maintained that Washington's accommodationist leadership had given African Americans just "the torch and the rope" as he built himself an educational empire and an admirable political reputation among whites, particularly segregationists. It was his confrontation with Washington in July 1903, the so-called Boston Riot, that led to Trotter's fame as a race leader and militant civil rights advocate. The Boston Riot also made Trotter the target of clandestine attempts by Booker T. Washington to destroy his newspaper.

Trotter's most significant contribution to civil rights for African Americans was his 1905 proposal that he and W. E. B. DU BOIS collaborate in creating a "national strategy board" to combat the worsening political conditions of African Americans. His proposal resulted in the founding of the NIAGARA MOVEMENT in 1905, which anticipated the NATIONAL ASSOCIATION FOR THE ADVANCEMENT OF COLORED PEOPLE (NAACP). The goal of the Niagara Movement, an all-black organization, was to take the offensive in striving for private and civil equality for African Americans. However, disagreement among the leaders, chiefly between Trotter and Du Bois, helped to weaken the movement. The failure of the Niagara Movement was also connected with the emergence of the white-led and better-financed NAACP, founded in 1909, which was committed to achieving equal rights through litigation in the nation's courts. Du Bois was one of the founding members of the NAACP, but Trotter was not a resolute supporter of the NAACP because it was white-led and advocated INTEGRATION. He believed that civil rights organizations dedicated to attaining equal rights for African Americans should be led by African Americans while having white members and forming alliances with white organizations. Trotter also believed in self-segregation, similar to that of Boston's Irish and Italians, for political and cultural purposes.

Trotter continually used the *Guardian* as a clarion to call his fellow black Bostonians to rally around him to protest racial discrimination. Nonetheless, Trotter's influence, and that of his newspaper, faded after the death of Booker Washington in 1916 and the death of his wife, Geraldine Pindell, in 1918. During the 1920s his influence and effectiveness further abated, and by the 1930s Trotter had fallen into deep despair, emotionally and financially. In 1934, Trotter died, after either jumping or falling from a building. Trotter's philosophy and tactics foreshadowed the modern civil rights movement, which emphasized nonviolent demonstrations and ideas of elective SEGREGATION and BLACK POWER as means of achieving full citizenship rights for African Americans.

BIBLIOGRAPHY

Cromwell, Adelaide M. *The Other Brahmins: Boston's Black Upper Class, 1750–1950.* 1994.

Fox, Stephen, R. *The Guardian of Boston: William Monroe Trotter.* 1970.

Gatewood, Willard B. *Aristocrats of Color: The Black Elite, 1880–1920.* 1990.

Harlan, Louis R., and Smock, Raymond W. *The Booker T. Washington Papers.* 1972.

Hixson, William B. *Moorfield Storey and the Abolitionist Tradition.* 1972.

Schneider, Mark R. *Boston Confronts Jim Crow, 1890–1920.* 1997.

Claude Hargrove

Truman, Harry S.

(1884–1972), U.S. president, 1945–1953.

Harry S. Truman, thirty-third president of the United States, issued an executive order desegregating the Armed Forces in 1948.

Truman was a relatively obscure Missouri senator before being selected Franklin Roosevelt's vice-presidential running mate in 1944. Shortly thereafter, in 1945, he ascended to the presidency upon Roosevelt's death. He ordered the detonation of atomic weapons on the Japanese cities of Hiroshima and Nagasaki, which led to the surrender of Japan, bringing World War II to an abrupt end. Truman finished out Roosevelt's term and was elected in his own right in 1948 after waging a stunning come-from-behind campaign to defeat Republican Thomas Dewey. Truman and his advisors were the architects of the American cold war policy, which was followed by every president through George BUSH. This is widely regarded as Truman's greatest legacy.

While Truman's reputation has been negatively affected by reports of his use of salty and sometimes derogatory language directed at African Americans, in fact he was the first national Democrat to take a strong position on civil rights issues of concern to African Americans. African Americans had first voted Democratic in large numbers for Franklin ROOSEVELT, largely because of the redistributive economic policies

President Harry S. Truman stands next to (from left): Mary McLeod Bethune, the founder of the National Council of Negro Women; Vijaya Lakshmi Pandit, ambassador to the United States from India; and Ralph Bunche, director of the trusteeship for the United Nations, in Washington, D.C., on November 15, 1949. The president had just presented them with citations for outstanding achievements. (AP/Wide World Photos)

of the New Deal. (See NEW DEAL AND DEPRESSION.) Truman and others feared that African Americans would return to the "party of Lincoln." Part of the reason for this fear were Republican gains among black voters in the off-year election of 1946, when the GOP captured the Congress. Some black leaders believed Truman was betraying them on labor and civil rights issues. The fear of losing the black vote motivated Truman to try to secure this crucial vote in large industrial cities in the north. (African Americans were still denied the vote in many places in the South, almost without exception in the counties with substantial black populations.)

Truman appealed to African Americans by becoming the first twentieth-century president to recommend major civil rights legislation to the Congress. He had formed the President's Committee on Civil Rights in 1946, which issued a report the following year recommending sweeping civil rights legislation and an executive order desegregating the armed forces. Truman ordered the latter and asked Congress in 1948 for legislation to eliminate the poll tax, increase protection against lynching, and desegregate interstate travel, among other things. An intraparty battle ensued at the 1948 Democratic convention between segregationists and northern liberals. Northern liberals prevailed with a platform plank with stronger procivil rights language than the compromise language Truman had proposed in an effort to mollify both sides. This dispute precipitated a walkout by some southern delegates and the protest candidacy of states' rights Democrat Strom THURMOND.

While Truman's strong position on civil rights confirmed the allegiance of a majority of African-American voters to the Democratic party, in fact very little of the civil rights legislation he proposed was enacted. His key contribution was his willingness to buck the traditional "hands-off" position on civil rights issues the party had always had. This changed the party forever from a party associated with segregation to a party that eventually became identified in Americans' minds with the civil rights movement. It also paved the way for the leadership position President Lyndon JOHNSON and the Democratic party took in the major civil rights legislation passed in the 1960s.

BIBLIOGRAPHY

Berman, William C. *The Politics of Civil Rights in the Truman Administration.* 1970.
Gaddis, John Lewis. *The United States and the Origins of the Cold War, 1941–1947.* 1972.
Gosnell, Harold F. *Truman's Crises: A Political Biography of Harry S Truman.* 1980.
Greenstein, Fred I. *Leadership in the Modern Presidency.* 1988.
Leuchtenburg, William E. *In the Shadow of FDR: From Harry Truman to Ronald Reagan.* 1983.
McCullough, David. *Truman.* 1992.
Milkis, Sidney M., and Michael Nelson. *The American Presidency: Origins and Development, 1776–1990.* 1990.
Ross, Irwin. *The Loneliest Campaign: The Truman Victory of 1948.* 1968.
Yarnell, Allen. *Democrats and Progressives.* 1974.

John Haskell

Tulsa Race Riot of 1921

On May 30, 1921, a young black shoe-shiner outside a white department store in Tulsa, Oklahoma, rode the elevator to the men's restroom. On his return, he apparently stepped on the foot of the young white female operator. She cried "Rape!" and the black lad fled into the Greenwood black district on the northeast edge of town. Arrested the next day, the youth was transferred to the safer county jail as the mayor and chief of police assured the community that no assault had occurred. In a few months the youth was released with no charges pressed. But in between these two events, a major race riot, initiated by the arrest, exploded in Tulsa, during which about one hundred blacks and whites were killed, and eleven hundred homes were burned, resulting in the tightening of segregation in an already segregated city.

Following the arrest of the shoe-shiner on May 31, 1921, the local press inflamed readers with inaccurate stories and references to a lynching. That night as hundreds of white males congregated around the courthouse, thirty to fifty armed black men marched to the jail offering their help to the besieged sheriff. He showed them that the youth was safe, and they returned to Greenwood. Later that night a larger group of black men, including World War I veterans, again marched to the jail and were again turned away by the sheriff. In an armed crowd of now thousands, some whites attempted to disarm some blacks. A shot was fired, and the riot exploded.

By the morning of June 1, at least three-fourths of Greenwood was looted and burned with $1,500,000 in damages. Six thousand blacks were interned in public facilities, but not a single white was arrested. For the next week blacks could walk the streets only if they wore special tags issued by the police. Deaths officially numbered thirty-four but were more likely seventy-five to one hundred. Despite the efforts of the Chamber of Commerce and realtor groups to condemn the burned district for a union railroad depot and industrial park, the black community rebuilt itself.

National Guardsmen lead black detainees to Tulsa's Convention Hall, in the aftermath of the June 1, 1921 race riot in Tulsa, Oklahoma. (AP/Wide World Photos)

BIBLIOGRAPHY

Alexander, Charles C. *The Ku Klux Klan in the Southwest.* 1965.

Ellsworth, Scott. *Death in a Promised Land: The Tulsa Race Riot of 1921.* 1982.

Halliburton, R. *The Tulsa Race Riot of 1921.* 1975.

Clifford H. Scott

Turner, Henry McNeal

(1834–1915), clergyman, African colonizationist.

Recognized as a spokesperson for nineteenth-century blacks, Henry McNeal Turner became a fiery proponent of BLACK NATIONALISM. As a free black itinerant minister for the Methodist Episcopal Church–South, he traveled throughout the region during the antebellum period, preaching to free blacks as well as slaves. In 1858 Turner joined the African Methodist Episcopal Church (AME), a religious organization administrated by and for blacks. He soon was appointed deacon, then elder, and later pastor of Washington, D.C.'s, largest African-American congregation. He used his pulpit to comment on the Civil War, applauding President Abraham Lincoln for the EMANCIPATION PROCLAMATION as well as the use of black troops in the Union Army. Lincoln in turn appointed Turner the first black army chaplain in U.S. history. After the war, Turner joined the Freedman's Bureau, traveling to Georgia to assist local blacks in the transition from slavery to freedom (see BUREAU OF REFUGEES, FREEDMEN, AND ABANDONED LANDS). Turner quickly discovered that RACISM remained virulent in the South, and that the Bureau was no exception. He resigned his

position and returned to the African Methodist Episcopal organization, convinced that he could accomplish more as the head of its newly formed Georgia mission. Turner's search for strategies to secure black independence focused on the AME and the REPUBLICAN PARTY, and he had remarkable success in encouraging blacks to join both groups. His own political ambitions were repeatedly thwarted by angry whites, however, and by 1870 Turner was completely disillusioned about the future of American race relations.

Turner had been intrigued by the idea of black repatriation to Africa since 1862, and he now turned his full attention to the prospect. Arguing that racism was so ingrained in the American character that blacks would never receive their rightful due, Turner insisted that the only hope for a decent life was to create a separate nation in Africa. In fact, Turner continued, God wanted blacks to return to Africa to help convert Africans to Christianity. Turner's emphasis on black nationalism and black pride dramatically altered the discourse around the emigration movement. He repeatedly asserted the inherent humanity of blacks, going as far as to insist that God Himself was black. While his fiery oratory infuriated many whites, blacks flocked to hear his message. In 1880 Turner was elected an AME bishop, and he used his increasing prominence to promote his migration project. He founded several magazines to circulate his views, called on the American government to help finance transportation to Liberia on the west coast of Africa, and tirelessly preached his vision throughout the South.

Although Turner made several trips to Africa to help build schools and churches, his dream of a large-scale migration was never realized. Delegates to an

1893 convention that he had organized refused to endorse his Back-to-Africa platform, and two disastrous test expeditions further eroded popular support. The rise of Booker T. WASHINGTON signaled both new black leadership and a retreat from Turner's aggressively defiant principles. Turner remained a powerful figure in religion and politics, however, becoming elder bishop of the AME and leading the Georgia Equal Rights Association. When he died in 1915, twenty-five thousand mourners attended his funeral.

BIBLIOGRAPHY

Angell, Stephen W. *Bishop Henry McNeal Turner and African-American Religion in the South.* 1992.

Redkey, Edwin S. *Black Exodus: Black Nationalist and Back-to-Africa Movements, 1890–1910.* 1969.

Trimiew, Darryl M. *Voices of the Silenced: The Responsible Self in a Marginalized Community.* 1993.

Wilmore, Gayraud S. *Black Religion and Black Radicalism: An Interpretation of the Religious History of Afro-American People.* 1983.

Rochelle C. Hayes

Tuskegee Experiment (1932–1972)

Impetus toward the Tuskegee Syphilis Experiment began with a 1930 Julius Rosenwald Fund grant to help the United States Public Health Service (USPHS) diagnose and treat syphilitics in six southern counties, including Macon County, Alabama. Tuskegee Institute's medical facilities and black medical personnel, who could assist white USPHS clinicians, attracted the agency to Macon County. After the Rosenwald Fund withdrew funding in 1932, Dr. Taliaferro Clark, director of USPHS's Venereal Disease Division, convinced Surgeon General Hugh S. Cumming of the value of studying untreated syphilis in males among the high percentage (36 percent) of Macon County blacks tested and found positive. Many doctors then suspected that syphilis produced different cardiovascular and neurological effects in blacks and whites.

The experiment made a mockery of informed consent. Doctors told the sample of 399 syphilitic men merely that they had "bad blood." Although Clark envisioned a short-term study, Dr. Raymond Vonderlehr, the initial director of field work in Macon County, extended the experiment indefinitely upon filling the retired Clark's directorship in 1933. Vonderlehr exploited the poorly educated subjects, promising special treatment if they returned for checkups. Eunice Rivers, an African-American nurse from Tuskegee, drove the men for free to subsequent annual checkups. The men received aspirin, placebos, and iron tonic for various ailments but no syphilis treatments. Burial stipends to the poor subjects' families encour-

Ninety-four-year-old Herman Shaw, a victim of the Tuskegee Syphilis study, stands smiling next to President Bill Clinton on May 16, 1997, in Washington, D.C. Clinton had just issued a long-delayed formal government apology to all those black men whose syphilis was deliberately untreated as part of a long-term government medical-research experiment. (AP/Wide World Photos)

aged continued participation. Harmful side effects from commonly used remedies of arsenic compounds and mercury became USPHS's excuse for lack of early treatment. This rationalization faltered when penicillin became widely used in the 1940s.

The experiment was extralegal as well as unethical. To keep subjects untreated, USPHS gained cooperation from private physicians through the Macon County and Alabama State Boards of Health and from Tuskegee Institute's John Andrew Hospital, where checkups and autopsies occurred. Surgeon General John Parran's 1934 campaign against venereal diseases did not help the men, nor did the U.S. Army and State of Alabama requirements of testing and treating draft-eligible men for venereal diseases during World War II.

Although reports concerning the Tuskegee Experiment were frequently published in medical journals, few physicians questioned its ethics. The American

Heart Association challenged the experiment's validity, citing subjective diagnoses of cardiovascular effects. Associated Press reports, informed by USPHS investigator Peter Buxtun, finally provoked public outrage in 1972. Health, Education, and Welfare Secretary Caspar Weinberger pledged free medical care for the men and future guidelines for human experimentation. Senator Edward Kennedy chaired subcommittee hearings on the experiment. In 1975 civil rights attorney Fred GRAY won a class-action suit against the federal and Alabama state governments. Subjects and their heirs each gained free medical care and thousands of dollars in damages.

The Tuskegee Syphilis Experiment intensified African Americans' distrust of their federal government. In the 1980s, polls revealed that many African Americans believed the government created acquired immunodeficiency syndrome (AIDS) as an instrument of genocide. President Bill CLINTON officially apologized to surviving subjects in 1997, but Senate rejection of Surgeon General nominee Henry Foster amid questions about his knowledge of the experiment demonstrated that suspicions persist.

BIBLIOGRAPHY

Clinton, William J. "Remarks in Apology to African-Americans on the Tuskegee Experiment." *Weekly Compilation of Presidential Documents* 33 (May 19, 1997): 718–720.

Fraley, Colette. "Foster's Answers Keep His Bid for Surgeon General Alive." *Congressional Quarterly Weekly Report* 53 (May 6, 1995): 1244–1247.

Jones, James H. *Bad Blood: The Tuskegee Syphilis Experiment.* 1993.

Rivers, Eunice, Stanley H. Schumann, Lloyd Simpson, and Sidney Olansky. "Twenty Years of Followup Experience in a Long Range Study." *Public Health Reports* 68 (April, 1953): 391–395.

Smith, Susan L. "Neither Victim nor Villain: Nurse Eunice Rivers, the Tuskegee Syphilis Experiment, and Public Health Work." *Journal of Women's History* 8 (1996): 95–113.

Wes Borucki

Tuttle, Elbert Parr

(1897–1996), judge.

Elbert Tuttle was a judge of the United States Court of Appeals for the Fifth Circuit and then the Eleventh Circuit from 1954 to his death in 1996. He played a significant vote in shaping and enforcing civil rights law. He was born in California and raised in Hawaii. Educated at Cornell, he moved to Atlanta, where he practiced law from 1923 until 1952, except for combat service in the Pacific during WORLD WAR II, when he was seriously wounded. While in private practice, he handled several prominent civil rights cases as pro bono (free-of-charge) matters. In 1952 Tuttle led the fight at the Republican National Convention to seat the pro-Eisenhower delegation from Georgia. His victory, along with those of Eisenhower delegations in Louisiana and Texas (headed by John Minor WISDOM and John Robert BROWN, his future colleagues on the Fifth Circuit), secured the Republican presidential nomination for Eisenhower. In 1954 President Eisenhower appointed Tuttle to serve on the Fifth Circuit Court of Appeals, which handled all appeals of cases from federal courts in Texas, Louisiana, Mississippi, Alabama, Georgia, and Florida. (In 1981, Congress split the Fifth Circuit by creating a new Eleventh Circuit, with jurisdiction over Alabama, Georgia, and Florida, where Tuttle served for the remainder of his career.) Because of their position in the Deep South, the Fifth, and later the Eleventh, Circuit were essential for making the Supreme Court's civil rights decisions, and later Congress's civil rights acts, real for millions of Americans. A conservative Fifth Circuit judge dubbed Tuttle, along with Judge John Brown of Texas, Judge Richard RIVES of Alabama, and Judge John Minor Wisdom of Louisiana, one of "the Four." This label, intended disparagingly, came to identify these four Fifth Circuit judges as committed to protecting the rights of black Americans, in spite of the personal risks to themselves and their families. As Chief Judge of the Fifth Circuit from 1960 to 1967, Tuttle issued decisions and actions that were essential in ensuring that civil rights litigants were able to receive timely relief from the courts. Although Judge Tuttle took senior status in 1968, which allowed him to hear fewer cases, he continued to hear and decide appellate cases until shortly before his death in 1996. Tuttle was a formal and ascetic man of unquestionable integrity. His decisions were clear and concise, cutting through to the essential issues in the cases before him. In 1981 he received the Presidential Medal of Freedom. As Justice William Brennan said of Tuttle and his colleagues in the Fifth Circuit, "They changed the face of a nation."

BIBLIOGRAPHY

Bass, Jack. *Unlikely Heroes.* 1981

Couch, Harvey C. *A History of the Fifth Circuit 1891–1981.* 1984.

Emanuel, Anne S "Lynching and the Law in Georgia Circa 1931: A Chapter in the Legal Career of Judge Elbert Tuttle." *William and Mary Bill of Rights Journal* 5 (Winter 1996): 215–248.

Read, F., and L. McGough. *Let Them Be Judged.* 1978.

Tuttle, Elbert P. "Equality of the Vote." *New York University Law Review* 41 (1966): 245–266.

Henry T. Greeley

U

Unions

Unions have been among the most vigorous opponents of and advocates for civil rights. Until well into the twentieth century, many unions acted as white, male "job trusts," prohibiting all people of color and white women from membership and by so doing limiting their access to many trades. Other unions, however, strongly supported racial and gender equality in the workplace and in society.

Craft unions, the most common unions in the United States in the late nineteenth and early twentieth centuries, typically enforced some form of racial and gender exclusion. Some craft unions, such as the Brotherhood of Locomotive Firemen and Engineers, explicitly restricted membership to white men. Others, such as the International Association of Machinists, had no formal bar against people of color but allowed their local lodges to discriminate freely. Still other craft unions maintained a color or gender line by manipulating dues levels, access to training programs, and other union policies. Craft unions also led legislative efforts to prohibit Chinese immigrants from entering the United States in the 1870s and 1880s.

Many of these discriminatory practices were carried over into the most important labor organization of the period, the American Federation of Labor (AFL). Formed in 1886 as an umbrella organization for craft unions, the AFL initially refused membership to any union that barred African Americans. Within ten years of its founding, however, the AFL had abandoned the principle, accepting into its ranks at least eight unions that refused blacks admission. The AFL itself, more-over, endorsed the practice of organizing African-American workers into separate, all-black union locals. The AFL leadership thus brought the labor federation into line with the JIM CROW system then emerging in the American South.

At times, the craft union's racial practices fanned the flames of racial hatred. In the spring of 1917, for example, the Aluminum Ore Company of East St. Louis, Illinois, defeated an AFL-led strike of white workers by hiring a small number of African-American strikebreakers. Union leaders responded not by trying to swing black workers to the union cause but rather by mounting a political campaign to drive African Americans out of the city. The unionists' campaign heightened already escalating racial tensions in East St. Louis, tensions that exploded on the evening of July 2, 1917. The result was a two-day pogrom that left at least thirty-nine African Americans dead. (See RED SUMMERS OF 1917–1921.)

Some late nineteenth- and early twentieth-century unions, in contrast, pursued policies that challenged racial and gender barriers. During its heyday in the 1880s, the Knights of Labor, the nation's first great labor organization, maintained some interracial lodges and mounted challenges to racial segregation. Three decades later, the radical Industrial Workers of the World (IWW) organized thousands of African-American workers, many of whom labored in the lowest-paying and most dangerous sectors of American industry. Even some AFL unions rejected the federation's exclusionary practices for more egalitarian policies. The unions of the needles trades, most notably the International Ladies Garment Workers Union and

745

Striking United Parcel Service Workers and sympathizers from other unions hold a rally at Liberty State Park in Jersey City, New Jersey, on August 13, 1997. (AP/Wide World Photos)

the Amalgamated Clothing Workers, worked assiduously to unionize women workers; and the United Mine Workers, the AFL's largest affiliate union, organized biracial locals, fought for repeal of the poll tax in Southern states, and battled against the Ku Klux Klan.

Even these unions, however, equivocated on civil rights issues. Local Knights of Labor chapters often divided black and white workers into segregated units, while the national organization barred Asian workers from membership. At times, IWW organizers used racist appeals to attract workers. The United Mine Workers and the needle trades unions by and large denied African Americans and women any leadership roles in their organizations. Furthermore, they did little to change the racist ideas that ran through the white rank and file.

The explosion of unionism in the 1930s changed the racial and gender dynamics within the labor movement. For its part, the AFL continued to be dominated by the skilled trades. But it also added to its ranks the all-black Brotherhood of Sleeping Car Porters, whose leaders and members would play a pivotal role in advancing racial justice in the United States. The schism within the labor movement in 1935 proved to be even more momentous. For years, the leaders of some AFL unions had been urging the federation to reach out to the vast number of semi- and unskilled workers who labored in the nation's great industries. Committed to maintaining the craft tradition, the AFL leadership consistently refused. Deeply frustrated by the AFL's inaction, the dissident union officials, led by United Mine Workers' president John L. Lewis, formed their own union federation, the Congress of Industrial Organizations (CIO), in 1935. In a series of dramatic strikes and legal challenges over the next five years, the CIO organized two and a half million workers into forty-one unions spread across industrial America.

Unlike the AFL, the CIO's member unions pledged to organize all workers, regardless of race, and to fight for an end to racial discrimination. A number of forces pushed CIO leaders to this position. In contrast to the crafts, which were almost exclusively white, the automobile, steel, and other mass production industries had a significant minority of African Americans in their work forces. The CIO could not ignore the needs and demands of African Americans. Once black workers were organized, they prodded their unions to take more aggressive action on racial issues. Many of the CIO's early leaders and organizers also pushed their unions on racial issues because of their own ideological commitments: communists or socialists, they had long favored racial equality. Some CIO leaders, finally, endorsed racial justice as a way of pushing southern conservatives out of the Democratic party, the CIO's political home.

CIO unions thus established strong records on civil rights issues. The United Automobile Workers (UAW), the United Packinghouse Workers of America (UPWA), the United Rubber Workers (URW), the Food, Tobacco, and Agricultural Workers Union (FTA), the United Steelworkers of America (USWA), the United Furniture Workers of America (UFWA), the United Electrical Workers (UE), and other CIO unions all maintained integrated union locals. Those unions with large Southern memberships, like the FTA, openly challenged the Jim Crow system. Northern-based unions, like the UPWA and the UAW, often tried to combat racism within their own ranks. During World War II, for example, the UAW refused to support white members who went on strike to protest the integration of their factories. Black workers within many CIO unions, moreover, used their unions as political training grounds and bases for civil rights activism, inside their factories and in their communities.

Many CIO unions also allied themselves with civil rights organizations and vigorously supported civil rights legislation. The UAW maintained close ties with the NATIONAL ASSOCIATION FOR THE ADVANCEMENT OF COLORED PEOPLE from the late 1930s onward, for example, while the United Furniture Workers of America built close connections with the NATIONAL NEGRO CONGRESS. CIO unions supported voter registration drives in the South during the 1940s, and they used their political influence to lobby for the abolition of the poll tax and the peacetime extension of the FAIR EMPLOYMENT PRACTICES COMMITTEE, the federal commission established during World War II to combat discrimination in hiring.

Unions extended their activism as the civil rights movement entered its most vibrant phase in the 1950s and 1960s. A local official of the Brotherhood of Sleeping Car Porters, E. D. NIXON, served as a co-organizer of the 1955–1956 MONTGOMERY BUS BOYCOTT in Alabama, and the union gave the boycott invaluable aid. The United Packinghouse Workers became a major source of financial and logistical support for the SOUTHERN CHRISTIAN LEADERSHIP CONFERENCE. The United Automobile Workers lent the movement its considerable political weight at numerous pivotal moments, most notably during the legislative struggle to secure passage of the CIVIL RIGHTS ACT OF 1964, when the union helped to organize and direct the lobbying campaign for the bill. Unions also catalyzed the Hispanic civil rights movement, given life by the struggles of migrant laborers to organize under the banner of the United Farm Workers. Civil rights activists, in turn, offered their support for union efforts. To cite the most dramatic example, Martin Luther KING, JR., was murdered as he campaigned in Memphis, Tennessee, on behalf of that city's striking sanitation workers.

For all their activism, however, the CIO unions did not have unblemished records on racial issues. Both the UAW and the United Steelworkers of America allowed some of their locals to maintain discriminatory seniority and job classification systems. They also did nothing to challenge the exclusionary practices of the skilled workers within their ranks, thus denying African Americans access to the most lucrative of blue-collar jobs. When the CIO and the AFL merged in 1955, the CIO leadership accepted, albeit grudgingly, the discriminatory practices of its new AFL partners, though the CIO unions helped to soften those practices in the 1960s. Nor did even the most liberal unions support all forms of civil rights activism. When the African-American freedom struggle adopted a more militant tone in the mid-1960s, most unions condemned the militants as irresponsible.

Labor's compromises on civil rights issues set off a number of conflicts within unions and between unions and black activists, particularly in the 1950s and 1960s. African-American workers determined to win equal treatment in their unions and on the job repeatedly battled against white workers determined to maintain discriminatory practices. Black workers and activists also criticized white labor leaders for their willingness to accept racial injustice, while white union officials lashed out at and tried to suppress their critics. In one of the most publicized of such clashes, in 1961 the AFL-CIO Executive Board censured A. Philip RANDOLPH, the president of the Brotherhood of Sleeping Car Porters, for criticizing the labor federation's temporizing on civil rights. The next year, the NAACP offered a scathing critique of the AFL-CIO's racial record, which strained relations between the civil rights organization and several major unions. Tensions grew in the late 1960s, nowhere more noticeably than in Detroit, where militant African-American auto workers formed the Revolutionary Union Movement as a BLACK POWER challenge to the United Automobile Workers, and in New York City, where black community activists clashed with the American Federation of Teachers over control of the Ocean Hill-Brownsville school district.

The CIO unions' commitment to gender equality was marked by a similar ambiguity. As in the case of black workers, CIO leaders recognized the need to bring women workers, white and nonwhite, into their organizations. But many CIO unions supported blatantly discriminatory practices, including separate seniority lists for men and women and pay differentials based on gender. In the immediate aftermath of WORLD WAR II, moreover, CIO unions used these discriminatory practices to purge thousands of women workers from the factories, so as to make room for male workers returning from military service. At the same time, however, unions served as an important base for feminist activism. Long before the resurgence of feminism in the 1960s, female unionists built powerful political networks within the labor movement, networks they used to demand equal treatment. Some of the most important figures in the feminist revival of the 1960s, including Betty FRIEDAN, worked in the union movement at some point in their careers, and they carried the lessons they learned there into the new movement they built. Several of the founders of the NATIONAL ORGANIZATION OF WOMEN were union officials.

Today, unions continue to promote social justice issues. The rising percentage of women and people of color in labor's ranks, moreover, has made it more difficult for unions to equivocate on racial and gender issues. Even in the skilled trades, discrimination has faded as racial and gender barriers in those unions have broken down under the force of civil rights law. The unions' ability to act as a vehicle for social change has been sharply limited, however, by their dramatic loss of power in the last two decades. Barely representing 14 percent of the American workforce at the close of the twentieth century, unions must struggle for their own survival as they struggle for a more just America.

BIBLIOGRAPHY

Arenesen, Eric. *Waterfront Workers of New Orleans: Race, Class, and Politics, 1863–1923*. 1991.

Arnesen, Eric. " 'Like Banquo's Ghost, It Will Not Down': The Race Question and the American Railroad Brotherhoods, 1880–1920." *American Historical Review* 99 (1994):1601–1633.

Asher, Robert, and Charles Stephenson, editors. *Labor Divided: Race and Ethnicity in United States Labor Struggles, 1835–1960*. 1990.

Boyle, Kevin. *The UAW and the Heyday of American Liberalism, 1945–1968*. 1995.

Draper, Alan. *Conflict of Interest: Organized Labor and the Civil Rights Movement in the South*. 1994.

Faue, Elizabeth. *Community of Suffering and Struggle: Women, Men, and the Labor Movement in Minneapolis, 1915–1945*. 1990.

Foner, Philip S. *Organized Labor and the Black Worker, 1619–1973*. 1974.

Gabin, Nancy. *Feminism in the Labor Movement: Women and the United Auto Workers, 1935–1975*. 1990.

Goldfield, Michael. "Race and the CIO: The Possibilities for Racial Egalitarianism During the 1930s and 1940s." *International Labor and Working Class History* 44 (1993): 1–32.

Halpern, Rick. *Down on the Killing Floor: Black and White Workers in Chicago's Packinghouses, 1904–54*. 1997.

Harris, William. *Keeping the Faith: A. Philip Randolph, Milton P. Webster, and the Brotherhood of Sleeping Car Porters, 1925–37*. 1977.

Honey, Michael K. *Southern Labor and Black Civil Rights: Organizing Memphis Workers*. 1993.

Korstad, Robert, and Nelson Lichtenstein, "Opportunities Found and Lost: Labor, Radicals, and the Early Civil Rights Movement." *Journal of American History* 70 (1988): 786–811.

Meier, August, and Elliot Rudwick. *Black Detroit and the Rise of the UAW*. 1979.

Milkman, Ruth. *Gender at Work: The Dynamics of Job Segregation by Sex During World War II*. 1987.

Nelson, Bruce. "Class, Race, and Democracy in the CIO: The 'New' Labor History Meets the 'Wages of Whiteness.'" *International Review of Social History* 41 (1996): 351–374.

Norrell, Robert J. "Caste in Steel: Jim Crow Careers in Birmingham, Alabama." *Journal of American History* 73 (1986):669–694.

Northrup, Herbert. *Organized Labor and the Negro*. 1994.

Rachleff, Peter J. *Black Labor in Richmond, 1865–1890*. 1984.

Roediger, David. *The Wages of Whiteness: Race and the Making of the American Working Class*. 1991.

Trotter, Joe William, Jr. *Coal, Class, and Color: Blacks in Southern West Virginia, 1915–32*. 1990.

Kevin Boyle

United Farm Workers of America

Throughout his career, César CHÁVEZ's critics, especially in U.S. agribusiness, reviled his United Farm Workers of America (UFW) as something other than a union. "Those who attack our union often say, 'It's not really a union. It's something else: a social movement, a civil rights movement. It's something dangerous.' They're half right," Chávez observed in a 1984 speech, "although it's never been dangerous if you believe in the BILL OF RIGHTS."

The UFW was born in the tumult of the 1960s' civil rights struggles, and millions of Americans came to see it as much more than a union. That was one key to establishment of the first successful farm workers union in American history.

For more than a hundred years before César Chávez, others tried and failed to organize the nation's poorest laborers. They ranged from the radical Wobblies, the INDUSTRIAL WORKERS OF THE WORLD, of the early 1900s to the more staid American Federation of Labor (see AFL-CIO) in the 1950s. But every strike was broken; every union was crushed. Chávez, a former migrant worker who had to quit school after the eighth grade, was literally struggling against history when he founded what would become the UFW in 1962 with $1,200 in life savings and ten members— himself, his wife, Helen, and their eight small children.

The union's success can be credited to three innovations: volunteerism, nonviolence, and the boycott. They originated in the UFW founder's careful study of labor history, the social doctrine of the Catholic Church, and the works of Mohandas K. GANDHI, as well as the strategies and tactics of Dr. Martin Luther KING, JR., and the civil rights movement.

Chávez was convinced that he could not organize the poor unless he was willing to share in their plight. He also concluded that all the previous efforts to organize farm workers ultimately failed when the unions quit after running out of money. He embraced voluntary poverty and adopted subsistence pay for UFW leaders and staff, what he termed "volunteerism." Chávez was the lowest-paid national union president in America, never earning more than $6,000 a year.

Angry farm workers demonstrate in the streets of San Francisco in 1988 on behalf of the United Farm Workers' "Wrath of Grapes Boycott" campaign. (© Marvin Collins/Impact Visuals/PNI)

Yet even though Chávez's union endured many setbacks over the decades, and almost saw its membership wiped out in 1973, the UFW survived.

Chávez's Catholic faith and the writings of his hero, Gandhi, turned the farm labor leader into a stalwart champion of nonviolence, even as others in civil rights organizations were abandoning the principle by the late 1960s. But Chávez's commitment also had a practical side. As with other social and political institutions in rural California that they dominated, the growers also controlled the courts and law enforcement agencies. Consequently, farm worker strikers who had responded in kind to grower violence in the past always came up short.

In the hungry winter of 1968, midway into the five-year-long Delano, California, grape strike, some young male strikers were talking about fighting back against those who had abused them and their families. Chávez responded with a twenty-five-day water-only fast to recommit his movement to nonviolence. The late Senator Robert F. KENNEDY flew to be with him in Delano when he broke the fast on March 10, 1968, describing Chávez as "one of the heroic figures of our time." Nonviolence drew widespread public support for the union cause.

Although the two men never met, Chávez and King corresponded, and Chávez closely followed the minister's career, starting with the King-led MONTGOMERY BUS BOYCOTT. Chávez knew he could not win in the fields alone, where the odds were stacked against farm workers during strikes. So he transferred the scene of battle to the cities, where farm workers could tap allies such as church, labor, minority, and student activists. He was the first to successfully apply a boycott to a major labor conflict, and it worked. The initial boycott of California table grapes forced these growers to sign their first UFW contracts in 1970. During a second grape boycott, a nationwide Louis Harris survey showed that seventeen million Americans were boycotting the fruit in 1975.

Chávez engineered other firsts. From the beginning, he insisted that Latino and Filipino grape strikers join together in the same picketlines and union halls, reversing a cynical decades-old tactic by growers who used one ethnic group to break the strikes of other minority workers.

Before César Chávez, all the experts said farm workers could not be organized. He spent thirty-one years proving them wrong. He organized, struck, marched, boycotted, and fasted. He won passage of the first and only law in the nation protecting—and even encouraging—the right of farm workers to organize, vote in secret-ballot union elections, and bargain with their employers: California's historic 1975 Agricultural Labor Relations Act. He led the UFW to victory in elections. He negotiated union contracts that provided farm workers with gains that were unimaginable only a short time before.

Chávez witnessed both victories and defeats. After grape and vegetable strikes and boycotts, UFW membership soared to around eighty thousand by the early 1970s; but it plummeted to less than five thousand in spring and summer 1973, when growers signed "sweetheart contracts" with the Teamsters Union, sparking thousands of workers to protest by walking out on strike. Farm workers won the right to vote in union elections with enactment of the California farm labor law after Democratic Governor Jerry Brown took office in 1975. Most of them voted for Chávez's UFW. Union membership rose again, to about forty-five thousand by the early 1980s, only to fall once more when enforcement of the law was effectively shut down under two Republican governors, George Deukmejian and Pete Wilson. Union membership had shrunk to around twenty thousand when Chávez died in 1993 at age sixty-six. Some forty thousand people, at least half of them farm workers, marched behind Chávez's plain pine casket during funeral services in Delano.

A year later Chávez's son-in-law and successor as UFW president, Arturo Rodriguez, kicked off a major new field organizing drive. Since then, the UFW has won numerous elections and signed many new contracts with growers. By 1999, there were more than twenty-seven thousand UFW members in three states.

The influence of Chávez and his union continues to stretch far beyond the fields. They are credited with inspiring generations of Latinos and other Americans to social and political activism. "The UFW was the beginning," Chávez once declared. "We attacked that historical source of shame and infamy that our people in this country lived with"—the exploitation that is the historical underpinning of farm labor in America. Therein lies a secret of the UFW's success and of Chávez's growing stature as an icon of Latino America even years after his death. "Once social change begins, it cannot be reversed," Chávez said. "You cannot uneducate the person who has learned to read. You cannot humiliate the person who feels pride. You cannot oppress the people who are not afraid anymore."

BIBLIOGRAPHY

Ferris, Susan, and Ricardo Sandoval. *The Fight in the Fields: César Chávez and the Farmworkers Movement.* 1997.
Hammerback, John C., and Richard J. Jensen. *The Rhetorical Career of César Chávez.* 1998.
Levy, Jacques E. *César Chávez: Autobiography of La Causa.* 1975.
Matthiessen, Peter. *Sal Si Puedes: César Chávez and the New American Revolution.* 1969.
McWilliams, Carey. *Factories in the Fields.* 1939.
Ross, Fred. *Conquering Goliath: César Chávez at the Beginning.* 1989.

Marc Grossman

Universal Negro Improvement Association

The Universal Negro Improvement Association (UNIA) was the first mass movement of African Americans for racial pride and economic independence. Founded by Marcus GARVEY in 1914 in Jamaica in response to the exploitation of black West Indian migrant workers in Central and South America, it was conceived from the beginning as an international, pan-African group. The New York division was established in 1917. Its tenets included a commitment to end COLONIALISM in Africa and white oppression in America.

UNIA's teachings were Washingtonian in theme; that is, it urged black Americans to work hard for economic autonomy. Garvey, however, also added a proud history, emphasizing not slavery but African accomplishment. Although he did encourage repatriation to Africa, the UNIA never expected large numbers of African Americans to leave the United States. Instead, it sought independent African nations. Black pride was to be accompanied by an advocacy of racial separation. Garvey preached against skin lighteners and hair straighteners and against miscegenation.

The UNIA held weekly meetings in cities across the United States during the 1920s. Clergy featured prominently among the leadership, and meetings had strong religious overtones. Ritual and pageantry played an important part in attracting attention to the

A follower of Marcus Garvey stands outside the Garvey Club, Inc., in New York City, April 1943. (CORBIS/Gordon Parks)

organization and instilling a sense of belonging in its members. There were over seven hundred branches in the United States and two hundred more in the Caribbean. Garvey estimated that the organization had six million devotees at its highest point. It published a newspaper, the *Negro World*, which circulated around the globe and was often banned by colonial governments.

Understanding that access to capital was crucial for black economic development, Garvey sold $5 shares of stock in order to set up a corporation. UNIA sponsored several business enterprises, most notably the Black Star Line, a steamship network established in 1919. The dream of black independence was so important that within a year the corporation had raised enough capital to buy three ships. These ships were greeted with celebration in ports and harbors around the United States, as symbols of black economic autonomy. Although the Black Star Line was destined to collapse as a result of weak management, it raised the promise of economic self-sufficiency among African Americans throughout the country and the Caribbean.

The 1920s were a period of rejuvenation for blacks in America, and the UNIA was not the only group working toward that end. However, the UNIA did not work with the NATIONAL ASSOCIATION FOR THE ADVANCEMENT OF COLORED PEOPLE (NAACP), and instead the two groups became competitors for black allegiance. W. E. B. DU BOIS and Garvey were intensely critical of one another, for example, although other black leaders turned Garvey into the authorities, alleging fraud connected with the steamship company. Garvey was convicted and spent over two years in jail, being released only to be deported in 1927. The UNIA continued to exist throughout the 1930s, but without Garvey's leadership and charisma it was a shadow of its former self. However, the message of racial pride and the sense of possibility that this huge movement inspired were its most important accomplishments and legacy.

BIBLIOGRAPHY

Hill, Robert A., and Barbara Bair, eds. *Marcus Garvey, Life and Lessons: A Centennial Companion to the Marcus Garvey and UNIA Papers.* 1987.

Levine, Lawrence W. "Marcus Garvey and the Politics of Revitalization." In *Black Leaders of the Twentieth Century,* edited by John Hope Franklin and August Meier. 1982.

Noeleen McIlvenna

Urban Habitat Program

The mission of the Urban Habitat Program (UHP) is to promote the development of multicultural, multiracial environmental leadership for building sustainable, socially just communities in the San Francisco Bay Area. As part of the environmental justice movement, UHP seeks to expand the civil rights agenda to include: the fight against suburban sprawl, equal protection in controls over land use, transportation reform, and community reinvestment in inner cities. Acknowledging a crisis of leadership within both the social justice and environmental movements, UHP is seeking to build capacity within communities of color for a twenty-first-century cosmopolitan vision that acknowledges the human rights of all and the urgency of reversing ecological collapse. The Urban Habitat Program was founded in 1989 by Carl Anthony and landscape architect Karl Linn. During its early years, as a project of the Earth Island Institute, UHP raised consciousness about environmental issues in communities of color and injected social justice issues into the environmental movement. UHP assigned priority status to identifying community-based groups exploring environmental justice and sustainability issues, as well as to developing a common language about the environment. UHP expanded the capacities of these groups to intervene in environment-related decisions affecting their communities.

UHP grew by directly engaging in community struggles, supporting and complementing the organizing efforts of other grass-roots groups, and initiating community-based projects that linked environmental, economic development, and civil rights issues. These projects fostered proactive strategies for long-term change, especially around issues of land use and transportation. To date, its programs have included advocacy efforts to win a community-designed lightweight rail system, intended to promote the economic development of San Francisco's Bayview/Hunter's Point District; the mobilization of community participation in military base conversion activities; and the establishment of the Bay Area Brownfields Working Group. UHP also helped to found EDGE, an alliance of environmental and civil rights groups.

In 1991, Urban Habitat led a delegation representing forty organizations from the San Francisco Bay Area to the first People of Color Environmental Leadership Summit under sponsorship of the United Church of Christ Commission on Racial Justice. While much of the summit focused on expanding civil rights agendas that address Native Americans' land rights and the disproportionate impacts on communities of color that result from the siting of hazardous waste facilities in residential neighborhoods, UHP presented reports on sustainable communities as well as environmental justice issues at the metropolitan scale, including transportation and urban abandonment.

The work of Urban Habitat has contributed to a nationwide awareness that public investment in sub-urban highways disproportionately benefits wealthier populations and disproportionately burdens poorer socio-economic groups, contributing to racial and economic polarization in metropolitan communities.

In 1993 and 1995, Urban Habitat provided leadership for California statewide conferences that opened public debate on the intersection between population policies and the civil and human rights of recent IMMIGRANTS; UHP showed the ways environmental information is misused to scapegoat undocumented workers, to rationalize the withholding of social services from immigrants, and to encourage the militarization of the southern U.S. border.

Urban Habitat also works on military conversion, brownfields (properties that are abandoned or underused because of environmental contamination), environmental literacy, and urban environmental restoration, strengthening community capacity and attracting resources to grass-roots organizations. In collaboration with the California Rural Legal Assistance Foundation, UHP publishes the nationally recognized journal *Race, Poverty and the Environment*. The organization pursues new strategies that unite the civil rights and environmental movements and are useful to metropolitan communities of color, working people, and the urban poor.

BIBLIOGRAPHY

Anthony, Carl. "Making Brownfields Bloom." In *Land and People*, Vol. 8, No. 2 (Fall 1996).

Bullard, Robert, ed. *Unequal Protection, Environmental Justice and Communities of Color*. 1994.

Hernandez, Lizette. *Clean As It Ought to Be*. 1998.

Parks, Munsun. *Working for Sustainable Communities*. 1998.

Yee, Cameron. *Congestion Pricing and the Right to Access: A Social Justice and Ecological Sustainability Framework and Analysis*. 1998.

Carl Anthony

Urban Indians

Urban settlement had a long tradition among Native North Americans, with Indian groups residing in pre-seventeenth century cities in the Southwest and the Mississippi River Valley. With the establishment of European colonies, Indians often became a part of the colonial villages. However, by the early nineteenth century the United States had adopted policies to isolate Indian peoples from westward-expanding settlement, often on remote reservations. Despite many Indians seeking wage labor in newly established towns, most lived in rural settings through the early twentieth century. In 1930 only 10 percent of Indians lived in cities.

With thousands of Indians in military service abroad in WORLD WAR II or working in defense plants, the exposure of these Indians to mainstream society made life on poverty-ridden reservations less acceptable upon their return after the war. Also, the G.I. Bill provided new educational opportunities to them. Adding impetus to Indian urbanization was an introduction of U.S. government assimilation policies in the 1950s, marked by aggressive efforts at terminating federal recognition of many tribes. In that decade, government programs such as the Adult Vocational Training Program and the Employment Assistance Program focused on urban relocation. From 1952 to 1972 over 100,000 Indians were sent to urban job-placement centers. As a result the percentage of Indians living in cities expanded from 13 percent in 1950 to almost 30 percent by 1960. By 1990 the majority, 56 percent, of American Indians lived in urban settings.

Though many became successful professionals and key contributors to various spheres of mainstream American life, racial discrimination and poverty became endemic for urban Indians. Underemployment led to homelessness, rampant substance abuse, and unusually high injury, disease, death, and infant mortality rates. To provide support for the expanding Indian urban population, Indian centers, clubs, and churches appeared in many cities. However, funding for urban Indian social services became controversial as tribal leaders did not want limited funds for reservation services siphoned away for nonreservation Indians. However, in 1976 Congress passed the Indian Health Care Improvement Act to ameliorate the urban Indian plight. Exposure to the civil rights movement of the 1950s and 1960s in the cities also inspired Indian radicalism, the AMERICAN INDIAN MOVEMENT, and the RED POWER movement. Such activism, generally begun by urban Indians, spread later to the rural reservations.

An important sociocultural result of Indian migration to the cities was the mixing of Indian peoples from many tribes. The growth of PAN-TRIBALISM resulted, further altering American Indian identity. Traditional ways of life were lost, native languages forgotten, and tribal connections often broken. Intermarriage with non-Indians became more common. With the resurgence of tribal economies in the 1980s and corresponding growth in political strength, some urban Indians moved back to their rural tribal communities. There they applied their education and skills to further propel Indian resurgence in America. Urbanization and reservation revitalization constituted conflicting trends in late twentieth-century Indian life. Questions and issues related to tribal membership and rights, claims to Indian ancestry or tribal affiliation, and intellectual property issues, such as who has the right to represent Indian interests to the mainstream society, became major concerns.

BIBLIOGRAPHY

Champagne, Duane, ed. *Contemporary Native American Cultural Issues.* 1999.

Grossman, David C., James W. Krieger, Jonathan R. Sugarman, and Ralph A. Forquera. "Health Status of Urban American Indians and Alaska Natives: A Population-Based Study." *Journal of the American Medical Association* 271 (1994): 845–851.

Sorkin, Alan L. *The Urban American Indian.* 1978.

Sugarman, Jonathan R., and David C. Grossman. "Trauma Among American Indians in an Urban Community." *Public Health Reports* 111 (1996): 321–328.

Thornton, Russell, Gary D. Sandefur, and Harold G. Grasmick. *The Urbanization of American Indians: A Critical Bibliography.* 1982.

Weibel-Orlando, Joan. *Indian Country, L.A.: Maintaining Ethnic Community in Complex Society.* 1991.

Richard C. Hanes

U.S. Commission on Civil Rights

The U.S. Commission on Civil rights is an independent advisory agency that was created when Congress passed the CIVIL RIGHTS ACT OF 1957. The Commission was initially established on a temporary basis to provide a bipartisan forum to study problems of voting discrimination against African-American citizens in the South. Congress directed the Commission to investigate complaints of voting discrimination and to collect information concerning the denial of equal protection of the laws on account of race, color, religion, and national origin. In its advisory role the Commission was directed to assess the effectiveness of federal laws and policies against discrimination and make policy recommendations to the president and Congress. The Commission lacks enforcement authority, but is empowered to hold hearings, subpoena witnesses, publish reports, issue findings, and submit recommendations.

The Commission's first decade coincided with the heroic era of the civil rights movement. The moral issues were posed with stark clarity: racist white governments in the Southern states challenged by impoverished, disfranchised black citizens. The Commission, an independent, bipartisan body chaired during its first dozen years by John Hannah, president of Michigan State University, was effective in policy persuasion largely because it was not an enforcement or policymaking arm of government. In an era of COLD WAR competition and televised racial violence, the Commission appealed to the nation's sense of fairness, to the American creed of equal rights for all. Commission reports won high visibility in the national media, where editorials reinforced Commission proposals for desegregating schools, enforcing voting rights, and banning discrimination in employment.

The Commission in its first years concentrated on the denial of voting rights to African Americans. Holding hearings in the Deep South, the Commission used its single coercive weapon, the authority to subpoena witnesses, to require testimony from recalcitrant local officials. In 1959 and 1961 the Commission issued hard-hitting reports, demonstrating the failure of the voting rights laws and proposing the kind of direct federal intervention in voter registration that made the Voting Rights Act of 1965 both radical and effective. Commission reports on employment discrimination and education helped shape the breakthrough CIVIL RIGHTS ACT OF 1964, especially Title VII, establishing the EQUAL EMPLOYMENT OPPORTUNITY COMMISSION (EEOC), and Title VI, prohibiting discrimination by businesses and state and local governments receiving federal financial assistance.

Commission reports on housing segregation contributed to the FAIR HOUSING ACT (CIVIL RIGHTS ACT of 1968). This law, the last of the great civil rights statutes of the 1960s, marked a transition in the civil rights movement and in the Commission's history as well. The urban riots of 1965–1968, which scorched major cities throughout the North and West but rarely occurred in the South, signaled a sea change in race relations. For Southern blacks, the civil rights legislation of the mid-1960s had produced immediate benefits. But segregated stores, voting barriers, and "whites-only" jobs were not pressing issues for African Americans outside the South. On the other hand racial concentration in housing, less pressing in the rural South, was increasing in the urban North.

In the 1970s the policy agenda of the Commission expanded and shifted to reflect a nationwide emphasis on school desegregation and equal employment opportunity for African Americans, and also the addition by Congress, the federal courts, and regulatory agencies of new protections and remedies. In addition to race, religion, and national origin, the Commission monitored discrimination by sex, age, and disability. In addition to nondiscrimination policies, the Commission supported controversial affirmative action remedies, including school busing for racial balance, minority hiring preferences, "comparable worth" standards to reduce gender differences in pay, the EQUAL RIGHTS AMENDMENT, and "race norming" in employment test scores. By the late 1970s the Commission was attacked by conservatives and Republicans as a "captured" agency serving the interests of liberal advocacy groups, especially African-American, feminist, Hispanic, and Native American organizations.

Following the elections of 1980, the Reagan administration attempted to replace sitting commissioners with appointees critical of "reverse discrimination." The result was a political battle during 1981–1982 that split the agency and damaged its credibility and effectiveness. In 1983 Congress compromised with the president, expanding the number of commissioners from six presidential appointees to eight, four of them appointed by the president and four by Congress.

The 1980s were years of turmoil for the Commission. Its agenda showed greater ideological variety and a wider range of policy debate, but weaker programmatic coherence and less civility. Leaks to the media from warring factions damaged the Commission's prestige. Yet despite the conservative counteroffensive, by the end of the Reagan–Bush regime there appeared to be more continuity than change in federal civil rights policy. Congress in 1988 passed the CIVIL RIGHTS RESTORATION ACT over REAGAN's veto. That same year Reagan signed a fair housing enforcement law that looked remarkably similar to the strong, but unsuccessful bill championed by the Commission in the Carter years. In 1990 President George BUSH signed the AMERICANS WITH DISABILITIES ACT, extending new protections to an estimated 43 million Americans. And the following year, Bush signed a civil rights law that greatly expanded protections and remedies available to women.

As civil rights policy has grown more complex in the 1980s and 1990s, constituency groups benefiting from federal civil rights policies have grown in number and competition for enforcement attention between protected groups has increased. As a consequence, the ideological clarity of civil rights disputes has become blurred. Controversy over the Civil Rights Commission has declined, but its visibility and moral authority has declined as well. The American "Rights Revolution" of the final third of the twentieth century produced a proliferation of conflicting rights claims and expanding federal authority—for example, protection from hate crimes and sexual harassment. In such an environment, the Commission's role has shifted from the race-centered, moral conscience, and policing focus of the 1960s to function as a forum for debate, codifier of statutory and administrative rights and remedies, clearinghouse for information, and battleground for conflicting rights claims.

BIBLIOGRAPHY

Ball, Howard. "United States Commission on Civil Rights." In *Government Agencies*, edited by Donald R. Whitnah. 1983.

Dulles, Foster Rhea. *The Civil Rights Commission, 1957–1965.* 1968.

Graham, Hugh Davis. "The Civil Rights Commission: The First 40 Years." *Civil Rights Journal* (Fall 1997): 6–8.

Lawson, Stephen F. *Black Ballots: Voting Rights in the South, 1944–1969.* 1976.

Hugh Davis Graham

U.S. Court of Appeals for the Fifth Circuit

See Fifth Circuit.

U.S. Court of Appeals for the Fourth Circuit

See Fourth Circuit.

Utah

The presence of African Americans in Utah Territory dates back to the early 1800s, when blacks were members of exploratory and fur-trapping expeditions. When Brigham Young arrived in Utah in 1847, his group included three slaves, owned by southern Mormons. With the arrival of additional Mormon caravans, the number of slaves grew to about 60 by 1850. Slavery was sanctioned by territorial law in 1852 but officially ended in 1862, when the U.S. Congress abolished the practice in all U.S. territories, regardless of geographic latitude. As the black population grew, racial discrimination increased throughout the state. Much of it was fueled by the Church of Jesus Christ of Latter Day Saints (LDS), or Mormons, which held that blacks were inferior to whites. Racial tensions grew in the early 1900s, culminating in the 1925 LYNCHING of Robert Marshall in Price. After World War II, Utah's blacks heightened their focus on racial injustice, becoming increasingly willing to openly express their opinions in public forums. Ogden, Utah, became a center of Utah civil rights activities.

Efforts continued through the turbulent 1950s and 1960s with nonviolent demonstrations supporting civil rights. In 1974, the NATIONAL ASSOCIATION FOR THE ADVANCEMENT OF COLORED PEOPLE (NAACP) filed suit against the LDS church on behalf of two black Boy Scouts who were denied leadership positions in a church-sponsored troop. The suit was dismissed when the church agreed not to discriminate against Boy Scouts because of race. The racial atmosphere improved with passage of the federal CIVIL RIGHTS ACT OF 1964 and a U.S. Supreme Court ruling striking down bans on interracial marriage. The LDS church opened the priesthood to black males in 1978. In 1976 the Reverend Robert Harris became the first black elected to the Utah state legislature, and in 1986 Martin Luther KING, JR.'s, birthday became a state holiday.

LDS teachings regarded the Native American tribes of Utah (the Utes, Paiutes, Shoshone, and others) as descendants of a tribe of ancient Israel; hence there was less prejudice against Native Americans than against blacks. Even so, as the Mormon population of Utah expanded rapidly into southern Utah, conflicts arose, the largest of which was the Black Hawk War with the Utes of 1863–1868. In the forty-three years following passage of the DAWES ACT in 1887, Utah's Native American land holdings declined by more than 80 percent. In 1934, the INDIAN REORGANIZATION ACT was passed, with favorable results, as part of Franklin D. ROOSEVELT's NEW DEAL. However, in the 1950s Utah Senator Arthur V. Watkins, chairman of the Senate Indian Affairs Subcommittee, sponsored legislation to cut off all U.S. government aid to Native American tribes and to terminate official recognition of many of Utah's smaller tribal groups. In recent years Utah's Indians have increasingly sought relief through the state and federal courts, winning a series of cases culminating in a 1986 Supreme Court decision granting them legal jurisdiction over a substantial amount of the land they had lost after 1887. In 1999 the Native American population in Utah approached what it was when the Mormons arrived (20,000), although the Navahos, who entered the state after WORLD WAR II, are now the largest tribe rather than the Utes.

The Mormon Church itself came into conflict with the U.S. government during the 1870s and 1880s because of its endorsement of bigamy and polygamy. Bigamy/polygamy had been prohibited under English statutory law since 1604. In 1862 the U.S. Congress passed the Morrill Act, making bigamy a felonious crime in all U.S. territories. Subsequently the Edmunds Act of 1882 prohibited "bigamous cohabitation," a misdemeanor that was less difficult to prove than outright bigamy. Over 1,300 LDS members were jailed for such cohabitation during the 1880s. Continuing conflict between the government and the Mormons over this issue spread to surrounding territories and delayed the admittance of Utah into the union, but in 1890 Mormon leader Wilson Woodruff claimed to have received a divine revelation. A manifesto issued shortly thereafter by the Mormon Church officially ended its endorsement of multiple marriages, and conflict with federal authorities subsided.

The rights of women, like those of blacks and Native Americans, were greatly influenced by the Mormon church. The church supported suffrage early on. Utah women were first granted the right to vote in 1870 by the territorial legislature, but it was revoked by the U.S. Congress in 1887. When Utah became a state in 1896, the right of women to vote and hold public office was written into the state constitution. The issue of women's rights again came to the forefront in the 1970s with the proposed Equal Rights Amendment (ERA) to the U.S. Constitution. Although previously supportive of women suffrage, the Mormon church felt that the ERA went too far. The church expressed its opposition to the ERA. The Utah legislature voted down ERA ratification in 1973 and again in 1975.

Gay and lesbian civil rights have not been embraced by the state, again in large part due to the Mormon church's uncompromising condemnation of homosexuality, Utah does not have a hate crimes law; nor does it recognize gay domestic partnerships. Much of the current debate on gay and lesbian rights centers on schools. In 1995, the Salt Lake Board of Education banned all gay, African-American, Latino, and Native-American student groups in city schools. A year later, the state banned gay student groups from all public schools. In 1998, the U.S. District Court for Utah ruled in *Wendy Weaver v. Nebo School District* that the district had acted illegally when it fired a teacher because she is lesbian. Despite the gains made by blacks, Utah is one of the most politically conservative states in the nation, especially involving the civil rights of ethnic minorities, women, and gays and lesbians. The Mormon church still strongly influences state policies on civil rights.

BIBLIOGRAPHY

Beeton, Beverly. *Women Vote in the West: The Woman Suffrage Movement 1869–1896.* 1986.

Coleman, Ronald G. "A History of Blacks in Utah, 1825–1910." Ph.D. dissertation, University of Utah. 1980.

Davis, Ray Jay. "The Polygamous Prelude." *American Journal of Legal History* 6 (1962): 1–27.

Embry, Jessie L. *Black Saints in a White Church: Contemporary African American Mormons.* 1994.

Kelen, Leslie G. and Stone, Eileen Hallet. *Missing Stories: An Oral History of Ethnic and Minority Groups in Utah.* 1996.

Papanikolas, Helen, ed. *The Peoples of Utah.* 1976.

Powell, Allan Kent. *Utah History Encyclopedia.* 1994.

Weiler, Kathleen (producer). *Utah's African American Voices,* KUED (PBS) television documentary. 1999.

Ken R. Wells

V

Vega, Bernardo

(1885–1965), social activist and labor organizer.

Bernardo Vega was born in Cayey, Puerto Rico, in 1885. As a young adult, he became active in the island's *Federación Libre de Trabajadores,* one of the island's most prominent labor organizations. He was also a founding member of Puerto Rico's Socialist Party, which was formed in his hometown of Cayey in 1915. Vega was a cigar maker *(tabaquero)* by trade, an occupation that placed him in the social and political vanguard of the working class. An important early milestone in his career as a labor activist was his recognition that to achieve lasting changes in the island's economic structure the efforts of the workers needed to be directed not only against the local bosses and the colonial elite of Puerto Rico, but also at the United States. Vega emigrated to the U.S. in 1916 and settled in New York City, where he continued as a cigar worker and labor organizer and activist. His efforts on behalf of organized labor soon resulted in his being recognized as one of a handful of leaders within New York's El Barrio.

In 1926, Vega helped form the *Liga Puertorriqueña y Hispana,* which was one of the first organizations founded to provide a public voice to the concerns of New York's growing Latino community. He went on to create the weekly magazine *Gráfico,* and served as its editor for several years. A compelling and humorous writer, he became a regular contributor to both *Nuevo Mundo* and *Liberación,* two of the most powerful Spanish-language papers in the nation. In the late 1940s Vega was a member of Henry WALLACE's PROGRESSIVE PARTY, and served as national director of its Hispanic division.

After Vega returned to Puerto Rico, he was gradually drawn into the political infighting that was wracking the Socialist Party. Becoming disenchanted with the unceasing internecine bickering that was taking place, he redirected his efforts into the Party for an Independent Puerto Rico. Vega also threw his support behind the MOVEMENT FOR INDEPENDENCE (MPI), and served as its organizational secretary from 1961 until his death in 1965.

BIBLIOGRAPHY

Iglesias, Cesar Andrew, ed. *Memoirs of Bernardo Vega: A Contribution to the History of the Puerto Rican Community of New York City.* 1984.

Robert W. Nill

Velásquez, William C.

(1944–1988), social activist and voting rights leader.

Born on May 9, 1944, in Orlando, Florida, where his father was stationed during WORLD WAR II, "Willie" Velásquez grew up in San Antonio, Texas. He earned a bachelor's degree in economics from St. Mary's University in 1966 and almost immediately began a career of group organizing. While an assistant to the executive director of the Bishop's Committee for the Spanish-speaking of the United States Catholic

Conference, Velásquez became a founder and charter member of the Mexican American Youth Organization (MAYO).

His personal aim, and MAYO's, was social action, which he took to another stage when he became the Texas coordinator of El Movimiento Social de La Raza Unida, the forerunner of the LA RAZA UNIDA PARTY. In February 1968, Velásquez joined the UNITED FARM WORKERS (UFW) to help organize a strike in Texas's Rio Grande Valley. He became the UFW's San Antonio–area boycott coordinator before moving on to found and direct the Mexican American Unity Council (MAUC) in San Antonio. In June 1970, he became the Phoenix-office field director for MAUC's parent, the National Council of La Raza.

In 1971, Velásquez became La Raza's assistant director of field organizing and fund raising. Working from the national office in Washington, D.C., he focused particularly on developing what in 1974 became the SOUTHWEST VOTER REGISTRATION EDUCATION PROJECT (SVREP), to increase Latinos' political participation in the region where they were most populous. In 1984, he founded the Southwest Voter Research Institute (SVRI) in San Antonio, to further his vision of Latino empowerment in the democratic process.

Velásquez died of complications of kidney cancer on June 15, 1988. He was awarded a posthumous Presidential Medal of Freedom in 1995, and SVRI was renamed the William C. Velásquez Institute (WCVI) in his honor in 1997.

BIBLIOGRAPHY

"Central Los Angeles; Late Latino Leader Velasquez Honored." *Los Angeles Times*, October 4, 1995, B4.

Sanchez, Carlos. "William Velasquez, 44, Dies; Founder of SW Voter Project." *Washington Post*, June 16, 1988, D6.

William C. Velásquez Papers. WCVI, San Antonio, Texas.

Thomas J. Davis

Vermont

As one of the smallest states in the Union, in both land mass and population, Vermont is also known as the "whitest state" in the nation. With an economic and cultural base overwhelmingly rural, its citizens participate in a two hundred-year-old tradition of town meetings. Gathering in a central location on the first Tuesday in March, Vermonters still conduct their towns' annual business the old-fashioned way. Citizens exercise their individual right to voice an opinion and vote on important issues in a public forum. This pursuit of democracy at the grass-roots level may be at the core

of understanding civil rights in the Green Mountain State. Such traditions notwithstanding, the state's record on civil rights is filled with contradictions.

With the adoption of its first constitution in 1777, Vermont became the first state to prohibit slavery. In 1823, when Alexander Lucius Twilight received a degree from Middlebury College, he became the nation's first African-American college graduate. Between 1830 and 1845, blacks could be found holding elected office in the state legislature while elsewhere other blacks were being held in slavery.

In the decade following the Civil War, the question of women's right to participate in public affairs was openly argued. Passage of an act enabling taxpaying women to vote and hold office in school districts in 1870 opened the flood gates of change. New goals for women were the right to vote in town meetings and ultimately complete suffrage. In 1917, Vermont granted women the right to vote, as it became the first state in New England to expand women's suffrage beyond the right to vote in school elections. In 1985, Vermonters elected their first woman governor (Madeline Kunin), returning her to that office for three consecutive terms.

In spite of this history, Vermont has not been a near utopia of expanding rights for all citizens. Although spared the discord experienced by much of the nation in the 1960s, Vermont has had many of the same racial problems found in other states. In August 1964, one month following congressional passage of the CIVIL RIGHTS ACT OF 1964, Vermonters created their first Civil Rights Union. Joining with local chapters of the NATIONAL ASSOCIATION FOR THE ADVANCEMENT OF COLORED PEOPLE (NAACP) and the National Conference of Christians and Jews, the Vermont Civil Rights Union began the work of documenting and eradicating discrimination against blacks and Jews. The organization also established and supported the first licensed integrated day care center in Mississippi. Such projects were accompanied by endless debates in both the state legislature and local newspapers, which suggested widespread and deep-seated animosity and race hatred.

At the dawn of the twenty-first century, Vermont can still boast of being relatively free of open confrontation over civil rights, but that does not mean the state is problem-free. In fact, the most recent self-studies and national reports have suggested the opposite. With a nonwhite population at an all-time high of less than 2 percent but climbing, in all likelihood the story of civil rights in the state is still unfolding.

BIBLIOGRAPHY

Guyette, Elise A. "Black Lives and White Racism in Vermont." Master's thesis. University of Vermont, 1992.

McCray, Denise A. "Blacks in Vermont: A Geographical Analysis." Master's thesis, University of Vermont. 1993.

Muller, Nicholas H., and Samuel B. Hand. *A State of Nature: Readings in Vermont History*. 1992.

True, Marshall. "Slavery in Burlington? An Historical Note." *Vermont History* (1982).

Wrinn, Stephen M. *Civil Rights in the Whitest State: Vermont's Perceptions of Civil Rights 1945–1968.* 1998.

Willi Coleman

Victims' Rights

The victims' rights movement, a diverse coalition of organizations representing a variety of political views, seeks to protect the welfare of crime victims by providing them with support services and by securing for them a permanent place in the U.S. criminal justice system. The movement began as an outgrowth of the women's movement of the late 1960s and 1970s. Rape crisis centers, established by feminists to provide counseling, information, and legal advice to rape victims, were the first groups to offer support services to crime victims on a large scale. Soon, grass-roots organizations proliferated around the country, providing assistance to victims of a wide variety of crimes. In the early 1980s new types of victims' rights organizations emerged: led by individual crime victims or their relatives, organizations such as Mothers Against Drunk Driving waged national publicity campaigns to increase public awareness of the impact of crime on both victims and their families.

As support for victims' rights grew, advocates began to embrace a legislative and political agenda. Fueled by the belief that the criminal justice system protected the rights of the accused at the expense of the rights of victims, victims' rights leaders sought to give crime victims a role in the justice system's processing of the crimes that were committed against them. Specifically, the movement's supporters demanded: victims' right to an order of financial restitution from the offender; their right to be present and to speak at offenders' sentencing, parole, and bail hearings; and their right to notification of all court proceedings, including the release of the offender.

In 1982 this legislative component of the victims' rights movement received federal approval with the release of the Final Report of President Ronald Reagan's Task Force on Victims of Crime. The task force recommended a variety of legal protections for crime victims, including a federal constitutional amendment guaranteeing their rights. By 1989, forty-two states had passed victims' rights legislation packages, sometimes known as "Victims' Bills of Rights," and twenty states went even further by adding victims' rights amendments to their constitutions. In 1990, Congress granted its support to the victims' rights platform, passing the first federal Victims' Bill of Rights—known officially as the Victims' Rights and Restitution Act.

In 1996, the issue of victims' rights again rose to the forefront of American politics with the trial of accused Oklahoma City bomber Timothy McVeigh. The hundreds of victims of the 1995 bombing of the Murrah federal building in Oklahoma City successfully lobbied for federal legislation that overturned judicial orders barring them from witnessing and speaking at McVeigh's trial. On the heels of this victory, Congress again turned its attention to the issue of victims' rights. In 1996, Senators Diane Feinstein (D-Calif.) and John Kyl (R-Ariz.) introduced a proposal to add a victims' rights amendment to the United States Constitution; Henry Hyde (R-Ill.) introduced a similar proposal in the House of Representatives. Congress has yet to act on the proposal, however, and a constitutional amendment remains an elusive goal for the victims' rights movement.

Timeline

1963 The world's first crime victim compensation statute is passed (New Zealand).

1965 California passes first state law allowing victim compensation.

1972 First rape crisis center is established, Berkeley, California.

1975 The National Organization of Victim Assistance (NOVA) is founded.

1980 Wisconsin passes the first state Victims' Bill of Rights.

1980 Mothers Against Drunk Driving (MADD) is founded by Candy Lightner.

1982 The Final Report of the President's Task Force on Victims' of Crime recommends a constitutional amendment.

1984 The Federal Victims of Crime Act establishes a crime victim fund.

1984 The Justice Assistance Act funds two hundred new victim-service programs.

1985 The National Victim Center is founded.

1986 Rhode Island passes the first state constitutional amendment guaranteeing victims' rights—financial restitution, submission of victim impact statements, to be treated with dignity.

1990 The Federal Victims' Rights and Restitution Act (Victims' Bill of Rights) gives victims the right to be notified of and be present at court proceedings and the right to be kept apprised of an offender's conviction, sentencing, imprisonment, and release status.

1994   A "Victims' Rights package" is part of a larger crime bill (Violent Crime Control and Law Enforcement Act).

1995   The National Victims' Constitutional Amendment Network begins lobbying for federal amendment.

1996   A constitutional amendment is proposed in both Houses (Feinstein and Kyl; Hyde).

1996   The first federal law is passed mandating restitution to crime victims.

1996   A federal law ensures victims' access to closed-circuit TV broadcasts of relevant trials relocated as part of a court-ordered change of venue.

1997   The Victims' Rights Clarification Act is passed.

BIBLIOGRAPHY

McMurry, Kelly. "Victims' Rights Movement Rises to Power." *Trial* 33, no. 7 (1997): 12–15.

Reske, Henry J. "Constitutional Cooperation: Bipartisan Support Creates Momentum for Victims' Rights Amendment." *ABA Journal* 82 (October 1996): 26–7.

Shapiro, Bruce. "Victims and Vengeance: Why the Victims' Rights Amendment Is a Bad Idea." *The Nation* 264, no. 5 (February 10, 1997): 11–19.

Toobin, Jeffrey. "Victim Power." *New Yorker* 73, no. 5 (March 24, 1997): 40–43.

Weed, Frank J. *Certainty of Justice: Reform in the Crime Victim Movement.* 1995.

Jill Ginstling

A returning Vietnam veteran passes through the arrival area at Oakland Army Base, California. In spite of the poster, no bands played and no crowds cheered returning G.I.s in the United States' most controversial war. (AP/Wide World Photos)

Vietnam War

The Vietnam War began in support of the American-sponsored Republic of South Vietnam, which by 1960 was coming under heavy pressure from communist North Vietnam. American advisers could not stem the tide, and during 1965 President Lyndon B. JOHNSON in effect took over the war from the South Vietnamese. Within three years, however, Johnson realized that he could not win an increasingly unpopular war of attrition without further escalation that might trigger retaliation from the Soviet Union or from China. President Richard M. NIXON, who succeeded Johnson in 1969, sought to liquidate the war with a cease-fire that took effect in January 1973, by which time American battle deaths had exceeded 47,000.

The long and costly war aroused organized opposition, fed not only by lengthening lists of casualties but also by obvious inequities in the Selective Service System, which had loopholes, such as educational deferments, that worked against the sons of working-class families. Also, local draft boards, overwhelmingly composed of middle-class whites, proved arbitrary in awarding exemptions, which lent substance to charges that the Vietnam conflict was a rich white man's war but a poor man's and a black man's fight. Nevertheless, large numbers of blacks continued to serve, ignoring opposition to the war on the part of many African-American leaders and organizations, and often getting fairer treatment in uniform than they received as civilians.

White campaigners for civil rights in the South who resided on college campuses used their organizing skills to oppose the war. Teach-ins on university campuses, mass rallies, and CIVIL DISOBEDIENCE—effective against institutionalized RACISM—now were being used to attack a war that seemed equally unjust. Those leading the charge, however, tended to enjoy the protection conferred by existing draft law, engendering an aura of self-interest that did not escape the notice of those blacks and whites actually conscripted to fight the war.

A loosely coordinated but rapidly expanding ANTIWAR MOVEMENT challenged official justifications for the war and urged the avoidance of military service. The nonviolent civil rights movement and the opponents of the war drew closer when Dr. Martin Luther KING, JR. challenged the war, charging shortly before his assassination in April 1968 that the fighting absorbed resources that otherwise could have created opportunities for black and poor Americans. After King was assassinated, the civil rights movement splintered, and various factions resorted increasingly to violence, trying, like the BLACK PANTHERS, to take what society would not willingly yield. This militancy caused whites to resist further change and at times to attack the programs designed to ensure equal access to jobs and EDUCATION. Antiwar activists sometimes resorted to vandalism and worse in their crusade—for example, blowing up a laboratory at the University of Wisconsin. Perhaps their best remembered gesture of protest was flag-burning, which led ultimately to agitation for a constitutional amendment to punish the practice long after it became a relic of a troubled past. Whatever its tactics, the anti-war movement may well have stopped the draft—President Nixon launched a draft lottery in 1969 and announced an all-volunteer peacetime force as the Vietnam fighting was nearing an end—but the disaffection of parents, rather than that of their sons and daughters, probably contributed more toward ending the war.

Racial violence erupted after the murder of Dr. King and soon spread to the armed forces, shattering a calm that had prevailed since the Korean War. The ideal of equal treatment and opportunity regardless of race, creed, or ethnic origin seemed in jeopardy, as did the determination of the Department of Defense to protect the remaining civil rights of those who had voluntarily accepted some restrictions by donning the uniform. To restore racial amity within the services, the armed forces embarked on a program of education in race relations, using a specially designed curriculum and trained instructors. The program contributed to the return of racial harmony, but the end of the draft and the war also helped, since the services now needed fewer recruits and could screen them more carefully.

BIBLIOGRAPHY

Appy, Christian G. *Working-Class War: American Combat Soldiers and Vietnam.* 1993.

Boettcher, Thomas D. *Vietnam, The Valor and the Sorrow: From the Home Front to the Front Lines in Words and Pictures.* 1985.

Foner, Jack D. *Blacks and the Military in American History: A New Perspective.* 1974.

MacPherson, Myra. *Long Time Passing: Vietnam and the Haunted Generation.* 1984.

Bernard C. Nalty

Violence Against Women Act of 1994

The Violence Against Women Act of 1994 (VAWA) classified anti-female violence as a civil rights violation and enabled victims of sexual assault and other gender-related violence to sue their alleged attackers in federal court to recover damages. At the time of its passage, VAWA was applauded as a groundbreaking triumph in the area of women's rights, although parts of VAWA were subsequently found unconstitutional by the U.S. Court of Appeals for the FOURTH CIRCUIT. While VAWA has still not been applied on a widespread basis, and its status will not be fully clear until it is reviewed by the SUPREME COURT, it has nonetheless introduced valuable new strategies in the struggle against domestic violence and rape.

The Act was passed unanimously by the U.S. House of Representatives, where it had 223 sponsors, and received bipartisan support in the Senate. In the four-year hearings that led to passage of the bill, state officials, including 41 state attorneys general, offered in-depth analysis that stressed the deficiencies of the existing state-based mechanism for dealing with crime based on gender. So, the Violence Against Women Act introduced federal measures for handling felonies that specifically target women. In response to state limitations in the prosecuting of interstate domestic violence cases, VAWA created a vehicle for federal involvement in such cases. Among other remedies, it offered victims the ability to sue in federal court for compensatory, punitive, or other damages, even when they were not pressing criminal charges. Furthermore, the act enhanced the options available to law enforcement and prosecutors of rape, domestic violence, and child abuse cases. With $1.6 million, the Act funded, through 1999, a variety of programs, including a toll-free hotline which offered assistance to women who were victims of domestic violence. Because of testimony at congressional hearings about the reduced productivity and consumer spending on the part of abused women, VAWA was principally predicated on the right of Congress to regulate interstate trade; it was also based on the FOURTEENTH AMENDMENT, which requires states to provide all individuals with equal protection under the law. In 1998, VAWA II was proposed to continue to maintain funding for established programs, as well as to develop new ones, and to extend protection to new groups.

From its inception, VAWA was repeatedly challenged in court. Although it withstood the first eleven such tests, on March 5, 1999, the U.S. Court of Appeals for the Fourth Circuit, in a seven-to-four ruling, declared unconstitutional the civil rights–based protection in VAWA, although it let stand the Act's funding of victims' programs for other provisions (see VIC-

TIMS' RIGHTS). In the case of *Brzonkala v. Virginia Polytechnic Institute*, former Virginia Tech student Christy Brzonkala charged two student athletes with raping her three times in her dorm room in 1994. She also accused the school of failing to provide her with a safe, non-hostile environment as required by Title IX of the 1972 Higher Education Act. She was represented in part by Judy Goldscheid of the National Organization for Women's Legal Defense and Education Fund. In overturning the civil-rights aspect of VAWA, Judge J. Michael Luttig described the Act as an inappropriate extension of federal power. The court also rejected the argument that VAWA could be founded on the federal government's ability to regulate commerce, stating that the matter in question pertained to private conduct and thus was not closely enough related to commerce. In dissenting, Justice Diane Gribbon Moltz emphasized the detrimental effects of violence on economic activity. Shortly after the *Brzonkala* ruling, a New York federal district judge upheld VAWA and condemned the Fourth Circuit for ignoring evidence at the congressional VAWA hearings that demonstrated the link between violence against women and commerce.

VAWA continues to be the subject of extensive debate. Opponents of the bill maintain that there is no reason to believe that state governments are unsympathetic to women's claims, and that moreover they are better equipped to deal with enforcement of criminal law. To construe domestic violence and rape as economic in nature, they argue, would dilute the characterization of economic activity so that *all* activity could be labeled economic. Furthermore, they believe the Fourteenth Amendment refers to state activity rather than individual criminal conduct.

Feminists, many of whom view violence against women as a hate crime, continue to ardently defend VAWA. Kathy Rogers of the National Organization for Women's Legal Defense and Education Fund in New York points to the unevenness and bias of state laws and the obstacles that impede interstate prosecution of abusive partners. She cites the following figures to underscore the seriousness of the problem of anti-female violence in limiting employment and consumer spending, and in increasing health expenditures: three to five billion dollars are lost to absenteeism caused by domestic violence, which also results in an additional five to ten billion dollars in national costs in health care, criminal justice, and other areas; and an estimated half of the women who are raped end up losing their jobs.

BIBLIOGRAPHY

Campbell, Bonnie. "Breaking the Silence on Domestic Violence." *State Government News* 38, issue 8 (August 1995).

Gelhous, Lisa. "Constitutional Challenge to VAWA Raises Ire." *Trial* 35 (1999): 14–16.

Hanson, Mark. "Crossing the State Line." *ABA Journal* (1999).

Idelson, Holly. "A Tougher Domestic Violence Law." *Congressional Quarterly Weekly Report* 52, no. 25 (June 25, 1994).

McDonnell, Michael. "Let the States Do It, Not Washington." *Wall Street Journal* (March 29, 1999).

Rogers, Kathy. "States Limited in Relief for Battered Women." "Letters to the Editor." *Wall Street Journal* (April 6, 1999).

Sarah Kurian

Virginia

It is ironic that a colony and state very influential in the fight for liberty and individual rights would deny those rights to much of its population for a long period of its history. The home of George Mason's Declaration of Rights, Thomas Jefferson's Declaration of Independence and Statute of Religious Freedom, and James Madison's Bill of Rights, Virginia discriminated against its Native-American, African-American, and female citizens from its founding to the late twentieth century.

The exclusivity of white male power was breached temporarily in the years after the Civil War when the Underwood Constitution of 1869 secured the vote, office-holding, and education—albeit of the segregated variety—for black Virginians. But such advances were short-lived, as the post-RECONSTRUCTION era witnessed attempts to limit the black vote through use of separate voting lists, gerrymandering of districts, and the poll tax. Although William Mahone's Readjusters repealed the poll tax in 1882, eliminated the whipping post, and established the Petersburg teacher training school for blacks, they were stigmatized by the race issue and were run out of office by conservative Democrats, who secured their ascendancy through electoral laws that reduced Republican and black participation.

These trends culminated in the passage of a new state constitution in 1902 that effectively eliminated the black vote altogether. Publicly acknowledging that its purpose was to disfranchise Negroes, the all-white constitutional convention approved a grandfather clause, literacy and understanding clauses, and a poll tax that within two years reduced the black vote by 80 percent and much of the white vote as well.

Over the next thirty years, the Old Dominion, following the pattern of other Southern states, instituted a system of JIM CROW laws that separated the races in all public conveyances and facilities, prevented interracial marriages and liaisons, and defined the races by blood content. Virginia's registrar of vital statistics, Walter Plecker, even went so far as to classify Native Americans living in the state as "Negroes." In 1922, the Anglo-Saxon Clubs of America was founded in Richmond to find "final solutions of our racial problems. . . . " Although the state passed one of the toughest antilynching statutes in the country in 1928, blacks still could not sit on juries and suffered gross inequities in school funding. Nonetheless, they continued to press for justice, winning access to the Democratic Party primary in 1929 and the right to equal pay for black teachers.

Virginia women enjoyed only marginally better opportunities than African Americans during this period. In spite of gaining limited access to the professions and the right to hold property in their own names (1877), they could not enter all institutions of higher learning, serve on juries, or vote. The latter disability was removed by the passage of the WOMAN SUFFRAGE AMENDMENT in 1920, with no thanks to the Virginia General Assembly, which refused to ratify the amendment until 1952, two years after it finally granted women the right to serve on juries.

In the post–World War II years, encouraged by significant economic and demographic changes, black Virginians tested the barriers of discrimination, overcoming segregated interstate bus transportation (*Morgan v. Virginia*, 1946), electing Oliver HILL to the Richmond City Council in 1948, and protesting inferior schools in Prince Edward County, an action that led to the celebrated *Brown* decision in 1954. That case (BROWN V. BOARD OF EDUCATION) promised a new era in American race relations, but Virginia's political leadership moved to obstruct its implementation, leading to one of the most dismal chapters in state history.

In 1955 the Gray Commission, appointed by Governor Thomas Stanley to formulate a response to the *Brown* decision, called for local pupil assignment schemes and tuition grants for children wishing to avoid integrated schools. But the local option features of the Gray Plan that would have permitted a degree of integration were too flexible for segregationist groups such as the Defenders of State Sovereignty and Individual Liberties. Pleas from the Defenders along with the interposition doctrines of Richmond *News Leader* editor James J. Kilpatrick convinced Senator Harry F. BYRD, Sr., the longtime leader of the state Democratic Party, to adopt a stronger anti-integration position.

Calling for a campaign of "massive resistance" to desegregation, Senator Byrd, who had fought President TRUMAN's civil rights legislation and had opposed elimination of Virginia's poll tax, supported the SOUTHERN MANIFESTO in CONGRESS and directed state leaders to create a statewide plan to preserve segregated schools. The Stanley Plan, approved by a special session of the General Assembly in September 1956, established a State Pupil Placement Board to circumvent federal court decisions by assigning students to schools on criteria other than race and authorized the governor to close schools threatened by integration. The legislature also vindictively passed bills to harass and undermine the work of the NATIONAL ASSOCIATION FOR THE ADVANCEMENT OF COLORED PEOPLE (NAACP), which, under the direction of lawyers Oliver Hill and Samuel Tucker, was pursuing equal rights litigation across the state. Subsequent legislation, in 1958, provided for the closing of schools patrolled by U.S. military forces (the "Little Rock" bill) and made voting by poorly educated voters more difficult.

Confronting federal court orders to desegregate schools in Warren County, Charlottesville, and Norfolk, Governor J. Lindsay Almond, in accordance with the Stanley Plan, closed those schools to 13,000 white students in September 1958. Pressure now mounted on the governor from parent–teacher groups, civic associations, and business leaders who were shocked at this threat to public education. On January 19, 1959, the Virginia Supreme Court of Appeals and a federal district court ruled that the closings violated, respectively, the state's constitutional requirement to maintain free schools and the equal protection clause of the FOURTEENTH AMENDMENT to the U.S. Constitution. Within two weeks a few black children entered previously all-white schools in Norfolk and Arlington, and Governor Almond moved to create a new commission to deal with the issue. The Perrow Plan, similar to the old Gray Plan, was approved by the legislature in April; it established a "freedom of choice" program that included local-option desegregation, new pupil placement laws, and tuition grants that would keep race-mixing to a minimum. Although the pace of integration over the next few years would be glacial, the process had begun.

A last act of defiance occurred in Prince Edward County. Faced with a final court order to desegregate, the Board of Supervisors chose to withhold funding for its schools, effectively closing them in September 1959. White citizens of the county immediately opened a private academy for their children, while black children were forced to do without public schooling for five years, the last year of which some education was provided through a privately funded free school. In 1964 the U.S. SUPREME COURT ordered the schools to reopen.

Elsewhere, citizen protests, congressional legislation, and additional Supreme Court decisions challenged the policies of the Byrd Machine and paved the way for an end to the remaining vestiges of Jim Crow in Virginia. Sit-in demonstrations, picketing, and public marches, notably in Danville and Farmville in

1963, highlighted the need for change. The public accommodations act of 1964 (CIVIL RIGHTS ACT OF 1964) ended segregation in public facilities and discrimination by sex as well as race; and the combined effects of the Twenty-fourth Amendment to the U.S. Constitution, which eliminated the poll tax in federal elections, and the VOTING RIGHTS ACT OF 1965 opened the door for thousands of black Virginians to participate in the electoral process for the first time. The Court's "one man, one vote" dictum increased urban representation in the General Assembly and curtailed the rural authority of the Byrd Machine, which was now confronting a revived Republican Party as well. In a 1966 ruling the Court also ended application of the poll tax in state elections. In *Loving v. Virginia* (1967), it overturned the law against racial intermarriage, and in *Green v. School Board of New Kent County, Virginia* (1968), it ordered faster school desegregation, leading to the considerable busing of students that effectively ended a decade-long policy of tokenism but contributed to a resegregation of urban schools.

Under the leadership of Governor Mills Godwin, a former massive resister, and Linwood Holton, the state's first Republican governor since Reconstruction, Virginia followed the nation's lead in bringing an end to its history of public discrimination. A new state constitution, approved by the voters in 1970, guaranteed every Virginia child the right to a quality public education, guaranteed the civil rights of all Virginians, and ended discrimination based on sex. The University of Virginia admitted blacks (1960s) and women (1970) to its undergraduate programs, and the General Assembly terminated laws ending different treatment for women and repealed SEGREGATION and racial definition laws; even so, it also chose to follow in the footsteps of its predecessor and refused to ratify the EQUAL RIGHTS AMENDMENT. Nevertheless, as a testament to the progress made in the field of civil rights, Virginians elected as governor in 1989, Democrat L. Douglas Wilder, the first African American ever elected chief executive of a state.

BIBLIOGRAPHY

Buni, Andrew. *The Negro in Virginia Politics, 1902–1965.* 1967.

Ely, James. *The Crisis of Conservative Virginia: The Byrd Organization and the Politics of Massive Resistance.* 1976.

Gates, Robbins L. *The Making of Massive Resistance: Virginia's Politics of Public School Desegregation, 1954–1956.* 1964.

Heinemann, Ronald L. *Harry Byrd of Virginia.* 1996.

Lassiter, Matthew D., and Andrew B. Lewis, eds. *The Moderates' Dilemma: Massive Resistance to School Desegregation in Virginia.* 1998.

Lebsock, Suzanne. *Virginia Women, 1600–1945: "A Share of Honour."* 1987.

Moger, Allen W. *Virginia: Bourbonism to Byrd, 1870–1925.* 1968.

Murray, Pauli. *States' Laws on Race and Color.* 1950.

Rountree, Helen C. *Pocahontas's People: The Powhatan Indians of Virginia Through Four Centuries.* 1990.

Rubin, Louis D. *Virginia: A History.* 1977.

Salmon, Emily J., and Edward D. C. Campbell, Jr., eds. *The Hornbook of Virginia History.* 1994.

Sherman, Richard B. "'The Last Stand': The Fight for Racial Integrity in Virginia in the 1920's." *Journal of Southern History* 54 (February 1988): 69–92.

Smith, Bob. *They Closed Their Schools. Prince Edward County, Virginia, 1951–1964.* 1965.

Wynes, Charles E. *Race Relations in Virginia, 1870–1902.* 1961.

Younger, Edward, and James T. Moore, eds. *The Governors of Virginia, 1860–1978.* 1982.

Ronald L. Heinemann

Voter Education Project

The Voter Education Project (VEP) was a program implemented by the Kennedy administration in the early 1960s that was intended to increase voter registration among Southern blacks. This endeavor was conducted under the auspices of the SOUTHERN REGIONAL COUNCIL (SRC), a nonprofit, nonpartisan civil rights organization formed in 1943 for the stated purpose of gathering data on discrimination against blacks attempting to vote in the South. By increasing the number of blacks participating in both local and general elections, the administration felt it would be possible for the Democratic Party to loosen the hold of the segregationist DIXIECRATS on the Southern United States.

In 1962, the SCR opened its Voter Education Project with a study intended to determine the level of registration among Southern blacks. Overseeing VEP efforts was Wiley A. BRANTON, a civil rights attorney of considerable repute who had previously served as legal counsel for the students of the Little Rock, Arkansas desegregation case (see LITTLE ROCK NINE). In addition to conducting numerous studies, the VEP gave seed money to civil rights groups and to nonpartisan local groups in the South. These grants were intended to promote voter registration and education among disfranchised blacks.

Pleased with the results of this endeavor, in 1965 the SRC acted to give the Voter Education Project greater autonomy by allowing it to select its own board of directors. While implementing these changes, the SRC appointed Vernon JORDAN to succeed Wiley Branton as executive director. Under Jordan's leadership, the VEP placed its voter education efforts on an equal footing with voter registration. After the passage of the VOTING RIGHTS ACT OF 1965, Jordan helped to create a program intended to instruct black political candidates in how to conduct an effective election campaign. The result of these efforts was a marked increase in political participation among blacks throughout the South.

A tax reform bill passed in 1969 placed considerable restrictions on the use of tax-exempt funds for voter registration, necessitating the severing of all ties between VEP and its parent organization, the Southern Regional Council. As voter registration became almost universal among the nation's blacks, the organization saw its role reduced somewhat to that of a group attempting to raise political awareness among those blacks who felt they had little stake in the political process.

The Voter Education Project's most important contribution to civil rights in the United States was found among the hundreds of thousands of newly registered voters that resulted from its efforts. A secondary legacy was the assistance it provided to numerous eager but inexperienced black political candiadates who stood little chance without the resources of VEP to help educate and support them. Both achievements helped to hasten the opening up of the political process to the nation's African Americans.

BIBLIOGRAPHY

Bass, Jack. *The Transformation of Southern Politics.* 1995.

Lawson, Steven F. *Black Ballots: Voting Rights in the South.* 1976.

Robert W. Nill

Voting Rights

Americans of African origin have lived in what is today the United States for nearly four centuries, but have obtained the right to vote only over the past 130 years. RECONSTRUCTION after the Civil War marked a revolutionary change in the political status of African Americans by granting southern black men the right to vote. Military Reconstruction acts passed by Congress in 1867 required former Confederate states to enfranchise adult black males before the states could be readmitted for representation in Congress. Furthermore, congressional lawmakers designed the FIFTEENTH AMENDMENT, ratified in 1870, to prohibit any state from abridging the right to vote on the basis of race, color, or previous condition of servitude. The amendment, however, did not directly confer the right to vote on African Americans; instead, it prohibited

states from excluding blacks from the ballot for overtly racial reasons. This distinction proved catastrophic.

Blacks saw their voting rights whittled away throughout the late nineteenth century. As whites regained control over Southern governments, they gradually found ways around the FIFTEENTH AMENDMENT. The height of retrenchment occurred during the 1890s and early 1900s, when state after state in the South disfranchised African Americans through a variety of legalistic means. Led by Mississippi in 1890, Southern politicians enacted literacy tests that kept most blacks from qualifying to vote. To underscore their intention, lawmakers exempted whites whose fathers or grandfathers had fought in the Civil War from taking suffrage exams. Legislators devised poll taxes as voting requirements to make it difficult for poor blacks to find money to participate in an election. These regulations also limited a sizeable number of poor and uneducated whites from voting, but passage of white primary legislation barred blacks alone from casting ballots in the election that counted most in the one-party South: the Democratic primary. The rise in LYNCHING during this period made it even less likely that black Southerners would attempt to seek the franchise.

Yet African Americans in the South never lost a desire for recovering cherished suffrage rights and managed to sustain a legacy of electoral participation. Mainly in urban areas, a small number of registered blacks cast ballots in nonpartisan municipal elections that did not require membership in the Democratic Party. In 1909, African Americans joined white progressives to launch the NATIONAL ASSOCIATION FOR THE ADVANCEMENT OF COLORED PEOPLE (NAACP), which became the leading organization seeking to petition the courts to strike down biased suffrage laws. Thirty-five years later, their efforts paid off when the SUPREME COURT outlawed the white primary (SMITH V. ALLWRIGHT). In the decade following this ruling in 1944, the proportion of African Americans enrolled to vote climbed from 3 percent to over 20 percent. This figure included black women, who had become eligible to vote with ratification of the NINETEENTH AMENDMENT in 1920, but who subsequently had faced the same obstacles as black men. The electorate swelled as an outcome of suffrage drives in local communities waged by black WORLD WAR II veterans, progressive clergy, NAACP branches, civic and women's clubs, sympathetic white labor union organizers, including communists, and interracial groups such as the SOUTHERN CONFERENCE FOR HUMAN WELFARE.

These gains notwithstanding, in 1954, four-fifths of African-American adults in the South remained disfranchised. The emerging civil rights movement of the 1950s exerted political pressure on the national government to remove racial barriers to enfranchisement. Washington responded slowly. Voting rights measures signed by President Dwight D. EISENHOWER in 1957 and 1960, expanded federal power to file lawsuits against voter registrars who thwarted blacks from the franchise. As the national government litigated, civil rights groups fanned out throughout the South to conduct voter registration drives. Under sponsorship of the VOTER EDUCATION PROJECT (1962–1964), the NAACP, STUDENT NONVIOLENT COORDINATING COMMITTEE (SNCC), SOUTHERN CHRISTIAN LEADERSHIP CONFERENCE (SCLC), and CONGRESS OF RACIAL EQUALITY (CORE) helped boost black voter registration figures to 43 percent in 1964 from 27 percent in 1992 (white registration increased to 63 percent in 1964 from 53 percent in 1962). In addition, the Twenty-fourth Amendment (1964) abolished the poll tax in national elections.

The push to restore the right to vote reached a climax in 1965. Although reformers had made considerable progress, blacks continued to encounter discriminatory administration of literacy tests and face white resistance in many areas of the South. Consequently, in January 1965, the Reverend Martin Luther KING, JR., head of the SCLC, launched a voting crusade in Selma, Alabama, to bring national attention to the plight of unregistered blacks. After a three-month struggle culminating in a mass march from Selma to Montgomery, President Lyndon B. JOHNSON introduced legislation to remove lingering barriers to black enfranchisement. Among its powerful provisions, the 1965 Voting Rights Law suspended literacy tests for voting and authorized deployment of federal registrars to enroll blacks. (See VOTING RIGHTS ACT OF 1965.) The Act was hugely successful, and by the end of the 1960s, over 60 percent of black Southerners had signed the voter rolls.

The voting rights battle has shifted to expanding opportunities for electing African-American officeholders. Beginning in 1969 (*Allen v. State Board of Elections*), the SUPREME COURT interpreted the scope of the Voting Rights Act to overturn discriminatory procedures that limit chances for black candidates to win office. These include election districts drawn to hinder black minority candidates from overcoming opposition from the majority-white electorate. Fueled by judicial decrees and enforcement by the Justice Department, the number of black elected officials in the South jumped from less than 100 in 1965 to over 4,900 in 1993. At the same time, Congress has renewed the Voting Rights Act, most recently in 1982, extending coverage until the year 2007.

However, during the 1990s, the Supreme Court has backed away from some of its earlier decisions. In a series of cases, the justices ruled against so-called "ra-cial gerrymandering." They concluded that the Voting Rights Act does not require states to shape legislative districts based primarily on race to give blacks an advantage in electing African-American representatives. The high court's views reflect opposition to affirmative action programs that are considered by whites to give special preference to blacks, whether job seekers, university applicants, or candidates for electoral office. Though the future of affirmative action appears threatened, there seems less danger that African Americans will once again lose the right to vote as happened following Reconstruction.

BIBLIOGRAPHY

Dittmer, John. *Local People: The Struggle for Civil Rights in Mississippi.* 1994.

Garrow, David J. *Protest at Selma: Martin Luther King, Jr., and the Voting Rights Act of 1965.* 1978.

Gillette, William. *The Right to Vote: Politics and the Passage of the Fifteenth Amendment.* 1969.

Gilmore, Glenda Elizabeth. *Gender and Jim Crow: Women and the Politics of White Supremacy in North Carolina, 1869–1920.* 1996.

Guinier, Lani. *The Tyranny of the Majority: Fundamental Fairness in Representative Democracy.* 1994.

Hamilton, Charles V. *The Bench and the Ballot: Southern Federal Judges and Black Voters.* 1973.

Hine, Darlene Clark. *Black Victory: The Rise and Fall of the White Primary in Texas.* 1979.

Key, V. O. *Southern Politics in State and Nation.* 1949.

Kousser, J. Morgan. *The Shaping of Southern Politics: Suffrage Restriction and the Establishment of the One Party South, 1880–1910.* 1974.

Lawson, Steven F. *Black Ballots: Voting Rights in the South, 1944–1969.* 1976.

Lawson, Steven F. *Running for Freedom: Civil Rights and Black Politics in America Since 1941,* 2nd ed. 1997.

Matthews, Donald R., and James W. Prothro. *Negroes and the New Southern Politics.* 1966.

Sullivan, Patricia. *Days of Hope: Race and Democracy in the New Deal Era.* 1996.

Watters, Pat, and Reese Cleghorn. *Climbing Jacob's Ladder: The Arrival of Negroes in Southern Politics.* 1967.

Voting Rights Act of 1965

Following passage of the CIVIL RIGHTS ACT OF 1964, which dealt mainly with desegregation and equal employment opportunities, President Lyndon B. JOHNSON instructed the Justice Department to explore the possibility of drafting proposals to combat lingering suffrage discrimination. Less than a majority, 43 percent, of eligible Southern blacks were registered to vote and continued to face longstanding barriers of literacy tests, poll taxes, discriminatory enrollment practices, intimidation, and violence. The president did not have a specific legislative timetable in mind, perhaps seeking to give Congress a political respite after the protracted battle to enact the 1964 law.

Black activists succeeded in pushing up the schedule. Selma, Alabama, became the focal point of their attempts and the spark that ignited vigorous national action. The force of resistance from the city and from Dallas County where it was located had frustrated prior suffrage drives and kept the overwhelming majority of blacks off the registration rolls. Consequently, in January 1965, Dr. Martin Luther KING JR., head of the SOUTHERN CHRISTIAN LEADERSHIP CONFERENCE (SCLC), launched mass demonstrations to secure the right to vote. The campaign continued for three months, resulting in numerous arrests and the death of several civil rights workers. On March 7, a scheduled walk from Selma to Montgomery to highlight the voting rights cause resulted in further bloodshed, which kept the demonstrators from getting very far on their journey. This violence, televised before a national viewing audience, prompted President Johnson in

mid-March to ask Congress to pass legislation based on proposals Justice Department lawyers had been crafting. Later that month, Dr. King rallied further support for legislation by undertaking once again the pilgrimage to Montgomery, this time completing it successfully under the watchful eyes of federal troops.

Support for the voting rights bill was widespread. Pressure exerted by the Selma campaign persuaded the national government, backed by Northern public opinion, that acting forcefully and quickly was a necessity. The traditional opponents of civil rights, white Southern Democrats, were clearly on the defensive. The grievances highlighted in Alabama and publicized throughout the country left them with very little room to maneuver against the proponents of extending to African Americans a constitutional right that clearly and so visibly had been denied them.

The Johnson administration's proposal provided tough remedies to break down remaining obstacles to black enfranchisement. It featured a formula that automatically covered jurisdictions that used literacy tests for voting and in which less than a majority of eligible adults had registered or voted in the 1964

In 1965, some two million African Americans were registered to vote in the South. In rural Wilcox County, Alabama, voters line up in front of a polling station at the Sugar Shack, a local general store. (CORBIS/Bettmann)

presidential election. This included the Southern states with the worst records of black voter registration: Alabama, Georgia, Louisiana, Mississippi, North Carolina, South Carolina, and Virginia. In addition, literacy tests were suspended for five years and the attorney general would have the power to appoint federal registrars to enroll blacks if the states did not voluntarily do so. Moreover, no state or locality could adopt changes in electoral procedures without first clearing them with the Justice Department. Affected jurisdictions could escape by proving in federal court in Washington, D.C., that they had not discriminated against black registration during the previous ten years.

Congressional debate focused on the poll tax and coverage of the bill, not the desirability for legislation. Liberals in Congress wanted the bill to include a ban on the poll tax, but the administration refused because it questioned the constitutionality of such a provision. (The Twenty-fourth Amendment barring use of the poll tax in federal, but not state, elections was ratified in 1964.) Moreover, Johnson's legislative leaders needed the support of congressional Republicans to pass the measure over the threat of a Southern filibuster in the Senate, and GOP leaders likewise doubted the validity of eliminating the poll tax without a constitutional amendment. Republicans also questioned the triggering formula that targeted seven Southern states. They proposed instead to combat disfranchisement only where it could be shown actually to exist, and thereby favored authorizing the attorney general to dispatch federal registrars to any county upon receiving twenty-five certified complaints of voter bias. At the same time, they opposed dropping literacy tests as a registration requirement.

President Johnson refused to budge because he wanted the focus of enforcement to remain on hardcore areas of the South and considered literacy exams the root of the problem. Backed by a coalition of Northern Democrats and moderate Republicans, the final bill contained the administration's provisions intact and included a compromise that directed the attorney general to bring suit against the constitutionality of the poll tax. Traditional Southern Democratic opponents refrained from mounting a prolonged and concerted attack, and within a relatively speedy five months after its introduction, the voting rights bill passed Congress overwhelmingly. Indeed, reflecting the growing legislative consensus, four senators and forty-three congressmen from the South joined the majority for the bill. The president signed it into law on August 6.

The act proved an immediate success. In 1966, the Supreme Court not only affirmed the constitutionality of the Voting Rights Act, but also outlawed the use of the poll tax as a suffrage requirement. By 1968, 62 percent of black adults had registered to vote. The most striking change occurred in Mississippi where black registration leaped from 6 percent to around 60 percent in three years. The increase in black voters also encouraged the election of African-American officeholders. Fewer than twenty-five in 1964, the number of black elected officials in the South had climbed to over 700 in 1970.

Since 1965, Congress has renewed the provisions of the Voting Rights Act three times, and they will remain in effect until the year 2007. The courts have also increased the scope of the act to range beyond voter registration. The law has been used to challenge electoral rules, such as at-large elections, which limit the impact of black ballots. However, since the mid-1990s the Supreme Court has decreed that whereas race cannot be used as a negative means of curtailing electoral possibilities for African Americans, neither can race be used affirmatively to enhance the chances of blacks winning public office. Thus, at the dawn of the twenty-first century, the Voting Rights Act of 1965 remains in place as a safeguard of electoral participation for African Americans, though not as firmly as it once did.

BIBLIOGRAPHY

Ball, Howard, Dale Krane, and Thomas P. Lauth. *Compromised Compliance: Implementation of the 1965 Voting Rights Act.* 1982.

Fairclough, Adam. *"To Redeem the Soul of America": The Southern Christian Leadership Conference and Martin Luther King, Jr.* 1987.

Garrow, David J. *Protest at Selma: Martin Luther King, Jr. and the Voting Rights Act of 1965.* 1978.

Graham, Hugh Davis. *The Civil Rights Era: Origins and Development of National Policy.* 1990.

Grofman, Bernard, and Chandler Davidson, eds. *Controversies in Minority Voting: The Voting Rights Act in Perspective.* 1992.

Lawson, Steven F. *Black Ballots: Voting Rights in the South, 1944–1969.* 1976.

Lawson, Steven F. *In Pursuit of Power: Southern Blacks and Electoral Politics, 1965–1982.* 1985.

Parker, Frank R. *Black Votes Count: Political Empowerment in Mississippi After 1965.* 1990.

Stern, Mark. *Calculating Visions: Kennedy, Johnson, and Civil Rights.* 1982.

Thernstrom, Abigail. *Whose Votes Count? Affirmative Action and Minority Voting Rights.* 1987.

Steven F. Lawson

Voting Rights Amendment of 1970

The 1970 extension of the Voting Rights Act of 1965 was signed into law by President Richard M. Nixon on

June 22, 1970, renewing the 1965 Act until 1975. The 1970 Act (1) provided a nationwide ban, until 1975, on the use of literacy tests and other discriminatory devices used to hinder voting; (2) weakened residency requirements for participation in presidential elections; and (3) established national standards for absentee registration and balloting in presidential elections. In addition, it extended Sections Four and Five of the 1965 Act to states and political subdivisions which maintained a literacy test as of November 1, 1968, and had less than a 50 percent turnout or registration for the 1968 presidential elections. Sections Four and Five required states subjugated to the Act, due to previous discriminatory activity, to prove to the Justice Department that any new actions or legislation surrounding voting would not have a discriminatory impact. Challengers to the 1970 extension, such as Attorney General John N. Mitchell and the Nixon Administration, argued unsuccessfully that the progress achieved since 1965 in extending the right to vote did not justify the retention of sections manifesting regional bias. Title III of the 1970 Act granted voting rights to eighteen- to twenty-one-year-old citizens in all primary and general elections. Because the Supreme Court, in *Oregon v. Mitchell* (1970), ruled that Congress can only change voter qualifications for federal elections, not for state and local, this ruling resulted in the Twenty-sixth Amendment to the United States Constitution.

BIBLIOGRAPHY

"Background and Provisions of the Voting Rights Act of 1965." *Congressional Digest* (June/July 1975): 163–166, 192.

"Congress and Voting Rights Controversy." *Congressional Digest* 48 (November 1969): 257–265.

Mitchell, John N., Joseph H. Tydings, William M. McCulloch, William F. Ryan, Richard H. Poff, Fletcher Thompson, Stephen J. Pollak, and Charles H. Griffen. "Pro/Con: Should Nixon Administration Proposals to Modify the Voting Rights Act be Enacted Now?" *Congressional Digest* 48 (November 1969): 266–287.

"110 years of Voting Rights Legislation." *Congressional Quarterly Weekly Report* (April 11, 1981): 634.

Oregon v. Mitchell 400 U.S. 112 (1970).

Paper, Lewis J. "Notes: Legislative History of Title III of the Voting Rights Act of 1970." *Harvard Journal on Legislation* 8 (1970): 123–157.

Voting Rights Act of 1970 (Public Law 9-285, Statute 318).

"Voting Rights: Civil Rights Battle Focuses on Voter Bill." *Congressional Quarterly Weekly Report* (August 1, 1969): 1411–1415.

Michelle Donaldson Deardorff

Voting Rights Amendment of 1975

A seven-year extension to the 1965 VOTING RIGHTS ACT, this amendment changed Section Four's trigger mechanism, which determines which states or political subdivisions fall under Section Five's requirement of preclearance by the Justice Department of any legislative change. Under the 1975 amendments, political subdivisions using a literacy test in 1972 and having an electorate with less than 50 percent of eligible voters registered by November 1, 1972 would be placed under the Justice Department's jurisdiction. Advocates for the extension testified favorably before House and Senate subcommittees, emphasizing the continued need for federal supervision of state electoral activities, the continued existence of discrimination and intimidation against African-Americans voters, and the unique needs of language minorities and the illiterate. Opponents focused on what they perceived to be the inherent regional bias of Sections Four and Five, which are applied based on the evidence of past discriminatory actions. In addition, opponents noted the inherent problems of a federally appointed body (the Justice Department) determining the legitimacy of the decisions of locally elected bodies.

Title II of the Act was expanded to include state and political subdivisions with a significant percentage of language minorities, statutorily defined as individuals of Spanish heritage, Native Americans, Native Alaskans, and Asian Americans. Title III required states with English-only registration and voting materials to fall under the requirements of the 1965 Voting Rights Act, if they possess a single-language minority comprising 5 percent of the voting population and manifest an English illiteracy rate higher than the national norm.

BIBLIOGRAPHY

Cohen, Richard E. "Justice Report: Changing Racial Conditions May Shape 1975 Voting Rights Act." *National Journal Reports* (October 26, 1974): 1606–1613.

"Controversy Over Voting Rights Act Extension." *Congressional Digest* (June/July 1975): 163.

Gottron, Martha V. "Voting Rights Act Extension Approved." *Congressional Quarterly Weekly Report* (May 3, 1975): 925–926.

1975 Voting Rights Act, Amending the Voting Rights Act of 1965 (Public Law 94-73).

Rodino, Jr., Peter W., James B. Allen, William L. Scott, League of Women Voters of the United States, David E. Satterfield, III, American Civil Liberties Union, Voter Education Project, Inc., James W. Rane. "Pro/Con: Should the Expiring 'Special Provisions' of the Voting Rights Act Be Further Extended?" *Congressional Digest* (June/July 1975): 170–191.

770   Voting Rights Amendment of 1985

United States Commission on Civil Rights. "The Voting
Act: Ten Years After." Report to the President and Congress (January 1975).

Michelle Donaldson Deardorff

Voting Rights Amendment of 1985

In 1980, the Supreme Court rendered the decision of
City of Mobile v. Bolden, regarding the constitutionality
of an at-large local election. The Court ruled that challengers of a discriminatory electoral practice are required to demonstrate an intent to discriminate
against black candidates. Because merely showing that
African Americans had not won elections despite their
size in the general population, was not sufficient, civil
rights advocates were concerned about the implications for interpreting the Voting Rights Act. In response to this decision, the 1965 VOTING RIGHTS ACT
was amended to lessen the burden of proof for challengers. The 1985 amendment stated that evidence of
discriminatory results could demonstrate a constitutional violation.

In addition, Congress amended Section Two of the
Voting Rights Act to guarantee that no voting practice
can result in a "denial or abridgment of the right of
any citizen of the United States to vote on account of
race or color" (42 USC § 1973). Section Two, unlike
the preclearance requirement of Section Five, applied
to all states and political subdivisions regardless of a
past history of discriminatory practices. It also allowed
citizens to challenge election practices that deny or
dilute votes on the basis of color, race, or membership
in a language minority group. In 1986, the Supreme
Court interpreted this amendment in *Thornburg v. Gingles,* ruling that any voting system that has the impact
of discrimination is in violation of the law, regardless
of intent. Section Two and *Thornburg v. Gingles* in combination have resulted in numerous challenges to state
redistricting practices.

BIBLIOGRAPHY

City of Mobile v. Bolden 446 U.S. 55 (1980).
Cohen, Richard E. "Will the Voting Rights Act Become a
Victim of Its Own Success?" *National Journal* (August
1, 1981): 1364–1368.
Forman, James, Jr. "Victory by Surrender: The Voting
Rights Amendments of 1982 and the Civil Rights Act
of 1991." *Yale Law and Policy Review* 10 (1992): 133–
176.
Rodino, Jr., Peter W., James M. Collins, Mario Biaggi, M.
Caldwell Butler, Harold Washington, Thomas J. Bliley,
Jr. "Pro/Con: Should Congress Approve House-Passed
H.R. 3112 Extending the Voting Rights Act of 1965?"
Congressional Digest (December 1981): 298–313.
Thornburg v. Gingles 478 U.S. 30 (1986).
Witt, Elder, and Nadine Cohodas. "Reagan, Congress at
Odds over Voting Rights Changes." *Congressional Quarterly Weekly Edition* (November 23, 1985): 2429–2433.

Michelle Donaldson Deardorff

VV Campaign

See Double V Campaign.

W

Walker, Maggie Lena

(1867–1934), businesswoman.

Maggie Lena Walker was a prominent businesswoman and community leader in Richmond, Virginia. As a response to the rising tide of segregation and disfranchisement at the turn of the century, Walker advocated self-help and economic cooperation within the African-American community. Yet she remained politically active and protested against discrimination and segregation. Born and raised in Richmond, Walker attended the Colored Normal School, graduating in 1883. She taught in the public schools for three years, while also taking courses in accounting and sales. Virginia law prevented Walker from teaching after her marriage in 1886 to Armstead Walker, a contractor and builder.

After her marriage, Walker directed her energies to raising her children and to the community organizations to which she belonged.

At the age of 14, Walker had joined the Independent Order of St. Luke, a mutual benefit society that aided the sick and provided burial insurance for its members. Starting as a local recruiter for the Order, Maggie Lena Walker moved up through its ranks, and in 1899, was elected to the position of Right Worthy Grand Secretary. Walker used the Order to encourage unity and to create economic opportunities for African Americans. Under Walker's leadership, the Order grew from 1,080 members to over 100,000 members. She organized a juvenile division of the Order, and in 1902, established a newspaper, the *St. Luke Herald.* In 1903, Walker founded and served as president of the St. Luke Penny Savings Bank, an institution dedicated to the small depositor. Many of the bank's customers included African-American washerwomen and children. The Penny Savings Bank flourished and later merged with another black-owned bank in Richmond to become the Consolidated Bank and Trust Company. Walker retired from the presidency of the bank in 1932, but served as chairperson of its board of directors until her death in 1934. With the founding of the Penny Savings Bank, Walker became the first woman bank president in the United States.

While promoting self-help and economic cooperation within the black community, Walker continued to protest discrimination and segregation. She and other St. Luke members played a leading role in the 1904 streetcar boycott in Richmond. After the passage of the NINETEENTH AMENDMENT, Walker led efforts to register black women to vote. Furthermore, in 1921, when Virginia Republicans moved to exclude African Americans from the party, black leaders ran their own slate of state officers. Walker ran for superintendent of public instruction.

Along with her work with the Order of St. Luke, Maggie Lena Walker served in other organizations dedicated to community uplift. She founded the Richmond Council of Colored Women and was a member of the Virginia Federation of Colored Women's Clubs. She also worked with the International Council of Women of the Darker Races, the National Training School for Girls, and the Virginia Industrial School for Girls. She served at various times as an officer in the Richmond branch of the NATIONAL ASSOCIATION FOR

THE ADVANCEMENT OF COLORED PEOPLE (NAACP) and was a member of the NAACP's national board of directors.

BIBLIOGRAPHY

Branch, Muriel Miller, and Dorothy Marie Rice. *Pennies to Dollars: The Story of Maggie Lena Walker.* 1997.

Brown, Elsa Barkley. "Womanist Consciousness: Maggie Lena Walker and the Independent Order of Saint Luke." *Signs* 14 (1989): 610–633.

Dabney, Wendell P. *Maggie L. Walker and The I. O. of Saint Luke: The Woman and Her Work.* 1927.

Maggie Lena Walker Papers. Maggie Lena Walker National Historic Site, Richmond, Va.

Larissa M. Smith

Wallace, George C. (Corley)

(1919–1998), Alabama governor.

George Wallace served five terms as Alabama's governor, including his wife Lurleen's term, between 1962 and 1986. Wallace was elected to the Alabama state legislature in 1947 and to the circuit court in 1952,

Alabama Governor George Wallace smiles at a rally in support of Republican presidential candidate Barry Goldwater at Glen Burnie, Maryland, on October 19, 1964. (AP/Wide World Photos)

where he became known as the "fighting judge" for his defense of segregation. However, he lost his first gubernatorial bid, in 1958, because he was seen as "soft" on the race question, as he had refused to walk out with the Alabama delegates when the civil rights plank was passed at the 1948 Democratic National Convention, although he personally opposed its passage, nor did he endorse the DIXIECRATS in the presidential election that year. In order to overcome that image, he began using support of racial segregation to win elections. Although Wallace did not have a clear racist ideology and opposed conspiracy theories, his political associates included members of the KU KLUX KLAN, the National States Rights Party, the Liberty Lobby, and WHITE CITIZENS COUNCILS. Perhaps the words of his inaugural speech in 1962 were his most famous, when he declared "segregation now . . . segregation tomorrow . . . segregation forever" (Carter, 1995, p. 108). Wallace was also known for his extreme, yet unsuccessful, resistance to the integration of the University of Alabama, which led to a confrontation with the National Guard sent in by Attorney General Robert KENNEDY.

George Wallace made three bids for the presidency of the United States. He ran as the candidate for the American Independent Party in 1968, winning only 58 electoral votes in the "Deep South" and Arkansas. However, Wallace had made a great impact on Republican politics. Richard NIXON employed a "Southern strategy," which coopted issues that Wallace had articulated, such as law and order and school desegregation. In the 1972 campaign for the presidency, Nixon was advised by Pat Buchanan, his speech writer, to draw Wallace voters by opposing integration. While campaigning in Maryland for the presidency in 1972, Wallace was shot by Arthur Bremer and left paralyzed from the waist down. He attempted to run again in 1976, but failing health led him to support Jimmy CARTER after a loss in the North Carolina primary. After the assassination attempt, George Wallace's racial attitudes changed, and he begged forgiveness from those who had been harmed. However, some skeptics doubted the sincerity of his pleas, as Wallace was seen as a political opportunist.

Although George Wallace did not win a presidential election, he is credited with bringing the Dixiecrats back to the REPUBLICAN PARTY. Republican candidates from Nixon to George BUSH were able to win the South with campaigns based on racial division. Although Wallace's candidacies articulated the fear of whites in the wake of the civil rights movement after the passage of the CIVIL RIGHTS ACT OF 1964 and the VOTING RIGHTS ACT OF 1965, his values remained popular through the 1980s and 1990s. A long economic downturn in America that began in 1973 fanned cultural and racial fears, creating a receptive political climate for the right-wing proto-populist presidential candidacy of Pat Buchanan, David Duke's election to the Louisiana House of Representatives, and Newt Gingrich's 1994 "Republican Revolution." Paleoconservative Republican candidacies continue to push the Republican Party toward NATIONALISM and racial division with cries for "America First!"

BIBLIOGRAPHY

Carter, Dan T. *The Politics of Rage: George Wallace, the Origins of the New Conservatism, and the Transformation of American Politics.* 1995.

Carter, Dan T. *From George Wallace to Newt Gingrich: Race in the Conservative Counterrevolution 1963–1994.* 1996.

Clark, E. Culpepper. *"The Schoolhouse Door": Segregation's Last Stand at the University of Alabama.* 1995.

Diamond, Sara. *Roads to Dominion: Right-Wing Power and Political Movements in the United States.* 1995.

Egerton, John. *Speak Now Against the Day: The Generation Before the Civil Rights Movement in the South.* 1994.

Kazin, Michael. *The Populist Persuasion: An American History.* 1995.

Phillips, Kevin. *Boiling Point.* 1993.

Stephanie Shanks-Meile

Wallace, Henry Agard

(1888–1965), U.S. vice president.

Henry A. Wallace at the time of his bid for the presidency. (© Archive Photos)

Henry Agard Wallace served as U.S. Secretary of Agriculture from 1933 to 1941 and as vice president of the United States 1941–1945. After Wallace's defeat for renomination as vice president, President FRANKLIN D. ROOSEVELT named him Secretary of Commerce—a position he held until September 1946. And many historians think that Wallace's presidential run in 1948 as standard bearer of the PROGRESSIVE PARTY was a landmark in the civil rights struggle.

Wallace was born on October 7, 1888, on a farm near Orient, Iowa. The family had long been prominent in agricultural politics and journalism. After receiving a B.S. in animal husbandry from Iowa State College in 1910, Wallace went on to develop the first commercially usable variety of hybrid corn and, in 1926, founded the Hi-Bred Corn Company. After his father, Henry Cantwell Wallace, became Secretary of Agriculture in 1921, the younger Wallace took over editorship of the family-owned newspaper, *Wallace's Farmer.*

A strong advocate of government intervention to raise farm prices, Wallace abandoned his family's traditional Republican allegiance to back Democrat Al Smith for president in 1928 and Franklin D. Roosevelt four years later. Named Secretary of Agriculture, Wal-

lace became point man for implementing the NEW DEAL's agricultural recovery program. As an emergency measure in the summer of 1933, he moved to reduce price-depressing surpluses by paying farmers to plow up ten million acres of growing cotton and slaughter six million pigs. Thereafter, the Agricultural Adjustment Administration (AAA) worked to achieve that goal by giving farmers benefit payments in return for reducing their acreage.

Up to this time, Wallace's vision appears not to have extended beyond the problems of commercial farmers. And there is no evidence that he had given any attention to the special difficulties of blacks, despite close personal ties when he was a youngster with George Washington Carver. On the contrary, the AAA program had a gravely adverse impact upon Southern tenants and sharecroppers—with blacks the worst sufferers. Thousands were forced off the land, while landlords, more typically than not, failed to share benefit payments with those workers who remained. When a group of urban liberals in the AAA's General Counsel's

Office tried to assure tenants and sharecroppers fairer treatment, Wallace agreed to their "purge" in February 1935.

The turning point in Wallace's hands-off attitude toward racial issues was a trip that he made through the South in fall 1936 accompanied by W. Will ALEXANDER, new head of the Resettlement Administration, and his assistant, C. B. ("Beanie") Baldwin. Moved by the poverty he saw, Wallace forged an alliance with a biracial group of Southern progressives that would be centered, after its founding in spring 1938, in the SOUTHERN CONFERENCE FOR HUMAN WELFARE (SCHW).

The SCHW joined with the nascent Congress of Industrial Organizations in a campaign for federal legislation to repeal the poll tax as a voting prerequisite. Wallace, after Roosevelt tapped him as his vice-presidential running mate in 1940, became the Conference's great hope for making the federal government an activist force for the radical transformation of the Southern political, economic, and social systems. Those hopes were frustrated by Wallace's defeat for renomination as vice president in 1944. The escalating COLD WAR with the Soviet Union was the final blow. Wallace's break with President Harry S. TRUMAN over the administration's containment policies and his decision to run as a third-party nominee for president brought to a head the simmering conflict within liberal ranks over the role of Communist Party members and fellow travelers.

With the anti-anti-communist faction headed by Clark FOREMAN ascendant in the SCHW, that organization became the backbone of the Progressive Party in the South. While placing his primary emphasis on foreign-policy issues, Wallace did make the call for racial equality a leading theme of his campaign. His threatened appeal to black voters is widely believed to have played a major role in pushing Truman to take a stronger stand in support of civil rights than he probably would have otherwise done.

After the 1948 election, Wallace withdrew from political activity. By the time of his death on November 18, 1965, he appears to have returned to his Republican roots.

BIBLIOGRAPHY

Blum, John Morton, ed. *The Price of Vision: The Diary of Henry A. Wallace, 1942–1946.* 1973.
Conrad, David E. *The Forgotten Farmers: The Story of Sharecroppers in the New Deal.* 1965.
Schapsmeier, Edward L., and Frederick H. Schapsmeier. *Henry Wallace of Iowa: The Agrarian Years, 1910–1940.* 1968.
Schapsmeier, Edward L., and Frederick H. Schapsmeier. *Prophet in Politics: Henry Wallace and the War Years, 1940–1965.* 1970.
Sullivan, Patricia. *Days of Hope: Race and Democracy in the New Deal Era.* 1996.

John Braeman

Waring, J. Waties (Julius)

(1880–1968), judge.

J. Waties Waring served as a U.S. District Judge for the Eastern District of South Carolina from 1942 to 1952. From the bench he wrote important legal decisions in favor of black civil rights. As an eight-generation white Charlestonian, Waring's decisions represented a break from his own and his state's racial history.

In 1913 Waring married a well-connected Charlestonian woman and a year later was appointed assistant U.S. attorney for South Carolina's eastern district. Through much of his adult life Waring adhered to the South's JIM CROW practices. But by the time of his appointment to U.S. District Judge in 1942, Waring had come to view the southern system of segregation as anachronistic. In a series of important legal decisions, Waring ruled in favor of equal pay for black and white public school teachers. In *Elmore v. Rice* (1947) and *Brown v. Baskin* (1948), Waring struck down the rules of South Carolina's Democratic party that barred blacks from membership and participation in the party's white primaries. "It is time," Waring wrote, "for South Carolina to rejoin the Union." In a 1951 dissenting opinion Waring exclaimed that "segregation is per se inequality," which helped set the course for the NATIONAL ASSOCIATION FOR THE ADVANCEMENT OF COLORED PEOPLE's (NAACP) legal victory in BROWN V. BOARD OF EDUCATION (1954).

Waring's legal and personal transformation during his judicial tenure provoked the anger and dismay of many white Carolinians. In 1952 he retired from the bench and retreated to New York City, where he lived the remainder of his life in exile from South Carolina.

BIBLIOGRAPHY

Yarbrough, Tinsley E.. *A Passion for Justice: J. Waties Waring and Civil Rights.* 1987.

Peter Lau

War on Poverty

In its "equal opportunity" programmatic focus, the War on Poverty can be viewed as both a symbolic manifestation and a political public-policy response to the civil rights movement's goal of economic justice for

African Americans and other racially oppressed peoples. The phrase "War on Poverty" was first used by President Lyndon B. JOHNSON to refer to programs sponsored by his administration that were designed to eliminate poverty in the United States. The phrase "Great Society" referred, initially, to the ideal social order that Johnson hoped would arise from the successful completion of the War on Poverty. But "Great Society" soon came to be an umbrella term describing a wide variety of Johnsonian social initiatives of which the War on Poverty formed one major aspect. In his initial speeches on the subject, Johnson promised that the War on Poverty and related programs would have a scope and impact comparable to that of Franklin D. ROOSEVELT's NEW DEAL. Sadly, Johnson's War on Poverty was started as the United States was becoming deeply enmeshed in the VIETNAM WAR and as a result was never undertaken on the scale that Johnson had originally envisioned. In assessing the War on Poverty's practical historic significance, it is clear that in both its relatively meager appropriations and the nature of its programs it was not designed to keep Johnson's bold initial promises of an "all-out" and "unconditional war on poverty," whose goal was nothing short of "total victory."

There has been a major academic debate about the importance of the African-American vote in presidential politics and of the civil rights movement in the origins and development of the War on Poverty. Some scholars note that when President John F. KENNEDY initiated social programs that benefited low-income inner-city residents of color, they constituted an essential political constituency. This was especially true in the Northern cities and states that were key to victories by Democratic presidential candidates. Other scholars observe that the War on Poverty was planned during the peak of the civil rights movement and was executed at a time when the civil rights struggle was being transformed into an increasingly militant BLACK POWER movement.

However, the midlevel government officials who planned the War on Poverty strategically tended to underplay the role of RACE in the planning of the program and to deny that the War on Poverty was targeted to help African Americans. This denial was a major tactic in seeking approval of the initiative from a Congress that included powerful Southern racial segregationists. This argument carried over into early policy-planning insiders' accounts of the origins of the War on Poverty.

More recent scholarship suggests, however, that less important than whether racial politics and the civil rights movement were determining factors in the origins of the War on Poverty was their profound impact in shaping the War on Poverty once the program was implemented. Some scholars suggest that indeed the economic focus of the War on Poverty itself was a circumspect way of addressing the growing concerns and militancy of an important political constituency of African Americans without evoking a WHITE BACKLASH.

Among the major antipoverty programs established with the enactment of the Economic Opportunity Act of 1964 were those intended specifically to aid youth: the Job Corps (which included a Youth Conservation Corps), state-level and community-based work training programs to provide work experience for unemployed youth, and work-study programs for college students (the Economic Opportunity Act of 1964).

In addition to general Community Action Programs, which were to be "developed, conducted, and administered with the maximum feasible participation of the residents of the areas," there were Adult Basic Education and the Volunteers In Service To America (VISTA) program. Special Programs to Combat Poverty in Rural Areas included grants and loans for low-income families and cooperatives organized to serve their needs, as well as assistance for migrant workers. There were also investments and employment-related incentives such as Small Business Administration loans, and work experience programs for the hard-core unemployed (the Economic Opportunity Act of 1964).

The meager expenditures for the War on Poverty (its initial new money appropriation was less than 1 percent of the total federal budget); and its focus on changing individuals and reforming the local agencies and government that served them, rather than addressing the socially structured roots of poverty and inequality, meant that major causes of African-American impoverishment such as racial discrimination in HOUSING, EDUCATION, and EMPLOYMENT went unchallenged. Consistent with the focus on changing the poor, the War on Poverty stressed job preparation, not job creation. Consequently, the War on Poverty and Great Society programs—such as the Medicaid program, which provided health care for the poor, and Title I of the ELEMENTARY AND SECONDARY EDUCATION ACT OF 1965, which offered compensatory education for low-income schoolchildren—were not effective tools in reducing the very high rates of poverty among the racially oppressed. A dramatic drop in poverty rates from the mid-1960s through the 1970s cannot be directly attributed to the War on Poverty or Great Society programs. A more important factor was government policy changes that brought increases in direct monetary payments to the poor through increased public assistance and Social Security benefits.

The War on Poverty was much more successful as a political rather than as an economic war. Its community action agencies provided meeting places, staff, equipment, and other resources that supported militant social protest activity that made local social-service agencies and governments more responsive to the needs of the poor. This success, along with frequent urban riots, helped provoke a white backlash and ultimately the program's demise. In the meantime, however, the agencies also served as bases for the emergence of African Americans, and to a lesser extent, Latino/a Americans, as significant forces in urban electoral politics.

Symbolically, the Economic Opportunity Act's "maximum feasible participation" of the poor mandate legitimated the view that poor people should be involved in making decisions that affect their lives. In this way the War on Poverty helped fuel expectations of participatory democracy in decisions affecting local communities that are still characteristic of America's urban politics today.

In brief, like the civil rights movement, a major accomplishment of the War on Poverty was its role in the expansion of the base of democratic participation for many African Americans and other racially oppressed peoples who had previously been locked out of that process.

BIBLIOGRAPHY

Davies, Gareth. *From Opportunity to Entitlement: The Transformation and Decline of Great Society Liberalism*. 1996.

Donovan, John C. *The Politics of Poverty*. 1967.

Johnson, Lyndon B. "Annual Message to the Congress on the State of the Union." January 8, 1964. *Public Papers of the Presidents of the United States, Lyndon B. Johnson*. Vol. 1. 1965.

Katz, Michael B. *The Undeserving Poor: From the War on Poverty to the War on Welfare*. 1989.

Lemann, Nicholas. *The Promised Land: The Great Black Migration and How It Changed America*. 1991.

Matusow, Allen J. *The Unraveling of America: A History of Liberalism in the 1960s*. 1984.

Moynihan, Daniel P. *Maximum Feasible Misunderstanding: Community Action in the War on Poverty*. 1970.

Patterson, James T. *Grand Expectations: The United States: 1945–1974*. 1996.

Piven, Frances Fox, and Richard A. Cloward. *Regulating the Poor: The Functions of Public Welfare*. 1993.

President Johnson's Message on Poverty. To the Congress of the United States. March 16, 1964. The War on Poverty. The Economic Opportunity Act of 1964. A Compilation of Materials Relevant to S. 2642. Prepared for the Select Committee on Poverty of the Committee on Labor and Public Welfare. United States Senate, 88th Congress 2nd Session Document No. 86. July 23, 1964.

Quadagno, Jill. *The Color of Welfare: How Racism Undermined the War on Poverty*. 1994.

Stone, Clarence N., Robert K. Whelan, and William J. Murin. *Urban Policy and Politics in a Bureaucratic Age*. 1986.

The Economic Opportunity Act of 1964. Public Law 88-452. 88th Congress, 2nd session, Aug. 20, 1964.

U.S. Bureau of the Census. *Current Population Reports*, Series P-60, Nos. 138 and 140. 1984.

Yarmolinsky, Adam. "The Beginnings of OEO." In *On Fighting Poverty: Perspectives From Experience*, edited by James L. Sundquist. 1969.

Zarefsky, David. *President Johnson's War on Poverty: Rhetoric and History*. 1986.

Timeline

May 13, 1957   The Mobilization for Youth program to combat juvenile delinquency is initiated at a board meeting of the Henry Street Settlement House in New York City's Lower East Side. This program is generally considered to be a precursor to the War on Poverty community action programs.

September 22, 1961   President John F. Kennedy signs the Juvenile Delinquency and Youth Offenses Control Act of 1961, providing federal funding for the Mobilization for Youth project as well as matching funding to supplement the not-yet-announced Ford Foundation-sponsored Gray Areas Project.

December 28, 1961   The Ford Foundation announces the grant of funding to the city of Oakland in its efforts to combat juvenile delinquency and street crime—the first of six such grants under the Gray Areas Project, a further precursor to the War on Poverty.

November 19, 1963   Three days before his assassination in Dallas, Texas, President Kennedy appoints Walter Heller, chair of the president's Council of Economic Advisors, to prepare anti-poverty legislation for the next session of Congress.

January 8, 1964   President Lyndon Johnson, in his first annual State of the Union message to Congress, announces his commitment to an "unconditional War on Poverty." (Later that year, in an address to the graduating class at the University of Michigan, he outlines his vision of a "Great Society.")

July 2, 1964   Johnson signs the Civil Rights Bill of 1964.

July 18, 1964   Riots erupt in New York City's Harlem. These and subsequent riots in cities like Detroit, Newark, and Los Angeles (Watts) help sow the seeds of an eventual white backlash against the War on Poverty and similar programs.

August 20, 1964   Johnson signs the Economic Opportunity Act of 1964, providing funding for the Job Corps youth training program, the Community Action Program, and others.

November 25, 1964 Sargent Shriver, director of the newly formed Office of Economic Opportunity (OEO), announces funding for various War on Poverty projects.

April 11, 1965 The Elementary and Secondary Education Act is signed into law, providing funding for compensatory education for low-income students.

June 2, 1965 U.S. mayors express concern about the social protest activity sponsored by some of the more militant community action agencies and request that the War on Poverty be more closely administered by city governments and not by autonomous agencies. Vice President Hubert Humphrey meets with Chicago's Mayor Richard Daley and strives to attain a workable compromise solution.

July 30, 1965 Johnson signs the Medicare Bill into law. Of special significance to civil rights is the Medicaid portion of the bill, which provides health care to low-income people who could not afford it otherwise.

October 18, 1967 The Green Amendment is approved. Introduced by Congresswoman Edith Green, the amendment is designed to reduce the impact of militant protest activities originating in various War on Poverty-related Community Action Program agencies by transferring jurisdiction over the programs from independent agencies to local governments. As a compromise, the amendment also provides an extension of the charter of the Office of Economic Opportunity for an additional two years. Its existence would eventually be prolonged up to the end of 1974.

May 2, 1968 Several weeks after the assassination of Dr. Martin Luther King, Jr., the Poor People's Campaign, under the leadership of Reverend Ralph Abernathy, sets up its Resurrection City camp in the vicinity of the Washington Monument in the nation's capital. Poor weather and the active opposition of the Johnson administration (perhaps motivated by the escalating anti-war protest, which had become interwoven with civil rights activism) contribute to the failure of Abernathy's campaign.

December 20, 1974 Congress sends legislation to President Gerald Ford authorizing the phase-out of the Office of Economic Opportunity, effectively ending the War on Poverty. President Richard Nixon in 1973 had attempted to dismantle the OEO, but Congress had refused to go along, though Nixon subsequently managed

to transfer many OEO programs to other departments and to down-size the organization before the Watergate investigation rendered him politically powerless.

Noel A. Cazenave

Warren, Earl

(1891–1974), Chief Justice of the United States.

Born in Los Angeles and raised in Bakersfield, California, Earl Warren graduated with a law degree from the University of California before going on to serve as state attorney general, California's only thrice-elected governor, Chief Justice of the United States, and chair of the Warren Commission, which investigated the assassination of President John F. KENNEDY.

Warren was born in 1891 to Methias (Matt) and Chrystal Hernlund Warren, who had both immigrated as children to the United States from Norway and Sweden, respectively. Young Earl Warren, a lackluster student, earned an undergraduate degree in political science in 1912 and a law degree in 1914. He worked first as a junior lawyer for an oil company, then for a private law firm, before joining the U.S. Army in August 1917

Supreme Court Chief Justice Earl Warren. (Library of Congress)

and serving briefly during World War I. After his discharge in December 1918, Warren resumed his career as an attorney in northern California before serving as an assistant attorney for the City of Oakland; he soon became an assistant district attorney for Alameda County and, later, district attorney. In 1938, Californians elected Warren to serve as the state's attorney general. In this capacity Warren supported President Franklin D. Roosevelt's February 1942 Executive Order 9066, calling for the evacuation and internment of Japanese Americans—a decision that he later regretted (see Japanese American Internment Cases). That same year, Warren was elected as a moderate Republican to the first of three terms he would serve as governor of California (1942–1953). As governor, Warren supported a bill for a payroll-tax supported health insurance program for California workers and their families as well as a State Fair Employment Practices Bill; both of these were defeated by the Republican-dominated legislature. Governor Warren was successful in getting other legislation passed, however, such as a gasoline tax to improve public highways and construct freeways. He also directed an appropriation of funds to support an array of social programs and increased financial support for the University of California.

In 1948 Warren ran for vice-president as Thomas E. Dewey's running mate and in 1952 Warren campaigned for the presidency. In 1953 President Dwight D. Eisenhower appointed Warren to serve as the fourteenth Chief Justice of the United States (1953–1969). What became known as the "Warren Court" is renowned for its role in protecting and expanding civil rights and civil liberties. Warren was the driving force in guiding the High Court toward its liberal decisions. As a result, he was admired and respected by liberals but hated by many conservatives, who believed that he and his court were eroding states' rights. The rulings of the Warren Court prompted the conservative Eisenhower to remark that appointing Warren to the Supreme Court was "my biggest damn-fool mistake." During his tenure as Chief Justice, Warren also served as chairman of the Warren Commission, which investigated the Kennedy assassination.

Perhaps the most famous Warren Court decision was one of its earliest: *Brown v. Board of Education of Topeka, Kansas* (1954). (See Brown v. Board of Education.) The *Brown* case challenged the doctrine of Jim Crow segregation prevalent in the American South, which had been supported by the Supreme Court's earlier ruling in Plessy v. Ferguson (1896). The Court's unanimous 1954 decision rejected *Plessy* and postulated that segregated schools were a violation of the Fourteenth Amendment's equal-protection clause. On May 17, 1954, Earl Warren himself read the famous verdict. The ruling sparked protests from conservatives throughout the South. The Court, however, provided little direction on implementation of the law, allowing in 1955 that desegregation should proceed "with all deliberate speed."

Other Warren Court rulings prompted criticisms of the Court and accusations that Warren aided and abetted communists. In a series of cases between 1955 and 1957 in which communism and communists were an issue, the Court protected individual rights while defining the limits that Congress and state legislatures had in investigating individuals. Later landmark cases included *Mapp v. Ohio* (1961), which concluded that evidence seized unlawfully could not be used against a defendant; *Baker v. Carr* (1962), a reapportionment case that had a far-reaching effect on how voter representation was determined; *Engel v. Vitale* (1962), which affirmed the separation of church and state by holding that compulsory prayer and reading of the Bible in public schools were unconstitutional; *Gideon v. Wainwright* (1963), which ruled that defendants were entitled to legal counsel regardless of whether they could afford an attorney; *Escobedo v. Illinois* (1964), which further expanded the rights of the accused by ruling that confessions extracted without due process were not admissible in court. All of these rulings prompted protests from conservatives nationwide.

Miranda v. Arizona (1966) was yet another controversial case. This landmark case further defined and protected the rights of the accused. Ernesto Miranda, a Mexican American, had been accused of kidnap and rape. While in police custody, Miranda signed a confession which also stated that he fully understood his legal rights. Miranda's attorney, however, argued that his client had not been informed of his rights, including the right under the Fifth Amendment to not be compelled to incriminate oneself. In the majority opinion, delivered by Warren, the High Court overturned Miranda's conviction and explained that the accused must be informed of their rights—including the right to remain silent—immediately after being apprehended and must be allowed to speak with a lawyer before police questioning. *Katz v. United States* (1968) reversed the 1928 decision of *Olmstead v. United States*; the Court ruled that evidence obtained through wiretapping or other forms of electronic eavesdropping was not admissible in court unless authorized by a prior warrant. This ruling as well as those in *Escobedo* and *Miranda* prompted law-enforcement officers across the country to charge that the Warren Court's decisions "handcuffed" police and "coddled" criminals.

Following his retirement from the Supreme Court in 1969, Warren remained an activist and traveled around the world and throughout the United States speaking before various groups and organizations. He died in 1974 in Washington, D.C., of cardiac arrest.

BIBLIOGRAPHY

Cray, Ed. *Chief Justice: A Biography of Earl Warren.* 1997.

Katcher, Leo. *Earl Warren: A Political Biography.* 1967.

Pollack, Earl Warren: *The Man Who Challenged America.* 1979.

Schwartz, Bernard. *Super Chief: Earl Warren and His Supreme Court.* 1982.

Earl Warren Oral History Project. Bancroft Library. University of California at Berkeley.

Alicia E. Rodriquez

War Resisters League

The War Resisters League (WRL) was formed in 1923 by pacifists and socialists (see CONSCIENTIOUS OBJECTION; PACIFISM; SOCIALIST PARTY) who abhorred the attacks on critics of U.S. foreign policy during WORLD WAR I (1914–1918). Many of those who had protested U.S. involvement in that war were intimidated, beaten, and even murdered at the hands of anti-labor and anti-immigrant mobs. Far from protecting the victims of this xenophobic reign of terror, the Woodrow Wilson Administration (1913–1920) used its authority to clamp down on dissidents and on draft resisters. The Espionage Act (1917) and the Sedition Act (1918) were designed to stamp out dissent. The federal government had helped shape an intolerant public culture of "100 percent Americanism" and now stripped those who held unpopular beliefs of their main defense, the First Amendment right of free speech.

The entire political establishment seemed to have forgotten the BILL OF RIGHTS. Even the noted progressive Supreme Court Justice Oliver Wendell Holmes ruled (in upholding the Espionage Act) that Congress could limit free speech in times of war. Socialists, populists, pacifists, advocates of the WOMAN SUFFRAGE MOVEMENT, isolationists, and the radical wing of the trade union movement were all vulnerable if criticism of the government could be suspended. Socialist Party leader Eugene Debs was sentenced to ten years in prison for making a speech in favor of socialism and against the war. The legal struggle against this repressive atmosphere proceeded under the leadership of the AMERICAN CIVIL LIBERTIES UNION (ACLU), formed in 1917. The War Resisters League eventually took a different approach.

The War Resisters League preached pacifism during both WORLD WAR II (1941–1945) and the KOREAN WAR (1950–1953). Its members resisted the draft and many were imprisoned. By the time of the VIETNAM WAR (1965–1973), which the War Resisters League was among the first organizations to denounce, the group had adopted more confrontational tactics. Its leadership had absorbed the philosophy of nonviolent resistance preached by the leader of the struggle to free India from British colonial rule during the 1940s, Mohandas GANDHI. Gandhi's message resonated with the nineteenth-century teachings of nonviolent protest found in the writings of Henry David Thoreau. This lesson was underscored by the campaigns of the U.S. civil rights movement and by Martin Luther KING, JR.'s message of the transforming power of nonviolent protest undertaken in a spirit of brotherly love. During the Vietnam War, the League organized anti-war rallies, burned draft cards, and aided draft resisters.

In the years after the Vietnam War, the War Resisters League continued the struggle for peace. The group protested against U.S. intervention in Latin America during the 1980s. It backed disarmament efforts and gave support to the anti-apartheid movement in South Africa (see ANTI-APARTHEID MOVEMENT for a discussion of the movement in the United States). In the 1990s, the League applauded the end of that authoritarian institution, as well as the end of the COLD WAR. However, it also faced new challenges as conflict arose in Kuwait-Iraq, Somalia, Bosnia-Kossovo, and East Timor.

BIBLIOGRAPHY

DiCanio, Margaret B. "War Resisters League (WRL)." *Encyclopedia of Activism, 1960 to the Present.* 1998.

Isserman, Maurice. "The Irony of American Pacifism." *Peace and Change 11, no. 3.* (1989): 47–65.

Murphy, Paul L. *World War I and the Origin of Civil Liberties in the United States.* 1979.

David R. Riddle

Warrior, Clyde

(1939–1968), Native American activist.

Clyde Warrior was an activist on behalf of Indian rights and a founder in 1961 of the NATIONAL INDIAN YOUTH COUNCIL (NIYC). Warrior challenged the ideas, methods, and values of traditional tribal groups in their relationships with the mass of Indian people. He was very radical and nationalistic in his proposals for direct action to solve Indian problems. He was born near Ponca City, Oklahoma, in 1939. His grandparents raised him according to traditional Ponca customs. He spoke the native language and as a teenager became an accomplished pow-wow fancy dancer. In July 1965 he married Della Hopper (of the Otoe tribe). They had two daughters. Warrior graduated from Northeastern State University in Tahlequah, Oklahoma, in 1966. During his college years, he became increasingly active in programs for Indians. He took great pride in his heritage and expressed the Indian desire for freedom from the paternalism of the government's termination, relocation, and assimilation policies of the 1950s.

At the American Indian Chicago Conference in June 1961, over four hundred delegates from sixty-five Indian nations met to discuss issues and develop an agenda for presentation to the administration of John F. KENNEDY. Another purpose of the conference, sponsored by the Anthropology Department of the University of Chicago, was to examine the conditions of Indians and update the *Meriam Report* of 1928 (see Henry Roe CLOUD). Clyde Warrior was among the number of young radicals who came representing a rising tide of militancy in the Indian community. The radicals declared their belief in Indians' "inherent right of self-government" and expressed their intention to keep native lands and retain their cultural identities (see also SOVEREIGNTY).

Warrior led a youth caucus that split away from the Chicago Conference. This caucus met at Gallup, New Mexico, in August 1961, drew up a constitution and bylaws, and formed the NATIONAL INDIAN YOUTH COUNCIL. Warrior served as its president. Other founders and officers included Herb Blatchford, Mel Thom, Shirley Hill Witt, Joan Noble, Mary Natani, and Vivian One Feather. They recruited a growing membership estimated at 5,000 by 1964 and published a periodical entitled *ABC: Americans Before Columbus.*

Hundreds of young Indians joined the movement, which organized protests, demonstrations, civil disobedience, and direct action campaigns in the 1960s, marking the beginning of the RED POWER movement. Warrior's leadership gave direction to a growing spirit of self-determination. Many older Native American leaders thought Warrior and NIYC to be extremists. His radical language and behavior in NIYC contrasted sharply with the more moderate approaches espoused by the NATIONAL CONGRESS OF AMERICAN INDIANS. Indeed, he not only criticized white politicians but denounced some older tribal leaders as "Uncle Tomahawks" and "sell-outs to the white establishment."

In the meantime, on August 15, 1962, a delegation from the American Indian Chicago Conference presented the *Declaration of Indian Purpose* to President Kennedy. The conference called for a reversal of the government's termination policies, increased educational opportunities, more economic development programs, better health care, protection of water rights, re-evaluation of the federal Kinzua Dam project, and abolition of the ten regional BUREAU OF INDIAN AFFAIRS offices.

In a 1964 essay, *Which One Are You? Five Types of Young Indians*, Warrior saw the necessity for Indians to reject the images of them created by white society. In order to solve Indian problems, he called for genuine democratic leadership and goals for Indians "based on true Indian philosophy geared to modern times." His radical position and violent language startled many Americans. He predicted conditions in American would worsen: "There are going to be more riots." If reforms did not happen in American society, "then . . . Indians might just smash it, and change it themselves." Warrior wondered how long Indians would tolerate abuse. When would "they start raising hell with their oppressors?" Warrior gave testimony entitled "We Are Not Free" at hearings of the President's National Advisory Commission on Rural Poverty. He outlined Indians' frustrations and hopes about living in America. Warrior reflected, "Our old people felt rich because they were free." But in 1967 Indians were poverty-stricken. As, he stated, "We are poor in spirit because we are not free." According to Warrior, the focus of Indian community improvement programs "must be Indian creations, Indian choices, Indian experiences."

One of Warrior's greatest achievements was assisting Indians in Washington state to protect their tribal fishing rights in March 1964 protests known as "fish-ins." Officials from Washington interfered with Indian TREATY RIGHTS to fish for salmon in their "usual and accustomed places." The federal government did not protect native people. Warrior, NIYC, and local tribal leaders sought to protect native fishing rights guaranteed in treaties with the United States, ensure Indian self-determination, and guarantee cultural survival. NIYC used lobbying techniques, demonstrations, marches, and SIT-INS, but the most effective direct-action method was the "fish-in." Physical confrontations with state and federal officials on the Quillayuate River, continued additional "fish-ins," and follow-up courtroom litigation reaffirmed fishing and tribal rights of the Quileute, Nisqually, Muckleshoot, and other Indian peoples. In 1974, after Warrior's death, Federal District Judge George H. Boldt decided that the Indians not only had a right to fish but a right to half of the annual fish harvest in the state of Washington, a decision upheld by the U.S. Supreme Court in 1978. Warrior's direct-action "fish-in" served to protect and enhance Indian rights.

NIYC not only defied authorities in the 1964 "fish-in" but arranged a protest march on the state capitol at Olympia, Washington, and conducted a meeting of fifty-six Indian nations from across the United States. The council also participated in the African American civil rights movement by joining FREEDOM RIDES, marching with Martin Luther KING, JR., to Montgomery in 1965, and serving as Indian coordinator of the POOR PEOPLE'S CAMPAIGN in 1968.

Warrior suffered from alcohol addiction. He gained much weight, gave up fancy dancing, and developed serious liver problems. Alcohol treatment efforts did not work, his liver failed, and Warrior died in July 1968 at the age of twenty-nine.

BIBLIOGRAPHY

Calloway, Colin G. *First Peoples: A Documentary Survey of American Indian History.* 1999.

Hauptman, Lawrence M. "The Voice of Eastern Indians: The American Indian Chicago Conference of 1961 and the Movement for Federal Recognition." *Proceedings of the American Philosophical Society* 132 (1988): 316–329.

Lurie, Nancy O. "The Voice of the American Indian Chicago Conference." *Current Anthropology* 2 (December 1961): 478–500.

Smith, Paul Chaat, and Robert Allen Warrior. *Like a Hurricane: The Indian Movement from Alcatraz to Wounded Knee.* 1996.

Warrior, Clyde. "We Are Not Free." In *Red Power: The American Indians' Fight for Freedom,* edited by Alvin M. Josephy, Jr., Joane Nagel, and Troy Johnson. 1999.

Warrior, Clyde. "Which One Are You? Five Types of Young Indians." *ABC: Americans Before Columbus* 2, no. 4 (December 1964): 1–3.

Rodger C. Henderson

Washington

U.S. exploration of Washington State began in the late 1700s, with settlement beginning after the 1804 Louisiana Purchase and the Lewis and Clark Expedition. Although initially part of the Oregon Territory, the Washington Territory was created in 1853. The settlement there of minorities was shaped by two factors. First, in 1844, the Oregon Territory forbade slavery but prohibited African Americans from settling in what is now Oregon, so most African-American settlers moved north to what is now Washington State. Further, the Donation Land Law of 1850 permitted only adult white males and their wives to acquire land, barring both Native Americans and other minority immigrants from land acquisition.

Washington is home to two forms of aboriginal culture, Coastal and Plateau Native Americans. Upon becoming Washington's first territorial governor and the Secretary of Indian Affairs in 1853, Gov. Isaac Stevens negotiated treaties. These established reservations that overlapped original settlements and provided "the right of taking fish at all usual and accustomed places . . . in common with all citizens of the Territory." Sporadic armed conflict with Native Americans ended with the war against the Nez Perce in 1877–1879. In the turbulent 1960s and 1970s, the western Washington tribes asserted aboriginal fishing rights under their treaties and sometimes met with violent resistance from state government and citizens. This dispute culminated in the federal court *Boldt* decision, granting Native-American tribes one-half of the catch at traditional sites.

The first new minority settlers to Washington were Asian. Washington Asian history is not monolithic but the story of several groups: Chinese, Japanese, Filipinos, Koreans, and Southeast Asians (Vietnamese, Laotians, and Cambodians). The first Chinese came to Washington from California to relieve labor shortages in the 1880s, but faced significant discrimination and violence as their numbers grew, culminating in the national CHINESE EXCLUSION ACT OF 1882. To replace Chinese labor, both Japanese and Filipino immigration was encouraged in the early 1900s to work in agriculture and the fishing industries. Both groups, however, met with discrimination as their numbers grew. By 1910, the Japanese were the largest racial minority in Washington. In 1919, businessmen in the largest city, Seattle, established the Anti-Japanese League, and many Japanese faced violence or the burning of their farms. In 1921, encouraged by the League, Washington State passed its own Alien Land Law, which made it illegal for noncitizens to own land. The national response soon followed, and Japanese were excluded from immigration into the United States in 1924. Filipinos were still allowed into Washington, however, because the Philippines were a United States territory; but by 1934, with the advent of Philippine independence, Filipinos were also excluded.

The state's most serious violation of Asians' civil rights occurred during World War II, when 13,400 Japanese were evacuated from Washington to internment camps under Presidential Executive Order 9066, issued February 19, 1942. Seventy percent of those removed were United States citizens. Gordon Hirabayashi, a student at the University of Washington, disobeyed the curfew and evacuation order imposed on Japanese and was arrested and convicted in 1942. It took until 1986 for his conviction to be overturned in the United States SUPREME COURT. At the conclusion of WORLD WAR II, the United States Supreme Court ordered the internment camps closed, and each family received $25 and a ticket home. As a result, the Japanese population in Washington plummeted from a high of 14,500 to just under 10,000 people. President Gerald FORD apologized in 1976 and rescinded Executive Order 9066. In the 1980s, the United States Congress backed REPARATIONS for interned Japanese families.

But conditions had improved for all Asian groups in the 1960s. In 1962, Wing Luke was elected to the

Seattle City Council, the first Asian to hold such a post outside of Hawaii. Meanwhile, the IMMIGRATION ACT OF 1965 was passed, and in 1966 the Washington State legislature repealed the Alien Land Law. While the 1973 study of the Asian American Advisory Council showed discrimination in HOUSING and EMPLOYMENT, new Asian groups such as Koreans, Samoans, Vietnamese, Cambodians, and Laotians began to arrive, particularly after the conclusion of the VIETNAM WAR. As of 1999, Asians are the largest minority in Washington State. (See ASIAN-AMERICAN MOVEMENT.)

African Americans first arrived in Washington in the late 1880s as mining strikebreakers. The biggest influx, however, occurred during World War II, when Boeing, a defense contractor, sought workers for its factories. As a result of this influx, African Americans became the largest ethnic group in the state during the 1950s. At the same time, they faced de facto segregated HOUSING and EDUCATION (see SEGREGATION). The 1960s civil rights movement forced state citizens to acknowledge discrimination in a state which had thought itself egalitarian. The civil rights groups in the African-American community now split between those who sought a more confrontational approach and those who preferred to work within the system. In the summer of 1968 there were four nights of riots in Seattle, and both white and black students at both area schools and colleges actively demonstrated. Several housing discrimination SIT-INS during the 1960s culminated in the 1968 Open Housing Ordinance in Seattle. The African-American community also targeted discriminatory labor union practices, particularly in the skilled trades and protective services.

Seattle and the African-American community also faced off over the issue of integrated schools. In 1966, Seattle began a voluntary school transfer program, but many argued that this was not enough and the NATIONAL ASSOCIATION FOR THE ADVANCEMENT OF COLORED PEOPLE (NAACP) filed suit against the city. Facing both the lawsuit and boycotts, the school system agreed to a comprehensive BUSING plan and the NAACP withdrew its suit, making Seattle the largest metropolitan school district in the nation to desegregate without court order. Although challenged by a successful anti-busing initiative, the United States Supreme Court ruled the initiative unconstitutional in 1982. The Seattle School district, however, is now in the process of returning to neighborhood schools. In 1989, the largely white electorate in Seattle elected Norm Rice, an African American, as their mayor. By 1999, African Americans were the third largest ethnic group in the state.

Hispanics began to settle in the agricultural areas of eastern Washington in the 1930s and soon became the largest minority in that part of the state. While welcomed as cheap farm labor, they were excluded from public accommodations. In 1942, farmers backed the "bracero," or worker, program in which Mexican farmworkers were brought to Northwestern American farms. This program continued until 1964 with the support of the Washington congressional delegation. The civil rights struggle for Hispanics has focused on the rights of farmworkers to vote, organize, and secure decent housing. They are now the second largest minority group in the state.

Movements for WOMAN SUFFRAGE began in Washington in the 1850s, and women lost their first legislative effort to acquire voting privileges by only one vote in 1854. After several subsequent attempts, women gained the right to vote in 1910. In 1926, Seattle was the first major city to elect a woman, Bertha Knight Landes, mayor. Women also benefited from World War II labor shortages, and during this time about one-half of the Boeing work force was composed of women. In 1972, the state added an EQUAL RIGHTS AMENDMENT to its constitution.

Finally, many gays and lesbians have found Washington to be a hospitable environment (see GAY AND LESBIAN RIGHTS), noting that in 1975 the state repealed its sodomy statute. In 1973, Seattle included sexual orientation in the list of protections in its employment discrimination law and later, in 1975, in its open housing law. In 1978, the state supreme court upheld the grant of custody to a lesbian couple, although in 1977 the same court had upheld the 1972 firing of an openly gay public school teacher. In 1978, a group called Save Our Moral Ethics attempted to overturn the Seattle ordinances but was unsuccessful.

Washington passed a Law Against Discrimination in 1949 that is the basic framework for civil rights enforcement in the state. It is more generous than the national CIVIL RIGHTS ACT OF 1964, covering more groups than the federal statute. Many local governments, too, have passed civil rights ordinances that are more generous than the state law. In 1969, state and local governments began minority contracting programs, and in 1974 the state issued its first formal AFFIRMATIVE ACTION report on state employment; but in 1998 state voters approved Initiative 200, which would prohibit affirmative action: "The state shall not discriminate against, or grant preferential treatment to, any individual or group on the basis of race, sex, color, ethnicity or national origin."

BIBLIOGRAPHY

Blair, Karen. *Women in Pacific Northwest History: An Anthology.* 1988.

Chin, Art. *Golden Tassels: A History of the Chinese in Washington, 1857–1977.* 1977.

Commission on the Causes and Prevention of Civil Disorder. *Race and Violence in Washington State: A Report of the Commission on the Causes and Prevention of Civil Disorder.* 1969.

Cordova, Fred. *Filipinos: Forgotten Asian Americans, 1763–1963.* 1983.

Gould, William B. "The Seattle Building Trades Order: The First Comprehensive Relief Against Employment Discrimination in the Construction Industry." *Stanford Law Review* 26 (1974): 779–813.

Halseth and Bruce Glasrud, eds. *The Northwest Mosaic: Minority Conflicts in Pacific Northwest History.* 1977.

Hildebrand, Lorraine. *Straw Hats, Sandals and Steel: The Chinese in Washington State.* 1977.

Mumford, Esther H. *Seattle's Black Victorians, 1852–1901.* 1980.

Pelz, Ruth. *The Washington Story: A History of Our State.* Rev. ed., 1993.

Ruby, Robert H., and John A. Brown. *Indians of the Pacific Northwest: A History.* 1981.

Sale, Roger. *Seattle: Past to Present.* 1976.

Takami, David A. *Divided Destiny: A History of Japanese Americans in Seattle.* 1998.

Taylor, Quintard. *A History of Blacks in the Pacific Northwest: 1788–1970.* Ph.D. dissertation, 1977.

Taylor, Quintard. *The Forging of a Black Community: Seattle's Central District from 1870 through the Civil Rights Era.* 1994.

Washington State Commission on Asian American Affairs. *Ten Years Later: A Public Hearing on the Issues Impacting Washington State's Asian Pacific Americans in the 1980's.* 1983.

White, Sid, and S. E. Solberg, eds. *Peoples of Washington: Perspectives on Cultural Diversity.* 1989.

Yoshitomi, Joan, et al. *Asians in the Northwest: An Annotated Bibliography.* 1978.

Lea B. Vaughn

Booker T. Washington in his study. (CORBIS/Bettmann)

Washington, Booker T.

(1856–1915), educator.

Booker Taliaferro Washington was born in April 1856 on a plantation located in Franklin County, Virginia. His mother served as a cook in the main house, while his father is believed to have been a local white man. After the end of the Civil War, Washington and his family relocated to Malden, a rough-and-tumble town in West Virginia, where Washington Ferguson, his black stepfather, was employed as a salt miner. By all accounts, Washington Ferguson was a shiftless, untrustworthy man who saw his children mainly as a source of income. It was while working in the mines himself that Booker T. Washington was first presented with an opportunity to receive something resembling a formal education, when a black Civil War veteran set up a primary school for the miners' children. Washington proved to be a quick study, and developed a voracious appetite for all manner of learning, a hunger he was able to sate partially by taking a job as a houseboy for a local mine owner's wife. His new job provided him with a chance not only to escape the drudgery of the salt mine but also gave him access to his employer's library—a benefit of inestimable value.

In 1872 Washington entered the Hampton Normal and Agricultural Institute in Virginia. While there, he made a favorable impression on the school's founder, Samuel C. Armstrong, a former Union general and lifelong friend to freed blacks. The feeling was mutual, and it was the effect this man had on the young scholar that proved to be decisive in the latter's decision to devote his life to improving the condition of his race. Graduating in 1875, he returned to Malden with the intent of opening the region's first sustained school for blacks—a challenge he relished. Two years later, he left Malden and traveled to Washington, D.C., to study at Wayland Seminary. Although Washington's time at Wayland was brief, it had a profound impact on the course of his life, for it was while he was enrolled there that he first began to recognize what he believed was the shortsightedness of those "colored schools" that emphasized a classical curriculum at the expense of more practical subject matter. An education in the classics, Washington believed, provided little of real merit when its graduates were forced to confront the mundane issues of sustaining oneself and one's family. In his estimation, many of these would-be scholars were often intellectual hothouse flowers, profoundly unsuited for life outside academia.

In 1879 Washington received an invitation from Armstrong to speak at Hampton's commencement. His address was so well received that it led to a job offer from the Institute. In the fall of that year, he took charge of the school's Indian education program. A difficult task, he nonetheless proved to be a capable administrator; and he also found time to create a night school for poor blacks, in which they could trade labor for tuition, then attend full-time once they had accumulated adequate funds with which to see them through the remainder of their program. In 1881, Armstrong inquired whether or not Washington might be interested in helping to start an all-black practical school in Tuskegee, Alabama. He soon agreed, and was hired, largely due to the strong recommendation he had received from Armstrong. It was soon apparent, however, that the school existed in name only; Washington would literally have to build it from the ground up. This he began by purchasing a run-down plantation, then using the newly formed Institute's students to construct the few facilities he needed to commence this noble effort.

From the outset, Washington's ambition was to raise up an entire race, not just to teach a few. He discerned three economic objectives that the Institute would work to achieve. First, he wanted to educate blacks on the importance of owning their own land or means of livelihood. Second, he strove to impart to them the need to be able to sustain themselves in a trade. Finally, Washington stressed the importance of inculcating some sense of the importance of keeping ahead of debt, usually by virtue of farming or laboring economically. It was these values that Washington would reiterate when he spoke in the U.S. Congress on behalf of a soon-to-be grant to help fund Atlanta's 1895 Cotton Exposition. He hammered home his belief that industry, skill, property, economy, intelligence, and character would act in unison not only to raise up blacks but the whole of society. It was the same message he used in front of a racially mixed audience in an address he gave when the Exposition opened later that year, in which he indicated to many that the time had indeed come for the African American to raise himself up through education and industry.

Washington's achievements went far beyond the Tuskegee Institute. In 1895 he helped to found the NATIONAL ASSOCIATION OF COLORED WOMEN, and he maintained a co-ed policy at Tuskegee from day one. In 1900 he aided in the formation of the National Negro Business League, and he helped create the Southern Education Board in 1901. This last body would prove to be of great importance because it acted as a funnel for the donations and grants that sustained both Tuskegee and Hampton. Washington also managed to function as an ad hoc advisor on racial issues to the Roosevelt and Taft administrations.

Despite his growing notoriety as a public speaker, Washington would gain his greatest acclaim with the publication of his book *Up From Slavery* in 1901. He would continue to write extensively about his views on race in works like *The Story of the Negro* and *The Man Farthest Down*. He never wavered from the position that blacks should strive for economic equality only, and should forego social and physical intermingling—a view that garnered him strong criticism from W. E. B. Du Bois and many others.

In his later years, Washington would devote much of his time to lecturing and fund-raising, but he still managed to carry through to fruition several noteworthy social-uplift efforts. One of these was a mobile agricultural exhibition that traveled throughout the rural South demonstrating the greater yields and larger livestock made possible by new agricultural techniques. He also marshaled public support for a "Negro Health Improvement Week," which educated blacks in nutrition, sanitation, and a host of other positive health practices. Both programs were so successful that they were incorporated into federal relief agencies, and they expanded their audience to include poor whites.

Recognizing that African Americans did not have the resources necessary to create an effective network of local schools in the South, he sought to interest Northern philanthropists in the endeavor. Eventually, he succeeded in getting philanthropist Julius Rosenwald to pledge matching funds to the construction of a series of primary schools for blacks, a commitment that would lead to the building of over five thousand schools during the following four decades (see Education). Washington carried his message of economic equality through to the very end of his life, which came when he fell ill on a speaking engagement in November 1915. He returned home to his beloved Tuskegee, where he died, surrounded by the institute he had created.

Despite all that he achieved, Booker T. Washington remains a controversial figure, mainly because he did not embrace a program of social equality, preferring instead to emphasize immediate economic gains in the hope that they could be translated into long-term social ones. Nevertheless, even Washington's critics admitted that his achievements were considerable. He may not have gone as far as some might have liked, but the inroads made by Washington provided the framework on which subsequent gains could be made. What is more, his Tuskegee Institute created a forum from which blacks could emerge better able to deal with both life and racism than their predecessors.

BIBLIOGRAPHY

Harlan, Louis R. *Booker T. Washington: The Making of a Black Leader, 1856–1901.* 1972.

Harlan, Louis R. *Booker T. Washington: The Wizard of Tuskegee, 1901–1915.* 1983.

Washington, Booker T. *The Future of the American Negro.* 1900.

Washington, Booker T. *Up From Slavery.* 1901.

Washington, Booker T. *Tuskegee and Its People.* 1905.

Washington, Booker T. *The Story of the Negro,* 2 vols. 1909.

Washington, Booker T. *The Man Farthest Down.* 1912.

Robert W. Nill

Washington, D.C.

See District of Columbia

Watts Uprising

At least thirty-four people died in Los Angeles during the Watts uprising of August 1965; a thousand more were injured, and four thousand arrested. Property damage was estimated at $200 million in the 46.5-square-mile zone (larger than Manhattan or San Francisco), where approximately thirty-five thousand adults participated directly and actively, and seventy-two thousand had an involvement of lesser intensity. On hand to oppose them were sixteen thousand National Guard, Los Angeles Police Department, highway patrol, and other law enforcement officers; fewer military personnel were used that same year to subdue Santo Domingo.

Participants were overwhelmingly African American, and the events were sparked by an incident of police brutality on one of the hottest days of the year, August 11. Order was not restored until August 18.

The black population in Southern California was mostly a post–WORLD WAR II phenomenon; streaming into Los Angeles from Texas, Louisiana, and Oklahoma, these migrants encountered a fierce and persistent HOUSING discrimination that locked them into "ghettos" such as Watts, where residences were mostly substandard. A high unemployment rate in this area was buoyed by the fact that the sprawling metropolis that was Los Angeles did not have an adequate public transportation system to carry those in Watts to jobs that at times were scores of miles away.

The tumultuous events that were centered in Watts came shortly after the passage of the VOTING RIGHTS ACT OF 1965, which increased the number of blacks voting in the Deep South. These newly minted voters

The Watts riots in progress in Los Angeles, California. A sign in the middle of the street reads, "Turn left or get shot." (UPI/CORBIS-Bettmann)

were widely expected to vote for the DEMOCRATIC
PARTY of incumbent President Lyndon B. JOHNSON;
however, as the image of meek, nonviolent blacks pas-
sively resisting JIM CROW was replaced by the image
of "rioting" blacks in the streets, a "white backlash"
against racial equality was fomented: this led to electoral gains for the REPUBLICAN PARTY and the election
in 1966 of their candidate for governor of California,
Ronald W. REAGAN.

In the aftermath of the rebellion, a number of new
ideological trends were created or accelerated in black
Los Angeles. There was "cultural nationalism," as symbolized by Maulana Ron Karenga, which stressed the
issue of identity, taking on West African names, adopting various forms of African dress, and so on. There
was also the form of nationalism symbolized by the
BLACK PANTHER PARTY, which was influenced by the
post–Nation of Islam MALCOLM X and emphasized
the fight against police brutality. The NATION OF ISLAM
itself also attained higher levels of popularity in black
Los Angeles after 1965. On the other hand, the NA-
TIONAL ASSOCIATION FOR THE ADVANCEMENT OF COL-
ORED PEOPLE, which had been derided on all sides for
losing touch with the constituency it was sworn to represent, maintained a bastion of middle-class influence
dominated at the leadership level by doctors, dentists,
and attorneys.

The Johnson administration appointed a committee headed by former Central Intelligence Agency
Director John McCone (assisted by future Secretary
of State Warren Christopher) to investigate the causes
of the unrest. Unsurprisingly, police brutality, inadequate housing, unemployment, and lack of transportation were singled out as factors. However, the
recommendations from the McCone Commission
were rather tame and mild, and as the century unfolded "South Central Los Angeles" became a national
symbol of urban decay. Thus, when this area erupted
again in 1992 in the wake of the failure to convict police officers captured on videotape beating black motorist Rodney King, long-time watchers of Watts were
not surprised.

BIBLIOGRAPHY

Horne, Gerald. *Fire This Time: The Watts Uprising and the
1960s.* 1995.

Gerald Horne

Weaver, Robert Clifton

(1907–1997), economist.

Adviser on race relations in the Franklin ROOSEVELT
administration and first African-American cabinet
member (Secretary of Housing and Urban Develop-

*Robert C. Weaver on February 2, 1966, while he was
serving as Secretary of Housing and Development
under President Lyndon B. Johnson.* (AP/Wide
World Photos)

ment), Robert Weaver was born in Washington, D.C.
Earning a scholarship to Harvard University, where he
befriended Ralph BUNCHE and William H. HASTIE.
Weaver earned all three of his degrees in economics
at Harvard. The last of these, a Ph.D., was awarded to
him in 1934.

In 1933 Clark H. FOREMAN, race relations adviser
to Secretary of the Interior Harold L. ICKES, selected
Weaver as his assistant. Two years later Weaver replaced Foreman as Ickes' adviser. In 1937 Weaver assumed a similar position as adviser on race relations
in the new Housing Authority. The Roosevelt administration was making subtle overtures to blacks in an
effort to reverse the policies of previous Republican
and Democratic administrations (see REPUBLICAN
PARTY and DEMOCRATIC PARTY). (It was President
Woodrow Wilson who had segregated the U.S. government's departments and limited blacks to marginal
jobs.)

During World War II, Robert Weaver worked for
several government agencies, primarily as an expert
on black labor and race relations. He and other blacks
opposed a suggestion that the FDR administration institute a Bureau of Negro Affairs. As a high-ranking

official of the Roosevelt government, Weaver was a key member of the "Black Cabinet," an informal group of African Americans who advised the administration on race questions and who worked to end racial discrimination in the federal government. Weaver left the Roosevelt administration before the end of the war and served in several political and administrative positions in Chicago. During this time he wrote two important monographs on racial discrimination: *Negro Labor: A National Problem* (1946) and *The Negro Ghetto* (1948).

In 1955 New York Governor Averell Harriman appointed Weaver to head the rent commission, a cabinet-level post. He held this post until he was summoned back to Washington by President John F. KENNEDY, who named him director of the U.S. Housing and Home Finance Agency. President Kennedy had planned to establish a department of Housing and Urban Development (HUD), but the Southern members of Congress opposed both elevating the agency to cabinet rank and Weaver to head it (see HOUSING). Weaver's support of integrated housing was anathema to Southern congressmen. President Lyndon JOHNSON was able to overcome Southern opposition and in 1966 established HUD as a cabinet-level department, appointing Weaver as its first secretary and the first African American to hold a cabinet position. Many of the imaginative programs Weaver backed were not realized during his administration of HUD, due to the nation's increasing involvement in the VIETNAM WAR and increasing war expenditure. In 1969, Weaver left government service for the presidency of Baruch College.

Robert Weaver was a consummate bureaucrat who in quiet ways promoted the welfare of African Americans and the poor. His splendid monographs argued convincingly for equitable pay and hiring practices for all Americans, regardless of color. He understood the complexity of urban living as it pertained to blacks and the poor. Perhaps Weaver's greatest accomplishment was his work in the 1930s, when he acted as an ombudsman for all African Americans.

BIBLIOGRAPHY

Kirby, John. *Black Americans in the Roosevelt Era.* 1980.
Weiss, Nancy J. *Farewell to the Party of Lincoln.* 1983.
Wolters, Raymond. *Negroes and the Great Depression.* 1970.

Claude Hargrove

Weber, Frederick Palmer

(1914–1986), civil rights activist and political organizer.

Palmer Weber was born in the tidewater town of Smithfield, Virginia. As a young boy, while being

treated for tuberculosis at the Blue Ridge Sanitorium, he became a dedicated student of philosophy, economics, and politics. After enrolling at the University of Virginia in 1931, he became a leading organizer of the Depression-era student movement that had emerged on campuses throughout the nation.

Race became a dominant factor in Weber's analysis of the South's economic and political structure and a defining element in his development as an activist and organizer. He attacked lynching in the pages of Virginia's student newspaper, and supported the campaign for federal ANTI-LYNCHING legislation. Weber raised support for the Scottsboro defendants (see SCOTTSBORO CASE) and supported the application efforts of Alice Jackson, a black woman who sought admission to the University of Virginia, as part of the NAACP's early campaign to equalize educational opportunities. He worked to organize the university's hospital and cafeteria workers, most of whom were black. In 1935 Weber, along with James JACKSON, led an interracial delegation of students to the state house in Richmond to submit a bill calling for an end to school segregation.

In 1940, after completing a Ph.D. in philosophy, Weber went to Washington, D.C., and joined the staff of the Tolan House Committee on Interstate Migration. He quickly became acquainted with liberal legislators and labor leaders, black government officials and activists, and Southern progressives such as Virginia DURR and Clark FOREMAN. Weber worked on several different government committees, including Senator Claude Pepper's Senate Subcommittee on Health and Education, and on a variety of issues concerning jobs, wartime MIGRATION, and fair EMPLOYMENT, as well as the expansion of VOTING RIGHTS. Weber joined forces with Durr in the campaign for legislation to abolish the poll tax and to secure a bill that would streamline voting requirements for soldiers serving overseas. Durr recalled, "Palmer had a brilliant ability to take hold of something, organize it, and set it in motion."

At the end of 1943, Weber moved to New York and joined the staff of the newly formed CIO Political Action Committee (CIO-PAC) as research director. He focused most of his attention on the South and on the effort to build on inroads that had been made by CIO unions (see AFL-CIO), NAACP branches, and groups like the SOUTHERN CONFERENCE FOR HUMAN WELFARE. Weber was most concerned with increasing black voter registration in the South and with expanding black and white cooperation in the political arena. The Supreme Court's 1944 ruling in SMITH V. ALLWRIGHT, overturning the white primary in the South, marked a major watershed—one which Weber was fully prepared to take advantage of. He accompanied Mary McLeod BETHUNE on a ten-day tour of major

Southern cities, a tour that included public rallies to get out the vote and private meetings with local black leaders. During the 1946 primary season, Weber worked closely with black organizers such as Luther Porter JACKSON, Ella BAKER, and Henry Lee Moon, and with NAACP branch leaders throughout the South. That year, the number of registered black voters in the South increased more than threefold over 1940 figures, making the black vote a factor in several key elections. In 1946, Weber was elected to the NAACP's national board, becoming the first Southern white man to serve on it.

In a speech to CIO members in SOUTH CAROLINA in 1946, Weber emphasized the importance of the CIO's no-discrimination policy and warned that the CIO was "doomed if the Negro and white workers fail to come to sympathetic understanding." Yet, after the war, CIO leadership was increasingly inclined to accommodate white RACISM in the effort to increase union membership. With the start of the COLD WAR, the CIO national leadership took a hard line against independent political action, further bolstering a conservative, top-down approach to organizing. As a result, in 1948, Weber resigned from the CIO-PAC and joined Henry Wallace's PROGRESSIVE PARTY as codirector of the Southern campaign.

Weber and codirector Louis BURNHAM organized Wallace's Southern campaign as "a head-on attack against the segregation system." They drew on the network of civil rights activists and community leaders who had come together around the South during the 1930s and 1940s. Weber and Burham, both veterans of the student movement of the 1930s, enlisted student volunteers as the backbone of the Southern campaign. College students, many of whom were veterans, helped organize Southern supporters and register voters. Northern students traveled South during the summer to help with the petition drive to get Wallace on the ballot and to aid with voter registration. Blacks and women participated in all phases of the campaign and sometimes launched their own campaign. In Virginia, for example, Jerry Gilliam, a black postal worker and NAACP activist, ran for the U.S. Congress from Norfolk and Virginia Durr challenged Harry BYRD for his seat in the U.S. Senate. Black newspaper publisher Larkin Marshall ran for the U.S. Senate from Georgia. The high point of the campaign came that fall, when Henry Wallace undertook a weeklong campaign tour from Virginia to Mississippi and refused to address segregated audiences. Wallace's historic challenge to racial segregation, and the violence that met it, captured national headlines.

In the aftermath of the election, and Wallace's dismal showing at the polls, Weber cautioned against defeatism and isolation. He urged young volunteers to return to the DEMOCRATIC PARTY and work in the primaries and with the NAACP. He reminded them that they were participating in a broad, ongoing effort to open up the electoral process to African Americans in the South, one that was essential "to truly realizing democracy and bringing about progressive change."

Association with the Progressive Party, however, tarred one as a "fellow traveler" of the COMMUNIST PARTY, and Weber himself faced a difficult time as Cold War repression heightened. With limited opportunities, he carved out a position as an investment analyst in New York. While he remained active on the NAACP board, Weber also devoted much of his energy to the defense of CIVIL LIBERTIES. In 1951, he helped establish the National Emergency Civil Liberties Committee, a New York–based organization whose defendants ranged from public school teachers fired by local school districts for their political affiliations to Paul ROBESON and others whose passports had been confiscated by the U.S. State Department.

By the 1960s Weber had established himself as a business analyst and investment adviser in New York. An active opponent of the war in VIETNAM, he helped organize Businessmen Against the War in Vietnam, and he continued to support civil rights activities, particularly in the area of voting rights, working with the NAACP, the AMERICAN CIVIL LIBERTIES UNION (ACLU), and the SOUTHERN REGIONAL COUNCIL. During the last years of his life he served on the advisory board of the University of Virginia's Carter G. Woodson Institute for African and African American Studies and helped establish the Woodson Institute's Center for the Study of Civil Rights in 1985.

BIBLIOGRAPHY

Sullivan, Patricia. *Days of Hope: Race and Democracy in the New Deal Era.* 1996.

Weber, Palmer. "The Negro Vote in the South." In *Virginia Spectator* (November 1938).

Patricia Sullivan

Webster, Milton P.

(1887–1965), union official.

Milton P. Webster served as the most significant organizer and administrator for A. Philip RANDOLPH and the BROTHERHOOD OF SLEEPING CAR PORTERS' (BSCP) struggle for union recognition from 1925 to 1937. Moreover, Webster fought for more than four decades to correct inequities for all black workers.

Born in Clarksville, Tennessee, in 1887, Webster was recognized early on for his outward criticism against racial injustice. His outspokenness and candor eventually led to his being expelled from Clarksville. After leaving the city, Webster moved to Chicago, where he worked as a Pullman porter for the next twenty years. Webster was fired from this job for his attempts to organize black porters and enlist them in the Railroad Men's Benevolent Association. By this time, his courage, conviction, and experience had earned him the respect of Chicago's African Americans and this resulted in his emergence as the REPUBLICAN PARTY leader of Chicago's Sixth Ward. Thus, when Randolph launched his 1925 campaign for the BSCP union in Chicago, it was recommended that he solicit the advice and support of Webster. Randolph followed this suggestion and Webster became one of the four founding officers of the BSCP and the leader of the union's Chicago division.

Although Webster and Randolph did not always agree on the direction in which to take the BSCP, Webster's organizational and administrative expertise, combined with Randolph's oratory skills, served as a mainstay for the organization. Webster's work ethic and commitment to black workers extended to the MARCH ON WASHINGTON MOVEMENT, in which he served as representative for the FAIR EMPLOYMENT PRACTICES COMMITTEE and President FRANKLIN ROOSEVELT's Committee on Fair Employment in the early 1940s. Webster's tireless efforts for black workers continued into the 1950s and 1960s, when he was appointed to the AFL-CIO Civil Rights Committee.

BIBLIOGRAPHY

Anderson, Jervis. *A. Philip Randolph: A Biographical Portrait.* 1972.

Brazeal, Brailsford. *The Brotherhood of Sleeping Car Porters.* 1946.

Harris, William H. *Keeping the Faith: A. Philip Randolph, Milton P. Webster, and the Brotherhood of Sleeping Car Porters, 1925–1937.* 1977.

Pfeffer, Paula. *A. Philip Randolph, Pioneer of the Civil Rights Movement.* 1990.

Russ Wigginton

Wells, Ida B.

(1862–1931), journalist, civil rights activist, anti-lynching crusader.

Ida Bell Wells was born a slave in 1862, became a leading African-American political activist, and is best known for her anti-lynching crusade. Wells was born to slave parents, Elizabeth, a cook, and James, a carpenter, in Holly Springs, MISSISSIPPI. Wells's parents sent her and her siblings to schools sponsored by the BUREAU OF REFUGEES, FREEDMEN, AND ABANDONED LANDS and urged the children to use their education to help build better futures for themselves. Tragedy

Journalist Ida B. Wells, editor and part owner of the Memphis Free Speech. (CORBIS/Bettmann)

struck in 1876, when a yellow fever epidemic took the lives of Wells's parents. At age fourteen, she took charge of her siblings and almost simultaneously began a career as a teacher, teaching at a rural school outside Holly Springs. A year later, she took a teaching position in Memphis, TENNESSEE, where she taught in the city's segregated black schools (see SEGREGATION).

Before long, Wells became a journalist and leading community activist, calling attention to such issues as the inequality of black and white public schools, JIM CROW segregation, and the horrors of LYNCHING. Wells first called attention to Jim Crow segregation particularly as it occurred on railroad cars. In 1884, while on a passenger train in Tennessee, Wells was approached by the conductor, who refused to take her ticket in the "ladies' car," informing Wells that she had to move to the forward "smoker" car. Wells bit the conductor's hand when he tried forcibly to remove her from the car, and she later filed suit against the Chesapeake and Ohio Railroad. A local court ruled in her favor, but the Tennessee Supreme Court reversed the decision in 1887. In a series of articles and editorials in black newspapers, Wells addressed the inequality of Memphis's segregated schools (for which the Memphis School Board subsequently discharged her) and the city's Jim Crow segregation. By 1889 she became co-owner of a Memphis newspaper, *Free Speech and Headlight* (it later became *Free Speech*). In May 1892, she published an editorial denouncing lynching, which marked the beginning of her career as an anti-lynching crusader.

Prior to March 1892, Wells had criticized the lawlessness of lynching but believed that it was rape and other heinous crimes that incited lynchings. Wells now began to change her thinking when whites lynched three of her friends—all of whom had been respected members of Memphis's black community. The men had owned a grocery store that was in competition with a white-owned store, and they had been jailed following an altercation initiated by the white store owner. The men were subsequently dragged from the jail and lynched. On May 21 Wells published an editorial in *Free Speech* denouncing the murders, and criticized the city for not protecting its black citizens from lawless whites. Wells, who left Memphis on business shortly after completing her editorial, learned in New York that in response to her critical editorial the office and equipment of *Free Speech* had been destroyed. Threats kept Wells from returning to Memphis and she did not return to the South for thirty years.

Wells accepted a position as a reporter for the *New York Age*, where she continued to call attention to lynchings and chronicled her forced exile from the South. In addition, Wells published three pamphlets that sought to educate the public about the horrors of lynchings and the circumstances in which they occurred. In her investigations, Wells concluded that lynchings were not in response to the rape of white women—which had been a popular misperception and the most common alleged "justification" for them. Rather, lynchings were the lawless actions of white mobs, rendered out of hatred, jealousy, rage, and a lack of respect for the legal system. Wells's investigations showed also that victims of lynchings were accused of a variety of crimes other than rape: sometimes black men (and even women and children) were lynched without being accused of a crime. For example, a successful black farmer or merchant might draw the ire of whites and become a victim. Wells criticized white mobs as well as Southern municipal, local, and state governments, and law enforcement agencies, for failing to protect blacks and failing to allow those accused of crimes to be judged in a trial rather than by mob law.

In 1895 Wells married Ferdinand L. Barnett in Chicago and went on to raise four children. After 1900, Wells went into "semi-retirement" from her activism; while she periodically addressed lynchings and other reform issues nationally, she devoted her main energies to her family and to issues concerning African Americans in Chicago. She died in Chicago in 1931.

BIBLIOGRAPHY

Duster, Alfreda M., ed. *Crusade for Justice: The Autobiography of Ida B. Wells.* 1970.

Royster, Jacqueline Jones, ed. *Southern Horrors and Other Writings: The Anti-Lynching Campaign of Ida B. Wells, 1892–1900.* 1997.

Sterling, Dorothy. *Black Foremothers: Three Lives.* 1979.

Ida B. Wells Papers. Regenstein Library, University of Chicago.

Alicia E. Rodriquez

"We Shall Overcome"

No song has had a more prominent role in the civil rights movement than "We Shall Overcome." The simple but moving song was transported from the influential HIGHLANDER FOLK SCHOOL in TENNESSEE to the movement for civil rights through student activists who had trained there, and it later was frequently sung during the SIT-INS in Nashville in April 1960. Commonly considered the anthem of that movement, the song was frequently sung during mass meetings, marches, and other protests. It was prominent in such major protest events as the 1961 FREEDOM RIDES throughout the South as well as during demonstrations in Birmingham, Alabama, in 1963 and the March to Selma in 1965 (see ALABAMA). Perhaps the most famous performance was given by folksinger Joan Baez, who led a massive crowd in an emotional version of the song on August 28, 1963, at the MARCH ON WASHINGTON.

Despite its notoriety, the origins of "We Shall Overcome" are unclear. According to Taylor Branch, author of *Parting the Waters: America in the King Years 1954–63*, the song is generally considered to be a modified version of the gospel song "I'll Overcome, Some Day," written by the Rev. C. A. Tindley. Tindley's song is also thought in turn to have been derived in part from the traditional spiritual "No More Auction Block for Me." Branch suggests that Tindley's song was transported to the Highlander Folk School by striking tobacco workers from SOUTH CAROLINA in the mid-1940s. It was refined and modified at Highlander over time, and folksinger Pete Seeger is usually credited with changing the words from "We will overcome" to "We shall overcome." In *"When the Spirit Says Sing!": The Role of Freedom Songs in the Civil Rights Movement*, Kerran L. Sanger identifies Guy Carawan, music director at the Highlander School in the 1950s, as the key figure who helped to give the song its currently recognizable form and taught the song to civil rights activists. Taylor

Branch credits Septima CLARK's direct-action training workshop at Highlander in April 1960 as the vehicle for the song's immediate adoption within the student sit-in protests and subsequently into the mainstream of the civil rights movement. As the most recognized song of the movement, "We Shall Overcome" exemplifies the critical role of MUSIC in that social protest. The song gave strength, courage, and hope to those who sang it during the protests of the 1960s. While the song's verses were often modified and changed to reflect the realities of the immediate situation, the basic sentiment of "We Shall Overcome" has always been that RACISM, racial injustice, and discrimination can be overcome through progressive collective action—"some day," if not today.

BIBLIOGRAPHY

Branch, Taylor. *Parting the Waters: America in the King Years 1954–63.* 1989.

Sanger, Kerran L. *"When the Spirit Says Sing!": The Role of Freedom Songs in the Civil Rights Movement.* 1995.

Joann D. Ball

West Virginia

West Virginia, the Mountain State, has a unique history in the area of civil rights. Along with the universal struggle by minority groups for winning civil rights, which has been mirrored in almost every state in the Union, West Virginia laborers have a proud heritage of working hard to ensure safe working conditions, benefits, and livable wages, particularly in the mining industry. The West Virginia state motto ("*Montana semper liberi,*" or "Mountaineers are always free") is indicative of the area's long-standing commitment to individual rights, a commitment that did not always spill over into the civil rights arena.

Civil rights issues were prevalent in the area now known as West Virginia while it was still a part of Virginia. Interestingly, the Virginia legislature went against the wishes of the Continental Congress and approved the enlistment of slaves into militias during the American Revolution, promising slavemasters $1,000 for each slave and promising the slaves themselves $50 and freedom at the conclusion of hostilities with Great Britain. African-American troops helped defend the colony and posted claims for landowners, including George Washington. Although former slaves played a valuable role in defending Virginia, the fallout from Nat Turner's 1831 rebellion led to restrictions on free blacks as well as on those who were still slaves, which caused many free blacks to go elsewhere.

The Civil War reshaped the lives of whites and blacks in western Virginia. As a Southern state and the home of the capital of the Confederacy, Virginia seceded from the United States in 1861. However, the western delegates to the Virginia legislature objected to secession. This move initiated the drive toward statehood and, in 1863, West Virginia was admitted to the Union, initially as a slave state, although the status of blacks there was somewhat ambiguous, and slavery was only phased out gradually. The black population of West Virginia was considerably smaller than that of Virginia, and West Virginia, although predominantly rural, was not primarily agricultural. Consequently there was somewhat less resistance to the abolishment of slavery in West Virginia than in its neighbor to the east. Following the war, West Virginia ratified the THIRTEENTH AMENDMENT to the Constitution, which abolished slavery in the United States. Within West Virginia, however, opposition to such measures as permitting African Americans to serve as witnesses and on juries in court remained vehement. The balance tipped again when a new state constitution enfranchised African Americans in 1872, but the political wrangling during the contentious debate left black adults without the right to serve on juries and left black children in segregated schools.

The era of RECONSTRUCTION following the Civil War ushered in a period of industrialization around the nation and in West Virginia. West Virginia workers had to make the drastic transition from a largely agrarian economy to the emerging dominance of the bituminous coal industry. The production of coal in West Virginia—particularly in the southern part of the state—increased dramatically between 1885 and 1910. Workers of all kinds came to the state and mined millions of tons of coal. Laborers also laid track for the major railroads, which helped carry coal to the nation, and many stayed behind to work in the mines once their work on the rails was completed.

Mining companies provided work for laborers, and many coal companies actively recruited both black and white workers. Yet working conditions in the mines were intolerable in many cases. The life of a miner was one of Herculean workdays, dangerously unhealthy work surroundings, and low wages, and the miner was at the complete mercy of his employer. Efforts to organize workers at first met with employer opposition, factionalism among the organizers, and anti-union violence (see UNIONS). On a national scale, the United Mine Workers of America formed in 1890. Under the leadership of John Mitchell, the union called several strikes to demand improved working conditions and higher wages. These strikes proved effective, including one in Colorado in 1902 that resulted in coal shortages in large Eastern cities. As summer turned into fall that year, the threat of no coal in the winter caused much concern, and President

Theodore Roosevelt had to intervene to settle the strike in favor of the workers in order to assure a warm winter for those who could obtain coal.

Though the efforts of the United Mine Workers were successful in a few states, the union's attempts to organize often met with violent recriminations from the coal companies and the local West Virginian police forces. In the spring of 1920, workers clashed with Baldwin–Felts Company forces in Matewan, West Virginia, when the company fired workers who had joined the United Mine Workers. Many of the workers lived in company-owned housing. The company evicted them and their families, often at gunpoint. Word spread among the workers, many of whom took up arms and tried to arrest the company detectives who were evicting people. As a showdown commenced, a shot was fired and nine people died from the ensuing fight. Fifteen months later, representatives of the company shot one of the miners who had been involved in the battle in cold blood. This touched off an armed rebellion of 10,000 workers, the largest insurrection in the United States since the Civil War. These conflicts led to greater union membership, and gradually unions gained more clout and companies were forced to recognize their rights.

As the rights of West Virginia laborers began to improve over time, the rights of West Virginia's minorities did not. The state was fertile ground for the KU KLUX KLAN, and the local courts and state government repeatedly suppressed the rights of black West Virginians, even though African Americans retained the vote in the state (see VOTING RIGHTS). As the coal industry began to mechanize, the number of jobs declined and many African Americans left the state; those who remained fought entrenched policies of discrimination as they attempted to attend desegregated schools (see SCHOOL DESEGREGATION) and gain EMPLOYMENT in new areas. Of course, eventual federal legislation mandated sweeping changes in the battle against discrimination in all areas, but integrating West Virginian society was often difficult. Many African Americans, whose numbers in the state began to dwindle, held tightly to their own churches, social, and political organizations. For the most part, the winning and subsequent enforcement of civil rights for African Americans in West Virginia has been a slow and arduous one at many levels. However, West Virginia has seen many important political and social victories, and its people have proved to be catalysts for change.

The WOMAN SUFFRAGE MOVEMENT in West Virginia was somewhat slow to gain momentum. Although the American observance of Mother's Day began in Crafton, West Virginia, on May 10, 1908, women's suffrage efforts only came to prominence in the state in the decade or so before the passage of the NINETEENTH AMENDMENT, granting women with the right to vote. Irene Drukker, the daughter of Jewish suffragist Sarah Drukker, moved to Huntington, West Virginia, from Cincinnati and soon became president of the Huntington Equal Suffrage Association, galvanizing it to new levels of activism. The right to vote for women was defeated in a statewide referendum in 1916, but shortly thereafter, Lena Lowe Yost of Morgantown, West Virginia, assumed leadership of the local Women's Christian Temperance Union (WCTU) chapter and expanded the organization's efforts to include not only lobbying for the prohibition of alcohol but also for the furtherance of the suffragist struggle. In appreciation of her involvement in the WCTU, Yost was appointed as the chair of the 1920 Republican National Convention (see REPUBLICAN PARTY); she was the first woman to serve in that capacity at a major-party political convention. West Virginia then became the thirty-fourth state to ratify the Nineteenth Amendment to the Constitution. In 1928, Minnie Buckingham Harper became the first black woman to serve as a member of a legislative body in the United States, when she was appointed to the state legislature.

In 1960, West Virginia helped permanently lay to rest the long-standing belief that a Roman Catholic could not be elected as president in the predominantly Protestant United States. This belief was rooted partly in outright anti-Catholic prejudice but perhaps more in a fear that a Catholic president would be unduly subject to the dictates of the Pope in Rome, violating the American tradition of separation of church and state. Although in 1960 West Virginia had, percentage-wise, one of the smallest Roman Catholic populations of any state in the union, Catholic Senator John F. KENNEDY of Massachusetts, running against Senator Hubert Humphrey of Minnesota (who, like Kennedy, never raised the Catholic issue during the campaign), won a decisive victory in the West Virginia DEMOCRATIC PARTY primary, which helped pave the way for Kennedy's nomination and eventual election as president.

BIBLIOGRAPHY

Hyde, Arnout. *A Portrait of West Virginia.* 1989.

Salzman, Jack, David Lioniel Smith, and Cornel West, eds. *Encyclopedia of African-American Culture and History,* Vol. 5. 1996.

Savage, Lon. *Thunder in the Mountains: The West Virginia Mine War, 1920–21.* 1990.

Sisung, Kelle, ed. *Special Interest Groups Profiles for Students.* 1999.

Matthew May

White, George Henry

(1852–1918), lawyer, congressman.

George White, the first black congressman to serve in the twentieth century, was born into slavery in North Carolina. As a youth, after EMANCIPATION he attended public schools while aiding in the family cask- and barrel-making business, then attended Howard University, where he received a certificate in 1877. Shortly afterward, following private study, White passed the North Carolina bar examination, opened a law office in New Bern, N.C., worked as a school teacher, and became politically active as a Republican. In 1880, he was elected to the state House of Representatives from a heavily black district, and four years later was elected to the state Senate. In addition to his Senate seat, White served as a county prosecutor and maintained a private law practice.

In 1896, with help from white Republicans, White was elected to the U.S. House of Representatives, and he won reelection in 1898. During his two terms, White was the only African American in Congress, and considered himself the representative of all black Americans. He spoke on behalf of black artillery regiments in the Army, denounced job discrimination, and called for federal enforcement of civil rights. However, all of these measures were unsuccessful. In his last weeks in Congress, White spoke out strongly against LYNCHING and introduced the first bill to make lynching a federal crime.

After leaving Congress, White participated in the founding of Whitesboro, an unsuccessful black town in New Jersey. He later moved to Philadelphia, where he practiced law and operated a savings bank.

BIBLIOGRAPHY

Clay, William. *Just Permanent Interests.* 1989.
"White, George." *Dictionary of American Negro Biography.* 1982.

Greg Robinson

White, Walter Francis

(1893–1955), NAACP leader.

Walter Francis White, executive secretary of the NATIONAL ASSOCIATION FOR THE ADVANCEMENT OF COLORED PEOPLE (NAACP) from 1931 to 1955, was one of seven children of George White, a mail carrier, and Madeline Harrison. In 1906, he watched a race riot from the family's eight-room house in Atlanta. It was then, the blond, blue-eyed White later wrote in his

Walter Francis White consoles the wife of a lynch victim. (CORBIS)

autobiography, *A Man Called White* (1948), that he realized that he was a Negro.

He attended the Atlanta Preparatory School and in 1916 was graduated from Atlanta University with an A.B. degree. He then worked for the Atlanta Life Insurance Company and began crusading against JIM CROW as a member of the Atlanta branch of the NAACP. There he caught the attention of James Weldon Johnson, the NAACP's first black executive secretary, who hired him in 1918 as his assistant to investigate lynchings in the South. The blueprint for his work was the NAACP's study, *Thirty Years of Lynching, 1889–1918*, published in 1919. White's own study of lynching, *Rope and Faggot*, was published in 1929. (See LYNCHING.)

He was a gregarious, effusive public relations officer whose friends included Mary McLeod Bethune, Harold Ickes, Governor Averell Harriman of New York, and Eleanor ROOSEVELT. He was in his heyday regarded as a national Negro leader, coming just after Frederick DOUGLASS and Booker T. WASHINGTON.

One of the forty-one lynchings he investigated was that in Elaine, Arkansas, in 1919, in which 3 whites and 200 blacks were killed. He barely escaped with his life after whites discovered that he was a black man posing as a white reporter collecting information on the crimes. In 1934, 1935, 1937, and finally in 1938, White led the fight for passage of an anti-lynching bill in Congress. Though the efforts failed, White won broadened support for his crusade from organizations representing more than 42 million people.

White also investigated eight urban race riots, one of which was in Detroit in 1943. In another that same year, in Harlem, he cruised the area with New York Mayor Fiorello LaGuardia all night in a limousine, attempting to calm the crowds.

In 1946, responding to another riot in Columbia, Tennessee, and a double lynching in Monroe, Georgia, White arranged a meeting between a small group of distinguished citizens and President TRUMAN. Truman, partially responding to the group's concerns, created the President's Committee on Civil Rights, in 1947. In that year also, White helped to create the National Committee Against Mob Violence. In late 1947, Truman's fledgling committee issued a report, *To Secure These Rights*, which served as the blueprint for the NAACP's legislative struggle that eventually resulted in passage of the 1957 Civil Rights Act, the first such measure passed in eighty-two years. Partially as a result of White's influence, Truman closely embraced the NAACP's position, and that support contributed to the DIXIECRATS' 1948 bolt from the Democratic Party over the party's civil rights plank.

Another example of White's influence was the 1939 open air concert given by Marian Anderson at the Lincoln Memorial in Washington, D.C., which he helped to organize after the Daughters of the American Revolution refused to let her sing at Constitution Hall. In addition to its being broadcast over radio, 75,000 people attended the event.

He first won recognition for his political acumen in 1930, by engineering the defeat of President Herbert Hoover's nomination of Judge John J. Parker, from North Carolina and widely believed to be racist, to the Supreme Court. In 1941, after A. Philip RANDOLPH, head of the BROTHERHOOD OF SLEEPING CAR PORTERS, threatened a national march by blacks on Washington to protest discrimination in the defense industry, White joined him in his meeting with President FRANKLIN D. ROOSEVELT. To avoid the march, Roosevelt issued Executive Order 8802, barring such discrimination and creating the FAIR EMPLOYMENT PRACTICES COMMITTEE to administer and enforce the order.

In 1943 White spent three months touring the European, Mediterranean, and Middle Eastern theatres, investigating discrimination against black American servicemen. Upon returning to the United States, he submitted a fourteen-point memorandum to the War Department, with recommendations for improving racial conditions in the armed services. In December 1943, he conducted a similar investigation in the Pacific Theatre.

White helped to garner international recognition and respect for the NAACP. In 1921 he attended the Second Pan-African Congress, in London, Brussels, and Paris, organized by Dr. W. E. B. DU BOIS. In 1945 he, Du Bois, and Mary McLeod BETHUNE represented the NAACP as consultants to the American delegation at the founding conference of the United Nations in San Francisco. In 1948, he attended the meetings of the U.N. General Assembly in Paris, as one of the nongovernmental organization representatives, and presented his views over worldwide radio on the hotly debated issues of genocide and human rights.

White created the NAACP's legislative bureau in Washington in 1942 and served as its two-day-a-week director until 1950, when he hired Clarence MITCHELL, Jr. to replace him. In addition to Mitchell, White hired Roy WILKINS as his assistant secretary, Thurgood MARSHALL as NAACP special counsel, Gloster B. Current as director of branches, and Henry Lee Moon as director of public relations. He thus created the team that led the NAACP through its most critical period of the civil rights struggle of the 1950s and 1960s. He helped to create the institutional framework and support that led to the NAACP's trailblazing court victories that held discrimination in housing, voting and education unconstitutional.

His awards include the NAACP's Spingarn Medal, presented on July 2, 1937, by Governor Frank Murphy of Michigan. He wrote two novels, *Fire in the Flint* (1924) and *Flight* (1926). He also wrote *A Rising Wind* (1945), which reported on the status of black troops in the European and Middle Eastern theatres of World War II, *How Far the Promised Land* (1955), and scores of articles.

In 1922 he married Leah Gladys Powell of Ithaca, New York. They had a daughter, Jane, and a son, Walter Carl Darrow. After their divorce in 1949, White married Poppy Cannon, a white woman and editor of *House Beautiful* magazine. White escaped the firestorm of negative reaction to the marriage by taking a year's leave of absence from the NAACP to recuperate from a previous heart attack. He and his bride visited Europe, Israel, Egypt, India, and Japan as members of the "Round the World Town Meeting of the Air." In 1950 he returned to the NAACP and finally succumbed to another heart attack in 1955.

BIBLIOGRAPHY

Reports of the Secretary to the NAACP National Board of Directors, 1939–1955.

Sitkoff, Harvard. *A New Deal for Blacks, the Emergence of Civil Rights as a National Issue: The Depression Decade.* 1978.

Watson, Denton L. *Lion in the Lobby, Clarence Mitchell, Jr.'s Struggle for the Passage of Civil Rights Laws.* 1990.

Denton L. Watson

White Backlash

Institutionalized inequality has been a bedrock of the United States since its inception. Barriers to opportunity have existed for people of color, women, and persons with physical and mental disabilities. Only elite white men were granted the full rights of CITIZENSHIP in the Constitution, which also excluded non-propertied whites from full access to America's social institutions. Historically the passage of civil rights policies for people of color and other minorities has led to the formation of white resistance movements attempting to reassert previously existing white-skin privilege. Civil rights policies have often been relatively small-scale reform measures, so changes in the social structure have not led to broad-scale sociocultural transformation. Alternative forms of institutional discrimination, such as redlining (the illegal practice of creating financial barriers for real estate purchase and investment in poor neighborhoods where residents are disproportionately people of color), and new cultural expressions of white supremacy have tended to hinder or stifle increased access for minorities. Backlash movements form in an attempt to reassert privileges that the powerful fear they will lose if new opportunities are opened to minorities, who are seen as competitors. Economic scarcity and income inequality caused by concentrations of wealth fan the flames of RACISM and SEXISM among less privileged whites as competition over societal resources escalates.

The history of the KU KLUX KLAN over the past 135 years has been shaped by civil rights legislation in the United States. Dating back to the end of the Civil War, many whites resisted RECONSTRUCTION efforts, hoping to regain the perceived benefits of slavery. Although only elite whites maintained large slave holdings, the culture of WHITE SUPREMACY was effective in casting Reconstruction as a war against all whites, including tenant farmers, who were led to believe that they had benefited from slavery and would be victimized by improvements in civil rights for blacks. The Ku Klux Klan was organized as a reactionary backlash resistance movement to terrorize blacks through cross burnings and LYNCHING campaigns. They hoped to revive the pre–Civil War South, which abolitionists referred to as the "Lost Cause of the Confederacy," to prevent blacks from asserting their newly granted citizenship rights.

However, the Klan encountered government prosecution for its night-riding terror and experienced a significant decline in membership by 1872. The resurgent Ku Klux Klan of the 1920s was organized in a xenophobic rage against the waves of immigrants, who were blamed for crime and poverty in America's cities. The civil rights movement of the 1950s and 1960s also sparked tremendous activity among far-right groups waging a white cultural war against DESEGREGATION, AFFIRMATIVE ACTION, and other related social programs. Much of the current propaganda of the Ku Klux Klan and other related groups still centers on the dangers of civil rights policies to the survival of the white race, and images of Martin Luther KING, JR. commonly provide the background for bull's-eyes used for shooting practice by Klan members. Each January, the commemoration of his life as a national holiday draws members of the Klan, neo-Nazis, and Skinheads together in protest of Dr. King's contribution to civil rights history.

Americans often prefer to think that white racism is restricted to extremist groups such as the Klan, but the ideologies of far-right groups have roots in mainstream values. The right wing has traditionally opposed civil rights policies, although usually without overt biologically determinist arguments about the racial superiority of whites. Studies of the racial attitudes of Americans show that a much larger percentage support far-right values than membership figures of those organizations would reflect. Racist attitudes also manifest themselves differently by social location, with the working class exhibiting more stereotypical expressions, such as the use of racial epithets, and middle class individuals tending toward more subtle expressions hidden behind a mask of class inegalitarianism. For example, middle class persons would be more likely to say that busing is too much trouble and is too time-consuming, but say they would not be opposed to middle-class blacks moving into their neighborhood. The use of symbolic racism, or using code words such as "welfare queens" for poor black women, introduces a variety of means of expressing racist values beyond traditional racial discourse.

Mainstream right-wing politics have long been appealing, especially for white Americans, as many of their racial concerns are articulated in that arena. After the Civil War, the Southern members of the DEMOCRATIC PARTY reacted against the abolitionists in the REPUBLICAN PARTY. However, race-based platforms were brought back to the Republican Party, polarized to a more conservative stance by the third-party presidential candidacy of George WALLACE in 1968 and 1972, which ushered in what is often termed the "Southernization" of American politics. From Richard NIXON to George BUSH, Republican candidates were successful in tapping into white resistance and the fear of white victimization. Pat Buchanan advised Nixon to take back the South by coopting Wallace's campaign strategy, in order to win the 1968 election for the Republican Party.

The "cultural wars" theme struck a chord in that period, which has persisted to the present time. Throughout the 1990s, Pat Buchanan pursued the U.S. presidency with cries for "America First" that date back to the nativist movements of the 1940s (see NA-TIVISM). Congressman Newt Gingrich's new right "Republican Revolution" and the "Contract with America" garnered national support in the mid-1990s, particularly among more affluent whites, with its anti–affirmative action, anti-welfare, and economic restructuring policies, which benefited the primarily white upper class. Welfare reform had been a cornerstone of Bill CLINTON's campaigns; so centrist Democrats joined hands with Republican new rightists in the mid-1990s in support of welfare reform to dismantle entitlements for the poor, who are disproportionately people of color. One spinoff from the Republican Revolution was the "English Only" campaign, which proposed the elimination of bilingual education and elimination of the printing of government documents in Spanish. New rightists strongly oppose MULTICUL-TURALISM and political correctness in an attempt to eliminate cultural change engendered by the civil rights and women's movements.

CALIFORNIA became a political hotbed of new right activity in 1994 with the passage of Proposition 187, which targeted illegal aliens. Governor Pete Wilson supported the initiative in his reelection campaign as he argued that welfare was drawing illegal immigrants into the state in unprecedented numbers. Proposition 187 denied immigrants the right to health care, public education, and other social services. Social workers, teachers, and health care providers were ordered to report illegal aliens to government officials, essentially functioning as para-INS Agents. The CALIFORNIA CIVIL RIGHTS INITIATIVE (CCRI) also was approved by backlash voters, who supported the dismantling of affirmative action created by the CIVIL RIGHTS ACT OF 1964. The CCRI was placed on the ballots of several other states. Opponents of the anti–affirmative action initiatives are faced with state grassroots political battles, since the U.S. SUPREME COURT refused to review the constitutionality of CCRI. These are two important examples of mainstream white backlash and moral panic over the fear of white victimization.

It is clear that the new right has brought racist and sexist values that were once underground and marginalized back into mainstream discourse. Many theorists have suggested that the right wing has survived a series of transformations as it has adapted to changing social and cultural conditions. They have also noted that America's political center has shifted to the right. Although political rhetoric has evolved to address persistent racial concerns by developing new code words for the racism of the past, the aim is still that of preserving white Eurocentrism from the perceived dangers of a pluralist and more egalitarian society.

BIBLIOGRAPHY

Ansell, Amy Elizabeth. *New Right, New Racism.* 1997.
Berlet, Chip, ed. *Eyes Right! Challenging the Right Wing Backlash.* 1995.
Carter, Dan. *From George Wallace to Newt Gingrich.* 1996.
Diamond, Sara. *Roads to Dominion.* 1995.
Diamond, Sara. *Facing the Wrath.* 1996.
Dobratz, Betty A., and Stephanie L. Shanks-Meile. *"White Power, White Pride!" The White Separatist Movement in the United States.* 1997.
Feagin, Joe R., and Hernan Vera. *White Racism.* 1995.
Ferber, Abby L. *White Man Falling.* 1998.
Wellman, David T. *Portraits of White Racism.* 1993.
Wilson, Carter A. *Racism: From Slavery to Advanced Capitalism.* 1996.

Stephanie Shanks-Meile

White Citizens' Councils

Elite segregationists formed the Citizens' Councils after the U.S. SUPREME COURT in *Brown v. Topeka Board of Education* (see BROWN V. BOARD OF EDUCATION) ruled against the constitutionality of separate-but-equal public schools in 1954. A second Supreme Court case in 1955 ordered local school boards and federal district courts to desegregate the schools although the enforcement was weak, and a timetable for compliance was not specified. Even though the goals of those two Supreme Court decisions were not realized until the CIVIL RIGHTS ACT OF 1964, SEGREGATION had been ideologically and symbolically challenged. KU KLUX KLAN organizations continued their campaigns of terror against blacks and white "race traitors," but they lacked the ability to attract the mass support and financial resources necessary to fight desegregation.

Formation of the White Citizens' Councils was set in motion by Mississippi district court judge Tom Brady, who delivered a speech to the Sons of the American Revolution that became a booklet for what the Councils called "Black Monday," referring to the day of the first Supreme Court ruling. In that speech Judge Brady used biological determinism to signal danger as whites faced amalgamation with the death of segregation. With anticommunism at its zenith, he argued that desegregation was caused by socialists, many of whom were immigrants. Judge Brady called for a separate territory for blacks, for the election of

Supreme Court justices, and for states to outlaw public schools. In an attempt to boycott blacks economically, he asked whites to fire their maids.

Robert B. Patterson, along with other prominent civic and business leaders, founded the Citizens' Councils in July 1954 after convening a town hall meeting attended by about seventy-five people. Council leaders traveled around MISSISSIPPI, giving speeches at Rotary and Kiwanis Clubs that led to larger meetings and a public rally. Membership in the White Citizens' Councils grew in response to civil rights struggles and victories. The Association of Citizens' Councils reached its peak in 1956, with 250,000 members in ten Southern states.

The Citizens' Councils fought INTEGRATION through propaganda and education campaigns with literature distribution and reliance upon radio programs and public speaking. The Councils could be categorized as part of the mainstream right-wing, along with the John Birch Society, which had some organizational ties with the Councils. They made appeals for traditional moral values, argued against government programs to redistribute resources on the basis of need rather than merit, and rejected aid to foreign countries. From a states' rights perspective, the Councils argued that states had the right to legislate against federal integration laws. They supported anti–civil rights measures in Southern states, such as passage of the 1954 Mississippi restrictive voting ballot initiative, which required a sophisticated literacy test to serve as a barrier to African-American suffrage. Voters also approved a provision for the Mississippi legislature to abolish the public schools if the federal government enforced integration.

The Federation for Constitutional Government was formed in 1955 by numerous U.S. and state legislators, governors, and other prominent Councilors to coordinate southern resistance to integration. Mississippi was followed by GEORGIA, LOUISIANA, and VIRGINIA in creating state commissions that cooperated with and donated large sums of public money to the Citizens' Councils to protect those states from "race-mixing." By 1962, one-fourth of the U.S. CONGRESS had given interviews in Congressional recording studios that were aired on the Councils' radio and television programs and were distributed free to stations. The White Citizens' Councils attracted middle-class segregationists and some elites who wished to distance themselves from the Ku Klux Klan, which attracted mainly working-class members. The Councils shared the ideologies of biological determinism and anticommunism with the John Birch Society and the Klan, but they relied on boycotts and intimidation that remained within the boundaries of democratic process, rather than resorting to underground terror campaigns. Although the White Citizens' Councils declined in the late 1950s, they continued through the 1960s, and published the last issue of their magazine, *The Citizen*, in 1985. Their relationship to the Klan is possibly best understood by noting that the eventual losses in Council membership corresponded to a growth in Klan rolls by 1957.

BIBLIOGRAPHY

Bridges, Tyler. *The Rise of David Duke.* 1994.
Chalmers, David M. *Hooded Americanism: The History of the Ku Klux Klan.* 1965.
Diamond, Sara. *Roads to Dominion: Right-Wing Movements and Political Power in the United States.* 1995.
George, John, and Laird Wilcox. *Nazis, Communists, Klansmen and Others on the Fringe.* 1992.
Wade, Wyn Craig. *The Fiery Cross.* 1987.

Stephanie Shanks-Meile

White Rights

The term "white rights" refers to a cluster of beliefs adhered to by a loose coalition of racist and white supremacist groups that ultimately seek the reinstatement of SEGREGATION and the disfranchisement of blacks and other racial and ethnic minorities. Some of the more prominent organizations that have embraced the cause of white rights include former KU KLUX KLAN leader David Duke's National Organization for the Advancement of White People (NAAWP), the White Aryan Resistance (WAR), and the neo-Nazi National Alliance, whose founder, William Pierce, wrote *The Turner Diaries.* Several mainstream conservatives share many of their views, especially those regarding IMMIGRATION and AFFIRMATIVE ACTION, perhaps the most notable of these individuals being sometime presidential candidate Pat BUCHANAN.

The white rights movement emerged in the 1970s and early 1980s in response to the expansion of affirmative action programs and the implementation of racial quotas and preferential hiring practices. Other factors that helped fuel white rights platforms included mandated BUSING and the court-ordered DESEGREGATION of institutions of higher learning. Proponents of white rights assert that the creation of these programs has resulted in blacks and other minorities being given greater opportunities at the expense of more qualified whites, creating conditions that give rise to de facto reverse discrimination. Although most of their views remain too extreme to gain much support among mainstream conservatives, many of their attacks on affirmative action and welfare have struck a chord in conservative circles.

White rights advocates endorse an end to all racial quotas in hiring and promotion and the removal of

A crowd of irate white Bostonians attending a "white rights" rally in protest of court-ordered busing. (CORBIS/Bettmann)

racial and ethnic considerations for college admissions and academic aid, as well as in union membership and acceptance to professional societies. The white rights program calls for an end to all or virtually all immigration, the elimination of bilingual education, and a policy of arrest and deportation of illegal aliens, regardless of individual circumstance. Some support the militarization of the Mexican border, and the adoption of shoot-to-kill policies for those crossing illegally. Welfare programs are also a target for white rightists, as they believe that welfare underwrites minority sloth and ignorance, which in turn feed urban crime and decay. The most extreme elements of this movement advocate the creation of an all-white homeland in the Pacific Northwest, and espouse a doctrine that views racial warfare as inevitable, although this is a minority view.

BIBLIOGRAPHY

Ridgeway, James. *Blood in the Face: The Ku Klux Klan, Aryan Nations, Nazi Skinheads, and the Rise of a New White Culture.* 1991.

Sargent, Lyman Tower, ed. *Extremism in America: A Reader.* 1995.

Robert W. Nill

White Supremacy

For all but the most recent era in modern world history, until the decolonization of the European sea-borne empires in Asia and Africa after WORLD WAR II, the global ascendancy of the so-called white race seemed normal and inevitable. In the "white man's countries," the former European colonies of settlement in the temperate zones of North and South America, Australasia, and South Africa, where white settlers enslaved, removed, exterminated, or otherwise suppressed the indigenous peoples, white supremacy has been not only a fact of life but the central political and ideological foundation; and its legacy endures.

RACE is one of the slippery words. According to the *Oxford English Dictionary* (*OED*), a race is "a group of persons, animals, or plants, connected by common descent or origin"—different categories of organisms, animal or vegetable, no matter how high or low in creation. Other derivations, some of them obsolete, help explain the slipperiness. It could mean a procession: a race of bishops. It was synonymous with a tribe, nation, or people: the German or Irish race. In South Africa around the turn of the twentieth century the "race question" was the conflict between English- and Afrikaans-speaking whites, with that between white and black being called the "color" or "native question." Race also has connotations of class (peasants as a race) and gender. In anthropology it is "one of the great divisions of mankind"—which may seem clear enough until one asks, how great or how many? The more precise the discussion of race, the more obscure it becomes.

The American Nazi Party, which unambiguously advocates white supremacy, holds a "white power" rally in Lafayette Park opposite the White House, on July 3, 1976, the day before the bicentennial of the signing of the Declaration of Independence. (© Archive Photos)

Yet the concept does have some scientific validity. Far in the distant past, when the world was younger and the human population relatively infinitesimal, small collections of people lived for long periods in comparative isolation, interbreeding largely among themselves. Thus dominant gene pools were established, fixing and perpetuating accidental variations in skin color, facial characteristics, hair texture, and the like, as well as less obvious but more important differences such as the frequency of blood types or the sickle-cell anemia commonly associated with endemically malarious regions in Africa, the Mediterranean, and elsewhere. Isolation was never absolute, as "mixing" occurred more or less continually; so "racial" groupings were never more than approximate, and were always more quantitative than qualitative. Most so-called white people are not the color of milk, and the colors of the black peoples of Africa range from yellowish-brown to coal-black. Races are imagined and constructed; race is an idea. Race has no historical reality apart from race consciousness, which is formed when more than one "race" meet and collide. Where only one race exists, as in precolonial Africa or the Americas before the sixteenth century, race is not a factor. Instead, it is a function of power and ideology. As the African-American scholar Alain Locke put it, "Much false race theory is orthodox history, as well as the apologia of prevailing practice."

In the quintessential white man's country the United States, white supremacy can be regarded as a long continuum composed of relatively distinct stages, the first and most important of these being slavery. It was also by far the longest, from the Jamestown settlement in Virginia in 1620 until it was finally ended by the passing of the THIRTEENTH AMENDMENT to the Constitution in 1865, just after the Civil War. It is not wrong to regard Abraham Lincoln's EMANCIPATION PROCLAMATION two years earlier as the effective end of slavery in the United States, but it was a war measure, designed to cause massive problems for the South; he actually freed no slaves in the Confederate States and did not liberate those in border states.

Although white race PREJUDICE was not a significant factor in the Roman Empire, where there were many Germanic, Celtic, and other white slaves, it does seem to have been well entrenched by at least the sixteenth century. By then, again according to the *OED*, "white" was associated with all things good, pure, and beautiful, "black" being associated with all things evil, polluted, and ugly. In the New World, where land was cheap and labor scarce, some sort of forced labor was economically essential; Native Americans and lower-class Europeans were difficult to enslave, whereas Africans were available and comparatively cheap. It was a vicious circle: as racial slavery became entrenched, as "black" or "Negro" became interchangeable with "slave," white RACISM had to increase in order to justify slavery. America in the nineteenth century was far more racially dominated and divided—economically, politically, legally, ideologically—than it had been two centuries earlier.

The end of slavery was far from the end of white supremacy. Following the Civil War the Southern states enacted so-called BLACK CODES, designed to maintain the freedmen in a condition of semiservitude, reinforced by a reign of terror conducted by an organization with an estimated half a million members, including many upper-class leaders, the KU KLUX KLAN. Under RADICAL REPUBLICAN leadership, the federal government negated these codes, enacted the FOURTEENTH and FIFTEENTH AMENDMENTS, and attempted to enforce RECONSTRUCTION under an occupation. Even the FREEDMEN'S BUREAU, however, often wound up being involved in a conspiracy to keep black labor docile. Nor did the federal government follow through on the wartime promise of a substantial transfer of capital to the former slaves, namely, forty acres and a mule. Then in 1877 came the historic compromise, in which the South gained home rule. For nearly a century, until the 1960s, white supremacy reigned unchallenged.

The final stage of white supremacy was SEGREGATION, in some ways more subtle and indirect than the oppression that preceded it. There was a substantial time gap: legal segregation came into force in the South not in 1877, when presumably it might have done so, but during and after the 1890s. Initially segregation was proposed by moderates, as an alternative to more violent solutions. Segregation was a Progressive reform. It was associated with industrialization, with the fast-growing cities of the New South. Supposedly, as the SUPREME COURT found in PLESSY V. FERGUSON (1896), segregated facilities would be equal and therefore not discriminatory. Throughout most of the American nation—informal in the North, legally enforced in the South—segregation remained in effect until the Supreme Court's BROWN V. BOARD OF EDUCATION decision (1954), the civil rights revolution of the 1960s, and beyond.

What must be emphasized is the overall continuity of white supremacy from 1620 down to the 1960s, and above all the culture of violence that has maintained and reinforced it. Under slavery the whip was ubiquitous; punishing a master for cruelty to slaves was rare indeed; slave patrollers permitted dogs to chew away on the legs of captured runaways; sexual violence, planters and their sons demanding that slave women serve them, was so common as to be the rule. After slavery, when destruction of valuable property was no longer a consideration, violence actually increased. By the time the South gained home rule in the 1870s, the

Klan had killed several thousand blacks and tortured many others; race riots in New Orleans, Memphis, and elsewhere were so well-organized and destructive, and local authorities so often implicated in them, that they were more like what in Russia were called pogroms. After 1877, although Klan terrorism gradually receded, LYNCHING increased, reaching its climax in the 1890s, when two hundred to three hundred people a year were lynched, 90 percent of them black. According to Tuskeegee Institute figures, the overall total in the former Confederate States amounted to more than three thousand lynchings. After the 1890s, lynching gradually receded; but as lynching declined, judicially imposed death sentences increased, with 75 percent of those executed black. The violence of white supremacy bred counterviolence. Young black males especially often saw themselves as being in a war with the police; in black neighborhoods, as in other communities, "bandits" often became folk heroes.

Two nations, largely estranged from one another; poverty, unemployment, and crime disproportionately concentrated among the blacks; an unbroken history of their violent conflict with the police; a vicious circle of violence begetting violence—all are the legacy of white supremacy in America.

BIBLIOGRAPHY

Cell, John W. *British Colonial Administration in the Mid-Nineteenth Century: The Policy-Making Process.* 1970.
Cell, John W. *The Highest Stage of White Supremacy: The Origins of Segregation in South Africa and the American South.* 1982.
Foner, Eric. *Reconstruction: America's Unfinished Revolution, 1863–1877.* 1988.
Nieman, Donald. *To Set the Law in Motion: The Freedmen's Bureau and the Legal Rights of Blacks.* 1979.

John W. Cell

Wilkins, Roy

(1901–1981), NAACP leader.

Roy Wilkins, executive director of the NATIONAL ASSOCIATION FOR THE ADVANCEMENT OF COLORED PEOPLE (NAACP), was born in St. Louis, Missouri, son of the Rev. William D. Wilkins of the African Methodist Episcopal Church, and Mayfield Edmonson Wilkins. Upon the death of his mother in 1906, his father sent him and his sister Armeda and brother Earl to live with their mother's sister Elizabeth and her husband, Sam Williams, in St. Paul, Minnesota.

Young Wilkins attended St. Paul's nonsegregated public schools. In his final year of high school and during his college years, he worked as a caddy, redcap, porter, dining-car waiter, and stockyards cleanup man.

Wilkins, Roy   801

Roy Wilkins, executive secretary of the National Association for the Advancement of Colored People, ca. 1960. (© Archive Photos)

He graduated from the University of Minnesota School of Journalism in 1923. After graduation, Wilkins joined the editorial staff of the Kansas City (Missouri) *Call*, where he became managing editor and wrote a column, "Talking It Over." He also joined the local branch of the NAACP. On September 15, 1929, Wilkins married Aminda Ann Badeau, also of St. Louis. They had no children.

In 1932, a year after he joined the NAACP national staff as assistant secretary, Wilkins and George Schuyler, a newspaper columnist, conducted an NAACP investigation of working conditions for blacks on a Mississippi flood prevention project in Vicksburg. The two men's findings and report helped improve working conditions for African Americans there.

From 1934 to 1944, Wilkins was editor of *The* CRISIS, the official journal of the NAACP. During Walter WHITE's leave of absence from June 1, 1949, to May 1, 1950, because of bad health, Wilkins was NAACP act-

ing secretary. Upon White's return and until his death, Wilkins served as administrator of the organization. He was named executive secretary (later changed to executive director) on April 11, 1955.

In 1949 Wilkins worked with White; Clarence MITCHELL, Jr., then labor secretary; Gloster B. Current, director of branches; Leslie S. Perry, administrator of the NAACP Washington Bureau; and other organizations to implement the goals of the Joint Committee on Civil Rights, which the NAACP organized on February 5. Later that year, Wilkins got the NAACP to create an Emergency Civil Rights Committee, which led an Emergency Civil Rights Mobilization in Washington from January 15 to 17, 1950. More than four thousand delegates, representing 100 organizations, participated and demanded that Congress pass the FAIR EMPLOYMENT PRACTICES COMMITTEE bill (FEPC) and other civil rights legislation. Wilkins was general chairman of the Mobilization, which founded the LEADERSHIP CONFERENCE ON CIVIL RIGHTS (LCRR), a coalition of civil rights, labor, religious, and civic groups.

Throughout his career, Wilkins built his influence on his skills as an administrator, pamphleteer, and persuasive pleader of the African American's cause in the halls of power. Fearing reprisal from the Internal Revenue Service—which in 1939 had forced the NAACP to create the Legal Defense and Educational Fund, Inc., as a semi-independent tax-exempt, legal arm—Wilkins rarely, if ever, acknowledged his skill as a politician. His principal political vehicles were the LCCR, of which he was chairperson, and the NAACP's nationwide branch network that extended to military bases in Germany and the Panama Canal. Under his leadership, the number of NAACP branches increased from 240,000 to a peak of more than 500,000 in 1963. In addition to nurturing the branches, Wilkins's other primary administrative concern was protecting the organization's integrity. That led him in 1966 to denounce "BLACK POWER" as fiercely as he had denounced communism in the previous decade.

Wilkins judiciously built the NAACP's programs on its egalitarian philosophy, whose central goal was an integrated society in the United States (see INTEGRATION). In 1944, he had expressed the group's goals in "The Negro Wants Full Equality," an incisive contribution to *What the Negro Wants*, edited by Rayford W. Logan. In 1961, on behalf of the LCCR, Wilkins presented President John F. KENNEDY with a sixty-page memorandum entitled "Federally Supported Discrimination," which documented extensive racial problems and urged the president to "promulgate," through executive action, "a general Federal civil rights code governing the operations of the whole executive branch of government."

Wilkins's leadership ensured passage of the CIVIL RIGHTS laws. He pursued full implementation of the SUPREME COURT's 1954 BROWN V. BOARD OF EDUCATION school DESEGREGATION decision. One of the NAACP's most notable victories in that battle was the desegregation of Central High School in LITTLE ROCK, Arkansas in 1957. In 1962, in conjunction with the now-independent NAACP Inc. Fund, Wilkins successfully fought for the admission of James H. MEREDITH to the University of Mississippi. Both battles were extremely violent and required, respectively, the direct intervention of President Dwight D. EISENHOWER and President Kennedy, both of whom used federal troops to quell opposition.

Under Wilkins, in 1963, the NAACP took the lead in organizing the celebrated MARCH ON WASHINGTON on August 28 for "Jobs and Freedom," which included passage of further civil rights legislation. In 1967 President Lyndon B. JOHNSON appointed him a member of the National Advisory Commission on Civil Disorders. Issued in 1968, its report affirmed that white racism was the root cause of the nation's racial tensions and conflicts. In 1969, Wilkins committed the NAACP to the successful struggle to block President Richard M. NIXON's successive appointments of H. Clement Haynsworth and G. Harrold Carswell to the Supreme Court.

Among Wilkins's awards is the Spingarn Medal, received in 1964. Wilkins's retirement from the NAACP was clouded by a bitter dispute over the date of his departure—whether it was to have been January 1, 1977, as the board of directors demanded, or July 31, 1977, as he insisted. He won the battle by triumphantly concluding his career at the NAACP Convention in St. Louis, Missouri.

BIBLIOGRAPHY

Bardolph, Richard. *The Negro Vanguard.* 1959.
Watson, Denton L. *Lion in the Lobby: Clarence Mitchell, Jr.'s Struggle for the Passage of Civil Rights Laws.* 1990.
Wilkins, Roy, with Tom Mathews. *Standing Fast: The Autobiography of Roy Wilkins.* 1982.

Denton L. Watson

Williams, Robert F.

(1925–   ), revolutionary black nationalist.

Ten years before the "BLACK POWER" militant civil rights movement, a NATIONAL ASSOCIATION FOR THE ADVANCEMENT OF COLORED PEOPLE (NAACP) branch president named Robert F. Williams made a press statement advocating that racial violence be met with violence. Whites and conservative blacks reacted strongly against this call to arms in 1959, but more

Robert F. Williams. (CORBIS/Bettmann)

than two decades of racial tension and violence followed.

Robert Franklin Williams was born in Monroe, North Carolina, on February 26, 1925. His attitudes about race relations were shaped at age ten, when he witnessed a policeman drag a black woman down Monroe's main street, a scene framed in his memory by the laughter of whites and the screams of the victim.

At age seventeen, Williams left high school for training as a machinist with the NATIONAL YOUTH ADMINISTRATION. Williams then lived in Detroit and San Francisco, working as a machinist. In Detroit, he was introduced to the COMMUNIST PARTY. He was drafted into the Army, an experience also tinged by racial animosities as he did not receive promised training and spent time in the stockade for insubordination—an experience in which he took pride.

After the war, Williams returned to Monroe, finished his high school diploma, and began writing. His poetry and prose were published in magazines; he had a weekly column in the *Monroe Enquirer.* Back in Detroit, Williams continued to write, and was published in the Communist Party's paper, the *Daily Worker.* Williams then spent several years at three colleges on the G.I. Bill, where he was introduced to the works of Karl Marx and Vladimir Lenin. Unable to find a job in 1954, he enlisted in the U.S. Marine Corps where he received training in special combat and weapons. At

Camp Pendleton, Williams spent 180 days in the brig for refusing to salute the flag at a parade ceremony.

Returning to Monroe in 1955, Williams became increasingly involved in civil rights activities and joined the Monroe chapter of the NAACP, where, as branch president, he made the statement about meeting racial violence with violence. Williams was an activist branch president, but he was increasingly frustrated with the NAACP's conservative ways. When the Monroe Police Department refused to curtail KU KLUX KLAN activities, Williams advocated armed defense of the African-American community and obtained a National Rifle Association club charter. On October 5, 1959, the club fired upon the Klan.

In August of 1959, accused by a white couple of kidnapping when he intervened to protect them from a mob of angry blacks, Williams fled to avoid arrest. He then spent the next ten years in Cuba and the People's Republic of China. While in exile, Williams wrote his militant newsletter, *Crusader*, and hosted a revolutionary radio program. In March 1968, Williams was elected president in exile of the Republic of New Africa (RNA), a revolutionary Marxist-Leninist organization dedicated to establishing a separate black nation within the United States.

Returning to Michigan in 1969, a disillusioned Williams resigned from the RNA. He continues to write and lecture. He helped form the People's Association for Human Rights and eventually rejoined the NAACP, where he earned the Lake/Newaygo chapter's Black Image Award in 1992.

BIBLIOGRAPHY

"Robert F. Williams." Biography Resource Center, Gale Group at GaleNet.com. http://galenet.com.

Cohen, Robert Carl. *Black Crusader: A Biography of Robert Franklin Williams.* 1972.

Meier, August, Elliot Rudwick, and Francis L. Broderick, eds. *Black Protest Thought in the Twentieth Century.* 1971.

Shapiro, Herbert. *White Violence and Black Response.* 1988.

Williams, Robert F. *Negroes With Guns.* Marzani & Munsell, 1962. Reprint 1973.

Michael Dawson

Williams v. Mississippi (1898)

Williams v. Mississippi (1898) was the last in a series of cases that limited the power of the post–Civil War constitutional amendments and withdrew federal support from the political revolution of RECONSTRUCTION in the South. In *Williams*, the U.S. SUPREME COURT ruled that the measures used by MISSISSIPPI to disfranchise the state's black population did not violate the FIF-TEENTH AMENDMENT, which in 1870 had made it unconstitutional to abridge a man's right to vote because of RACE or previous condition of servitude. In 1890, Mississippi Democrats had enacted the "Mississippi Plan" at the state's constitutional convention, a series of laws designed to keep blacks from voting without disfranchising poor whites.

Mississippi Democrats devised a variety of mechanisms to disfranchise blacks without referring directly to race. The poll tax, an annual tax that one had to pay in order to vote, kept many poor blacks from voting. High literacy and property requirements for voting also disfranchised most of the black population. In order to ensure that poor whites could vote, legislators included a "grandfather clause" that exempted from these tests voters whose grandfathers had voted or who themselves had voted before 1867. An "understanding" clause served to disfranchise blacks who could meet the other requirements, by allowing registrars to ask potential voters any question they wanted about the state constitution before they could register to vote. When a black Mississippian challenged the provisions of Mississippi's 1890 constitution, the U.S. Supreme Court ruled that these mechanisms were not racially discriminatory because they did not directly mention race by name. Like the more famous PLESSY v. FERGUSON, the *Williams* decision served as a legal foundation for SEGREGATION and white political supremacy in the twentieth-century South.

BIBLIOGRAPHY

McMillen, Neil. *Dark Journey: Black Mississippians in the Age of Jim Crow.* 1990.

Parker, Frank. *Black Votes Count: Political Empowerment in Mississippi after 1965.* 1990.

Renee Romano

Wisconsin

Wisconsin was admitted into the Union in 1848, intensifying a pattern of African-American immigration to the region that had begun decades earlier. Many blacks came to the state to work mining lead ores in the Wisconsin territory; still others came as members of three New York Indian tribes that were forcibly moved to the Green Bay and Fox River regions of the territory. By 1840, the small number of African Americans living in Milwaukee County established the center of the state's abolitionist movement. Following admission as a state, many African Americans and other newcomers gravitated to the major cities of Milwaukee, Racine, Beloit, and Madison. Minorities mainly worked in service occupations and the growing labor industry. As the years went by, African Americans and

National Guard Colonel Hugh Simondson with Native American activist members of the Menominee Warriors group during their 1975 occupation of the Alexion Brothers Novitiate in Wisconsin. (CORBIS/Bettmann)

other minorities made up an incredibly small percentage of the total population of Wisconsin. With the onset of the two world wars, however, migration to Wisconsin's major cities increased. The industrial necessities of producing war machinery opened up opportunities for work, and many Southern blacks were recruited to carry on the effort.

Historically, Milwaukee has been the focal point of civil rights advocacy and change in the state of Wisconsin, and an incident in Milwaukee was the impetus for African-Americans winning suffrage. When Wisconsin joined the United States in 1848, its state constitution provided for a popular referendum on suffrage for African American males. A vote was held the next year, but was declared to have failed by the state legislature. However, legal proceedings were commenced disputing the result. Ezekiel Gillespie, an African American from Milwaukee, claimed that a pollwatcher in the city turned him away as he attempted to cast his vote in the referendum. Gillespie fought his banishment from the ballot and in 1866, the Wisconsin Supreme Court reversed the referendum results and granted all African-American men the right to vote in Wisconsin.

Throughout most of its history as a territory and state, Wisconsin was mostly a segregated and discriminatory place. Slaves and those harboring slaves were jailed for breaking the various fugitive slave laws on the books, and there were lynchings of African Americans, although the latter practice was not nearly as prevalent as in the Southern states. Thus, Wisconsin was not immune to the need for state civil rights laws,

and such legislation was introduced and passed in the late 1880s and 1890s after an effort lead by William T. Green, an African-American law student at the University of Wisconsin. Voicing and publicizing the need for new civil rights legislation, African-American newspapers such as the *Wisconsin Afro-American*, the *Wisconsin Enterprise-Blade*, and the *Wisconsin Weekly Advocate* were established and flourished during this time period.

Following WORLD WAR I, Wisconsin began to experience the same kinds of racial difficulties as other states. When the war ended, many African-American workers who had migrated from the South and contributed to the war effort were displaced, causing frustration that sometimes turned into violent conflict. In 1919, the NATIONAL ASSOCIATION FOR THE ADVANCEMENT OF COLORED PEOPLE (NAACP) opened chapters in Milwaukee and Beloit, which coincided with the establishment of URBAN LEAGUE offices in both cities. These organizations immediately went to work to improve the lot of African Americans and other minorities. One of their first projects involved the wretched housing conditions and the lack of opportunities for better housing for African Americans that existed in Milwaukee. The NAACP's efforts in Milwaukee resulted in a state charter for the Columbia Savings and Loan Association, which assisted minorities with finding adequate housing. However, even into the 1990s, many black citizens of Wisconsin lived in isolated neighborhoods and in mostly inadequate housing.

The modern civil rights movement, of course, took on a different overtone in Northern states such as

Wisconsin. Although discrimination was quite prevalent all across the United States, discriminatory practices and policies were not codified as they were in the South. However, many businesses and individuals did indeed discriminate against African Americans and other minorities, especially in housing, which became the focal point of civil rights protest in Wisconsin in the tense period of the late 1960s. Housing discrimination had reached the point of frustration and from 1967 through 1968, a Catholic priest named James GROPPI, along with the support of Milwaukee's NAACP Youth Corps, led continuous marches through the streets of Milwaukee in support of an open-housing ordinance. In the middle of this protest, rioting broke out in the summer of 1967; Milwaukee was one of a handful of cities that experienced violence that summer—Detroit, Newark, Harlem, and other urban areas erupted as frustration over equal rights, the VIETNAM WAR, and other issues mounted.

Despite the violence, supporters of the open-housing ordinance marched through the city for two hundred consecutive days. City councilwoman Vel Phillips (who would go on to a distinguished political career in state government) led the political arm of the fight, which eventually ended in victory and a new open-housing ordinance in Milwaukee. The results of this hard-fought win are somewhat disappointing in the long run, however. The 1990 census revealed that housing in Milwaukee was still more segregated than many major urban centers in the United States. Desegregating the public schools in Milwaukee proved to be just as difficult; a lawsuit on behalf of black and white children took fifteen years to settle in federal court before Milwaukee schools were legally desegregated. As is plainly visible, the struggle for civil rights for all people has been just as much of a struggle in the North as in the South.

BIBLIOGRAPHY

Holzheuter, John. "Wisconsin." In *Encyclopedia of African-American Culture and History*. Volume 5, edited by Jack Salzman, David Lionel Smith, and Cornel West. 1996.

Sigler, Jay A., ed. *Civil Rights in America*. 1998. Gale Research. Detroit.

Trotter, Joe William, Jr. *Black Milwaukee: The Making of an Industrial Proletariat, 1915–45*. 1985.

Matthew May

Wisdom, John Minor

(1905–1999), judge.

John Minor Wisdom was a judge of the United States Court of Appeals for the FIFTH CIRCUIT from 1957 until his death in 1999. He played a pivotal role in promulgating and upholding civil rights law. Judge Wisdom was born into a prominent family in New Orleans, Louisiana. He graduated from Washington and Lee University in 1925 and from Tulane Law School in 1929. From 1929 to 1957 he was engaged in law practice in New Orleans, except for four years of military service during WORLD WAR II. Wisdom's experiences in Louisiana led him to believe strongly in the importance of a two-party system (see POLITICAL PARTIES), and so he worked strenuously to revive the REPUBLICAN PARTY in his state. In 1952, Wisdom led the insurgent Eisenhower delegation from Louisiana to the Republican National Convention in Chicago and managed their successful fight for recognition, which, with similar successes in Texas and Georgia (led by his future judicial colleagues, John Robert BROWN and Elbert TUTTLE), helped Dwight D. EISENHOWER to win the nomination. President Eisenhower appointed Wisdom to the United States Court of Appeals for the Fifth Circuit in 1957. This court dealt with all appeals of lawsuits from federal courts in Texas, Louisiana, Mississippi, Alabama, Georgia, and Florida. (In 1981, Congress split the Fifth Circuit by creating a new Eleventh Circuit with jurisdiction over Alabama, Georgia, and Florida and reducing the Fifth Circuit to Texas, Louisiana, and Mississippi.) Its location in the Deep South gave the Fifth Circuit a crucial role in implementing the Supreme Court's civil rights decisions and, later, the Congress's civil rights statutes. Wisdom, along with Judge John Robert Brown of Texas, Judge Richard RIVES of Alabama, and Judge Elbert Tuttle of Georgia, became known as one of "the Four." These four judges protected black American rights, although they exposed themselves and their families to personal risks by doing so. Judge Wisdom was both the most scholarly and the most verbally eloquent member of the group. He wrote many of the leading opinions protecting civil rights, including perhaps most notably *United States v. Jefferson County Board of Education*, which held that the Constitution required a school system to be "a bona fide unitary system where schools are not white schools or Negro schools—just schools." The *Jefferson County* decision, initially made in December 1966 and upheld in 1968, finally forced the Deep South to implement BROWN V. BOARD OF EDUCATION. In 1976, Wisdom took "senior status," allowing him to have a reduced case load, but he continued to hear and decide appeals for twenty-three more years, until a few weeks before his death in May 1999. Wisdom's intelligence, scholarship, and writing ability made him widely respected; his charm, zest for life, and genuine sympathy for all people made him widely loved. In 1996, he received the Presidential Medal of Freedom. As Justice William Brennan said of Wisdom and his colleagues in the Fifth Circuit, "They changed the face of a nation."

BIBLIOGRAPHY

Bass, Jack. *Unlikely Heroes.* 1981.

Couch, Harvey C. *A History of the Fifth Circuit 1891–1981.* 1984.

Read, F., and L. McGough. *Let Them Be Judged.* 1978.

Tulane Law Review 60 (December 1985). Issue commemorating Wisdom.

Tulane Law Review 69 (June 1995). Issue honoring Wisdom.

Washington and Lee Law Review 53, no. 1. Issue commemorating Wisdom.

Wisdom, J. M. "The Ever Whirling Wheels of American Federalism." *Notre Dame Law Review* 59 (1984): 1063–1078.

Wisdom, J. M. "The Friction-Making Exacerbating Political Role of Federal Courts," *Southwestern Law Review* 21 (1967): 411–428.

Henry T. Greeley

Woman Suffrage Movement

The earliest known call for female voting privileges in the United States came in 1648 from Maryland landowner Margaret Brent, who demanded that, like male freeholders, she be granted a vote in the House of Burgesses (the Maryland colonial legislature). Nonetheless, although some states allowed female taxpayers to vote for a time after the American Revolution, the issue of female enfranchisement was virtually dormant well into the nineteenth century. It was only in 1848, with the first women's rights convention in Seneca Falls, New York, that an organized effort to pursue the vote was formed. Elizabeth Cady STANTON and Quaker minister Lucretia Mott had first conceived of the convention years before, out of anger over the segregation of female abolitionists at the World Anti-Slavery Convention of 1840 in London, England. They were joined by three other women—Mary Ann McClintock, Jane Hunt, and Mott's sister, Martha Wright—in organizing the Seneca Falls convention. Attended by 300 men and women, the convention produced the "Declaration of Sentiments," a document outlining eighteen grievances regarding the status of women and twelve resolutions for future action, including one that proposed female enfranchisement. Although the call for the vote was controversial even to the convention attendees, the Declaration of Sentiments received one hundred signatures. Two weeks later, at a Rochester, New York, convention, there was even more solid support for suffrage; two years later, at the first national women's rights convention in Worcester, Massachusetts, it became clear that the suffrage movement had found a broad base of support.

In the early 1850s, Stanton met temperance worker Susan B. ANTHONY, who would soon match her passion for FEMINISM and rank beside her as a principal figure in the suffrage movement. The two worked both together and separately on a variety of reform causes, including abolition and married women's property rights. Like other suffragists, they were hopeful that female contributions to the Civil War victory would be rewarded with enfranchisement; as that hope failed to materialize, they became more adamant that female suffrage take equal priority with other reforms. Beginning in 1869, the suffrage movement experienced a deep, two-decade rift over the issue of ratification of the FIFTEENTH AMENDMENT, which would completely prohibit the disenfranchisement of African-American males, a right that had been merely discouraged by the FOURTEENTH AMENDMENT. Under the Fourteenth Amendment, states that did not grant African Americans the vote faced the prospect of suffering a relative reduction in their representation in the House of Representatives, a body which would be reformulated to reflect the overall number of male voters. Elizabeth Cady Stanton and Susan B. Anthony insisted that the Fifteenth Amendment expand its provisions to include women.

In the past, both Stanton and Anthony had worked ardently for the rights of African Americans—in fact, earlier in the decade they had helped found the National Woman's Loyal League, which produced a petition with 400,000 signatures in support of the THIRTEENTH AMENDMENT. That amendment freed slaves in states loyal to the union in 1865. Now, in 1869, however, they viewed the absence of a reference to women in the Fifteenth Amendment as a defect of such a magnitude that it interfered with their support for the earlier amendment. They stressed that women were just as qualified to vote as other disenfranchised groups and that it would be absurd for them to act as advocates for others and to neglect their own rights. Women, as longstanding supporters of the African-American cause, deserved to be simultaneously enfranchised, they argued.

Stanton and Anthony now exited an organization that had briefly united the objectives of both feminists and abolitionists to form a new organization that concentrated principally on feminist issues: the National Woman Suffrage Association (NWSA). In response to the formation of NWSA, more conservative feminists, led by Lucy STONE, formed the AMERICAN WOMAN SUFFRAGE ASSOCIATION (AWSA) later in 1869. Its disdain for the NWSA membership continued beyond the ratification of the Fifteenth Amendment in 1870. AWSA continued to accuse NWSA of RACISM. Comprised entirely of suffragists from existing groups, AWSA was dismayed by some of NWSA's suggested reforms—for

Suffrage parade in New York City, May 6, 1912. (Library of Congress)

example, the expansion of the grounds for divorce beyond adultery. Furthermore, it was outraged by NWSA's unconventional supporters, such as free-love advocate Victoria Woodhull, her sister Tennessee Claflin, and their friend Isabella Hooker, all of whom intertwined ideas of spiritualism and radical reform with feminist thinking. AWSA and NWSA were moreover divided on the question of which strategy to pursue in the suffrage battle. AWSA favored a state and local approach, whereas NWSA sought a federal amendment to the Constitution that would grant female suffrage.

The women's movement relied heavily on speech-making at civic clubs and other local volunteer organizations. There were numerous conventions and a stream of feminist articles, books, and periodicals. Another favorite tactic among all generations of suffragists was the petition drive, whereby petitions were circulated in support of various measures. Occasionally there were staged publicity-seeking events, including Susan Anthony's disruption of the 1876 centennial celebrations in Philadelphia and acts of CIVIL DISOBEDIENCE, such as Lucy Stone's 1858 refusal to pay property taxes on her New Jersey home. Even in the late nineteenth century, there were various female candi-

dacies for government, although these were often purely symbolic; in the early twentieth century, bolder feminists staged a number of marches, demonstrations, and pickets.

The suffrage movement, over its seventy-two-year history, was influenced by and came to influence many other social trends and political movements. Even the earliest suffragists had extensive prior experience as activists involved in volunteer or charitable work before becoming involved in the suffrage cause. Many had been abolitionists as well and saw female suffrage as a natural extension of the liberation of African Americans. A number of notable suffragists were of the Quaker faith, which had long promoted progressive ideals. Suffrage was also embraced by scores of noted writers or other women of accomplishment of the day—for example, pioneer female clergywomen Antoinette Blackwell and Olympia Brown; author Julia Ward Howe; American Red Cross founder Clara Barton; journalist and civil rights activists Ida Wells-Barnett (see Ida B. WELLS) and Mary Church TERRELL, who was the first president of the NATIONAL ASSOCIATION OF COLORED WOMEN. And there were prominent male supporters of female suffrage, including anti-slavery orator Frederick Douglass and poet-philosopher Ralph Waldo Emerson.

Suffrage became closely linked with the issue of temperance, especially during Frances Willard's leadership (1879–1898) of the national Woman's Christian Temperance Union (WCTU). WCTU was a force behind the drive to permit women to vote in municipal elections, because those local elections often involved referenda determining whether liquor could be sold. (This did, of course, at the same time make the suffrage movement a target of the liquor industry's retaliation.) Beginning in 1878 with the California State Grange organization, the Granger movement—a political-action group that had been representing the needs of farmers from 1867 onward—began offering support to woman suffrage through local bodies of the National Grange of the Patrons of Husbandry, the principal Granger organization. Although the suffragists' relationship with the LABOR MOVEMENT was initially checkered, they continued to court labor until 1890, when suffrage received a formal endorsement from the American Federation of Labor (see AFL-CIO). Further reform movements were to follow the AFL's lead, including ones promoting consumer rights and other progressive causes. Ultimately it was the trend toward greater female EDUCATION and the desire for more social freedom that strengthened the suffrage movement the most.

Throughout the suffrage campaign, some feminists suggested modified strategies for securing the vote. Because it was widely recognized that it was essential for mothers to have a voice in matters pertaining to education, suffragists were able to obtain for women a kind of limited so-called "school suffrage," which allowed them to vote only on certain issues—on school-related matters, in some states: Kansas, 1861; Michigan and Minnesota, 1875, for women who were both widows and mothers of school children; Vermont and New York, 1880. In 1898 tax-paying women in Louisiana were enfranchised on tax matters. Generally, Western states were more receptive to female suffrage, in part because of the hope that women's influence would promote law and order. In Utah female suffrage gained ground because it bolstered local support for the practice of polygamy, which Congress sought to prohibit. As U.S. territories Utah and Wyoming enfranchised women in 1869, as did Washington in 1883; Wyoming retained female suffrage after gaining statehood in 1890, although Congress reversed women's enfranchisement in Utah as part of the 1887 Edmunds-Tucker Act, and the vote for women was defeated in Washington in a state referendum in 1889. In 1915, Congress considered but did not pass a law to permit women who met state voting requirements to vote in congressional elections.

In 1890 the branches of the women's movement, NWSA and AWSA, united to form the NATIONAL AMERICAN WOMAN SUFFRAGE ASSOCIATION (NAWSA). NAWSA was the organization that probably deserved greatest credit for the enactment of the NINETEENTH AMENDMENT, which enfranchised women. NAWSA was first headed by Elizabeth Cady Stanton, although it would later repudiate her 1896 denunciation of the Bible. Susan B. Anthony followed Stanton as NAWSA president, with an eight-year tenure beginning in 1892. Both the Stanton and Anthony presidencies were marred by enormous frustration in the suffrage campaign. It was under the first presidency of Iowa educator Carrie Chapman Catt (1900–04) that NAWSA and the movement as a whole experienced a new infusion of energy and demonstrated more savvy. In her second presidency (1914–21), Catt enacted the "Winning Plan" (1916), which promoted the state-based strategy as a means to an ultimate federal suffrage amendment. NAWSA, however, still faced competition from a younger, more aggressive contingent of feminists including Alice Paul and Lucy Burns, whose Congressional Union (later the NATIONAL WOMAN'S PARTY) practiced a confrontational strategy and demanded the immediate enactment of a federal amendment. In 1917 Paul organized a picket of the White House, for which she and many followers were arrested and imprisoned. Public outrage over these arrests was another significant factor in creating momentum for the drive to pass the suffrage amendment.

The Nineteenth Amendment is worded as follows:

Section 1: The right of the citizens of the United States to vote shall not be denied or abridged by the United States or by any state on account of sex.
Section 2: Congress shall have power to enforce this article by appropriate legislation.

Suffrage amendments had been offered each year since 1868, and the wording of the amendment was unchanged from its 1878 version. In spite of support from President Woodrow Wilson, the amendment was still the subject of considerable controversy in Congress. Among the issues raised in congressional debate were fears in the North of detriment to business, distaste in the South for perceived damage to states' rights, and a widespread phobia of involving women further in the public sphere. Nonetheless, suffrage finally was passed by the 66th Congress: by the House of Representatives, 304–89 (May 20, 1919), and by the Senate, 66–30 (June 4, 1919). The amendment secured its thirty-sixth state ratification from Tennessee on August 18, 1920.

Following the enactment of the Nineteenth Amendment, some of the former suffragists reorganized into the LEAGUE OF WOMEN VOTERS to offer their advocacy of progressive reforms on issues such as child welfare and workers' rights. The League joined with other groups to form the Women's Joint Congressional Committee to enhance female voting solidarity. Many former suffragists, such as Carrie Chapman Catt and Jeanette Rankin (the first woman elected to Congress), stressed the importance of pacifism and saw it as an outgrowth of their feminist efforts.

BIBLIOGRAPHY

Anthony, Katharine. *Susan B. Anthony: Her Personal History and Her Era.* 1954.

Barry, Kathleen. *Susan B. Anthony: A Biography of a Singular Feminist.* 1988.

Blackwell, Alice Stone. *Lucy Stone: Pioneer of Woman's Rights.* 1971.

Catt, Carrie Chapman, and Nettie Rogers Shuler. *Woman Suffrage and Politics.* 1923.

DuBois, Ellen Carol. *Elizabeth Cady Stanton/Susan B. Anthony: Correspondence, Writings, Speeches.* 1981.

DuBois, Ellen Carol. *Feminism and Suffrage: The Emergence of an Independent Women's Movement in America, 1848–1869.* 1978.

Duniway, Abigail Scott. *Path Breaking: An Autobiographical History of the Equal Suffrage Movement in the Pacific Coast States.* 1914.

Flexner, Eleanor. *Century of Struggle: The Woman's Rights Movement in the United States.* Rev. ed., 1975.

Frost, Elizabeth, and Kathryn Cullen-DuPont. *Women's Suffrage in America: An Eyewitness History.* 1992.

Frost-Knappman, Elizabeth, with Sarah Kurian. *The ABC-Clio Companion to Women's Progress in America.* 1994.

Griffith, Elisabeth. *In Her Own Right: The Life of Elizabeth Cady Stanton.* 1984.

Grimes, Alan P. *The Puritan Ethic and Woman Suffrage.* 1967.

Gurko, Miriam. *The Ladies of Seneca Falls: The Birth of the Woman's Rights Movement.* 1974.

Harper, Ida Husted. *The Life and Work of Susan B. Anthony.* 1898.

Kerr, Andrea Moore. *Lucy Stone: Speaking Out for Equality.* 1992.

Kraditor, Aileen. *The Ideas of the Woman Suffrage Movement, 1890–1920.* 1981.

Lunardini, Christine A. *From Equal Suffrage to Equal Rights: Alice Paul and the National Woman's Party, 1910–1928.* 1986.

Wheeler, Leslie. *Loving Warriors: Selected Letters of Lucy Stone and Henry B. Blackwell.* 1981.

Sarah Kurian

Women and Civil Rights Struggles

In spite of the triple constraints of gender, RACE, and CLASS, women of color have been active agents in struggles for the rights of differently privileged racial groups, women, children, students, gays, lesbians, mi-

Sojourner Truth, American evangelist and reformer. (National Portrait Gallery, Smithsonian Institution)

grant farmers, garment workers, welfare recipients, and others. Seldom recognized as "leaders," women actually have made significant contributions and performed multiple leadership roles: articulating the needs and concerns of followers; defining and setting goals; providing ideologies justifying action; formulating strategies and tactics; initiating action; organizing and coordinating actions; mobilizing and persuading followers; leading and directing actions; raising funds and other material resources; teaching, educating, and training followers as well as other leaders; generating publicity; obtaining public sympathy and support; and serving as mediators of group interactions, especially competition and conflict.

African-American Women

From the 1600s through the 1900s, black women have been active participants and leaders in civil rights struggles, from ship jumping during the middle passage through slave rebellions on Southern plantations to SIT-INS at segregated public facilities and electoral politics at all levels of government.

During the 1800s and early 1900s, Harriet Tubman, Sojourner Truth, Anna Julia Cooper, Fannie Barrier Williams, and other women fought for freedom from

Fannie Lou Hamer testifying before the U.S. Senate. Her proclamation, "I'm sick and tired of being sick and tired!" made a resounding impact throughout the nation. (AP/Wide World Photos)

slavery and for the rights of African Americans as well as suffrage for U.S. women. Educational activists Mary McLeod BETHUNE, Nannie Helen Burroughs, Dee Mae Griffith McNair, Charlotte Hawkins Brown, Fannie Jackson Coppin, Hallie Quinn Brown, and others struggled to found schools for black children and youths. Anti-lynching crusader Ida B. WELLS and civil rights activist Mary Church TERRELL fought for justice and equality for African Americans. Black women activist-educators, including elementary school teachers Septima Poinsette CLARK and Modjeska Monteith Simkins from South Carolina, fought for racial equality in teacher salaries and public schools and for black political empowerment via EDUCATION. All these women utilized resources derived from their participation in black churches, schools, and colleges as well as civil rights organizations such as the NATIONAL ASSOCIATION FOR THE ADVANCEMENT OF COLORED PEOPLE (NAACP) and the NATIONAL URBAN LEAGUE.

During the 1940s and 1950s, NAACP youth leader Ella BAKER, who eventually became executive director of the SOUTHERN CHRISTIAN LEADERSHIP CONFERENCE (SCLC) in 1957 and organizer of the STUDENT NONVIOLENT COORDINATING COMMITTEE (SNCC) in 1960; seamstress Rosa PARKS, who sparked the MONTGOMERY BUS BOYCOTT in 1955; literacy pioneer Septima CLARK, who founded the first adult CITIZENSHIP SCHOOL in 1957; and other women worked tirelessly for civil rights in the NAACP and other male-dominated organizations, including the CONGRESS OF

RACIAL EQUALITY (CORE) and the Southern Christian Leadership Conference. At the same time, as a result of exclusionary race-based practices by white women's political organizations and gender-based practices by male-dominated black organizations, other African-American women founded their own civil rights organizations. For example, in Montgomery, Alabama, college professors Mary Francis Burkes and JoAnn Gibson Robinson founded the middle-class-based Women's Political Council (WPC) in 1946, and domestic-cook Georgia Gilmore founded the working-class-based Club From Nowhere (CFN) in 1955. Insurance agent Johnnie CARR worked with Burkes, Robinson, Gilmore, and other women leaders of both the WPC and the CFN as they planned, organized, strategized, mobilized, and raised funds that were crucial to the success of the boycott, which led to the court's declaring Montgomery's segregation laws unconstitutional.

The Montgomery women boycott leaders drew upon the previous year's successful educational struggle involving twelve unsung, virtually invisible women initiators of the landmark 1954 BROWN V. BOARD OF EDUCATION case. Moreover, the *Brown* case had been selected as the lead case among four previously filed 1951 cases that were consolidated by the SUPREME COURT, which heard complaints from Delaware (*Belton v. Gebhart*), Virginia (*Davis v. County School Board of Prince Edward County*), South Carolina (*Briggs v. Elliot*), and the District of Columbia (*Bolling v. Sharp*). These cases involved many women plaintiffs and paved the way for college student Autherine LUCY to attempt DE-SEGREGATION of the University of Alabama in 1956 and for Arkansas NAACP leader and teacher Daisy BATES to lead nine black students in the first successful post-*Brown* school desegregation at Central High School in 1957.

During the 1960s, 1970s, and 1980s, sharecroppers Fannie Lou HAMER and Victoria Gray cofounded the MISSISSIPPI FREEDOM DEMOCRATIC PARTY (MFDP), and other black women formed the National Black Feminist Organization (NBFO), the Cumbahee River Collective (CRC), the Third World Women's Alliance (TWWA), the Association of Black Women Historians (ABWH), and the National Coalition of 100 Black Women (NCBW). Allowing black women to address concerns for justice and equality on a variety of topics, these organizations built upon the tradition of activism by the black women's club movements and "racial uplift" organizations of the late 1800s and early 1900s, including the NATIONAL ASSOCIATION OF COLORED WOMEN (NACW) and the NATIONAL COUNCIL OF NE-GRO WOMEN (NCNW). Also in the 1970s, Congress-woman Shirley CHISHOLM declared herself "unbought and unbossed" and made history as the first woman to be a serious contender for nomination as president of the United States.

Perhaps the most youthful and openly revolutionary phase of African-American women's struggles for civil rights occurred in the direct confrontations of the 1960s and 1970s, when the Student Nonviolent Co-ordinating Committee and the BLACK PANTHER PARTY were founded. SNCC leader Diane NASH led student-ins in Nashville, Tennessee; SNCC freedom singer Bernice Johnson Reagon led protests in the ALBANY MOVEMENT; future journalist Charlayne Hunter-Gault desegregated the University of Georgia; and Ruby Doris Smith ROBINSON and other college student shock troops sought INTEGRATION and citizenship rights using CIVIL DISOBEDIENCE, nonviolent direct action, jail-ins, FREEDOM RIDES, and desegregation efforts on college campuses.

By 1966, many young women had become dissatisfied with the slow pace of change. Some eventually embraced revolution, racial separatism, and armed self-defense and joined the BLACK POWER movement and the Black Panther Party. These radicals struggled inside and outside the "revolution" as they founded liberation schools, established breakfast programs for poor children, were placed under surveillance by the FEDERAL BUREAU OF INVESTIGATION (FBI) and other law enforcement agencies, encountered SEXISM from male comrades in struggle, and had to engage in intellectual genuflection to keep the gendered status quo. The significance of revolutionary women leaders, including Kathleen Cleaver, Angela DAVIS, Elaine Brown, JoNina Abrams, Assata Shakur, and Erika Huggins, has been obscured, denigrated, or minimized by sensationalized media portrayals of violence, police confrontations, and love relationships with radical men. Yet, in spite of retaliation, arrest, imprisonment, sexism, racism, and classism, these and other black women of different generations and class locations risked their safety, lives, livelihoods, and personal relationships to lead many civil rights struggles.

Latinas–Chicanas

Latinas (Spanish-speaking) and Chicanas (of Mexican descent) have been active leaders in various U.S. struggles. In addition to gender equality and women's rights, Latina struggles have concentrated on six main issues: (1) migrant farm worker rights and labor unionization; (2) land grant rights, especially in New Mexico; (3) racially biased immigration laws; (4) Chicano student rights, bilingual education, and Chicano studies in higher education; (5) crusades for racial justice; and (6) political and economic self-determination.

During the 1930s and 1940s, Consuelo Espinoza, Mary Rose Garrido-Wilcox, and other women activists pushed for Americanization and political empowerment in struggles organized by the Mexican American Movement (MAM) and the LEAGUE OF UNITED LATIN AMERICAN CITIZENS (LULAC). In the 1950s and 1960s, working with César CHAVEZ in the COMMUNITY SERVICE ORGANIZATION (CSO) and later in the UNITED FARM WORKERS (UFW), Dolores Fernandez HUERTA as well as Jessie Lopez de la Cruz and Maria Elena Lucas organized boycotts, strikes, and demonstrations to obtain rights for migrant workers. As a lobbyist, Huerta served as a spokesperson and negotiator for the migrant workers movement and successfully persuaded politicians to pass legislation that eliminated the requirement for public assistance programs to be granted only to U.S. citizens. After retiring from her lobbying position, Huerta became vice president of the UFW from 1970 to 1973 and continued to struggle for workers' rights in the fields, canneries, and mines.

Emphasizing lawsuits and legislative advocacy, Vilma Martinez worked as a leader in the MEXICAN AMERICAN LEGAL DEFENSE AND EDUCATION FUND (MALDEF), a national organization founded to tackle civil rights litigation impacting on the Latino community. Promoted to president and general counsel of MALDEF in 1973, Martinez in 1975 succeeded in getting the VOTING RIGHTS ACT OF 1965 for African Americans and Puerto Ricans extended to Chicanos/as and promoted bilingual education in public schools for non-English-speaking children. Largely supported by the Southwest Council of La Raza (SCLR) and the

Ford Foundation, Martinez and other women of MAL-DEF and the massive SOUTHWEST VOTER REGISTRATION EDUCATION PROJECT (SVREP) organized, waged campaigns, and raised funds for voter registration and other actions instrumental in facilitating the political consciousness and political empowerment of Mexican Americans.

At the local level, Mexican American women and other Latinas founded and led many community-based organizations, such as the MOTHERS OF EAST LOS ANGELES (MELA), a network of four hundred working-class families of an Eastside Los Angeles barrio. Under the leadership of Juana Gutierrez, MELA women ("border feminists") successfully defeated state-sponsored and commercial projects that threatened the rights of their families and communities. Gloria Molina, who won election to the California assembly in 1982, and MELA activists were influential forces in their opposition to the Los Angeles County Men's Central Prison. At various times from the 1930s to the 1990s, Maria Varela, Dora Ibanez, Marta Cotera, and other Latinas served as leaders in local chapters of various regional and national organizations of the *movimiento*, such as the CRUSADE FOR JUSTICE, the La RAZA UNIDA PARTY, the MOVIMIENTO ESTUDIANTIL CHICANO DE AZTLAN (M.E.Ch.A.), the United Mexican American Students (UMAS), the pro-Mexican property rights ALIANZA FEDERAL DE PUEBLO LIBRES, and the self-styled paramilitary BROWN BERETS, a radical organization similar to African Americans' revolutionary Black Panther Party for Self-Defense.

Asian-American Women

Although much less visible than other women activists of color, Asian-American women have engaged in several struggles, including the fight for Asian-American garment workers' rights, bilingual education, Filipino farm workers' rights, African-American racial equality, New Left student free speech rights, Third World coalitions for ethnic studies on college campuses, repatriation for Japanese internment during WORLD WAR II, and an end to the VIETNAM WAR. During the 1930s and 1940s, some women held demonstrations and engaged in strikes to protest repressive aspects of Japanese relocation camp life. Some denounced their U.S. citizenship, pushed for repatriation, and used the courts to challenge the constitutionality of evacuation.

The Asian-American struggles for civil rights and the YELLOW POWER movement in general did not crystallize noticeably until after the mid-1960s. Visible Asian activism has been intermittent, short-lived, more limited, and much less publicized and researched than that of other racial/ethnic minority groups for a number of reasons, including the relatively small population of Asian Americans (less than 1 percent of the American population until the immigration law reforms of 1965), the great diversity of ethnicities, immigrant cultures, and identities among Asian Americans (especially Chinese, Japanese, Korean, Filipino, Pacific Islander, Southeast Asian, and East Indian), the localized and decentralized nature of Asian-American community-based struggles, and the lack of nationally recognized Asian-American leaders. Although activist Yuri Kochiyama and politician Patsy Mink have some name recognition, most women do not.

The development of a pan-Asian identity in the United States and Asian-American feminist organizing have been complicated not only by Asian immigrant patterns that historically have been shaped by intermittent anti-Asian immigration laws but also by differences in perceptions of their status by American-born (and/or U.S.-raised) and foreign-born (and/or raised in Asia) Asian Americans, by persistently biased media images of Asian immigrants as a middle class "model minority" with little reason to struggle, and by sexism and classism inside and outside of Asian-American communities.

The first significant number of Asians to emigrate to the United States came from China, going as laborers to California and Hawaii in the 1840s through the late 1880s. In 1882, the CHINESE EXCLUSION ACT became the first act to ban immigration on the basis of ethnicity. Chinese women, whose husbands and potential partners came to America to work on the railroads, were forced to remain in China (a relatively weak world power) and therefore were hindered in establishing families and stable immigrant communities in the United States. In contrast, Japanese immigrants of this period came from an emerging superpower with heightened status in the world polity and were not so vulnerable to U.S. exclusion acts. Therefore, Japanese immigrants were better able than Chinese immigrants to establish families and communities that included women.

Later, immigration acts were passed selectively to curtail or stop Asian immigration to the United States. The fear of a "yellow peril" prompted passage of the 1917 immigration act banning immigration from all Asian countries except Japan and the Philippines and passage of the 1924 immigration act, which banned all Asian immigrants. Asian-American women's visibility and their ethnic communities were affected by these laws, which resulted in local, state, and federal legislation producing racial barriers to citizenship and community empowerment of Asian immigrants.

In the 1950s, 1960s, and 1970s, Asian Americans were impacted by changes in anti-Asian immigration laws and other legislation. Because of their countries' support of the United States during World War II, Chinese and Filipino immigrants were naturalized in mass ceremonies as Japanese Americans were still trying to recover from their internment in the postwar era of the 1950s. During the 1960s, Asian-American women began to participate in electoral politics (primarily in Hawaii) and mass protest politics (primarily in urban areas of the West and East coasts). As the first Asian American woman to serve in the U.S. CONGRESS, as representative from Hawaii in 1964, Patsy Takemoto Mink pushed for passage of the IMMIGRATION ACT OF 1965, which removed "national origins" as the basis of American immigration legislation and would change the face of Asian-American communities and activism.

During the pre-1965 era, the majority of Asian Americans lived in working-class ethnic enclaves (such as the Chinatowns of California and New York) and were American-born as a result of the many anti-Asian exclusion acts. During the post-1965 era, more "Americanized" second- and third-generation Chinese and Japanese Americans became geographically and economically mobile, increased their intergroup communications, and entered college in record numbers, thus forming the basis of a solid Asian-American middle class. Also after the 1965 act, more foreign-born professional and middle- to upper-class immigrants from Asia and the Pacific Islands were allowed to enter the United States through family reunification and professional/managerial categories. Poverty, poor housing, overcrowding, bad police–community relations, low political participation, and lack of legal, health, and recreational services in Chinatowns, Manilatowns, and other working-class Asian-American communities became the objects of community organizing by mostly American-born second- and third-generation Chinese- and Japanese-American college student activists.

Utilizing confrontational protest tactics and organizing informal rap sessions, study groups, women's community projects, support networks, and consciousness-raising publications, Yuri Kochiyama, Miya Iwataki, Evelyn Yoshimura, Wilma Chan, Jackie Church, Helen Zia, Elaine Kim, Carol Ito, Anna Rhee, Sunita Mani, and other Asian-American women activists organized to guarantee the civil rights of Asian Americans, particularly those in ethnic enclaves, and to promote a pan-Asian identity, not only on college campuses but throughout Asian-American communities. Targeting education and voting rights, these women were founding leaders or members of the Organization of Asian Women (OAW), National Organization of Pan Asian Women (NOPAW), the National Network of Asian and Pacific Women (NNAPW), and the Asian American Women United (AAWU). These mostly college-educated and middle-class Asian-American women fought for the rights of both women and racial/ethnic minorities at the grassroots levels via changes in legislation, education, em-

ployment, and scholarship. The Los Angeles Asian Women's Center (LLAWC) was one of the most significant community outreach programs, established by Asian-American women activists to provide a drug-abuse program and an environment that promoted health, child care, education, and counseling, especially for low-income women.

While Asian-American women participated in race-centered movements as well as in a movement of their own to improve the role and status of women, those who founded explicitly feminist organizations aimed to promote an environment of strong Asian "sisterhood" and to intensify the role and participation of Asian women within the society as a whole. Efforts were made in legislation, education, and EMPLOYMENT; but women who participated in and led informal rap sessions, study groups, community projects, and new Asian feminist organizations of the late 1960s and 1970s were often viewed as too radical by their parents (an older generation with longer memories and experiences with discrimination) as well as by male activists and residents of the working-class communities where Asian women organized and focused much of their attention.

Women activists who participated in the 1968 San Francisco State student strike, considered a defining moment in Asian-American activism, helped to establish ethnic and Asian-American studies as legitimate programs on college campuses throughout the United States. The three most influential periodicals of the time—*Bridge, Gidra,* and *Amerasia Journal*—illustrated that women's activism was gendered and constrained by sexism. Those women revolutionaries in the I Wor Kuen (IWK), a radical collective formed by Chinese-American college and high school students in 1969 in New York, encountered sexism as they worked with men to overcome classism and capitalist class relations.

In the late 1970s, 1980s, and 1990s, Asian women activists focused on issues of ethnic diversity and needs within Asian-American groups of different socioeconomic class backgrounds, including immigrant status (American or foreign-born), educational needs of non-English-speaking children, reproductive rights, and legal remedies for women victims of domestic violence. Perhaps the most important and successful Asian-American educational struggle, which underscored the different issues caused by differences in immigration patterns, was the matter of educational resources for non-English-speaking students in public schools. In 1970, thirteen non-English-speaking Chinese-American students filed suit against the San Francisco Board of Education, which resulted in the 1974 Supreme Court LAU v. NICHOLS ruling that the school system had discriminated against students by not providing them bilingual education and other services to help immigrant students overcome language barriers. This ruling for bilingual education helped not only Asian Americans but also Latina Americans, Native Americans, and other groups in their struggles for the rights of all children, American- and foreign-born, to achieve equal education in America.

Native American Activists

Native American Indian women historically have performed crucial roles in American Indian society, although with a high degree of sex–gender segregation. Native women of the Iroquois Federation, for example, played a powerful political role among Native American tribes during the fourteenth and fifteenth centuries. In the twentieth century, however, Native women's acts of resistance and leadership in civil rights struggles became much more visibly national, direct, and confrontational. In general, their civil rights struggles have focused on nine main areas: (1) self-determination; (2) treaty rights, especially to land, fishing, water, and mineral resources; (3) land reclamation and acquisition by non-Indians; (4) education, schooling, and Native American studies; (5) religious rights and sacred burial grounds; (6) environmental racism and ecocide; (7) pan-Indianism (see PAN-TRIBALISM); (8) government and police treatment on reservations and in prisons; and (9) violence against and rape of women.

In the 1960s and 1970s, Native women fought to change federal Indian policies that terminated the rights of American Indians and demoralized reservation and urban Indian communities. Women served as leaders and participants in RED POWER (a militant pan-Indian movement) and in various movement organizations, such as the AMERICAN INDIAN MOVEMENT (AIM). Having experienced firsthand the poverty, discrimination, isolation, frustration, reservation alcoholism, and often hopelessness of their people in general and their children and families in particular, Native women were leaders in the quest for Indian self-determination and in the takeover of the national BUREAU OF INDIAN AFFAIRS (BIA) in 1967 in Washington, D.C.; sit-ins at BIA offices throughout the country; the ALCATRAZ OCCUPATION in 1969; armed confrontations on the Pine Ridge reservation; trials of Indian activists and protests at Pyramid Lake, and the WOUNDED KNEE OCCUPATION in 1973. Women were also activists in youth-led organizations, such as the NATIONAL INDIAN YOUTH COUNCIL (NIYC), the Young American Indian Council (YAIC), and the Organization of Native American Students (ONAS).

During the turbulent 1960s and 1970s, Wilma Mankiller began her civil rights struggle as a student activist, whose consciousness was raised after the 1969 Alcatraz Occupation. Mankiller worked to establish treaty rights, a legal defense fund to reclaim Native American lands, and an adult education program for Native Americans in California. In 1985, after returning to her Oklahoma roots, Mankiller became the first woman principal chief of the Cherokee nation. As a feminist leader, Mankiller initially posed a threat to the male Cherokee status quo and was attacked because of her gender. However, by the time of her re-elections in 1987 and 1991, Mankiller's womanist activism and leadership on behalf of her people had earned the respect of men and women throughout the Cherokee nation and the Intertribal Council of the Five Tribes. Other Native American women, such as Irene Stewart and Annie Wauneka, have also run for various government offices and toured the country to gather support for Native American causes.

Though not elected to political office, La Donna Harris, Grace Thorpe, Stella Leach, Mary Crow Dog, Belva Cottier, Karen Baird-Olson, and other Native women used a combination of legal strategies, direct action tactics, building occupations, caravans, and other means to fight for Native American self-determination as well as land, water, fishing, burial, religious, and educational rights. However, in fighting against environmental ecocide, Christianization, racially motivated violence and murder, non-Indian land acquisition, and broken treaties, Indian women sometimes experienced retaliation and were kept under surveillance, fired, beaten, jailed, and even killed.

In 1974, the Women of All Red Nations (WARN) was formed as an AIM affiliate and as an autonomous pan-Indian organization of Native American women activists. WARN leaders wanted to emphasize traditional leadership roles of women in Native American cultures. They also joined white environmental activists in 1979 to protest milling, water depletion, and contamination caused by nuclear mining of uranium in South Dakota. LaNada Boyer (Shoshone-Bannock) and Francis McKinley (Navajo-Ute) were two of the founding steering committee members of the NATIVE AMERICAN RIGHTS FUND (NARF), a nonprofit legal organization created in 1971 to defend, promote, and guarantee the legal rights of American Indian people. Boyer, McKinley, and other Native women activists used NARF and the courts to establish recognition and inherent sovereignty of Indian tribes and to protect Indian water, religious freedom, sacred burial grounds, and VOTING RIGHTS.

During the 1980s and 1990s, Native women concentrated on environmental racism as well as the rights of women in prisons and on reservations. Roberta Blackgoat traveled and protested environmental racism and destruction on Native American reservations throughout the United States. In 1994, for her role in publicizing the evils of ecocide by multinational corporations and other businesses, Blackgoat was named "America's Unsung Woman" by the National Women's History Project.

BIBLIOGRAPHY

Baca Zinn, Maxine, and Bonnie Thornton Dill, eds. *Women of Color in U.S. Society.* 1994.

Baird-Olson, Karen. "Reflections of an AIM Activist: Has It all Been Worth It?" In *American Indian Activism: Alcatraz to the Longest Walk*, edited by Troy Johnson, Joane Nagel, and Duane Champagne, pp. 225–241. 1997.

Barnett, Bernice McNair. "Sharecroppers, Domestics, and the Club From Nowhere: Poor and Working Class Women Organizing for Indigenous Collective Action." Paper presented at the annual meeting of the Southern Sociological Society, Louisville, Ky. March 1990.

Barnett, Bernice McNair, Rose M. Brewer, and M. Bahati Kuumba. "New Directions in Race, Gender, and Class Studies: African American Experiences." Special issue, *Race, Gender, & Class* 6 (2) (1999): 7–28.

Barnett, Bernice McNair. "Race, Gender and Class in the Personal–Political Struggles of African Americans: Reclaiming Voice." In *Race, Gender, and Class: Towards an Inclusive Curriculum*, edited by Jean Belkhir and Bernice McNair Barnett, pp. 34–36. 1999.

Barnett, Bernice McNair. *Sisters in Struggle: Invisible Black Women Leaders of the Civil Rights Movement, 1940–1975.* Forthcoming.

Bell-Scott, Patricia. *Life Notes. Personal Writings by Contemporary Black Women.* 1994.

Chavez, Jennie V. "Women of the Mexican American Movement." *Mademoiselle*, pp. 148–152, April 1972.

Chow, Ester Ngan-Ling. "The Development of a Feminist Consciousness Among Asian American Women." *Gender & Society* 1 (3) (1987): 284–299.

Chow, Ester Ngan-Ling, Doris Wilkinson, and Maxine Baca Zinn, eds. *Race, Class & Gender: Common Bonds, Different Voices.* 1996.

Crawford, Vickie, Jacqueline Rouse, and Barbara Woods, eds. *Trailblazers and Torchbearers: Women in the Civil Rights Movement.* 1990.

Garcia, Alma. "The Development of a Chicana Feminist Discourse, 1970–1980." *Gender & Society* 3 (1989): 217–238.

Giddings, Paula. *When and Where I Enter: The Impact of Black Women on Race and Sex in America.* 1984.

Gilkes, Cheryl Townsend. "Building in Many Places: Multiple Commitments and Ideologies in Black Women's Community Work." In *Women and the Politics of Empowerment*, edited by Ann Bookman and Sandra Morgan, pp. 54–76. 1988.

Higginbotham, Evelyn Brooks. *Righteous Discontent: The Women's Movement in the Black Baptist Church, 1880–1920.* 1993.

Hine, Darlene Clark. "Lifting the Veil, Shattering the Silence: Black Women's History in Slavery and Freedom." In *The State of Afro-American History: Past, Present, and Future*, edited by Darlene Clark Hine, pp. 224–249. 1986.

hooks, bell. *Aint I a Woman: Black Women and Feminism.* 1981.

Hull, Gloria T., Patricia Bell Scott, and Barbara Smith, eds. *All the Women Are White, All the Blacks Are Men, but Some of Us Are Brave.* 1982.

Mankiller, Wilma, and Michael Wallis. *Mankiller: A Chief and Her People, An Autobiography by the Principal Chief of the Cherokee Nation.* 1993.

McAdam, Doug. *Freedom Summer.* 1988.

McAdam, Doug. "Gender as a Mediator in the Activist Experience." *American Journal of Sociology* 97 (1992): 1211–1240.

Morris, Aldon. *The Origins of the Civil Rights Movement.* 1984.

Payne, Charles. *I've Got the Light of Freedom.* 1995.

Robinson, JoAnn Gibson. *The Montgomery Bus Boycott and the Women Who Started It.* 1987.

Terborg-Penn, Rosalyn. "Discrimination Against Afro American Women in the Women's Movement, 1830–1920." In *Afro American Woman: Struggles and Images*, edited by Sharon Harley and Rosalyn Terborg-Penn, pp. 17–27. 1978.

Bernice McNair Barnett

Women of All Red Nations

Influenced by the African-American civil rights movement, Native American activists in the 1960s sought to initiate a new era of political self-determination and indigenous rights. One of the more visible RED POWER organizations, the AMERICAN INDIAN MOVEMENT (AIM), was formed in 1968 as a pan-Indian organization. Escalating confrontation with the U.S. government was highlighted by the 1969 occupation of Alcatraz Island and the 1973 armed conflict at Wounded Knee, South Dakota (see ALCATRAZ OCCUPATION; WOUNDED KNEE OCCUPATION).

Noting that Indian males were consistently subjected to much harsher treatment than others by law authorities, a small group of women led by Lorelei DeCora Means, wife of AIM leader Russell MEANS and member of the Minneconjou Lakota, and Madonna Thunderhawk and Phyllis Young, both Hunkpapa Lakotas, formed Women of All Red Nations (WARN) in 1974. They realized that Indian women could pursue certain activist roles generally less available to Indian men and thus serve to hold AIM projects together while AIM leaders were dispersed and detained. The modern political equivalent of a traditional Indian women's society, WARN focused on the U.S. government's paternalistic and colonialistic treatment of Native American peoples. They sought to educate the public concerning reservation conditions suffered by women and children, including poverty, poor nutrition, government sterilization programs, inadequate health care, domestic violence, and emotional despair resulting from socially desperate conditions. They also organized protests against police brutality and the long prison terms meted to Indian male activists. Additionally, in the 1980s WARN combated environmental degradation that posed health hazards to Indian communities in the Northern Plains.

BIBLIOGRAPHY

Josephy, Alvin M., Jr., Joane Nagel, and Troy Johnson, eds. *Red Power: The American Indian's Fight for Freedom*, 2nd ed. 1999.

Means, Russell. *Where White Men Fear to Tread: The Autobiography of Russell Means*. 1995.

Weyler, Rex. *Blood of the Land: The Government and Corporate War Against the American Indian Movement*. 1982.

Richard C. Hanes

Wong Kim Ark, United States v. (1898)

United States v. Wong Kim Ark (1898) was a decision rendered by the U.S. Supreme Court upon review of a case initially heard in the U.S. District Court for the Northern District of California. Wong Kim Ark was born in San Francisco in 1873 of Chinese parents who were "domiciled residents" of the United States earning a living as merchants. Wong spent his entire childhood in the United States. In 1890, he went to China for a temporary visit and returned the following year. Though the 1882 CHINESE EXCLUSION ACT and its 1884 amendment, as well as the 1888 Scott Act and the 1892 Geary Act—laws that barred the entry of Chinese laborers—were in effect, the collector of customs at the port of San Francisco, who was responsible for enforcing these Chinese exclusion laws, allowed Wong to land because he was a "native-born" American citizen.

However, when Wong visited China a second time in 1894, he was denied reentry upon his return in 1895. His lawyer, Thomas Riordan, filed a writ of *habeas corpus* on his behalf and his case was heard in the District Court for the Northern District of California. There, Judge William Morrow, citing an 1884 decision of the lower federal court, *In re Look Tin Sing*, which had affirmed that anyone born in the United States was an American citizen, ordered Wong released from custody. Immigration officials appealed the decision, arguing that "the said Wong Kim Ark, although born in the city and county of San Francisco . . . is not . . . a citizen thereof, the mother and father of the said Wong Kim Ark being Chinese persons and subjects of the Emperor of China, and the said Wong Kim Ark being also a Chinese person and a subject of the Emperor of China. Because the said Wong Kim Ark has been at all times, by reason of his race, language, color and dress, a Chinese person, and now is, and for some time last past has been, a laborer by occupation," he was not exempted from the provisions of the exclusion laws, as were Chinese merchants, students, diplomats, and temporary visitors, who were still allowed entry after 1882.

After a careful review of the criteria for American citizenship, and of English common law upon which U.S. nationality laws were based, the SUPREME COURT decided that neither the Chinese exclusion laws nor earlier court rulings denying Chinese the right of naturalization applied to Wong Kim Ark. The justices declared: "A child born in the United States, of parents of Chinese descent . . . becomes at the time of his birth a citizen of the United States, by virtue of the first clause of the Fourteenth Amendment of the Constitution," which states that "All persons born or naturalized in the United States, and subject to the jurisdiction thereof, are citizens of the United States and of the State wherein they reside." Citing the precedence set by seventeen earlier cases, including several involving Chinese litigants, the majority opinion stated that the FOURTEENTH AMENDMENT forbade any state to "make or enforce any law which shall abridge the privileges or immunities of citizens of the United States"—an amendment that "was intended to bring all races, without distinction of color, within the rule which prior to that time pertained to the white race." Moreover, no principle of international law could "defeat the operation of the established rule of citizenship by birth within the United States." In short, even though Congress, various state legislatures, and some lower courts had denied persons of Chinese ancestry many rights—including the right to immigrate, to become naturalized, to vote, to live where they chose, to attend integrated schools, and to marry white persons—the highest court in the land took a stand against the attempt to abrogate the birthright citizenship of Chinese Americans, thereby protecting the civil rights of everyone.

BIBLIOGRAPHY

McClain, Charles J. "Tortuous Path, Elusive Goal: The Asian Quests for American Citizenship." *Asian Law Journal* 2, 1 (May 1995): 33–60.

United States v. Wong Kim Ark, 168 U.S. 649 (1898).

Sucheng Chan

Woodson, Carter Godwin

(1875–1950), African-American historian, writer, and editor.

Carter Godwin Woodson was born in Buckingham County, Virginia, to parents who were former slaves. He attended Berea College, receiving a bachelor's degree in 1903, the University of Chicago, where he received a second bachelor's and a master's degree in 1908, and Harvard University, where he received a Ph.D. degree in history in 1912. In 1915 he founded the Association for the Study of Negro Life and History. He taught from 1910 to 1922 in the District of Columbia Public Schools, Howard University, and West Virginia Collegiate Institute before turning his attention full-time to the Association and the *Journal of Negro History,* which he had founded in 1916. Woodson published four monographs, five textbooks on African-American history, five edited collections of source materials, and thirteen articles, as well as five sociological studies that were collaborative efforts.

Woodson's contribution to civil rights came through his involvement in and support of organizations like the NATIONAL ASSOCIATION FOR THE ADVANCEMENT OF COLORED PEOPLE (NAACP), the NATIONAL URBAN LEAGUE, the Friends of Negro Freedom, the Young Negro Cooperative League, the New Negro Alliance's DON'T BUY WHERE YOU CAN'T WORK CAMPAIGNS, and the NATIONAL NEGRO CONGRESS. Although political activism was secondary to his scholarly career, Woodson used his scholarship to inform politics and argued that African Americans needed to be better educated about their own history to agitate more effectively for equal rights.

He was a founding member of the Washington Branch of the NAACP in 1912. During the 1910s and 1920s he lobbied Congress and demonstrated in NAACP campaigns protesting lynching and against segregation on Washington streetcars and in government buildings. He also advocated that African Americans use their economic clout and boycott businesses that did not treat them fairly. In the 1930s Woodson retained his membership in mainstream black organizations but was more supportive of leftist organizations. He had ties with Marcus GARVEY and wrote columns for Garvey's newspaper the *Negro World.*

Woodson combined scholarly and political activity and brought his views to the black masses through columns in the black press. In 1930 he founded the Committee for Improving Industrial Conditions Among Negroes in the District of Columbia and directed a survey of black employment. Woodson was extremely critical of black education and asserted that the black

Carter G. Woodson in his office at Howard University. (AP/Wide World Photos)

masses needed to be taught at new vocational schools for urban industrial living. The black bourgeoisie, in turn, had a responsibility to provide economic opportunities for themselves and the working class. Promoting the use of segregation to end segregation, Woodson advocated black patronage of black businesses and the organization of neighborhood cooperatives. He also supported the National Negro Business League's establishment of Colored Merchants Associations.

Through the 1940s until his death in 1950, Woodson continued his advocacy of black political independence. He was critical of black leaders who allied with southern whites and formed the Southern Conference of Race Relations, the Southern Regional Council, and the COMMISSION ON INTERRACIAL COOPERATION. After World War II, Woodson tempered his criticism of white and black leaders of racial advancement organizations and praised the slow and steady progress of the NAACP's crusade to end desegregation of higher education through the courts.

BIBLIOGRAPHY

Goggin, Jacqueline. *Carter G. Woodson: A Life in Black History.* 1993.
Meier, August, and Elliott Rudwick. *Black History and the Historical Profession, 1915–1980.* 1986.

Jacqueline Goggin

Woodward, Comer Vann

(1908–   ), historian.

A white, Southern historian, C. Vann Woodward's transformative analyses of race relations in the United States, Southern regionalism, and the workings of modern capitalism suffused his integrationist activism (see INTEGRATION), and continue to shape scholarship on the American South. In 1952, he worked for the NATIONAL ASSOCIATION FOR THE ADVANCEMENT OF COLORED PEOPLE (NAACP), providing historical research for the *Brown v. Board of Education of Topeka, Kansas* case (1954). (See BROWN V. BOARD OF EDUCATION.) At that time he developed arguments for the book that stands as his most significant contribution to the civil rights movement: *The Strange Career of Jim Crow* (1955). In this immensely popular study, Woodward argued that legal SEGREGATION was relatively recent to the South, fraught with internal inconsistencies and local variation, and in need of elimination through federal law. Directing the book primarily to other white Southerners, Woodward dismantled segregationist arguments that the color line was the traditional basis of a regional "way of life." He concluded that ridding the South of legal apartheid and the state-sanctioned oppression of African Americans would not take away that which made it distinct, but would ensure the region's economic success and uniqueness.

Woodward became disenchanted with the direction of the civil rights movement after 1968, lamenting what he saw to be the fracturing of the liberal, biracial coalition for rights into a myriad of social causes. He was particularly disturbed by the rise of BLACK NATIONALISM, which he believed to be antithethical to the goal of integration.

BIBLIOGRAPHY

Roper, John Herbert. *C. Vann Woodward: Southerner.* 1987.
Roper, John Herbert, ed. *C. Vann Woodward: A Southern Historian and His Critics.* 1997.
Woodward, C. Vann. *Tom Watson: Agrarian Rebel.* 1938.
Woodward, C. Vann. *Origins of the New South.* 1951. With new introduction, 1971.
Woodward, C. Vann. *The Strange Career of Jim Crow.* 1955. Rev. ed. 1957. 2nd rev. ed. 1966. 3rd rev. ed. 1974.
Woodward, C. Vann. *The Burden of Southern History.* 1960. Rev. ed. 1968.

Micki McElya

World War I

World War I had a considerable impact on the social, economic, and political status of African Americans. Wartime employment and demographic changes, combined with the heightened mood of xenophobia and intolerance, increased racial tension and raised serious civil rights issues. Even before the United States entered the conflict in April 1917, the expansion of northern industry to meet allied war demands opened employment opportunities for African Americans and encouraged a large-scale migration out of the South. Encouraged by earlier migrants and by appeals in black publications such as the *Chicago Defender* and *The Crisis* (the NATIONAL ASSOCIATION FOR THE ADVANCEMENT OF COLORED PEOPLE [NAACP] journal), as well as by labor agents, approximately 400,000 African Americans seized the opportunity to escape from the South between 1915 and 1920.

Flocking mainly to larger industrial centers, the new arrivals found work in a variety of manufacturing occupations, but competition over jobs and housing led to outbreaks of racial violence. In July 1917 a riot in East St. Louis left thirty-nine blacks and eight whites dead. Despite a silent protest march by 10,000 African Americans in New York City on July 28, 1917, violence continued: the number of lynchings rose from thirty-eight in 1917 to eighty-three in 1919, and the RED SUMMER of that year witnessed over twenty riots or major racial incidents across America, including Washington, D.C. The worst riot occurred in Chicago between July 27 and August 2, 1919, when thirty-eight people, fifteen white and twenty-three black, were killed and over five hundred were injured.

African-American war veterans were among the many victims of racial violence. The very inclusion of African Americans in the military was a contentious issue. Although accepted for the draft, they were excluded from the Marine Corps, served in menial roles in the Navy, and were segregated in the Army. Persistent racial harassment of black troops in Houston, Texas, resulted in a riot in which fifteen white people were killed in August 1917. Sixty-four African Americans were quickly tried, and nineteen were executed.

Of the 400,000 black soldiers who served during the war, only 20,000 were in combat regiments. Although more than one hundred African Americans were recognized for bravery by the French, tales of cowardice and sexual misconduct were given prominence by U.S. authorities. The appointment of Emmett Scott, Booker T. WASHINGTON's former secretary, as assistant to the Secretary of War, and of George Haynes as director of Negro economics in the Department of Labor, was some recognition of the importance of black participation, but did little to affect white opinion. As a consequence there was some obvious disquiet among the black population. While W. E. B. DU BOIS urged African Americans to "close ranks" and forget their "special grievances," a conference of black newspaper editors called by the government in June 1918 expressed concern at "justifiable" grievances. A minority of black spokesmen, most notably A. Philip RANDOLPH, urged nonparticipation. Disillusionment at the lack of racial progress contributed to the emergence of a more radical spirit and a "New Negro" more prepared to fight back in the violence of 1919.

BIBLIOGRAPHY

Barbeau, Arthur E., and Florette Henri. *The Unknown Soldier: Black American Troops in World War I*. 1974.

Nielson, Gordon. *Black Ethos: Northern Urban Negro Life and Thought 1890–1930*. 1977.

Rudwick, Elliott M. *Race Riot at East St. Louis, July 2, 1917*. 1964.

Scott, Emmett J. *Scott's Official History of the American Negro in the World War*. 1919.

Tuttle, William M. Jr. *Race Riot: Chicago in the Red Summer of 1919*. 1996.

Neil A. Wynn

World War II

America's involvement in World War II as a shooting component of the Allied Forces began when the Japanese attacked Pearl Harbor on December 7, 1941. Beginning with the attack, America waged a winning military campaign against the Axis powers that ended with the Japanese unconditional surrender on August 15, 1945. It was indeed during this war-torn era that black Americans participated in and witnessed significant shifts in policies affecting their status both in and out of uniform. Unlike African Americans in World War I, World War II provided increased opportunities for black troops. For example, they went to integrated officer candidate schools; participated in the Army Air Corps for the first time, were allowed to join the Marine Corps, and the WACS (Women's Army Corps) and WAVES (Women Accepted for Voluntary Emergency Service) opened their ranks to black women. World War II was indeed a watershed for African Americans. It served as a catalyst in the struggle for civil rights, both in the military and larger society. As in previous wars, African Americans viewed World War II as an opportunity for a better day, despite long-held military, political, and white civilian beliefs that the military would not be used as a laboratory for effecting social change within and outside of the armed forces. Contrary to these beliefs, African Americans were on solid ground for thinking optimistically. Between WORLD WAR I and World War II, Marcus GARVEY, for example, had stimulated a great deal of black pride; several black scholars had begun an aggressive and

Members of the 99th U.S. Fighter Squadron, the first all-black unit of the U.S. Army Air Force to go into action, standing in front of their planes on January 30, 1944. (AP/Wide World Photos)

scientific surge of reconstructing a positive, contributory, and significant African-American past; the "New Negro" musicians, painters, and writers were busily reinforcing and enlivening African-American culture; the New Deal had appointed over one hundred African-American professionals by 1940 who were known as President ROOSEVELT's "black brain trust." The black vote had become increasingly significant, especially in the North; and the African-American press continued a more aggressive drumbeat for racial equality.

In economic matters, African Americans also celebrated some modest gains. After a long struggle, for instance, the American Federation of Labor (see AFL-CIO) granted a 1936 full-member charter to A. Philip RANDOLPH and the BROTHERHOOD OF SLEEPING CAR PORTERS and, in 1941, President Roosevelt issued Executive Order 8802, establishing the FAIR EMPLOYMENT PRACTICES COMMITTEE; thus initiating a federal stance for nondiscrimination in defense industries. These socioeconomic, cultural, and political gains were very strong indicators that World War II was a catalyst for making America's democratic rhetoric and the "American Dream" a reality for its black citizen-soldiers. Although World War II had a major influence, President TRUMAN's Executive Order 9981, issued on July 26, 1948, the official abolition of segregation and racial discrimination in the Armed Forces resulted from a long struggle and perhaps had the greatest impact on black America. But it was during the VIETNAM WAR era in the 1960s and 1970s that the American people, especially black America, witnessed and participated in the first, truly integrated American military.

BIBLIOGRAPHY

Buchanan, A. Russell. *Black Americans in World War II.* 1977.

Kennett, Lee. *G.I.: The American Soldier in World War II.* 1997.

McGuire, Phillip, editor. *Taps for a Jim Crow Army: Letters from Black Soldiers in World War II.* 1993.

Polenberg, Richard. *War And Society: The United States 1941–1945.* 1972.

Wynn, Neil A. *The Afro-American and the Second World War.* 1993.

Phillip McGuire

Wounded Knee Massacre (1890)

The Ghost Dance, an apocalyptic Native American religious movement that prophesied the destruction of the white man and the return of the buffalo, swept through the West during the year 1890. Followers performed an exhausting dance to invoke visions of their dead relatives living with the renewed Earth. Indian agents and U.S. Army officers were alerted to possible troubles, and tensions grew as the movement spread throughout the northern Plains. In early December, Major James McLaughlin, agent at the Standing Rock Reservation in NORTH DAKOTA, who feared Sitting Bull's possible endorsement of the Ghost Dancers, ordered him arrested. When the Hunkpapa religious leader was killed by Indian police, panic spread throughout the SOUTH DAKOTA reservations, and the frightened Indians began a trek to the Pine Ridge Reservation, where they believed Chief Red Cloud would protect them.

A band of Minneconjou Sioux, led by ailing Chief Big Foot, were intercepted before they reached Pine Ridge, and were detained by elements of the Seventh Cavalry at a small creek called Wounded Knee, less than twenty miles from the Pine Ridge agency. When the soldiers demanded that the Indians surrender their guns, a scuffle broke out, and a shot was fired. The nervous soldiers immediately began firing into the Indian camp with small arms and Gatling guns, continually sweeping the campsite and firing into the soldiers on the other side of the valley.

Some people suspect that revenge for the defeat at the Little Big Horn motivated the continuing slaughter, as the bodies of Indian women and children were found as far as three miles away from the camp. An estimated three hundred people were killed. In the late afternoon a blizzard began, and soldiers gathered the wounded as best they could, loaded them onto wagons and drove them to the agency. Confusion reigned in Pine Ridge, with the wounded left in open wagons in the blizzard until members of the Episcopal church opened its doors, removed its benches, scattered straw on the floor, and allowed the government doctors to care for the people.

Three days later when the blizzard was over, military details from the agency returned to the scene to bury the dead, who were frozen in grotesque poses indicating that some had been alive but were missed by the soldiers earlier. A baby was found still alive and was later adopted by one of the Army officers. A large trench was dug on the hillside, and the bodies of the Indians were thrown into it without much fanfare. Pictures of soldiers happily posing around the trench told the real story of the incident.

A flurry of hearings in CONGRESS that winter questioned whether the Department of War should have primary jurisdiction over the Indians because of Wounded Knee, but no action was taken. Over the years bills to compensate the Sioux have been thwarted by Army insistence that the conflict had been a battle, not a massacre. The casualty figures speak for themselves.

BIBLIOGRAPHY

Brown, Dee. *Bury My Heart at Wounded Knee: An Indian History of the American West.* 1971.

Mooney, James. *The Ghost-Dance Religion and the Sioux Outbreak of 1890.* 1991.

Vine Deloria, Jr.

Wounded Knee Occupation (1973)

In 1972 Indian activists decided to march on Washington, D.C., during election week to force the administration of Richard M. NIXON to initiate a new Indian policy built around the treaty relationship. After meeting with the Commissioner of Indian Affairs, they discovered that housing arrangements had not been made for them. When guards tried to close the doors, tempers flared and the Indians proceeded to occupy the BUREAU OF INDIAN AFFAIRS building. After several days' occupation, the government agreed to provide travel for the people to return home, and most did so after trashing the building.

Arriving back in SOUTH DAKOTA frustrated by their failure to get a clear statement from the administration, the group refused to disband and protested when an Indian was killed in an off-reservation bar near Custer, South Dakota. Their announcing that they would celebrate the Washington march at Pine Ridge brought an angry response from Oglala Sioux tribal chairman Dickie Wilson, and tribal members split on their allegiances. On February 27, 1973, a band of armed Indians representing both the marchers and local reform organizations occupied the church and surrounding areas at Wounded Knee.

Calling themselves the Independent Oglala Nation, the people demanded that the federal government restore their traditional government. Tribal police and federal officers set up a roadblock, and the siege began. It would last seventy-three days, during which sporadic skirmishes resulted in the deaths of several people on both sides of the conflict. The Indians easily kept themselves supplied by slipping through the government lines at night. The occupation became a celebrity event. Actor Marlon Brando and civil rights leader Ralph ABERNATHY announced they were going to Wounded Knee, and prominent lawyers William KUNSTLER and Mark Lane promised to defend the protestors in the forthcoming trials. Russell MEANS and Dennis BANKS quickly achieved fame as the leaders of the occupation through extensive television and press coverage of the occupation.

In early May, after intense negotiations, the occupation ended, as the Indians surrendered and were charged with a variety of crimes. Although the Indians appeared to be well armed during the standoff, few weapons were found, an indication that they had buried or hidden most of their weapons prior to

Two Native American protesters stand guard with rifles at Wounded Knee, South Dakota, on the Pine Ridge Indian Reservation during the Wounded Knee occupation in 1973. (CORBIS/Bettmann)

surrender. The forbearance of the government in allowing an armed force to hold an American village hostage was later seen by some people as an effort to keep Wounded Knee on the front pages of the newspapers and Watergate on the back page.

In trials following the occupation, only six of some 212 defendants were convicted, and they pled nolo contendere. The Means–Banks trial was the headline case coming out of the occupation, and it was dismissed because of government misconduct and the altering of evidence. In July, White House representatives had a formal meeting with the disgruntled Sioux of the reservation and agreed to certain administrative reforms and to review the treaty status of the Oglalas. A prominent feature of the occupation was the support given the protest by the religious leaders of the tribe, leading to a revival of its old religious ways.

BIBLIOGRAPHY

Burnette, Robert, and John Koster. *The Road to Wounded Knee.* 1974.

Matthiessen, Peter. *In the Spirit of Crazy Horse.* 1983.

Vine Deloria, Jr.

Wyoming

Because they believed that only "statehood would allow real economic and social development to progress," members of the Territorial Legislature of what would come to be known as "the Equality State," without waiting for the appropriate enabling legislation from Washington, called a constitutional convention to begin on September 2, 1889. Twenty-five days later, the drafters presented a fully crafted document that is noteworthy for its vision and inclusion of a declaration of rights that granted women the franchise. Wyoming was the first state to do so. In 1894, Estelle Meyer was elected Superintendant of Public Instruction, the first woman to be elected to office in the United States. Because there were and are, even today, so few people of color in the state—fewer than 40,000 out of a total population of 454,000 according to the 1990 Census—there has been little in the way of organized civil rights activity.

Spelled out in Article 1, Sections 2, 3, and 34, and in Article 6, Section 1 of the Wyoming Constitution, are phrases such as ". . . all members of the human race are equal"; ". . . the laws . . . affecting the political rights and privileges of its citizens shall be without distinction of race, color, sex, or any circumstances of condition whatsoever"; and "all laws of a general nature shall have a uniform operation." To some extent, these sections were reinforced in 1957 by the passage of a public accommodations act, not apparently because a specific case had been brought, but more because the climate in the country was changing. And finally, "the rights of citizens of the state of Wyoming to vote and hold office shall not be denied or abridged on account of sex. Both men and women citizens of this state shall enjoy all civil, political and religious rights and privileges," the section of the constitution that reaffirmed the right of women to vote and hold office first recognized in the territory in 1869.

Native Americans—almost all of them nomadic hunters—had been resident in Wyoming since at least 7000 B.C. They were driven out of the territory in massive numbers during the decade and a half following the Civil War until by 1879 only a few Shoshoni and Arapaho remained, confined to the Wind River Reservation, three million acres in west central Wyoming, existing largely in isolation from civil rights struggles and the nation-at-large until today. Although in 1998, only about 20 percent of the Native American population in Wind River had telephones, there are definitely hopeful signs. On July 31, 1998, a group of Arapaho students and teachers on the reservation established their site on the World Wide Web, announcing to the outside world, "We have only just begun . . ."

One further item that does mar the record, however, was the antimiscegenation statute first adopted during territorial days, repealed in 1882, reinstated in 1913, and not overturned until 1965. In the first instance it was the shortage of white women in the territory that led to its passage, in the second it was the rise of WHITE SUPREMACY and NATIVISM that in 1895 had seen the state legislature petition Congress to restrict immigration to the United States.

BIBLIOGRAPHY

Guenther, Todd R. "'Y' All Call Me Nigger Jim Now, But Someday You'll Call Me Mr. James Edwards': Black Success on the Plains of the Equality State." *Annals of Wyoming* 61, 2 (Fall 1989): 20–40.

Hardaway, Roger D. "Prohibiting Interracial Marriage: Miscegenation Laws in Wyoming." *Annals of Wyoming* 52, 1 (Spring 1980): 55–60.

Larson, T. A. *History of Wyoming.* 1978.

Miller, Tim R. *State Government Politics in Wyoming*, 2nd ed. 1985.

William M. King

X-Z

X, Malcolm

See Malcolm X.

Yellow Power

"Yellow Power" refers to the Asian-American political consciousness and activism that began during the late 1960s. The first known instance of the use of this term was by Larry Kubota in "Necessary but not sufficient: Yellow Power!," published in the inaugural issue of *Gidra* (April 1969), the first radical Asian-American newspaper. He defined "Yellow Power" as "Asian Americans seeking greater control over the direction of [their] lives . . . and the determination to effect constructive changes in society." Subsequently, in "The emergence of yellow power in America," also published in *Gidra* (December 1969), Amy Uyematsu defined it as "a collective ethnic political effort to achieve local self-determination through a unified Asian-American community." The phrase "Yellow Power" never captured the popular imagination and was rarely ever used, even among Asian-American activists. Instead, the name ASIAN-AMERICAN MOVEMENT is usually used when referring to political activism by Asian Americans during this period.

Influenced by the "Black Power" and "Brown Power" movements, the Asian-American movement was the last of the ethnic consciousness movements to emerge in the wake of the civil rights movement. Though inspired by these earlier social movements, the origins of the ASIAN-AMERICAN MOVEMENT can ac-tually be traced to the protests against the Vietnam War and the emergence of a generation of college-aged Chinese and Japanese Americans. Though it had revolutionaries in its ranks, the Asian-American movement was mainly a reform effort to achieve racial equality, social justice, and political empowerment through ethnic solidarity, political activism, educational and community development, and cultural expression. Among its lasting contributions was the founding of Asian-American Studies programs in colleges and universities around the nation.

BIBLIOGRAPHY

Amerasia Journal: Commemorative Issue, Salute to the 60s and 70s, Legacy of the San Francisco State Strike 15(1) (1989).
Chan, Sucheng. "The Asian-American Movement, 1960s–1980s." In *Peoples of Color in the American West*, edited by Sucheng Chan et al. 1994.
Espiritu, Yen Le. *Asian American Panethnicity: Bridging Institutions and Identities.* 1992.
Wei, William. *The Asian American Movement.* 1993.

William Wei

Yick Wo v. Hopkins (1886)

This decision marks the first time the United States SUPREME COURT overturned a law because of discriminatory enforcement. This ruling confirmed and extended the FOURTEENTH AMENDMENT's equal-protection clause to noncitizens as well as citizens, initially established by *Ho Ah Kow v. Nunan* (1879).

Yick Wo was one of 150 Chinese arrested in 1885 for operating a laundry in San Francisco without city permission. Reflecting anti-Chinese sentiment in the 1870s and 1880s, the San Francisco Board of Supervisors enacted fourteen laws regulating laundries, three-fourths of which were Chinese-owned. Two laws required any laundry located in a wooden building to obtain a special license. Although he had never violated health or safety regulations during twenty-two years of business, the board denied such a license to Yick Wo and two hundred other Chinese. The board granted all of the eighty non-Chinese applications.

The United States Supreme Court reviewed Yick Wo's case along with the similar case of Wo Lee. The city claimed the laws protected the health and safety of its citizens. Lawyers hired by the Tung Hing Tong (an association of San Francisco Chinese laundrymen to which Yick Wo belonged) persuaded the court, however, that these two laws granted the San Francisco board arbitrary power to shut down Chinese laundries.

The Supreme Court unanimously declared the laws unconstitutional. Justice Stanley Matthews expressed the Court's opinion that enacting a neutrally worded law against a particular race of persons violated the constitutional right of equal protection under the law. *Yick Wo* thus set an important precedent by allowing courts to examine a law's enforcement in addition to the wording of the law itself when determining its constitutionality.

BIBLIOGRAPHY

Gioia, John. "A Social, Political and Legal Study of Yick Wo V. Hopkins." In *The Chinese American Experience*, edited by Genny Lim. 1984.

McClain, Charles J., and Laurene Wu McClain. "The Chinese Contribution to the Development of American Law." In *Chinese Immigrants and American Law*, edited by Charles McClain. 1994.

McClain, Charles J. *In Search of Equality. The Chinese Struggle Against Discrimination in Nineteenth-Century America.* 1994.

Yick Wo v. Hopkins, 118 U.S. 356 (1886).

See also:

Chan, Sucheng. *Asian Americans. An Interpretive History.* 1991.

Hing, Bill Ong. *Making and Remaking Asian America Through Immigration Policy, 1850–1950.* 1993.

Karst, Kenneth I. *Belonging to America. Equal Citizenship and the Constitution.* 1989.

Karen J. Leong

YMCA

See Young Men's Christian Association and Young Women's Christian Association.

Young, Andrew

(1932–), civil rights leader.

Andrew Young, a leader in the SOUTHERN CHRISTIAN LEADERSHIP CONFERENCE (SCLC) in the 1960s, spent two terms as a Georgia congressman, was Ambassador to the United Nations, and led Atlanta as mayor.

Born in New Orleans in 1932 to Andrew Young and Daisy Fuller, Young embarked upon a career as a Congregationalist minister, social reformer, and public servant after graduating from Howard University. In 1954 he married Jean Childs, with whom he had three daughters. After Hartford Theological Seminary in Connecticut and ordination, Young led local blacks in a voter registration drive from his first pulpit in rural Georgia in 1955. Two years later he moved to New York as head of youth programs for the ecumenical National Council of Churches, an important ally in the widening civil rights struggle.

Young joined the Southern Christian Leadership Conference (SCLC) in 1961, working in its fledgling citizenship and voter education programs with Dorothy Cotton and Septima Poinsette Clark, two women with a wealth of experience who often went unheralded by the male-dominated leadership of the SCLC. Soon a close adviser to SCLC founder Martin Luther KING, Jr., Young participated in the Albany, Birmingham, St. Augustine, and Selma desegregation and voting rights campaigns between 1961 and 1965. He became the SCLC's executive director in 1964. Although ambivalent about expansion beyond the South, Young helped to organize the SCLC's contentious Chicago campaign, which generated few tangible concessions but highlighted King's growing attention to issues of poverty and economic racism.

Young brought effective leadership to the SCLC's chaotic operational structure, and his diplomatic skills served the organization equally well. King encouraged him to play the role of "conservative" counterweight to the ideological and strategic excesses of his peers. Young was able to command respect from whites and blacks and fostered dialogue across the increasingly fractious spectrum of protest organizations, but his faith in the essential goodness of southern whites earned him genial mockery from battle-hardened movement veterans. With a keen appreciation of the media's role in dramatizing racial injustice, Young urged King to hone his rhetoric to shape popular per-

Andrew Young in his office as Mayor of Atlanta. (CORBIS/Flip Schulke)

ceptions of the movement. While he recognized the galvanizing effect of mass meetings and marches, Young devoted equal attention to organizing African-American boycotts of discriminatory businesses, placing great value in economic leverage.

Following King's assassination, Young remained with the SCLC to participate in the POOR PEOPLE'S CAMPAIGN of 1968 and the Charleston hospital worker's strike of 1969. Resigning in 1970, he ran for Georgia's 5th Congressional District, winning the primary but losing the general election when thousands of white Democrats crossed party lines to vote for his Republican opponent. Young won the seat in 1972, the first African American to serve Georgia in Congress in the twentieth century, and was twice reelected. Jimmy CARTER contacted Young on the eve of Young's third term and asked him to represent the new administration as Ambassador to the United Nations. The first black to hold the post, Young was a forceful advocate for Carter's global human rights policies. However, he was forced to resign in 1979 after engaging in unauthorized discussions with members of the Palestine Liberation Organization. In 1981 white and black Atlantans elected Young to the first of two terms

as mayor, during which he helped to launch the city's successful bid to host the 1996 Olympic Games. Young lost in a gubernatorial primary election runoff against Zell Miller in 1990.

Andrew Young's career has mirrored civil rights battles waged along overlapping fronts, including racism, militarism and international human rights, and the endurance of poverty amidst affluence. His lifelong dedication to greater justice has been, he claimed in his autobiography of the same name, "an easy burden" to carry.

BIBLIOGRAPHY

Branch, Taylor. *Parting the Waters: America in the King Years, 1954–63.* 1988.

Branch, Taylor. *Pillar of Fire: America in the King Years, 1963–65.* 1998.

Fairclough, Adam. *To Redeem the Soul of America: The Southern Christian Leadership Conference and Martin Luther King, Jr.* 1987.

Garrow, David. *Bearing the Cross: Martin Luther King, Jr., and the Southern Christian Leadership Conference.* 1986.

Young, Andrew. *An Easy Burden: The Civil Rights Movement and the Transformation of America.* 1996.

Young, Andrew. *A Way Out Of No Way: The Spiritual Memoirs of Andrew Young.* 1994.

David C. Carter

Young, Whitney Moore, Jr.

(1921–1971), civil rights leader.

A social worker and civil rights leader, Whitney Young served as executive director of the National Urban League from 1961 to 1971.

Born in Lincoln Ridge, Kentucky, Young was the middle child and only son of Whitney Moore, Sr., and Laura Ray Young. His father was a member of the faculty and the first black principal of Lincoln Institute, a boarding high school for blacks. His mother served as the local postmistress. Whitney, Jr., graduated from Lincoln Institute in 1937 and earned a B.S. in 1941 from Kentucky State Industrial College in Frankfort.

Young served in the European Theater in World War II as first sergeant of a black army battalion, where he learned the art of interracial mediation through his informal role as a liaison between black soldiers and white officers. He earned a master's degree in social work from the University of Minnesota in 1947 and joined the NATIONAL URBAN LEAGUE, serving first as industrial relations secretary of the affiliate in St. Paul, Minnesota (1947–1950), and then as executive secretary in Omaha, Nebraska (1950–1953). In 1954, Young became dean of the Atlanta University School of Social Work, a move that gave him firsthand exposure to the emerging struggle for civil rights.

In January 1961, during a year's sabbatical at Harvard University, Young was named to succeed Lester B. Granger as executive director of the National Urban League, a post he held from that October until his death (apparently from drowning) a decade later in Lagos, Nigeria.

As the leader of the National Urban League, Young put the organization on a sounder financial footing, restructured the national office, tightened the national organization's control over its affiliates (which grew from sixty-three to ninety-eight during his tenure), and expanded the scope of the agency's programs in employment and social services. When Young took over, the League measured progress in employment in dozens of individual job placements. By the late 1960s, it reported 40,000 to 50,000 placements annually in new or upgraded jobs.

The League worked to improve the quality of black education and to motivate young blacks to stay in school, and it expanded its traditional housing, health, and welfare services. It undertook programs to give blacks a stronger voice in public affairs, including voter education and registration, labor education and advancement, leadership development, and, with the "New Thrust" of the late 1960s, community organizing.

Young brought the National Urban League into the civil rights movement and made it a force in the major events and public policy debates of the 1960s. A proponent of compensatory action to achieve equality for blacks, he argued for special efforts in employment, education, health and welfare services, and housing to make up for past discrimination. Although the federal government never directly embraced his proposal for a domestic Marshall Plan, the social programs of the New Frontier and the Great Society reflected some of his major themes.

Traditionally the most conservative of the organizations working for racial advancement, the National Urban League moved under Young's leadership toward a more activist stance. He met regularly with his counterparts from the other major organizations, helped to organize the MARCH ON WASHINGTON (1963), and participated personally in some of the major protests of the 1960s. Privately, he fashioned a distinctive role as strategist and mediator among members of the civil rights leadership.

Young's special role in the black movement was to sell civil rights to the nation's most powerful whites. Contemporaries described him as the "inside man" of the black revolution, the bridge and interpreter between black America and the business leaders, foundation executives, and public officials who comprised the white power structure. Consummate politician and salesman, he goaded and challenged the white establishment to redress the effects OF SEGREGATION, discrimination, and poverty. He lobbied the federal government on civil rights and social policy, and he hammered home the obligation of corporations, the professions, nonprofit institutions, and voluntary associations to promote integration and equal opportunity. His efforts yielded tangible payoffs in jobs, training programs, and government and foundation support for social programs in the ghettos.

At the same time, Young enjoyed close relations with the churches, fraternal and service organizations, business and professional associations, women's clubs, and educational institutions that provided the infrastructure for community life in black America. Their endorsement conveyed support for his integrationist leadership within the black population, made a tangible difference to the National Urban League, and enhanced Young's credibility and influence with powerful whites.

BIBLIOGRAPHY

Dickerson, Dennis C. *Militant Mediator: Whitney M. Young, Jr.* 1998.

Parris, Guichard, and Lester Brooks. *Blacks in the City: A History of the National Urban League.* 1971.

Weiss, Nancy J. *Whitney M. Young, Jr., and the Struggle for Civil Rights.* 1989.

Young, Whitney M., Jr. *To Be Equal.* 1964.

Young, Whitney M., Jr. *Beyond Racism.* 1969.

Nancy J. Weiss

Young Men's Christian Association and Young Women's Christian Association

Frequently overlooked, the YMCA and the YWCA played important roles in the civil rights movement. The YMCA and the YWCA were institutionally distinct but shared many characteristics. Each had a national coordinating body and autonomous locals. A study of the Ys discloses the significant roles played by black-controlled local organizations as well as a white-dominated liberal mainstream organization. Both became arenas for struggle over the meaning of racial justice in Christian organizations and in American society. Both were rooted in 19th-century evangelical Protestantism, a religious base shared by both whites and African Americans. Together, the associations reveal the importance of religion to twentieth-century racial reform, although both are now open to people of all faiths.

The United States YMCA was founded in 1851 to instill Christian values in young white men migrating to cities. African-American men lobbied to join these associations or, failing this, to start branches of their own. The first African-American association began in Washington, D.C., in 1853. In its early years the YMCA split over the issues of slavery and the Civil War. Some Northern associations remained active during the war while most Southern associations ceased to function. After the war, the organization rebuilt nationally and established a policy and a precedent of shunning controversy.

In the late 19th century, the YMCA increasingly turned away from a Protestant evangelical mission, directed toward men of all classes, and came to stress character-building activities for middle-class men and boys. William A. Hunton, the first national African-American YMCA staff member, hired in 1891, was responsible for the development of programs for African Americans in both cities and colleges. Subsequent black staffers, such as Jesse E. Moorland and George E. Haynes, promoted autonomous black-controlled local associations. Although they opposed segregation,

they recognized the unwillingness of most white YMCA members to integrate. They advocated a strategy of self-reliance for the achievement of racial equality, arguing that separate, albeit unequal, facilities were better than none. They also believed that autonomous, black-controlled branches could serve the needs of their constituencies better than as part of white-controlled associations. Funded by the black community with some support by whites (notably philanthropist Julius Rosenwald), these programs provided African Americans with recreational resources and often the only black-controlled quasi-public space outside of black churches. Frequently, they provided the only places for local Urban League or NAACP chapters to meet.

Prompted by black migration to cities and increasing racial violence during the World War I period, some white leaders such as Will W. ALEXANDER and Willis D. Weatherford, stressed the importance of interracial cooperation as a way of easing racial tension. Weatherford's book, *Negro Life in the South* (1910), published by the YMCA, became required reading in study groups in YMCAs and colleges across the country. YMCAs cooperated with the NATIONAL URBAN LEAGUE in the North and the COMMISSION ON INTERRACIAL COOPERATION in the South. Channing H. Tobias, the senior African-American national staffer beginning in 1924, worked to challenge segregation in the Association.

During mid-century the YMCA faced increasing criticism from the black community for its segregation policy and, in 1946, the YMCA National Convention voted to work "toward the goal of eliminating all racial discriminations." Aided by federal monies, local associations increasingly addressed racial problems as they faced changing urban demographics. Political unrest over the Vietnam War and Watergate as well as decreased federal funds led to the YMCA reconceiving its focus by the early 1970s, particularly as many associations followed their white members to the suburbs.

In the late 1800s, the Association had stressed the importance of being sex-segregated. During World War I, with men overseas, associations opened their facilities to women and girls, but did not eliminate gender from their constitution until 1957. By the 1960s and 1970s, a stress on family-oriented programs led to expanded offerings for women and girls (which may also have been a response to some characterizations of YMCAs as gay spaces). Today, the YMCA sees itself as a community service organization focusing on health and fitness and child care, having become the country's largest nonprofit provider of day care.

In 1858, the YWCA was started in the United States to meet the needs of self-supporting young white women migrating to cities. By 1870, there was a black women's association in Philadelphia. In the 1870s, a YWCA student movement (influenced by the YMCA) began work in colleges, with an association starting at Spelman College in 1884. The two movements—urban and student—merged in 1906. In 1907, an all-white meeting of the National Board of the YWCA sanctioned a policy of segregation at the local level. Described as a response to the desires of Southern white women, the policy also reflected the desires of some Northern white women who had pushed for segregated associations in cities like New York. Segregated branches, often more dependent upon white-controlled central associations than were black YMCAs, made for a situation that limited the power that black women held. On the other hand, they permitted black women employment and leadership in those branches. Like black YMCAs, these associations often became vibrant community centers in the black community. Conferences of black staff members created a national network of YWCA leaders, such as Addie Waites Hunton, who worked with women in other organizations, notably those in the NATIONAL ASSOCIATION OF COLORED WOMEN, to advance the race. The YWCA has also conducted programs for Native Americans, primarily in Indian schools, and offered scattered programs for Asians and Latinos. Until late in the 20th-century, however, race issues usually focused on black–white relations.

The YWCA expanded dramatically during World War I. By 1920, the YWCA was one of the largest autonomous women's organizations and the major one having substantial participation by black women, albeit in a biracial structure. During the 1920s black women, led by Lugenia Burns Hope, challenged the YWCA's racial policies. While segregated branches remained the norm, the women won some control over their own associations and won token representation on white governing bodies. Elizabeth Ross Haynes, an early black national staffer, was elected to the national governing body in 1924. Black and white women in the YWCA urged a strategy of interracial cooperation to confront racial problems. African-American national YWCA leaders such as Eva del Vakia Bowles argued that interracial fellowship would change the minds of white women. They established meetings between white women, including Katharine Du Pre Lumpkin, and black women such as Juliette Derricotte. Some of these white women became the backbone of white support for racial justice in the following years. Bowles and others argued against the African-American YMCA strategy of more racially separate associations, fearing that separation would lessen their ability to influence whites.

By the 1930s, the YWCA increasingly favored political strategies, not merely educational ones, in its civil rights struggle. Local black YWCA leaders, such as Anna Arnold HEDGEMAN, led campaigns to get black women jobs in local businesses. National black staffers such as Frances H. Williams pressured the Association to testify in favor of legislation to stop lynchings and the poll tax. Others like Grace Towns Hamilton sought to educate the larger membership through the YWCA's public affairs programs. Many of the white women who joined these efforts were students trained by the white women who had first joined with black women in the 1920s. The YWCA's 1946 convention endorsed the "Interracial Charter," calling for the "inclusion of Negro women and girls in the main stream of Association life." Some southern locals withdrew in protest, but others joined the civil rights struggle. The YWCA was one of the few organizations that white liberals could support as a way of endorsing civil rights in the South. YWCA cafeterias in cities such as Atlanta were among the first quasi-public spaces to permit interracial seating in the South.

In the 1950s and 1960s, campus YWCAs brought together white women like Mary King and black women like Ella BAKER. The YWCA had observer status with the STUDENT NONVIOLENT COORDINATING COMMITTEE after its founding in 1960. The YWCA endorsed the call for the 1963 MARCH ON WASHINGTON and former staffer Hedgeman was the only woman on the national organizing committee. Mary King and Sandra Cason (Casey HAYDEN), along with other women, participated in the reinvigoration of the women's rights movement. As YWCAs implemented the Interracial Charter by desegregating, the elimination of black branches often led to diminished leadership opportunities for African-American women. In cities like Charlotte, white-controlled boards relocated associations out of downtown areas and into white suburbs. Recognizing that the struggle for civil rights meant more than promoting desegregation, black women continued to challenge the YWCA over racism. Led by its first African-American president, Helen Wilkins Claytor, and long-time YWCA member Dorothy HEIGHT, the membership passed the "One Imperative" in 1970 calling for the Association to work "to eliminate racism wherever it exists and by any means necessary."

YWCA women had advocated the dissemination of birth control information as early as 1934 and, by 1967, a woman's right to choose an abortion. The organization has identified domestic violence as a key issue, with local associations becoming the largest provider of resources to battered women. The YWCA defines its goals today as the empowerment of women and the elimination of racism.

The histories of the YMCA and the YWCA shed light on strategies for racial justice employed by various groups of African Americans and their white allies in the twentieth century. The differences between the two organizations were the result of structural differences as well as the comparative abilities of key leaders to implement organizational change. They also reflected the fact that women had fewer organizations in which they could wield power and, as a result, the YWCA had a larger number of progressive women of both races. Their male counterparts frequently left the YMCA for organizations that placed greater priority on civil rights. The YWCA, in addition, provided a bridge between the civil rights and women's liberation movements, as well as between generations of activists struggling against racism and sexism.

BIBLIOGRAPHY

Archival sources: Records for the YMCA of the USA, its predecessors, and some locals can be found at the YMCA Archives, University of Minnesota Libraries, St. Paul, Minnesota. Records for the YWCA of the USA, its predecessors, and some locals can be found at the YWCA of the USA, National Board, New York, New York.

Chafe, William. *Civilities and Civil Rights: Greensboro, North Carolina, and the Black Struggle for Freedom.* 1981.

Chauncey, George, Jr. "Christian Brotherhood or Sexual Perversion? Homosexual Identities and the Construction of Sexual Boundaries in the World War One Era." *Journal of Social History* 19 (1985): 189–212.

Chochrane, Sharlene Voogd. " 'And the Pressure Never Let Up': Black Women, White Women, and the Boston YWCA, 1918–1948." In *Women in the Civil Rights Movement: Trailblazers and Torchbearers, 1941–1965,* edited by Vicki L. Crawford, Jacqueline Anne Rouse, and Barbara Woods. 1990.

Evans, Sara. *Personal Politics: The Roots of Women's Liberation in the Civil Rights Movement and the New Left.* 1979.

Lerner, Gerda, ed. *Black Women in White America: A Documentary History.* 1972.

Lynn, Susan. *Progressive Women in Conservative Times: Racial Justice, Peace, and Feminism, 1945 to the 1960s.* 1992.

Mjagkij, Nina. *Light in the Darkness: African Americans and the YMCA, 1852–1946.* 1994.

Mjagkij, Nina, and Margaret Spratt, eds. *Men and Women Adrift: the YMCA and the YWCA in the City.* 1997.

Robertson, Nancy Marie. " 'Deeper Even Than Race'?: White Women and the Politics of Christian Sisterhood in the YWCA, 1906–1946." Ph.D. dissertation. New York University. 1997.

Weisenfeld, Judith. *African-American Women and Christian Activism: New York's Black YWCA, 1905–1945.* 1997.

Nancy Marie Robertson

YWCA

See Young Men's Christian Association and Young Women's Christian Association.

Zoot-Suit Riots

In June of 1943, as men of all ethnicities shipped off to service in World War II, the city of Los Angeles witnessed a violent outbreak on its own shore in the form of the so-called "Zoot-Suit Riots." More appropriately labeled the Servicemen's Riots of 1943, these ten days of unrest arose as U.S. Navy recruits attacked Mexican-American youth throughout the predominantly Mexican East Los Angeles barrio. They beat them, sometimes stripping them of their clothing and shaving their heads. When the illegal assaults finally came to an end, the Navy command made the streets of the city off limits to their personnel and many Mexican Americans—the victims of the violence—found themselves arrested for no other crime than their race.

In some ways, the riots can be viewed as a battle between generations. The Mexican-American youth, who used the word *pachuco* to label themselves, asserted pride in their culture and generation through

Two young Los Angeleans reported to police that they were attacked by U.S. sailors who tore off their trousers, June 1943. (Anthony Potter Collection/ Archive Photos)

their distinct style of dress. Attired in their elaborate zoot suits and duck-tailed hairdos, the young men of this style shared fashions with other youth of color throughout the nation who danced to jazz and swing. Both young men and women celebrated and marked their generation through their dress and, sometimes, tatoos. They even spoke their own language called caló, something of a hybrid of Spanish and English. By wearing their own sort of uniforms and having their own customs of style and communication, the youth seemed foreign to servicemen who came from all over the nation (many never having seen a Mexican person). Fear of the unknown combined with a strong form of patriotism that labeled all "non-Americans" as enemies. The servicemen, swept up in a wartime anger at the "foreign" and perhaps also lashing out at the fear of death themselves, rushed to Mexican-American hang outs and initiated the violence on a rumor that one of "their own" had been assaulted by a *pachuco* in an argument having to do with a young woman.

At the same time, these events can also be seen as a natural outgrowth of racial fear and stereotyping. The local press depicted the *pachuco* fashions as unpatriotic and reflective of a nefarious element. They depicted Mexican-American juvenile crime as an infectious disease and as evil as a foreign attack. Many servicemen who read these accounts easily contrasted this social problem with their own enlistment as men trained to protect their nation. Not looking like these servicemen—not looking the way a "good American" should look—the *pachucos* embodied much of the racialized hatred of all persons of color.

Armed with clubs and loaded into taxi cabs, groups of servicemen descended upon the zoot-suitor night spots on June 3, 1943. Police usually got involved only after a beating had taken place, and then only to arrest or discipline the Mexican-American victims rather than arresting their attackers. The disturbances lasted until Navy officials declared downtown Los Angeles off limits to their men.

The violence of these ten days highlighted the racial problems of Los Angeles and the Mexican-American community in particular. Outcries for justice came from all over the nation and as far away as the Mexican government, who deplored the attacks as acts of racial bigotry.

BIBLIOGRAPHY

Acuña, Rodolfo F. *Occupied America: A History of Chicanos*, 3rd edition. 1988.

Mazón, Mauricio. *The Zoot-Suit Riots: The Psychology of Symbolic Annihilation*. 1984.

McWilliams, Carey. *North from Mexico: The Spanish-Speaking People of the United States*. 1948.

Tomas F. Sandoval, Jr.

Index

Note: Page numbers in **boldface** indicate main article on subject. Those in *italics* indicate illustrations.

Minnesota, **480–481**

Minnesota, Near v., 119

Miranda, Ernesto, 778

Miranda v. Arizona, 778

Miscegenation. *See* Interracial marriage

Mississippi, 87, **481–484**

Mississippi Freedom Democratic Party (MFDP), 58, 326, **484–485**, 713, 715

Mississippi, Williams v., **803**

Missouri, **485–487**

Mitchell, Clarence, Jr., **487–488**

Mitchell, J. E., *608*

MLN (Movimiento de Liberacíon Nacional), **498–499**, 621

MMDs (Majority-minority districts), 683

Montana, **488–489**

Montgomery bus boycott, 160, 394, **489–491**, 591, 616

Montgomery Improvement Association (MIA), 1, 115, **491**

Moore, Amzie, **492**

Moore, Harry Tyson, **492–493**

Mora, Magdalena, **493**

Moreno, Luisa, **493–494**

Morgan, Irene, 494

Morgan v. Virginia, 332, **494**

Mormons, 754–755

Morris, T. T. "Brack," 197

Morrow, E. Frederic, *247*

Moses, Robert Parris, **494–495**, 713

Mothers of East Los Angeles (MELA), **495**, 812

Mothers of East Los Angeles-Santa Isabel (MELA-SI), 495

Motley, Constance Baker, **495–496**, *496*

Moton, Robert Russa, **497**

Mott, Lucretia, 152

Mound Bayou, Mississippi, 87

Mount Rushmore protests, **497**

Movement for Independence-Puerto Rican Socialist Party, **498**, 620

Movement for National Liberation, **498–499**, 621

Movements. *See also* Protests and demonstrations

   Albany movement, **19**, 315

   anti-apartheid movement, **40–41**

anti-lynching campaign, **41**, 369

anti-war movements, **43–45**, *44*

Asian American movement, **52–54**

Birmingham campaign, **68–70**, *69*

Black arts movement, **73–75**

Black convention movement, **79–80**

black power, 82

brown power, **96–97**

Chicago freedom movement, **124–125**

Chicano movement, **125–127**, *126*

children's advocacy movement, **127–129**

children's rights movement, **127–129**

colonization movements, **178–179**, 250

free speech movement, **302–303**

freedom summer (1964), 121, **301–302**, 484–485, 715

homophile movement, **345–346**

Independent Living Movement (ILM), 367–369, 658–659

International Hotel episode, **378–379**

labor movement, **417–419**

March on Washington Movement (MOWM), 231, **451–452**, 560

Nashville student movement, 299, 712

Native American movement, **541–543**

Native Hawaiian sovereignty movement, **544–545**

Niagara movement, 237, 292, **561–562**, *562*, 739

poor people's campaign, 1–2, 469, *603*, **603–604**

Puerto Rican movement, **619–620**

red power, **642–643**

student movements, **712–714**

yellow power, **823**

Movies, 119, **282–285**

Movimiento de Liberacíon Nacional (MLN), **498–499**, 621

Movimiento Estudiantil Chicano de Aztlán (M.E.Ch.A.), **499**

Movimiento Pro Independencia (MPI), **498**, 620

MOWC. *See* March on Washington Committee (MOWC)

MOWM (March on Washington Movement), **451–452**

MPI (Movimiento Pro Independencia), **498**, 620

Ms. (magazine), 709

Muhammad, Elijah, 448–449, *500*, **500–501**, *538*, 539–540

Muhammad, Warith Deen, 539

Multiculturalism, **501–502**

Murieta, Joaquín, **502**

Murray, Anna Pauline "Pauli," **502–504**, *503*

Muscular Dystrophy Association (MDA), 392

Museum of African American History (MAAH), **504**

Music, **504–507**, 791

Muste, A. J., 44, 137–138, 585–586, *586*

Myrdal, Gunnar, 29–30, 598, 691

N

NAACP. *See* National Association for the Advancement of Colored People (NAACP)

NAACP Legal Defense and Educational Fund (LDF), 320, 452–453, **509–510**, *510*

NAAL (National Afro-American League), 292, **511**

Nabrit, James, Jr., 97

NACW (National Association of Colored Women), **519**, 725

NAGPRA (Native American Graves Protection and Repatriation Act), **540–541**

NARF (Native American Rights Fund), **543–544**, 814

Narragansetts (tribe), 656

Nash, Diane Bevel, **510–511**, 723

Nashville student movement, 299, 712

Nation of Islam, 24, 271–272, 448–449, 500–501, **538–539**

National Afro-American Council, 292

National Afro-American League (NAAL), 292, **511**

National American Woman Suffrage Association